AF516300

China and India

CHINA AND INDIA

Great Power Rivals

Mohan Malik

New Delhi | Mumbai | Chennai | Kolkata | Bengaluru | Hyderabad | Kochi | Guwahati

First Indian Edition 2012

VIVA BOOKS PRIVATE LIMITED

- 4737/23 Ansari Road, Daryaganj, New Delhi 110 002
  E-mail: vivadelhi@vivagroupindia.net, Tel. 42242200
- 76, Service Industries, Shirvane, Sector 1, Nerul, Navi Mumbai 400 706
  E-mail: vivamumbai@vivagroupindia.net, Tel. 27721273, 27721274
- Jamals Fazal Chambers, 26 Greams Road, Chennai 600 006
  E-mail: vivachennai@vivagroupindia.net, Tel. 28290304, 28294241
- B-103, Jindal Towers, 21/1A/3 Darga Road, Kolkata 700 017
  E-mail: vivakolkata@vivagroupindia.net, Tel. 22836381, 22816713
- 7, Sovereign Park Apartments, 56-58, K. R. Road, Basavanagudi, Bengaluru 560 004
  E-mail: vivabangalore@vivagroupindia.net, Tel. 26607409, 26607410
- 101-102 Mughal Marc Apartments, 3-4-637 to 641, Narayanguda, Hyderabad 500 029
  E-mail: vivahyderabad@vivagroupindia.net, Tel. 27564481, 27564482
- Beevi Towers, First Floor, SRM Road, Kaloor, Kochi 682 018, Kerala
  E-mail: vivakochi@vivagroupindia.net, Tel: 0484-2403055, 2403056
- 232, GNB Road, Beside UCO Bank, Silpukhuri, Guwahati 781 003
  E-mail: vivaguwahati@vivagroupindia.net, Tel: 0361-2666386

www.vivagroupindia.com

Published by arrangement with

Lynne Rienner Publishers, Inc.
1800 30th Street, Suite 314
Boulder, Colorado 80301
USA

ISBN : 978-81-309-2053-5

Published by Vinod Vasishtha for Viva Books Private Limited, 4737/23, Ansari Road, Daryaganj, New Delhi-110 002. Printed and bound by Saurabh Printers Pvt. Ltd., Noida.

Dedicated to Ellika and her generation

Contents

Acknowledgments

I am particularly indebted to Andrew Scobell, Tansen Sen, P. R. Kumaraswamy, and Denny Roy for their invaluable support in this endeavor. While researching and writing on China-India relations over the last quarter of a century, I have also incurred many debts of gratitude. In particular, I am grateful to many Chinese strategic experts who have shared their thoughts and ideas on this subject with me. I have had the privilege of discussing my ideas with a number of my colleagues at various institutions in China, India, Australia, Britain, Singapore, and the United States. This volume has also benefited immensely from my participation in numerous workshops, conferences, seminars, informal discussions, and conversations. Not least, I would like to express my gratitude to the diplomatic, military, and intelligence personnel of many Asia-Pacific countries for granting me interviews and providing me with valuable information and useful insights on this subject over the last two decades. Needless to say, none of them bears any responsibility for the views expressed in this book, for which I am solely responsible. The assistance of the Asia-Pacific Center for Security Studies library staff, Gayle Yoshikawa and David Coleman, is gratefully acknowledged. I also want to express my sincere gratitude to Lynne Rienner Publishers for all the support, especially Jessica Gribble for her outstanding help in improving the final product.

Acronyms

ADB	Asian Development Bank
ADMM+8	ASEAN Defense Ministers' Meeting Plus Eight
AEC	Asian Economic Community
AFRICOM	US Africa Command
AIFTA	ASEAN-India Free Trade Agreement
APEC	Asia-Pacific Economic Cooperation
APSCO	Asia-Pacific Space Cooperation Organization
APT	ASEAN Plus Three (ASEAN plus China, South Korea, and Japan)
ARF	ASEAN Regional Forum
ASEAN	Association of Southeast Asian Nations
ASEM	Asia-Europe Meeting
AWACS	Airborne Warning and Control System
BCP	Burmese Communist Party
BIMSTEC	Bay of Bengal Initiative for Multi-Sectoral Technical and Economic Cooperation
BJP	Bharatiya Janata Party
BRIC	Brazil-Russia-India-China
C^4ISR	Command, Control, Communications, Computers, Intelligence, Surveillance, and Reconnaissance
CAFTA	China-ASEAN Free Trade Agreement
CAMS	Chinese Academy of Military Sciences
CASS	Chinese Academy of Social Sciences
CBMs	Confidence-Building Measures
CCP	Chinese Communist Party
CENTCOM	US Central Command
CHIMEA	China, India, the Middle East, and Africa
CIA	Central Intelligence Agency
CICIR	China Institute of Contemporary International Relations
CIISS	China Institute for International Strategic Studies
CNPC	China National Petroleum Corporation
CoD	Community of Democracies
COIN	Counter Insurgency

CTBT	Comprehensive Test Ban Treaty
EAC	East Asian Community
EAS	East Asia Summit
ETIM	East Turkestan Islamic Movement
EU	European Union
FDI	Foreign Direct Investment
FEER	Far Eastern Economic Review
FTA	Free Trade Agreement
G-20	Group of Twenty
G-4	Group of Four
GCC	Gulf Cooperation Council
GDP	Gross Domestic Product
IAEA	International Atomic Energy Agency
IBSA	India-Brazil-South Africa bloc
IDSA	Institute for Defense Studies and Analyses
IHT	International Herald Tribune
IMF	International Monetary Fund
ICBMs	Influence-and-Confidence-Building Measures
IO	Indian Ocean
IONS	Indian Ocean Naval Symposium
IOR	Indian Ocean Region
IOR-ARC	Indian Ocean Rim Association for Regional Cooperation
IT	Information Technology
JeM	Jaish-e-Muhammad
JTF	Joint Task Force
JuD	Jamaat-Ud-Dawa
KMT	Kuomindang
LAC	Line of Actual Control
LeT	Lashkar-e-Toiba
LOC	Line of Control
MEA	Ministry of External Affairs
MGC	Mekong-Ganges Cooperation
MOD	Ministry of Defense
MOFA	Ministry of Foreign Affairs
MoU	Memorandum of Understanding
NIC	National Intelligence Council (US)
NATO	North Atlantic Treaty Organization
NFU	No-First Use
NLD	National League for Democracy
NNWS	Non-Nuclear Weapons State
NOCs	National Oil Companies

NPT	Nuclear Non-Proliferation Treaty
NSG	Nuclear Suppliers' Group
NWS	Nuclear Weapons State
OIC	Organization of Islamic Conference
OPEC	Organization of the Petroleum-Exporting Countries
ORBAT	Order of Battle
P-5	Permanent Five Members of the UN Security Council
PACOM	US Pacific Command
PLA	People's Liberation Army
PMO	Prime Minister's Office
PRC	People's Republic of China
PTBT	Partial Test Ban Treaty
QDR	Quadrennial Defense Review (US)
RSS	Rashtriya Swyamsevak Sangh
SAARC	South Asian Association for Regional Cooperation
SCO	Shanghai Cooperation Organization
SLOC	Sea Lanes of Communication
SLORC	State Law and Order Restoration Council
SPDC	State Peace and Development Council
SWF	Sovereign Wealth Fund
TAR	Tibet Autonomous Region
TYC	Tibetan Youth Congress
UAE	United Arab Emirates
UFC	Uniting for Consensus group
UN	United Nations
UNSC	United Nations Security Council
US	United States
USSR	Union of Soviet Socialist Republics
VIP	Very Important Person
WMD	Weapons of Mass Destruction
WPNS	Western Pacific Naval Symposium
WSJ	Wall Street Journal

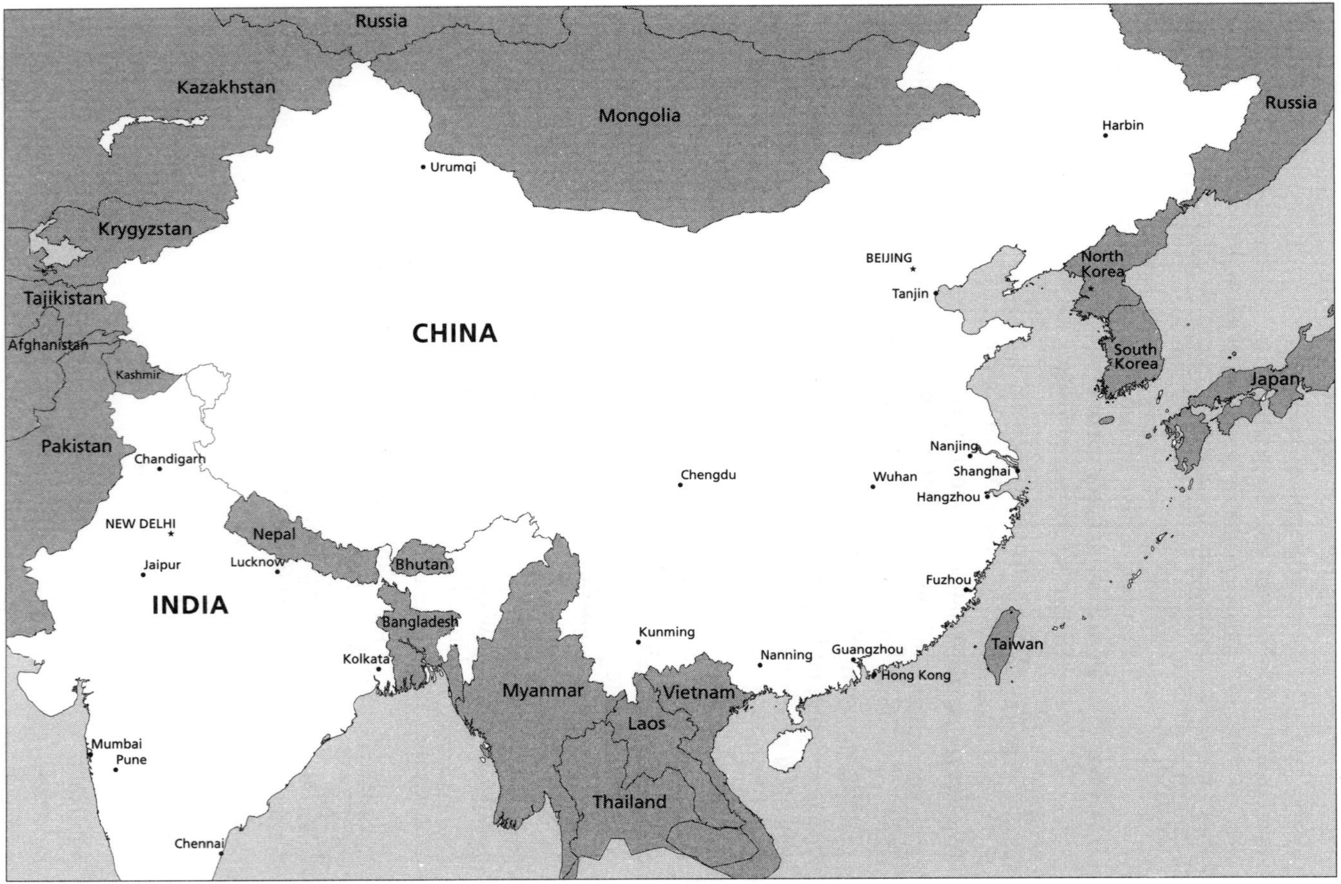

China and India

1
Introduction

This book has been long in coming. The state of bilateral relationship between China and India—two of the world's oldest civilization-states—has long intrigued me. I began writing on the China-India relationship soon after I landed in Beijing in 1983 to learn the Chinese language—that is, long before the comparative study of China and India became a growth industry in the West. It is indeed gratifying to see the China-India relationship gradually moving from the periphery toward the center stage of international politics over the last decade.

As newly independent states in the mid-twentieth century, China and India faced similar challenges of poverty, economic development, and national integration, but went on to chart completely different paths of socio-economic and political development over the next six decades. In particular, economic reforms in China (since 1979) and in India (since 1991), coupled with the globalization of the world economy, have unleashed forces that are reshaping the world's geostrategic, economic, and environmental landscape. Militarily and diplomatically, China and India will be powerful and influential but poor in terms of per capita income because of their large populations. Both have massive manpower resources: a scientific, technological, and industrial base. They also have two of the world's fastest-growing militaries. Both continue to grow while the economies of the West and Japan shrink. Both want to envelop neighbors with their economies. Both are competing for resources, foreign investment, trade, markets, and increasingly, overseas bases. Both are intent on acquiring comprehensive national strength.

There is no dearth of academic and policy works on China and India published over the last few years. Most of these works deal with politico-economic development models and go on to extrapolate implications for the world economy, sustainable growth, and environment. However, wishful thinking—not reality—characterizes much of the writing on the bilateral relationship between China and India.[1] There is reason to be skeptical of the highly optimistic pairing of China and India, as both face daunting economic, socio-political, demographic, and security challenges which could unravel them. Both confront a strategic future more uncertain, complicated, and potentially conflicted than is generally recognized.

China and India's growth is unfolding in the middle of a perfect storm: resource scarcity, global economic rebalancing, geopolitical shifts, environmental degradation, and transnational security threats that will have unforeseen consequences. China and India are in the early stages of a jarring economic transition that is creating new winners and losers within and without. China might find it easier to take off than take over. There is nothing inevitable about the rise of China or India at the cost of the West. Economic forecasts do not factor in unforeseen developments such as political disasters and game-changing technological advances that often upset calculations about international pecking order. It is possible that the West, and particularly the United States, may yet witness an unexpected surge. Besides, China and India have often demonstrated an uncanny knack for being their own worst enemies. The risks to China's rise are internal. But risks to India's economic growth are both internal and external. Unlike China, all of India's neighbors are weak, failed, or pariah states, at war within and without. Sustaining growth in an "arc of crisis" from Iran to Burma won't be easy.

Should China and India continue on their upward trajectory, their rise will change the world forever: the world economy, demography, geopolitics, resources, outer space, and environment. While the two countries are keen to learn from each other's economic experience, optimistic projections of bringing them together to form a "Chindia" of billions of entrepreneurs to power the global economy are misplaced. They remain two fierce competitors, determined to outdo each other, rather than two collaborators with common agendas. Despite burgeoning economic links, China and India harbor strong hostility and suspicions about one another.

This study seeks to temper the hyperbole that characterizes a lot of writing about the *simultaneous accommodation* of China and India in and by the international system. Most recent writings take it as a given that China has accommodated (or, that Beijing will accommodate) India's rise to create a multipolar world. The reality is far more complicated. Like other great powers, China seeks to recast its region, if not the world, in its own image. Having transformed the economies of the Asia-Pacific region, China would naturally want to transform the politics and security of the Asia-Pacific region. It remains to be seen how well Asia accommodates a rising China and how a rising China accommodates the rest of Asia that includes India, Japan, and Southeast Asia. As China grows more powerful, it is becoming more assertive in its relations with other Asian countries. China's primary rival on continental Asia remains India, another rising power with aspirations for an increased role and status in the international system. However, the ambition and power of the Chinese far outstrip that of India. China is also far ahead of India in all socio-economic indices. China's economy is now three times larger than India's, with a disproportionately larger footprint in global trade, capital flows, energy consumption, and carbon emissions. Chinese and Indian economies are more competitive than complementary. There is little or no mutual economic interdependence. In fact, India's is the only large economy that is not in debt to China. Nor is India's growth contingent upon Chinese economic growth. Neither growing trade and cultural ties nor participation in multilateral institutions have moderated their competition or resulted in the accommodation of deep-seated differences which are a function of their aspirations for power and influence at the regional and global levels.

Like China, India seeks greater international status, power, and influence commensurate with its growing economic power. However, like any other established great power, China wants to ensure that its position remains strong vis-à-vis challenger India. China's quest for global power and influence pits it against India's drive for strategic autonomy and regional influence. Great powers frown upon the rise of peer competitors. Determined to maintain its edge over its southern rival, Beijing resists any attempt by New Delhi to achieve strategic parity through a combination of military, economic, and diplomatic means. Already, New Delhi's initiatives designed to strengthen India's position in Asia have provoked protests, counter-measures, and dire warnings from Beijing. China's foreign policy behavior is thus no different from other great powers. For India's rise challenges China's power and status in the Asia-Pacific in much the same way as China's rise challenges US global dominance. If India is able to sustain its impressive economic growth over the next couple of decades, it will find itself engaged in an intense economic and security competition with China with considerable potential for conflict. Ancient rivalries and animosities could spoil their happy march toward prosperity.

The unequal strategic equation between China and India remains a major source of tension. Chinese Premier Wen Jiabao remarked in April 2003 that "in the last 2,200 years, China and India spent 99.9 percent of the time enjoying friendly relations. Only 0.1 percent of the time relations were not good." Left unsaid was the fact that these two "civilization-cum-empire states" were distant neighbors for much of their history. Their relations turned sour (0.1 percent of the time, to use Premier Wen's historical arithmetic) soon after the transformation of the traditional Indo-Tibetan frontier into what is now the 4,057 kilometer-long Sino-Indian disputed border with disputed histories. This very short period's shadow looms unusually large because as relatively new neighbors with little or no historical experience in dealing with each other politically, India and China have been unable to find equilibrium in their relations. Although both have managed to avoid conflict since 1962, adopting a pragmatic approach to managing their differences and seeking ways to manage their competition, several obstacles exist in forming a normalized, cooperative relationship which could make or mar either one's future as Asia's rising power.

Scarred by an old war and unresolved territorial dispute and jaded by rival alliance relationships, a whole range of new issues now bedevil bilateral relations as China and India engage in a worldwide scramble for resources, maneuver for advantage in their overlapping spheres of influence, plan for control of major sea lanes, and compete for influence in regional and global institutions. Each expresses disquiet over the other's rising defense spending. Concurrent with their rising economic might, both have set about modernizing their militaries to lend extra muscle to their growing strategic ambitions, thereby reigniting fears of a nuclear arms race. China and India are currently engaged in a geopolitical chess game across Asia and Africa. Their expanding geopolitical horizons and overlapping spheres of influence across oceans are creating frictions. Resource (oil, gas, and water) scarcity is adding new layers of strains and tensions. Geographic proximity has long been one of the main factors in conflicts between rising great powers sharing the same neighborhood. The fact of the matter is that China and India are locked in a classic security dilemma: one country sees its own actions as self-defensive, but the same actions appear aggressive to the other. India feels the need to take counter-balancing measures and launch certain initiatives to counter China's growing power—but these are perceived as challenging and threatening in China. Both want to focus on economic development and avoid overt rivalry or conflict. Still, the volatile agents of nationalism and history, ambition, strength, and size produce a mysterious chemistry. China's rapid economic growth, military power, and hyper-nationalism at home are shaping Chinese public expectations and limiting possibilities for compromise with other powers. Unless managed skilfully, nationalist pride in India could bring about a clash with Chinese nationalism. For Asia has never known both

China and India growing strong simultaneously in such close proximity with disputed frontiers and overlapping spheres of influence.

Hence, a thorough understanding of the nuts and bolts of the bilateral relationship—especially as perceived by the policymakers and strategic analysts of these two Asian giants—is vitally important. Despite some cooperation on economic, environmental, and transnational security issues, China and India remain locked in an intense geopolitical rivalry. As Shen Dingli, a well-known Chinese strategic thinker and deputy head of the South Asia Research Institute in Shanghai, points out: "The structural problem is leadership. The question is who leads in Asia?"[2] The stage is thus set for more competition than cooperation between Han and Hindu in the twenty-first century. Notwithstanding the leadership's pragmatism and priority on domestic stability and good relations abroad, both China and India may well find themselves drawn into future regional "hot spots" or possibly intervening in neighboring countries because of some instability or action that is perceived as threatening over the long term. This is, of course, a geopolitical perspective grounded in Power Transitions Theory. In a sense, this volume is along the lines of the argument presented in John Garver's study *Protracted Contest: Sino-Indian Rivalry in the Twentieth Century* (University of Washington Press, 2001). Those who are interested in the great Asian drama unfolding in the early twenty-first century will find much to ponder in this analysis of relations between the world's two most populous civilization-states in the world.

This book is divided into three parts. Part I provides a critical analysis of the similarities and differences in their strategic cultures and examines Chinese and Indian perceptions and expectations of each other. Part II focuses on the flashpoints and fault lines that exist in the China-India ties. The extension of the Sino-Indian rivalry for influence into regional and global multilateral forums is also discussed here. Part III focuses on energy and maritime security issues and concludes with a discussion of evolving tilts, alignments, and alternative strategic futures.

Notes

[1] A series of reports and books have come out over the past few years pairing their economic rise as a given, along with the spurious notion of "Chindia" coined by Jairam Ramesh in his *Making Sense of Chindia* (India Research Press, 2005). Other similar works include P. Engardio's *Chindia: How China and India Are Revolutionizing Global Business* (McGraw Hill,

2007); T. Khanna's *Billions of Entrepreneurs* (Harvard Business School Press, 2008); D. Smith's *The Dragon and the Elephant* (Profile Books, 2007); R. Meredith, *The Elephant and the Dragon* (W. W. Norton, 2008); R. Dulci Rahman and J. Miguel Andreu's *China and India: Towards Global Economic Supremacy?* (Academic Foundation, 2006).

[2] Quoted in Peter Ford, "Rivals China, India in escalating war of words," *Christian Science Monitor*, October 20, 2009 <http://www.csmonitor.com/2009/1020/p06s04-woap.html>.

Part 1

The Burden of History

2
Strategic Cultures: Pax Sinica vs. Pax Indica

As ancient civilizations, China and India coexisted in peace and harmony for millennia. As postcolonial modern nation-states, however, with the exception of a very short period of bonhomie in the early 1950s, relations between the two Asian giants have been marked by conflict, containment, mutual suspicion, distrust, and rivalry. Just as the Indian sub- continental plate has a tendency to constantly rub and push against the Eurasian tectonic plate, causing friction and volatility in the entire Himalayan mountain range, India's bilateral relationship with China also remains volatile and friction- and tension-ridden. Most observers of China-India relations believe that factors such as the border dispute, the Cold War alignments, power asymmetry, mutual distrust, and more recently, nuclear and resource security issues are the major causes of tortuous and uneasy relations between the two Asian giants. I maintain, however, that there is a fundamental clash of interests between China and India that is rooted in their strategic cultures, history, geo-economics, and geopolitics. The biggest obstacle to Sino-Indian amity is that both countries aspire to the same things at the same time on the same continental landmass and its adjoining waters.[1] This chapter argues that to understand the roles China and India want to play on the international stage in the twenty-first century, we first need to return to history to gain an understanding of their roles and relationship several millennia ago. Both China and India have gone through regular periods of decline and resurgence. In China's case the period of decline lasted for nearly two centuries, while in India's case, it lasted for a millennium. Much like China in eastern Asia, modern India has inherited, and recognizes, a long historical and cultural tradition of Indic civilization in southern Asia. Therefore, it is important to consider the influences of history and culture as well as the physical facts of geography and demography upon the Chinese and Indian governments' views of the world and of their own roles in the international system.

Strategic Culture

The way a country's interests are conceptualized, defined, and defended is influenced by its unique historical and cultural experiences.[2] Strategic culture consists of widely shared beliefs—including worldviews, traditions, attitudes, symbols, myths, self-image, and identity—related to a nation's self-representation and its "proper" role in world politics. Political and military elites socialized in different cultural contexts may behave in different ways and make different choices, even when placed in similar situations. For example, as a result of "beliefs" about "historic role," "self-image," and "identity," there is a powerful elite consensus in both China and India that as the two oldest civilizations and once-great powers which were subjected to centuries of European domination, they must acquire the *full* spectrum of economic, technological, and military (conventional, nuclear, information, and space) capabilities in order to be dominant regionally and influential globally. What eludes the Western understanding of Asia is the sense of national destiny that drives China and India's ambitions. Many maintain that there was no "India" or "China" before the twentieth century. Whether we can speak of an India or a China in the past or not, the fact is that China and India's strategic cultures are a function of historical experiences and perceptions of their appropriate roles in the world. Strategic culture is not a trivial variable in the description or explanation of strategic behavior. There is a degree of continuity in pre-modern strategic cultures of China and India into the modern age. It is the lack of understanding of Asian history and strategic cultures before the arrival of Europeans that has left many observers confused and perplexed as to what India is up to. Many analysts opine that India behaves as if it were the successor to the British Raj. While true, this does not take into account the fact that India (like China) had also existed both as an ancient civilization and as an empire (albeit, for much shorter periods than China) in southern Asia for centuries before it became a British colony. India's traditional historical and cultural ties with Central and Southeast Asia *do* influence Indian perceptions of, and more importantly, its ambitions for, its future role in Asia. It was this lack of understanding of India's strategic culture that led Therese Delpech to wonder why it is "poor and weak India," not rich Japan that is challenging China's role in the post-Cold War Asia.[3]

Before discussing the history of China-India relations and their strategic cultures, it is useful to point out that this approach does not assume that strategic culture is the sole determinant of decisions in national security policy, but that it is an important determinant. The future has a past but the future does not necessarily resemble the past. Also, this approach does not imply that domestic political and ideological variables or structural factors (such as relative power capabilities, alliance patterns, and external threats) do not explain Chinese or Indian foreign policy behavior. Finally, it does not follow that strategic culture is so unchanging and rigid that it is insusceptible to change over time in the face of conflicting reality and experience. This approach, however, does assume that strategic culture is powerful in influencing national roles, capabilities, interests, and ambitions. Alastair Johnston's study of Chinese strategic culture suggests that strategic culture is a key variable in the explanation of China's strategic behavior. There is, at least in the Chinese case, "a long-term, deeply rooted, persistent, and consistent set of assumptions about the strategic environment and about the best means of dealing with it."[4] And George Tanham's study of India's strategic culture shows that this is true of India as well.[5]

From Civilizations to Nation-States

China and India are two of the world's oldest continuing civilizations, each with the quality of resilience that has enabled it to survive and prosper through the ages and against all odds. In contrast, several other ancient civilizations either disappeared or were subsumed by others. During the past 3,000 years, every one of the Asian countries—some situated on the continental landmass, others being islands off the mainland Asia—has at some stage been directly influenced by one or both of these two great civilizations. Much like China in eastern Asia, modern India has inherited, and recognizes, a long historical and cultural tradition of Indic civilization in southern Asia. As the future originates in the impulses of the past, it is appropriate to consider some of the influences which that history and culture, and the physical facts of geography and demography, may have upon the Chinese and Indian governments' worldviews and their roles in the international system. The burden of history indeed weighs very heavily on China and India. Observers of China and India generally agree that the discourse of civilization is critical for the construction of Chinese and Indian identities as modern nation-states. Much like China, during the feudal age, India was divided into many states often at war with one another. These states maintained diplomatic relations with each other as if they were foreign countries. Both have a long, rich strategic tradition: both China's *Sun Zi Bingfa* (Sun Tzu's treatise on *The Art of War*) and

Kautilya's *Arthshastra* in India (a treatise on war, diplomacy, statecraft, and empire) were written over 2000 years ago.

If China and India had coexisted peacefully for over 2,000 years, it was mainly because they were distant neighbors. The mighty barrier of the Himalayas and Tibet separated the two countries and made political contacts few and far between. In the cultural sphere, it was mostly a one way street—from India to China. From India, Hindu and Buddhist religious and cultural influence spread to China (and Korea and Japan) around the second century AD. Chinese scholars were sent to Indian universities at Nalanda and Taxilla. Buddhism enriched and transformed Chinese thought, science, medicine, literature, and fine arts. Ancient India was the object of China's admiration, respect and awe.[6] A seventh century Chinese commentary on India described it as a "Middle Kingdom":

> Lying in the south of the snow mountain (Himalayas) is the Central State (*Zhong guo* in Chinese or *Madhyadesa* in Sanskrit). Her land is plain, her weather temperate regardless of winter or summer. Trees and flowers grow exuberantly all the year round. The land is never visited by flowing frost. How can a peripheral state (like China) be comparable to her![7]

During this period in history, from Kashmir to Kanyakumari and from Kandahar (in Afghanistan) to Kamrup (Assam), India was one civilizational entity.[8] The Hindu Kush mountain ranges in the northwest and Himalayas in the north that acted as the northern frontiers—Indian civilization's Great Wall—constituted the "sacred geographical limits of the Indian nation." B. K. Sarkar, in his stimulating work *Chinese Religion through Hindu Eyes*, wrote of the "Indianization of Confucianism" and the "Indianization of China" from the seventh to the tenth centuries.[9] Liang Jizhao told Nobel laureate Rabindranath Tagore in the 1920s: "India and China are like twin brothers. Before most of the civilised races became active, we two brothers had already begun to study the great problems which concern the whole of mankind ... India was ahead of us and we, the little brother, followed behind."[10] The Chinese image of India was not just as a Buddhist paradise (*xi tian*) but also as a source of scientific learning.[11] In the 1930s, Dr. Hu Shih, the leader of the Chinese intellectual renaissance, said: "When China was brought face to face with India, China was overwhelmed, dazzled, and dumbfounded by the vast output of the religious zeal and genius of the Indian nation. China acknowledged its defeat and was completely conquered."[12] On the whole, in the realm of ideas, the impact of India on China has been much greater than vice versa.

The texture of the Chinese-Indian relationship underwent a major transformation between the seventh and the fifteenth centuries. The religious exchanges of the first millennium (the years 0 to 1000) gave way to mostly commercial exchanges in the first half of the second millennium (1100 to 1500). As historian Tansen Sen points out: "While in the first millennium the sacred Buddhist sites in India were the pivot of Sino-Indian interactions, the lucrative markets of China and the expanding intercontinental commerce emerged as the main stimuli for the bilateral relations since the early eleventh century. In other words, the relations between India and China were realigned from Buddhist-dominated to trade-centered exchanges."[13] Furthermore, whereas the process of Buddhist religious-cultural interaction between China and India occurred overland in the first millennium, "communications between the two during the Song-Yuan-early Ming period took place primarily through the maritime routes" in the second millennium.[14] Apparently, the closure of the silk route (following the wave of Islamic invasions throughout Central Asia) and of the overland route via Tibet (by a powerful and expansionist Tibetan kingdom) to India and the West stimulated China's maritime trade and commerce with India through seaborne trade. In addition, Christopher Wake identifies three other factors that contributed to a significant growth in overseas maritime trade:

- The southward shift in the demographic and economic center of gravity of China under way at the beginning of the second millennium;
- the Song dynasty's decision to increase government revenue through import duties; and
- significant advances made in shipbuilding technology.[15]

A combination of these geopolitical, technological, and economic developments saw Chinese ships sailing all the way to Indian ports on the Malabar coast by the end of the eleventh century. It was at the ports of Kolam (Quilon), Cochin, Calicut, and Coromandel, which emerged as major transit points in the Indian Ocean region, that goods from Africa, Arabia, and other places were transferred onto Chinese vessels for shipment to Quanzhou.[16] The second millennium also saw India faced with internal disunity, internecine warfare, and repeated Islamic invasions. The ancient Indic civilization on the subcontinent lay in ruins.[17] China, in sharp contrast, emerged as a stronger military, political, and economic power under the Song, Mongol (Yuan), Ming, and Manchu (Qing) rulers.

The Chinese and Indian civilizations had also existed in close juxtaposition in Southeast Asia, greatly modifying the indigenous cultures of the region. These two great strains of culture flowed side by side and intermingled in many areas, but did not fuse in any major way. In fact, they represented two distinct attitudes of mind and conflicting worldviews, and exerted very little influence on one another. One extended in the direction of the material and practical, the other in the direction of the philosophical and intangible. To the Chinese mind, "this-worldly," practical, materialistic, and pragmatic—the commonsense of Confucius still had a far greater appeal than the metaphysical "other-worldliness" of Buddhism. The influence of the former is evident in Vietnam, which came under Sinic cultural influence, whereas the latter is more dominant in Burma, Thailand, Laos, and Cambodia, which still trace their Buddhist-Hindu religious roots directly to the Indic civilization.

Many scholars have long argued that neither Han nor Hindu rulers were territorially expansionist. Both seemingly lacked "martial" imperialist instincts. Both China and India were ravaged by foreign nomadic tribes that established "foreign" dynasties. In China's case, most threats to Chinese security certainly originated from the interior. Some China-watchers contend that "China's real cultural achievements historically had little to do with militarism and imperialism and that Chinese civilization reached its qualitative peaks during the relatively peaceful and culture-oriented (albeit small) Song and Ming Chinas." They claim that the Tang, Song, and Ming dynasties and Nationalist China represented the real China, unencumbered as they were by the martial spirit or messianic zeal of the Mongols, Manchus (Qing), and Communists.[18] This line of argument maintains that it was primarily non-Han dynasties—the Mongols and the Manchus—who conquered China and expanded traditional China's territories into central, south, southeast, and northeast Asia. Until the Chinese and Russian Empires met in Central Asia in the nineteenth century and China created the province of Xinjiang (New Territories), China could not subdue the nomadic armies on the Central Asian steppe. As Alastair Johnston pointed out: "So persistent was the nomadic threat that during the Ming dynasty (1368–1644) a strategic culture developed regarding relations with the Mongols, in which Beijing eschewed all thought of diplomacy and limited victories, seeking total annihilation of its nomadic adversaries."[19] In other words, it was Han contact with martial Mongols that brought about the culture of violence and martial spirit and whetted the Chinese appetite for territorial expansion. Likewise, Indian historians stress that most of their expansion in their extended neighborhood (whether in Central Asia or Southeast Asia) was mostly in the mercantile, cultural, and religious realms and was by and large peaceful.[20] They point out that Hindu India's empire building—with the exception of southern India's Chola dynasty, the Srivijaya Kingdom on the Malay peninsula, and the Kamboja empire—was undertaken mostly by Moghuls from Central Asia and the British from Europe.[21]

Many historians, however, criticize the view that "empire building in both China and India was undertaken mostly by foreign rulers" as historically and factually inaccurate. Based on new archeological research and historical sources, Nicola Di Cosmo's *Ancient China and its Enemies* questions the traditional Sino-centric interpretation of Chinese history as a contest between barbarous "martial" north (Hsiung-nu nomads) and the civilized south (Shang and Chou China).[22] Recent scholarship has shown that the Han dynasty clearly had an expansionist agenda when dealing with the Central and Inner Asians and the same was true with the Tang dynasty, not only in Central Asia, but also in Tibet and Korea.[23] Even Nationalist China under Chiang Kai-shek was plenty martial, Chiang himself saying he saw fascism as a model for China. He did not have the opportunity to be expansionist because the Japanese had him on the defensive.[24] The expansion of Han Chinese rule to Manchuria, Mongolia, Taiwan, Xinjiang, Tibet, and Yunnan over the last 2,000 years has been largely achieved through conquest, absorption, assimilation, and large-scale migration.[25]

Similarly, major territorial expansion in Southwest Asia, Kashmir, and Central Asia was undertaken during the reigns of Emperors Ashoka and Kanishka in India. At its greatest extent, the Mauryan Empire (322–185 BCE) stretched to the north along the natural boundaries of the Himalayas and to the east stretching into what is now Assam. From the tenth through the thirteenth centuries, several of the Pallava and Chola kings assembled large navies and armies to overthrow neighboring kingdoms and to undertake punitive attacks on the states in the Bay of Bengal region. They also took to the sea to conquer parts of what are now Sri Lanka, Malaysia and Indonesia. George Tanham observes: "In what was really a battle over the trade between China and India and Europe, the Cholas were quite successful in both naval and land engagements and briefly ruled [dominated] portions of Southeast Asia."[26] Suffice it to say, nearly all kingdoms and empires behaved in a more or less expansionist manner whenever strength allowed and opportunity arose.

No people are more history-conscious than the Chinese. The Chinese leadership nowadays pays rich tribute to the outward-looking policies of the Ming dynasty during the fifteenth century when Admiral Zheng He's (also spelled as Cheng Ho) voyages of exploration in 1405–1433 led to the exchange of knowledge and goods as far afield as the east coast of Africa, thereby suggesting that today's commercial engagement is in the same spirit of trade and openness, and that China's extension of its maritime power into Southeast and South Asia and the Indian Ocean region should not be feared or resisted. A growing body of evidence, however, questions the portrayal of Admiral Zheng He's seven voyages to Southeast Asia, India, Arabia, and Africa as benign missions of peace and friendship.[27] Many scholars argue that Zheng He's expeditions 600 years ago, which followed lesser ones by the Mongol Yuan dynasty, began a southward Chinese expansion that was driven as much by commercial as political hegemony motives.[28] This southward expansion, which paralleled China's territorial expansion in the north and west, had huge consequences not only for the geopolitics of the region but also for its demographics, the region having hitherto been more subject to Indian than Chinese cultural influence.

> On land this included the annexation of Yunnan, a partially successful attempt to control Vietnam and interference in the affairs of Burma. By sea it took the form of expeditions to achieve "regime change" among the small political entities of Southeast Asia, including detaching the trading states of Sumatra from allegiance to the Java-based Majapahit empire. The military forces of Zheng He and others overthrew rulers as far away as Sri Lanka who would not submit to Ming hegemony, installing puppets in their place.... Ming policy expanded China's geographical and tributary claims. These are found in its claims to the whole of the South China Sea, used to justify its seizure of islands from Vietnam, and Ming-era assumptions of the superiority of Chinese civilization over its Malay and Indian counterparts.[29]

Admiral Zheng He's naval expeditions to Southeast Asia and the Indian Ocean in the fifteenth century not only demonstrated the might of the Chinese empire but also ensured Chinese imperial domination of the trade routes linking the Middle East and East Asia. The Yuan and Ming rulers forced many Southeast Asian kingdoms to pay tribute to China's emperors as a precondition for preferential trade treatment, thereby achieving a *Pax Sinica* throughout the known world. Southeast Asian states that regularly sent tributes included Annam (North Vietnam), Siam (Thailand), Sulu (South Philippines), Burma, and Laos. Sinologist

Geoff Wade argues that these military missions had strategic aims, and thus amounted to "what might be called maritime proto-colonialism: that is, they were engaged in that early form of maritime colonialism by which a dominant maritime power took control (either through force or the threat thereof) of the main port-polities along the major East-West maritime trade network, as well as the seas between, thereby gaining economic and political benefits."[30] Given this historical backdrop, it is not surprising that China's re-emergence as a great power is causing regional unease and discomfort in East Asia where the memories of the tributary state system or "the Middle Kingdom syndrome" have not completely dimmed.

Maritime Asia (Southern China, Annam, Srivijaya, Sumatra, Siam, and Southern India) in the first half of the second millennium was bound by economic interdependence and seaborne trade and saw the establishment of preferential trade-cum-tributary arrangements and of trading diasporas at major ports in Southeast and South Asia. Despite trade and tributary arrangements, this region was neither peaceful nor conflict-free. For example, despite strong religious and cultural ties, the desire to control lucrative maritime trade between China and the Indian Ocean region is said to have caused the Cholas to launch punitive raids on the Srivijayan ports on the Malay peninsula.[31] Does the conduct of Ming rulers' maritime strategy or the linkage of tribute with trade have any bearing upon the state of China-Southeast Asia and China-India relations in the third millennium? The Ming voyages are now an inextricable part of Chinese nationalist lore—and its populist claim to the Indian Ocean. Imperial hubris or nostalgia for a return to the past can have unpredictable consequences. As noted earlier, trade and maritime exchanges between China and the kingdoms along the southern Indian coast saw dramatic growth in the first half of the second millennium. While promoting trade and maritime linkages, the Yuan and Ming court officials also became involved in dispute resolution involving feuding kingdoms in Calicut, Cochin, and Bengal. Even the mighty kingdom of Vijayanagar in southern India sent an embassy to China in 1374 to serve as a warning to the Tughluq Sultanate of Delhi against any further Muslim intrusions into the Hindu South. (This was not the first time an Indian ruler had sent an embassy to China to seek support. The Indian diplomatic mission of 720 specifically mentioned the threat from the Tibetans and Muslim Arabs as the main reason for seeking help from the Tang Court. Apparently, this was so because northern India had fallen to the Muslim invaders. In contrast, China's Tang dynasty had successfully defeated and repulsed the Islamic armies.) Tansen Sen's study on Chinese maritime networks to southern Asia outlines the politico-strategic nature of China-India interactions during the first half of the second millennium:

> For the Ming court, the expeditions of Zheng He, the tributary missions that ensued, the granting of titles to or writing imperial proclamations for the local rulers, and the involvement in the political disputes, all formed an integral part of its ideology to underscore the leadership of the Ming emperor in the known world. Moreover, the Ming court through these actions wanted to demonstrate its supremacy over previous Chinese dynasties in regard to controlling and civilizing foreign states. The activities of the Ming emissaries in the Indian subcontinent suggest that the region was considered an integral part of the "Great Unified [Empire]" doctrine.... The Yuan court, under Qubilai Khan, explored the Indian coast to establish tributary, commercial, and strategic relationship as part of his imperialistic endeavor. The early Ming rulers, on the other hand, tried to use their superior naval force to bring the Indian kingdoms within the folds of the rhetorical Chinese world order.[32]

In short, the period between the twelfth and fifteenth centuries in the second millennium witnessed a major transformation in India's relations with China. The predominantly commercial exchanges of the second millennium brought about a shift in Chinese perceptions of India, which were markedly different from Chinese views of India in the first millennium when religion and culture ruled the roost. Direct trade between China's Quanzhou and India's west coast ceased sometime around the middle of the fifteenth century due to a shift in regional trade patterns and internal political upheavals. It may not be an oversimplification to argue that if the first millennium was the age of *Pax Indica*, the second millennium was the age of *Pax Sinica*. In the first millennium (during the years 0 to 1000), India was the world's pre-eminent economic power, closely followed by China. In the first half of the second millennium (1100 to 1500), China overtook India as the world's largest economy, relegating India to second place. This is corroborated in economic historian Angus Maddison's pioneering study, *The World Economy: A Millennial Perspective*, which shows that India was the world's largest economy with a 32.9 percent share of the worldwide GDP in the first century and 28.9 percent in the eleventh century. During the years 1500–1600 as well, India was second only to China in terms of world GDP share and remained among the top until as late as seventeenth century.[33] Even as recently as 1820, China and India accounted for 49 percent of the world economy.

Until the fifteenth century, China and India were still far ahead of Europe in almost all aspects of life, and the flow of manufactured goods and technological know-how was mostly from East to West. Before the age of European colonization, China accounted for about 33 percent of the world's manufactured goods and India for about 25 percent. China under the Song (960–1267) and Qing (1644–1911) dynasties was the world's greatest power. Under the Guptas (320–950 AD) and Moghuls (1526–1857), India's economic, military, and cultural prowess was the object of envy. Then in a complete reversal of fortune, the mighty Asian civilizations suddenly declined and disintegrated, and were eventually conquered by European powers. While India's experience of threats from European maritime powers occurred in the seventeenth century, China's came only in the nineteenth century. In the eighteenth century, by increasing its hold over India, the British East India Company managed to squeeze most of its European rivals out of the trade with China. Initially, the company's chief line of trade was selling raw cotton from India and importing silk from China. In the early nineteenth century it began to engage in opium smuggling in a big way, growing the opium in India and selling it in China, culminating in the two Anglo-Chinese Opium Wars in 1840 and 1857, which broke the back of the Manchu China.[34] In the last three centuries of the second millennium, first India and then China were reduced to mere economic appendages of the industrialized West. After a hiatus of nearly 300 years, both are once again on their growth trajectories, and the economic contest between China and India has resumed once again in the third millennium.

Hierarchy: Tribute and the Doctrine of *Mandala* ("Concentric Circles")

Whereas modern nation-states need clearly *defined* and *demarcated boundaries*, pre-modern states, empires and kingdoms existed within *temporary* and *undefined frontiers*. Just as in any traditional hierarchical society, rulers and the ruled have assigned places; in international society, the big and powerful and small and weak have their assigned places. Imperial China had regulated its relations with other states by a tribute system, under which foreign rulers were treated like vassals of the emperor. When China was weak, tribute ceased; when strong, it was resumed. A tributary relationship did not necessarily imply a Chinese military presence or direct administrative control. Strategically, the tributary system was essentially a defensive measure insofar as it created a zone of buffer states on the empire's periphery. It also helped identify potential allies in the event of a conflict against common adversaries. Economically, it was profitable because the tribute bearer would invariably receive from the benevolent emperor gifts worth more than the tribute given to the emperor. The Song Court's decision to link maritime trade to the tributary system was one of the key reasons for the increased competition among foreign traders who outdid each other in paying obeisance to China's rulers in order to win preferential trade concessions.[35] The skilful use of economic carrots in return for an acceptance of suzerain or subordinate status seems to be at work today in China's liberal trade arrangements with countries that strictly abide by the "One China" policy and toe Beijing's line on global issues.

The tributary system was based on power asymmetry or an institutionalized inequality in relations between the Middle Kingdom and the tributaries, which served to reinforce the belief in the superiority of Chinese civilization amongst its neighbors. This power asymmetry was intrinsic to the stability of the Sino-centric tributary system for many centuries before the arrival of more advanced European powers in Asia.[36] Other empires in history have employed similar measures. While the Chinese nationalist view recollects the Chinese sphere of influence in territories from the Russian far east across Southeast Asia and the Tibetan plateau into the Himalayas, the Indian nationalist worldview counts among India's tributaries peoples and states variously influenced by the Hindu and Buddhist religious traditions and languages (Pali and Sanskrit) stretching from Afghanistan to Indonesia.[37] This hierarchical way of conceptualizing foreign relations dominated Asian people's thinking at least until the late nineteenth century. So the Westphalian state system based on the concept of legal equality or state sovereignty distinguished itself not only from the old feudal system in Europe, but also from other forms of suzerainty that existed at that time in Asia—in China, India, and the Arab Islamic world.

The traditional Chinese concept of international relations was also based upon concentric circles from the imperial capital outwards through variously dependent states to the barbarians, which stands in sharp contrast to the theory of equal sovereign states developed by the West.[38] As Rafe de Crespigny notes: "The relationships may be described in intimate style, as father and mother, elder and younger brother, or even lips and teeth, but there is a hierarchy, and the relationship may be confirmed by force. In this respect, natural Chinese interest in East and Southeast Asia is influenced not only by a sense of good order but also by expectations of control and guidance."[39] This theory of international relations based on concentric circles resembles the concept of *Mandala* as outlined in Kautilya's *Arthashastra* more than 2,000 years ago. Inter-state relations in Ancient India were of the most Machiavellian character. Much as in Imperial China, the rightful fruits of victory in ancient India were tribute, homage, and subservience, but not annexation. The basic concept which governed the relations of one king with another was the doctrine of the "circles" (*Mandala*), which postulated that a king's neighbor is his natural enemy, while the king beyond his neighbor is his natural ally. As noted Indologist A. L. Basham observed: "The working of this principle can be seen throughout the history of Hindu India in the temporary alliances of two kingdoms to accomplish the encirclement and destruction of the kingdoms between them."[40] The Chinese dynasties had followed a similar policy of encircling and "attacking nearby neighbor and maintaining friendly relations with more distant kingdoms" (*yuan jiao jin gong*).

The Concept of Centrality: "The Middle Kingdom Syndrome"

Before the nineteenth century, "China can reasonably be considered to have been 'more equal' than the other countries of East Asia; in South Asia, the same applied to India under the Moghuls" (and much earlier, under the Guptas and Mauryas).[41] When Chinese and Indian elites speak of restoring their country's rightful place in the world, they give expression to a concept of "centrality" in Asia and the wider world. This concept reflects their perception that as the foundation of regional cultural patterns, their rightful place is at the apex of world hierarchy. The notion of Chinese supremacy is illustrated by the manner in which alien rulers once in power, including the Mongols and the Manchus, invariably adopted Confucian culture and institutions.[42] Both China and India, wrote Austin Coates, "share the same concept of their own centrality."[43] Apparently, the diffusion of Chinese culture in East Asia and Indian religions and culture throughout Asia supports their perceptions of "centrality". Since there was not much interaction between the two Asian centers of civilizations and power despite their proximity, each had developed, by and large, in its own isolation, with its own sphere of influence and worldview regarding its place in the wider world. Historically and civilizationally, China in eastern Asia and India in southern Asia enjoyed supremacy, thereby reinforcing their notion of "centrality." Coates further notes that:

> The concept of centrality is politically—in the widest sense of that word—the most fundamentally important fact about these two countries, since it is the basis of their entire outlook on life, toward

> themselves, toward their neighbors, toward other lands, toward the world, and toward the universe. *Without understanding and taking account of the concept of centrality, no harmonious and profitable economic and political relations with these two countries are possible....* Chinese and Indians, individually and en masse, think and speak from a position of absolute centrality.... Viewing the world and all human activity from this standpoint of centrality inevitably brings with it a certain sense of superiority.... *Where the Indian centrality is of the mind, the Chinese centrality is material and terrestrial*, personified in the Chinese race, and supremely embodied in former times by kings, later by emperors.... The truth is that each centrality has known of the other's existence for considerably more than two thousand years. Yet neither has ever realized that the other is a centrality similar to itself, with the same comprehensive, changeless, and absolute view of itself, the world, and the universe.... *The concept of centrality is itself responsible for the blindness China and India exhibit in regard to each other's nature*. The concept is enormous and noble, it is the roots and trunk of a great tree of civilization. Yet in a certain sense it can be compared with pride, which similarly contains an unusual measure of blindness.... Whenever the concept is damaged, one may expect reactions similar to those of a man of excessive pride when the myth of his cleverness or power is exploded.[44]

Whenever China has been ascendant in its history, its emperors as well as discreetly assenting rulers of neighboring small states have assumed the country to be a kind of "universal" center. The small-state rulers were expected to and did offer tribute and homage. This notion of centrality, however, which lies at the heart of the concept of "Middle Kingdom" (*Zhong guo*) in China, was "damaged" severely as it came in contact with other non-Chinese civilizations. As Martin Jacques notes: "China lives in and with its past to such an extent that it is tormented by its failure during the late twentieth century to stay at the top of the international system."[45] This largely explains the CCP's obsession with "catching up with the West" or "leapfrogging" to emerge as Number One Power in the world (*Zhongguo di yi*) so as to restore China to its lost grandeur. Anyone who has lived in China and reads Chinese language sources is well aware of this great patriotic national obsession.[46] Its roots go back to the late nineteenth century "Self-Strengthening Movement" (*ziligengshen*), to Mao's "Great Leap Forward" in the late 1950s (which sought to displace Britain as the world's largest steel producer but ended in a disastrous famine that took millions of lives), and to Deng Xiaoping's "Four Modernizations" strategy outlined in 1978 (which finally succeeded in beating the West at its own game). As in the past, China's re-emergence as the fulcrum of the world economy in the twenty-first century is meant to restore its traditional supremacy in the world.

A strong and powerful Imperial China, much like Czarist Russia, became expansionist in Inner Asia as opportunity arose and strength allowed. This gradual westward expansion over the centuries extended Imperial China's control over Tibet and parts of Central Asia (now Xinjiang). Modern China is, in fact, an "empire-state" masquerading as a nation-state. The People's Republic of China's present geographical limits reflect the frontiers established during the spectacular episode of eighteenth century Qing (Manchu) expansionism, which were then hardened into fixed national boundaries (except outer Mongolia) following the imposition of the Westphalian nation-state system over Asia in the nineteenth and twentieth centuries. The Chinese Communist Party (CCP) leadership consciously conducts itself as the heir to China's imperial legacy, often employing the symbolism and rhetoric of empire. From primary school textbooks to television historical dramas, the state-controlled information system has force-fed generations of Chinese on a diet of nationalist bluster and imperial China's grandeur. The writing and rewriting of history from a nationalistic perspective to promote national unity and regime legitimacy has been accorded the highest priority by China's rulers, both Nationalists and Communists. The Chinese are firm believers in the notion that those who have mastered the past control their present and chart their own futures along with those of others. In its diplomacy as well, Beijing places a very high value on "the history card" (often a revisionist interpretation of history) for achieving its foreign policy objectives, especially to extract territorial and diplomatic concessions. As Martin Jacques puts it: "Imperial Sinocentrism shapes and underpins modern Chinese nationalism."[47]

It was only as a result of the extension of Imperial China's borders to Tibet and Xinjiang (a.k.a. Eastern Turkestan) that the modern nation-states of China and India came in close physical contact. Unlike Imperial China, however, India never developed a pro-active defense of its strategic frontiers. A case in point is the building of the 1,500 mile-long Great Wall by successive Chinese dynasties to keep out nomadic invaders from the north. Despite the fact that nearly all of India's invaders—Alexander of Macedonia, the Scythians, Mohammed of Ghori, Mahmud of Gaznavi, Tamurlane, Nadir Shah, Babur the Moghul—came down the same Khyber and Bolan mountain passes to loot, rape, and pillage every few years or so, no attempt was made to erect impenetrable defenses (i.e., a Great Wall of India). Therein lay a key difference between the strategic cultures of China and India: the former's preference for clearly defined and protected hard borders versus the latter's acceptance of undefined and unprotected, soft frontiers.

In contrast with China, India also lacked a central authority and did not engage in the physical subjugation of neighboring countries. As China moved south, some races vanished altogether, while others were subjected to a process of absorption and assimilation into the broader Chinese identity. As John Garver observes, "China's history has seen a process of gradual expansion in which more numerous, richer, and better-organized Han settlers have assimilated lesser non-Han peoples."[48] This process of expansion, assimilation, and pacification mainly via demographic penetration of nearby lands and buffer states accelerated in Manchuria, Inner Mongolia, Xinjiang, and Tibet during the twentieth century. Today the homelands of China's old conquerors, the Mongols and Manchus—"the barbarians from the north"—are both overwhelmingly Han. This Sinification process is now reportedly under way in northern Burma, Laos, Central Asia, and the Russian Far East. In India, on the other hand, no deliberate attempt could be made to change the demographic balance either in Kashmir or the northeastern states. Coates offers a philosophical explanation: "The Indian centrality is of the mind, [whereas] the Chinese centrality is material and terrestrial." The concept of India as a political entity was as hazy as ideas of what lay beyond its borders. India's capitulation to invaders has historically been ascribed to the fractious nature of its polity. That tradition holds true of India today. Unlike the Chinese, Indians are not known for thinking and acting strategically.[49] India's territorial boundaries shrank following the 1947 partition that broke up the civilizational unity of the subcontinent going back 2,000 years to the first Mauryan Empire. Soon thereafter, the occupation of Tibet in 1950 allowed China to extend its reach and influence into a region where it had, in terms of culture and civilization, previously exercised little or no influence in the past. Whereas India is non-status-quoist in terms of *status*, power and influence, China remains non-status-quoist in terms of *territory*, power and influence. It is well known that the idea of national sovereignty goes back to the sixteenth century Europe. However, the idea of maritime sovereignty is largely a mid-twentieth century American concoction that has now been seized upon by China and others to extend their maritime frontiers in the South China Sea. Beijing reportedly claims around 80 percent of the South China Sea as its "historic waters" and has now elevated it to "core interests" (along with Taiwan and Tibet).[50] The continued reinterpretation of history to advance contemporary political, territorial, and maritime claims coupled with the CCP's ability to turn "nationalistic eruptions" on and off like a tap during moments of tension with the United States, Japan, India, and Vietnam makes it difficult for Beijing to reassure its neighbors that China's peaceful rise does not require balancing or hedging strategies.

It was the task of conversion of the *undefined frontiers of ancient civilizations* into clearly *defined* and *demarcated boundaries of modern nation-states* that brought about the armed clashes in the late 1950s. China-India relations have been tense ever since a border dispute led to a full-scale war in 1962 and armed skirmishes in 1967 and 1987. Several rounds of talks held over more than a quarter of a century (since 1981) have failed to resolve the disputed claims. An unsettled border provides China the strategic leverage to keep India uncertain about its intentions and nervous about its capabilities, while exposing India's vulnerabilities and weaknesses and ensuring New Delhi's "good behavior" on issues of vital concern to China. More importantly, unless and until Beijing succeeds in totally pacifying and Sinicizing Tibet as it has Inner Mongolia, China is unlikely to give up the "bargaining chip" that an unsettled boundary vis-à-vis India provides it with.

Chinese strategic thinkers perceive the emerging multipolar world similar to that of the Warring States era (475–221 BC), which was characterized by power rivalries, conflicts, shifting alliances, and betrayals, with some states competing to become a hegemon and others forming alliances to prevent any state from attaining that dominant status. This outlook necessitates distrust of strong, powerful neighbors (e.g., India) and preference for small, weak, and subordinate or client states. John Garver in his *Protracted Contest: Sino-Indian Rivalry in the Twentieth Century* reaches the same conclusion:

> China's long-term security interests and the long-term growth of Chinese prominence in Asia would be best served by having more, smaller states rather than one larger state on China's southern border. Thus, Chinese policy has sought to prevent the possibility of Indian domination or unification of the South Asian region. An Indian-led South Asian bloc would be far more dangerous (because it would be more powerful) if it pursued policies antithetical to Chinese interests.[51]

Historically, China sits as the equal of no one. The Middle Kingdom does not *see* others as equal.[52] The Chinese refer to their nation as "*Tian-xia*," or "all-under-heaven," implying a belief in cultural superiority based on virtue (*de*).[53] It reinforces belief in China's greatness and supposedly unique place in international relations. To imply equality with China is to offend the Chinese sense of what is "right." During a speech in the Parliament on November 25, 1959, India's Prime Minister Jawaharlal Nehru noted: "From fairly early in history, they [Chinese] have had a sense of greatness. They call themselves the 'Middle Kingdom,' and it seemed natural to them that other countries should pay tribute to them. Their thinking was that the rest of the world occupied a lower grade. That has made it difficult for us to understand the working of their mind, and what is more to the point, for them to understand the working of our mind."[54]

Classic Chinese statecraft dictates that there is no such thing as friendly foreign powers. "All states are either hostile or subordinate."[55] Subordinate states (North Korea, Burma, Cambodia, Pakistan) are allies and dependents who need to be protected and provided with economic, diplomatic, and military support, whereas hostile states, who either do not kowtow to the Celestial Emperor or have close military ties with foreign powers (Japan, South Korea, Taiwan, India, and Vietnam), are enemies who need to be subdued by involving them in troublesome embroilments and/or by "teaching them a lesson." Whether Imperial, Nationalist or Communist, China has long sought either to install buffer states or to cultivate friendly, and preferably pliant, regimes or tributary states along its periphery. As Austin Coates states:

> The fact is that since 1949 [Beijing] has dictated a border policy identical with that which has been pursued at all times in the imperial past, whenever the country was in an internally strong position.... Actually, it is a very old story. The aim of Chinese imperial policy (as of Communist policy) was that neighbor states must be respectful, obedient, and in areas immediately adjacent to the Chinese lands, preferably impotent [and] sufficiently weak.[56]

Beijing's preference for friendly, pliant regimes all along the maritime chokepoints in the Indian Ocean sea lanes is not much different from the Ming Court's past attempts to dominate the maritime lanes by changing political regimes at various places (in Malacca, Sumatra, and Sri Lanka) so as to facilitate free trade and maritime commerce. Old attitudes remain well-entrenched. China's future power projection capabilities are likely to be influenced by ancient Chinese statecraft, in particular, the strategic tradition of punishing those who fail to pay tribute and show respect and deference to the Middle Kingdom. Apparently, politically subservient and compliant regimes on its borders add to Beijing's sense of security because "most Chinese strategists believe that China is more secure if other states are weaker and thus less secure."[57] A survey conducted in China in 2005 revealed that most interviewees thought that "a stronger China will try to restore its traditional vassal system." Once China emerges as an "unrivalled regional power and a major global actor, it will use its enhanced power to grant assistance and protection to 'the faithful countries,' in return for their alliance, obedience and inevitable submission and compliance."[58] It is true that all great powers (democratic or authoritarian) tend to behave in a similar hegemonic fashion once they reach the pinnacle of power. Nonetheless, China has a long historical track record of this behavior. Two sinologists have succinctly summed up Chinese attitudes toward interstate relations, war, and strategy, based as they are on Chinese strategic tradition:

> In Chinese eyes, the values of this cultural framework describe Chinese identity and reflect a self-perception of cultural superiority over China's lesser neighbours. The Chinese not only want to restore China's dominant role at the centre of Asia, but seek to establish their country as one of the major poles—second to none—in a multipolar world.... This conceptualisation of interstate relations based upon a hierarchical system with China at the top is ingrained in their cultural worldview. *Today, this sense of hierarchy is expressed in notions of comprehensive national power based on culture, economics and organisational power and military power...* The Chinese generally employ their military for limited purposes, usually to strengthen the credibility of Chinese power, shore up their status as the natural leader of Asia, test their opponent's will and intentions opportunistically, or teach a political lesson. Forces are employed at a time and place of Beijing's choosing, assuring surprise and overwhelming force. Moreover, *this strategy also reinforces the point that China's interests cannot be ignored, and emphasises that China's role in regional issues must be recognised as essential to their resolution. In this way, China assumes a dominant role in relation to its neighbours....* Although abjuring 'hegemonic' ambitions, Beijing's growing power in the region raises fears among its neighbours that it will inevitably pursue hegemonic ambitions at their expense.[59]

Having said that, it is worth noting here that the much-talked-about "Middle Kingdom syndrome" is not essentially Sino-centric or unique to China alone. All great centers of civilization and great powers have at times displayed elements of the Middle Kingdom: that is, a belief in universalism, a civilizing mission, and a sense of superiority. Even in the modern world there is an element of the Middle Kingdom in the attitude of the United States. This was true of Britain in the age of *Pax Britannica*. Before the age of the national territorial state and international law, non-egalitarian inter-state relations were not uncommon. As one observer points out: "The world order of Rome, Christendom, India, and the various Islamic empires of West Asia all shared unequal interstate relations.... Even in the most modern period of international law, the categories of less than sovereign states and vassal states have been recognized."[60]

Fundamentally, the key point is that historically and civilizationally, while China was the "Middle Kingdom" of eastern Asia, India sees itself as the "Middle Kingdom" of southern Asia. Much like the Chinese, the Indians' view of society as a hierarchy serves as a basis for their view of the world. India's elite sees "a hierarchical layering of nations according to wealth and power," and believes that "India should be in the top ranks of the world hierarchy—a Brahmin idea of the world."[61] Indian leaders since independence have believed that India was once a world power and therefore it *should* be the preeminent power in the South Asian/Indian Ocean region even though it lacks a clear strategy, determination, and many of the resources needed to achieve that objective in the future.

Furthermore, it is in China's and India's dealings in their immediate neighborhoods that the patterns and perceptions of the past appear most obvious, and provide contradictions and conflicts for the present and future. Both China and India have sought to establish a sort of Monroe Doctrine in their regions with mixed degrees of success. Both claim that their attitude toward their neighbors is essentially benevolent while making it clear that they must not make policies or take actions, or allow other nations to take measures in their countries that would impinge on, respectively, Chinese or Indian interests and security. If they do so, China and India are willing to apply pressure in one fashion or another to bring these neighboring states into line.[62] Both are, however, unable to reassert their traditional suzerainty over their smaller neighbors in East and South Asia respectively, as any attempt to do so encounters resistance from regional and extra-regional powers.

Geopolitical Shifts

Clearly, China and India are as much "civilization-states" as pre-modern "empire-states" and modern "nation-states." Their strategic cultures require both to regain the power and status their leaders consider appropriate to their countries' size, population, geographic position, and historical heritage. Their common desire to regain lost greatness has created grandiose ambitions, but geopolitical shifts, historical patterns, and contrasting perceptions have brought those ambitions into conflict. More importantly, the historical reference points for nationalist narratives in both capitals are different. The Indian nationalist narrative harks back to "the golden age" in the first millennium—between the second and eighth centuries—when religious, linguistic, and other cultural influences emanating from the subcontinent had fostered a wide sphere of influence that "extended from the Himalayan Mountains in the north to the seas in the south, into Southeast Asia on the east, to Persia in the West, and into Central Asia in the northwest."[63] This was the period when "India found itself occupying a unique place in the Chinese world order: a foreign kingdom that was culturally and spiritually revered as equal to the Chinese civilization."[64] In contrast is the modern Chinese nationalist narrative, wherein China's traditional tributary system encompassed large parts of Inner and Central Asia, Northeast Asia, Southeast Asia, and parts of South Asia (Nepal, Kashmir, Bhutan, Sikkim, Bengal, and Burma) prior to "the century of humiliation." In Chinese dynastic histories, "India is presented as one of many far-away regions that occasionally sent tribute missions to China and, thereby, acknowledged her status as a vassal state."[65] Stated simply, while India's elite looks back in history to the first millennium, the mandarins in Beijing have their country's superior position in the second millennium on their minds when they deal with India.

Both countries are focusing on increasing comprehensive national strength on a solid economic-technological base. The domestic political and economic developmental processes of India and China have tended to reinforce the competitive aspects of their relationship. Both suffer from a siege mentality borne out of their elites' acute consciousness of the fissiparous tendencies that make their countries' present political unity so fragile. To a considerable extent, this drive explains China's and India's national security policies and their competitive or conflictual relations with each other. Since India is one of the oldest civilizations and a former world power, the Indian elite believes their country has as much, if not more, right to great power status as China. Since the days of Prime Minister Jawaharlal Nehru, independent India has entertained hopes of a joint Sino-Indian leadership of Asia as a counter to Western influence, but the Chinese have shown no enthusiasm for sharing leadership of Asia with anyone, least of all India. For the main objective of China's Asia policy is to prevent the rise of a rival to challenge its status as the Asia-Pacific's sole "Middle Kingdom." As an old Chinese saying goes, "one mountain cannot accommodate two tigers." Checkmated in East Asia by three great powers—Russia, Japan, and the United States—Beijing has long seen South and Southeast Asia as its sphere of influence. Recognizing that strategic rival India has the size, might, numbers, and, above all, the intention to match China, Beijing has long followed a "*hexiao, gongda*" policy in southern Asia: "supporting and uniting with small (Pakistan, Bangladesh, Burma, Nepal, and Sri Lanka) to fight the big (India)." The "strategic space" in which India traditionally operated has become increasingly constricted due to Beijing's forays into Burma and the Indian Ocean region since the 1990s. From New Delhi's perspective, much of Beijing's penetration deep into the South Asian region in the second half of the twentieth century has been primarily at India's expense—a bitter pill to swallow as ancient India did not play second fiddle to China historically and civilizationally. This is one of the root causes of volatility and strain in the relationship.

If the past is a guide to the future, one can argue that the China-India rivalry has its roots in the desire of each for restoration of its historic status and influence (which prevailed before the arrival of European powers in Asia) and China's determination (albeit, for reasons mostly of India's own making) to deny India a role on the world stage commensurate with its size, population, military capability, economic potential, and civilizational attributes.[66] When Indian observer Rakshat Puri lamented in the late 1990s the fact that a sound "appreciation, and knowledge about each other's histories, traditions and cultures do not at present seem to exist in the policy-making circles of either the Chinese or the Indians,"[67] he was, in fact, echoing Austin Coates' view that "neither has ever realized that the other is a centrality similar to itself.... The concept of centrality is itself responsible for the blindness China and India exhibit in regard to each other's nature." Puri's view that "real peace between China and India can come only when relations between them are founded on equality," laudable as it is, may however be unrealistic. The Chinese have a deeply hierarchical view of the world and insist that India's growth must be "conducive to the equilibrium of the current international order" (translation: India must not equal or surpass China).[68]

There have been numerous occasions in history when China and India were simultaneously weak; there have been occasional moments of simultaneous cultural blossoming. But for more than half a millennium, Asia has not seen the two giants economically and militarily powerful and pursuing a policy of expansion at the same time. As Austin Coates pointed out: "This [expansion] ... is intrinsic to both in their relations with each other.... Each essentially exerts pressure on the other, China because she simply *does*, India because she simply *must*.... What would happen if both these civilizations were ever to become anything like equally powerful at the same time?"[69] Well, that time is now approaching fast, and it is likely to result in significant new geopolitical realignments. Both China after a "century of humiliation" and India after a millennium of decline are keen to assume the great power roles they believe to be their historical and civilizational right. Both want a new international status that is commensurate with their growing strength. Both remain suspicious of each other's long-term agenda and intentions, and both see themselves as newly rising great Asian powers whose time has finally come. The rise of Han nationalism is matched by the rise of Hindu nationalism. As India combines its potential economic might with strategic might, its foreign policy is becoming increasingly assertive. This means that a resurgent India will face a rising China, which will ensure a conflict of interests between the two giants unless their power competition is managed carefully. It is not so much a clash of civilizations as a clash of the two "Middle Kingdoms" which had historically dominated in southern Asia and eastern Asia respectively—a clash of identical worldviews, similar aspirations, and interests. All the indications point to a geopolitical contest between China and India over domination of South, Southeast, and Central Asia and the Indian Ocean region. Just as Sino-Indian interactions invariably affected the intermediary kingdoms in Central and Southeast Asia in the first and second millennia, the state of Sino-Indian relations will inevitably affect small and middle powers in the third millennium as well. The emergence of China and India as economic giants undoubtedly will throw a huge new weight onto the world's geopolitical balance. The nature of the rivalry will be determined by how domestic political and economic developments in these two countries affect their power, their outlooks, and their foreign and security policies.

Future Tense

All great powers are shaped by their own histories, values, and experiences and behave in distinct ways. The burden of history weighs heavily on Chinese and Indian elites. A desire to regain the lost glory and status, a sense of superiority, and the linkage between domestic and external security are common to both. For India, a fractious polity and the lack of strategic thinking continue to bedevil foreign policy-making. China confronts the historical problem of holding together a geographically large empire, as evident from the present government's attempt to create the sense of a united Chinese nationality in the face of perceived threats of internal unrest and foreign aggression (*nei luan wai huan*). The old tradition of stratagem and deception in strategic policy remains in vogue. The preceding analysis of Chinese and Indian strategic traditions indicates that as the preeminent and pivotal power in southern Asia, India perceives itself much as China has traditionally perceived itself in relation to eastern Asia. As in the past, the strategic cultures of China and India continue to influence their bilateral relations and how each handles its growing power and relates to other nations.

There exists a sharp political and cultural chasm between the two civilization-states. India embraces heterogeneity, accommodation, and pluralism. China worships homogeneity and uniformity. Its sense of superiority is based on a combination of cultural, political, and economic hubris. As China's power grows, a millennia-old sense of superiority will manifest itself in Chinese foreign policy behavior as it seeks to impose its will and leave its imprint in different parts of the world. Their underlying power rivalry and their self-images as natural great powers and centers of civilization and culture continue to drive them to support different countries and causes. Asia has never known both China and India growing strong simultaneously in such close proximity with overlapping spheres of influence. New economic prosperity and military strength is reawakening nationalist pride in India, which could bring about a clash with Chinese nationalism, if not handled skillfully. The existence of two economically powerful nations will create new tensions as they both strive to stamp their authority on the region. In the short to medium term, their priority on domestic stability, economic development, and pragmatism in foreign policy would keep ambitions in check. It is possible that economically prosperous and militarily confident China and India will come to terms with each other eventually as their mutual containment policies start yielding diminishing returns, but this is unlikely to happen for a few decades. Since China and India have often shown an uncanny knack of being their own worst enemies, it is also possible that the two Asian goliaths may not make it and instead break up into several independent states. After all, much of Chinese and Indian history is made up of long periods of internal disunity and turmoil when the centrifugal forces brought down even the most powerful empires.

Notes

[1] See J. Mohan Malik, "India copes with the Kremlin's fall," *Orbis*, 37:1 (Winter 1993), 69-87 and "China-India relations in the Post-Soviet era: the continuing rivalry," *China Quarterly,* 142 (June 1995), 317-55.

[2] Y. Klein, "A theory of strategic culture," *Comparative Strategy*, 10:2 (January-March 1991), 5; P. J. Katzenstein (ed), *The Culture of National Security: Norms and Identity in World Politics* (New York: Columbia University Press, 1996).

[3] See T. Delpech, "Nuclear weapons and the 'new world order': early warning from Asia?" *Survival*, 40:4 (Winter 1998-99), 57.

[4] A. I. Johnston, Cultural Realism: Strategic Culture and Grand Strategy in Chinese History (New Jersey: Princeton University Press, 1995) 258.

[5] G. Tanham, "India's strategic culture," *Washington Quarterly*, 15:1 (Winter 1992), 129-142.

[6] Chinese monk Xuanzang's arrival in India in the early 630s coincided with the establishment of a vast empire in northern India by King Harsha (r. 606-647), with its capital at Kanauj, which extended from north-western Bengal in the east to the river Beas in Punjab in the west.

[7] *Daoxuan: Shijia Fangzhi* (Accounts of the land of Sakyamuni), written in 650, published in 1924 by Ye Gongzhuo), juan 1, 3B, cited in Tan Chung, "The changing Indian images in the Chinese mind during the nineteenth and twentieth centuries," Chapter 14, in Rita Sil (ed), *Images of India in World Literatures* (New Delhi: National Publishing House, 1987), 120, 119-150. Historians believe that Daoxuan's (596-667) passionate portrayal of India as a civilized and sophisticated society was perhaps overstated and apparently necessitated by the frequent criticisms levelled against Buddhism by the Daoist and Confucian rivals in his home country.

[8] India's Hindu-Buddhist civilizational identity underwent dramatic change after the Muslim invasions of India. "India" of the 15th century was not the same as "India" of the 3rd century BCE.

[9] B. K. Sarkar, *Chinese Religion through Hindu Eyes* (Shanghai: Commercial Press, 1916), 252.

[10] R. Tagore, *Talks in China* (Calcutta: Arunoday Art Press, n.d.), 2-3.

[11] D. Wilson, *China: The Big Tiger* (London: Abacus, 1997), 437, 515.

[12] "Indian influence on Chinese thought," Chapter XXIII in S. Radhakrishnan et al (ed), *History of Philosophy: Eastern and Western,* Volume 1 (London: George Allen & Unwin, 1952), p. 574, 573-589.

[13] Tansen Sen, *Buddhism, Diplomacy, and Trade: The Realignment of Sino-Indian Relations, 600-1400* (Honolulu: Association for Asian Studies and the University of Hawai'i Press, 2003), 2.

[14] See T. Sen, "The formation of Chinese maritime networks to Southern Asia, 1200-1450," *Journal of the Economic & Social History of the Orient*, 49:4 (2006), 448, 421-453.

[15] C. Wake, "The great ocean-going ships of Southern China in the age of Chinese maritime voyaging to India, Twelfth to Fifteenth Centuries," *International Journal of Maritime History*, 9:2 (December 1997), 73, 51-81.

[16] Wake, "The great ocean-going ships. . . ," 78-79.

[17] The southern parts of the subcontinent retained their Hindu heritage, as exemplified by the Chola kingdom.

[18] See Cao Changching and J. D. Seymour (eds), *Tibet Through Dissident Chinese Eyes: Essays on Self-Determination* (New York: M. E. Sharpe, 1998), xxiii.

[19] Johnston, *Cultural Realism*; cited in R. S. Ross, "The geography of peace: East Asia in the twenty-first century," *International Security*, 23:4 (Spring 1999), 103-4.

[20] Tanham, "India's strategic culture," 135.

[21] R. Roy-Chaudhury, *Sea Power and Indian Security* (London: Brassey's 1995), 15; G. Coedes, *The Indianized States of Southeast Asia* (University of Hawaii Press, 1968) 46-47, 30-31.

[22] See Nicola Di Cosmo, *Ancient China and its Enemies* (Cambridge University Press, 2002). The hitherto popular interpretation was based mostly on the great Chinese historian Ssu-ma Chien's "Records of the Grand Historian" (99 BC).

[23] See Pan Yihong, *Son of Heaven and Heavenly Qaghan* (Bellingham: Western Washington University Press, 1997).

[24] See D. Roy, *The Pacific War and Its Political Legacies* (Westport, CT: Praeger, 2009), pp. 11-13.

[25] The term "Han Chinese" is a latter-day invention (named after the Han dynasty that followed the Qin empire but lasted a much longer 400 years). The Han Chinese are, in fact, "a racial mix of the northern Chinese and the nomadic steppe tribes." See M. Jacques, *When China Rules the World* (New York: The Penguin Press, 2009), 244; F. Dikotter (ed), *The Construction of Racial Identities in China and Japan* (London: Hurst and Company, 1997), 20.

[26] See Tanham, "India's strategic culture," 137.

[27] G. Wade, "The Zheng He voyages: a reassessment," *Journal of the Malaysian Branch of the Royal Asiatic Society*, 78:1: (2005), 37-58; G. Wade, "Ming China and Southeast Asia in the 15th century: a reappraisal," *ARI Working Paper* No. 28, July 2004 <http://www.ari.nus.edu.sg/docs/wps/wps04_028.pdf>.

[28] Sen, "The formation of Chinese maritime networks to Southern Asia, 1200-1450."

[29] P. Bowring, "China's growing might and the spirit of Zheng He," *International Herald Tribune* (*IHT*), August 2, 2005, 7.

[30] Wade, "The Zheng He voyages: a reassessment," 78, 51.

[31] For details, see T. Sen, "The military campaigns of Rajendra Chola and the Chola-Srivijaya-China triangle," Unpublished paper, 2008.

[32] Sen, "The formation of Chinese maritime networks to Southern Asia, 1200-1450," 445, 447.

[33] A. Maddison, *The World Economy: A Millennial Perspective* (OECD Development Centre, 2001).

[34] It was during the British rule that Chinese tea ("*cha*" pronounced as "*chai*" in Hindi) was introduced in India.

[35] Sen, "The military campaigns of Rajendra Chola and the Chola-Srivijaya-China triangle."

[36] Jacques, When China Rules the World, 375.

[37] J. W. Garver, *Protracted Contest: Sino-Indian Rivalry in the Twentieth Century* (Seattle and London: University of Washington Press, 2001), 12-16.

[38] R. de Crespigny, "Tradition and Chinese foreign policy," in S. Harris and G. Klintworth (eds), *China As a Great Power* (Melbourne: Longman, and NY: St Martin's Press, 1995), 43.

[39] de Crespigny, "Tradition and Chinese foreign policy," 43.

[40] A. L. Basham, *The Wonder that was India* (Fontana, Collins, 1967), 128; Kautilya, *The Arthashastra* (New Delhi: Penguin Books, 1987), 541-680.

[41] H. C. Hinton, "China as an Asian power," in T. W. Robinson and D. Shambaugh (eds), *Chinese Foreign Policy: Theory and Practice* (Clarendon Press, 1994), 359.

[42] Jacques, *When China Rules the World*, 239; Wang Gungwu, *Joining the Modern World* (Singapore: Singapore university Press, 2000), 11.

[43] Austin Coates, *China, India and the Ruins of Washington* (New York: The John Day Company, 1972), 16.

[44] Coates, China, India and the Ruins of Washington, 49-54. Italics mine.

[45] Jacques, When China Rules the World, 418.

[46] "China's big goal in the 21st century is to become world's number one, the top power," argues Senior Colonel Liu Mingfu in *China Dream [Zhongguo meng]* (Beijing: Zhongguo youyi chuban gongsi, 2010).

[47] Jacques, When China Rules the World, 244.

[48] J. W. Garver, Protracted Contest: Sino-Indian rivalry in the Twentieth Century, 69.

[49] Tanham, "India's strategic culture," 130; R. Puri, "India and the 'Middle Kingdom'," *Hindustan Times*, March 17, 1999.

[50] Minxin Pei, "An assertive China the 'new normal'?" *The Diplomat*, November 24, 2010 <http://www.carnegieendowment.org/publications/index.cfm?fa=view&id=42011>.

[51] Garver, Protracted Contest, 30.

[52] Coates, China, India and the Ruins of Washington, 233.

[53] I. C. Ojha, *Chinese Foreign Policy in an Age of Transition* (Boston: Beacon Press, 1971), 4-5.

[54] Cited from N. Menon, "State, strategy, power, and policy analyzing China and India," *Indian Defence Review*, 23:3 (July-September 2008), 95.

[55] Coates, China, India and the Ruins of Washington, 293.

[56] Coates, China, India and the Ruins of Washington, 349.

[57] B. N. Garrett & B. S. Glaser, "Chinese perspectives on nuclear arms control," *International Security*, 20:3 (Winter 1995/96), 75.

[58] S. Sartori, "How China sees India and the world," *Heartland: Eurasian Review of Geopolitics*, 3 (Hong Kong: Cassan Press, 2005), 57.

[59] M. Weisenbloom and R. Spotswood, "China's emerging strategic doctrine," *China Strategic Review*, 3:1 (Spring 1998), 24-53. Empahsis added.

[60] Ojha, Chinese Foreign Policy in an Age of Transition, 17.

[61] Tanham, "India's strategic culture," 131.

[62] As Coates puts it: "Apart from the Indians, whom the Chinese mind simply cannot cope with, the Chinese regard the rest of Asia as lesser people, deserving of benevolence by virtue of the plain fact that they *are* lesser people." Coates, *China, India and the Ruins of Washington*, 216. On India's claim that its attitude toward its neighbors is essentially benevolent, see Tanham, "India's strategic culture," 133.

[63] Garver, Protracted Contest: Sino-Indian Rivalry in the Twentieth Century, 11-12, 15.

[64] Sen, Buddhism, Diplomacy, and Trade: The Realignment of Sino-Indian Relations, 600-1400, 8.

[65] Sen, Buddhism, Diplomacy, and Trade: The Realignment of Sino-Indian Relations, 600-1400, 53.

[66] K. Subrahmanyam, "Understanding China: Sun Tzu and Shakti," *Times of India*, June 5, 1998, 7.

[67] R. Puri, "India and the 'Middle Kingdom,'" *Hindustan Times*, March 17, 1999, 7.

[68] See Editorial, "India's surprising but welcome message," *Global Times*, February 22, 2010 <http://opinion.globaltimes.cn/editorial/2010-02/506893.html>.

[69] Coates, *China, India and the Ruins of Washington*, 17, 347.

3
India's China Debate: Eyeing the Dragon

Just as the Indian sub-continental plate constantly rubs and pushes against the Eurasian tectonic plate, causing friction and volatility in the entire Himalayan mountain range, India's relations with China also remain volatile, friction-, and tension-ridden because of past experience, a war, territorial disputes, a paucity of parallel interests, conflicting worldviews, and divergent geopolitical interests. Today, India and China are rising powers engaged in a competition for natural resources and supremacy in overlapping areas of influence in Asia. In India's policy circles and media, "the China debate" is the most active than at any time since the 1962 Sino-Indian War. How to deal with China plugs into a wider debate in India—a debate about India's role in Asia and the world. For Indians, "the China challenge" comes in four forms—enmity, envy, awe, and emulation: the territorial dispute along the 4,057-kilometer China-India border and the intensifying geopolitical rivalry with China that may one day lead to another war between the two Asian giants, the economic reality of a China ahead of India by all economic measures, ideological self-doubt about the "virtues" of India's democratic experiment compared with China's "Market-Leninist" (free market plus authoritarian) model, and the quest to emulate Beijing's strategy of accumulating "comprehensive national power" while sidestepping contentious issues. India's economic reforms, in particular, have gained a big boost from the fear that it may fall behind China. This chapter first offers a brief overview of key issues and principal drivers in India's bilateral relations with China. It then identifies major stakeholders in India's policy-making process and examines three different schools of thought in India's China debate.

Key Issues and Developments

India's relations with China have been soured by territorial disputes, notably the rejection by the Chinese of the British-drawn McMahon Line of 1914 separating Tibet and India, the flight of the Dalai Lama to India in 1959, and the dispute remaining from the 1962 Sino-Indian border war, in which China occupied 14,500 square miles of territory in the Ladakh region of the Jammu and Kashmir state. Since the 1962 War, relations have been characterized by mutual antagonism, rivalry, distrust, and hostilities. The Sino-Soviet split of the 1960s and the Indo-Pakistani animosity and subsequent Sino-Pakistani alliance further exacerbated tensions and rivalry. Border skirmishes took place in 1965 during the India-Pakistan War and in 1967 on the Sikkim-Tibet border. The bilateral relationship nosedived during the India-Pakistan war of 1971, which led to Bangladesh's independence. Interactions were revived in 1976 with an exchange of ambassadors; however, until 1979, there was no meeting of minds, and the countries' belligerency was pronounced in counter-strategies each adopted to thwart the influence of the other.

Soon after independence from the British, India signed treaties with the Himalayan kingdoms of Bhutan, Nepal, and the small princely protectorate of Sikkim in 1949–50, which drew them closer into India's security orbit, thereby signaling to China that the security of their northern borders was India's responsibility. Since the 1962 War, India has kept a watchful eye on China's relations with Nepal and Bhutan. Whenever Nepalese rulers have tried to play "the China card" in their relations with India, problems have arisen (for example, the 1989–90 blockade and the Maoist government's fall in 2009) and tremendous pressure has been brought to bear on Nepal to conform. Sikkim was annexed by the Indira Gandhi government in 1975 to bolster India's defenses against China. India's involvement in the Sinhalese-Tamil ethnic conflict in Sri Lanka during the 1980s was another prime example of New Delhi's attempts to realize its twin objectives of enhancing its strategic position and containing the geopolitical fallout from Tamil ethnic separatism threatening India's unity and integrity. Through the Gandhi-Jayewardene agreement of 1987, New Delhi coerced Sri Lanka into giving India a veto over the use of its port facilities. Throughout the 1970s and 1980s, China aligned itself with Pakistan and cultivated closer ties with the small states of Sri Lanka, Nepal, and Bangladesh to undermine India's attempts to establish regional predominance in South Asia. India responded by establishing closer ties with the Soviet Union

(1971–1991) and China's rival in Indo-China, Vietnam, and supported the Hanoi-backed Hun Sen government in Cambodia.

Following visits by Indian and Chinese Foreign Ministers to each other's capitals in 1979 and 1981 respectively, both sides agreed to find a mutually acceptable solution to the boundary dispute through negotiations. Eight rounds of talks were held between 1981 and 1987, but failed to find a solution. The period from June 1986 to May 1987 once again saw a marked deterioration in relations over alleged Chinese intrusion in Sumdorong Chu Valley in Arunachal Pradesh in June 1986, renewed tension on the border resulting in armed clashes, and led to a fresh spate of accusations, counter-accusations, and warnings of "serious consequences" from Beijing. However, tensions were defused through high-level dialogue, and a decision was made to upgrade the level of talks from the bureaucratic to the political level. During Indian Prime Minister Rajiv Gandhi's official visit to China in December 1988, both sides agreed to establish a joint working group to create conditions for "a fair and reasonable settlement" and "to maintain peace in the border region."[1] They also agreed to work toward improving overall bilateral relations. Agreements were signed to establish direct commercial flights and to increase scientific, technological, and cultural exchanges between China and India. In September 1993, China and India signed an agreement "to maintain peace and tranquility" along their disputed Himalayan border. This agreement between the two Asian giants—which required both sides to respect the Line of Actual Control (LAC), that is, to maintain the status quo pending a peaceful, final boundary settlement, and to reduce military forces along the border in accordance with the principle of "mutual and equal security"—was widely perceived as a "landmark agreement" and "a significant step forward" in their uneasy relations since the 1950s.[2] This breakthrough was a logical culmination of a series of developments since the late 1980s, especially the visit of India's premier to Beijing in 1988 and the reciprocal visit of China's premier to New Delhi in 1991, the end of the Cold War and the bipolar system following the Soviet collapse, the consequent dramatic changes in the global strategic environment, and the overall improvement in bilateral relations between China and India. Throughout the 1980s and 1990s, the conventional wisdom was that since neither China nor India would ever give up the areas they occupied, the most feasible settlement would be the acceptance by both sides of the existing LAC, with some minor adjustments in the eastern and western sectors. The "peace and tranquility" agreement signed by Premier Li Peng and Prime Minister Narasimha Rao in September 1993 was widely interpreted as an acceptance of "ground realities" by both Beijing and New Delhi.

In the early 1990s, India and China found themselves at the receiving end of the post–Cold War changes in global strategic environment in general and US strategy in particular, whose stated objective was "to prevent the emergence of any great power that can challenge American dominance in Europe or in Asia." India, long allied with the Soviet Union, was thrown off balance by the disintegration of its former ally and came under pressure from Washington on a range of issues—from nuclear weapons and missile proliferation to intellectual property rights and economic liberalization.[3] According to the Pentagon's "Defense Planning Draft, 1994–1999," Washington proposed to "discourage Indian hegemonic aspirations over the other states in South Asia and on the Indian Ocean."[4] Faced with a serious economic crisis, India followed China's example and embarked upon a similar path of export-oriented and investment-driven economic prosperity. The economic crisis effectively brought India's military modernization to a halt. India's declining defense expenditure contrasted sharply with double-digit increases in China's defense budgets post–Tiananmen Square massacre. The growing internal security preoccupations also constrained New Delhi's ability to play a wider role in the broader Asian region. For its part, China—isolated and ostracized by the West in the aftermath of the 1989 Tiananmen massacre—was sulking over what it perceived as the highly unbalanced, US-dominated unipolar world of the post-Soviet era. Beijing resented Washington's pronouncements on the issues of human rights, weapons sales and nuclear technology transfers, and trade issues. Hence, China saw some benefit in making common cause with India to resist "arm-twisting" by the United States. The Chinese leaders reportedly told the visiting Indian president in 1992 that "if Third World countries like China and India did not unite and co-operate they would be 'left behind,' and 'bullied' by others."[5]

At any rate, India's deteriorating relationship with Pakistan since the late 1980s provided additional incentive to improve relations with China.[6] A durable peace with China was supposed to help India concentrate on the more vexatious internal security problems in Kashmir, Assam, and elsewhere. Like India, China was also faced with its own separatist problems in Tibet and Xinjiang and the growing independence movement in Taiwan. At a time when the whole of Central and Inner Asia was in flux, Chinese leaderships worried about the resurgent nationalist movements based on ethnicity and religion in the border provinces of Tibet, Inner Mongolia, and Xinjiang receiving a boost from the collapse of the Soviet Union and the gaining of independence by the Baltic states, the Ukraine, and the Central Asian republics, which shared similar historical experiences. Unrest in Tibet in 1988 showed how vulnerable and tenuous the Chinese hold was over that country. India had as much interest in the stability and sustenance of multi-ethnic, multi-cultural, multi-religious states as China.

In short, post-Cold War realism coupled with the focus on economic development dictated that their common interests outweighed their differences at least for a decade or so. This realization led to a significant warming of Sino-Indian relations: Beijing promised not to use "the Pakistani card" against India and offered "flexibility" on Sikkim. The Chinese also adopted a somewhat neutral stance on the Kashmir dispute, favoring a bilateral India-Pakistan negotiated solution. More importantly, beginning in the late 1980s, the Chinese made public and private efforts to dissuade South Asian countries from assuming Beijing's partisan involvement in their disputes with India. For example, in 1990, the Chinese kept New Delhi informed of the Sri Lankan and Nepalese requests for arms transfers and of the scale and delivery details.[7] In return, India reassured China on the Tibetan question.[8] Signs of a "new era" became evident in the establishment of educational, cultural, and economic links. For the first time, in December 1993, Chinese naval vessels called at Indian ports. These positive developments led some observers to speculate whether Beijing had finally come round to accepting the idea of some sort of cross-recognition of spheres of influence: China's acceptance of Indian pre-eminence in South Asia in exchange for Indian acceptance of Chinese pre-eminence in Southeast Asia.[9] One analyst wondered whether the next logical step would be to reach a similar tacit understanding to delineate naval spheres of influence between the northern Indian Ocean and the South China Sea.[10]

However, veteran China-watchers ruled out a genuine *détente* between India and China in the post-Cold War era and predicted more competition and rivalry than cooperation. Pointing out that the dramatic improvement in Sino-Indian relations occurred in the immediate aftermath of the Tiananmen Square massacre when the Communist regime in Beijing was feeling isolated and vulnerable, they pointed to China's tendency to befriend enemies in times of adversity.[11] Besides, China was perceived as willing to co-operate with India only on specific issues considered important to Beijing, such as human rights, environment, and US hegemony, while doing little to assuage India's security concerns in its vicinity by curbing arms sales to Pakistan or making its intentions clear in Burma. All of India's neighbors remained

China's top five largest arms buyers: Pakistan, Burma, Bangladesh, Iran, and Sri Lanka. Significantly, Chinese leaders continued to balance high-level visits to India with tours in the region.[12] Further, Beijing's nuclear and missile assistance to Pakistan emerged as a major bone of contention throughout the 1990s and nearly overshadowed the territorial dispute. In 1995, China amended its No-First-Use (NFU) of nuclear weapons pledge to make it applicable only to nuclear-weapons-free zones and to countries that had signed the Nuclear Non-Proliferation Treaty (NPT), thereby effectively excluding India from its NFU pledge until New Delhi signed the NPT as a non-nuclear weapon state. For its part, Beijing had its own India concerns, most notably, India's hosting of the Tibetan government-in-exile and the growing warmth in India's relations with the United States.

The Sino-Indian relations weathered another serious downturn over India's 1998 nuclear tests when the nationalist Bharatiya Janata Party (BJP)-led coalition government cited "the China threat" as the main reason for going nuclear. During the 1999 Kargil War, even as Beijing cautioned Islamabad against escalating the level of conflict, the People's Liberation Army (PLA) increased both the intensity and frequency of its cross-border intrusions along the LAC in the Ladakh area of Kashmir. This was apparently aimed at keeping the Indian military under pressure on two fronts. It was during this period that President Jiang Zemin authorized a ten-year plan (1998–2008) to upgrade infrastructure and enhance military capabilities in Tibet and Xinjiang as part of the "Great Western Development Project," littering the barren terrain with highways, airports, and railways capable of moving large numbers of goods and troops at a short notice. Simultaneously, a diplomatic charm offensive to tighten China's embrace of India's smaller neighbors was also launched. India's size and power in South Asia make it an object of continuing resentment among its neighbors, who welcome China's embrace to balance Indian structural predominance. Civil wars in Sri Lanka and Nepal and the rapid radicalization of Pakistan and Bangladesh also opened space for Beijing to expand its footprint.[13] Consequently, the first decade of the twenty-first century saw Beijing elevating its ties with Burma, Bangladesh, Nepal, Sri Lanka, Mauritius, and the Maldives both to counter India's "Look East" policy that was bringing Indian economic and military interests into China's claimed sphere of influence in Southeast and East Asia and to gain access to naval bases in the Indian Ocean as part of Beijing's "Go South" strategy. High-level defense exchanges and joint military exercises between New Delhi and Washington ruffled feathers in Beijing. China voiced concern over the possible emergence of an "axis of democracy" (or the so-called

"Asian NATO") in the Asia-Pacific involving India, the United States, Japan, and Australia upgrading their defense ties.[14] As they began rubbing up against each other in Africa, Central Asia, the Middle East, the Indian Ocean region, and the South China Sea in competition for access to resources and markets, both China and India unveiled plans to expand their navies to protect the sea lanes of communication (SLOCs).

Simultaneously, a number of measures were taken to strengthen economic, political, and military ties between India and China. In July 2006, the two countries reopened the historical Nathu La Pass that had been closed since the 1962 War to further promote border trade. Since 2003, their militaries have started conducting joint exercises. A regular bilateral security dialogue has begun and meetings at the prime minister and foreign minister levels take place more frequently. India's trade with China has grown exponentially and could cross $60 billion in 2010 and more than double again by 2020.

However, friction and tension continue to simmer below the surface. Several rounds of talks at official and political levels over the last three decades have failed to resolve the border dispute. The two governments demonstrated their commitment to settling the territorial issue by appointing special representatives during Indian Prime Minister A. B. Vajpayee's 2003 visit to China. After 14 rounds of talks between the special representatives, progress remains painfully slow as the two sides remain deadlocked, with little prospects of breakthrough in sight.[15] Periodic violent eruptions in Tibet against the Chinese rule and the looming battle over the next Dalai Lama's succession add to stresses, strains, and mistrust. Since 2006, Beijing has adopted a hard line on its claim to Arunachal Pradesh, especially to Tawang. New Delhi has made it clear that public opinion would not allow any Indian government to give up any populated areas that elect representatives to the Indian Parliament now or in the future. Since 2000, the Indian military has been reporting frequent PLA incursions (170 in 2007 and 210 in 2008) all along the border from Ladakh to Arunachal Pradesh.[16] Intrusions along the Sikkim-Tibet border signal this supposedly "settled issue" remains unsettled. For their part, the Chinese Foreign Ministry spokespersons deny any incursions "because the border has never been demarcated between India and China."[17] This stance implies that the border patrols are free to go across the Line of Actual Control, and is purportedly in violation of the 1993 agreement on "peace and tranquility" along the disputed frontier. This agreement had specified that "both shall strictly respect and observe the Line of Actual Control between the two sides," and "no activities of either side shall overstep" this line and, in case they do, they "shall immediately pull back to their own side" on being cautioned by the other side.[18] Beginning in 2006, India started taking several measures to build up its defenses along its disputed frontier with China and address its infrastructural and logistical disadvantage in its long-neglected border areas. The Indian military decided to reinforce its strength by raising two additional army mountain divisions and stationing missiles and advanced Sukhoi-30 MKI aircraft in Assam. Moreover, the media became more vocal about China as a rising strategic threat to India. All this prompted Beijing to angrily remind New Delhi of its perceived superiority in terms of military strength, economy, and diplomatic heft.[19]

There is a disconnect between how the publics in both countries perceive each other. Indian wariness rubs up against Chinese disdain. The tenor of state-run Chinese media's rhetoric about India has changed perceptibly since 2006, indicating an internal shift toward a hard line within China *vis-à-vis* India. Since the Tibetan uprising of March 2008, Beijing has sought to elevate the Indian state of Arunachal Pradesh (now called "southern Tibet" in Chinese) as a core issue to its sovereignty, just like Taiwan, that must be returned to the motherland's fold. The year 2008-09 thus saw a steady escalation of tension over a range of issues—from Tibet to trade and the civil nuclear energy deal to separate visas to Indian citizens from Kashmir.[20] Consequently, tensions between the two giants started mounting just when the rest of the world had taken the peaceful, simultaneous rise of China and India for granted. Not surprisingly, those analysts who had claimed that "a border deal with China was more amenable to an early solution than the Kashmir dispute with Pakistan" seemed puzzled and disappointed with the turn of events.[21]

A dramatic increase in bilateral trade and exchange of high-level visits notwithstanding, there remain deep, and widening, fractures within the current India-China relationship. In the absence of mutual accommodation of each other's interests and core security concerns, the power rivalry between Asia's rising giants is intensifying. As in the past, so in the future China's failure to pacify Tibet and the looming battle over the next Dalai Lama's selection coupled with Beijing's strategic imperative to pre-empt India's rise as a peer competitor could possibly bring about a clash. Officially, Beijing and New Delhi repeatedly declare that neither country would view the other as a security threat. They characterize their relationship as "strategic and cooperative partnership" and professions of friendship and cooperation are regularly made in both capitals. They also cooperate to mutual advantage in international forums—especially when pitted against the developed world—on issues such as climate change, labor standards, and trade.

Principal Drivers in India's China Debate

India's China debate thus remains scarred by the bitterness over both the 1962 War and the territorial dispute—the principal "driver" shaping India's policies and attitudes toward China. Strategically, Indian defense planners keep close eye on China's growing military strength. Given the history of threatening Chinese military moves during India's wars with Pakistan in 1965, 1971, 1999, and the continuing Sino-Pakistani military nexus, Indian defense planning takes into account China's military support for Pakistan in times of crisis under certain scenarios by opening a second front against India in the east. Developments in Chinese-Indian relations are central to India's internal debate about the reliability of its strategic deterrent and whether to test nuclear weapons again. Even if the territorial dispute were resolved, India and China would still compete in the Asia-Pacific region. Other "drivers" or factors that contribute to the fractious and uneasy relationship include power asymmetry; Beijing's military alliances with Pakistan and Burma; Beijing's alleged support to insurgents in north-eastern India; nuclear proliferation and terrorism issues; the future status of Tibet, Kashmir, and Sikkim; economic and resource competition (oil, gas, and water); China's opposition to an Indian permanent seat in the UN Security Council; Chinese and Indian encroachments into what each sees as its "sphere of influence," as evident in Beijing's plans for a naval presence in the Indian Ocean and India's counter-moves to establish closer strategic ties with "China-wary nations" (such as Tajikistan, Mongolia, Japan, Vietnam, Taiwan, the Philippines, Indonesia, and Australia); and last but not least, each country's relations with the United States.

Further, the traditional India-China rivalry has now acquired a maritime dimension. Beijing harbors long-term ambitions to build a navy with a capability that matches both its role as a great power and its growing global economic interests. The deployment of Chinese naval vessels off the coast of Somalia in the Indian Ocean, an area New Delhi regards as its backyard, to fight piracy since 2008 has demonstrated Beijing's will and capability to conduct sustained missions far from its homeland. Defense analysts want the government to be on "guard against the dragon in the water [as] India is critically dependent on the SLOCs for economic growth and energy needs."[22] Unlike the United States or the European Union, India bristles at the prospect of an increased presence of the Chinese Navy in the Indian Ocean.

In the economic sphere, Indian and Chinese economies are competitive rather than complementary. Both look to the West and Japan for advanced technology, capital, and investment. China has long regarded India as a large potential market for Chinese goods. However, Indians see China as predatory in trade and look with worry at China's robust growth rates, fearing being left behind. Over the last 30 years, China's GDP has grown at about 10 percent a year, compared with India's 7 percent growth rate. Even in the information technology (IT) sector, Indians fear that just as the Chinese left India behind in the nuclear arena (where India had an edge in the 1950s), China would leave India behind in the IT software sector as well. Both are also increasingly competing for access to resources across the Indian Ocean from Africa, the Gulf, and from Australia. China's single-mindedness in gaining access to natural resources, capital, markets, and bases around the world—all greased by arms, money, and diplomatic protection—contrasts sharply with disjointed, half-hearted measures by India's government-owned and private sector companies. Trade between the two countries has been growing at more than 30 percent a year but their burgeoning commercial relationship is heavily skewed in Beijing's favor. Nearly 90 percent of India's exports to China are raw materials and iron ore that then come back as higher-value finished goods and undercut India's small and medium enterprises. The growing trade deficit is a cause of disagreement. New Delhi wants Beijing to allow greater market access to Indian goods and services and to remove a variety of non-trade barriers in the area of IT, pharmaceuticals, energy, Bollywood movies, and agricultural produce. Following a spate of anti-dumping measures initiated by the Indian government against Chinese goods and Beijing's threats of retaliation against trade protectionism, economic frictions are rising.[23] India also keeps a wary eye on the strategic consequences of the integration of South Asian economies with the much larger Chinese economy through economic and trade dependencies, diplomatic protection, resource relationships, and investments in infrastructure.

In addition, China's use of regional and international organizations to institutionalize its power while either denying India access to these organizations or marginalizing India within them adds a new competitive dynamic to the bilateral relationship. In the past decade, India has found itself ranged against China at the United Nations (UN) Security Council, the East Asia Summit (EAS), the Asia-Europe Meeting (ASEM), the Asia-Pacific Economic Cooperation (APEC), the Nuclear Suppliers' Group (NSG), and the Asian Development Bank (ADB). With China's influence in global and regional institutions growing, Indian diplomats expect many more "Made-in-China" roadblocks in the future: "China could use its position in multilateral financial institutions to hold back funds for countries that take a position that is more sympathetic and supportive of Tibetan leader the Dalai Lama for instance, or of Taiwan."[24] In a tit-for-tat response, New Delhi has kept Beijing out of the Bay of Bengal Initiative for Multi-Sectoral Technical and Economic Cooperation (BIMSTEC) and the Mekong Ganges Cooperation (MGC) forums, which bring together countries in South Asia and Southeast Asia, and rejected China's request to be included as observer or associate member into the 33-member Indian Ocean Naval Symposium (IONS) initiative started by India in 2008. With the possible exception of environment and trade issues, there are not many issues of multilateral collaboration and cooperation between China and India.

On the positive side, India and China now have a more substantive relationship today than in the previous decades. Both desire a peaceful security environment to concentrate on acquiring comprehensive national strength underpinned by a solid economic-technological base. Both have begun to behave like normal neighbors—allowing trade and investment and promoting people-to-people contact. Bilateral trade flows have risen rapidly from a paltry $350 million in 1993 and $3 billion in 2000 to nearly $60 billion in 2010. In 1994, India displaced Pakistan to become China's largest trading partner in South Asia, and in 2003, China displaced Japan as India's largest trading partner in East Asia. Unlike in the past, growing economic ties provide a cushion in times of crisis over territorial, nuclear, and military security issues in the future. The reality of the rapidly expanding bilateral engagement could provide a different template for addressing the boundary dispute.

Having said that, the forces impelling India and China toward continuing suspicion and competition are much more powerful and deeply rooted in their very different domestic political systems, competing interests, and in their positions in the international system. China is a reference point for India's economic, security, and diplomatic policies, and India's strategic planners have always emphasized the need to keep up militarily with China. There exists in the Indian mind a deep distrust of China. China has advanced much further than India in the achievement of its goals. To a considerable extent, this power asymmetry explains the Asian giants' competitive relations with each other. The combination of internal issues of stability and external overlapping spheres of influence forestall the chances for a genuine Sino-Indian rapprochement.

Major Stakeholders and Actors: Interests and Agendas

India's major "stakeholders" regarding China are the Prime Minister's Office (PMO), the military and intelligence community, and the Ministry of Defense (MOD), the Ministry of External Affairs (MEA), political parties, academia, media, and the hitherto non-existent but increasingly influential business lobby. The PMO acts on the collective advice of the intelligence agencies, MEA, MOD, and the military. In reality, political (and increasingly, economic) considerations prevail over the cautious assessments of the national security bureaucracy.

There are also sharp differences on China within the policy establishment. The MEA oscillates between the political line set by the elected leadership (which is often optimistic about good relations with China), and its own instincts, which are to mistrust China. The MOD favors a hawkish policy *vis-à-vis* China, recognizing that the PLA remains a bastion of anti-Indian sentiment in the Middle Kingdom's ruling apparatus. The military establishment cautions against lowering its guard if India wants to avoid a repeat of a 1962-type defeat. The burden of history still weighs heavily on the policy-making elite in India. The MOD maintains that China's policy of *détente* is intended to lull India into a false sense of security. The MOD's annual reports point to the growing military asymmetry between India and China (especially the threat from Chinese nuclear missiles to Indian cities), China's continued close military nexus with Pakistan, especially in northern Kashmir, and Beijing's expanding strategic ties with India's neighbors. The MOD's 2009 Annual Report noted that:

> China's development of strategic missile and space-based assets and of rapidly enhancing its blue-water navy to conduct operations in distant waters, as well as the systematic upgrading of infrastructure, reconnaissance and surveillance, quick response and operational capabilities in the border areas, will have an effect on the overall military environment in the neighbourhood of India.[25]

In June 2009, India's Minister of State for Defense, M. M. Pallam Raju, stated that India was well aware of China's efforts to "encircle India" by recruiting its smaller neighbors: "Chinese influence is not just in Pakistan. They are trying to develop a port in Sri Lanka and in Myanmar (Burma). And we are well aware of all these developments. We are taking steps that Chinese influence does not pose a threat."[26] India's navy chiefs routinely express concern about the Chinese navy's close interaction with Indian Ocean states. Senior Indian naval officers make no secret of their intention to counter the expansion of Chinese naval power in the Indian Ocean by controlling choke points in the Malacca Straits, nor that the establishment of a permanent naval presence in the Andaman Islands on the vital trade routes between Suez and Singapore is a step in that direction. The intelligence community believes that "China respects power and competition, not weakness and cooperation," and laments successive governments' attempts to soft-pedal differences with China and favors finding a powerful lever against China (for example, playing "the Taiwan card" to counter China's "Pakistan card"). India's Foreign Minister has described the rise of China as one of India's foremost security challenges. The Indian Planning Commission's "Vision 2020" document contends that India would be growingly threatened by the rising economic and military strength of China, and calls on the leadership to join regional or global defense pacts.

Since the late 1990s, a degree of bipartisanship has emerged in the approach to China between the Bharatiya Janata Party (BJP) and Congress Party, although how to handle China remains the subject of political point scoring. The BJP-led coalition's attempts during 1999–2004 to improve ties with China received multi-partisan support across the Indian political spectrum. Even though all parties recognize that Tibet was an independent nation for much of its history, no major political party wants to make Tibet an issue in bilateral relations.

Although the aspirations for great power status are held by almost all Indian political parties (barring the Communists who fear provoking their Chinese masters), the nationalist BJP ardently covets that status. The BJP has been critical of the successive Congress-led governments for fine-tuning Sino-Indian bilateral relations by playing a secondary role to an assertive China. It was not a coincidence that Sino-Indian relations deteriorated sharply after the BJP-led coalition came to power in 1998. In the past, successive Indian governments had carefully avoided publicly raising controversial issues with a view to maintaining cordiality in bilateral negotiations. Though the BJP gradually moved toward more cooperative relations with China while in power, it subscribes to the belief that only a firm policy based on comprehensive strength, strategic alliances, and proactive containment of China will force the Chinese to abandon their hostility toward India. Interestingly, the BJP's slogan of "prosperous and powerful country" bears remarkable resemblance to the CCP's national goal of "rich country, strong military" (*fuguo qiangbing*).[27] The Congress-led coalition governments have continued the policy of engaging and balancing China. Unlike in the past, India's leaders are now increasingly pragmatic when it comes to their dealings with China, and India's elite understands profoundly that New Delhi would gain little from direct confrontation with Beijing.

There has been a proliferation of policy think-tanks and academic centers of Chinese studies in India since the early 1990s. While the former—dominated by retired generals, intelligence community and diplomats—tend to be wary of China, the latter—run mostly, but not exclusively, by left-wing academics, journalists, and mostly pseudo-China experts—push a pro-China line. On national security issues dealing with China and Pakistan, the Indian print and electronic media tends to be nationalistic in its tone. Elements in the media are often manipulated by the government. In 2009, a series of news stories quoting "official sources" charged China with cross-border incursions. These were seemingly aimed at generating populist pressure on Beijing, which had suddenly turned hostile.

Finally, since the mid-1990s, the Indian business lobby has started influencing India's China policy, pushing for closer economic ties. Initially, there were alarmist cries in India Inc. of the Chinese flooding Indians out in their own market through large-scale dumping of Chinese consumer goods. During 2004–2006, however, with the trade balance in India's favor, envy and awe gave way to new confidence in both cooperating with and even besting the dragon. Several joint ventures in power generation, consumer goods, chemicals, minerals, mining, infrastructure construction, IT, and telecommunication sectors are in the pipeline. However, the rapid accumulation of trade deficit with China since 2007 has worried the Indian government and industry.

The distrust of China in the Indian civil society runs deep. With the Chinese perceptions of India also turning increasingly negative, Indians are less enamored with collaborating with China. A 2008 Pew attitude survey found that a majority of Indians view China's increasing economic and military power negatively.[28] This marked a noticeable deterioration in Indian perceptions of China compared to only three years ago. The ranks of Indian strategists who see China as a near-term security threat have grown in numbers and policymakers seem willing to publicly express their concerns about China's growing strategic influence in India's immediate neighborhood. Reflecting the popular mood, the Indian Parliament has weighed in on two occasions—first in 2007 following the Chinese anti-satellite test and then in 2008 in the aftermath of violent anti-China protests in Tibet—by allowing discussions on the ramifications of the Chinese actions for India. India's strategic community often bemoans the lack of a long-term, hard-nosed and coherent strategy to deal with China. A fragmented state like India certainly lacks the long-term strategic vision, perseverance, and patience that guide a highly centralized China in its relentless pursuit of power and national goals.

Three Schools of Thought: Engagement, Concirclement, and Appeasement

Broadly speaking, the chasm in India's China debate divides those who want to proceed based on Beijing's words and those who want policy to be founded on Chinese deeds. This divide has led to three main views on China: the pragmatic (or "balanced engagement") school, the hyperrealist (containment-cum-encirclement or what I call "concirclement") school, and the appeasement school. The composition of these groups is not fixed, but, in general, elements of the Congress party and India's business community, as well as the Ministries of Finance and Commerce, incline toward the pragmatist view; segments of the BJP and the Ministries of Defense and Home Affairs fall into the hyperrealist camp; while India's vocal Communist Party of India (Marxist), Maoists, and other left-wing parties ascribe to the appeaser view.[29] The pragmatic school is the dominant, mainstream view. The second hyperrealist school has gained new adherents in the 2000s as the official Indian perception of China has undergone a dramatic shift, with China now being widely seen as posing a major security threat in the short to medium term (five to ten years). Ironically, this change took place not long after the conclusion of a "strategic partnership" agreement between the two countries in April 2005. The third school of thought is now held by a small percentage of Indians, mostly die-hard China supporters. The triumph within the policy establishment of "the China hawks" over "the China doves" shows not only the growing trust-deficit but also that there will always be limits to the embrace with China as long as the border dispute remains unresolved.

Pragmatists: "Engage but Balance China"

Pragmatists, who represent India's dominant school of thought on China, hold that China is a long-term threat and that the Sino-Pakistan nuclear/missile nexus is of immediate concern. This threat is to be dealt with through dialogue, multi-faceted engagement, and power balancing. Meanwhile, economics should be the key factor in bilateral relations because intensifying trade and commerce would eventually raise the stakes for China in its relationship with India, and thus bear on Beijing's ties to Pakistan and the rest of South Asia. The key assumption is that greater exposure and interaction at all levels will help make light of some of history's burdens. Pragmatists believe that a world in which China and India grow together would be an ideal one, with their interdependent economies and powerful militaries acting as deterrents to a potential military conflict. A desire for stability on its south-western flank and fears of an India-United States alliance have caused Beijing to take a more even-handed approach, while still favoring Islamabad. Pragmatists acknowledge the huge gap between China's rhetoric and reality in its dealings with India and see the need for robust defenses to guard against future power projection once China reaches the pinnacle of its economic and military power. However, with its current focus on economic progress coupled with the desire to project "peaceful rise," China is likely to be a restrained power interested in managing, if not resolving, conflict. Therefore, it is in India's interests to promote peace and tranquility on disputed borders, resolve the border issue realistically, and promote cooperation with China on issues of mutual interest.

Pragmatists do not deny that India and China are competitors but believe their aspirations are manageable. Just as the United States and the Soviet Union did not go to war to counter each other's power or spheres of influence, India and China can learn to co-exist with each other's aspirations. The Asia-Pacific region is large enough to accommodate both India and China.[30] Both share common interests in maintaining regional stability (for example, combating the Islamist fundamentalists), exploiting economic opportunities, and maintaining access to energy sources, capital, and markets. Some advocate leveraging Chinese power to restrain and reform Pakistan because both "India and China have a common stake in ensuring that Pakistan follows the course of political moderation and economic modernization."[31] On economic, environmental, and cultural issues, it is argued that China and India may have far more reason to cooperate than to collide. Besides, cooperation could allow them to balance US influence and increase their negotiating positions with the sole superpower.

Pragmatists agree that Beijing's foreign policy behavior is driven by a long-standing ambition to see China play a role of a superpower in Asia and the world. Their major concern is not that China will invade other countries, but rather that it will use its growing comprehensive national strength—economic, diplomatic, military, cultural, and institutional resources—to shift the overall balance of power in Asia to influence others' policy preferences and shape outcomes in China's favor. To hedge against that scenario, pragmatists favor internal and external balancing in line with India's traditional preferences—a self-reliant build-up of economic and military power and pursuit of good relations with all major powers, including China, and to avoid strategic relationships that might limit its strategic maneuverability. Growing ties with the United States, Japan, Russia, the Association of Southeast Asian Nations (ASEAN), and the European Union have also given India more confidence in dealing with China. India needs the capital, technology, markets, and natural resources of the West, Japan, and Russia as well as China to reduce the power gap between China and India. Pragmatists do not want India to align itself overtly with forces inimical to China, which is now India's largest trading partner. They contend that emerging multipolarity would provide incentives for China to pursue a moderate, cooperative foreign policy that promotes stability and growth in Asia.

Not all Indian experts agree, though, and some argue that as long as China is ruled by the Chinese Communist Party, it is self-contained. By pursuing short-sighted domestic and foreign policies that undermine China's "peaceful rise" image and interests (for example, with respect to periodic protests in Tibet and Xinjiang, anti-foreign nationalist eruptions, support for unsavory militarist regimes in North Korea, Pakistan, Burma, and Sudan, unresolved territorial/maritime disputes, and mercantilist policy), the CCP itself does a great job of containing China from time to time. In this context, pragmatists also draw attention to India's growing economic and military strength and soft power that give India a significant advantage in its long-term competition with China. They point to several diplomatic defeats suffered by China in its attempts to deny India membership in the ASEAN Regional Forum (ARF), the UNSC, the EAS, and the NSG.[32] More importantly, India enjoys the support of the West while China is a lonely rising power. Democratic India's rise certainly does not evoke much concern in the United States, European, or Asian countries in the manner that many countries view authoritarian China's rise negatively. Apart from the weak, failing, and pariah states of Burma, Iran, North Korea, Pakistan, and Sudan, Beijing has very few, if any, true friends in the world.[33] Pragmatists also discount the alarmist scenarios of Chinese naval presence in the Indian Ocean, claiming that all major economies—the United States, Japan, China, India and others—have common interests in keeping SLOCs open and would seek to dampen maritime competition.

Interestingly, the "engage China" school also emphasizes the need to "emulate China." Much like China, India should have a long-term "calculative strategy," which allows rapid accumulation of economic-technological-military power while sidestepping difficult issues. Like China, India should pursue mutual economic dependencies among Asian nations through increased trade, investment, and infrastructure development to bolster India's economic and political ties across Asia that will temper Chinese ambitions and countervail Chinese power. Like China, India too should pursue the goal of achieving the status of an autonomous, self-reliant power in the international system.[34] In short, "India must emulate China to be secure against its neighbor in the decades to come, and more importantly, to manage its relations with other great powers as Beijing does."[35] Pragmatists want to leverage the economic opportunities from China's rise because China's rise has been good for India in that it provided a template for the world's second most populous country to follow to lift millions out of poverty trap. Even "China pessimists" amongst pragmatists concede that both sides need rapprochement to buy time to consolidate their respective economic and strategic positions:

> Beijing needs a few more years to integrate Tibet irrevocably into the mainland through new railway lines and flooding the plateau with Han Chinese in order to consolidate its position along its newly-acquired borders with South Asia, while India wants to reach cruising heights of economic progress and military security before it can stand up to Chinese dominance.[36]

This strategy of "balanced engagement" or *interim entente* with China has many takers in official circles, especially with the business lobby rooting for such a path. Even an avid China baiter like George Fernandes, India's Defense Minister in the BJP-led coalition government (1998–2004), abandoned much of his steam on China, pursuing a chastened moderate tone as a consequence of the official "China policy consensus," which lies somewhere between the "balanced engagement" and "concirclement" schools.

Hyperrealists: "Contain and Encircle China"

Hyperrealists are mostly China hawks or hardliners whose views on China as a great power, as a trading partner, or as a military threat and on India's China policy are vastly different from those of pragmatists and appeasers. Hyperrealists perceive China as an irredentist and expansionist power that presents a "clear and present danger" to India. They point out that no country with borders with China is satisfied with its gargantuan neighbor because "China will never be territorially satiated."[37] They contend that China would not be sitting on India's western and eastern flanks today (in Pakistan, Bangladesh, and Burma) if Nehru had successfully resisted Tibet's incorporation into China in the

1950s. They ridicule the notion of joint Sino-Indian management of Asian security as illusion. Hyperrealists cannot conceive of friendly relations with Beijing, because given its Middle Kingdom complex and the hubris of Han superiority, China will always undercut India militarily or economically. They draw attention to the vast gap between Beijing's declaratory and operational policies *vis-à-vis* India. Despite its professions of amity and goodwill, Beijing's saccharine talk often gives way to snarls, threats, and intimidation whenever New Delhi has asserted its rights.[38] They describe China as "the biggest roadblock to India's rise in the world." As R. Jagannathan observes:

> China … has pursued military superiority with doggedness since the 1980s. It has opposed India formally, and behind the scenes, at every forum. At the Nuclear Suppliers' Group [in 2008], China tried its best to scuttle the Indo-US deal. At the UN, China was the only country (apart from Pakistan) to steadfastly spike our dreams of permanent membership. The Middle Kingdom is clearly the rogue state behind the clandestine transfer of nuclear and missile technology between Pakistan and North Korea. A nuclear and terror-supporting Pakistan is critical to Chinese plans to keep India bogged down in local insurgencies. A rogue North Korean state enables China to keep both South Korea and Japan off-balance. At the Asian Development Bank, China's was the hand that nearly stopped a loan for Arunachal Pradesh.…We have to dump the Nehruvian mindset of fooling ourselves into believing that China is a benign power. It is not. It is a rogue state under wraps.[39]

Hyperrealists contend that China's military has never fundamentally changed its containment policy toward India since its occupation of Tibet and has worked hard to tie it down south of the Himalayas to ensure a favorable pro-China balance of power. Since China aspires to be Asia's sole superpower, it would not countenance a peer competitor in India. China's Asia policy seeks to wean India's neighboring countries away from Indian influence by creating conditions that promote local hostility toward India and its regional interests.[40] In the 1950s, China occupied Tibet. In the 1960s, it attacked India and befriended Pakistan. In the 1970s and 1980s, Beijing transformed Pakistan into its surrogate and transferred Chinese nuclear-armed missiles to Pakistan to target Indian cities. In the 1990s, Beijing moved into Burma. In the first decade of the twenty-first century, China started wooing Bangladesh and the strategically located Indian Ocean island nations of Sri Lanka, Mauritius, and the Maldives in search for allies in order to gain advantage in any future confrontation in the region. India's former UN ambassador Arundhati Ghose states that Beijing's maneuvering in South Asia is causing "a lot of disquiet." China is "flexing its muscles" and its message is that "we are the big boys here and Asia can only afford one power…and China is the one which will determine what is going to happen here."[41] Hardliners deride China's attempts to "have its nukes and proliferate too" while asking India to disarm and sign the NPT. In addition to arming India's neighbors, Beijing has also kept New Delhi under pressure by supporting insurgency movements in India's minority regions.[42] As a former defense minister noted, "China has encouraged or endorsed a revisionist agenda on the Indian periphery and this causes deep anxiety—more so when this heightens state-sponsored terrorism."[43] Much to India's chagrin, the Chinese ambassador to the UN Security Council opposed the declaration of the Lashkar-e-Toiba (LeT) as a terrorist organization until the LeT attacked in Mumbai in November 2008 and blocked India's proposal to place sanctions on Jaish-e-Mohammed (JeM) head Maulana Masood Azhar.[44] This stance and the fact that the state-controlled Chinese media has never ever acknowledged Pakistan's role in terrorist activities in India "is viewed by many as amounting to collusion."[45]

Hyperrealists maintain that Chinese nationalism or Han chauvinism could be more threatening to its Asian neighbors than was Chinese Communism, and that a wealthy, powerful China will assert itself in world affairs as every other powerful nation has done. They believe that there are only two alternatives before the Asian countries: either accept Chinese hegemony or take steps to contain and balance Chinese power. They hope that the latter would be more acceptable to China's neighbors, and India, which has the size, might, and numbers of China, should seek to "manoeuvre itself into a dominant position in order to offer itself and, more importantly, be seen as a counterweight to the Chinese power in Asia."[46] A shared interest in balancing China's growing economic and military influence in Asia has already led to a great improvement in Indian-United States, Indian-Japanese and Indian-ASEAN ties. They maintain that only Indian military power and a containment-cum-encirclement strategy or "concirclement of China" by a ring of Asian powers will hold Beijing in check. India must take a lead in forming an alliance of "China-wary" countries along China's periphery, especially maritime powers to contain China's continental power. Put simply, "India must do to China what China has done to India," that is, containment and encirclement. Just as China is unwilling to concede India's primacy in South Asia and the Indian Ocean region, India cannot accept Southeast and East Asia as China's sphere of influence. From this perspective, India's "Look East" policy is a manifestation of its strategic intent to compete with China for influence in the wider Asia-Pacific region.

Hyperrealists decry pragmatists' belief in "trade over security" as irrational. They note that growing India-China economic interaction has not made Beijing abandon its "concircle India" policy because of the Chinese assessment that India (in addition to the United States) poses a major obstacle to the realization of China's ambitions in the twenty-first century. Despite all the hype over India's burgeoning (in fact, skewed in Beijing's favor) trade with China, it consists mostly of raw materials, iron ore, and steel to fuel China's economic growth while China exports manufactured goods, electronics, and machinery to India. This is not much different from what the British did during the colonial era to India. China and India remain economic and energy competitors and Beijing is determined to erode India's share of global IT exports. They add that it is by design, not default, that India, the United States, Japan, and Vietnam—countries that Chinese strategists variously describe as China's enemies, rivals, and competitors—have come to post huge trade deficits while every other country in the Asia-Pacific region enjoys huge trade surpluses with China. The latter is especially true of those US friends and allies (Canada, Australia, South Korea, Thailand, the Philippines, and Indonesia) that Beijing wants to wean away from Washington. They advocate protectionist measures to protect India's manufacturing and knowledge industries. Further, hyperrealists envision a happy family of democracies stretching from Mongolia, South Korea, Japan, Taiwan, Indonesia, Australia, Singapore, and Thailand to India that would counter the China-led "coalition of autocracies" and the alternative "Beijing consensus" (development-without-democracy) developmental model that China advocates in the developing world.

Just as Chinese strategists advise their government to nurse its grievances and bide its time *vis-à-vis* the United States, India's "China-wary" watchers want their country to nurse its grievances *vis-à-vis* China, bide its time, and acquire comprehensive power. While supporting *interim détente*, the concirclement school of thought cautions against rushing into a border settlement with China from a position of weakness, citing the examples of Kyrgyzstan, Tajikistan, and Vietnam, which had to surrender huge chunks of their territories to China as part of "unequal treaties imposed on them in the 1990s." One China-watcher comments:

> India should be buying time. Another decade of strong economic reforms and growing cooperation with the United States could give

> India the necessary leverage and self-confidence to deal with China. Given the unsustainable contradiction between China's communist autocracy and market capitalism, time is on India's side.[47]

In addition to the old territorial dispute, China's naval forays into the Indian Ocean lend credence to the concirclement school's arguments succinctly summed up in the following analysis:

> India's ability to avert the emergence of a China-oriented Asia will hinge on its success in retaining its domination in the Indian Ocean. A China that expands its presence in the Indian Ocean and exerts increasing influence over the regional waterways and over Burma, Bangladesh, Sri Lanka, Pakistan and Nepal will pave the way for a Sino-centric Asia and for a greater squeeze of India.... If India does not guard the various gates to the Indian Ocean–through its exercise of power and through strategic partnerships with key players–it will confront the Chinese Navy in the Bay of Bengal and the Arabian Sea.[48]

Though still small but no longer on the margins, the ranks of the concirclement school have swelled since the late 1990s with the emergence of the so-called "baby hawks"—a new generation of young nationalists who oppose any accommodation with China except on equal terms because of what they perceive to be "the second betrayal" (the war of 1962 being the first) of their country by China during the "rapprochement phase (1988–98)" in the form of Chinese transfers of nuclear-armed missiles to Pakistan and Beijing's concerted efforts to turn Burma, Bangladesh, Nepal, and Sri Lanka into China's surrogates. They ask: "Is China willing to treat India as an equal? And will India settle for anything less? Unless these questions are answered, how can the strategic competition be avoided in the longer term? China's Middle-Kingdom impulse makes it intolerant of Indian competition in Asia and the Indian Ocean region."[49] As Brahma Chellaney observes:

> While singing the virtues of a multipolar world, China aspires to be the sole pole in Asia, so it is free to limit US influence, contain India, bully Taiwan, shame Japan, divide ASEAN, and make use of semi-failed States that serve as its clients—Pakistan and Burma against India, and North Korea against Japan. New Delhi has to engage China on equal terms, which would mean that Beijing could no longer be allowed to one-sidedly pursue a strategy of engagement with containment. Nobody is suggesting India adopt an aggressive posture. But India can surely nuance its position on Tibet and Taiwan to help checkmate Chinese designs and gain leverage.[50]

Hardliners, who only a few years ago were losing ground to pragmatists and appeasers, feel vindicated by the downturn in Sino-Indian relations since 2006. With the Chinese official media launching an anti-India tirade during 2007–09 (for example, pronouncements about "a repeat of the 1962 War" and threats to disintegrate India),[51] and Beijing using international forums to apply pressure on New Delhi, even a mainstream liberal newspaper like *The Times of India* has now joined the ranks of those who call upon the government to "take a leaf out of Beijing's book when it comes to formulating a muscular response." It argues that "a deliberately confrontationist policy would be counterproductive but there is nothing to be gained from restraint based on a false perception of ground realities or needless appeasement...It must be made clear to Beijing that the relationship with New Delhi is based on *quid pro quo*."[52] The alleged increase in PLA's incursions across the LAC since 2000 and Beijing's re-opening of settled issues (such as Sikkim and separate visas for Kashmiris) have emboldened the hyperrealists to justify upgrading of ties with Taiwan to "force moderation in China's position *vis-à-vis* India."[53] As one commentary noted:

> The more you give, the more it takes. China only understands competition.... Philosophically, India is more attuned to Taiwan than China, and they have complementary strengths. Taiwan has huge capital and high-tech in IT, electronics ... while India has cheap labour, top professionals, and a massive market. A little friendliness to Taiwan will rattle China, and that is not a bad beginning.[54]

Hyperrealists believe it is time for India to counter China's "special all-weather relationships" with "India-wary" countries in South Asia. They see in the geostrategic location of the two countries—India south-west and Japan north-east of China—as a facilitating factor in bringing the two together to contain the rising power of China.[55] They welcome a greater Japanese military profile in the Asian region to counter the Chinese. The conclusion of the Joint Declaration on Security Cooperation between Japan and India in 2008, proclaiming that the two nations will form an "essential pillar for the future [security] architecture" essentially fulfilled a long-standing demand of hyperrealists. Further, they would like New Delhi, Tokyo, Hanoi, and Jakarta to co-operate on policy toward the world's fastest-rising power, which is "a challenge as much in military terms as in economic terms."[56] Hardliners want New Delhi to take the lead in establishing an anti-China alliance system with Tajikistan, Mongolia, South Korea, Japan, Taiwan,

Vietnam, Australia, Indonesia, and Burma, all of whom in the end worry about China more than any other major power. Hyperrealists also favor an Indian naval presence in the South China Sea and the Pacific Ocean to counter future Chinese naval presence in the Indian Ocean. Some insist that India must play "the Tibet card" and support the Tibetan independence movement to convince Beijing to avoid belligerence.[57] Others want to help Taiwan and Vietnam go nuclear and ballistic.[58]

For the concirclement school, pragmatism in Chinese foreign policy during the period of economic modernization is merely tactical, and will be dispensed with when Beijing feels strong enough to use force to settle scores. Hyperrealists believe that rising powers India and China are likely to come into conflict as their capabilities, ambitions, and influence grow.[59] For China cannot establish its predominance on the Asian continent without subduing India. To many China observers, India's rise as a potential peer competitor indicates the failure of China's South Asia policy of the last four decades. India's growing economic and military strength—particularly one that is backed by the West and Japan—on its restive south-western frontiers (Tibet and Xinjiang) is seen not only as posing a direct challenge to China's territorial integrity but also as a major obstacle in China's expansion southwards. As Air Commodore (retd) Jasjit Singh observed: "Factors beyond our control could propel the two countries into a possible conflictual situation. After all, the Chinese premier was reported to have told another head of state shortly after the war in 1962 that *the war had not been about (disputed) territory*!"[60] Hardliners envisage six types of conflict scenarios involving China:[61]

- Border incursions erupting in a short war;
- Chinese intervention in an India-Pakistan war;
- Proxy wars in Nepal, Burma, Bangladesh, and Sri Lanka and overt support for insurgencies in India;
- Diversion of the Brahmaputra river to China's north;
- Naval skirmishes in the Indian Ocean or the South China Sea; and
- Anti-satellite and cyber attacks.

Therefore, they want India to ensure that the overall military balance of power does not tilt in China's favor, especially in air, naval, nuclear, cyber, and space capabilities. Nuclear deterrence is seen as vital to secure India against China. For hyperrealists, India's faith in an India-US strategic partnership to deal effectively with the China-Pakistan nexus is misplaced. Washington could easily trade cooperative interests with India for larger geo-strategic interests with New Delhi's primary competitors—China and Pakistan. They worry about India's marginalization in the event of a Sino-US condominium in the context of a long global economic crisis. A former minister and parliamentarian, Arun Shourie, warns against "India's precarious dependence on the United States for dealing with Pakistan and China" at a time when Washington is dependent on Pakistan militarily for preventing another 9/11 and on China economically for its economic recovery.[62] Others argue that an anti-China alliance with the United States is welcome in the near-term, but over the long-term, India must acquire military, diplomatic, and economic strength to emerge as an independent pole and the linchpin of a new alliance system, stretching from Turkey and Israel in the west to Taiwan and Japan in the east, to combat the twin threats of the twenty-first century: Chinese expansionism and Islamic fundamentalism.[63] In short, hyperrealists advocate "tit-for-tat" policy to put an end to the "take-take nature of Chinese diplomacy." They prefer a down-to-earth, result-oriented, business-like balance-of-power-based concirclement strategy toward China.

Appeasers: "China Is No Threat"

India's pro-China lobby (consisting of Communists, left-leaning academics, pseudo-Sinologists and journalists at China-funded think-tanks and media outlets, pacifists, anti-nuclear and anti-US elements, and idealists) has historically exercised far greater influence on policymaking than their small numbers would warrant. The advent of coalition/minority governments in India has given small communist parties with limited parliamentary seats enormous power to advance Beijing's foreign policy agenda and demand non-confrontational diplomacy with China. Appeasers view China very differently indeed. They see China as a giant, cute and cuddly panda, not a fire-breathing dragon. From their perspective, China is no threat at all. Appeasers support whatever China says and does 100 percent.[64] To them, China is not an irredentist, aggressive power that threatens or bullies its neighbors. Rather, China is a developing country seeking to improve the lives of its billion-plus people, much like India. The problem, in their view, is India, not China.

China apologists have a ready explanation to justify any Chinese action. The 1962 War is attributed to New Delhi's own mistakes and the Cold War dynamics. The border dispute is of India's making, and the key to building a durable India-China partnership is to "de-territorialize their bilateral relations." According to Kanti Bajpai, "China ceased being a threat more or less the day it got what it wanted, which was Aksai Chin. China is the satisfied power with respect to the border, and it is not interested in hostilities, conventional or nuclear."[65] Appeasers mouth platitudes and regurgitate Chinese statements of good intent and goodwill. They maintain that China and India share the same perspective on the need for a stronger UN, a multipolar world, the World Trade Organization, the environment, and other transnational security issues. To end the US hegemony, appeasers want India to think what it can do to make China strong and powerful, not what China can do for India. They hold that engagement with China and giving China its due in the world will mollify Beijing and modify Chinese policies toward India. They support minimalist and non-provocative defense and favor constructing a bilateral relationship based on common security that jettisons the push and shove of balance-of-power politics. The pro-China lobby was very critical of the Vajpayee government's citing of "the China threat" to justify nuclear tests in 1998, it supported China's sabotage of India's bid for a permanent seat on the UN Security Council in 2005, and spearheaded domestic opposition to the US-India nuclear energy deal that complemented the opposition being mounted internationally by China against the termination of international nuclear sanctions on India in 2008.

Conclusion

India's relations with China have witnessed numerous twists and turns over the last half century. The key players in India's decisionmaking about China are the Prime Minister's Office, the military and intelligence community, the Ministry of External Affairs and the Ministry of Defense, political parties, and business lobbies. Though officially India is committed to engaging China on multiple levels, there exist serious differences on how to deal with China. Pragmatists, hyperrealists, and appeasers have different perspectives on China. Pragmatists believe that economic engagement and wary cooperation can occur between the two countries. While India does need to take steps to guard against Chinese power, cooperation should be the first priority. Pragmatists tend to view the Sino-Indian border dispute as a test for proponents of China's "peaceful rise" theory. In line with India's traditional preferences, pragmatists favor internal balancing—a build-up of economic and military power. Conversely, hyperrealists view China as an immediate threat to India. They argue that increased economic engagement has not led to a reduction in China's support for Pakistan or its broader efforts to encircle India. As a result, they advocate an aggressive strategy of alliance building with other "China-wary" states to constrain Beijing's ability to dominate the region. For hyperrealists, the probability of some kind of military confrontation in the near future is much higher. In contrast, pragmatists think that a more likely near-term scenario than an open conflict between India and China will be a jockeying for economic and political influence in the region. However, both pragmatists and hyperrealists see India's three core interests—preservation of territorial integrity, strategic autonomy based on credible nuclear deterrent, and maritime pre-eminence in the Indian Ocean—increasingly coming under assault from a rampant dragon on the prowl.[66]

Therefore, for both schools of thought, the India-US partnership is an important component of India's strategy to balance China, albeit more for pragmatists and less for hyperrealists who want India to look beyond the US fixation to safeguard its interests. Both schools believe that Beijing's assessment of the United States as being overextended militarily (with wars in Iraq and Afghanistan) and weakened economically (post-financial crisis) has imbued Chinese policy-makers with the confidence to be more assertive in ways that are inconsistent with Indian interests. However, hyperrealists discern a major policy shift underway, and they attribute increased global assertiveness under President Hu Jintao to a new evolving Chinese strategy, which is transitioning from the late Chinese patriarch Deng Xiaoping's directive of "hiding real capabilities to bide our time" (*taoguang yanghui*) to "making contributions by seizing opportunities" (*yousuo zuowei*), taking the lead and showing off China's capabilities to shape others' choices in Beijing's favor.[67] Both engagement and concirclement schools of thought believe that India can only become a great power by raising its economic growth rates, and this is feasible if India works not against, but rather with, the great powers as a way of increasing trade, technology transfers, and investment. India prefers a US-led unipolar world to a China-dominated Asia—but ultimately seeks a multipolar world with itself as a constituent pole. Pragmatists and hyperrealists differ on the type of the nuclear deterrent: pragmatists are nuclear moderates, while hyperrealists are nuclear maximalists. Both schools believe that China will not willingly accept India's rise on the world stage. Both see China, much like the United States, using global norms and conventions and manipulating its position in multilateral international institutions for its own purposes and to clip India's wings. A third group of appeasers believes that China is a fundamentally peaceful state that does not pose a threat to India.

Interestingly, though they may not state it quite as strongly and publicly, most Indian mainstream strategic analysts and policymakers share some hyperrealist positions to some extent. For both pragmatists and hyperrealists, the adage "Do unto others as you would have them do unto you," and not meaningless rhetorical declarations of peace and friendship, provides a solid foundation for Sino-Indian amity. Negative developments in Sino-Indian relations since 2006 have bolstered the credibility of hawkish arguments and effectively silenced the pro-China lobby. The bottom line of India's China debate thus tends more toward the China-skeptic position. Overall, while acknowledging the inevitability of competition, the Indian government's approach has been to steer a pragmatic course ("balanced engagement") between the hyperrealist ("China as threat") and appeasement ("China as benign power") schools of thought. India's evolving Asia policy reflects the desire to build an arc of strategic partnerships with China's key neighbors, and with the United States, to help neutralize the continuing Chinese military assistance and activity around India and to ensure that China's growing power does not slide into belligerence.

Notes

[1] For details, see J. Mohan Malik, "Hands across the Himalayas," *Pacific Defence Reporter,* March 1989, 43-45.

[2] S. Gupta and S. Chakravarti, "Sino-Indian relations: vital breakthrough," *India Today*, September 30, 1993, 22; "China and India paving way for peace," *Beijing Review,* September 20-26, 1993, 6; L. Kaye, "Bordering on peace," *Far Eastern Economic Review* (hereafter *FEER),* September 16, 1993, 13.

[3] Kaye, "Bordering on peace"; J. Mohan Malik, "India copes with the Kremlin's fall," *Orbis,* 37:1 (Winter 1993), 69-87.

[4] *FEER,* April 15, 1993, 10-11. See *New York Times,* March 8, 1992. Also see *Indian Defence Review,* April 1992, 26.

[5] Zheng Ruixiang, "Shifting obstacles in Sino-Indian relations," *Pacific Review*, 6:1 (1993), 65.

[6] N. Mitra, "Coming closer," *Sunday* (Calcutta), August 23-29, 1992, 59.

[7] "India tipped off," *FEER,* August 9, 1990, 5; Editorial, "China's non-interference," *Hindustan Times,* November 18, 1989.

[8] BBC, *Summary of World Broadcasts: The Far East* (hereafter SWB/FE), No. 1789 (September 9, 1993), G/2; Gupta and Chakravarti, "Sino-Indian relations," 23.

[9] J. W. Garver, "Chinese-Indian rivalry in Indochina," *Asian Survey,* 27:11 (November 1987), 1216-17.

[10] R. Thakur, "Normalizing Sino-Indian relations," *Pacific Review,* 4:1 (1991), 15.

[11] See arguments presented in J. Mohan Malik, "China-India relations in the Post-Soviet era: the continuing rivalry," *The China Quarterly*, 142 (June 1995), 317-355.

[12] For example, Chinese Foreign Minister Qian Qichen's July 1994 visit to New Delhi "coincided" with Defense Minister Chi Haotian's visit to Pakistan and the arrival of a high-powered military delegation in Burma in the same month.

[13] V. Sharma and V. K. George, "China is fishing in troubled waters in Lanka," *Hindustan Times*, April 25, 2009.

[14] B. Loudon, "Indo-US military links spook Beijing," *Australian*, April 12, 2007.

[15] K. Sibal, "Talks with China head nowhere," *Rediff.com*, August 13, 2009 <http://news.rediff.com/column/2009/aug/12/talks-with-china-head-nowhere.htm>.

[16] J. M. Smith, "The China-India border brawl," *Wall Street Journal*, June 24, 2009 <http://online.wsj.com/article/SB124578881101543463.html>.

[17] Xinhua, "Foreign Ministry spokesman refuses Indian allegations," *China Daily*, May 13, 2009, 1.

[18] Cited from J. Ranade, "It takes two to tango," *Times of India*, July 16, 2009.

[19] S. Ramachandran, "Indian might met with Chinese threats," *Asia Times online*, July 10, 2009 <http://www.atimes.com/atimes/South_Asia/KG10Df01.html>.

[20] This shift in Chinese stance coincided with the dismal performance of Beijing-backed Communist Party of India (Marxist) in the May 2009 parliamentary elections that deprived China of its major source of influence within the Indian government.

[21] See, for example, C. Raja Mohan, "Coonoor cunundrum," *Indian Express*, April 20, 2007.

[22] T. Mathew, "Mighty dragon in the sea," *Hindustan Times*, June 23, 2009.

[23] S. Dasgupta, "India to question China on market access, balance of trade," *Times of India*, January 18, 2010, 1; "China slams India for protectionism," *South Asia Media Net*, June 26, 2009.

[24] Quoted in S. Ramachandran, "Chinese antics have India fuming," *Asia Times online*, May 5, 2009 <http://www.atimes.com/atimes/South_Asia/KE05Df01.html>.

[25] V. Raghuvanshi, "India sounds another caution on China force upgrade," *Defense News*, July 20, 2009, 54.

[26] AsiaInt, "India wary of China's friends," *AWA*, June 5, 2009.

[27] "In the BJP, the Chinese Communist Party's (CCP) seems to have met its match. Just as the CCP believes in the superiority of the Han race, Han civilisation and the Han culture while displaying patronising and condescending attitude towards minorities such as Tibetans, Mongols and Muslims and downplaying the repeated colonization of the Han race first by Inner Asian tribes such as Mongols, Manchus and then by the Europeans, the BJP believes in the superiority of the Hindu race, Hindu civilisation and Hindu culture while downplaying the repeated colonisation of India by Greek, Muslim and European

invaders as a result of Hindu disunity and their contributions to Indian culture," see J. Mohan Malik, "The India-China Divide" *Hindustan Times*, May 24, 1999, 13.

[28] Pew Research Center, "Global economic gloom–China and India notable exceptions," *Pew Global Attitudes Project*, June 12, 2008, 43.

[29] See W. C. Ladwig, "Delhi's pacific ambition," *Asian Security*, 5:2 (2009), 87-113.

[30] IANS, "India, China not rivals, but partners in emerging Asia: S M Krishna," *Times of India*, July 22, 2009, 1.

[31] C. Raja Mohan, "Sino-Indian boundary talks," *The Hindu*, October 23, 2003.

[32] Indian leaders expect many more similar hurdles but prefer to deal with such Chinese tactics quietly and diplomatically, instead of lashing out at Beijing publicly. P. D. Samanta, "China says no but US, Japan help ADB clear India's plan," *Indian Express*, June 16, 2009; "China 'dissatisfied' with ADB Document involving China-India border dispute," *Xinhua*, June 18, 2009.

[33] J. E. Keating, "Beijing's most embarrassing allies," *Foreign Policy*, May 24, 2010 <http://www.foreignpolicy.com/articles/2010/05/24/beijing_s_most_embarrassing_allies>.

[34] J. MacDonald, B. Danyluk and A. Donahue, *Perspectives on China: A View from India*, Prepared for Director, Net Assessment, Office of the Secretary of Defense, (Booze, Allen & Hamilton, December 2005), v-vii.

[35] Raja Mohan, "Sino-Indian boundary talks."

[36] V. Kranti, "China and the central issue," *The Pioneer*, June 23, 2003; B. Chellaney, "China frets over Indo-US ties," *Washington Times*, February 2, 2002.

[37] "No silk road," *Newsinsight.net*, November 7, 2003 <http://www.newsinsight.net/archivedebates/nat2.asp?recno=757&ctg=>.

[38] Ramachandran, "Indian might met with Chinese threats"; On Tibet, Beijing's public language still matches the crudeness and callousness with which it sought in 1962 to "teach India a lesson." See A. Shourie, *Are we deceiving ourselves again?* (New Delhi, ASA/Rupam, 2009) 214.

[39] R. Jagannathan, "The China challenge," *Daily News and Analysis Online*, June 17, 2009 <http://www.dnaindia.com/opinion/column_the-china-challenge_1265849>.

[40] MacDonald, Danyluk and Donahue, *Perspectives on China,* 27.

[41] Quoted in J. Lamont and A. Kazmin, "Fear of influence," *Financial Times*, July 12, 2009.

[42] "China plans to dismember North-East: CIA," *Newsinsight.net*, November 13, 2003 <http://www.intelligenceonline.net/allintelligencefull.asp?id=3052453302413011&recno=2419>.

[43] "George to raise India's concerns in China," *The Tribune*, January 30, 2003, 1.

[44] P. D. Samanta, "Sanctioning jaish chief: UK blinks, China lone dissenter," *Indian Express*, June 25, 2009.

[45] B. Raman, "Obama's failure to understand Indian distrust of China," *Saag.org*, No. 3511, November 19, 2009 <http://www.southasiaanalysis.org/%5Cpapers36%5Cpaper3511.html>.

[46] J. Singh, "Post-Cold War security situation in Southern Asia," *Strategic Analysis,* 17:1 (April 1994), 18.

[47] B. Chellaney, "Vajpayee kowtows to China," *Japan Times*, July 9, 2003.

[48] B. Chellaney, "Dragon's foothold in Gwadar, *Asian Age*, April 11, 2007.

[49] Conversations with retired Indian military officers and diplomats in New Delhi, 2007-08. Also see K. Sibal, "India should stand up to China as an equal," *Rediff.com*, February 22, 2008 <http://www.rediff.com/news/2008/feb/22guest.htm>.

[50] B. Chellaney, "The 100 percenters," *Hindustan Times*, June 19, 2003.

[51] I. Bagchi, "Chinese media on India-bashing spree," *Times of India*, June 24, 2009, 1.

[52] Editorial, "The China tantrum," *Times of India*, April 17, 2009.

[53] AFP, "Taiwan, India in secret military cooperation: Report," *Hindustan Times*, January 2, 2002. Full report in "Wo he Yindu mimi zhan kai junshi hezuo," *Lianhe xinwen* [Taipei], <http://udnnews.com/CB/NEWS/FOCUSNEWS/POLITICS/647735.shtml>.

[54] "No silk road," *Newsinsight.net*.

[55] Lt Gen K. S. Khajuria (Retd), "Security in south west Asia region post-Cold War…," *Indian Defence Review*, (July 1993), 44. Conversations with India's Japan experts, 1992.

[56] See D. Jaishankar, "Foreign policy challenges for UPA 2.0," *Pragati: The Indian National Interest Review*, July 2009 <http://pragati.nationalinterest.in/2009/07/foreign-policy-challenges-for-upa-20/>.

[57] R. Sikri, *Challenge and Strategy. Rethinking India's Foreign Policy* (New Delhi: SAGE Publications, April 2009), 104, 109.

[58] "Enemy's enemy: China won't ever befriend India," *Newsinsight.net*, September 16, 2003 <http://newsinsight.net/archivedebates/nat2.asp?recno=721&ctg=>.

[59] PTI, "Nervous China may attack India by 2012: Expert," *Hindustan Times*, July 12, 2009, 1.

[60] J. Singh, "The arc in the sky," *Indian Express*, November 10, 2003. Italics added.

[61] Former National Security Adviser wants India to be "prepared militarily to defend on two fronts if they (Pakistan and China) become active simultaneously." See B. Mishra, "China's positioning on the border is very aggressive," *Rediff.com*, April 3, 2010 <http://news.rediff.com/report/2010/apr/03/chinas-positioning-on-the-border-is-very-aggressive.htm>; MacDonald, Danyluk and Donahue, *Perspectives on China,* 27; S. Padmanabhan, "China is working towards diverting Brahmputra river away from India," *Hindu Business*, April 14, 2009.

[62] A. Shourie, "New beginnings?" Speech delivered on the Address of the President, June 2009 in the Rajya Sabha (Indian Parliament's upper house), June 8, 2009.

[63] Jagannathan, "The China challenge."

[64] See, for example, V. V. Paranjpe, "Climb over the wall," *Hindustan Times*, June 17, 2003, 8; For an excellent critique of India's pro-China lobby, see S. Chaulia, "Mental slaves," *The Statesman*, May 1, 2009 <http://www.thestatesman.net/page.arcview.php?clid=4&id=284531&usrsess=1%20<>.

[65] K. P. Bajpai and A. Matoo (eds), *Securing India: Strategic Thought and Practic*e (New Delhi: Manohar, 1996), 21. India's pro-China lobbyists have long argued that Beijing's diplomacy is primarily economics-driven, and its burgeoning ties with India's South Asian neighbors pose no strategic threat. However, they cannot explain as to why would Beijing then not provide nuclear reactors and missiles to Taiwan, Vietnam, Mongolia or the Philippines—countries in China's neighborhood that have much closer and mutually beneficial economic ties with Beijing than Bangladesh and Pakistan.

[66] See Indian Navy Chief Admiral S. Mehta's speech in *The Hindu*, August 11, 2009.

[67] J. Ranade, "Enter the dragon," *Times of India*, June 11, 2009.

4
China Perceives India: "Great Power Dreamer"

In inter-state relations, perceptions often matter more than reality and influence policy. A country's foreign policy is often a function of perceptions, beliefs, and images. Put simply, what a country's leaders think matters as much as a country's interests. One's particular set of beliefs about "the other" usually defines and shapes a specific policy course. This chapter focuses primarily on Chinese views and perceptions of India and South Asia from the 1960s to the present, seeking to derive the roots of current Chinese policy toward India and to provide policy-relevant analysis as to how past events and perceptions may affect present and future developments in Sino-Indian relations in five areas: mutual suspicion and distrust, the unresolved border conflict, ties with the West (Washington and Moscow), India's great power ambitions, and the Sino-Indian geopolitical rivalry. Given the important role of perceptions, biases, and worldviews in shaping interstate relations, the views of Chinese leaders and strategic analysts are the focus of discussion. This chapter begins with a brief historical background to outline the broader international and domestic contexts. It sets the scene with Mao and Zhou's views on the origins of the 1962 War and territorial dispute—both of which continue to bedevil the China-India bilateral relationship. It then reconstructs an episode during the Cold War to explain not just what Mao and Zhou thought of India and South Asia in the early 1970s but also how their understanding and expressions were conditioned by the geostrategic environment at the time. The 1971 India-Pakistan War not only helped facilitate and hasten the Sino-US rapprochement but also laid the foundation of the Sino-US-Indian triangular relationship. The last part of the chapter analyzes changes and continuities in China's perspectives on India in the post-Cold War era. The key argument is that while significant changes have taken place in Sino-US relations since 1971, China's relationship with India, in contrast, is characterized more by continuities than changes, with the past continuing to exercise strong influence on China's present and future policy toward India. There remains a major perceptual gap which creates persistent instability in bilateral relations. Consequently, relations between Asia's two old civilization-states at the beginning of the third millennium remain stymied by a paucity of parallel interests, are dogged by nationalism on both sides, and are marred by conflicting worldviews and divergent interests.

Chinese leaders' views on India in the 1960s are captured in the author's analysis of declassified US documents of President Richard Nixon and his National Security Advisor Henry Kissinger's conversations with Chairman Mao Zedong and Premier Zhou Enlai—first published as a journal article in 2002.[1] A critical content analysis of these transcripts—a total of seven verbatim documents on the Nixon-Zhou talks of February 1972 and forty-one documents on the Beijing-Washington back-channel and Kissinger's secret trip to China in 1971, classified as "Top Secret" up until 2000—reveals much that is useful for policymakers today in Beijing, Washington, and New Delhi as they fashion their policy responses to the security challenges of the early twenty-first century.[2] For instance, in his first meeting with Kissinger in July 1971, Zhou described the South Asian subcontinent as a prime area of "turmoil under heaven"[3]—this remains the case forty years later.

These documents fill in major gaps in the existing literature on Chinese views of India as well as on Washington's triangular diplomacy with Beijing and Moscow.[4] They reveal the American motives and attempts to use the 1971 India-Pakistan War to build their strategic alliance with China, as well as Chinese objectives and dilemmas at that time. A look at the historical origins of the great power triangular diplomacy in the early 1970s—the Washington-Beijing quasi-alliance to counter the Soviet threat—is timely and useful in a period when the United States is seen in Beijing as engaged in triangular diplomacy of a different kind in the early twenty-first century—the Washington-New Delhi quasi-alliance to counter the perceived China threat. In addition, any long-term assessment of bilateral ties must be based on a sound understanding of the perceptions and attitudes of the past. Secondly, these transcripts provide scintillating details on the personalities of leaders like Khrushchev, Mao, Nehru, Nixon, Kissinger, Indira Gandhi, and Yahya Khan that helped shape Asian geopolitics during the Cold War era.[5] The role that domestic politics plays in interstate negotiations is also revealing.[6] Furthermore, the transcripts demonstrate how the mutual and intra-deception/misperception between the United States and China and between the Soviet Union and India contributed to miscalculation and, in turn, led to a security dilemma. Last but not least, these transcripts serve as a useful reminder of the games great powers play, more often than not at the expense of small and weak states in the international system.

Given that US documentation provides only a partial and somewhat biased record of a more complex reality, other important sources have been used in the argumentation. Since the early 1990s several Chinese works on the 1962 War have been published which provide insights into China's decision-making process. The official PLA history of the 1962 War harps on India's aggressive intentions and actions that led to the conflict and details PLA's military operations.[7] Other useful sources that further illustrate, illuminate, and provide an objective analysis of some of the issues discussed here are William Burr's *The Kissinger Transcripts* (1999), Raymond Garthoff's *Détente and Confrontation* (1994), Allen S. Whiting's *The Calculus of Chinese Deterrence, India and Indochina* (1975), Y. Vertzberger's *Misperceptions in Foreign Policymaking* (1984), Steven Hoffman's *India and the China Crisis* (1990), and John Garver's *Protracted Contest: India-China Rivalry in the Twentieth Century* (2001) and "China's Decision for War with India in 1962" (2006).[8] The first decade of the twenty-first century saw a significant surge in Chinese strategic writings on India (and other countries) in open sources, both print and electronic. These writings, presented in the last section of this chapter, reveal mostly negative, suspicious, and stereotyped views and image of India. Not surprisingly, Chinese and Indian leaders continue to talk at, rather than to, each other. At the official level, however, both claim that there is enough space in the Asia-Pacific region and beyond for both China and India to be ascendant as they once were in history for a long period of time.

The Historical Context

Before discussing Chinese leaders' views of India, it is important to keep in mind the international and domestic political contexts and the motives, interests, and aspirations of key actors involved in order to understand their full import. Chinese leaders' perceptions of India have been shaped by the Tibetan rebellion and the subsequent flight of the Dalai Lama to India in 1959, Chinese territorial claims, and China's victory over India in the border war of 1962. Beijing's support to Pakistan in its wars with India in 1965 and 1971 added to strains and tensions. The visit of US President Richard Nixon to China from February 21–28, 1972 was—as Nixon himself later opined—"the week that changed the world."[9] This was the first visit by an American president to the People's Republic of China (PRC) to hold substantive discussions on international security issues in a series of conversations with Chairman Mao Zedong and Premier Zhou Enlai.[10] Nixon was instrumental in opening up a new political relationship between the United States and Communist China after decades of mutual estrangement, hostility, and conflict.

President Nixon landed in China two months after the India-Pakistan War of December 1971, which led to both the dismemberment of Pakistan (an ally of both the United States and China, and more importantly, a facilitator of the Sino-US rapprochement),[11] and the emergence of Bangladesh as an independent state (with the help of India backed by the Soviet Union). Natural, therefore, was that the two sides spent a considerable amount of time discussing the new security situation in South Asia and the need to coordinate their future responses. That is why five out of seven documents on the Nixon-Zhou talks held in February 1972 deal with India and South Asia. In sharp contrast, only three (nos. 35, 36, and 40) out of a total of forty-one documents deal with India and South Asia during Kissinger's talks with Zhou in July 1971.[12] This was also the time when the Vietnam War was at its peak—despite the Nixon administration's plans to bring a negotiated settlement. The Soviet Union was seen as a rising, expansionist power, lending its military and diplomatic support to allies such as India and Vietnam. On top of it all, the Nixon-Zhou meeting was preceded by a tense stand-off between China and the Soviet Union following both several bloody skirmishes on their disputed border in 1969 and the Soviet threat to take out China's nuclear arsenal in a preemptive strike. The domestic situation in China was volatile, with the turmoil and chaos unleashed by the Cultural Revolution having brought economic and social development to a standstill. The power struggle between moderate and radical factions of the CCP was still raging, and the central leadership was badly shaken by the fallout of the purges of Lin Biao's associates within the defense establishment.

An analysis of the Zhou-Nixon transcripts reveals two major reasons for the Chinese and American distrust and dislike for India during the Cold War: New Delhi's close ties with the Soviet Union and Beijing's alliance with Pakistan, especially Islamabad's pivotal role in putting Chinese leaders in touch with the Americans. This analysis demonstrates that, as in the past, China's alliance relationship with Pakistan and Beijing's security concerns vis-à-vis India—coupled with territorial disputes and the need to protect its "soft strategic underbelly," Tibet—continue to determine Beijing's South Asia policy in general and its India policy in particular. That is why, despite significant improvement in bilateral relations, mutual distrust and suspicion still continue to shape Chinese perceptions and policy toward India.

Mao, Zhou, and Nixon Assess India of the 1960s and 1970s

Kissinger had informed Nixon about the "Chinese detestation of the Indians" and China's "historical distrust of India" after his first meeting with Zhou Enlai in July 1971.[13] By the time he visited China in February 1972, Nixon had also developed a personal dislike for India, and particularly Prime Minister Indira Gandhi because of her open defiance of the American will during the December 1971 India-Pakistan War, which resulted in Pakistan's dismemberment.[14] Comparing the Germans, the Japanese, and the Chinese (who, in Nixon's view, had the qualities of drive and hard work), Nixon made derogatory remarks about the Indians' breeding habits, laziness, and their lack of sense of purpose and determination. (Not surprisingly, the rest of the statement is censored.) Nixon opined that "the money goes down a rat-hole in countries like India," and regretted that "the more aid we have given, the less influence we have." Zhou echoed Nixon: "And India actually is a bottomless hole."[15] This point about the futility of US economic assistance to India was also taken up by Mao Zedong in his conversations with Nixon and Kissinger, and was reproduced in *The Kissinger Transcripts*. While Nixon seemed ignorant of Indian history, Zhou was suspicious of Indian designs.[16] Nixon said: "As I look at India's brief history, it has had enough trouble trying to digest West Bengal. If now it tries to digest East Bengal, it may cause indigestion which would be massive." His host, Zhou Enlai, concurred:

> That's bound to be so. It is also a great pity that the daughter [Mrs. Gandhi] has also taken as her legacy the philosophy of her father embodied in the book *Discovery of India*. Have you read it?... Yes, he [Nehru] was thinking of a great Indian empire—Malaysia, Ceylon, etc. It would probably also include our Tibet.... Chen Yi called it to my attention. He said it was precisely the spirit of India that was embodied in the book.[17]

If Zhou found Nehruvian interpretation of Indian history so difficult to digest, one wonders what he would have made of the ultra-nationalist view of India's history (which is, in many respects, similar to the Chinese Communist Party's [CCP] own view of Chinese history), propounded by the Rashtriya Swyamsevak Sangh (RSS) and its political wing, the ruling Bharatiya Janata Party (BJP), which looks toward restoring India's glorious past as a civilization and a great world power. It was not a mere coincidence that Sino-Indian relations deteriorated sharply soon after the BJP-led coalition came to power in March 1998, labeled China as "potential enemy number one," tested nuclear weapons, and signaled its intention to engage China in tit-for-tat diplomacy.[18]

Furthermore, Zhou is reported as having said that "the biggest challenge after the Second World War was the liberation of China."[19] From the perspective of Chinese nationalists, the independence of India or Indonesia from colonial rule was largely a non-event. This was not surprising because Chairman Mao harbored doubts about India's independent status more than two decades after the British had left. Mao told Kissinger on November 12, 1973: "India did not win independence. If it does not attach itself with Britain, it attaches itself to the Soviet Union. And now, more than one-half of their economy depends on you (the United States)."[20] For the Mao-Zhou duo, Nehru was first a British and then a Soviet stooge, incapable of acting on his own and India was first a British colony and later a Soviet colony.[21] Mao also made light of Gandhi and Indian philosophy which "was never meant to have a practical application." In other words, while China's socio-cultural values are highly materialistic, the Indian value system is spiritual and otherworldly, causing economic backwardness. As will be shown below, Nixon was a self-confessed "hard-liner on India" and took credit for all the anti-India decisions during the 1971 Indo-Pakistan War. It was a complete meeting of the minds among known India-baiters at the time. Nixon later summed up Chinese attitudes toward their neighbors: "The Russians they hate, the Japanese they fear and as for the Indians, they feel contempt."[22]

Interestingly, John Garver's *Protracted Contest: Sino-Indian Rivalry in the Twentieth Century* draws attention to a 1974 poem by Mao which gave a clear, if poetic, description of the scorn with which he viewed India's aspirations for greatness. In this poem, which outlined Mao's worldview at the time, Mao described the United States as the tiger, Britain as the lion, the Soviet Union as the bear, the Islamic countries as the moon, the rich West as the sun, and India as a cow. A cow, moreover, is "only food or for people to ride and for pulling carts; it has no particular talents. The cow would starve to death if its master did not give it grass to eat.... Even though this cow may have great ambitions, they are futile."[23] Even to date, the CCP stereotype of India is of a loathsome, backward neighbor that sold opium to China, sent soldiers to crush the Boxer rebellion, provided Sikh policemen for the pre-1949 international settlements in Shanghai, copied British parliamentary democracy, adopted English as its official language, gave refuge to the Dalai Lama and Tibetan "splittists," and, last but not least, laid claim to British India's expansionist policies.

Zhou also did not view India as a fully sovereign nation but as a satellite state with imperial ambitions. Interestingly, in the course of conversation, Zhou went on to make an important point about India's inability to exercise hegemony:

> From our point of view, even if the subcontinent were under one country there would still be turmoil there, because they have nationality problems there even more complicated than yours [USA] which are now covered up. If India took over all of the subcontinent, there would be even more trouble. India is not able to exercise hegemony—this is our philosophy.[24]

This view contrasts sharply with official China's frequent warnings about India's hegemonic designs since the early 1960s. In their bilateral meetings with smaller South Asian countries, Chinese leaders and policymakers have long bemoaned India's "hegemonic aspirations" and "big brotherly attitude" especially when contrasted with China's "peace-loving, brotherly, and good-neighborly attitude."[25] As will be shown later, on the one hand, this disparity reflects the uncertain nature of China's India policy, and on the other, demonstrates that debate within the Chinese policymaking community about India's future capabilities and intentions and the challenges for China is far from over.[26]

Territorial Dispute and China's India War of 1962

The unresolved Sino-Indian territorial dispute has long been both a cause and an effect of the negative images and attitudes that China and India have held of and toward each other; Zhou's conversations with Nixon are quite revealing in this regard. Recalling the origins of the 1962 War with India, Zhou Enlai noted that "the events actually began in 1959." However, he then went on to attribute the war entirely to the US-Soviet summit at Camp David in June 1959 and Khrushchev's unilateral decision to tear up the nuclear agreements between China and the Soviet Union prior to his departure for Camp David. Zhou observed: "After that there were clashes between Chinese and Indian troops in the western part of Sinkiang [Xinjiang], the Aksai Chin area, … India was encouraged by the Soviet Union to attack. We fought them and beat them back, with many wounded. But the TASS News Agency said that China had committed aggression against India." Then Chinese Foreign Minister Chen Yi took Khrushchev to task for endorsing the Indian version of events. He asked Khrushchev: "Why did you rely on the Indian press over the Chinese press? Wasn't that a case of believing in India more than us, a fraternal country (that is, China)?" Zhou told Nixon that "the TASS Agency account had the effect of encouraging India. And also Neville Maxwell mentioned in the book that in 1962 the Indian government believed what the Russians told them that we, China, would not retaliate against them."[27]

In reality, Zhou's account of the origins of the Sino-Indian War in 1962 as narrated to Nixon and Kissinger was at best subjective and partially correct and at worst a distortion or a selective narrative of historical facts. Zhou was correct in saying that "the events actually began in 1959," but they had nothing to do with the Camp David summit (held in June 1959) or the Soviet decision to renege on its promise to provide China with a nuclear bomb. The origins of the war lay in an event that had occurred three months earlier—in the March 1959 Tibetan uprising which ended with the Dalai Lama's flight into exile in India and the renunciation of the Seventeen-Point Agreement which had "legalized" China's incorporation of Tibet in 1951. Zhou, however, cleverly sidestepped the single most important issue of national uprising in Tibet and Mao's subsequent decision to punish Nehru for granting asylum to Tibet's spiritual leader; Mao blamed it all on the Soviet Union, apparently to emphasize the common security concerns that Beijing at that point in time shared with Washington vis-à-vis Moscow (and New Delhi).

Zhou cited Maxwell[28] in support of his claim that "in 1962 the Indian Government believed what the Russians told them that we, China, would not retaliate against them."[29] However, it was not just the Russians who told the Indians so. Chen Yi had himself said so twice, once in response to a question in Karachi. As Steven Hoffman argues, the Indian leadership relied too much on a private assurance given to Defense Minister Krishna Menon by Chen Yi in July 1962 in Geneva that "there may be skirmishes between forces of the two countries along the border, but full-scale hostilities were unthinkable."[30] Zhou was therefore being disingenuous in scapegoating the Soviet Union for encouraging Indian hostilities because he later acknowledged that the real motivation behind the war was China's concern about Tibet.

Both Chinese leaders and scholars blamed India's Tibet policy and actions as the root cause of the 1962 War. Mao told a visiting delegation from Nepal in 1964 that the major problem between India and China was not the McMahon line, but the Tibet question. Mao said: "In the opinion of the Indian government, Tibet is theirs."[31] According to the official PLA history of the 1962 War, the Chinese leadership perceived

India's policies as part of an effort to undermine Chinese rule and seize Tibet and turn it into an "Indian protectorate" or "buffer zone" (*huanzhongguo*) because control over Tibet was seen as essential for India's "mastery over South Asia," and "for guaranteeing India's security." This line of argument is summed up in Xu Yan's history of the 1962 War: "Nehru aspired and worked consistently throughout the 1950s to turn Tibet into a 'buffer zone'.... Nehru imbibed British imperialist ideology, and believed that India should dominate neighboring countries.... Congress Party leaders [entertained] aspirations that India should lead and organize the Indian Ocean region.... The 'decisive factor' in the deterioration of Sino-Indian relations was Nehru's policy of 'protecting' the Tibetan 'splittists' after the Lhasa rebellion of March 1959."[32] In addition to India's perceived desire for "achieving hegemony in Asia" by subduing its smaller neighbors, Chinese leaders found other reasons to justify their war decision: "India's desire to gain increased US and Soviet military support by becoming a part of their anti-China campaign; a desire to divert class and national contradictions within India; and a belief that China was weak and bluffing."[33]

This led India to needlessly provoke China with its Forward Policy when it could have done a deal over Aksai Chin. The turning point was Nehru's rejection of a swap proposal made by Zhou Enlai during his April 1960 visit to India that China would drop its claims in the eastern sector (Arunachal Pradesh) in exchange for India giving up its claims in the western sector (Aksai Chin). Such a swap would have given each country legal right to territory already in its possession. Nehru, however, rejected the swap deal and insisted that China abandon its claim in the east and withdraw from Aksai Chin in the west.[34] Chinese leaders viewed Nehru's rejection of the swap proposal as unreasonable. Zhou acknowledged China's decision to up the ante on the border dispute: "We sent three open telegrams to Nehru asking him to make a public reply, but he refused. *He was so discourteous; he wouldn't even do us the courtesy of replying, so we had no choice but to drive him out.*" Zhou also claimed that "actually the five principles [of peaceful coexistence, i.e. *Panchsheel* Agreement of April 29, 1954] were put forward by us, and Nehru agreed. But later on he didn't implement them."[35] Obviously, Nehru had incurred Zhou's wrath for being discourteous and arrogant, and a punitive military action against India, from Beijing's perspective, was a logical step. That is how the Celestial Emperor of the Middle Kingdom had traditionally reacted to the discourteous and arrogant rulers of tributary states and hostile regimes in Chinese history.[36] Besides, this was also the time when "Mao became convinced that the US and India, along with China's erstwhile ally the USSR, were all working together against China.... Forceful blows were necessary to foil this anti-China conspiracy."[37] Many commentaries on the era concede not only that Nehru was exceedingly arrogant but also that Indian decision-making at the time was hardly a model of reason.[38] In a well-researched study of "China's Decision for War with India in 1962," Garver argues that "*both sides* bear onus for the 1962 war, China for misconstruing India's Tibetan policies, and India for pursuing a confrontational policy on the border."[39]

When discussing the Sino-Burmese boundary settlement which required China's acceptance of the McMahon Line, Zhou outlined one of the principles of China's boundary settlements: China tended to be more accommodative toward smaller countries than toward big powers. Zhou told Nixon: "The boundary settlement of the Sino-Burmese boundary line was one of mutual accommodation, but actually the result was that Burma gained a bit more, which was reasonable. Since they are a smaller country than us we gave them the benefit of the doubt."[40] However, it would be misleading to draw the conclusion that China is more likely to make territorial concessions to the smaller countries than to the larger ones because this argument does not account for the border war and armed skirmishes between China and Vietnam that lasted from the late 1970s to the late 1980s, or China's claim over the Spratlys. Clearly there are major factors other than the difference in the size of the country to be dealt with that explain the variation in Chinese border negotiation behavior. Apparently, Beijing's preference was to settle borders with smaller and weaker states, and if need be, make territorial concessions to them; at the same time, however, the desire was also to force territorial concessions from larger and stronger states perceived either as threats to China or as China's potential rivals. Zhou believed that the two big countries—the Soviet Union and India—were not keen on settlement and were cooperating against China: "They want to leave a pretext so that they can take the opportunity to make provocations against us when they need it." He then let the cat out of the bag by implying that China had provoked border incidents to pressure the Soviet Union to open boundary question negotiations in the late 1960s—a slip which throws new light on China's crisis behavior.[41]

There appear to be some interesting parallels between the origins of the Sino-Soviet in the late 1960s and the Sino-Indian border clashes of the early 1960s that deserve critical scrutiny. As regards the 1969 clashes on the Sino-Soviet border, Zhou admitted that the PLA had provoked border incidents in order to pressure the Soviet Union to begin boundary question negotiations in the late 1960s.[42] This contradicts what

Maxwell argued in a 1973 article which claimed that the Chinese engaged "only after taking sustained fire from the Russians," and held Moscow responsible for the conflict just as Maxwell had earlier held New Delhi responsible for the Sino-Indian border conflict in the early 1960s.[43] Newly available archival evidence and testimony from Russia, East Germany, and China, however, contradicts Maxwell's account and confirms what Zhou had indirectly hinted at in his conversations with Nixon but was ignored by the president and his national security advisor:[44] the Chinese had initiated the armed clashes on the Ussuri River in 1969. Based on interviews with a number of China's Cold War historians, the commander of the Shenyang Military Region during the crisis, and Russian area specialists, Lyle Goldstein's recent study reveals that "in 1968, China began preparations to create a small war on the border.... The Soviets were really panicked [because] they were absolutely unprepared.... It was a complete surprise [to them]." The clashes were motivated by "Mao's need for an external threat" to both unite the faction-ridden CCP and a country torn by the class warfare that the Cultural Revolution had unleashed.[45] This "diversionary theory of conflict," wherein leaders create international conflicts to divert public attention from domestic conflicts, could also in part explain what happened in the early 1960s on the Sino-Indian border. Just as the unprepared Soviets were easily outnumbered by superior and well-trained Chinese forces in 1969, so were the unprepared Indians easily outnumbered and outgunned by well-equipped, well-trained, and battle-hardened Chinese forces in 1962. Unless archival evidence to the contrary is made available on the 1962 clashes, the "diversionary theory" could partly explain the Sino-Indian conflict, which came as it did soon after the Great Leap Forward fiasco, Tibet's revolt and the Dalai Lama's flight to India, and Mao's attempts to reassert his control over the party and the government. Mao had predicted that "[i]f China fought successfully and in an awe-inspiring way, this will guarantee at least thirty years of peace with India."[46] The 1962 defeat did mark a huge setback in India's confidence and international standing and tilted the regional power balance in China's favor. Many analysts contend that "China's ambition to become the pre-eminent power of Asia, a dream that Nehru had usurped on behalf of India, was back on course after 1962."[47] More importantly, it was the 1962 China-India War which laid the groundwork for the Cold War-era geopolitical alignments in South Asia, with Beijing firmly aligning itself with New Delhi's *bete noire*—Islamabad—and New Delhi tilting initially toward Washington and later aligning itself with Beijing's nemesis, Moscow.

The 1971 India-Pakistan War

If armed clashes on the Sino-Soviet border in 1969 had prompted Beijing and Washington to set up secret channels of communication, the 1971 India-Pakistan War provided the first instance of Sino-US strategic cooperation and paved the way for a public US-PRC kiss and make up. It was the Nixon administration's decision to tilt US policy toward Islamabad at the height of the 1971 India-Pakistan War which convinced the Chinese leadership of Washington's "seriousness and reliability" as an ally and its commitment to rapprochement.[48] This tilt, engineered secretly by Nixon and Kissinger (who saw India as a Soviet proxy and China as an ally against the Soviet threat), drew widespread opposition, however, within and without the Nixon administration. The shift was based partly on the erroneous assumption that Indian Prime Minister Indira Gandhi had the will or the capability to destroy West Pakistan after dismembering its eastern wing; it also was partly an expression of gratitude to Beijing's ally, President Yahya Khan of Pakistan, for playing an important role in facilitating secret communications with China during 1970 and 1971.

Zhou told Nixon that after the complete rupture in Sino-Soviet relations in 1960, the Chinese used to convey their messages to Moscow (during 1964-65) through Pakistani military ruler Ayub Khan.[49] This was an interesting revelation insofar as it showed that General Yahya Khan was not the first Pakistani leader to act as an intermediary for the Chinese. His predecessor Ayub Khan's services were also used in a similar capacity to keep the channels of communication open with the Soviet Union. General Ayub Khan might have acted as a messenger during the Tashkent Agreement, which was facilitated by Khrushchev after the 1965 India-Pakistan War over Kashmir. This earns Pakistan the unique distinction of having acted as an intermediary for the Chinese in their secret dealings with both superpowers at the height of the Cold War—a fact that should make Pakistani diplomacy an object of envy for leader of the "non-aligned" movement and arch-rival, India. The transcripts reveal that the Chinese premier was quite impressed with the Pakistanis' military prowess and fighting spirit but was scathing in his criticism of General Yahya Khan's leadership qualities. Zhou told Nixon:

> Yahya really did not lead his troops in East Pakistan well. Even though we assisted with armaments.... At the time of the ceasefire, they [the Pakistanis] still had 80,000 troops in East Pakistan. It was not a situation in which they couldn't keep fighting. We know the Pakistanis are good fighters, and the men wanted to keep on. The trouble was the

> Commanders were terrible—they really just scattered the troops.... Yahya should have concentrated his troops to win a victory, and once the Indian side had suffered a defeat they would have stopped because West Bengal was not very secure either ... [with] a force of 40,000 against one Indian division, they would have been able to win and that would have demoralized the Indians.... Yahya was a good man, but did not know how to lead an army, how to fight.[50]

Zhou then referred to Kissinger's secret meeting with China's UN Ambassador Huang Hua on December 10, 1971, in New York. The remaining part is censored, but the full account is presented in William Burr's *The Kissinger Transcripts*.[51] It was at this meeting that Kissinger provided sensitive intelligence information, derived from reconnaissance satellites, on Soviet military deployments along the Sino-Soviet border.[52] Kissinger told Ambassador Huang (who later visited India as foreign minister in 1981) how the White House was sustaining its tilt toward Pakistan via veiled threats to the Soviets, secret requests to Middle Eastern governments to provide military equipment to Pakistan, and instructions to send an aircraft carrier fleet through the Straits of Malacca into the Bay of Bengal "to ensure 'maximum intimidation' of India and the Soviet Union."[53] At this meeting, Huang launched a strong anti-India tirade which led Kissinger to conclude incorrectly that the Chinese were about to enter the conflict as India's military moved in to decimate West Pakistan. Demanding strong condemnation of India, Huang said:

> Because if India, with the aid of the Soviet Union, would be able to have its own way in the subcontinent then there would be no more security to speak of for a lot of other countries, and no peace to speak of. Because that would mean the dismemberment of and the splitting up of a sovereign country and the creation of a new edition of Manchukuo, the Bangladesh.... The Soviet Union and India now are progressing along on an extremely dangerous track in the subcontinent. And as we have already pointed out *this is a step to encircle China*.[54]

Kissinger fully agreed with Huang Hua, saying that "if nothing was done to stop India, then East Pakistan will become a Bhutan and West Pakistan will become a Nepal, and India with Soviet help would be free to turn its energies elsewhere" [that is, Tibet].[55] Although Huang did not mention Tibet, because "the discussion was about Soviet-Indian collusion to partition other countries, the implication was obvious."[56] Nor had Kissinger forgotten Zhou's warning to India during his secret visit to Beijing five months before: "India is committing aggression against Pakistan. They have also committed aggression against us, too.... This was because India had long ago under Nehru adopted an expansionist philosophy.... *The turmoil in East Pakistan in a very great way is due to India.... If they [the Indians] are bent on provoking such a situation, then we cannot sit idly by.*"[57] Zhou had also "recalled the Chinese defeat of India in 1962 and hinted rather broadly that the same thing could happen again."[58]

It was in this context that Kissinger offered US support to deter the Soviet Union in case China decided to mount an attack on India in support of Pakistan. Kissinger told Huang Hua on December 10, 1971: "[I]f the People's Republic were to consider the situation on the Indian subcontinent a threat to its security, and if it took measures to protect its security, the U.S. would oppose efforts of others [read, the Soviet Union] to interfere with the People's Republic.... "[59] This assurance of American support for Chinese intervention in the war was carefully omitted by Kissinger from his memoirs. He later argued that this action had been "the first decision to risk war in the triangular Soviet-Chinese-American relationship."[60] (Fortunately, a week after this meeting, on December 17, Pakistan acquiesced to India's unilateral cease-fire.)

Nixon also confirmed this account by saying: "In December, when the situation was getting very sensitive in the subcontinent—I'm using understatement—I was prepared.... "[61] The rest of the statement is blacked out but its content is no longer a secret as it was alluded to in Nixon's memoirs and numerous other works. He was referring to the dispatch of the *USS Enterprise* aircraft carrier to the Bay of Bengal and nuclear coercion if India had continued its advance into West Pakistani territory and if the Soviet Union had not pressured India to halt its aggression after the liberation of Bangladesh. The Chinese were also keeping a close watch on the US-Soviet moves and counter-moves. As Zhou told Nixon: "When your navy ships were moving toward the Indian Ocean they [the USSR] also very quickly sent nuclear subs down from Vladivostok to the Indian Ocean."[62] The next paragraph is blacked out wherein the two sides apparently discussed their support for each other's intimidation of India and the Soviet Union, pressure designed to bring a quick end to the war. Nixon described himself as a "hard-liner on India" (and this was music to his Chinese hosts' ears), saying "all the Indian decisions were mine ... [though] Dr. Kissinger was a [co-]conspirator with me."[63] Kissinger later admitted in his memoirs: "We also wanted to have forces in place in case the Soviet Union pressured China."[64]

Nixon and Kissinger's handling of the 1971 crisis came in for sharp criticism from several observers who held that the two men had misconstrued Chinese intentions and inflated the Soviet and Indian war objectives.[65] Apparently, Kissinger underestimated Chinese leaders' tendency to engage in hyperbole and high-pitched rhetoric whenever China was perceived as weak and vulnerable. Caught in the turmoil of the Cultural Revolution and facing a hostile Soviet Union on its northern borders, China lacked the capability (and intention, many would argue) to intervene militarily on Pakistan's behalf.[66] Raymond Garthoff captures the essence of the White House decisionmaking in 1971:

> The war involved multiple and complex considerations.... The underlying fallacy in Kissinger and Nixon's thinking is that they persisted in assessing Soviet aims in terms of presumed Indian aims, and vice versa. Moreover, they attributed maximum offensive aims to both.[67]

The transcripts reveal that the Chinese also interpreted developments in terms of their prejudgments. Therefore, a more plausible explanation is that given Nixon and Kissinger's main preoccupation with China's role within the framework of the emerging triangular diplomacy, the two were overly influenced by Chinese rhetoric, and their biases toward India and the Soviet Union led to a misinterpretation of intelligence reports. From Nixon's perspective, threatening and intimidating India and the Soviet Union during the December 1971 war was meant to send a signal to the Soviets to refrain from helping Washington's adversaries in regional or internal conflicts in the Third World. Equally importantly, the pressure was also meant to demonstrate US reliability to the Chinese as a prelude to Nixon's talks with Zhou and Mao.[68] The transcripts show the Chinese government and Nixon administration's reluctance/failure to judge the issue of the military's brutal repression in East Pakistan purely on its own merits,[69] that is, without looking at it through the prism of the US-Soviet-China Cold War rivalry.

As John Garver notes, Mao's view of India was that of a neo-colonialist regime propped up by the Anglo-American imperialists and/or the Soviet revisionists as a way of encircling China, and that the Soviet-supported Indian intervention in Bangladesh could serve as a precedent for possible intervention in Tibet.[70] While India could create difficulties in Tibet, the Soviet Union could pose problems for China's only Muslim majority province of Xinjiang, formerly known as East Turkestan. Zhou himself acknowledged China's nightmare scenario in February 1972: "The worst possibility is what I told Dr. Kissinger … the eventuality that you all would attack China—the Soviet Union comes from the north, Japanese and the U.S. from the east, and India into China's Tibet."[71] Zhou recalled the conversation that Soviet Foreign Minister had held with Japanese leader Fukuda regarding the possibility within the next five years of a greater conflict between China and the Soviet Union than there was at Zhenbao Island: "Perhaps they want to do as they did in Bangladesh, and maybe they will try to create a Republic of Turkestan.... "[72] To allay Beijing's concerns about any future American-Soviet deals detrimental to China's interests, Nixon and Kissinger also repeatedly assured Zhou that "we will make no, have no understandings with the Soviet Union...[without] informing your government."[73] Both sides also agreed to coordinate their stance on the recognition of Bangladesh and delay it as long as possible because, as Zhou stated:

> Both of us owe something to Yahya, although he didn't show much statesmanship in leading his country, for bringing the link between our two countries.... As for us, our recognition of Bangladesh will be later than yours and we may be the last. But that does not mean that we will refuse to have any contact whatsoever with an area with so huge a population.... Islamic countries haven't recognized Bangladesh, and we must respect their views.[74]

This stance indicated Beijing's early recognition of the need to keep the Islamic world on its side. Since the 1980s, the Islamic countries have established mutually beneficial relations with Beijing in arms (conventional and nuclear) purchases, trade, and energy supplies and never condemned Beijing's "strike hard" campaigns in its restive Muslim-majority province of Xinjiang.

If Zhou's narration of events leading up to the 1962 India-China War and the 1969 Sino-Soviet clashes was full of half-truths, it was so because his primary objective at the talks was to emphasize the commonality of interests between the United States and China vis-à-vis the Soviet Union and India. In their zeal to counter the perceived Soviet threat, both had decided to put the Taiwan issue on the back burner, with the United States making significant concessions to the Chinese. The two sides not only used the Soviet and Indian threats to find common ground but also emphasized their common interests vis-à-vis Japan. Emphasizing that "both China and the U.S. have had very difficult experiences with Japanese militarism," Nixon expressed the fear that should the United States pull out of Japan, Japan could develop nuclear weapons.[75] He then offered to take on the responsibility of protecting China's interests vis-à-vis Japan and India. On several occasions, Nixon conceded the primacy of Chinese interests in the Indian subcontinent ("we believe your interest here is greater than ours").[76] In real policy terms, this statement signaled to the Chinese an American acknowledgement that South Asia was China's sphere of influence.[77] Interestingly, the transcripts reveal that Zhou was considering restoring ambassador-level ties (severed since the 1962 War) with India in 1971 (that is, just before the Bangladesh crisis erupted) and the Indian government was informed of this move. However, the Sino-US rapprochement and the Bangladesh War in 1971 served to delay the normalization of Sino-Indian relations by almost a decade, though ambassador-level ties were eventually restored in 1976. Throughout the 1970s and 1980s, India's close ties with the Soviet Union as well as China's military alliance with Pakistan and quasi-alliance with the United States (forged after the Soviet invasion of Afghanistan in 1979) hampered the development of Sino-Soviet, Sino-Indian, and Indian-American ties. Sudden, dramatic changes in major power alignments have unintended consequences for other actors in the international system. The Sino-American rapprochement in the early 1970s was no exception. The state of Sino-US relations has always heavily influenced India's foreign policy orientation. For instance, President Nixon's courting of Mao's China in 1971 heightened New Delhi's sense of international isolation in regard to India's looming war against Pakistan; pushed non-aligned India firmly into the Soviet embrace leading to the signing of the Indo-Soviet Treaty of Friendship, Peace, and Cooperation in August 1971 as a guarantee against Chinese military intervention; and later influenced New Delhi's decision to carry out a nuclear test in May 1974 to counter any future US or Chinese nuclear blackmail.[78]

Chinese Perspectives in the 1980s and 1990s

In 1986, India's granting of statehood to Arunachal Pradesh sparked violent skirmishes between China and India at Sumdurong Chu Valley in 1987 and again brought the nations to the brink of another war before tensions were defused and a Joint Working Group established to resolve the territorial dispute. A series of developments in the late 1980s and early 1990s—Indian Premier Rajiv Gandhi's 1988 Beijing visit, the cooling of China-US relations following the unrest in Tibet and violent crackdown on pro-democracy protests in Beijing's Tiananmen Square, Beijing's pre-occupation with domestic stability and economic development, and last but not least, China's fears of increased instability and turbulence, both internal and external, following the Soviet fragmentation in 1991—added incentive to Beijing's search for a tranquil environment with India. With India's support, China obtained observer status in the Non-Aligned Movement. Faced with the emergence of the United States as the sole superpower post–Cold War, China's leaders in their summit meetings with Indian leaders began proposing a "united front" for opposing Western interference in the internal affairs of developing countries, for upholding the principle of inviolable state sovereignty, for working toward the establishment of a multipolar world, and for opposing the Western stance on human rights and environment protection.

While China and Pakistan continued to loom large in Indian policy considerations, India barely appeared on China's radar screen. Official China perceived itself as a global player while India was bracketed with Pakistan and perceived "as weak and divided and economically such a catastrophe."[79] The Soviet Union's collapse led to speculation about a possible Indian disintegration into several states. In 1994, Chinese Foreign Minister Qian Qichen reportedly told his Pakistani counterpart Sardar Asseff that "if India continued to increase its defense expenditures at the cost of its social sectors, it would collapse like the Soviet Union."[80] From Beijing's perspective, a great power must have multidimensional capabilities—economic, military, technological, political, and diplomatic—or what Chinese call the "comprehensive national strength" (*zonghe guoli youshi*). By these standards, China's India-watchers did not think much of India's desire to become a great power like China since it fell short because of its poor economic performance, weak political system, chronic social instability, and failure to convince other Asian nations of its paramountcy.[81] Chinese analyses of the 1990s on the emerging multipolar world did not mention India as one of the poles or as an influential regional power. In the power competition game, China was surging far ahead of India while the latter was mired in socio-political instability.

During this period, Beijing remained apprehensive about India's backing for the Dalai Lama and Tibetan resistance. Chinese strategic writings listed India as one of China's most likely opponents in regional conflicts on its southern borders in the 1990s and beyond (the others being Vietnam and Taiwan).[82] A Chinese strategist told *Far Eastern Economic Review* (*FEER*): "We still regard India as a threat because they still occupy Chinese territory, *though not as ominously as a few years ago*."[83] China's South Asianists, such as Ye Zhengjia, cautioned against India's regional hegemonic policies (vis-à-vis Nepal, Sri Lanka, and Bangladesh) and New Delhi's desire "to isolate Pakistan in the new international environment."[84] Courting "India-wary" smaller countries in South Asia to contain India became an integral part of China's strategic calculus. Throughout the 1990s, Beijing made inroads into India's backyard through cross-border economic and strategic penetration of Bangladesh, Burma, Nepal, Pakistan, and Sri Lanka. Chinese leaders and diplomats called upon India to "change its attitude toward China." While Indians continued to benchmark themselves against China, the Chinese, masters of self-projection, did not project their country as just an Asian power but a rising global power comparable to the United States while making disparaging comments about India's "unrealistic and unachievable 'big power dreams' (*daguomeng*)."[85] At best, India was seen, in Chinese eyes, as an emerging South Asian "regional power" (but one that could be easily contained) rather than a potential global player. Aware of the growing power differential, China's leaders insisted on India abiding by informal understandings that laid the basis for the Sino-Indian rapprochement in the early 1990s:

- Don't peddle "the China threat theory";
- Don't support Tibet or Taiwan's independence;
- Don't oppose the Sino-Pakistani "all-weather relationship" or Sino-Burmese "special relationship";
- Don't align with the United States to contain China; and
- Don't see or project India as an equal of China.

As long as New Delhi followed these "five Nos" (or, "five principles"), Beijing was willing to develop its relations with India as part of its "peaceful periphery" strategy to have good relations with all its neighbors. Peace and tranquility prevailed on the LAC for a decade from 1988 to 1998. However, bilateral relations nosedived when India cited Chinese threat as its primary reason for going nuclear in 1998. Beijing responded by playing a leading role in the UN Security Council and other international forums to isolate and sanction India for going nuclear.

India in China's Eyes in the 2000s: More Continuity Than Change

There has been a dramatic increase in Sino-Indian bilateral exchanges since 2001 at the political, economic, military, and cultural levels—including high-level visits at regular intervals and an overall improvement in the rhetoric and atmospherics. Both conduct a regular security dialogue, joint military exercises, and cooperate to mutual advantage in multilateral forums such as the G-8, the G-20, BRIC, and the Russia-China-India trilateral on transnational issues such as trade;

environment; and reform of international institutions of financial governance, the World Bank, and IMF. In January 2008, the two countries issued a joint document on a "Shared Vision for the 21st Century," pledging to promote a harmonious world of peace and stability and further strengthen the Sino-Indian "Strategic and Cooperative Partnership for Peace and Prosperity."

Unlike in the past, Chinese strategic analysts, retired diplomats, and official media are no longer shy of expressing different viewpoints on India—albeit within the bounds of official policy. The broad divide is between those who want to nip "the India challenge" in the bud before it becomes a serious threat and those who want China to come to terms with a rising India and partner with it whenever opportunity presents. The first viewpoint is represented by the PLA hardliners and the second by old India hands and moderates in the Foreign Ministry–backed think-tanks and the Chinese Academy of Social Sciences. While hardliners are convinced that "India possesses an ambitious, belligerent, and expansionist strategic culture,"[86] moderates are optimistic about China and India maintaining peace and stability and coming together to promote Asian solidarity in their own self-interest. They point to burgeoning trade ties and collaboration on issues like climate change which have shown the benefits of cooperation. They accept the reality of cooperation whenever Chinese and Indian interests converge and competition whenever their interests are at odds. The Chinese decisionmaking system allows reconciliation of differing viewpoints and schools of thought. It is worth noting that even moderates turn hawkish on issues such as the Dalai Lama, the territorial dispute, Pakistan, and nuclear proliferation. The dominant viewpoint holds that the rivalry between Asia's giants has its roots in history and global power structure which needs careful management and conflict avoidance strategies.

On balance, for all the millennial talk about friendship and strategic partnership, little seems to have changed in China's view of India since the 1960s. If anything, the gulf between the two countries—in terms of their perceptions, attitudes, and expectations of and toward each other—has widened in recent years. There exists in the Chinese mind a deep distrust of India—with the converse also holding true. Still both exhibit a shared interest in not allowing tensions to overwhelm the relationship as a whole.

"India's Future Is Uncertain"

Chinese leaders and officials in the early twenty-first century remain as contemptuous of India's socio-economic achievements and as dismissive of New Delhi's claims of being "the world's largest democracy" as were Mao and Zhou in the 1960s and 1970s. In a meeting with American academics in 2001, Vice-Foreign Minister Wang Yi dismissed as meaningless all talk of learning from India's democratic experience, describing India as "a tribal democracy whose long-term existence was far from a certainty."[87] A powerful section of the Chinese national security bureaucracy entertains doubts about the prospects of India's survival as a nation-state over the long term, seeing it as a "soft state characterized by abject poverty, religious and linguistic cleavages, and regional fault lines."[88] Many assume that plagued with insurgencies, terrorism, and separatist movements internally and under strategic pressure on multiple fronts externally, the Indian state would eventually unravel. A provocative article entitled "China can dismember the so-called 'Great Indian Union' with one small stroke" posted on China International Strategy Net (www.iiss.cn) in August 2009 argued that "India as a nation never really existed in history," and urged China to remove an emerging security threat by initiating the balkanization of India into 20-30 independent states with the aid of friendly countries like Pakistan, Bangladesh, and Nepal and thereby recover the 90,000 sq km territory in southern Tibet.[89] The author claimed that "China and India cannot really deal with each other harmoniously" because "there cannot be two Suns in the sky." Though officials in Beijing downplayed it as an expression of individual opinion, the opinion piece provided an insight into a well-known realist strand in Chinese thinking on India.[90] Suffice it to say, China's India-watchers believe that India's fractious polity will limit its economic and military potential, and Chinese leaders remain skeptical about India's future prospects.

"India Cannot Compete with China" ("Yindu neng bi ma?")

Another dominant belief in China's strategic circles is that, as in the 1950s, there is more hype than substance to India's rise, generated mostly by the Western media. Official China loathes being spoken of in the same breath as India. Chinese media commentaries deplore Indian economy, society, polity, and military. India plays no part in the vision projected by Beijing of the twenty-first century as a Chinese one. Whilst China already struts the world stage as a superpower, India remains far behind in all indices of power. Traditionally, China has never looked at India as an equal, but merely as an upstart wannabe that likes to punch above its weight and needs to be constantly reminded of its place. One of the objectives of "Mao's India War," as Roderick MacFarquhar called it, was political: to cut India down to size by demolishing what it represented—a democratic alternative to Communist China. The PLA's rapid victory did help discredit the Indian model and boost China's global standing and dealt a severe blow to Nehru's ambitions for leadership of the Third World.[91] As in the pre–1962 War period, many Chinese analysts find the growing global tendency to compare their country with India as "offensive" and "demeaning." One letter-writer to *Asia Times Online* noted derisively: "China is not competing with India … it is competing with the USA. Who wants to compete with India?"

What irks the Chinese elite apparently is the international praise showered on India's democratic model. The Chinese contend that their economic success proves that China's political cultural and governance system are far superior to India's. China's political system has succeeded in lifting 400 million people out of poverty between 1981 and 2001—an unprecedented, historic achievement in itself. The successful weathering of the economic crises of 1997 and 2008 has further reinforced this belief. A commentary published in June 2009 in the Communist Party mouthpiece *Renmin Ribao*, that serves as a window into the thinking of Beijing's insular leadership, mocked India for failing to keep pace with China's economic growth: "In 1947, when India won independence, it was one of the global industrial powers, ranking Top 10 in the world and far ahead of the then backward China. But today, China's GDP has tripled that of India and … the wealth gap between China and India has increasingly widened."[92] This is the reason, says Li Hongmei, Indians harbor a mix of "awe, vexation, envy, and jealousy." Chiding "Western powers for inciting India to challenge China," Li laments: "To feed its ambitions, the West has gone so far as to devise ways to extol India as a potentially No. 1 democracy in Asia, but intentionally plays down China's social and economic progress."[93] In a similar tone, an editorial in *Global Times* (*Huanqiu Shibao*) asked "frustrated India" to back off: "India likes to brag about its sustainable development, but worries that it is being left behind by China. China is seen in India as both a potential threat and a competitor to surpass. But India can't actually compete with China in a number of areas, like international influence, overall national power, and economic scale. India apparently has not yet realized this."[94]

As in the past, the PLA judges the Indian military inferior to the Chinese in combat, logistics, equipment, and war-fighting capability. In a conversation with French President Jacques Chirac in late 1999, President Jiang Zemin took a dig at the Indian army. Referring to PLA forays aimed at testing Indian preparedness across the LAC in mid-1999 Kargil War between India and Pakistan, Jiang mockingly told Chirac: "Each time we tested them by sending patrols across, the Indian soldiers reacted by putting their hands up." Jiang raised his own hands up to drive home the point to President Chirac. Blaming the 1962 War on "Indian aggression," Jiang warned: "If India were to attack China again, we will crush it." He then "squeezed his hands together to stress the word 'crush.'"[95] In the aftermath of India's nuclear tests of 1998 and the Kargil War of 1999, President Jiang had issued a directive to the PLA to prepare for 45-day long war with India.[96] A decade-long growth in military capabilities and infrastructure underwritten by a defense budget 3 to 4 times the size of India's apparently tilted the military balance in China's favor.[97] An editorial in June 2009 reprimanded India for "unwise military moves" of marshalling forces and deploying elite fighter aircraft in the northeast. It described India's moves as "dangerous" and asked India to "consider whether or not it can afford the consequences of a potential confrontation with China." China is not afraid of India, the editorial taunted, while reminding New Delhi that Beijing had friends in Pakistan, Sri Lanka, and Nepal, but most importantly, it left no doubt about Beijing's future position on Arunachal Pradesh: "China won't make any compromises in its border disputes with India."[98]

The steady emergence of India as a powerful player in Asia is not looked upon favorably by Beijing. As noted earlier, China's strategic culture necessitates distrust of strong, powerful neighbors and a preference for small, weak, and subordinate or client buffer states.[99] Since late 2005, there has been an internal shift within China to a harder line toward India (discussed below). In their exchanges with Americans, Chinese interlocutors insist that if Washington wants Beijing's cooperation on economic, environment, proliferation, and other issues, "the existing hierarchy of power in Asia must be maintained." This formulation means that India (and Japan) must not be allowed to raise their profile and power regionally or internationally. Says Ma Jiali: "For a long time, India has been dreaming of playing a more dramatic role on the world stage, and obtaining the sixth VIP seat on the UN Security Council."[100] Ma argues that "the enhancement of India's strategic position will reduce China's strategic influence to some extent," and "will weaken China's strategic role."[101] Maintaining that India's rise is not in China's interests because acceptance of South Asia as India's sphere of influence would constrain China's growth and stature as the preeminent power in Asia, Chinese analysts advocate drawing Pakistan, Bangladesh, Nepal, Sri Lanka, and Burma firmly into China's security and economic orbit so as to contain India if it indeed manages to emerge as a powerful economic and military power.[102] A high degree of suspicion, mistrust and conflictual relations between India and its smaller South Asian neighbors provides Beijing with enormous strategic leverage vis-à-vis its southern rival and thus prevents India from achieving optimal economic growth and spreading its wings on the global stage.[103] As one Chinese official quipped: "If India doesn't give up its 'great power dreams' (*daguomeng*), China can turn every neighbor of India into another Pakistan. That would turn India's 'great power dream' into a nightmare."[104] Playing the barbarians off against each other has long been a core tenet of traditional strategic posture since imperial times.

"India as a Western Stooge Would Shift Power Balance"

Chinese exhortations to India not to become a pawn of the West to contain China are not new but have gained new currency since the turn of the century. China's "peaceful rise" diplomacy has long sought to prevent Asian countries from banding together and/or entering into alignment with the United States in order to countervail China's power. India's high economic growth rates and New Delhi's efforts to forge strategic ties with the United States, Japan, and other "China-wary" countries in Asia since the late 1990s have forced Beijing's mandarins to focus on the strategic implications of India's rise for China. Apparently, Chinese leaders were led to believe that China's growing economic and military might would eventually enable Beijing to re-establish the Sino-centric hierarchy of Asia's past as the United States saps its energies in fighting small wars in the Islamic world and Japan shrinks economically and demographically, while India remains subdued by virtue of Beijing's "all-weather relationships" with its South Asian neighbors. As Yang Dali and Zhao Hong wrote: "In the face of India's growing strategic influence, China's approach is to develop economic and strategic ties with South Asian nations, ensuring that India is surrounded by countries friendly toward China."[105] Overawed by China's growing wealth, might, presence, and influence, India and others were expected to acquiesce to China's primacy in the Asia-Pacific, paving the way for the re-emergence of a hierarchical order resembling the traditional Sino-centric tributary system. Only those who sought to balance China by banding together or aligning with the United States would invite Beijing's wrath and retribution.

Seen from Beijing's perspective, a number of "negative developments," especially since 2005—the Indian and Japanese bids for permanent seats on the UN Security Council; the formation of the East Asia Summit that includes India, Australia, and New Zealand; the US-India nuclear deal; and the strategic dimension of India's "Look East" policy—have upset Chinese calculations. Jing-Dong Yuan concurs: "Gone are the days when China could look down upon India as a lightweight and a regional power confined to South Asia. Indeed, India's rise presents serious challenges to China's security interests with regard to territorial disputes, energy security, and regional and global power realignment."[106]

Apparently, India's nuclear tests of 1998 did not cause as much concern in Beijing as India's success in sustaining a high economic growth rate of 8–9 percent since 2004. Though India's 1.6 trillion dollar economy is three times smaller than China's, should it keep growing at 7–8 percent per year, and should China's economy stumble or slow down, the gap between India and China would narrow. In other words, a possible Japanization of the Chinese economy with India emerging as the next China is quite troubling. A *Renmin Ribao* commentary articulated this concern: "Since India declared independence in 1947, it has always been determined to become a big power.... *Although there are still people questioning the possibility,* India did make 'good achievement' in the following 60 years." The commentator accused New Delhi of seeking "big power status with Washington's backing" and "even stretch[ing] its tentacles outside Asia," and "actively chas[ing] after strategic cooperation with some African countries."[107] Most economists believe that India is unlikely to catch up with China, let alone outpace China, which has already emerged as a manufacturing giant. Nonetheless, the prospect of India raising its power, stature, and profile regionally or globally has begun to cause some unease. Much like Zhou, his successors remain uncomfortable with India's "great power dreams" (*daguomeng*), especially the ultra-nationalist view of history propounded by India's right-wing forces.[108]

In particular, the strategic consequences of India's economic resurgence coupled with Washington's offer in March 2005 to "help make India a major world power in the twenty-first century" worried the Chinese. This offer, and the long-term India-US defense cooperation framework and the July 2005 US-Indian nuclear energy deal that followed soon thereafter, drew comparisons by Chinese strategic analysts to "the strategic tilt" toward China executed by President Richard Nixon in 1971 to contain the common Soviet threat. A month after Rice's offer, Premier Wen Jiabao visited India in April 2005 and asked India not to sign a long-term military cooperation agreement with the United States.[109] Perceiving these developments as "destabilizing" for their country's future, China's India-watchers began warning their government that Beijing "should not take India lightly any longer."[110] Lan Jianxue of the Chinese Academy of Social Sciences observed:

> India's position in China's foreign affairs has become increasingly important. Now India has become an object to be roped in by big countries or groups of countries, while India also uses its relations with big countries to expand its own influence. In the foreseeable future, relations between the two countries [China and India] will enter into a crucial period.... As both sides increase their deterrent power [*wei she*] against each other, problems that involve core interests of the two countries will gradually emerge.[111]

So, after a hiatus of a few years, Chinese media commentaries resumed their criticism of Washington's "hegemonic ideas" of drawing "India in as a tool for its global strategic pattern," while accusing India of becoming an American monitoring station to collect intelligence on China. Not all were on board with this line of thinking. Some old India specialists expressed reservations about Washington's ability to draw "India in as a tool for its global strategic pattern," arguing that "India's DNA doesn't allow itself to become an ally subordinate to the US, like Japan or Britain."[112] Nonetheless, most saw India as a "future strategic competitor," that would be an active member of an anti-China grouping due to the structural power shifts in the international system. They advocate putting together a comprehensive "contain India" strategy based on economic tools (aid, trade, infrastructure and resource development), coercive diplomacy and enhanced military cooperation with "China-friendly" countries.

More importantly, an internal study on India undertaken in mid-2005 (with inputs from China's South Asia watchers such as Cheng Ruisheng, Zhou Gang, Ma Jiali, Sun Shihai, Rong Ying, Wang Dehua, Shen Dingli, amongst others) at the behest of the Chinese leadership's "Foreign Affairs Group" recommended that Beijing take all measures to maintain its current *strategic leverage* (in terms of territory, membership of the exclusive Permanent Five and Nuclear Five clubs); *diplomatic advantages* (special relationships, membership of regional and international organizations); and *economic lead* over India.[113] Although the evidence is inconclusive, the most plausible deduction is that this internal re-assessment of India lies behind the recent hardening of China's stance on the territorial dispute and a whole range of other issues in China-India relations.[114]

In particular, the US-India nuclear deal and related defense agreements—once implemented—could bring about a major shift in the power balance in South Asia that is currently tilted in China's favor. In their writings, Chinese analysts seem upset over their southern neighbor's all-consuming passion to become "a big power," and see the nuclear deal as its key to unlocking the door leading to the big league in world politics. A *People's Daily* commentary noted:

> The US-Indian nuclear agreement has strong symbolic significance for India in achieving its dream of a powerful nation.... In recent years, it introduced and implemented a 'Look-East' policy and joined most regional organizations in the East Asian region.... In fact, the purpose of the United States to sign civilian nuclear energy cooperation agreement with India is to enclose India into its global partners' camp, so as to balance the forces of Asia [read, China]. This fits in exactly with India's wishes.[115]

Initially, many Chinese did not expect the India-US nuclear cooperation agreement to cross all the "four big hurdles" (staunch opposition from Beijing-backed Communist parties in India, negotiations on International Atomic Energy Agency safeguards, approval by the Nuclear Suppliers Group (NSG), and its passage by the US Congress). However, its successful passage in September 2008 (despite Beijing's last-minute efforts to sabotage it at the NSG meeting[116]) was received with trepidation and hostility. Official Chinese media described the nuclear deal as "dangerous," because it would allow India to enhance its nuclear capabilities to "check China and serve the US new geopolitical strategy." Even worse, it was seen as ending the nuclear symmetry between New Delhi and Islamabad (or, de-hyphenate the sub-continental rivals) and putting India on par with nuclear China (re-hyphenate China with India). In addition, the regional security situation is seen as having changed to India's benefit with New Delhi now getting American and European support in "pressuring Pakistan to abandon its India obsession" by moving forces to the Afghan border, which, in turn, has the effect of "restricting China's military." All these developments, from Beijing's perspective, are quite disconcerting because a major objective of China's South Asia policy has been to perpetuate parity between India and Pakistan."[117]

Apart from the nuclear deal, India's growing defense expenditure and the evolving India-US military ties that span from arms sales to joint military exercises, maritime, and space technology collaboration have come in for sharp criticism in the official Chinese media.[118] An oft-repeated theme in the CCP mouthpiece, *People's Daily*, is that the US sale of armaments and high technology to India is motivated by a covert American design to provoke armed conflict with China.[119] China's India-watchers warn that Beijing "should not take India lightly any longer." Said one leading commentator: "At present, India is still a lesser power than China in terms of economy and military, both conventionally and unconventionally. *But it is evident that the US has been tipping the balance between China and India*, seeking to woo India away from Russia and China and, in the mean time, feeding India's ambition to match China force for force by its ever burgeoning arms sales to India."[120] In an article in *Guoji Wenti Yanjiu* in March 2008, Cheng Ruisheng, former Chinese ambassador to India, cautioned that the US offer to sell India the advanced F-16 and F-18 fighter planes, P-3C antisubmarine patrol planes, and the Patriot antimissile system, and the transfer of other advanced military technology would not only "substantially promote the fighting capacity of Indian military … but also make India become an important strategic stronghold to guard against China." All this would, according to Cheng, "*deter China from gaining the dominant role in Asia*."[121] Ambassador Cheng warned that "[s]hould India enter into a new rivalry with China upon India's forming an alliance with America and Japan, that would spoil India's peaceful environment, and make it difficult for India to realize its goal of becoming a developed country in the twenty-first century."[122] A China News Network analysis called India "the new favourite concubine of the United States since 2005."[123] Commenting on a slew of agreements in the fields of military, space, and civil nuclear power generation signed during Secretary of State Hillary Clinton's July 2009 India visit, an analytical piece by Li Qiulin in the CCP organ, *Qiu Shi*, said that an economically humbled Washington realizes the limits to its power to guide the world order, but is counting on allies and partners like India to prolong its hegemony. Therefore, the United States is focusing on big power status and geopolitical role for India and considering the latter as a "strategic partner for changing the Asian power balance."[124] Li opined that the United States seeks to utilize India's bases, ports, and military training facilities for facilitating its activities in the Middle East and other regions. This suits India, which wants to acquire US advanced military technology and diversify arms supply sources and use the US support for attaining big power status and maintaining hegemony over the Indian Ocean and South Asia. More intriguingly, *Qiu Shi* commentary speculated about the strengthened US-India cooperation leading to their "unified strategy" on major regional issues, which would not only change the strategic balance but also influence India's military operations and border disputes (presumably with China) due to the availability of American weaponry and advisers.[125]

Despite protestations to the contrary that New Delhi is unwilling and unlikely to play the role of a closely aligned US surrogate as Japan or Britain, China's Asia strategy has come to be based upon the premise that democratic maritime powers such as the United States, Japan,

Australia, and India would eventually form an informal quadrilateral alliance to countervail continental China.[126] As a commentary in *Huanqiu Shibao* noted: "The fact is that Japan, Australia, and India are respectively located at China's northeast, southeast, and southwest, and all are Asian powers, while US power in the Pacific is still unchallengeable. Hence, should the 'alliance of values' concentrating military and ideological flavours in one body take shape, it will have a very great impact on China's security environment."[127] Given its troubled ties and territorial disputes with both Tokyo and New Delhi, Beijing also saw in the conclusion of the Japan-India Declaration on Security Cooperation in October 2008 a strategic design to curb its regional influence. Describing Japan and India as China's "twin challenges" in the next decade, one Chinese expert argued that "Japan is economically stronger today but a declining power over the long term. In contrast, India is economically and militarily weaker at present but a rising power over the long term. So, a carrot and stick policy might induce Japan to cut a deal with China to safeguard its future, but a rising India could be more difficult [as a potential peer competitor] to contend with unless counter-measures are taken now."[128] Add to this India's military exercises with the United States, Japan, and Australia, the US and Indian naval cooperation in the Indian Ocean support, and attempts to establish strategic ties with countries that supposedly fall within China's sphere of influence (Mongolia, South Korea, Vietnam, the Philippines, Taiwan, and Burma)—all of these "new irritants" reinforce Beijing's fears about India's growing role in the US-led containment of China.[129]

A serious escalation in tensions and warnings to India to mend its ways from the Chinese state-controlled media during 2008–09 should be seen against this background. *People's Daily* cautioned that "if India seeks to suppress China" by "taking advantage of its friendship with the West,"[130] then China would not cave in. Its sister publication, *Global Times*, chimed in:

> Indian politicians these days seem to think their country would be doing China a huge favor simply by not joining the 'ring around China' established by the US and Japan. *India's growing power would have a significant impact on the balance* of this question, which has led India to think that fear and gratitude for its restraint will cause China to defer to it on territorial disputes. But this is wishful thinking.... While China wishes to coexist peacefully with India, this desire isn't born out of fear. *India's current course can only lead to a rivalry between the two countries.*[131]

Evidently, these contemporary assessments of India mirror the views of China's leaders and media commentaries circa 1958–1962. The notion that India can be easily manipulated by the United States to adopt anti-China posture seems quite popular in public and strategic circles. It has the advantage of downplaying the root causes of tensions that originate from Beijing's own South Asia policies. Not surprisingly, a distinct chill ("cold peace," in the words of China's ambassador to India) has descended on India-China relations at least since 2007.[132] Although neither side seeks overt competition or open confrontation, the future of China's relations with India appears unpredictable. Given the negative image of India held by most strategic thinkers and leaders in China, it is indeed remarkable that the two emerging Asian powers have kept their diplomatic engagement on course by downplaying irritants and highlighting the positives, particularly their fast-growing bilateral trade figures.

"Territorial Dispute: A Leftover from History"

The unresolved territorial dispute coupled with the unending blame-game on the origins of the 1962 War continues to bedevil bilateral relations. The entire frontier from Kashmir to Burma remains in dispute. No Chinese government has recognized "the so-called MacMahon Line" that defines Arunachal Pradesh's border with Tibet. Premier Zhou Enlai's 1960 offer of a territorial status quo—the swap deal of Arunachal Pradesh for Aksai Chin—is now off the table. Border talks have been going on continuously since 1981 with the Chinese side insisting on the need for "mutual accommodation and mutual adjustment." The PLA, which enjoys considerable clout, seems reluctant to an early compromise on the border issue with India. A major complicating factor in the Sino-Indian equation is that tensions caused by the territorial dispute have been compounded by rivalry between the two giants for power and influence in Asia and beyond. The fear that India will turn its "attention and energies to China's Tibet after subjugating Pakistan and other smaller South Asian neighbors" (as Zhou Enlai and Huang Hua told Kissinger) permeates Chinese thinking about India and has been one of the key elements of China's South Asia policy. Aiding such a perception is the growing American footprint in Pakistan, which has the potential of robbing China of its most steadfast regional proxy to contain India. Apparently, many Chinese strategists see in the unresolved border an invaluable tool to keep India in check. Furthermore, China cannot brush aside third-party (i.e., its ally, Pakistan's) interests in the Sino-Indian territorial dispute.[133] This was not the case with the settlement of China's territorial boundaries with Russia or Vietnam. A resolution of the Sino-Indian border dispute would lead to the deployment of India's military assets on the India-Pakistan border, thereby tilting the military balance decisively in India's favor, much to Pakistan's disadvantage. This, in turn, would deprive Beijing of powerful leverage in its relations with Pakistan and undermine its old strategy of keeping India under strategic pressure on two fronts, particularly by creating border incidents on the India-China frontier (whenever the India-Pakistan border flares up or the Pakistan army is occupied on its western frontier with Afghanistan and internal security operations) so as to assist Beijing's "all-weather friend" Pakistan. Aggressive patrolling keeps India on tenterhooks all along the disputed border as well as tests India's resolve and preparedness, heightens its anxiety, and exposes its strategic vulnerabilities.

Since 2006, their territorial dispute is back in the limelight. Chinese diplomats have been publicly asserting claims to the entire state of Arunachal Pradesh, nowadays called "Zangnan" (Southern Tibet). Tawang, which witnessed fierce fighting in the 1962 War, is considered strategically important. It provides the shortest route from Tibet into India and connects Tibet with the Brahmaputra Valley in India's northeast. Militarily, control over Arunachal—and Tawang in particular—renders the Brahmaputra Valley and India's entire northeast region vulnerable to Chinese penetration. Much to Beijing's chagrin, the Dalai Lama announced for the first time in 2008 that Tawang is a part of India, infuriating China but bolstering India's territorial claims.[134] However, China's construction of road and rail networks across the Tibetan plateau has tilted the balance of forces along the contested frontier in China's favor. The Tibetan uprising in 2008 and riots in Xinjiang in 2009 exacerbated the Chinese sense of insecurity. Following the worldwide pro-Tibet protests in March 2008, fierce anti-India rhetoric was allowed to rage in the closely monitored blogosphere. The deployment of a large number of forces in Tibet and Xinjiang is aimed at both suppressing popular unrest, and if need be, teaching India another lesson. In a throwback to the 1960s-era rhetoric, *People's Daily* on August 12, 2009, launched a vituperative attack on "the aggressive attitude of the Nehru government," holding him responsible for "provoking the 1962 War" with the backing of "the then imperialist world, in particular, the U.S." It lamented that "[e]ven today, some Western powers still choose to side with the right-wing extremist elements in India as against China on the decades-long border disputes."[135] Several commentaries in the state-controlled media have made it clear that Beijing would not make any concessions on the territorial dispute. Such writings have not appeared in China's official press for decades. More importantly, as it has done in the case of Taiwan and Tibet in the past, Beijing is internationalizing its territorial dispute with India so as to force countries and international (esp. financial) institutions to choose sides. From Beijing's perspective, even adoption of a posture of neutrality on the "Zangnan" (Arunachal Pradesh) issue by countries would be a triumph for Chinese diplomacy and defeat for India. Although China claims India a third-tier security priority, far behind internal insecurity and challenges in the East Asian littoral, the Dalai Lama's presence in India and Beijing's fears of losing control over Tibet seem to elevate India to China's first-tier threat.

"Admiral Zheng He's Armada Returns to the Western (Indian) Ocean"

As noted earlier, China's leaders since the days of Mao have been wary of India's ambition to "lead and organize the Indian Ocean region." An unintended consequence of Washington's "gunboat diplomacy" during the 1971 India-Pakistan War was the gradual emergence of the Indian Navy as a formidable force in the Indian Ocean region. During the 1980s and 1990s, the Indian Navy's area of interest was defined as the northern Indian Ocean, from the Persian Gulf to the straits of Malacca. As China's dependence on overseas energy and trade routes grew in the 1990s, Beijing publicly began questioning India's view of its status in the Indian Ocean. A high-ranking PLA officer and director of the Chinese Academy of Military Sciences, General Zhao Nanqi, was quoted in 1993 as saying that China would extend its naval operations farther than the South and East China Sea to check attempts by India to "dominate" the Indian Ocean and other regional waters. Accusing India of seeking to develop a navy to rival that of "large global powers," General Zhao said that "this is something which we cannot accept … we are not prepared to let the Indian Ocean 'become India's Ocean.'"[136] The writings of Chinese experts refer to Indian military posturing in the Indian Ocean and to strategic partnerships India is developing with several countries in Southeast Asia and East Africa. From China's perspective, India's naval strategy restricts China's strategic space and attempts to extend influence and establish outposts in the region.[137] As a global maritime trading power, China is now seeking to once again project force into the Indian Ocean in the manner of the fleets sent out under the command of Admiral Zheng He nearly 600 years ago during the Ming dynasty. A naval analyst, Zhang Ming, describes India as "China's most realistic strategic adversary." Zhang worries that the

Indian islands of Andaman and Nicobar Archipelago could be used like a "metal chain" to block Chinese access to the Straits of Malacca. Zhang warns: "Once India commands the Indian Ocean, it will not be satisfied with its position and will continuously seek to extend its influence, and its eastward strategy will have a particular impact on China."[138]

Beijing is particularly concerned about the maritime dimension of India's ""Look East" policy, striving to push forward toward the Pacific Ocean with the goal of making itself a "colorful big power."[139] Since the late 1990s, India's navy has been conducting regular exercises with and making port visits in South Korea, Japan, the Philippines, Vietnam, and Indonesia. The geopolitical rationale for expanding India's maritime horizons beyond the Straits of Malacca into the South China Sea, according to one analyst, is to "secure the peace and stability in Southeast Asia, ensuring that this region will not be under the influence and control of any big power (read, China)."[140] Naval exercises between the Indian Navy and the Vietnamese Navy in 2000 in the South China Sea drew protests from Beijing. (To allay Beijing's concerns, the Indian Navy's joint naval exercises and port visits were extended to China in 2003.) According to Zhang Guihong: "One of the main motives for Indian navy force entering into Southeast Asia and South China Sea is to curb China's growing military influence in this region, containing China in terms of security, so as to raise its own international status and strengthen the negotiating position in its competition with China."[141] Much to China's chagrin, India's naval activism has encouraged many countries in the region to "view India as a possible counterweight to future China in Southeast Asia."[142] Growing angst over Indian naval forays in the Pacific Ocean led one Chinese analyst to ask: "Are we all ready to accept India as a Pacific power?"[143] Significantly, India's naval expansion is taking place at a time when China is itself pushing out into the Pacific and beyond into the Indian oceans.

"Teach India a Lesson Again"

Until 2005, while Beijing was expanding its strategic space in southern Asia, Chinese public perceptions of India were generally benign, even bordering on neglect and indifference. Topics such as Bollywood, Buddhism, India's English-language and info-tech (IT) prowess, instability, and the widespread poverty dominated Chinese public perceptions of India. The 1962 War was rarely mentioned in strategic circles or discussed in official Chinese media commentaries prior to 2006. However, a radical change in Chinese public attitudes toward India has noticeably taken place since then. Chinese Netizens' views of their southern rival have turned increasingly negative. This shift can be attributed in part to an increasing number of Chinese strategic experts, bloggers, retired diplomats, and even officially sanctioned websites and PLA-linked think tanks ratcheting up an "India threat" scenario. Beginning in early 2006, some strategic journals and pro-Beijing Hong Kong media published commentaries discussing the possibilities of a "limited border war" to "teach India a lesson again."[144] The Tibetan riots of March 2008—which refocused the world's attention on Tibet as China was preparing for Olympic glory—provided an additional impetus.[145] As in the past, Beijing laid the responsibility for the Tibetan unrest on exiled Tibetan leader the Dalai Lama and India. The Chinese media and strategic experts raised their anti-India rhetoric, calling New Delhi "arrogant" and warning it not to "misjudge the situation as it did in 1962," and to "stay away from a path of confrontation."[146] Though official Beijing expressed satisfaction over India's handling of Tibetan protests during the Olympic torch rally in New Delhi, the Chinese strategic community criticized India's continued support for the Dalai Lama "under the pretext of democracy, human rights, and religious freedom." Accusing the Indian government of "walking today along the old road of resisting China," the PLA leadership, through an article posted on the website of the China Institute of International Strategic Studies, cautioned that India should "not requite kindness with ingratitude."[147] In sharp contrast with the past, Chinese participants at international conferences began articulating their country's security concerns vis-à-vis India. And public reminders from the Communist Party's media of China's decisive victory over India in the 1962 War spiked during 2008–09.[148] For example, in June 2009, a *People's Daily*'s leading strategic expert warned that a fresh border dispute between China and India could "plunge the two neighbors again into a 'partial military action.'"[149]

A major theme in media commentaries was the desire to "capture the lost lands" and crush India for daring to compete with China.[150] Other themes included India as a paper tiger, the blunder supposedly committed by Mao in withdrawing after occupying the Arunachal Pradesh area in 1962, the need to avenge the historical wrongs in the event of another military conflict, no bartering of territory for friendship, and the Chinese society's comparative advantage because of its homogenous character as against the fissiparous tendencies in the Indian society.[151] Many of the commentaries and web postings seem to be penned by "insiders," as they displayed intimate knowledge of military operations, logistics, terrain, ORBAT (order of battle: number, location, weaponry, and strengths of army divisions), and a solid understanding of India's vulnerabilities and history of China-India border talks. Many of China's India specialists claim that the war-mongering rhetoric was not representative of China's official policy and that sensational press articles represented the shrill voice of a disgruntled minority which advocated a tougher line toward India but felt marginalized in the policymaking community. After all, similar commentaries have appeared against Japan, Vietnam, and South Korea in the recent past. However, it is worth noting that this media campaign coincided with a number of negative developments in China-India relations on a whole range of issues from membership in international institutions to territorial dispute and maritime and resource security issues. Besides, the fact that the CCP organ *Renmin Ribao* (*People's Daily online*) and its sister publication, *Global Times* (which represents ultra-nationalist viewpoint), took the lead in publishing hard-hitting articles castigating India pointed to a concerted anti-India media campaign that enjoyed some degree of official support. As an article in London's *Sunday Times* observed: "Not everyone in Beijing speaks in the silky language of the foreign ministry. Curiously, the enemy most often spoken of is India. Interestingly, the censors permit alarmingly frank discussion on the Internet of the merits of another war against India to secure the Tibetan plateau."[152] The most plausible explanation is that the Chinese government tolerates and perhaps encourages this nationalistic outpouring to pressure New Delhi to comply with its demands and desist from balancing China by tilting toward Washington and Tokyo. In part, it also reflects a breakdown in consensus on how to deal with a rising and globalizing India.

The print and electronic media campaign against India permitted by the Chinese government censors—unusual in its sarcasm and ridicule of Indian aspirations of becoming a global power but similar to the public fury unleashed against Japan in 2005—has had a negative impact on large sections of Chinese public opinion. The 2008 survey by the Pew Research Center's Pew Global Attitudes Project found 24 percent of Chinese ranking India as an "enemy."[153] In June 2009, an online poll conducted by *Global Times* showed that 90 percent of respondents believed India, more than any other country, threatened China's security.[154] All top four "Most Commented" opinion pieces on *People's Daily online* in 2009 were on India—written mostly in jingoistic tone and highly critical of Indian foreign policy and defense posture.[155] In a survey conducted by Beijing-based Horizon Research Consultancy in 2010, Chinese regarded Pakistan as a better ally, and placed India next only to the United States and Japan in the list of nations that threatened their country the most.[156] With most Chinese now perceiving India as a major threat—nearly 50 years after they fought a border war—China's nationalists have found in India a new chimera against whom to direct their energies. Thus, after half a century of preparing the nation against threats from the Soviet "social imperialism," the US hegemony, Japanese militarism, and Taiwan and Tibetan separatists, China has found a new threat in the new century: it happens to be none other than the "same ol' India"!

The Indian media (especially TV channels), always wary of China, did not take long to join the battle of sensationalizing alleged Chinese border incursions and by hyping "the China threat."[157] One reason China's leaders have long regarded India's democracy with contempt is because of its media, which is also partly blamed for the 1962 War. Foreign Minister Pranab Mukherjee was asked by his hosts during his 2009 China visit to "rein in the Indian media that was trying to spoil bilateral ties." When Mukherjee tried to explain how the media works in a democracy, he was curtly told: "We know how things work in India."[158] Strategic analysts in Beijing voice concern over what they perceive as an aggressive anti-China campaign by the Indian media over disputed borders, Tibet, UN reforms, unfair trade practices, terrorism, and nuclear issues. According to Hu Shisheng, an expert at the China Institute of Contemporary International Relations: "Most Indian elite are hostile to China due to the hype of the 'China threat theory' in Indian media, even though senior officials of the two countries have quite a good relationship."[159] From the Chinese perspective, the Indian media's negative portrayal of China bolsters the credibility of hawkish arguments, which state that China and its allies harbor hostile intent toward India. The media in India is also accused of collaborating to "curry favour with the Western anti-China forces by presenting their readers with biased information and fabricated stories about China."[160]

With the war in "Chindia" media raging on, some commentators drew parallels to the situation in 2008–09 and in the pre-1962 period. In a replay of events of 1958 when the PLA launched an "all out war" against the Tibetan rebels following the Lhasa uprising that culminated in the 1962 War, Beijing is now engaged, by its own admission, in a "life and death struggle" over Tibet and has launched a vilification campaign against the Dalai Lama. And India is again under greater Chinese pressure to proscribe his supporters' activities.[161] Many Chinese see the unrest in Tibet as instigated by the Indian government at the behest of the Americans, which uses the Tibetan government-in-exile to destabilize the Chinese hold on Tibet and open the door to Indian expansion. As they did from 1958 to 1962, the armed forces of both sides are once again pushing into remote and previously (for the most part) unoccupied mountainous frontier regions. India's plans to bolster its defenses along the LAC are labeled a "new forward policy" in the Chinese media. Even the rhetoric sounds familiar. One commentary claimed that the ghost of 1962 has not been exorcised from the memories of a small, but influential, category of retired Indian generals and diplomats, who still harbor ambitions of "giving it back to the Chinese."[162] While refuting one Indian defense analyst's warning of a Chinese attack by 2012, noted journalist Chen Xiaochen went on to caution India against "deploy[ing] more troops in the border area, similar to its Forward Policy 50 years ago," and wondered as to whether "India's 'New Forward Policy,' as the old one did 50 years ago, [would] trigger a '2012 war'?"[163] The Chinese Ministry of National Defense routinely denies carrying out "provocative actions" along the India-China border, maintaining that Chinese border patrols strictly abide by the relevant agreements on the Line of Actual Control (LAC).[164]

China's diplomats have reportedly discerned a certain degree of assertiveness, confidence and arrogance in their Indian counterparts that was missing in the 1980s and 1990s. Thus, as in the 1950s, India is again being viewed as a growing, ambitious, and nationalistic power with whom China may have to have a day of reckoning. According to one China-watcher, the 1962 War, ostensibly fallout of a contentious boundary dispute, was in reality the interim finale of an intense rivalry, with the purpose of cutting India down to size. This is corroborated in an authoritative biography of Nehru with a quote from a Chinese official who explained that the prime objective of the 1962 War was to demolish India's "arrogance" and "illusions of grandeur" and that China "had taught India a lesson and, if necessary, they would teach her a lesson again and again." Apparently, "the emphasis on 'again and again' indicates that China may not be averse to using a military option in the future."[165] More importantly, just as Nehru insisted on treating the McMahon Line as an "established fact" in the pre-war period, the Singh government is now insisting that "Arunachal Pradesh as an integral part of India" is a truth, thereby leaving little room for compromise.[166] There is a history to this: in the months leading up to the 1962 War, India also took fairly strident positions in public against China, only to be humiliated in the brief conflict.

Last but not least, China perceives India as the weakest link in an evolving anti-China coalition of democratic and maritime powers (the United States, Japan, Australia, and India). Apparently, some Chinese strategic thinkers feel that a limited war with India would send a resounding message to those who are again courting and counting on India as a balancer or counterweight to China in the twenty-first century.[167] Historically, rising powers have chosen to attack the most vulnerable or weaker power ("easy prey") in order to effect a shattering blow to the rival coalition. After all, a coalition is only as strong as its weakest link. As an old Chinese saying goes: "Kill the chicken to scare the monkey" (*shaji jinghou*)—(kill the weaker enemy to scare the stronger enemy). Some hardliners assume that should an action-reaction cycle escalate, the PLA is better-placed to control the levers of escalation. One commentary on the pros and cons of a war concluded that China would win any conflict and reap broader strategic rewards: "In the short term, India does not have the ability ... to launch a war against China.... This implies that in a conflict with China, India will be the one to suffer the most."[168] As China's power grows, the PLA might be tempted at some point in the future ("when conditions are ripe") to give a crushing blow to India's great power aspirations by occupying Tawang and giving India's military a bloody nose, as in 1962, the Chinese thinking goes, so Beijing need not worry about the "India challenge" for another half of a century. Instead of challenging China, Indian leaders would then be much more deferential in dealing with China. It would give Beijing a free hand in the exclusive use of the Brahmaputra river waters that could be diverted to China's parched northeast regions. A short and swift victory would also underscore the need for other countries in Asia, especially US friends and allies, to accommodate China's growing power by aligning with, rather than against, Beijing.

Having said that, there are several striking dissimilarities as well, the most important being that today's China and India are nuclear-armed nations with enormous stakes in maintaining peace in building a post-American world order. Though India is no match for China in force-on-force posture, it is no pushover militarily. Unlike the PLA that has not seen combat since the Vietnam War of 1979, India has a battle-hardened and experienced military. If Beijing is determined to gain the "lost territory" in Arunachal Pradesh, India is equally determined not to see a replay of the 1962 War by losing large chunks of territory. With India embarking upon a massive military modernization plan, a punitive war may well be too costly and its outcome unpredictable, especially after 2015. Besides, the CCP leadership may not find persuasive the idea put forward by hardliners that "teaching India a lesson" would buy a few decades of Indian quiescence and deference toward China.[169] For the reaction in India the last time that happened was quite the opposite. For Beijing, a hard-line approach to India could backfire and drive India and its other Asian neighbors into stronger opposition to China and deeper alignment with Washington and Tokyo, culminating in the emergence of an Asian NATO. And finally, the pursuit of aggressive foreign adventures would destroy the benign "peaceful rise" image that China is so assiduously striving to achieve. For the foreseeable future, it is safe to conclude that the India-China border will continue to be characterized by incursions, tensions, and perhaps skirmishes, interspersed with endless border talks. A conflict will cost India dearly in terms of economic developmental objectives and the political ambition of emerging as a great power in a multipolar Asia.

Beijing's India Strategy: "Chinese Checkers 2.0"

An analysis of Chinese perspectives on India over the last half century proves the age-old adage that "the more things change, the more they remain the same." From Beijing's perspective, as long as India understands that China is the preeminent great power in Asia, and New Delhi keeps her subordinate place in the hierarchy, both will enjoy a mutually beneficial relationship. However, should India aspire to emerge as China's equal or peer competitor—and that too with help from the West, then the entire gamut of issues are open for review and recasting. Convinced that India has opted for the latter course, Chinese analysts and diplomats caution that "certain changes adverse to India are likely to take place," which "would spoil India's peaceful environment, and make it difficult for India to realize its goal of becoming a developed country in the twenty-first century."[170] Not surprisingly, a long dormant border dispute, which had not flared up in decades, has been re-ignited, supposedly "settled" issues of Sikkim and Kashmir are being re-opened, and Beijing is blocking India's efforts to play a greater role in regional (e.g., East Asian Community) and international institutions (the UN Security Council). China's fears of India's participation in wider forms of strategic encirclement—real or imagined—have led Beijing to unveil a comprehensive "Chinese Checkers 2.0" strategy. Its cumulative effect is to deny India a peaceful environment on its periphery that is crucial to sustaining India's high economic growth rates for the next couple of decades in order to close the power gap with China. Beijing's revamped India strategy incorporates timeless tactics of speed, surprise, maneuver, deception, preemption, engagement, and harassment on multiple fronts simultaneously. The salient features of Beijing's new India policy are as follows:

- *Encirclement*: strengthen China's strategic presence in Tibet, Pakistan, Nepal, Sri Lanka, Bangladesh, Burma, and in the

Indian Ocean island states, and keep the territorial dispute and the threat of two-front war alive in ways that make India shift priorities and scarce resources from its economic development goals to an arms build-up that stunts India's economic growth.

- *Envelopment*: China's strategic and economic envelopment of South Asia through alliances, military build-up, trade, arms sales, and bases in the region. Integration of South Asian economies with the larger Chinese economy via aid, trade dependence, and investment in resource extraction and public infrastructure projects (highways, ports, railroads, pipelines, economic zones) would provide Beijing with greater leverage in bilateral relations.
- *Entanglement*: exploit India's domestic contradictions and religious and regional fault lines to keep India preoccupied with multiple security concerns within the confines of South Asia.[171]

Apparently, the major objective is to undermine India's will and sap its energy to compete with China, preferably without striking a blow. More importantly, it signals to Asia and the world that India falls short in being a "balancing power" so that no country looks toward India as a counterweight to China. For the foreseeable future, it is safe to conclude that the India-China relations will continue to be characterized by competition, perhaps tensions, interspersed with endless border talks and limited cooperation on issues of mutual concern. According to one Chinese analyst, Dai Bing, "while a 'hot war' is out of the question, a 'cold war' between the two countries is increasingly likely."[172] Although neither side seeks overt competition or open confrontation, the future of China's relations with India appears uncertain.

Conclusion

Despite dramatic changes in the domestic and international contexts since the early 1960s, little seems to have changed in Chinese attitudes toward and perceptions of India. In Beijing's view, a mutually beneficial partnership with India can be established if the Dalai Lama and the territorial dispute issues dividing them are resolved and India gives up its hegemonic aspirations in the region. As in the past, Chinese leaders entertain doubts about the historical authenticity of the Indian nation, show contempt for India's great power ambitions, perceive India as a pawn in Western designs to encircle and contain China, and worry about the strategic ramifications of India's growing power for Tibet's future. Interestingly, these perceptions and concerns have led four successive generations of Chinese leadership to contemplate or hint broadly about "teach[ing] India a lesson again" (apparently, to force India to be deferential) at least once in every decade since the 1962 War (Zhou Enlai in 1971, Deng Xiaoping in 1987, Jiang Zemin in 1999, and Hu Jintao in 2009), while refraining from actually doing so. Given the dominance of the realist zero-sum approach in Chinese strategic thinking, India's great power dreams constitute China's nightmare. Their burgeoning economic ties notwithstanding, the steady emergence of India as a powerful player is not looked upon favorably in Chinese strategic circles. Though leaders from both countries often rule out rivalry and repeat the ritualistic talk of enough space for both India and China to grow, such platitudes cannot obliterate the trust deficit that dates back to the bruising 1962 War, Tibet, and the unresolved territorial dispute. Chinese strategists keep a wary eye on India's military spending and weapons acquisitions, global aspirations, and the developments in India's naval and nuclear doctrines for their impact on China's primacy in Asia. New Delhi's development of strategic links and assets, in particular, is raising anxiety in Beijing. A theme dominant in all Chinese commentaries circa 2000 is that India's growing power—backed by the United States—would bring about a shift in the Asian balance of power detrimental to China. Chinese official media portrays India as a "big power" with "hegemonic ambitions" posing a threat from the Middle East to East Asia.

There is a great diversity of views on India in today's China. The hawkish PLA views usually tend to drown out more moderate Chinese voices in Indian and international media. How far such views reflect official thinking is debatable. What is not debatable is that the history of Sino-Indian relations rules out the possibility of any leadership divisions on India; in particular, any inference that the Chinese foreign policy establishment is not in agreement with the "contain India" policy of the country's military would be erroneous. Given the negative attitudes and perceptions, it is indeed remarkable that China and India have kept their diplomatic engagement on course by downplaying irritants and highlighting the positives. Despite the sparring on stapled visas for Kashmiris, harsh words on the Dalai Lama, border disputes, and denial of market access, temperatures have cooled and saner voices have prevailed. More importantly, leaders in both countries exhibit a shared interest in not allowing tensions and frictions to overwhelm the relationship as a whole. Bilaterally, the two sides insist on viewing each other as partners, not as a security threat, so as to build a relationship based on equality, in which each is sensitive to the core concerns and aspirations of the other. There is a growing realization that this bilateral relationship is critical to the world order as both countries try to position themselves as drivers and pivots of global institutions and the world economy. Hopefully, contacts at all levels will reduce misperceptions, misunderstandings, and miscalculation. And increasing economic interdependence would constrain any foreign policy behavior that would jeopardize foreign investment, trade flows, market access, and energy supplies.

Nonetheless, the fact of the matter is that China and India are locked in a classic security dilemma: one country sees its own actions as self-defensive, but the same actions appear aggressive to the other. Few if any of China's strategic thinkers seem to hold warm or positive views of India for China's future. Faced with exponential growth in China's power and influence, India feels the need to take counter-balancing measures and launch strategic initiatives to emerge as a great power, but these are perceived as challenging and threatening in China. Like any other established status quo great power, China wants to ensure that its position remains strong vis-à-vis challenger India for strategic, economic and geopolitical reasons. To this end, Beijing's India policy resists attempts by India to undermine China's influence or to achieve strategic parity (via military and economic expansion and membership in the UN Security Council) through a combination of strategic, economic, and diplomatic means. Through closer strategic ties with India's neighboring countries, China is warning India not to take any counter-measures to balance Beijing's growing might. Several developments during 2008–09 led to a rapid deterioration in China-India relations, verging on a pre-1962 scenario. The misperceptions of each other's intensions and fears—real or imagined—could set in motion a chain of reactions escalating toward a zero-sum contest. In the foreseeable future, any substantive change in the India-China bilateral relationship seems unlikely because "beneath the diplomatic niceties and rhetoric for strategic partnership … lurks the strong negative images Chinese hold of India (and vice versa)."[173] Sino-Indian ties remain fragile, unstable, and as vulnerable as ever to sudden deterioration as a result of misperceptions, misconceptions, accidents, and eruptions of unresolved issues. As in the case of Sino-US ties, Sino-Indian competitive tendencies rooted in geopolitics and nationalism are unlikely to be easily offset or overcome, even by growing economic and trade links. For the foreseeable future, China-India relations will continue to be characterized more by rivalry, competition, and containment and less by cooperation and engagement. Although India-China ties at government levels remain stable, the possibility of a renewed confrontation between two simultaneously rising Asian giants at different levels of growth cannot be completely ruled out as they seek to constrain the other through engagement, alliances, proxies, and regional entanglements.

Notes

[1] J. Mohan Malik, "Zhou, Mao, and Nixon's 1972 conversations on India," *Issues & Studies: An International Quarterly on China, Taiwan & East Asian Affairs*, 38:3 (September 2002), 184-219.

[2] The records of Nixon and Kissinger's conversations with Zhou and Mao are available online at the National Security Archives of George Washington University website <http://www.gwu.edu/~nsarchiv/NSAEBB/NSAEBB70/>; <http://www.gwu.edu/~nsarchiv/NSAEBB/NSAEBB70/>. Significant excisions appear in the Nixon-Zhou discussions of India, the former Soviet Union, Japan, and Taiwan, demonstrating that even today some of the information is regarded as sensitive by US government agencies. Nonetheless, these documents go well beyond the accounts of the talks that Nixon and Kissinger both provided in their respective memoirs which, while focusing on the Vietnam War and the Soviet threat, did not reveal much on the India-Pakistan-China triangular relationship. See R. Nixon, *RN: The Memoirs of Richard Nixon* (New York: Grosset & Dunlap, 1978), 559-80; and H. A. Kissinger, *White House Years* (New York: Little Brown, 1979), 1049-96.

[3] Kissinger's memorandum on "My talks with Chou En-lai" to Nixon of July 14, 1971, Document 40, 19-20 <http://www.gwu.edu/~nsarchiv/NSAEBB/NSAEBB66/ch-40.pdf>.

[4] W. Burr's book, *The Kissinger Transcripts*, shows that Kissinger was very careful about what he included and excluded in his memoirs of the Nixon years in his *White House Years* (1979) and *Years of Upheaval* (1982). "The biggest omission is the extraordinary degree to which Nixon and Kissinger tilted U.S. policy towards China, to the point of offering the Chinese sensitive intelligence information on Soviet military deployments, in their effort to cement a 'tacit' alliance against the Soviet Union." For details, see W. Burr (ed), *The Kissinger Transcripts: The Top Secret Talks with Beijing and Moscow: A National Security Archive Document Reader* (New York: The New Press, 1999).

[5] Some of the transcript conversations would not only irritate or disappoint the Indians, Pakistanis, Japanese, and Russians today but could also prove embarrassing to the Chinese and the Americans themselves. Flattery and disparaging comments about Soviet and other Asian leaders are one common characteristic. For example, the Nixon-Zhou conversation is peppered with scorn and contempt for the then Soviet ambassador to the United Nations, Jacob Malik (see <http://www.gwu.edu/~ nsarchiv/nsa/publications/DOC_readers/kissinger/nixzhou/12-01.htm> [hereafter, Document 2], 18-19.

[6] Interestingly, while Nixon took great delight in taking a dig at his domestic political opponents (both Republican and Democrat), the Chinese premier, true to form, did not utter a single word about the deteriorating health of Chairman Mao, the domestic political situation (e.g., the fall of Lin Biao), or

the intense power struggle that was going on in the faction-ridden CCP at that time.

[7] Zhong Yin bianjiang ziwei fanji zuozhanshi [History of the China-India Border Self-defensive War], (Beijing: Junshi kexue chubanshe, 1994), 37-40. Xu Yan, Zhong Yin bianjie zhi zhan lishi zhenxiang [True History of the China-India Border War], (Hong Kong: Cosmos Books Ltd., 1993), 28, 29-30, 50, 53. Xu's study, based mostly on primary documents, deals with China's decisionmaking process. Liu Xuecheng's The Sino-Indian Border Dispute and Sino-Indian Relations (Lanham, Md.: University Press of America, 1994) and Wang Hongwei, "Zhong yin bianjie wenti de lishi yu 1962 nian Zhong Yin bianjie zhanzheng" ["Historical background of the Sino-Indian border problem and the 1962 Sino-Indian War"], Yatai ziliao [Asia Pacific materials], No. 1, March 18, 1989, 1-13. For the Indian version, see P. B. Sinha, A. A. Athale, with S. N. Prasad (eds), History of the Conflict with China, 1962 (History Division, Ministry of Defence, Government of India, 1992).

[8] Burr, *The Kissinger Transcripts*, pp. 59-65; R. L. Garthoff, *Détente and Confrontation: American-Soviet Relations from Nixon to Reagan* (Washington, D.C.: Brookings Institution, 1994), esp. chap. 8: "Triangular diplomacy and regional conflict: the Indo-Pakistani war, 1971," 295-322; J. W. Garver, *Protracted Contest: India-China Rivalry in the Twentieth Century* (Seattle and London: University of Washington Press, 2001); J. W. Garver, "China's decision for war with India in 1962," Chapter 4 in A. I. Johnston and R. S. Ross (eds), *New Directions in the Study of China's Foreign Policy* (Stanford University Press, 2006), 86-130; and S. A. Hoffman, *India and the China Crisis* (Berkeley/London: University of California Press, 1990). The "cultural wall" and Chinese Sino-centric arrogance and its consequences are discussed in Y. I. Vertzberger, *Misperceptions in Foreign Policymaking: The Sino-Indian Conflict, 1959-1962* (Boulder, Colo.: Westview Press, 1984).

[9] Nixon, RN: The Memoirs of Richard Nixon, 559.

[10] A preliminary round of discussions between Zhou Enlai and Nixon's then National Security Adviser, Henry Kissinger, had taken place six months earlier, during the latter's secret visit to Beijing via Islamabad in July 1971, which paved the way for Nixon's historic visit. For the Kissinger-Zhou talks in July 1971, see W. Burr (ed), *Henry Kissinger's Secret Trip to China: The Beijing-Washington Back-Channel September 1970-July 1971* (National Security Archive Electronic Briefing Book No. 66, February 27, 2002) <http://www.gwu.edu/ ~nsarchiv/NSAEBB/NSAEBB66/>.

[11] For Pakistan's role in facilitating the Sino-U.S. rapprochement, see F. S. Aijazuddin, *From a Head, Through a Head, To a Head: The Secret Channel Between the U.S. and China through Pakistan* (Oxford: Oxford University Press, 2000).

[12] In October 1971, there was hardly any discussion on the India-Pakistan situation despite the threat of a looming war.

[13] Kissinger's memorandum on "My talks with Chou En-lai" to Nixon of July 14, 1971, Document 40:9-20, 22 <http://www.gwu.edu/~nsarchiv/ NSAEBB/NSAEBB66/ch-40.pdf>; and Kissinger, *White House Years*, 914, 848-49.

[14] Document 4 of the Nixon-Zhou transcripts—which also happens to be one of the more heavily excised documents—further confirms this. Among the excisions is an aspersion by Nixon against the Indians. See <http://www.gwu.edu/~nsarchiv/nsa/publications/DOC_readers/kissinger/nixzhou/14-01.htm> [hereafter, Document 4], 28.

[15] See <http://www.gwu.edu/~nsarchiv/nsa/publications/DOC_readers/kissinger/nixzhou/13-01.htm> [hereafter, Document 3], 10.

[16] At the height of the polemics in 1962, after China had attacked Indian frontier posts in proclaimed self-defense, the Chinese government issued a statement claiming that the "goal pursued by this ambitious Nehru is the establishment of a great empire unprecedented in India's history." Government of the People's Republic of China, *The Sino-Indian Boundary Question* (Peking: Foreign Languages Press, 1965), 39.

[17] Ibid. Italics added.

[18] J. Mohan Malik, "The India-China divide," *Hindustan Times*, May 24, 1999.

[19] Document 2, 17. Italics added.

[20] Burr, The Kissinger Transcripts, 195-96.

[21] Garver, Protracted Contest, 113.

[22] Burr, The Kissinger Transcripts, 42-43.

[23] Garver, Protracted Contest, 113.

[24] Document 3, 6. Italics added.

[25] J. Mohan Malik, "South Asia in China's foreign relations," *Pacifica Review*, 13:1 (February 2001), 73-85.

[26] See Jing-dong Yuan, "India's rise after Pokhran II: Chinese analyses and assessments," *Asian Survey,* 41:6 (November/December 2001), 978-1001.

[27] Discussion here draws on Nixon-Zhou Document 3, 4; and Kissinger-Zhou Document 36, 5-6 <http://www.gwu.edu/~nsarchiv/NSAEBB/NSAEBB66/ch-36.pdf>. Maxwell's *India's China War* (New York: Anchor Books, 1972) gave a pro-Beijing account of the 1962 war by an Australian journalist based in India. The major flaw was that Maxwell accepted the official Chinese statements at face value while attributing ulterior motives to the statements and actions of the Indian leadership. Most objective observers concede that both sides bore responsibility for escalating the dispute to the point of open war. See, for example, Vertzberger, *Misperceptions in Foreign Policymaking*; Hoffman, *India and the China Crisis*.

[28] A former Singaporean diplomat who accompanied Lee Kuan Yew on his first visit to China told this author that Zhou Enlai (and later his successor, Deng Xiaoping) used to give a copy of Maxwell's *India's China War* to visiting leaders and dignatories. Nixon had read the book (on Kissinger's advice) and when Prime Minister Indira Gandhi held talks with Nixon just before the outbreak of the 1971 war, he said the book provided a very interesting account of the beginning of the war between India and China. Predictably, Nixon told a laughing Zhou that "she didn't react very favorably when I said that." Document 3, 3.

[29] Document 3, 4.

[30] Hoffman, India and the China Crisis, 125.

[31] "*Mao Zedong sixiang wansui*" ["Long Live Mao Zedong Thought"], in *Miscellany of Mao Tse-tong Thought* (1949-1968), 2, No. 61269 (February 20, 1974), Joint Publication Research Service, 573; Garver, "China's decision for war with India in 1962," 96.

[32] Discussion here is based on Garver, "China's decision for war with India in 1962," 89-90; and Xu Yan, *True History of the China-India Border War.*

[33] Garver, "China's decision for war with India in 1962," 109-114.

[34] Garver, "China's decision for war with India in 1962," 104-5

[35] Document 3, 2. Italics added.

[36] In his authoritative study on *India and the China Crisis*, Steven Hoffman gives, however, another explanation for Nehru's intransigence and angst over Zhou's negotiating stance. A theme pursued in this book, and one which has been ignored in the earlier studies of the China-India conflict, is the importance of Indian nationalism, which influenced the Indian leadership's basic worldview and its response to China's demands for territorial concessions from India. Hoffman argues that the "Nehru government ... perceived in the Chinese negotiating stance an attempt to denigrate the historical authenticity of the Indian nation." In other words, the view was that unlike China, India was an artificial construct put together by the departing British colonialists. That is why "China never understood the psychological dimension of India's handling of the border dispute." (Hoffman, *India and the China Crisis*, 113-4). Coming as it did soon after India's independence from centuries of colonialism, the Chinese demand for territorial concessions was seen as demeaning and humiliating by Indian nationalists led by Nehru.

[37] Garver, Protracted Contest, 57.

[38] A retired major general and a respected military historian, D. K. Palit (upon whom Hoffman relies very heavily), began his own book on the 1962 war with these words: "[This book] records the inept handling of political and military affairs by the government and the army during that crisis—so inept that it verged on the bizarre.... It is incomprehensible that a government headed by so highly regarded a statesman as Jawaharlal Nehru could have made such gross misjudgments and breaches of established procedure." See D. K. Palit, *War in High Himalayas: The Indian Army in Crisis, 1962* (New Delhi: Lancer International, 1991), 1-2.

[39] Garver, "China's decision for war with India in 1962," 87.

[40] Document 3, 25.

[41] Ibid, 26.

[42] See W. Burr, *Cold War History*, "Sino-American relations, 1969: Sino-Soviet border conflict and steps toward rapprochement," at the National Security Archives website.

[43] N. Maxwell, "The Chinese account of the 1969 fighting at Chenpao," *The China Quarterly*, 56 (October/December 1973), 730-39; and Maxwell, *India's China War.*

[44] After all, Kissinger and Nixon would not have liked to see the US opening to China tainted by the perception that China was the aggressor on the Ussuri. It was in their interest to portray China as the victim of Soviet aggression.

[45] L. J. Goldstein, "Return to Zhenbao Island: who started shooting and why it matters," *The China Quarterly*, 168 (December 2001), 989, 995.
[46] Sun Shao, Chen Zhibin, Snows of the Himalaya Mountains: The True Record of the China-India War [Ximalaya shan de xue, zhong yin zhanzheng shilu], (Taiyuan: Bei Yue wenyi chubanshe, 1991), 99-100.
[47] M. J. Akbar, *Nehru: The Making of India* (Penguin, 1990).
[48] Burr, The Kissinger Transcripts, 57-59.
[49] Document 5, 2-3.
[50] Document 3, 7-8.
[51] Burr, The Kissinger Transcripts, 50-59.
[52] Raymond Garthoff suggests, however, that Kissinger had provided intelligence data to the Chinese as early as during his October 1971 visit to Beijing. See Garthoff, *Détente and Confrontation*, 262.
[53] Burr, The Kissinger Transcripts, 43, 47.
[54] Ibid, 53. Italics added.
[55] Ibid, 51.
[56] Garver, *Protracted Contest*, 214; and Kissinger, *White House Years*, 906.
[57] Document 35, 6, 11-12, <http://www.gwu.edu/~nsarchiv/NSAEBB/NSAEBB66/ch-35.pdf>. Italics added.
[58] Kissinger's memorandum on "My talks with Chou En-lai" to Nixon of July 14, 1971, Document 40, 19-20, 22 <http://www.gwu.edu/~nsarchiv/NSAEBB/NSAEBB66/ch-40.pdf>.
[59] Burr, The Kissinger Transcripts, 51.
[60] Kissinger, *White House Years*, 909.
[61] Document 3, 21.
[62] Ibid, 39.
[63] Ibid, 22.
[64] Kissinger, *White House Years*, 905.
[65] See the works of former Deputy Assistant Secretary of State C. Van Hollen, who presented a strong rebuttal to many of Kissinger's contentions in his "The tilt policy revisited: Nixon-Kissinger geopolitics and South Asia," *Asian Survey*, 20:4 (April 1980), 339-61. Seymour M. Hersh, *The Price of Power* (Summit, 1983), challenged Kissinger's thesis that an aggressive Indian policy backed by the Soviet Union threatened American interests, including the US opening to China and the prospects for American-Soviet détente.
[66] The only action the Chinese took to remind the Indians of the Chinese military presence and potential was to initiate some military alert measures and move forces closer to the line of actual control along the Chinese-Indian border from December 8-16, 1971. See Garthoff, *Détente and Confrontation*, 316.
[67] Ibid, 295, 300-301.
[68] Burr, *The Kissinger Transcripts*, 15. "In the minds of Kissinger and Nixon the publicized tilt toward Pakistan was but a natural corollary of the tilt toward China. The China tilt skewed the entire diplomacy of the United States toward South Asia," writes Garthoff, *Détente and Confrontation*, 320.
[69] Examples of which include the military's refusal to transfer power to the popularly elected leader, Sheikh Mujibur Rahman; ten million refugees fleeing

to India; and thousands massacred by West Pakistani troops before the Indians began arming resistance forces. See Garthoff, *Détente and Confrontation*, 319.

[70] See Garver, *Protracted Contest*, 199.

[71] Document 2, 18. Zhou Enlai also expressed regrets over Chiang Kai-shek's decision to grant independence to Mongolia.

[72] See <http://www.gwu.edu/~nsarchiv/nsa/publications/DOC_readers/kissinger/nixzhou/15-01.htm> [hereafter Document 5], 4.

[73] Document 3, 22.

[74] Ibid, 7, 11. Italics added.

[75] Document 2, 12.

[76] Burr, *Henry Kissinger's Secret Trip to China,* at <http://www.gwu.edu/~nsarchiv/NSAEBB/ NSAEBB66/ch-35.pdf> Document 35, 11-12.

[77] Document 2, 11.

[78] According to Garthoff: "As early as July 1971, Nixon and Kissinger in secret policymaking sessions referred to the president's desire to 'tilt toward Pakistan.'" Moreover, a few weeks before the signing of the treaty, "Kissinger had advised India's Ambassador L. K. Jha that India would not receive American support in case of Chinese intervention." See Garthoff, *Détente and Confrontation*, 298-300; Hersh, *The Price of Power*, 452-53.

[79] *India Today,* 30 September 1993, 26, 22-37; Lin Xia, "Indo-Russian relations enter a new era," *Beijing Review,* February 15-21, 1993, 11-12.

[80] "No change in complexion of Sino-Pak relations," *Asian Defence Journal,* February 1994, 122.

[81] Conversations with Chinese analysts Liu Jinkun, IIS (Beijing) and Hua Di (Stanford), May 1991.

[82] Ye Zhengjia, "India's foreign policy in the restructuring international relations," *Guoji wenti yanjiu (International Studies),* 3 (1992). A book *Can the Chinese Military Win the Next War?* saw the US, India, Vietnam, and Taiwan as potential military enemies. *Weekend Australian,* November 20-21, 1993, 16.

[83] Tai Ming Cheung, "Smoke signals," *FEER*, November 12, 1992, 29-30. Italics added.

[84] Ye, "India's foreign policy," 13.

[85] Scobell, "'Cult of defense' and 'Great power dreams,'" Chapter 13, in M. R. Chambers (ed), *South Asia in 2020: Future Strategic Balances and Alliances* (PA: U.S. Army War College, Strategic Studies Institute, November 2002), 329-359.

[86] Scobell, "'Cult of defense' and 'Great power dreams,'" 342.

[87] Conversation with an American academic, January 2002. Similar views are often expressed by Chinese diplomats and policy analysts at various forums.

[88] Shao Zhiyong, "India's big power dream," *Beijing Review*, April 12, 2001, 10; Scobell, '"Cult of defense" and "Great power dreams"…,' 347.

[89] "Zhongguo yi ge xiao dong zuo jiu chai san le suowei 'da Yindu lianbang'" ["China can dismember the so-called 'Great Indian Federation' with one small stroke,"], www.iiss.cn, August 8, 2009; J. Lamont and K. Hille, "Chinese essay sparks outcry in India," *Financial Times*, August 12, 2009.

[90] Beijing's reluctance to block the website even after the Indian Foreign Ministry's protest was quite telling. The website's owner-editor, Kang Lingyi,

denied any relationship between his and the PLA think-tank, the China International Institute for Strategic Studies. But sites such as Kang's are part of the regime's strategy to allow nationalism to grow to strengthen its political legitimacy. See Liang Chen, "Chinese Web post causes ire in India Source," *Global Times*, August 20, 2009 <http://globaltimes.cn/www/english/top-news/2009-08/459440.html>.

[91] Cited from B. Chellaney, "India's growing China angst," *FEER*, September 4, 2009, 31-35; See S. Guha, "India and China: a clash of ideologies," *UPI Asia online*, September 16, 2009 <http://www.upiasia.com/ Politics/2009/09/16/india_and_china_a_clash_of_ideologies/7684/>.

[92] Li Hongmei, "Veiled threat or good neighbor?" *People's Daily online*, June 19, 2009 <http://english.peopledaily.com.cn/90002/96417/6682302.html>.

[93] Li, "Veiled threat or good neighbor?"

[94] Editorial, "India's unwise military moves," *Global Times*, June 11, 2009 <http://opinion.globaltimes.cn/editorial/2009-06/436174.html>. This was written before the Xinjiang riots erupted in July 2009.

[95] Cited from B. Chellaney, "Jiang Zemin ridicules India: belligerence unprovoked," *Hindustan Times*, January 31, 2000, 1.

[96] J. Mohan Malik, "India in a China shop," *Hindustan Times*, February 24, 2000, 12.

[97] Li Hongmei, "What is beyond the physical line?" *People's Daily Online*, August 12, 2009 <http://english.people.com.cn/90001/90780/index.html>.

[98] Editorial, "India's unwise military moves." J. M. Smith, "The China-India Border Brawl," *Wall Street Journal*, June 24, 2009.

[99] H. McDonald, "Beijing content with the devil it knows," *Age* (Melbourne), January 14, 2003.

[100] Ma Jiali, "Drive for nuclear energy," *Beijing Review*, September 3, 2009, 15.

[101] See Ma Jiali, *Notice India: A Big Rising Country on the Rise* (Tianjin: People's Press, 2002), 14; Pillsbury, "Japan and India: dangerous democracies," 70-73.

[102] Even in the information technology's (IT) software sector, most Chinese are contemptuous of India's growth prospects over the long term, believing that just as they left India behind in the nuclear arena (where India had an edge in the 1950s), they would be able to supersede India in the IT software sector as well. See "We will defeat India in software battle: China," *Sifynews.com*, March 10, 2002; Ye Zhengjia, "Buru 21 shiji de Yindu" ["India enters the twenty-first century"], *International Studies* (English edition) 61:3 (July 1996), 20; and Hua Biyun, "Yindu lizheng chengwei xia shiji de jingji daguo" ["India: Striving to be an economic power in the next century"], *Xiandai Guoji Guanxi* [*Contemporary International Relations*], 75:1 (January 1996), 21.

[103] Mohan Malik, "China's strategy of containing India," *Power and Interest News Report*, February 6, 2006 <http://www.pinr.com/ report.php?ac=view_report&report_id=434>.

[104] Private conversation between Chinese and Pakistani military officers, June 2006.

[105] Dali Yang and Zhao Hong, "The rise of India: China's perspectives and responses," Paper presented at the Third International Conference on South Asia "Socio-political and economic challenges for South Asia." Meritus Mandarin, Singapore, October 25, 2007.

[106] Jing-dong Yuan, "Chinese perspectives on a rising India," November 30, 2008 <http://www.worldpoliticsreview.com/article.aspx?id=2983>; Zhao Gancheng, "Zhongguo dui Yindu zhanlue qianxi" ["An analysis of China's strategy toward India"], *Nanya Yanjiu* [*South Asian Studies*], No. 1 (2008), 3-8.

[107] Commentary, "Nuclear agreement and big power's dream," *People's Daily online*, August 30, 2007 <http://english.people.com.cn/90001/90780/91343/6251506.html>. Italics mine.

[108] See Chen Tieyuan, "People are concerned over India's 'dream of becoming a great power'," *Zhongguo Qingnian Bao* [*China Youth Daily*], May 8, 2001, trans. in *FBIS-CHI*; Shao Zhiyong, "India's big power dream," *Beijing Review*, April 12, 2001, 10; and Malik, "South Asia in China's foreign relations"; Scobell, '"Cult of defense" and "Great power dreams,"' 347.

[109] P. Bidwai, "Ties with China sour as alliance with US grows," *Inter Press Service*, July 6, 2007 <http://www.ipsnews.net/news.asp?idnews=38444>.

[110] Discussions and conversations with China's South Asia specialists in Beijing, Shanghai, Honolulu, 2006-2007.

[111] Lan Jianxue, "Zhong yin duiwai zhanlue yitong yu shuangbian guanxi" ["Differences and similarities in foreign strategies of China and India and their bilateral relations"], *Waijiao Pinglun* [*Foreign Affairs Review*] (Beijing), No. 103 (June 2008), 37-43.

[112] Opinion, "Washington draws India in against China," *People's Daily online*, July 7, 2005 <http://english.people.com.cn/200507/07/eng20050707_194676.html>.

[113] Discussions and conversations with China's South Asia specialists, 2005-08.

[114] Mohan Malik, "India-China competition revealed in ongoing border dispute," *Power and Interest News Report*, October 10, 2007.

[115] Commentary, "Nuclear agreement and big power's dream."

[116] A demarche to Beijing from New Delhi (after Premier Wen and President Hu refused to take phone calls from Prime Minister Singh on the eve of the NSG vote on September 5, 2008) and President Bush's telephone to President Hu reportedly led Beijing to shift position. Despite its strong disapproval of a pact that would narrow the power gap between India and China, Beijing could not take a stance that pushed India further into Washington's camp.

[117] See for example, Zhao Gancheng, "India's nuclear plan needs to be transparent," *Global Times*, September 16, 2009 <http://opinion.globaltimes.cn/commentary/2009-09/468107.html>.

[118] Editorial, "Why India is pursuing military strength," *People's Daily online*, August 20, 2009. Liu Li, "Gongtong erzhi zhongguo: meiyin qiaoding shinian junshi hezuo" ["Jointly containing China: US and India nail ten-year military cooperation package"], *Dongfang Zaobao* [*Oriental Morning Post*], June 30, 2005, 5.

[119] Li Hongmei, "What is beyond the physical line?"

[120] Li Hongmei, "Indian media stinks up public opinions," *People's Daily Online*, September 15, 2009, <http://english.peopledaily.com.cn/90002/96417/6758363.html>. Italics added.

[121] Cheng Ruisheng, "Yindu de waijiao zhanlue zouxiang" ["Trends in India's foreign strategy"], *Guoji Wenti Yanjiu*, (March 2008), 50-54. Italics added.

[122] Cheng, "Trends in India's foreign strategy," 53-54.

[123] Li Yincai, "Yindu waijiao neng zou duo yuan?" ["How far will India's diplomacy go?"] *Zhongguo Xinwengang*, February 17, 2009 <http://world.people.com.cn/GB/14549/8817892.html>.

[124] Li Qiulin, "Mei In jia qiang junshi he zuo gaibian nanya zhan lue geju" ["Strengthened US-India military cooperation will change strategic pattern in South Asia"], *Xueshi Shibao* [*Study Times*], reproduced in *Qiu Shi*, September 14, 2009 <http://www.qsjournal.com.cn/gj/gjgc/200909/t20090914_11445.htm>; *C3S Paper*, No. 372, September 23, 2009 <http://www.c3sindia.org/strategicissues/930>.

[125] Li, "Strengthened US-India military cooperation will change…"

[126] Rajat Pandit, "China's growing military clout worries India, US," *Times of India*, April 10, 2007, 1.

[127] "Japan still pushing the 'four-state alliance,'" *Huanqiu Shibao* [*Global Times*], August 6, 2007.

[128] Conversation with an analyst from CIISS, Beijing, June 2008.

[129] For a review of Chinese media articles on India, see D. S. Rajan, "China: media fears over India becoming part of Western Alliance," *Saag.org*, Paper No. 2350, August 29, 2007 <http://www.saag.org/papers24/paper2350.html>.

[130] Li Hongmei, "Veiled threat or good neighbor?"

[131] Editorial, "India's unwise military moves." Italics added.

[132] See interview in *Ifeng* journal, June 21, 2008, 11.

[133] In an ever-expanding notion of "forward defense," fifty years ago China did not feel secure if Tibet was not secure and under Beijing's control. Now China does not feel secure if Pakistan and Burma are not under Beijing's influence and control. See John W. Garver, "The future of the Sino-Pakistani entente cordiale," in Chambers, *South Asia in 2020*, 385-447.

[134] E. Wong, "Uneasy engagement China and India dispute enclave on edge of Tibet," *IHT*, September 4, 2009.

[135] Li Hongmei, "What is beyond the physical line?"

[136] "China's plan to build up navy," *Hindustan Times,* January 13, 1993, 14. Also see *Time,* May 10, 1993, 39.

[137] Xu Hua, "Yindu zhongshi haiyang junshi weishe," ["India emphasizes maritime deterrence"], *Xiandai Junshi* [*Conmilit*], (April 2000), 54-56.

[138] Cited from Robert Kaplan, "Center stage for the 21st century: rivalry in the Indian Ocean," *Foreign Affairs*, 88:2 (March/April 2009), 23.

[139] "US, Japan, ROK and India want to enter Southeast Asia," *People's Daily*, December 15, 2003.

[140] G.V.C. Naidu, *Indian Navy and Southeast Asia* (New Delhi: Knowledge World, 2000), 192.

[141] Zhang Guihong, "Competition and cooperation: Sino-India's relations in regional perspectives" *Contemporary Asia-Pacific* (Beijing), (December 2006).

[142] "Lee Kuan Yew reflects," *TimeAsia*, December 5, 2005.

[143] Zhao Gaocheng, "Commentary," in Symposium on Japan and India: Challenges and Prospects in Asia and Pacific in the 21st Century, March 10, 2006 <http://210.163.22.165/region/asia-paci/india/ sympo0603.pdf>, 36.

[144] The Chinese media's war talk was first discussed by Mohan Malik, "India-China competition revealed in ongoing border disputes," *The Power & Interest News Report*, October 9, 2007, <http://www.gees.org/documentos/ Documen-02608.pdf>; and D. S. Rajan, "China: strategic experts talk about a partial Sino-Indian war," *C3S Paper*, No. 230, Chennai Centre for China Studies, November 24, 2008 <http://www.c3sindia.org/strategicissues/419>.

[145] It was the most significant eruption of the Tibet issue since 1959. Earlier uprisings (e.g., 1988) were not on the same scale and did not have the same international impact.

[146] Zhanlue, "Zhenggao Yindu zhengfu: Buyao yiyuan baode" ["A warning to the Indian Government: don't return evil for good"], *Chinaiiss.org*, March 26, 2008 <http://str.chinaiiss.org/content/2008-3-26/26211952.shtml>; D. Chaudhuri, "China think-tank attacks India, calls it 'arrogant," *Hindustan Times*, April 13, 2008, 1.

[147] Lai Yuan, "Injun zai zhongyin bianji..." March 16, 2008 <http://www.warchina.com/n53470c41.aspx>; <http://str.chinaiiss.org/content/2008-3-26/26211952.shtml>; D. S. Rajan, "China: military media attacks on India-a Tibet issue fall out?" *C3S* Paper, No. 136, March 28, 2008 <http://www.c3sindia.org/tibet/222>.

[148] D. S. Rajan, "India is a paper tiger and will be trounced if it uses force against China," experts warn," *C3S Paper*, No.288, June 12, 2009 <http://www.c3sindia.org/india/588>.

[149] Li Hongmei, "Veiled threat or good neighbor?"

[150] On 7 ways to destroy India, see "Yindu xiang he zhongguo dou, women zhengkua ta you duozhong banfa" ["India wants to compete with China, we have many ways to destroy it"], <http://www.armsky.com/BbsJunshi/ bbsgaojing/200811/11653.html>.

[151] Mohan Malik, "War talk: perceptual gaps in 'Chindia' relations," *China Brief*, 9: 20 (October 7, 2009), http://www.jamestown.org/programs/ chinabrief/single/?tx_ttnews%5Btt_news%5D=35589&tx_ttnews%5BbackPid%5D=25&cHash=127f567fb8

[152] Michael Sheridan, "China reaches out on 60th anniversary," *Sunday Times*, September 27, 2009 <http://www.timesonline.co.uk/tol/news/world/asia/ article6850841.ece>. PTI, "Many Chinese still see India as their main enemy: report," *Times of India*, September 27, 2009, 1.

[153] Pew Global Attitudes Project, "The Chinese celebrate their roaring economy...," July 22, 2008 <http://pewglobal.org/reports/ display.php?ReportID=261>; PTI, "24% Chinese view India as an enemy," *Times of India*, July 28, 2008, 1.

[154] Zhu Shanshan, "90% in online poll believe India threatens China's security," *Global Times*, June 11, 2009 <http://china.globaltimes.cn/top-photo/2009-06/436320.html>.

[155] Editorial, "India's unwise military moves"; Li Hongmei, "Veiled threat or good neighbor?" *People's Daily online*, June 19, 2009 "What is beyond the physical line?" *People's Daily Online*, August 12, 2009; "Indian media stinks up public opinions," *People's Daily Online*, September 15, 2009. The media campaign prompted speculation as to whether the Chinese leadership was rallying domestic and global support for a further deterioration in the bilateral relationship.

[156] R. Patil, "Chinese think India backward," *Hindustan Times*, May 16, 2010, 1.

[157] A. Baruah, "'China bashing' in the Indian media," *BBC News*, September 16, 2009 <http://news.bbc.co.uk/2/hi/south_asia/8258715.stm>.

[158] Cited from S. Saxena, "Why do we fear the Chinese dragon?" *Times of India*, September 13, 2009, 7.

[159] Quoted in Liang Chen, "Chinese Web post causes ire in India Source," *Global Times*, August 20, 2009 <http://globaltimes.cn/www/english/top-news/2009-08/459440.html>.

[160] Li Hongmei, "Veiled threat or good neighbor?"

[161] B. Chellaney, "India's growing China angst," *FEER*, September 4, 2009, 31-35.

[162] Rajan, "India is a paper tiger and will be trounced…"

[163] Chen Xiaochen, "Illusion of 'China's attack on India before 2012,'" July 17, 2009, <http://www.chinastakes.com/2009/7/illusion-of-chinas-attack-on-india-before-2012.html>. The Indian media claims that unlike in the 1950s, it is now China that is engaged in a "new forward policy" in order to "provoke India into retaliatory action" which could then be justified to take military action.

[164] B. Raman, "Chinese military 'greatly displeased' by Indian media campaign against China," *C3S Paper*, No. 354, September 10, 2009 <http://www.c3sindia.org/india/853>.

[165] S. Gopal, *Jawaharlal Nehru: A Biography* (Oxford University Press, 1979) cited in V. Gumaste, "India and China: It was a stab from the front," *Rediff.com*, August 25, 2009 <http://news.rediff.com/slide-show/2009/aug/25/slide-show-1-a-stab-from-the-front.htm>.

[166] "Arunachal can't be parted with at any cost," *Times of India*, September 30, 2009, 1.

[167] Zhanlue, "Zhongguo yi ge xiao dong zuo jiu chai san le suowei 'da Yindu lianbang'" [Strategy: "China can dismember the so-called 'Great Indian Federation' with one small stroke"], www.iiss.cn, August 8, 2009.

[168] Shi Ren, "China, India hold border talks to resolve boundary disputes," *Zhongguo Tongxun She*, August 4, 2009.

[169] For instance, a *China Daily* editorial took to task both the Indian and Chinese media for misrepresenting facts on the ground. See Editorial, "Truth about India ties," *China Daily*, September 10, 2009, 8 <http://www.chinadaily.com.cn/opinion/2009-09/10/content_8674482.htm>.

[170] Cheng, "Trends in India's foreign strategy," 53-54.

[171] Beijing has reportedly stepped up weapon supplies to various insurgent groups in northeastern India. "China denies selling arms to Indian rebels: Xinhua," November 3, 2008 <http://www.chinadaily.com.cn/china/2008-11/03/content_7165601.htm>; AsiaInt Reference Library, "China accused of north-east India terror," *AWA*, December 12, 2008 <http://www.asiaint.com/arl/arl20058.asp>. China was reportedly "supporting ULFA for Tibet-related issues."

[172] Dai Bing, "India building a security barrier against China," *China.org.cn*, February 8, 2010 <http://www.china.org.cn/opinion/node_7078634.htm>.

[173] Scobell, "'Cult of defense' and 'Great power dreams,'" 343.

PART 2

FLASHPOINTS AND FAULT LINES

5
Tibet and the Territorial Dispute

Tibet lies at the heart of China-India relations. It is the key to understanding Beijing's stance on the China-India territorial dispute. The origins of the China-India rivalry date back to the "peaceful liberation of Tibet" (as the Chinese call it) or the "forcible occupation of Tibet" (as the rest of the world sees it) in 1950–51, which brought the two Asian giants in close proximity for the first time in history by transforming the traditional Indo-Tibetan frontier into the Sino-Indian boundary. Sixty years later, Tibet remains "a sensitive issue" (in Premier Wen Jiabao's words) between China and India. Since China's territorial dispute with India is inextricably linked with the past, present, and future status of Tibet, this chapter examines the central role that Tibet plays in defining China's relations with India and vice versa.

Tibet: History in Dispute

The Chinese claim to have exerted "undisputable and effective administration over Tibet since the beginning of the Yuan [Mongol] Dynasty (1271–1368)."[1] The Mongols, who entered China as conquerors, are claimed as Chinese, and their subjugation of Tibet is portrayed as a Chinese subjugation. Claiming to have governed Tibet since the thirteenth century, Beijing regards it as just as inalienably integral to its territory as Taiwan. To question Tibet's status is to revive painful memories of the humiliation China suffered in the nineteenth century when colonial powers, armed with gunboats and opium, devoured chunks of the Middle Kingdom. For China, Tibet is an entirely domestic issue that does not require external attention or interference. China sees Tibet as part of the larger fabric of Chinese civilization, or what Beijing calls the "big family of the Chinese nation" with a history of thousands of years as a unified multinational state.[2] This narrative is consistent with the Chinese construct of the "motherland" that sees all of its minority nationalities—Mongol, Manchu, Tibetan, Han, and

Muslim—as Chinese. As Ashild Kolas argues: "The 'Middle Kingdom' is not meant to be comprised of 'one nation, one state,' but rather of a territory corresponding to the 'Chinese Empire'."[3] The Tibetan issue also constitutes one of the CCP's core security concerns: territorial integrity and national unity. From Beijing's perspective, any weakening of the Chinese stand on Tibet could mark the beginning of their losing control over China's restive periphery consisting of Tibet, Xinjiang, and Inner Mongolia.

However, the "history question" is very complex and defies an easy interpretation.[4] For the problem with history is where and when to draw the line, and more importantly, why. Since there is little agreement between the Chinese and Tibetans over how to interpret their shared past, a brief account of the historical Sino-Tibetan relationship is in order.

Historically, culturally, ethnically, and linguistically, the Tibetans view themselves as quite distinct from the Chinese. Tibetans claim a recorded history of more than 2000 years. As an independent kingdom in the pre-Mongol era, Tibet had a militarily glorious past holding sway over an Inner Asian empire up until 822 AD. Tibetans controlled much of their region, including parts of Nepal, Burma, India, and present-day Xinjiang (China), and they did it the old-fashioned way, through warfare.[5] They refused to defer to Tang Dynasty emperors (618–907), and in the late eighth century even briefly captured Changan, the Chinese capital, and a Tibetan nominee was put on the Chinese throne. The Sino-Tibetan conflict led to bilateral negotiations for demarcation of borders between the two kingdoms. In 783 AD and 821 AD, two treaties were signed between Tibet and China. The latter allowed the Tibetan conquests in Central Asia and demarcated the boundaries between China and Tibet. It read: "Tibet and China shall keep the country and frontiers of which they are now in possession. All to the East is the country of Great China; and all to the west is assuredly the country of Great Tibet; from either side of the frontier there shall be no warfare, no hostile invasions, and no seizure of territory."[6]

From the seventh to ninth centuries, Tibet came under Indian religious and cultural influence—a development that turned out to be a game-changer for Tibet. During King Songtsen Gampo's reign, Tibetans converted to Buddhism and adopted a written language based on the Ranjana script.[7] It was the import of Buddhism from India that turned Tibet's erstwhile warrior culture into a pacifist society and made Tibet dependent on external military powers for dealing with threats from both within and outside. In 1247, the Tibetan abbot Sakya Pandita is said to have subordinated Tibet to the expanding Mongol Empire. However,

Tibet was brought under control by the Mongols only in 1267. Then in 1270, the Mongol ruler Kublai Khan proclaimed the Yuan Dynasty (1270–1368) after gaining control of much of China, but Tibet continued to be administered separately from China. Just as Greece inspired the Romans, Tibetan religious and cultural values seemingly captured the admiration and acceptance of the Mongols.[8] Given this sequence of events, "Tibet might be seen as belonging as much to the conquering as the conquered camp."[9] Though present-day China insists that "Chinese sovereignty over Tibet" was exercised in an unbroken line from the thirteenth century onward, historical records show that China's intervening Ming Dynasty (1368–1644) had no control over Tibet.[10] During much of the sixteenth and seventeenth centuries, China and Tibet enjoyed a relationship of "equality and mutual independence."[11] In the seventeenth century, the great fifth Dalai Lama visited Beijing and was received by the Ming emperor as an equal leader of an independent state. As Michael Davis noted: "The Ming court appeared to value the Tibetan religious leaders less for any spiritual role than as intermediaries who could help China to deal with the still threatening Mongols."[12]

However, later during the Manchu reign, the relationship got more complicated, with some Chinese military campaigns in Tibet. In the eighteenth century, the Manchu Qing Dynasty (1644–1911) first conquered China and then extended its reach over Tibet in 1724. (The Mongols, in contrast, had made Tibet a part of their empire *before* conquering China.) When Mongolian Dzungars intruded and began to assert themselves in Lhasa in 1717, a counter invasion was launched in 1719 by the Manchus who dispatched mainly ethnic Chinese forces to Tibet. Again, in 1724, Tibet sought Chinese military help against the Mongols. In 1728, Tibet accepted the Qing Court's decision to appoint permanent representatives (*Ambons*) in Tibet to bolster military protection. In 1793, a combined Chinese-Tibetan army marched on Kathmandu to chastise a Nepalese king for invading Tibet in 1788 and in 1790–91. The Chinese took this opportunity to tighten their grip on Tibet further.[13] The Qing emperors also enjoyed close association with Tibet and the Dalai Lama, with the emperor acting as patron of Tibetan Buddhism.[14] In the eighteenth century, "Chinese suzerainty over Tibet became an established fact."[15] Nonetheless, as Melvyn Goldstein and Cynthia Beall argue, China-Tibet relations under the Qing Dynasty were less formal than presumed; there were no treaties or other written agreements. Essentially, Tibet was "loosely subordinate to China" but at the same time, it administered itself with its own body of laws and officials.[16] Tibetan lamas often served as spiritual mentors to the emperors—thereby forming what the Tibetans called a *cho-yon* or patron-priest relationship—with the lamas mostly enjoying free rein in Tibet.[17] Under the Qing imperial tutelage, Tibet was never a province of the Qing Empire, unlike Taiwan and Xinjiang, which were declared as provinces in late nineteenth century. Further, Tibet enjoyed treaty-making rights that were recognized by the Qing imperial rulers of China.[18]

When the Manchu Qing Dynasty's rule ended in 1911, China became a republic. The collapse of the Manchu Empire saw both Mongolia and Tibet declaring their independence. Nonetheless, the new Nationalist (*Guomindang*) government in China remained wedded to the "Manchu notion" that treated the Tibetans as one of the minority nationalities along with the Manchus, the Chinese, the Mongols, and the Muslims within the framework of a multinational Chinese state.[19] The Republic of China claimed sovereignty over Tibet, but was simply too weak and pre-occupied with internal crisis and Japanese aggression to be in a position to actively exercise sovereignty claims.

Whereas Outer Mongolia's independence was supported by Tzarist Russia in 1913 and secured through an agreement between Nationalist China and the Soviet Union in 1945, Tibet failed to secure such recognition primarily because Britain needed to keep China on its side. At that time, the British policy toward Tibet was shaped by "the Great Game" in Central Asia and the strategic imperative to prevent an expanding Russian empire from posing a threat to British India. The British government preferred a strong presence in Tibet, but simultaneously, in pursuing its great power rivalry with Russia, it needed China's support and approval. In 1907, Britain and Russia signed a treaty that recognized Chinese suzerainty over Tibet for the first time in history, thereby insulating Tibet from the Tsarist Russian sphere of influence in Central Asia. For Britain, a weak China with nominal, ineffective suzerainty over Tibet was preferable to Imperial Russia exercising control over the Tibetan plateau. This move also negated the need for the deployment of Chinese forces in Tibet. It was against this backdrop that British India called for the tripartite Simla Conference in October 1913 to settle the boundary between British India and Tibet on the one hand and between Tibet and China on the other. The Simla Conference was attended by Henry McMahon from British India, Chen Yifan from Republican China, and Lonchen Shatra from Tibet. During the negotiations, the British proposed a solution—similar to one that China and Russia had framed to deal with Mongolia—of an Inner and Outer Tibet, suggesting that central and western Tibet could remain largely independent under nominal Chinese "suzerainty" while eastern Tibet would fall under Chinese "sovereignty." The result was the Simla

Agreement of 1914, which divided Tibet into Inner and Outer Tibet, with China gaining sovereign control over Inner Tibet but only suzerainty over Outer Tibet. The boundary between India and Tibet was demarcated, with British India retaining trading and extra-territorial rights in Outer Tibet. (This distinction between the two concepts—sovereignty and suzerainty—offered legal basis for the Tibetan claims for a special relationship with Beijing and unique political dispensation within modern China.) Independent India inherited this arrangement, which sought to sustain Tibet as a buffer zone with *de facto* independent status under Chinese suzerainty. The Agreement was initialed by all, presumably under British pressure, but the Chinese later refused to ratify it mainly because of disagreement over the boundary line between Inner and Outer Tibet (i.e. between China and Tibet).[20]

Since then, the Chinese have castigated the Simla Agreement as one of the "unequal treaties" imposed by colonial powers when China was weak. They contend that China's pre-occupation from 1911 to 1950 with revolution, civil war, and the Japanese invasion forced it to leave Tibet to its own devices. Despite their sharp differences over other issues, both the Nationalists and the Communists refused to accept Tibet's independence and kept alive China's claim of sovereignty while promising a special status for Tibet. The PLA's "peaceful liberation of Tibet" in 1950–51, presumably from foreign influences, ended Tibet's *de facto* independence. Faced with a powerful Communist China and lacking international support for Tibetan independence, the Dalai Lama signed a Seventeen-Point Agreement with Beijing in May 1951 that promised genuine autonomy and local self-rule under Tibet's established system of governance.[21]

For China, the next step was to eliminate India's inherited privileges and rights in Tibet arising from the British colonial period. To this end, the Panchsheel Agreement was signed between India and China in 1954 wherein, for the first time, Tibet was referred as "Tibet region of China." It nullified all the previous agreements of Tibet with India. However, harsh communist agrarian policies and popular discontent against Chinese rule erupted in a Tibetan uprising in March 1959 that led to a fierce Chinese crackdown and the exile of the Dalai Lama along with some 80,000 refugees to India (the diaspora now numbers approximately 130,000). In 1965, the Tibet Autonomous Region (TAR) was proclaimed following the redrawing of Tibet's borders by the Chinese Communist leadership that hacked off Tibetan areas in Kham and Amdo provinces to Sichuan, Qinghai, Gansu, and Yunnan.

Thus, prior to the thirteenth century and during the Ming dynasty rule (1368–1644, i.e., after the collapse of the Mongol Yuan Dynasty but before the Manchu Qing conquests), Tibet was itself an independent imperial power. Then following the collapse of the Qing Dynasty but before the Communist takeover of China, Tibet enjoyed a short period of independence from 1911 to 1950. Therefore, Tibet's relations with China since the thirteenth century have been characterized by varying degrees of association spanning the spectrum from suzerainty to independence to sovereignty.[22] In the Tibetan narrative, Tibet—much like Han China—was invaded and conquered by invaders such as the Mongols or the Manchus, and for some periods of its history was forced to be part of empires that included China or ruled from Beijing (as in the case of the Manchus), but it did not voluntarily become "a part of China." Elliot Sperling, historian and director of Tibetan Studies at Indiana University, concurs: "The idea that Tibet became part of China in the 13th century is a very recent construction. In the early part of the 20th century, Chinese writers generally dated the annexation of Tibet to the 18th century. They described Tibet's status under the Qing with a term that designates a 'feudal dependency,' not an integral part of a country." He adds: "Marxist China adopted the linguistic sleight of hand that asserts it has always been a unitary multinational country, not the hub of empires."[23] The fact of the matter is that modern China is more of an "empire-state" than a nation-state.

In the late nineteenth and early twentieth centuries, Tibet became the fulcrum of great power rivalry. Following the victory of Chinese Communists in 1949, Tibet acquired major geopolitical significance, impinging upon the interests of major powers. From 1947 to 1950, newly independent India dealt directly with Tibet as if it were a *de facto* independent state for all practical purposes. Representatives of the Tibetan government participated in the Inter-Asian Conference in 1947 and the Afro-Asian Conference in 1948 in Delhi. In 1949, Nepal cited its relationship with Tibet in support of its own sovereign status when applying for UN membership. Despite India's opposition to the use of force in Tibet in 1950–51, the Nehru government adopted a conciliatory posture toward China in the interests of friendship and Asian solidarity. While recognizing China's rule over Tibet, Nehru also encouraged the Tibetans to uphold their autonomy granted under the Tibetan government's 1951 agreement with China. From the mid-1950s to 1969, the US Central Intelligence Agency (CIA) offered financial support and training to Tibetan resistance fighters at bases along Tibet's porous borders with India and Nepal. These American activities, aimed at undermining Chinese rule in Tibet, were in the context of the Cold War.[24] This was the time when the United States maintained diplomatic ties with Taiwan and refused to recognize the government of the

People's Republic of China as the legitimate Chinese government. However, foreign intelligence activities amidst growing instability in Tibet convinced China's leadership that India, acting in collusion with the United States, was attempting to separate Tibet from China. This fear was an important factor in the resurrection of the border dispute and the deterioration of Sino-Indian relations in the late 1950s. The eruption of the 1959 rebellion in Tibet soured relations and culminated in the 1962 War. Beijing's victory in the war with India followed by the Sino-US rapprochement of the early 1970s and China's emergence as a great power since the 1980s led to a gradual decline in the geopolitical significance of Tibet. The eruption of widespread protests and anti-Chinese riots in Tibet from time to time coupled with the Dalai Lama's prestige as a Nobel peace laureate and support from human rights organizations and global civil society have kept the Tibetan issue alive in the media.

The Dalai Lama has travelled the world seeking support for the cause to pressure Beijing to reach a negotiated settlement. However, the dispute between China and the Dalai Lama is not only on their future vision for Tibet but mainly on Tibet's past. Having dropped the demand for Tibetan independence—since 1988, to be precise—the Dalai Lama has repeatedly indicated his willingness to accept Tibet's future within China with a certain degree of autonomy. However, the disagreement over Tibet's past has emerged as one of the most contentious issues in the stalled talks between the Dalai Lama's representatives and Chinese negotiators. Beijing insists that Tibetans acknowledge that "Tibet has always been an inalienable part of China." Though willing to compromise on Tibet's future, the Dalai Lama refuses to be party to the falsification of Tibetan history. For, it is "not only inaccurate but also unreasonable. We cannot change the past no matter whether it was good or bad."[25]

It is not only Tibet's contested past; the two sides cannot even agree on what constitutes Tibet today, despite several rounds of negotiations since the 1980s. When the Chinese talk of Tibet, they mean the 2.8 million Tibetans that live only in the TAR. However, a major component of the Dalai Lama's idea of autonomy is to unite under a single administrative entity the entire Tibetan plateau populated by 7 million ethnic Tibetans. More specifically, the regions of Kham and Amdo that currently fall under four different Chinese provinces (Sichuan, Yunnan, Gansu, and Qinghai), should be grouped with the area that is now called TAR as a means of preserving the Tibetan identity. This will double the total area claimed by Tibetans to 2.5m sq km from the 1.2m sq km that is in the TAR. This conception of Tibetan autonomy arouses Beijing's suspicions of Tibetan nationalism. Perceiving the Dalai Lama's "autonomy only" stance as tactical, Beijing fears that the creation of such an entity would serve as a stepping-stone to eventual independence for Tibet. Therefore, Beijing denies that "Greater Tibet" ever existed and contends that the exiled community does not represent the views of most Tibetans.

China's Tibet: The Cultural and Ideological Divide

Faced with a vastly changed geopolitical landscape since the late 1980s, the Dalai Lama has successfully transformed the Tibetan quest for self-determination into part of the larger international dialogue about global peace, human rights, environmental protection, democracy, and freedom.[26] In an address to the European Parliament in 1988, the Dalai Lama formally abandoned the goal of Tibetan independence in favor of "genuine autonomy" within the Chinese nation. Also known as the Strasbourg Proposal, the "Middle Path" (between the present status and full independence) was based on a five-point approach:

- Transformation of Tibet into a zone of peace;
- An end to the Han population transfer policy;
- Respect for fundamental human rights and democratic freedoms;
- Restoration and protection of Tibet's natural environment; and
- Cessation of nuclear weapons deployment and dumping of nuclear waste in Tibet.

However, this shift in stance has failed to evoke a positive response from the Chinese government. For one, the Dalai Lama's airing of his autonomy proposals in Western capitals does not impress a Beijing that continues to portray him as a "separatist" leader. For another, Beijing insists that the Dalai Lama's real plan is to break Tibet away from China. The dramatic growth in China's power and global influence over the last three decades has seen Beijing applying a muscular approach to pressure countries that support the Tibetan cause. Making it clear that Tibet is an internal issue, China routinely warns against allowing the Dalai Lama to visit other countries. The huge economic dependence of the US and other major economies on the Chinese market and financial investments has made most Western countries toe a soft line toward China on issues like Tibet and human rights. The Dalai Lama's rise to global stardom and the continued existence of his "government-in-exile" in India rankles Beijing.

The Chinese narrative debunks the utopian image of Tibet as a political and social Shangri-La prior to 1951.[27] China portrays Tibet as a backward, undeveloped, and feudal society prior to 1951, which featured a hierarchical and downtrodden serf class. Beijing claims that reforms introduced since 1959 have "abolished theocratic feudal serfdom, while ending the monopoly of the minority of nobility and senior monks over culture and education."[28] Beijing maintains that the Tibetan spiritual leader presided over a feudal system that kept the majority of Tibetans enslaved.

The state-controlled media has intensified personal attacks on the Dalai Lama and his supporters. For much of the world, he is the embodiment of Tibet in all its dimensions—spiritual, cultural, civilizational, and political. For his followers, the Dalai Lama is a living Buddha. But for the CCP leaders such as Zhang Qingli, head of the Communist Party in Tibet, the Dalai Lama is "a wolf in monk's robes, a devil with a human face but the heart of a beast."[29] In 2009, China declared March 28 a new holiday: "Serf Emancipation Day" (a reminder of the feudal system that existed in Tibet before the Chinese "liberation"), that commemorates the day in 1959 when the Tibetan government was dissolved "after the Chinese government foiled an armed rebellion staged by the Dalai Lama and his supporters, most of whom were slave owners attempting to maintain serfdom and the Dalai Lama went into exile."[30] Beijing stresses that it has not only "democratized" Tibetan society, but also brought about significant economic progress to Tibet in the last sixty years. Beijing hopes that economic development, improved infrastructure and steady demographic shifts will gradually ease the ethnic tensions that periodically erupt into violence. There is no denying that China has invested heavily in recent decades to improve the overall quality of life in Tibet, resulting in a doubling of life expectancy and higher living standards.

While Beijing projects a positive image of contemporary Tibet, Tibetan exile groups complain about serious human rights violations, cultural suppression, environmental destruction, economic domination, discrimination in jobs and education, and minority policies that have resulted in Tibet's cartographic dismemberment, revisionist history, systematic undermining of traditional institutions, and the militarization of Tibet.[31] Speaking on the anniversary of the rebellion in 2009, the Dalai Lama accused Beijing of turning Tibet into a "hell on Earth."[32] However, the issue that provokes the most visceral response is the "demographic subversion": supplanting Tibetan culture with the dominant Chinese Han culture. Tibetan exile groups portray the policy of Han immigration into Tibet since 1983 as China's "final solution" to the Tibetan problem. Exile estimates put the total number of Tibetans in the Tibetan parts of China today at 6 million against 7.5 million Han Chinese in the same regions.[33] Tibetan fears of being swamped are not entirely unfounded when one looks at what has happened in Xinjiang, where the population ratio is now 40 percent Han to 45 percent Uyghur; and Inner Mongolia, which is now 80 percent Han and fewer than 17 percent Mongol.

Xi Zang—"Western Treasure House": The Resource Dimension

Whilst geostrategic advantages accruing to China from its control over Tibet—especially in linking China with South Asia—are well understood, Tibet's future strategic value may well lie in the realm of resources. Tibet has everything that China lacks: vast, unpopulated land, abundant water, and invaluable natural resources. Interestingly, Tibet is called *Xi Zang* in Chinese, which literally means "Western Treasure House." Moreover, Tibet is indeed a treasure trove of natural resources and minerals. In fact, the Tibetan region is home to 40 percent of China's mineral resources, including coal, gold, silver, lithium, magnesium, iron, cobalt, copper, and one of the world's largest uranium deposits.[34] Having a large and diverse mineral base is one of China's major comparative advantages in its quest for wealth, power, and security.

More importantly, the Tibetan Plateau is the source of ten of Asia's major rivers, including the Brahmaputra, Ganges, Indus, Yellow, Yangtze, Irrawaddy, Mekong, and Salween.[35] Tibetan rivers bring water to 11 countries, to over 85 percent of the Asian population, approximately 50 percent of the world's population. Ninety percent of the Tibetan rivers' runoff flows downstream to China, India, Bangladesh, Nepal, Pakistan, Thailand, Myanmar, Laos, Cambodia, and Vietnam. Accelerated melting of Himalayan glaciers due to global warming would affect river water flows, thereby further adding to Asian countries' water woes. In a sense, the water issue between China and South Asia and Southeast Asia is geostrategic in nature. With China controlling the Tibetan plateau—the source of Asia's major river system—Beijing possesses a mighty powerful geopolitical lever over all of Asia.[36] As P. Stobdan opines: "Water may not become a catalyst for a direct conflict, but China could leverage Tibet's water as a politico-military tool vis-à-vis other riparian states."[37] At present, there is no international law to protect downstream nations.

China and India share the waters of the Indus, the Brahmaputra, and the Sutlej rivers, and are upper and lower riparian states, respectively. So here are Asia's two largest countries with disputed borders, competing worldwide for resources, and booming economies that need ever more water for drinking, farming, industrial expansion, and urbanization. Both see water as a strategic commodity. A book, *How Tibet's Water Will Save China*, written by former PLA soldier Li Ling, has been one of the bestsellers in China. It popularizes the *Shuo-tian* (reverse flow) proposal to end China's chronic water shortages, made first by hydrologist Guo Kai. The idea is to divert the Brahmaputra and Mekong rivers' waters from the South to the North for use in the arid provinces of northern China. If implemented, this would make India vulnerable to manipulation of the river water supply by China at a time of fast-depleting water reserves. The ecological impact on the Indian subcontinent of Chinese plans to divert the Brahmaputra (Yarlung Tsangpo in Tibet) or Sutlej rivers for irrigation purposes in China has emerged as a new divisive issue. Though Beijing has reportedly given assurances that it would ensure the "protection and rational use of water resources" in the trans-Himalayan rivers that flow to India from the upper reaches of the Himalayas on the Chinese side, many wonder if China would "use water as a threat multiplier."[38] To date, Beijing has not consulted downstream states before undertaking dam constructions upstream, whether on the Sutlej or the Mekong. Despite the November 2006 agreement on establishing an Expert Level Mechanism to exchange trans-border river issues and flood season data, Beijing has shown little enthusiasm on sharing information on river water flows with India. As Stobdan notes: "No downstream country has any legal arrangements or provisions of international law to deal with China's river manipulation. China has refused to join the Mekong River Commission, and has also not ratified the UN convention on Non-Navigable Use of International Watercourses (1997)."[39] Some analysts warn that China's green light for the diversion or northward rerouting of the Yarlung Tsangpo/Brahmaputra River would be akin to a "declaration of war" against India and Bangladesh.[40]

Given China's voracious appetite for natural resources to sustain its economic growth and Tibet's wealth of resources, Beijing cannot afford to loosen its grip over its "Western Treasure House." The broader strategic context and resource needs help explain Beijing's massive (albeit seemingly uneconomical) investments in the development of a network of railways, roads, highways, and airports in remote parts of Tibet.[41] The huge financial investments in the resource extraction sector further reduce the likelihood of Tibet ever gaining the kind of genuine autonomy to which most Tibetans aspire. George Ginsburg and Michael Mathos succinctly summed up the importance of Tibet: "He who holds Tibet dominates the Himalayan piedmont; he who dominates the Himalayan piedmont, threatens the Indian subcontinent; and he who threatens the Indian subcontinent may well have all of South-East Asia within his reach, and all of Asia."[42]

China's Tibet: India Caught in the Middle

Tibet casts a long shadow on China-India ties. As the successor of the British Raj, India inevitably is drawn into the dispute between the Dalai Lama and China not only on the future of Tibet but also on its past. The Dalai Lama is an old thorn in India's relationship with China. Beijing has long resented the protection afforded by India to the exiled Tibetan spiritual leader and a substantial Tibetan refugee population. India maintains that the Dalai Lama is a revered spiritual leader who is not allowed to engage in political activities on Indian soil. The Dalai Lama often characterizes India's policy as "excessively cautious," bordering on appeasement of China. While he and his followers advocate a more assertive and engaged Indian policy on Tibet, the Chinese diplomats never miss an opportunity to remind New Delhi about its promise not to allow Tibetans to conduct anti-China activities in India. Over time, the Tibet question has become embroiled in the domestic debate in India on how New Delhi should deal with Beijing. Broadly speaking, three schools of thought in India's strategic circles posit different trajectories for Tibet's future.

The first school favors "playing the Tibet card" to force moderation in China's India policy and to resolve the territorial dispute on terms favorable to India. Several articles in Indian media and strategic analysts in recent years have called upon the government to keep its options open on Tibet. Many argue that India's repeated declarations that "Tibet is an autonomous region of China" are unnecessary given that the Chinese have actually made no effort to fulfill their promise of autonomy to Tibet.[43] They are convinced that Beijing will not abandon its "contain India" policy regardless of whether or not New Delhi appeases Beijing on the Dalai Lama issue. For China's Tibet posture is part of a well-conceived frontier strategy that sees India as the only threat to its supremacy on the Asian continent. This school maintains that the long-term security of India's northern frontiers is inextricably intertwined with the existence and survival of Tibet as a buffer state and to the survival and strengthening of Tibetan culture and religion. Culturally and civilizationally, India is bound with Tibet, which is also home to two of the holiest Hindu shrines, Mount Kailash and Lake Manasarovar, revered by 800 million Hindus. Moreover, Tibet is the source of four great rivers that flow into India. Politically, abandonment of Tibet is not a viable option because it goes against the historic Indian tradition of offering refuge to those escaping oppressive rulers. Further, the Dalai Lama's presence represents India's civilizational soft power, its democratic values, culture, and the identity of the state. Following the Tibetan protests in March 2008, opinion polls showed that two-thirds of Indians found their government's response to China to be weak and inadequate, and a majority wanted their government to assert its support for the Tibetan struggle more vocally. Strategically, the presence of the Dalai Lama and his recognition of the McMahon Line as the border between India and Tibet bolsters New Delhi's negotiating stance on its border dispute with Beijing.[44] Ambassador (retd) G. Parthasarathy believes that "Tibet does give us a moral authority in dealing with China. Here are a people being pushed, *a la* American Indians, into reservations, and we are the ones who have provided them a haven. If we use this authority, China may be less aggressive about its border claims."[45] Or, perhaps not. Even those who believe that it is "too late to play the Tibet card" after Prime Ministers Rajiv Gandhi and Narasimha Rao's acknowledgement of "Tibet as part of China" advocate a more nuanced policy. As former foreign secretary A. P. Venkateswaran opined: "We can legitimately question the ruthless use of force recently against the Tibetans [in 2008] and against the Uighurs in Xinjiang [in 2009]. After all China keeps advising India on our relations with Pakistan, Bangladesh, Nepal etc., etc."[46] New Delhi also accuses Beijing of abetting separatist insurrections in India's troubled northeast and turning a blind eye to Pakistan-sponsored *jihadi* terrorism against India.[47] Overall, this "pro-Tibet" school holds that the expulsion of hostile influences from Tibet and the establishment of a friendly or neutral government in Lhasa would go a long way in ushering in a peaceful and stable environment in South Asia.

At the other end of the spectrum is a powerful school of thought that favors consigning the Tibetan issue to the dustbin of history for the last time. For Tibet's fate is already sealed. Even with overt Indian support (which is highly unlikely), the Tibetans cannot achieve their goals. This view holds that hosting the Tibetan spiritual leader has been disastrous for India-China relations, and that it is time for the Dalai Lama to leave India. The key proponents of this school are Beijing-backed Indian Communist parties, some influential politicians belonging to the Congress and smaller regional parties, and some leftwing journalists such as N. Ram of *The Hindu* group. They echo the Chinese view that

Beijing cannot solve its Tibet problem as long as India provides shelter to the Dalai Lama and his "Free Tibet" supporters or helps keep the Tibetan political and cultural identity alive. From their perspective, Tibet is strictly China's domestic matter and India must not do anything that raises Chinese suspicions. Whatever understanding the Dalai Lama wants to have with China is strictly a matter between himself and the Chinese, and none of India's business. Perceiving China as a peace-loving country that has solved land boundary disputes with all its neighbors except India and Bhutan, they predict that Beijing will be flexible in settling the border dispute with India as well "if the Dalai Lama leaves India or his activities are curtailed" to China's satisfaction.[48] Otherwise, they warn that continued support of the Dalai Lama could boomerang should Beijing retaliate by giving sanctuary to Kashmiri, Assamese, Maoist, Naga, and Mizo rebels in its territory. Therefore, from this "anti-Tibet" school's perspective, "it is worth sacrificing the Dalai Lama to avoid a future conflict and possible joint attack by Pakistan and China."[49]

In between these two extreme viewpoints ("play the Tibet card" versus "discard the Tibet card") lies India's official stance on "Tibet as an autonomous region of China," which has not changed much and is unlikely to change. Faced with China's growing assertiveness, the debate in India is really all about "the value of small steps, nuances, inflections and calculated omissions."[50] Despite all the talk of standing up to China and supporting the Tibetan cause, there is a tacit understanding across the political spectrum that the broad contours of India's Tibet policy, laid down in the Panchsheel Agreement of 1954 and successive bilateral agreements, should not be changed. In fact, successive Indian governments have bent over backwards to reassure and appease the Chinese on Tibet. India never recognized the Tibetan government-in-exile. As S. Kondapalli points out: "The Indian establishment strongly believes that taking in the Dalai Lama was very costly to India, that it led to the 1962 War with China. That is why successive generations of Indian bureaucrats have wanted to wash off the Tibet card."[51] It surely was washed off gradually. During Prime Minister Rajiv Gandhi's 1988 visit to China, India reiterated that the "Tibet region is an autonomous part of China." As a further gesture of goodwill, the 1988 position was given up during Prime Minister A. B. Vajpayee's visit in 2003 when India recognized the TAR "as part of the territory of the People's Republic of China," without linking it to the settlement of the disputed borders.[52] Repeated Indian assurances on not allowing Tibetans to engage in anti-China political activities aim at pleasing the Chinese, defusing the potential for trouble over Tibet.

Nonetheless, the Tibetan spiritual leader's immense popularity means that New Delhi can neither completely distance itself from the Tibetan cause nor can it clamp down too hard on Tibetans in violation of its own political and cultural values.[53] His presence, along with nearly 130,000 Tibetan refugees, complicate India's tightrope walk on Tibet.[54] The risks are much too high for India to contemplate anything more than the kind of humanitarian succor it provides to the Dalai Lama and exiled Tibetan community. If for China the Tibetan issue poses a crisis of integrity and image, for India, it poses a dilemma—how to avoid offending China without appearing to appease it. Thus, over the last 100 years, India's official position has evolved from viewing "Tibet as an independent country" (1911–1949) to accepting Chinese "suzerainty" (1950–54) to "sovereignty" (1955–1988) to accepting "Tibet as an autonomous region of China" (1988–2003), and finally recognizing "Tibet as part of China" (2003–present).[55]

Chinese Concerns: Future Tense

Yet the Chinese still worry. Given the history and complexity of relations, the Chinese remain skeptical of India's disavowals on Tibet. For one thing, they know that India has contiguity and historical-religious ties with Tibet, and more importantly, the Dalai Lama and a large Tibetan diaspora keen to go back one day. The Chinese regard the Dalai Lama as an Indian puppet. From their perspective, the Indians could shut "the Dalai shop" down if they wanted to, and that they do not signals Indian complicity. For another, what worries the Chinese most is the possibility that India, flush with economic success and US support, might one day decide to roll back China's influence in South Asia by choosing to play "the Tibet card" with the help of Tibetan separatists operating from havens located in India, Bhutan, and Nepal.[56] As Peter Lee points out, Beijing "views New Delhi's continued restraint in not playing the 'Tibet card' … increasingly as a matter of tactics rather than conviction."[57] Hua Han, a South Asia specialist at Beijing University, says the Chinese "don't want the Indian side to do anything to play the Tibet card."[58] Beijing regards the March 2008 unrest in Tibet and the accompanying worldwide protests as orchestrated by the Dalai Lama, India, and some Western countries. Consequently, China's mistrust of the Dalai Lama has deepened lately and its negotiating position hardened. A commentary in the CCP mouthpiece in October 2009 alleged that India was colluding with the Dalai Lama to split China.[59] This anxiety explains China's claims on Tawang in Arunachal Pradesh, home to some of the holiest sites in Tibetan Buddhism, including the biggest and most sacred monastery after the Potala Palace in Lhasa.[60] The Dalai Lama's visits there not only reinforce India's claim on Arunachal Pradesh, but also boost the Tibetan struggle and undermine Chinese territorial integrity.

Although the Chinese government labels the Dalai Lama a traitor and separatist intent on achieving independence, the Dalai Lama retains his commitment to the "Middle Path" approach of negotiated autonomy. The current stalemate can be ended only if all parties look to the future rather than the past. The consensus is that it is in Beijing's interests to end the prevailing impasse by starting meaningful negotiations aimed at reaching reconciliation with the Dalai Lama for several reasons:[61]

- One, the Dalai Lama is not seeking independence for Tibet but only the true autonomy offered in the 1951 Seventeen-Points Agreement and under the constitution of China.
- Two, he has explicitly rejected violence as a means to pursue greater Tibetan autonomy within China.
- Three, he alone has the authority to restrain advocates of violence. Containing advocates for belligerence and more radical political goals will be difficult once the Dalai Lama passes from the scene.
- Four, whoever succeeds the Dalai Lama, and however he is chosen, increased militancy by proponents of Tibetan independence cannot be ruled out. At any rate, any successor is unlikely to enjoy the Dalai Lama's stature and authority among Tibetans inside or outside of China.

To forestall Chinese interference in the selection process,[62] the Dalai Lama has indicated that his successor may be found outside of China (perhaps in the Tibetan Buddhist belt that stretches across northern India into Bhutan and Nepal), or may even be anointed before his death, thus marking a break with tradition. Nevertheless, China would refuse to accept any such candidate. Certainly, no successor anointed by Beijing would be regarded as legitimate. A lengthy and divisive succession to the Dalai Lama succession battle would not only sharpen internal political divisions on Tibet, but India would also inevitably be caught in this crossfire, perhaps bringing it into a confrontation with China.

Obviously, Beijing could reap immense benefits from an early-negotiated settlement. Notwithstanding Chinese official claims about "the Dalai clique" being in cahoots with hostile foreign powers, Tibet is essentially an emotional issue for Beijing that has the potential to damage China's aspirations for a peaceful emergence as a global great power, if not handled properly. The reality is that while Tibet is recognized as part of China by all countries in the world without exception, the Tibetan "government-in-exile" is recognized by none. As China acquires global power and influence, an uncompromising, *realpolitik*-based hard line stance raises legitimate questions and concerns about Chinese foreign policy behavior. Beijing is under pressure to ensure that its treatment of ethnic minorities meets global standards and norms of the twenty-first century because we no longer live in the nineteenth or early twentieth century world when brutal suppression of indigenous people (such as in the United States or Australia) evoked no outcry and response. By granting autonomy in Tibet's cultural, religious, and politico-economic affairs while retaining sovereign control over foreign and defense matters, the Chinese government could lend credence to its oft-repeated professions of being a peaceful and non-hegemonic power. The CCP's worries that such an arrangement would generate similar demands in Xinjiang or Inner Mongolia ignore significant differences in historical contexts between Tibet and other parts of China. More importantly, it would attract ethnic Tibetans back from India, thus reducing the role of exiled Tibetans in fostering Sino-Indian rivalry and neutralizing the potency of New Delhi's "Tibetan card."[63] As Paul Smith points out: "In this way, Beijing would be in a position to demonstrate convincingly that its political and economic ascendancy on the world stage is something to be celebrated and welcomed, as opposed to being feared and opposed."[64] In short, a compromise with the Tibetans would not only gain Beijing a great deal of international goodwill and influence but also give a major boost to China's soft-power diplomacy.

Nonetheless, Beijing remains unmoved. The Chinese do not buy the argument that the Dalai Lama is China's best bet or that it is better to deal with a pacifist moderate Dalai Lama than risk what comes after, believing that the threat of increased militancy once the Dalai Lama has left the scene is an empty one. For its part, Beijing seems convinced that time is on its side, not on the aging Dalai Lama's side, and therefore, it does not need to make any concessions.[65] Beijing has instead tried to entangle the Tibetan government-in-exile in endless and fruitless negotiations. Writer Wang Lixiong argues, "China really doesn't have any intention to solve this issue." Wang, like many others, believes that "China is content to play a game that involves meeting with delegations of exiled Tibetans when the demands of public relations require it, while patiently awaiting the Dalai Lama's death."[66] Besides, Beijing recognizes that, given China's rising economic and military power, few countries are willing to sacrifice their larger interests—economic, political, commercial, and military—to the agenda of Tibetan activists. Most Western countries and Japan have started taking a softer approach to human rights in China. Even in Sino-American relations, human rights and religious freedom are increasingly side issues in a relationship now driven by wider concerns over the global economic crisis, global warming, terrorism, and nuclear proliferation. Senior Chinese officials make no secret of their conviction that once the Dalai Lama passes on, the Tibetan cause will lose its sting: it will have neither a charismatic leader nor the current traction with the international community. They assume that it would be easier to deal with the next generation of Tibetans who may be less religious-minded and more progressive and materialistic in outlook.[67]

Making matters worse, there is a growing belief that the Tibetan refugees in India and elsewhere are the source of all of China's problems in Tibet, not Beijing's domestic policies. Beijing understands that as in the past so in the future; once unrest erupts in Tibet, India cannot completely wash its hands of Tibetan affairs. Chinese are irked by what they see as a pro-Tibet bias in Indian media and the "duplicitous nature of India's policies." New Delhi acknowledges that Tibet is a part of China. Nonetheless, Indian governments permit all kinds of "anti-China words and deeds" that erode China's sovereignty and image. Indian politicians and strategic affairs analysts often sympathize with Tibet's struggle while the government allows the Dalai Lama to travel abroad and meet foreign media and leaders. The discussion on the Tibetan unrest in the Indian Parliament in March 2008 and Foreign Minister Pranab Mukherjee's appeal to Beijing to address "the causes of trouble in the autonomous region of China through dialogue and non-violent means," allowing pro-Tibet rallies, and instigating an "anti-China campaign" in the Indian media—all these acts constitute, from Beijing's perspective, gross interference in the domestic affairs of China.[68] To most Chinese, India's support for Tibetans is all the more vexing at a time when China's growing global clout has made most Western countries either snub the Dalai Lama or merely pay lip service to the Tibetan cause.

Apparently, growing border tensions are related to Beijing's concerns over Tibet's future. The Chinese media's diatribe against India and a "calibrated escalation" of the border dispute since 2008 reflect Beijing's wider concern about a younger, restive generation of Tibetans the Dalai Lama does not control.[69] Beijing would obviously like to ensure that this new generation of Tibetan exiles based in northern India is not used as a bargaining chip by New Delhi in future. Indications are that China is no longer inclined to accept the Tibetan presence in India and might compel New Delhi to dismantle the Tibetan "government-in-exile" based in Dharamsala, especially after the death of the Dalai Lama. China's positioning of large military forces on the Tibetan plateau is aimed at both suppressing popular unrest and "teaching India a lesson" should New Delhi cross certain red lines. Some strategists envision that China may act to preempt, or respond to, an announcement of the Dalai Lama's chosen successor in India—particularly in Tawang—by deploying the PLA to occupy contested territory along the Sino-Indian border, thereby creating a risk of military conflict between the now nuclear-armed Asian giants.[70]

Faced with Beijing's uncompromising stance, sections of the Tibetan émigrés decry the Dalai Lama's dialogue posture as "ineffectual appeasement" of China. Many argue that Tibetan moderation has run its course. Though spiritually they still hold the Dalai Lama in esteem, some radical groups in exile (for example, the Tibetan Youth Congress) see his "Middle Way" as a constraint on their radical thinking and action, and show discontent with his approach to seeking autonomy instead of independence for their homeland.[71] They may feel freer to pursue their goal of "Free Tibet" through non-peaceful means once the Dalai Lama passes away. There exists widespread support amongst followers of Tibetan Buddhism for the "Free Tibet" movement across the Himalayas—from Ladakh to Nepal, Darjeeling, Sikkim, Bhutan, and Arunachal Pradesh. The results of a poll conducted among Tibetans reveal that most prefer full independence. It was against this backdrop that the Dalai Lama held a conclave of Tibetans from around the world in November 2008 to debate the future course of action. Though the final statement expressed support for the "Middle Way," it also declared, more ominously, that if there was no progress on autonomy then the goal could be shifted to complete independence.

Unlike the Chinese, Tibetans are convinced that the Tibet issue will not die with His Holiness. They caution that just as Christians could not be subdued after Jesus Christ's death, Beijing's posture of negotiating on its terms only after the Tibetan God King's death is flawed and dangerous. Nor will the Tibetan community accept a CCP-chosen successor to the Dalai Lama. Tibetan rules of reincarnation mean that the Dalai Lama dilemma may be deferred, but it is unlikely to go away. Should the Dalai Lama's reincarnation be "discovered" in Bhutan or somewhere in India, especially in Sikkim, Tawang, or Arunachal Pradesh, India will come under intense pressure from China on a range of issues.[72]

Stated simply, there is no meeting of minds. China's dislike for the Dalai Lama and his supporters is rooted in two contrasting worldviews.

Internally, Beijing's attempts to impose national unity and homogeneity to dilute ethnic identity via Han migration add to alienation and undermine China's national integration efforts as exemplified by the 2008 Tibetan uprising and the 2009 Uighur riots. Externally, Beijing's game plan to bring the entire Buddhist Himalayan belt within its security orbit faces opposition from India. Thus, a major crisis over Tibet may be in the making.[73] As one long-time observer puts it:

> The brutal truth is that in the past three millennia, imperial dynasties in China have known no other way to deal with their minorities than to "Sinify" them. Despite 60 years of effort and the expenditure of close to a trillion dollars on the development of "Greater Tibet," Beijing has failed with the Tibetans and is holding India responsible. It will only be a matter of time before it concludes that it will never succeed in Sinifying Tibet, so long as India keeps the Tibetan cultural identity alive by sheltering the Dalai Lama and his supporters. *The conflict of interests is potentially a mortal one.*[74]

In conclusion, Beijing's reluctance to negotiate meaningfully with the Dalai Lama could make Tibet unstable in the future and foster a younger generation of Tibetans in exile who prefer complete independence. Short of a dramatic breakthrough, the outlook for Tibetans looks bleak. Tibet may not be the pivot of the Sino-Indian relationship, but this single issue has the potential to rock and unravel the entire relationship. China's rhetoric and strategic posture suggest that it has increasingly started linking the Tibetan issue with the future of bilateral relations with India.

Territorial Dispute

Closely linked to the issue of Tibet's contested past and controversial status is the territorial dispute that has simmered for more than fifty years, threatening to disrupt relations between Asia's two giants. Nearly five decades after the 1962 War that erupted over their disputed border and three decades of negotiations, the 4,057 kilometer (2,520 mile) frontier between India and China, one of the longest inter-state borders in the world, remains the only one of China's land borders not defined, let alone demarcated on maps or delineated on the ground. The dispute stretches back to the British Raj, when colonial Foreign Secretary Henry McMahon drew the boundary between India and Tibet—based primarily on the highest watershed principle—at the 1914 Simla Convention. The McMahon line pushed British control northwards, which the Chinese refused to accept. Additionally, the PLA occupied large parts of Aksai

Chin during the 1962 border conflict beyond Beijing's original claim line. Then there is the contentious issue of the 5,180 sq km area of Shaksgam Valley in Kashmir that Pakistan handed over to China as part of the Sino-Pakistani border settlement in 1963, which China's Foreign Ministry spokespersons now claim is a non-issue between India and China.

Talks for a settlement have gone on since 1981 at diplomatic, expert, and political levels. Eight rounds of negotiations were held from 1981 to 1987. A "big push" was given to them first by Prime Minister Rajiv Gandhi's visit to China in 1988, the second one by Atal Behari Vajpayee's sojourn in Beijing in 2003, and a third one by Manmohan Singh's talks with Premier Wen Jiabao in 2005 and President Hu Jintao in 2006—without producing any worthwhile result. Fourteen meetings of a Joint Working Group, supported by boundary experts, were held from 1988 to 2002. The two sides exchanged maps of the relatively less contentious Middle Sector in 2001, but no "agreed Line of Actual Control" (LAC) has yet been negotiated along the borders of the Indian states of Himachal Pradesh and Uttarakhand. Marked maps showing the LAC are yet to be exchanged in the Eastern Sector (Arunachal Pradesh) and the Western Sector (Ladakh-Aksai Chin). Only after marked maps are exchanged can discussions take place to resolve the differences in these sectors. In 2003, border talks were elevated to a higher political dialogue of special representatives, who have held fourteen rounds of talks to date. Yet, there has been little progress, with both sides refusing to budge from their stated positions. While Chinese question Indian leaders' will and capacity to settle the dispute in a "give-and-take" spirit, Indians doubt China's sincerity in border negotiations. Whereas Chinese leaders counsel patience in resolving the boundary dispute "left over from history," Indians want the dispute to be resolved expeditiously and "not left to history again."[75] The Chinese formulation that "the border dispute with India will be resolved when the conditions are ripe" is often interpreted to mean, "when the overall military and economic balance of power has shifted in China's favor" (as it did in the case of Russia, Central Asian Republics, and Vietnam).[76]

Up until 2005, there was a great deal of optimism about a possible breakthrough. Evidence of this came during Prime Minister Vajpayee's China visit in June 2003 when New Delhi's readiness to address Chinese concerns on Tibet was matched by Beijing's willingness to resolve the Sikkim issue by recognizing the trade route through the Nathu La pass on the China-Sikkim frontier with India and later showing Sikkim as part of India in its maps. For its part, New Delhi reiterated its stance on the Tibetan Autonomous Region as part of China. This visit also paved the way for border talks to be held through special representatives of the leaders to find an early "political solution" to the boundary question, rather than going only by the legal and historical claims of the two sides. India indicated its willingness to settle for the territorial status quo by giving up claims to the Aksai Chin in Ladakh, and hoped China would give up its claims to Arunachal Pradesh in the eastern sector and recognize the McMahon Line just as Beijing had accepted Xinjiang/Tibet's boundaries with Afghanistan and Burma drawn by the British during the colonial era. In order to give a new thrust to the ongoing border negotiations, an "Agreement on the Political Parameters and Guiding Principles for the Settlement of the Boundary Question" was signed during Chinese Prime Minister Wen Jiabao's visit to India in April 2005. The joint statement issued at the end of the visit talked of a "Strategic and Cooperative Partnership" between India and China.

However, beginning in 2006, Beijing upped the ante by demanding major territorial concessions in populated areas of Arunachal Pradesh on terms that were seen in New Delhi as "humiliating and non-negotiable."[77] Tawang, in particular, has emerged as a sticking point since the Chinese claim it to be central to Tibetan Buddhism given that the sixth Dalai Lama was born there.[78] Much to Beijing's chagrin, the Dalai Lama has endorsed India's stance that Tawang in Arunachal Pradesh is part of India, thereby acknowledging the validity of the McMahon Line as per the 1914 Simla Agreement signed by Tibetan and British representatives.[79] The Chinese are adamant that Beijing will not accept the territorial status quo in the eastern sector partly because it would amount to Beijing's recognition of the McMahon Line, and acceptance of Tibet's de facto independence in the early twentieth century.[80] Ties between China and India were strained even further in May 2007 when the Chinese government refused a visa to an Indian official from disputed Arunachal Pradesh to visit China, and by the Indian government's invitation soon thereafter to Taiwan's then opposition Kuomintang (KMT) Party presidential candidate, Ma Ying-jou, to visit India in June 2007 to hold talks with senior Indian officials. China voiced its opposition to Ma's visit and called on India to abide by the "one China policy." Thereafter came media reports of the PLA encroachments across the LAC, indicating that nearly three decades of diplomatic efforts at resolving the border issue had come to naught. In August 2007, Beijing's demand for the removal of two Indian Army bunkers near the tri-junction of Sikkim, Bhutan, and Tibet on the grounds that these were located on China's territory raised questions about China's declared policy of treating Sikkim as part of Indian territory.[81] Periodic intelligence reports of Chinese small arms supplies to insurgents in India's volatile northeast via Bangladesh, Burma, and Nepal added to trust deficit. Repeated Chinese intrusions across the LAC, strident criticisms of visits to Arunachal Pradesh by Indian leaders and the Dalai Lama, and veiled threats to "split" India led to a war of words during 2008–09. The Indian military recorded well over 140 intrusions in 2007 in all three sectors—western (Ladakh), middle (Uttarakhand, Himachal) and eastern (Sikkim, Arunachal). There were nearly 270 border violations and 2,300 instances of "aggressive border patrolling" by Chinese soldiers in 2008, with "no significant increase" in the 2009 level.[82] For their part, the Chinese routinely deny any military incursions across the LAC. Hu Shisheng of the China Institute of Contemporary International Relations states: "The border has not been delimited. How can anyone claim that there have been incursions when the border issue has not been settled."[83] Nor do Chinese analysts see any sinister designs in western China's railroad development projects close to the disputed borders.

Discord over Accord

In a major policy shift, Chinese Foreign Minister Yang Jiechi told his Indian counterpart Pranab Mukherjee in May 2007 that the "mere presence of populated areas in Arunachal Pradesh would not affect Chinese claims on the boundary." This formulation was a repudiation of Article VII of the "Agreement on Political Parameters and Guiding Principles" signed during Chinese Premier Wen Jiabao's India visit in April 2005. This agreement stated: "In reaching a border settlement, the two sides shall safeguard populations in border areas." The inclusion of the phrase "settled population in the border areas" was then interpreted in India as a diplomatic concession that India had extracted from China as it protected Indian interests against Chinese claims to Tawang and other areas in Arunachal Pradesh.[84] New Delhi reacted by conveying to Beijing that it could not be pushed beyond a point on Tawang mainly because India has no intention of creating a precedent that would bolster similar Pakistani claims to Kashmir. This backtracking has resulted in a virtual stalemate in the talks between the designated special representatives. Describing the Chinese move as "a serious retrograde step," Mukherjee publicly rebuffed Beijing, saying that New Delhi would not part with populated portions of the state of Arunachal Pradesh: "Any elected government of India is not permitted by the constitution to part with any part of our land that sends representatives to the Indian Parliament."[85] Sending a clear signal against any Chinese designs over Arunachal Pradesh, India's Foreign Minister added:

> The days of Hitler are over. After the Second World War, no country captures land of another country in the present global context. That is why there is a civilised mechanism of discussions and dialogue to sort out border disputes. We sit around the table and discuss disputes to resolve them.[86]

Indian Prime Minister Manmohan Singh's visit to Arunachal Pradesh in late January 2008, soon after his return from China, to unveil major infrastructural construction projects further riled the Chinese. Zhao Gancheng, director of South Asia Studies at the Shanghai Institutes of International Affairs, saw Singh's visit to the disputed territory as a serious "provocation and unfavorable to the virtuous development of China-India relations and to the efforts for an early solution to the border issue."[87] The Chinese also took umbrage at the permission given to the US military to search for American airmen missing in action in Arunachal Pradesh during World War II.

The widespread Tibetan riots of March–April 2008, a few months before the Beijing Olympics, took place just when the rest of the world had started believing Beijing's official line that China had finally succeeded in co-opting Tibetans by raising living standards and building infrastructure projects in Tibet, and that China was one big happy family, with all nationalities living in harmony and working together to make China rich and strong. Turmoil in Tibet meant a big loss of face for the Chinese leadership as it showed that internal unity was still fragile. More importantly, it weakened Beijing's negotiating leverage with India over Tawang. Coinciding with the Tibetan unrest in 2008, several articles highly critical of India appeared in the Chinese media and strategic journals.

In May 2008, China opened a new front by contesting Indian control of a 2.1 sq km area, known as the Finger Area, in the northernmost tip of Sikkim state, whose border with China had never been disputed in the past. Foreign Minister Mukherjee was reportedly furious when the Chinese brought Sikkim, and not Arunachal Pradesh, to the negotiating table a month later. He refused to discuss the Sikkim issue, claiming that there was no dispute concerning that portion of the boundary with China, as the border in that sector had been settled along historical treaties and periodic exchanges of maps.[88] Beijing's belligerent rhetoric coupled with unrest in Tibet and Chinese military forays into Sikkim led India to beef up defenses in the vulnerable Siliguri Corridor and reactivate several abandoned airstrips along the Himalayas.[89] Some saw the Chinese move as signaling Beijing's retreat from its declared position on Sikkim while others thought Beijing was playing "the

Sikkim card" to pressure India over Tawang.[90] In a seemingly tit-for-tat response, Foreign Minister Mukherjee visited the 400-year-old Buddhist monastery in Tawang in November 2008 and once again ruled out ceding it to China: "China is often making claims on Arunachal Pradesh, but Arunachal Pradesh has a special place in our heart. People of Arunachal Pradesh regularly elect two representatives to the Lok Sabha [Parliament] and there is an elected state assembly carrying out the responsibility of administration like any of other 27 states. The question of parting company of Arunachal or any of its part does not arise." He added that China is "fully aware" the province is an "integral part of India." Beijing publicly denounced these comments, which the Foreign Ministry spokesperson stated "take no regard of the historical facts."[91] The Indian riposte to "the historical facts" argument by the Chinese was given by Sujit Dutta:

> Much of the historiography of [Beijing's territorial] claims is singularly unidimensional and self-serving. While advancing its territorial claims, the PRC has often consciously blurred the distinction between what was no more than hegemonic influence, tributary relationships, suzerainty, and actual sovereignty. Most of its claims are, therefore, not rooted in the exercise of the actual jurisdiction, continuity of rule through the post-imperial period, ethnicity, or the popular will in the areas claimed. . . China's unmitigated irredentism [is] based on the Qing imperial conquests of large non-Han territories in order to safeguard the security of core Han China. The theory that the periphery must be occupied in order to secure the core is an essentially imperial notion that was internalized by the Chinese nationalists—both Guomindang and Communist. The regime's attempts to reach its imagined geographical frontiers often with little historical basis have had and continue to have highly destabilizing strategic consequences.[92]

The year 2009 saw Beijing and New Delhi engaged in tit-for-tat moves that culminated in a war of words and heightened tensions. In June 2009, China blocked a $1.3 billion loan to India by the Asian Development Bank, part of which was meant for a watershed project in Arunachal Pradesh. India responded by publicly asking China to keep off developmental projects in Pakistan-occupied Kashmir. Beijing's public rebuke to Prime Minister Manmohan Singh for his October 2009 visit to campaign for Arunachal Pradesh legislature elections apparently led New Delhi to approve the Dalai Lama's visit to Tawang a month later in November. Chinese Foreign Ministry Spokesperson Qin Gang's reaction to this "provocation" was fast and furious: "The Indian side disregarded the solemn position of China in allowing the Dalai Lama to visit the disputed area of the eastern section of the China-India border region. China expresses strong dissatisfaction about that." Condemning the Dalai Lama's visit to Tawang, a *Global Times* commentary quoted Hu Shisheng, a researcher at the China Institute of Contemporary International Relations, as saying that India seemed to have "forgotten the lesson of 1962, when its repeated provocation resulted in military clashes. India is on this wrong track again."[93] Irked by the Chinese practice of using state-controlled media to air provocative views, India's Deputy Foreign Minister Shashi Tharoor retorted: "Such language will not help bilateral ties." Tharoor described Hu's comment as a "bit silly" that India had not learnt its lessons from the 1962 War, and added: "We are far from 1962 and history does not always repeat itself. We are not woefully prepared as we were in 1962 ... China's articulations in recent weeks have been nothing but an irritant."[94] There was also a shift in China's stance over Kashmir from one of neutrality to being pro-Pakistan by calling for external mediation. The Chinese Embassy in New Delhi began issuing Chinese visas to Indian nationals from Kashmir on loose sheets of paper, instead of stamping or pasting them on their passports as was the norm with other Indian citizens. This move indicated that along with Arunachal Pradesh, China considered the Jammu and Kashmir state as disputed.[95] Beijing also showed its displeasure over the Dalai Lama's high-profile visit to Tawang by inviting Mirwaiz Umar Farooq—an influential Kashmiri separatist leader affiliated with the largest mosque in Kashmir—to visit China.[96] For its part, India has made it clear that Kashmir is a "core issue" for India just as Tibet and Taiwan are core national interests for Beijing. In a subtle, yet strong, signal to China for not treating Jammu and Kashmir as an integral part of India, the Indian side held back its explicit commitment to the "One China" policy for the first time in a joint communiqué issued during Chinese premier Wen Jiabao's visit in December 2010. Instead, the principle of "mutual respect and sensitivity for each other's concerns and aspirations" was stated as the basis for carrying forward strategic cooperation.[97]

Resurrecting old issues and manufacturing new disputes to put the other side off balance and enhance negotiating leverage is an old negotiating tactic in Chinese statecraft. The Chinese foreign minister's claim in May 2008 that "Sikkim was a disputed area" (even though the issue had been resolved during Prime Minister Vajpayee's visit in 2003, and official Chinese maps, reversing a half century-old policy, had begun depicting Sikkim as part of India since 2006) is a case in point. Another one is the sharper focus on Tawang as part of a shriller claim over Arunachal Pradesh, which Beijing now calls "South Tibet" (a new

Chinese term for Arunachal Pradesh since 2005). It is worth noting that prior to 2005, there was no reference to "Southern Tibet" in China's official media or any talk of the "unfinished business of the 1962 War." Nor did the Chinese government or official media ever claim that the PLA's "peaceful liberation of Tibet in 1950 was partial and incomplete" or that "a part of Tibet was yet to be liberated." With China now insisting on the return of Tawang on religious grounds, Indians argue that they have a more powerful case for the return of the Mount Kailash-Mansarovar in Tibet, since it is a sacred religious place associated with the Hindu religion.

In short, China's increasing assertiveness over the disputed Arunachal Pradesh and India's refusal to concede ground has led to a remarkable meltdown in bilateral relations since 2006, despite public protestations of amity. The war of words somewhat subsided after Chinese and Indian prime ministers met in October 2009 in Thailand on the sidelines of the East Asia Summit to reiterate their mutual commitment to maintaining peace and tranquility on the border. However, an unresolved territorial dispute provides fuel for nationalists in both countries who criticize their governments for being soft or being weak. Some observers argue that Hu Jintao's desire to control the choice of the next Dalai Lama has led to pressuring India to concede access to the Tawang Monastery, which is crucial to this choice.[98] The deterioration in Sino-Indian relations under Hu need not have come as a surprise given his reputation as a hardliner over Tibet. (After all, Deng Xiaoping had groomed him for the CCP leadership because of his claim to fame for the successful suppression of the Tibetan revolt in 1988.) Others attribute the recent downturn in Sino-Indian relations more to a domestic power struggle within the CCP and the Tibetan unrest than to the Dalai Lama succession issue or to Chinese concerns about India's growing tilt toward the United States.[99] Some China-watchers maintain that China is signaling to India that if a sector-by-sector approach to dispute resolution is pursued, China expects concessions in both western and eastern sectors from India. The majority view is that New Delhi's unwillingness to show deference to the next superpower has long been a sore point with Beijing and inflames their territorial disputes. Whatever the case, the PLA seems to be back in the driver's seat in formulating China's policy toward India.[100]

New Chinese Perspectives on Territorial Dispute

Several commentaries in Chinese language sources published during 2006–2009 indicate a shift toward a tougher Chinese stance on the territorial dispute with India. Articles on "Future Directions of the Sino-Indian Border Dispute" published in *Guogji Zhanlue* in November 2006; Liu Silu's "Beijing Should Not Lose Patience in Chinese-Indian Border Talks" in *Wen Wei Po* on June 1, 2007; Professor Wang Yiwei's interview "Helping US May Derail Border Talks" with the *Asian Age* on July 25, 2007; "A Warning to the Indian Government: Don't Return Evil For Good," posted on the PLA-run China Institute of International Strategic Studies (CIISS) website on March 26, 2008; and Zuo Xuan's "India covets Dalai Lama's visit," in *Global Times* on November 9, 2009 are broadly representative of the official thinking in China's national security establishment on this subject. The key arguments and major themes presented in these and other similar writings are summarized below.

First, since India controls 90,000 square kilometers of the richest part of Tibet and the Himalayan region, equivalent to two and a half Taiwans and as large as Jiangsu Province, "the Chinese government will not easily give up its territory." *Wen Wei Po* commentator Liu Silu contended that as "it is equally difficult to get India to spit out the fatty meat it is chewing ... Beijing had better be patient at the negotiation table [because] time is on China's side." Apparently, many Chinese strategic thinkers believe that China's comprehensive national power vis-à-vis India is likely to increase over time, and that would enable Beijing to drive a better bargain on the boundary question in the future.[101]

Second, as Professor Wang Yiwei put it, "China showed 'greatness' once, after the 1962 Indo-China war, when it gave up the land it controlled [in Arunachal Pradesh] and it could not be expected to show magnanimity again ... India 'lost an opportunity' to settle the boundary question when Deng Xiaoping and Mao Zedong were alive. President Hu Jintao is not Deng or Mao. He is strong but cannot be compared with them."[102] What is left unsaid here is that China, having by now far outstripped India in terms of comprehensive national power, is no longer willing to make the kind of concessions today that Zhou and Deng had offered in 1960 and 1980 respectively for the sake of a secure border. From the Chinese perspective, the ball is clearly in India's court. If New Delhi wants a settlement, it must hand over a large chunk of territory in Arunachal Pradesh to China.

Third, a resource dimension has now been added to the old land border dispute which did not exist before. Apparently, many in China's strategic circles now seem to regret giving up the "resource-rich territory" of Arunachal Pradesh that the PLA had captured during the 1962 War ("the fruits of victory"), and signal a new determination not to repeat "the mistakes of the past" (i.e., show magnanimity by vacating conquered territory) in the event of another border war with India. Following the widespread Tibetan unrest in March 2008, one PLA analyst, assuming the pseudonym *Zhan Lue* (Strategist), went to the extent of warning India of another 1962-style invasion. He cautioned an "arrogant India" not "to be evil" or else Chinese forces in war "will not pull back 30 kilometers" as in 1962.[103]

Fourth, the Sino-Indian border issue is linked as much with sovereignty and territorial integrity as with the respective status of the two countries in the global hierarchy. Placing the boundary issue in strategic power transitions context, one commentary observed that "the border issue is only a symbol of Sino-Indian friction; the basic point concerns New Delhi's thinking that Beijing is the 'greatest obstacle' to India's rise." Claiming that India's occupation of "Southern Tibet" (i.e., Arunachal Pradesh) is a security threat to China, it advocated adopting a counter-strategy "*aimed at weakening the control of the Indian central government through steps like 'splitting' and 'dismembering' India. In that way, India, which is inferior to China in terms of comprehensive national strength, cannot challenge the PRC in future*."[104] Some in the PLA see an opportunity in establishing a strategic foothold in India's northeastern states that would bring the Chinese presence closer to the Bay of Bengal and also enable them to cut off militarily, if necessary, the narrow Siliguri corridor that connects the rest of India with the northeast. Hence, a *Guogji Zhanlue* commentary advises that Beijing "should not adopt any hasty step or make big compromises on principles" because this issue, "if approached in a hurry, could impact the respective rise of the two nuclear powers." Apparently, a major Chinese concern is that a border settlement, without significant Indian territorial concessions, could potentially augment India's power position and thus impact negatively China's rise.[105]

Fifth, a "fair and reasonable settlement" implies that "India will need to give up something to get something."[106] Ideally speaking, *Wen Wei Po* argued that China should "recover the entire area. But it is negotiable for the disputed territory to be split equally between China and India, as was the case of Heixiazi [Bolshoy Ussuriysky] Island in the northeast [on the Russian border]. A third option would be for Beijing to recover at least the 2,000 square kilometers covering Tawang and Takpa Shiri. It is argued that this is Beijing's last resort and it will not accept any deal worse than this."[107] An India expert at the Shanghai Academy of Social Sciences maintains that unless India is ready to make territorial concessions, "[the border issue] cannot be solved for the next 1000 years."[108] Apparently, having wrested substantial territorial concessions from Russia, Tajikistan, and Vietnam in their land border disputes with China, Beijing expects the same from India.

Sixth, China should economically harmonize/integrate Tibet, Nepal, and the border regions with India into China's economic sphere through increased economic links and infrastructure projects, such as the Qinghai-Tibet railway, before proceeding for a boundary settlement with India. Underlying this is the belief that economic envelopment would soften India's position, leading to a settlement on China's terms.

Last, if negotiations, coercive diplomacy, and economic harmonization (a carrot and stick policy) fail to produce the desired outcome, the use of force at an appropriate time in the future to recover "China's Southern Tibet" is not ruled out.[109] Many Chinese analysts believe that the military balance has shifted in their favor with the completion of the 1,118-kilometer (695 miles) Qinghai-Tibet railway and other military infrastructure projects in Tibet and that negates the need for any territorial concession to India in the eastern sector.

These views and arguments clearly (a) advocate a "containing India" strategy; (b) foretell a long and torturous course of future border negotiations; (c) point to the possible eruption of a "limited border war" between the two countries; and (d) indicate an uncertain and unpredictable future for India's relations with China.

For its part, the Indian government has responded by unveiling plans for economic development and major infrastructure projects (the building of 72 roads, several airstrips, and numerous bridges) in the border areas along the undefined LAC that would enable the Indian military to "swiftly move forces into the region and sustain them logistically in the event of any untoward trouble or emergency." Indian Defense Minister A. K. Antony told the Combined Commanders' Conference that "China has been building a lot of infrastructure—railways, airports and roads [along the Indian border]. We are also doing the same thing."[110] In response to the establishment of several new airbases in Tibet and three in southern China, the Indian Air Force is reportedly beefing up its presence by deploying two squadrons of Sukhoi-30MKIs near the Chinese border and reactivating old airfields.[111] The Indian Army is also raising two additional division-sized mountain warfare formations to give more teeth to its war-fighting capability in the Himalayas.[112] Indian military commanders contend that since the Chinese won such a clear and decisive victory in 1962, "India's dissuasive posture aims at denying China a repeat of its 1962 land-grab, thereby ensuring that a future war ends either in a stalemate or in a denial of clear victory for the PLA which will be tantamount to defeat for China and victory for India."[113] Most analysts concede that

China has escalated tensions over the territorial dispute to force India to make new concessions at a time when power asymmetry between the two is growing and to forestall India's rise as a potential peer competitor.[114]

In short, there is little or no sign of an early resolution to the conflicting claims, despite continuing negotiations and the recent upswing in diplomatic, political, commercial, and even military ties (including joint military exercises) between the world's two most populous countries. Both are amassing forces on the Tibetan border to prepare for all contingencies. Analysts from both countries see a possible reversion back to the period between the 1960s and the 1980s: the era of military confrontation and high tensions in Sino-Indian relations.[115] Both sides accuse each other of not negotiating in good faith on the boundary question. Both seem unable to look at the problem from the other side's perspective.

Pessimists rule out an early border settlement. They draw attention to the growing talk of a "limited border war" to grant China dominant position in the region and to settle the boundary dispute once and for all. As in the past, Chinese suspicions of Indian involvement in the unrest in Tibet have contributed to a hardening of the PRC's position on border issues. Unless and until Tibet is totally pacified and completely Sinicized as Inner Mongolia has been, Beijing is unlikely to give up the "bargaining chip" that an unsettled boundary vis-à-vis India provides it with. Beijing's ultimate goal is to extend its influence in the entire Himalayan belt in order to consolidate its grip on Tibet. In the meantime, an unsettled boundary suits Chinese interests for the present because China's claims in the western sector are complicated by the Indo-Pakistan dispute over Kashmir, Pakistan's interests in the Sino-Indian territorial dispute, and Beijing's interest in keeping India under strategic pressure on two fronts.[116] An unsettled border also provides China the strategic leverage to keep India uncertain about its intentions and nervous about its capabilities, while exposing India's vulnerabilities and weaknesses and ensuring New Delhi's "good behavior" on issues of vital concern to China.[117] Pessimists also note that historically Beijing has negotiated border disputes with neighbors in their moment of national weakness (Pakistan, Burma in the 1960s, and the Central Asian Republics in the 1990s) or only after the overall balance of power had shifted decisively in China's favor and/or after they had ceased to be a major threat (land border settlements with Russia and Vietnam in the 1990s). However, it has not negotiated with those who are perceived as China's present rivals and future threats (India, Japan, and Vietnam). Not only that, even if the territorial dispute were somehow resolved,

India and China would still compete over energy resources, markets, and bases for geo-strategic reasons. Additionally, a new potentially divisive issue for the future appears to be the ecological impact on the Indian subcontinent of Chinese plans to divert the rivers of Tibet for irrigation purposes in China.

In a commentary published in 2007, this author had predicted that although the probability of an all-out conflict is low, the prospect that some of India's road building projects in disputed areas could lead to tensions, clashes and skirmishes with Chinese border patrols cannot be completely ruled out.[118] By mid-2009, the Chinese were objecting to construction of roads and airstrips in Ladakh and Arunachal Pradesh amidst escalated war rhetoric on both sides of the Himalayas.[119] Should a conflict break out, the PLA's contingency plans emphasize a "short and swift localized" conflict (confined to the Tawang region, along the lines of the 1999 Kargil conflict initiated by Pakistan) with the following objectives in mind: (i) capture the Tawang tract; (ii) give India's military a bloody nose; and (iii) deliver a knockout punch that punctures India's ambitions to be China's equal or peer competitor once and for all. The ultra-modern civilian and military infrastructure in Tibet is expected to enable Beijing to exercise the military option to achieve the above-mentioned objectives should that become necessary at some stage in the future.

Conversely, optimists are confident that political will and increased mutual trust can break the impasse. As far as Tibet's future is concerned, it will ultimately be determined more by what happens inside Tibet than by what India says or does. Despite heightened tensions and tit-for-tat exchanges, neither side can afford to allow their disagreements to spin out of control because of both countries' focus on economic development for the next couple of decades. In particular, the adoption of a pragmatic approach based on ground realities would facilitate dispute resolution. An east-west swap (Arunachal Pradesh in the east for Aksai Chin in the west), with both sides making smaller territorial adjustments and giving up claims to territory controlled by the other, could be the most feasible way out. A future border settlement will need to ensure that in return for China's respect for Indian interests in Tibet, especially in Mount Kailash-Mansarovar, India would respect Chinese interests in Tawang. Negotiating these issues will test diplomatic skills, but a mutually agreed settlement will help curb jingoism and ultra-nationalist sentiment on both sides. In the meantime, both sides may have to learn to live without an early resolution to the dispute.

Conclusion

For nearly a thousand years now, attempts by Mongols, Manchus, and Hans to conquer, control, and subdue the Tibetans have encountered resistance of varying degrees. Much to Tibetans' chagrin, the imperatives of great power politics have always trumped support for the cause of Tibetan independence. Still, frequent disturbances and protests in and outside Tibet make the issue more acute insofar as they show how vulnerable the Chinese hold is over that region. The gap between the Chinese leadership and the Dalai Lama followers remains as wide as ever. The centrality of Tibet in Sino-Indian relations is best summed up in the following observation: "When there is relative tranquility in Tibet, India and China have reasonably good relations. When Sino-Tibetan tensions rise, India's relationship with China heads south."[120] As Tibet, the Dalai Lama succession issue, and the territorial dispute become more and more intertwined, frictions are growing in Sino-Indian relations.[121]

Despite several agreements and joint declarations, the Chinese still suspect that India prefers an independent Tibet and covertly supports Tibetan separatists. The belief that growing trade, cultural, and political ties would dampen Sino-Indian tensions over Tibet seems unfounded. Chinese denunciations of Tibetan leaders and activists in exile have become ever more harsh and shrill. The Dalai Lama's "Middle Way" approach to reconciliation has not placated Beijing, which sees it as just another ruse for Tibetan independence. From Beijing's perspective, political visits to Tawang, Indian troop increases in Arunachal, the refurbishment of border infrastructure, and greater political exposure to the Dalai Lama are grave provocations. Unless a negotiated settlement is reached, the loss of the Dalai Lama's moderating influence and an increase in rhetoric and violence by radical Tibetan émigrés would create problems between New Delhi and Beijing. India's growing power and closer relations with the United States also add to Chinese worries about the future of Tibet. Further, the Tibetan issue and the border dispute have now become linked to the broader China-India geopolitical rivalry in Asia. Perhaps an even more dangerous area of looming conflict is emerging in the sharing of Himalayan-based water resources.

Some in China's strategic circles feel that a limited war with India would send a resounding message to Tibetans that theirs is a lost cause. Both sides have begun reinforcing their military forces along their long, disputed border. The irony is that China and India could stumble into another war in the future for the same reasons that led them to a border war half a century ago in 1962. However, unlike in the past, both China and India are now nuclear-armed nations with enormous stakes in maintaining peace. Burgeoning trade ties and collaboration on issues like climate change have shown both capitals the benefits of cooperation even as border tensions rise. For Beijing, a hard-line approach to India could backfire and drive India (and other Asian neighbors) into stronger opposition to China. The pursuit of aggressive foreign adventures would destroy the benign "peaceful rise" image that China is so assiduously striving to achieve. A conflict will cost India dearly in terms of economic developmental objectives and the political ambition of emerging as a great power in a multipolar Asia.[122] Given their current focus on economic growth and prosperity, one hopes that saner voices will prevail in both capitals and both will find ways to resolve their disputes in the interests of regional peace and stability.

Notes

[1] "China says no compromise on national sovereignty, refute Dalai's so-called 'middle way,'" *Xinhua News Service,* November 10, 2008.

[2] "Text of China's white paper on 'protection,' 'development' of Tibetan culture," (Information Office of China's State Council), reported in *BBC Monitoring Asia Pacific-Political,* September 25, 2008.

[3] A. Kolas, "Tibetan nationalism: the politics of religion," *Journal of Peace Research,* 33:1 (1996), 64.

[4] P. Smith, "Tibet: at the crossroads of ethnic nationalism and geopolitics," in R. Wirsing (ed), *Fixing Fractured Nations* (Palgrave, 2010), 206-227.

[5] H. French, "Separating fact from image on Tibet," *IHT*, October 26, 2007.

[6] G. Sioris, "A Tibetan history lesson for China," *Japan Times*, July 28, 2003, 10.

[7] French, "Separating fact from image on Tibet."

[8] Sioris, "A Tibetan history lesson for China."

[9] M. C. Davis, "The quest for self-rule in Tibet," *Journal of Democracy*, 18:4 (October 2007), 165. Also see, W. W. Smith, Jr., *Tibetan Nation: A History of Tibetan Nationalism and Sino-Tibetan Relations* (Boulder, Colo.: Westview, 1996); and C. I. Beckwith, *The Tibetan Empire in Central Asia* (Princeton University Press, 1987).

[10] E. Sperling, "The Mongols, Mao and the Dalai Lama." *IHT*, April 13, 2008, 10.

[11] C. H. Alexandrowicz-Alexander, "The legal position of Tibet," *American Journal of International Law,* 48:2 (April 1954), 267.

[12] Davis, "The quest for self-rule in Tibet."

[13] M. Jang Kunwar, *China and War in the Himalayas, 1792–1793* (Oxford University Press, 1962), 283.

[14] Alexandrowicz-Alexander, "The legal position of Tibet."

[15] Alexandrowicz-Alexander, "The legal position of Tibet."

[16] M. C. Goldstein and C. M. Beall, "The impact of China's reform policy on the nomads of Western Tibet," *Asian Survey,* 29:6 (June 1989), 620. Pamela Crossley also characterizes the Qing connection with Tibet as a loose imperial

association featuring indirect rule through Tibetan monastic leaders. See P. Crossley, *A Translucent Mirror: History and Identity in Qing Imperial Ideology* (Berkeley: University of California Press, 1999), 327–36.

[17] Davis, "The quest for self-rule in Tibet," 157–171.

[18] S. Dutta, "Revisiting China's territorial claims on Arunachal," *Strategic Analysis*, 32:4 (2008), 549–81.

[19] For Indian historians, if Tibet is claimed as part of China because it was brought under control by the Mongols, then by the same logic, India could claim Afghanistan, Burma, Nepal, Sri Lanka, or Malaya as "integral parts of India" because they were all parts of either the Chola or Mughal Empire or British colonies and protectorates.

[20] "The reluctance of the British—concerned about their own imperial claims in India—to recognize more independence than a state of Chinese "suzerainty" appeared to be the only thing that held the Tibetans back." See M. C. Goldstein, *A History of Modern Tibet, 1913–1951* (Berkeley: University of California Press, 1989), 68–80, 832–41.

[21] This was the only agreement that the PRC has ever made with any of its designated 55 national minorities, clearly acknowledging Tibet's distinctive historical status. For details, see J. W. Garver, *Protracted Contest: Sino-Indian Rivalry in the Twentieth Century* (Seattle: University of Washington Press, 2001).

[22] D. Twining, "Could China and India go to war over Tibet?" *Foreign Policy,* March 10, 2009 <http://shadow.foreignpolicy.com/posts/2009/03/10/could_china_and_india_go_to_war_over_tibet>.

[23] Sperling, "The Mongols, Mao and the Dalai Lama."

[24] C. McGranahan, "The CIA and the Chushi Gandrug Resistance," *Journal of Cold War Studies,* 9:3 (Summer 2006), 113–114.

[25] Cited in D. Nelson, "Dalai Lama warns Tibetans are 'near extinction' at 50th anniversary of exile," *Telegraph*, March 10, 2009.

[26] Smith, "Tibet: At the crossroads of ethnic nationalism and geopolitics."

[27] "West in dark on Tibet, basic facts shed light," *China Daily,* February 20, 2009.

[28] "China issues white paper on Tibet, denies 'cultural genocide'," *BBC Monitoring International Reports,* September 25, 2008.

[29] C. Bodeen, "Dalai Lama 'wolf in monk's robes': China," *Associated Press*, March 19, 2008 <http://www.thestar.com/News/World/article/347839>.

[30] E. Wong, "Dalai Lama's defeat to be holiday in Tibet," *IHT*, January 19, 2009.

[31] China has several nuclear installations in Tibet.

[32] E. Wong, "Dalai Lama says China has turned Tibet into a 'hell on Earth,'" *New York Times*, March 10, 2009.

[33] Information here is from AsiaInt Reference Library, "China: A bleak future for Tibetans," *NAR*, September 2008 <http://www.asiaint.com/arl/arl19227.asp>.

[34] "Tibet," Jane's Sentinel Security Assessment—China and Northeast Asia, May 2, 2008.

[35] M. Zhao and O. Schell, "Tibet: plateau in peril," *World Policy Journal,* (Fall 2008), 174.

[36] "Melting glaciers threaten Indus, Ganges," *Southasiamedia.net*, July 25, 2007, <http://www.southasianmedia.net/index_story.cfm?id=409988&category=frontend&Country=main&pro=0>.

[37] P. Stobdan, "China should not use water as a threat multiplier," *IDSA Strategic Comment*, October 23, 2009.

[38] Stobdan, "China should not use water as a threat multiplier"; S. Dasgupta, "China rolls out water diversion project, Indian experts worried," *Times of India*, October 19, 2009.

[39] Stobdan, "China should not use water as a threat multiplier."

[40] TNN, "India to check if China is building Brahmaputra dam," *Times of India*, October 16, 2009.

[41] T. Mathou, "Tibet and its neighbors: moving toward a new Chinese strategy in the Himalayan region," *Asian Survey,* 45:4 (July–August 2005), 506.

[42] G. Ginsburg and M. Mathos, *Communist China and Tibet: The First Dozen Years* (The Hague: Martinus Nijhoff, 1964), 210.

[43] Dutta, "Revisiting China's territorial claims on Arunachal."

[44] P. Nanda, "Dalai Lama is India's boon, not bane," *UPI Asia online*, November 16, 2009, <http://www.upiasia.com/Society_Culture/2009/11/16/dalai_lama_is_indias_boon_not_bane/2011/>.

[45] A. Puri, "The Dalai Lama His Holiness...the dilemma," *Outlook*, April 14, 2008.

[46] Agencies, "Deal firmly with China: ex-foreign secy," *Indian Express*, October 20, 2009.

[47] M. Nalapat, "China and Pakistan's ISI," *The Diplomat*, July 19, 2010 <http://the-diplomat.com/indian-decade/2010/07/19/china-firms-aid-pakistans-isi/>.

[48] B. S. Raghavan, "Ending Tibetan impasse," *The Hindu BusinessLine*, October 12, 2009.

[49] Nanda, "Dalai Lama is India's boon, not bane"; Raghavan, "Ending Tibetan impasse."

[50] See Puri, "The Dalai Lama His Holiness...the dilemma."

[51] Puri, "The Dalai Lama His Holiness...the dilemma."

[52] This new formulation is silent on the history of the relationship between Beijing and Lhasa. However, as Dutta argues: "It was not realized that the TAR included Arunachal in the Chinese maps, nor was any reciprocity sought. Such unilateral concessions and postures have compromised India's negotiating edge." See his "Revisiting China's territorial claims on Arunachal."

[53] Puri, "The Dalai Lama His Holiness...the dilemma."

[54] "PM tells off Wen, says Dalai free to travel in India," *Times of India*, October 26, 2009, 1.

[55] A. Shourie, "India's Tibet policy," unpublished paper (2008); Arun Shourie, *Are we deceiving ourselves again?* (ASA/Rupa, 2008).

[56] Lee, "Dalai Lama at apex of Sino-Indian tensions."

[57] Lee, "Dalai Lama at apex of Sino-Indian tensions."

[58] Quoted in Puri, "The Dalai Lama His Holiness...the dilemma"; "Do not use the Dalai Card against China," *Huanqiu*, 8 November 2009.

[59] "Dalai Lama goes further down traitorous road," *People's Daily online*, October 23, 2009, <http://news.xinhuanet.com/english/2009-10/23/content_12304152.htm>.

[60] Tawang is said to be "a virtual treasure trove of Tibetan Buddhist religion and culture," and is seen as the repository of the last remnants of a Tibet which has been inundated with an influx of Han Chinese culture. S. Ramachandran, "Dalai Lama caught in Sino-Indian dispute," *Asia Times online*, September 18, 2009, <http://www.atimes.com/atimes/South_Asia/KI18Df02.html>.

[61] T. J. Christensen, "Shaping the choices of a rising China: recent lessons for Obama," *Washington Quarterly*, 32:3 (July 2009), 89–104.

[62] China played foul when the Dalai Lama recognized the 11th Panchen Lama (the second highest monk after the Dalai Lama) in the late 1990s. Beijing not only put the genuine Panchen Lama in prison, but also propped up its own parallel Panchen Lama. Beijing has long tried to exploit the latent discontent and factional disputes within the various Tibetan Buddhist religious sects.

[63] D. Norbu, *China's Tibet Policy* (Richmond, UK: Curzon Press, 2001), 294.

[64] Smith, "Tibet: at the crossroads of ethnic nationalism and geopolitics."

[65] Kent Ewing, "China closes the door on Tibet," *Asia Times online*, February 26, 2009, <http://www.atimes.com/atimes/China/KB26Ad01.html>.

[66] Wang quoted in Howard French, "Separating fact from image on Tibet," *IHT*, October 26, 2007.

[67] Discussions with Chinese officials, diplomats and South Asia specialists. "Dalai should seize chance provided by talks," *Global Times*, January 28, 2010 <http://opinion.globaltimes.cn/editorial/2010-01/501637.html>.

[68] Beijing was also disturbed by the sight of Indian Foreign Minister Mukherjee and US Secretary of State Condoleezza Rice jointly addressing the Tibet issue in Washington. Agencies, "Dalai Lama accuses China of cultural genocide," *Hindustan Times*, March 18, 2008, 1.

[69] Reuters, "Tibet at heart of new India-China border tension," *National Post*, October 21, 2009, <http://www.nationalpost.com/nationalpost/story.html?id=2127528>.

[70] Twining, "Could China and India go to war over Tibet?"

[71] S. Sehgal, "Succession worries unsettle Tibetans," *Asia Times online*, February 20, 2009, <http://www.atimes.com/atimes/South_Asia/KB20Df03.html>.

[72] J. Ranade, "India and next Dalai Lama," *Indian Express*, November 11, 2009.

[73] AsiaInt Reference Library, "Into the mountains with China," *AsiaInt South Asia Review* (SAR) November 2008 <http://www.asiaint.com/arl/arl19897.asp>.

[74] P. S. Jha, "An old Chinese proverb...," *Outlook*, 30 June 2008. Italics added.

[75] *Xinhua*, June 3, 2000; "China ready to expedite talks with India on LAC delineation," *The Hindu*, June 5, 2000.

[76] A. K. Joseph, "India, China fail to exchange border maps of western sector," *Rediff.com*, June 19, 2002.

[77] See R. Sharma, "China jams DD, AIR signals in border area," *Tribune*, June 26, 2007.

[78] India annexed the town and monastery of Tawang in February 1951, partly in response to China's military takeover of Tibet in 1950 and partly because the Simla Convention transferred it to India, despite Tibetan objections.

[79] "Tawang is part of India: Dalai Lama," *Times of India*, June 4, 2008, 1.

[80] A Chinese foreign ministry researcher quoted in D. S. Rajan, "China: an internal account of 'startling inside story of Sino-Indian border talks'," *C3S Paper No. 168*, June 10, 2008, <http://www.c3sindia.org/uncategorized/258/china-an-internal-account-of-%e2%80%9c-startling-inside-story-of-sino-indian-border-talks/>.

[81] R. Sharma, "China objects to Sikkim bunkers," *Tribune*, September 3, 2007. To date, China has made no formal public declaration that it recognizes Sikkim as Indian territory. R. Velloor, "China's position on issues with India 'hardening,'" *Straits Times*, June 12, 2007.

[82] E. Wong, "China and India dispute enclave on edge of Tibet," *New York Times*, September 3, 2009, 1.

[83] Hu quoted in S. Dasgupta, "Anti-Chinese sentiment hampering border talks," *Times of India*, September 19, 2008, 1.

[84] I. Bagchi and S. Dasgupta, "India red-faced as China gets tough," *Times of India*, May 27, 2007; S. Mustafa, "New PRC foreign minister hardens border dispute," *Asian Age*, August 4, 2007.

[85] Reuters, "India rebuffs Beijing on disputed border," *IHT*, June 17, 2007.

[86] "Pranab says can't give any part of Arunachal," *Indian Express*, June 17, 2007; Raman, 'Tawang: Some Indian plain-speaking at last!'

[87] Qian Pingguang, "Xinge dao Zhong In lintu zhengyi qu tiaozhan," ("The Indian prime minister visits Zangnan area"), *Shanghai Dongfang Zaobao*, February 2, 2008, 4.

[88] "China, India conclude border talks without agreement," *Xinhua*, September 19, 2008; S. Dasgupta, "No talks on Sikkim issue: India tells China," *Times of India*, June 6, 2008, 1; S. Ramachandran, "China toys with India's border," *Asia Times online*, June 27, 2008, <http://www.atimes.com/atimes/South_Asia/JF27Df01.html>.

[89] "India to raise Sikkim incursion with China," *Times of India*, June 19, 2008, 1.

[90] P. Stobdan, "Chinese checkers in the Himalayas: revisiting Sino-Indian relations," *Strategic Analysis,* 32: 5 (September–October 2008), 703–711.

[91] PTI, "Pranab's message to China: Arunachal is ours," *Times of India*, November 9, 2008, 1; "PRC FM spokesman says China regrets Indian FM's remarks on 'Arunachal Pradesh'," *Xinhua*, November 11, 2008; Chen Jia, "China firm on border issue: Qin," *China Daily*, November 12, 2008.

[92] Dutta, "Revisiting China's territorial claims on Arunachal."

[93] Zuo Xuan, "India covets Dalai Lama's visit," *Global Times*, November 9, 2009, <http://world.globaltimes.cn/asia-pacific/2009-11/483521.html>.

[94] IANS, "It's not 1962, India tells a China fuming at Dalai Lama visit," *MSN.com*, November 10, 2009 <http://news.in.msn.com/international/article.aspx?cp-documentid=3313381>.

[95] "India fumes as China issues loose-sheet visas to J&K residents," *Times of India*, October 2, 2009, 1.

[96] S. Dasgupta, "China looking to use stake in PoK as bargaining chip?" *Times of India*, October 21, 2009.

[97] P. D. Samanta, "No mention of 'One China' is New Delhi reply to Beijing for its silence on J&K," *Indian Express*, December 17, 2010, 1.

[98] Raman, "Tawang: Some Indian plain-speaking at last!"

[99] R. Sharma, "India-China border row—no headway expected this year," *Tribune*, June 8, 2007.

[100] B. Raman, "Why I am wary of China," *Rediff.com*, November 14, 2006, http://in.rediff.com/news/2006/nov/14raman.htm>.

[101] Liu Silu, "Beijing should not lose patience in Chinese-Indian border talks," ("Zhongyin bianjie tanpan, Beijing bu neng ji"), *Wen Wei Po* (Hong Kong), June 1, 2007.

[102] See interview with Prof. Wang Yiwei of Fudan University's Center for American Studies, in R. Ramachandran, "Helping US may derail border talks," *Asian Age,* July 25, 2007.

[103] Zhongguo Zhanlue, "Zhenggao Yindu zhengfu: Buyao yiyuan baode" (CIIS, "A warning to the Indian government: don't return evil for good"), March 26, 2008 <http://str.chinaiiss.org/content/2008-3-26/26211952.shtml>.

[104] D. S. Rajan, "China: strategic experts talk about a partial Sino-Indian war," *C3S Paper No. 230*, Chennai Center for China Studies, November 24, 2008 <http://www.c3sindia.org/strategicissues/419>. Italics mine.

[105] "Future directions of the Sino-Indian border dispute," *International Strategic Studies* [*Guogji Zhanlue*], November 2006.

[106] Prof. Wang Yiwei's interview in Ramachandran, "Helping US may derail border talks."

[107] Liu, "Beijing should not lose patience…"

[108] S. Bhatt's interview with Professor Wang Dehua, director of the Centre for South Asia Studies at the Shanghai Academy of Social Sciences, "If India and China cooperate…," *Rediff.com*, October 13, 2009 <http://news.rediff.com/special/2009/oct/13/china-and-india-parnership-is-good-news-for-world-says-chinese professor.htm>.

[109] "Future directions of the Sino-Indian border dispute."

[110] R. Bedi, "India develops infrastructure on Chinese border,' *Jane's Defence Weekly*, July 18, 2007.

[111] B. Majumdar, "China in mind, India to boost eastern air power," *Reuters*, August 8, 2007; A. Chang, "India boosting air force at China border," *UPI Asia online*, August 15, 2008 <http://www.upiasiaonline.com/Security/2008/08/14/india_boosting_air_force_at_china_border/8337/>.

[112] N. C. Bipindra, "India plans to strengthen mountain warfare machinery," *Rediff.com*, June 13, 2008 <http://www.rediff.com/news/2008/jun/13war.htm>.

[113] Discussions with senior military officers, June 2008; PTI, "No complacency on Chinese border, Antony tells Army," *Indian Express*, April 28, 2008, 1.

[114] See "India: Tibet issue complicates China ties," *Oxford Analytica*, April 14, 2008 <https://www.opensource.gov/providers/oxan/display.aspx?StoryDate=20080414&ProductCode=OADB&StoryNumber=3&StoryType=DB>.

[115] B. Raman, "Tibetan diaspora and India–China relations," *Saag.org*, Paper no. 2945, November 27, 2008 <http://www.southasiaanalysis.org/papers30/paper2945.html>; Rajan, "China: strategic experts talk about a partial Sino-Indian war"; CIIS, "A warning to the Indian government: don't return evil for good."

[116] A resolution of the Sino-Indian border dispute would lead to the deployment of India's military assets on the India-Pakistan border, thereby tilting the military balance decisively in India's favor, much to China's ally Pakistan's disadvantage.

[117] G. Parthasarathy, "Disturbing signs flow from across the Himalayas," *The Pioneer*, July 1, 2007; N. N. Jha, "Dealing with the dragon," *The Pioneer*, October 8, 2009.

[118] Mohan Malik, "India-China competition revealed in ongoing border disputes," *The Power & Interest News Report*, October 9, 2007 <http://www.pinr.com/report.php?ac=view_report&report_id=695&language_id=1>.

[119] Mohan Malik, "War talk: perceptual gaps in "Chindia" relations," *China Brief*, IX:20 (October 7, 2009), 6–9. <http://www.jamestown.org/uploads/media/cb_009_52.pdf>; Agencies, "China asks India to stop construction activity along border," *Indian Express*, December 1, 2009.

[120] C. Raja Mohan, "India's Tibet ambiguity," *Indian Express*, November 27, 2008 <http://www.indianexpress.com/news/India-s-Tibet-ambiguity/391206>.

[121] D. S. Rajan, "Dalai Lama in Arunachal-Chinese media build up anti-India rhetoric," *C3S Paper*, No. 402, November 10, 2009, <http://www.c3sindia.org/tibet/1029>.

[122] Mohan Malik, "Bordering on danger: A Sino-Indian boundary dispute risks flaring up," *Wall Street Journal*, October 15, 2009.

6
The China-Pakistan-India Triangle

Of all of China's relations with Asian neighbors, those with Pakistan outweigh and overlay any other bilateral relationship. The Beijing-Islamabad "special relationship" is part of China's grand strategy that molds the South Asian security environment. Despite some improvement in Chinese-Indian relations, Pakistan remains the linchpin of Beijing's South Asia policy. In fact, Beijing has long been *the* most important player in the India-Pakistan-China triangular relationship. The China-Pakistan relationship is akin to the US relationship with the United Kingdom or the US-Israel relationship.[1] Beijing's *entente cordiale* with Islamabad continues to flourish, underpinned by military, economic, and infrastructure development and diplomatic cooperation.[2] Chinese leaders regularly visit Islamabad (and other South Asian capitals) to reassure them that improvement in China-India relations would not be at their cost. No one put it better than Chinese President Hu Jintao himself during his November 2006 Pakistan visit: "We can give up gold but we cannot give up our friendship with Pakistan ... Pakistan and China's relationship is higher than the Himalayas, deeper than the Indian Ocean and sweeter than honey." For his part, Pakistani President Asif Ali Zardari has hailed China as "the future of the world" and Xinhua quoted him stating that "[a] strong China means a strong Pakistan."[3] Rhetorical flourishes aside, the reality is that the China-Pakistan relationship has not only survived the Cold War but has also thrived in the era of China-India rapprochement, Pakistan's re-emergence as a frontline ally in the US-led War on Terror, and the growing US-India strategic convergence.

However, Pakistan today is facing a "perfect storm" of crises, with its US-backed fight against al-Qaeda and the Taliban faltering and the country lurching toward bankruptcy (Islamabad's third economic meltdown since the mid-1990s). Despite Beijing's disenchantment with the current state of its "all-weather and time-tested ally," China remains strongly committed to its vital long-term alliance relationship with

Pakistan. If anything, Pakistan's transformation from being an ally to a battleground in the US-led War on Terror is forcing Islamabad into an ever-tighter embrace of China.[4] This chapter traces the ideational, historical, geopolitical, and strategic roots of the Sino-Pakistan nexus and its implications for India. It argues that their "all-weather" relationship, which has its roots in the geopolitical imperative of containing India, has now expanded into a broader partnership that encompasses the non-traditional security issues (*jihadi* terrorism, sea lanes safety, economic and resource security) and countering US hegemony. None of Pakistan's bilateral relationships is as robust and strong as its China tie nor can it match the scope and depth of the strategic benefits that flow from it. For Islamabad, China's rise as a global superpower and Beijing's growing challenge to American hegemony are welcome developments that work to the advantage of a strategically located middle power like Pakistan. Islamabad hopes to continue to benefit not only from the intensifying Sino-Indian geopolitical rivalry in Asia but also from the coming showdown between China and the United States, which will further increase the significance of Pakistan's strategic ties with China.

Meeting of Minds: Shared Interests, Values, and Worldviews

Every major event in history has unintended consequences. Historians will record that an unintended (and unsettling, from India's standpoint) consequence of two unrelated but major events in the middle of the twentieth century—first the 1947 partition of India creating the Islamic Republic of Pakistan that broke up the geostrategic unity of the subcontinent, and then the 1950 Chinese occupation of Tibet—was to bring about two erstwhile warring Islamic and Chinese civilization-empires into a solid compact against secular but predominantly Hindu India. These two developments allowed China to extend its reach and influence into a region where it had historically and civilizationally exercised little or no influence at all. Soon after the 1962 border war with India, China aligned itself with Pakistan to contain the common enemy. Since then this tactical alignment has turned into an "all-weather," time-tested, multi-dimensional strategic alliance relationship. Beijing's gradual penetration deep into Southern Asia since the middle of the twentieth century has been primarily at India's expense, thus making China the largest beneficiary of the partition in a manner that its authors would have never anticipated or imagined. To grasp the real meaning of China's *entente cordiale* with Pakistan, an understanding of psychological and ideological roots is as important as its geopolitical imperatives and strategic motivations.

At the ideational level, both the Chinese and the Pakistanis are motivated by a sense of grievance and injustice driven by their interpretation of the history between the West on the one hand and the Chinese and the Islamic world on the other. Imbued with a belief in the superiority of their race and religion respectively, China and Pakistan (or, more specifically, Islam) both share "dual psychology" in which they want both "domination and victimhood." The Pakistani apprehension about India's hidden agenda of undoing the partition shares space with a grandiose dream of Muslims once again ruling the entire subcontinent, as before the British. Likewise, the Chinese are paranoid about India's hidden agenda in Tibet, believing that India wants to split their country by supporting Tibet's independence. Chinese textbooks emphasize their country's victimization at the hands of foreign powers during "the century of humiliation" (but carefully omit or underplay Imperial China's long history of domination of and wars against its neighbors). While China's carefully cultivated sense of victimhood combined with a deep-rooted sense of cultural superiority breeds "inferiority-superiority complex" and a siege mentality, China's spectacular economic success over the last quarter century has contributed to the rise of hyper-nationalism. As for Pakistan, a series of military debacles coupled with the growing power imbalance between an economically booming India and a politically dysfunctional and economically bankrupt Pakistan since the early 1990s has added to Islamabad's sense of insecurity and vulnerability. Just as many Chinese dream about restoring their country's status as "the Middle Kingdom," many Pakistanis dream of restoring the Mughal Empire over the entire subcontinent. These two contradictory feelings of "fear and hope" and "victimhood and domination" account for the China-Pakistan alliance and their hostility toward India.

Ideologically, China—an atheist state ruled by the Communist Party—and Pakistan—an Islamic state—do not seem to have much in common. However, their beliefs systems share some striking commonalities. Much like other global ideologies, Islamists divide the world into two regions: the world of believers, *Dar-ul Islam*, or the House of Islam, and *Dar-ul Harb*, or the House of Infidels and non-believers containing all territories ruled by non-Muslims, against whom no-holds-barred *jihad* (holy war) is to be waged by the believers (the true followers of Islam) who are destined to dominate and rule over the non-believers.[5] In their purest form, both Communist and Islamic ideologies yearn for a utopia. The Islamist division of the world into two blocs is similar to the one made by the followers of other totalitarian ideologies—Communism and Fascism—which ruled out peaceful coexistence with other belief systems. Such concepts promote the idea of "us versus them" and generate hostility, enmity, and a permanent state of war. Interestingly, this concept of continuous struggle (*jihad*) against non-believers bears remarkable resemblance to Chairman Mao's concept of permanent revolution against his perceived enemies—rightists and capitalists—during the tumultuous Cultural Revolution (1967–76) in China. Much like the Communists of yesteryears, the long-term objective of Islamists is to spread the frontiers of Islam eastward to the whole continent of Asia and beyond. As Cathy Young observes: "Perhaps every belief system that lays claim to the ultimate truth carries the seeds of violent fanaticism and intolerance. This is true not only of religions but of secular ideologies such as Communism."[6] Having said that, it is worth adding that ideologically China is no longer a Communist state and Pakistan is not an Islamist state. The most important commonality between Beijing and Islamabad is the geopolitical challenge posed by New Delhi.

The masses in China and Pakistan have long been fed on a staple diet of assertive nationalism (in the form of Han racial superiority) and Islamization (that is, Islam's superiority over all other religions) respectively. Pakistan has built a self-image of itself as a state that defeated a superpower (the Soviet Union) through *jihadi* means and became the first Islamic country to acquire nuclear weapons by outwitting the international community. Such a worldview has given rise to grandiose ambitions and grievances that result in great expectations. In an interview with the *Los Angeles Times*, Khalid Rahman, executive director of the Institute for Policy Studies at Islamabad, noted: "A feeling is emerging in Pakistani society that we have a special role to play in uniting Muslims all over the world."[7] For its part, China claims a historical entitlement to superpower status, publicly enunciating its ambition to be a "world power second to none." Interestingly, Pakistan's "enlightened moderation" concept or repeated assurances to the international community about being a "moderate Islamic country" are not dissimilar from China's "peaceful rise" concept.[8] Both have authoritarian regimes where the military plays an important role in key decision-making processes.

Opinion polls show that Chinese and Pakistanis view each other much more positively than Americans and Indians, who are seen as "untrustworthy, arrogant, and unfriendly."[9] In China, Pakistan is seen as an "old friend" (*lao pengyou*) that gave China a "helping hand during the difficult Cold War years" (by opening an air corridor linking China to the outside world in the 1960s and 1970s and serving as a bridge for the normalization of China's relations with the United States).[10] Pakistani leaders have long offered strong and unequivocal support for Beijing's position on every single issue, from Tibet and Taiwan to Xinjiang and human rights—a welcome respite from international denunciations for Beijing which therefore receive much play in the state-controlled Chinese media. As Rong Ying, a South Asia expert at the China Institute for International Relations, commented in the aftermath of Tibetan riots in March 2008: "The contrast between President Musharraf's statements on Tibet and the attitude we see in the Indian media to the issue is very noticeable to us."[11] The vast majority of Pakistanis see their other great power ally, the United States, as "a fickle friend." Even though Washington has provided substantial economic and military assistance over the last 60 years (approximately $87 billion since the 1950s), Islamabad views friendship with the United States as one-sided based on short-term needs and expediency, driven primarily by American security concerns at any given time. Washington's abandonment of Pakistan following the Soviet collapse because of its nuclear weapons program, in particular, remains a sore point. The denial of a nuclear energy deal similar to the one offered to India has also strained ties, despite post-9/11 re-engagement with Washington. Beijing and Islamabad are concerned over the growing talk in Washington's policy circles of India as emerging as a counterweight to China on the one hand and the fragile, radical Islamic states of Southwest Asia on the other, viewing a potential US-Indian alignment with horror.[12] Pakistanis criticize US attacks into the tribal areas of Pakistan—both drone strikes and raids by US special forces—as a violation of their country's sovereignty. Washington has pressured Islamabad to refocus its military strategy on fighting the militants instead of devoting most of its resources to confronting India. Tarique Niazi explains the reasons behind the virulently anti-US sentiments prevailing amongst Pakistanis:

> China is the only country, when it comes to the national security of Pakistan, which Islamabad trusts. No one else. Pakistan does not trust the United States as much as China, and the reason for that is India. Pakistan's defence policy is Indo-centric. Who is going to support Pakistan when it goes up against India? Of course it is going to be China.[13]

For Pakistan, Beijing looms large in alliance calculations because it "fully identifies with its anti-India goals."[14] China has long been the most important security guarantor vis-à-vis India, the most important source of conventional and nuclear weaponry, and a vital source of trade and investment. Unlike the United States, China also enjoys geographical contiguity with Pakistan. China's "no-strings attached" economic aid to Pakistan is more appreciated than the substantially larger amount received from the United States and other countries. As one senior Pakistani military officer remarked: "The Chinese don't use and dump their allies like the Americans. North Korea is a good example. China is the only country in the world that will never abandon Pakistan."[15] For their part, many Americans are now questioning the durability of Washington's ties with Islamabad, despite the granting of "major non-NATO ally" status since 2004. They accuse Pakistan of "double-dealing" the United States on counterterrorism. The United States indeed has too little to show for its post-9/11 re-engagement and largesse (approximately $17 billion since 2001 including clandestine aid), which far outweighs any financial assistance Pakistan has ever received from China.[16] Despite the generous US aid, the *2010 Failed States Index* ranks Pakistan as the tenth most failed state in the world.

Further, the Chinese and Pakistani interpretations of history are also similar. For both Chinese and Islamists, territory—once conquered—is regarded as immutably theirs. Both see India as an "artificial construct" put together by the departing British colonialists in 1947. Apparently, this stance underpins the Chinese and Pakistani negotiating position on their territorial disputes with India, which is identical: "Whatever we have is rightfully ours, whatever you have is open to a negotiated settlement." To both, a border settlement in Arunachal Pradesh or in Kashmir that freezes the status quo with India is unacceptable. In contrast, New Delhi favors freezing the territorial status quo and opposes any map-making exercise. Indians see Sinic and Islamic civilizations as inherent expansionists that seek to dismember India to expand their control over the entire subcontinent.

What India sees as its strengths—democracy and secularism—are, in fact, viewed as its greatest weaknesses by the Chinese and Pakistanis. For these serve to perpetuate religious, linguistic, and regional fault lines in a country that lacks national unity and social cohesion. Many in the Chinese national security bureaucracy and the Pakistani establishment have long entertained doubts about India's survival as a nation-state over the long-term. They are convinced that India, like its erstwhile friends the Soviet Union and Yugoslavia, is doomed to further partition and Balkanization.[17] If the Chinese believe that Indian power contradicts Chinese power in Asia, many Pakistanis recall their founding father M. A. Jinnah's warning in 1947 that a strong and prosperous Hindu India would spell the end of Islam in the subcontinent.[18] Internally, India is ravaged by the alien ideologies of Maoism and jihadism. Externally, New Delhi sees the China-Pakistan duo coordinating their activities to contain India regionally and deny it a worthwhile role in global institutions. When China—at Islamabad's behest—blocked the UN Security Council's move to declare *Jamat-ul Dawa* (formerly *Lashkar-e-Tayyeba*, involved in numerous terrorist attacks in India) as an international terrorist organization under UN Security Council Resolution 1373, Prime Minister Manmohan Singh retorted: "We cannot also ignore the strategic cooperation that Pakistan secured from China in many ways. We cannot rule out the desire of some countries [read, China] to keep us engaged in low-intensity conflict with some of our neighbours as a means of getting India bogged down in a low equilibrium."[19] The Chinese and Pakistani security agencies cooperate to support anti-India activities and movements in Afghanistan, Bangladesh, Burma, Nepal, Sri Lanka, and the Maldives.[20] India's Home Minister P. Chidambaram lamented that "[e]ven as they [hostile forces] challenge our borders and our boundaries, terrorism and militancy are being fanned to destabilize the economy of the country which is at the threshold of a double digit growth."[21] One Australian journalist noted that "[t]here are elements within Pakistan's military and intelligence circles who subscribe to the devilish theory that once Kashmir is wrested away, the whole edifice of multi-ethnic, multi-religious India will collapse into a chaos of warring fiefdoms over which Pakistan will somehow prevail."[22] Islamabad has a longstanding policy of using *jihadist* proxy forces to attain "strategic depth" in Afghanistan and to pursue a revisionist agenda in Kashmir. Many Western analysts are convinced that *jihadi* (Islamist) and left-wing extremist (Maoist) organizations are instruments in the larger stratagem to re-draw the map of South Asia.[23] While there is little evidence of direct material support, the advent and growth of the Maoist movement certainly does serve China's goal of weakening its largest rival to the south. Andrew Small, a fellow at the German Marshall Fund, accuses China of providing "tacit support [to Pakistan] for the *jihadi* strategy that has helped to bind half a million troops in Kashmir."[24] All insurgencies from Afghanistan to Kashmir to Assam are sustained by Chinese small arms, while anti-India *jihadi* groups freely meet, train, and raise funds throughout Pakistan. As the *Pakistan Policy Working Group's Report* points out:

> Militancy in Pakistan is not a new phenomenon nor even a development since the Afghan *jihad* in the 1980s, as is often claimed. Since independence, the country has relied on a menagerie of Islamist

> militants and tribal armies to prosecute its foreign policies abroad, especially in India, Indian-administered Kashmir, and Afghanistan. Pakistan's use of militants as a foreign policy tool has had a profoundly destabilizing impact on the region....[25]

The UN Population Fund's projection of the doubling of India's Muslim population to 300 million (along with 300 million each in Pakistan and Bangladesh) by the middle of the twenty-first century is seen by some as facilitating "the secession of northeastern states from India to form a greater Islamistan in another 30 to 40 years."[26] The scenario of another Muslim state's emergence south of Arunachal Pradesh and east of Bangladesh apparently dampens any desire in Beijing for a negotiated border settlement with India.

In short, India's size, power, and ambitions are seen as representing an existential threat to the core interests of China and Pakistan. Neither rules out the possibility of a renewed confrontation with India over Tibet, Kashmir, Nepal, Burma, or in the Indian Ocean region. The Chinese-Pakistani perspectives on India center mainly around three major themes:

- India is a hegemonic and expansionist power that intends to undo the 1947 partition as a prelude to re-establishing India's dominance over the entire subcontinent and impose an Indian version of the "Monroe Doctrine" in southern Asia.
- The Indian navy wants to dominate and control the Indian Ocean.
- India aspires to become a great world power in league with the United States, Russia, and China armed with nuclear weapons and a UN Security Council veto.

This analysis of ideational, historical, and geopolitical perspectives explains why Pakistan and China, with seemingly different political systems, dissimilar religious beliefs, and divergent cultural aspects have had such a close relationship for such a long period.[27] This enduring alliance was formalized in 2005 with the conclusion of the China-Pakistan "Treaty of Friendship and Cooperation and Good Neighbourly Relations," whereby both sides committed that "neither party will join any alliance or bloc which infringes upon the sovereignty, security and territorial integrity" of either country, while simultaneously positing that both parties "would not conclude treaties of this nature with any 3rd party."[28] The future of this relationship depends a great deal on the evolving US relations with India, Pakistan, and China. Everything China does in Pakistan may not be with India in mind, but it inevitably impacts India because all of Pakistan's policies are quintessentially India-centric.

The Ties That Bind

The convergence of interests and identical worldviews, especially with respect to India, explains why the Sino-Pakistan partnership has not only survived but also thrived during the ups and downs and numerous twists and turns in China's foreign relations since the 1950s. Despite steadily improving relations with India since the early 1990s, China has not become less friendly to Pakistan, primarily because the combined strategic and geopolitical advantages China receives from its relationship with Pakistan (and, through Pakistan, other Islamic countries) easily outweigh any advantages China might receive from a closer relationship with India. From Beijing's perspective, Pakistan is vitally important to China for several reasons:

- *Geostrategy* (given its geostrategic location at the intersection of South Asia, Central Asia, and the Middle East) and *military security* (by keeping India's military engaged on its western frontiers);
- *National unity and territorial integrity* (in helping maintain control over Xinjiang and Tibet);
- *Maritime strategy and resource security* (by providing access to and bases in the Persian Gulf);
- *As a buyer and supplier of conventional and unconventional weaponry*;
- *As a partner in economic and infrastructural development*;
- *As a staunch diplomatic ally* (in regional and international forums, especially the Islamic world); and
- *As a bargaining chip* in China's bilateral relations with India and the United States.

Geostrategy and Military Security

First and foremost, China's geostrategic objectives and military security concerns vis-à-vis India, coupled with territorial disputes and the need to protect its "soft strategic underbelly"—Tibet and Xinjiang—underpin Beijing's Pakistan policy. Within months of the Dalai Lama's flight to India following a failed uprising in Tibet, Chinese ambassador Pan Tzu-li wrote to Prime Minister Nehru in May 1959 warning that China would make common cause with Pakistan, thereby forcing India to face military and diplomatic pressure on two fronts.[29] To this end, Beijing found in Islamabad a very willing partner, disillusioned as the latter was by the US arming of India post-1962 War and inaction during the 1965 Pakistan-India War over Kashmir.[30] Since the 1960s, China has made heavy strategic and economic investments in that country. Through Pakistan, China also retains the option of creating momentums that sap India's military power. In 1965, Beijing was ready to fight India on behalf of Pakistan. In 1971, the Indo-Soviet Friendship Treaty and domestic convulsions caused by the Cultural Revolution constrained China's military ability to intervene directly to save East Pakistan. During the 1980s and 1990s (at the height of China-India rapprochement), it was the provision of Chinese nuclear and missile shields to Pakistan that emboldened Islamabad to wage a "proxy war" in Kashmir without fear of Indian retaliation. During the Kargil War in 1999 and the military confrontation of 2001–02, China made "demonstrative [military] support" to Pakistan and its forces almost sparked off a standoff on the Sino-Indian border in Arunachal Pradesh.[31] New railroad infrastructure projects in Pakistani-held Kashmir and Tibet are aimed at bolstering China's military strength and intervention options against India should another war between sub-continental rivals threaten the very existence of Pakistan.

The Chinese calculate that as long as the one-million-strong Indian army is preoccupied with Pakistan on its western frontier and fighting insurgents in various parts of the country, it will not stir up trouble on the Tibetan border. In contrast, a secure and strong India at peace with Pakistan would allow New Delhi to focus its diplomatic energies and military against China and in East Asia—an unwelcome development from Beijing's perspective. John Garver succinctly sums up China's Pakistan policy:

> China's overriding strategic interest is to keep Pakistan independent, powerful, and confident enough to present India with a standing two-front threat.... Were India able to dissolve this two-front threat by subordinating Pakistan, its position against China would be much stronger.... [This would amount to] conceding South Asia as an Indian sphere of influence. Such a move would spell the virtual end to Chinese aspirations of being the leading Asian power and would greatly weaken China's position against Indian power.[32]

During the early 1990s, a desire for stability on its southwestern flank and fears of an Indian-Pakistani nuclear arms race caused Beijing to take a more evenhanded approach on Kashmir, while still favoring Islamabad. Since the mid-2000s, Beijing has been voicing open support to Pakistan and the Kashmiri separatists through developmental projects in northern Kashmir, offers to mediate, and the issuance of separate visas to Indian citizens of Kashmiri origins. One Chinese analyst maintains that "Beijing would not abandon its 'Kashmir card.' The Kashmir issue will remain active as long as China worries about its southern borders."[33] Although a certain degree of tension in Kashmir and Pakistan's ability to pin down Indian armed forces on its western frontiers enhances China's sense of military security vis-à-vis India, neither an all-out India-Pakistan war nor Pakistan's collapse would serve Beijing's grand strategic objectives. Most war-gaming exercises on the next India-Pakistan war end either in a nuclear exchange or in a Chinese military intervention to prevent the collapse of Beijing's "all-weather ally" in Asia.

Since Pakistan is the only country that stands up to India and thereby prevents Indian dominance over the region, Islamabad fulfils the key objective of China's South Asia policy. The Sino-Pakistan relationship also provides a good example of using China as a counterweight to what smaller South Asian countries (Bangladesh, Bhutan, Nepal, Sri Lanka, and the Maldives) perceive as India's attempts at bullying them. It demonstrates that much like Pakistan, other South Asian countries too *can*:

- follow an "independent" policy;
- benefit from China's economic and military largesse;
- enjoy China's diplomatic protective umbrella (via UN Security Council veto and arms sales);
- safeguard their sovereignty from interventionist policies of major powers (read, the United States); and
- counter Indian attempts to dominate or influence their decisionmaking.

In short, mutual suspicions, geopolitical tensions, and a zero-sum mentality add to a very competitive dynamic in the China-Pakistan-India triangular relationship. The fear of losing control over restive Tibet coupled with the geostrategic imperative to balance growing Indian power explain why China's efforts to improve ties with India are always accompanied by parallel efforts to bolster the Pakistani military's nuclear and conventional capabilities. During his July 2010 visit to China, Pakistani President Asif Zardari reportedly assured Chinese President Hu Jintao that Pakistan would continue "to act as a force multiplier for China" in the region.[34]

National Unity and Territorial Integrity

Their self-projections notwithstanding, both Pakistan and China are also fragile states. The Pakistani military's historic quest for a compliant regime in Afghanistan to gain "strategic depth" vis-à-vis India led it to nurture and employ militant Islamic *jihadi* forces in the west and east. These same forces are now threatening the very existence and survival of Pakistan.[35] The writ of the Pakistani government does not run over a large swath of territory along its border with Afghanistan, which provides sanctuary to al-Qaeda and Taliban. More fundamentally, the unifying power of those domestic and geopolitical forces—Allah, Army, America, and hostility to India—that have held Pakistan together since its creation in 1947 has weakened considerably over the last two decades.[36] For one, "Islam, from a source of strength, has [now] become Pakistan's most divisive factor." For another, the military has been eclipsed by a rising India and demoralized by its new mission to fight internal enemies of the state.[37] Pakistan's leaders and strategic analysts now concede that *jihadist* militancy now poses an existential threat to Pakistan's security that is greater than any conventional threat scenario involving India. More ominously, these terrorist groups are now infiltrating Pakistan's big cities. Amidst spiraling violence on both sides of the Pakistan-Afghanistan border, a surge in suicide bombings, terrorist attacks, and armed insurgency in Balochistan is engulfing the country at a time when the Pakistani government is facing simultaneous economic and political crises that could further imperil its role in the war against extremist forces.[38] Fears are being expressed over the world's only Islamic nuclear-armed state's nuclear weapons falling into the hands of al-Qaeda-Taliban should they succeed in overthrowing the government in Islamabad either through coup or an Islamic revolution.[39] Geopolitically, China's rise has resulted in a distinct pro-India tilt by the United States, leaving Pakistan out in the cold.

The spillover effects of rabid Talibanization of Pakistani society have been worrying the Chinese for quite some time.[40] Much like Tibetan Buddhism, Beijing views radical Islam as a strategic threat to China's national integrity, particularly in Xinjiang (formerly East Turkestan), where the East Turkistan Islamic Movement (ETIM) has been fighting to carve out China's Xinjiang province and other parts of Central Asia to re-create an independent East Turkistan nation for several decades. China's "all-weather" relationship with Pakistan is also aimed at containing the separatist threats it perceives in its western Muslim-majority Xinjiang province. Beijing has repeatedly impressed on Islamabad the importance of tightening control over its border with

China. The Chinese leadership has placed a premium on integrating China's western regions into the booming economies of its east. Beijing is investing billions in oil-rich Muslim-majority Xinjiang province and in Pakistan, in order to build an economic corridor between western China and the Persian Gulf. A significant rise in Chinese financial investments in Pakistan has coincided with Pakistan's emergence as a safe haven and training ground for Uyghur Muslim separatists from Xinjiang province. The past few years have also seen a series of Chinese civilians working in Pakistan kidnapped and killed by Islamic militants, partly in retaliation against Beijing's "strike hard" campaigns against Uyghur Muslims and partly in protest against Beijing's resource extraction and infrastructure development projects in Pakistan's Wild West.

Beijing has started demanding better protection of its citizens in Pakistan in unusually forceful language. In October 2008, within days of Pakistan President Zardari's visit to Beijing, China's Ministry of Public Security indicated that most of the ETIM terrorists operating on its soil have close links with similar groups and base camps in a "south Asian country" (Pakistan) for the purpose of training and exchange of arms and ammunitions. The statement was seen as exerting pressure on Pakistan "to do more" to crack down hard on anti-Chinese extremist groups taking shelter on Pakistani soil at a time when Islamabad was desperately seeking financial and nuclear assistance from Beijing.[41] For its part, the Pakistani government has been much more responsive to such demands from the Chinese than their Western counterparts, worried as it is about the negative fallout on Pakistan's strategic alliance with China. In October 2004, Pakistani troops killed Beijing's Osama bin Laden, the ETIM leader Hasan Mahsum, who had taken refuge in South Waziristan. China and Pakistan have established the Joint Task Force (JTF) to protect the 10,000 Chinese working in Pakistan. In early 2007, when seven Chinese women working in a massage parlor were kidnapped, President Pervez Musharraf acknowledged that his controversial decision to raid Islamabad's Red Mosque compound under the control of extremists was made under pressure from China. Pakistani leaders have repeatedly made appeals to Xinjiang Muslims to eschew extremism and cooperate with China for peace and progress and lent their support to Chinese efforts to combat Uyghur and Tibetan separatism.

Discussions with Chinese analysts reveal Beijing's growing anxieties about the *jihadi* tendencies within the Pakistani military. China is committed to "doing everything it can to back moderate or non-*jihadi* factions in the military." To this end, engaging Pakistan's government and maintaining good relations with even its fundamentalist religious parties (such as *Jamat-e-Islami* and the *Jamiat Ulema-e-Islam*) is an important part of keeping control in China's own restive Muslim northwest. Countering terrorism is one area where China's interests *seemingly* converge with the United States. Neither can afford to see Pakistan fail, nor can they ignore the radical Islamists operating in Pakistan's tribal areas. Geostrategically too, a stable, strong, and prosperous Pakistan serves Chinese and US interests better than a failing and weak Pakistan. Publicly, Beijing has called for multilateral cooperation (involving China, the United States, Pakistan and Afghanistan) to deal with the problem of Islamist militancy in Afghanistan and Central Asia. Nonetheless, China seems to make a distinction between those *jihadi* elements that threaten it directly and those that affect its perceived rivals—the United States or India. This is evident from China's stated opposition to US air strikes and ground operations in Pakistan's tribal areas on the grounds that such attacks violate Pakistan's sovereignty. The Sino-US interests may converge on counter-terrorism but their conflicting geostrategic objectives hinder genuine counter-terrorism cooperation in the Af-Pak region.[42] China is suspicious of the strategic expansion moves of rival major powers under the cover of counter-terrorism. Likewise, Pakistani support for the Taliban owes a great deal to Islamabad's concerns about Indian encirclement via Afghanistan. The US military bases in Afghanistan and Pakistan and India's growing footprint in Afghanistan and Tajikistan are viewed with concern in Beijing and Islamabad.[43] Chinese strategists caution India against using the War on Terror as a pretext to isolate and subdue Pakistan.[44] The Chinese may be paranoid about Islamic separatism in their Muslim-majority Xinjiang province, but they ignore Islamist opponents of India. As noted earlier, China provided direct protection to *LeT/JuD* and *Jaish-e-Mohammed* terrorist groups at the UN Security Council's 1267 committee, blocking efforts to sanction them ostensibly for want of evidence.[45] As Andrew Small put it: "Beijing sees leveraging, not severing, Pakistan's ties to extremists as vital to China's own interests."[46] Finally, China's reluctance to cooperate with the United States and others can be attributed to Beijing's fear of becoming a primary target of Islamist terror groups and extremists. China does not want the Xinjiang problem to be seen as an Islamist issue that attracts the attention of *jihadis* from across the world. China's South Asia specialists are content with using China's strategic leverage over the Pakistani government to safeguard Chinese interests. A hostile stance toward India also reassures the Pakistani establishment of China's unstinted support in Islamabad's domestic and external struggles.

Unless the Pakistani state implodes under the weight of its own internal contradictions or a radical Islamist regime comes into power that seriously undermines Chinese interests by supporting the ETIM and other *jihadi* outfits in the region, there will be no rupture in China's relations with Pakistan.[47] Despite its discomfort with the growing anarchy in Pakistan, China remains committed to its enduring alliance with Pakistan.[48] Beijing needs Islamabad's support and cooperation to ensure the stability and security of its restive far western region. Hu Shisheng, a Chinese specialist in South Asian politics at the China Institute for Contemporary International Relations in Beijing, sums it up: "We will contribute to its stabilization. A stable Pakistan is essential for building a stable Xinjiang. A disintegrated or dismantled Pakistan will be a disaster for us.... Without close cooperation with Pakistan, how can China ensure stability there?"[49] In short, China has developed strategic equities in Pakistan that do not allow it to let Pakistan go under.

Maritime Strategy and Resource Security

Given its location on the Arabian Sea, Pakistan's value as Beijing's steadfast ally has increased and so has China's stake in that country over the last two decades. Pakistan provides China with secure access to naval bases (Karachi, Ormara and Gwadar) close to the entrance of the Persian Gulf, allowing Beijing to extend its sphere of influence to the Middle East and Central Asia. During his February 2006 visit to China, Pakistani President General Pervez Musharraf invited his hosts to "fully use Pakistan's geographic advantages and use Pakistan as a trade and energy corridor in the region" to meet Beijing's energy requirements.[50] As part of energy supplies diversification strategy, Beijing plans to build an oil pipeline, oil refinery, and oil-reserve depots from the Gwadar port to Xinjiang to transport oil and gas imports from the Persian Gulf—a route that will not only cut freight costs and supply time but also lower China's reliance on US-policed shipping lanes through the Malacca and Taiwan Straits. The port will also give the landlocked Central Asian states access to the Arabian Sea for commercial shipping purposes and become a transit terminal for Iranian, Saudi and African crude-oil imports.[51] As John Garver puts it: "The Gwadar port combined with the modernization of Pakistan's rail system will substantially enhance China's ability to move goods and people between its western regions via Pakistan to the Arabian Sea—and as importantly from Gwadar to Central Asia."[52] China is a major investor in the Dalbandin-Gwadar railway that connects with the Karakoram Highway and another highway that links Gwadar with Karachi.

China insists that its interest in Gwadar port is purely commercial, but it will have a strategic-multiplier effect. It is as significant as Beijing's construction of the Karakorum Highway in the 1960s and its arming of Pakistan with nuclear and missile capabilities in the 1980s and 1990s. A presence in Gwadar provides China with a "listening post" from where it can monitor US naval activities in the Persian Gulf, Indian activities in the Arabian Sea, US-India maritime cooperation in the Indian Ocean, and patrol the Indian Ocean sea lanes, as well as with an alternative land-based route for crude-oil imports.[53] For Pakistan, the Gwadar port provides its navy strategic depth along its coastline and the tactical benefits of having a new port as an alternative to the vulnerable Karachi port, which the Indian Navy has blockaded during past conflicts.[54] In 2002, Musharraf had observed that Pakistan would benefit from China's involvement in the port because "as and when needed, the Chinese Navy would be in Gwadar to give befitting reply to anyone." The Pakistani government has designated the port area as "a sensitive defense area."[55] It is the western-most pearl in China's "string of pearls" strategy, which envisages building strategic relations with several countries along the SLOCs from the Middle East to the South China Sea to protect China's energy interests and other security objectives.[56] The Gwadar port, like other Chinese-developed ports in Sri Lanka, Burma, and Cambodia, will eventually allow the Chinese Navy to hedge against the US (and Indian) dominance over major sea lanes. John Garver outlines the geostrategic rationale underlying China's gigantic infrastructure development projects in the west and east of India:

> Development of robust over-land transportation systems between Yunnan and the Bay of Bengal, and between western Xinjiang and Gwadar could substantially strengthen the PLA's ability to sustain intense military operations in the eastern and western Indian Oceans ... [In the event of a conflict with India,] If the PLA-N [People's Liberation Army-Navy] could obtain bases on the Indian Ocean littoral (perhaps at Gwadar and Kyaukpyu), and link those forward bases to China by robust road and rail lines, India's geographic advantages would be substantially diminished to the PLA-N's advantage.[57]

However, the best-laid plans might come unstuck if Pakistan fails to pacify and stabilize Balochistan province, where Gwadar is located. The growing Balochi independence movement, which has repeatedly targeted Chinese engineers since 2004, makes the Chinese nervous about implementing their proposals for investment in the construction of a petrochemical complex, a pipeline. and a railway line.

China is also set to play a central role in Pakistan's plans to increase its nuclear energy to 8000 megawatts (MW) by 2030, more than ten times the 770MW yielded by its two existing Chinese reactors and a smaller Canadian one. Failing to secure the same exemption from US laws banning nuclear co-operation with non-signatories to the nuclear Non-Proliferation Treaty that India has been granted because of the role played by Pakistan's top scientist, A. Q. Khan, in a nuclear proliferation scandal involving Libya, Iran, and North Korea, Pakistan has asked China to fill the void. In fact, Beijing has long played a lead role in Pakistan's nuclear program. The Chinese do not buy Washington's argument against extending nuclear co-operation to Pakistan because India and Pakistan are "different countries, with different histories and different needs."[58] In a meeting of the Nuclear Suppliers' Group (NSG) at Vienna in September 2008, which granted India the right to trade in civilian nuclear fuel and technology, China had spoken out against the "discriminatory nature" of that agreement and demanded a similar concession for Pakistan.[59] The US-India nuclear deal rankles the Chinese because it fulfils two of India's key strategic objectives that are vociferously opposed by Beijing: ending the nuclear parity with Pakistan and establishing strategic equivalence between India and China.[60] Seen from Beijing's standpoint, if India is a "unique case" for the United States, then Pakistan is a "special case" for China in the nuclear sector. Pakistan has asked China to build it up to six reactors of 600 to 1000 megawatts, at least twice the size of the 300-megawatt reactor China built at Chashma in Pakistan's Punjab province. During President Zardari's visit to China in October 2008, a deal was signed for China to build two nuclear energy plants in Pakistan.[61] Having "fathered" Pakistan's nuclear weapons program, China has a legitimate right to "grandfather" its civilian nuclear energy program as well. In short, China's burgeoning cooperation in the maritime, resource, and nuclear spheres will further tighten its bonds with Pakistan even as rising militant violence strains Islamabad's anti-terror alliance with the United States.[62]

Military Hardware Buyer and Supplier

In addition to assistance with strategic infrastructure projects, China is also Pakistan's largest arms supplier, selling everything from aircraft to missiles to naval vessels. Beijing's long-standing policy is to arm Islamabad with every weapon system that India has (and will have) in order to maintain a favorable balance of power in South Asia.[63] China has assisted Pakistan in developing its defense industry so that the two sides can collaborate in the joint development of the F-22P frigate, the *Al-Khalid* and *Al-Zarar* tanks, an airborne early warning radar system (AWACS), Land Attack Cruise Missile, K-8 jet trainers, J-10 fighter planes, and JF-17 Thunder combat aircraft, which is being sold to several Asian and African countries.[64] China has also established a Defense Electronics Complex in Pakistan that will develop electronic equipment and communication technology for military use.[65] With its growing space, satellite, and intelligence capabilities, Beijing has offered a C^4ISR (command, control, communications, computing, intelligence collection, surveillance, and reconnaissance) umbrella to Pakistan. Nearly 70 percent of Pakistani military hardware originates from China.

China also remains involved in upgrading Pakistan's nuclear weapons capabilities. Beijing has not only provided Islamabad with nuclear bombs, uranium, and plants (all three Pakistani nuclear plants—Kahuta, Khushab and Chasma—have been built with Chinese assistance) but also their delivery systems: ready-to-launch M-9 (*Ghaznavi/Hatf*), M-11 (*Shaheen*), and a number of *Dong Feng* 21s (*Ghauri*) ballistic missiles. India's nuclear weapons program continues as a source of concern for China and Pakistan as China's and Pakistan's do for India, thereby adding to their mutual suspicions. An article by Zhang Weiwei in *Guoji Guanxi* (*International Studies*, February 6, 2006) of the Chinese Foreign Ministry-affiliated China Institute of International Studies acknowledged that "Pakistan enjoys an edge over India in the nuclear sector"—a feat difficult for Islamabad to accomplish without Chinese inputs.

However, this is not to say that the Sino-Pakistan military relationship is a one- way street. The Chinese have benefited enormously over the decades from partnering with the Pakistani armed forces that possess and operate advanced conventional military hardware.[66] Pakistan has long served as a conduit for Western technology to flow into China, particular military technology related to avionics, radar systems, sidewinder missiles, tanks, fighter aircraft, Stinger shoulder-fired missiles, Tomahawk cruise missiles, and uranium enrichment technology that was stolen by A. Q. Khan from Holland in the late 1970s.[67] China has also used Pakistan as a front in the arms trade with several Middle Eastern states where Beijing seeks to project itself as an ally against the US-Israeli domination of the Middle East. A close military-to-military cooperation with recipients of advanced Western weaponry in the Islamic world helps the Chinese undermine the arms embargo imposed by major Western suppliers since the 1989 Tiananmen massacre. This strategy earns China goodwill, advanced technology, foreign exchange, and access to energy resources in the oil-rich Gulf states.

Some Chinese strategists worry about the destabilizing consequences of a prolonged US military presence in Pakistan on the future of Sino-Pakistan ties as well as on Pakistan's domestic stability. The US military presence in Pakistan is said to have sharpened the divide within the Pakistani military into pro-West and pro-Beijing factions. Since the conclusion of the "China-Pakistan Treaty of Friendship, Cooperation and Good-Neighbourly Relations" in April 2005—which binds the two nations to desist from "joining any alliance or bloc which infringes upon the sovereignty, security and territorial integrity of the other side,"—the military relationship seems to be acquiring anti-US overtones. The Chinese believe that "a Treaty of this sort with Pakistan could mean that in any eventuality in future of China-US strategic competition in South Asia becoming acute, Islamabad would be treaty-bound in not supporting the US."[68] That Islamabad does not disagree with this interpretation is evident from the statement made by Pakistani Information Minister Rashid Ahmad in an interview with Chinese television (February 20, 2006) during his trip to Beijing that "Pakistan will stand by China if the US ever tries to 'besiege' it."[69] This signals a clear preference for China over the United States if Pakistan is ever asked to choose between the two. As the War on Terror has expanded into Pakistan, there has been a corresponding surge in defense cooperation between Beijing and Islamabad.

Since 2004, both sides have stepped up their bilateral cooperation in military training and conduct joint military exercises.[70] The Chinese navy is a major participant in the large multinational AMAN series of exercises hosted by the Pakistan navy. The two allies plan to base their naval strategy around a large submarine fleet and possess a variety of ballistic and cruise missiles in large numbers in their arsenals. The net effect of ongoing and planned military hardware co-development and co-production projects will be to make Pakistan an integral part of China's fast-expanding military-industrial complex in the decades to come. Beijing has also signaled its desire to establish military bases in overseas locations that would possibly include Pakistan. The growing military nexus between China and Pakistan, in turn, has raised the specter of a two-front war in India.[71]

Economic Integration and Infrastructure Development

A stable, powerful, and prosperous Pakistan balancing India's growing power serves China's grand strategic objective while a weak, failing, and economically bankrupt Pakistan is detrimental to Chinese interests. Pakistan's descent into chaos would rob China of its premier surrogate instrument against India. Recognizing that Pakistan was in an economic mess, China has stepped in thrice since the mid-1990s (in 1996, 2000–01 and 2008), using "bail-out diplomacy" to provide economic assistance to help the country stave off bankruptcy.[72] Beijing also welcomed post-9/11 US re-engagement with Pakistan that has resulted in billions of dollars worth of economic and military assistance to its ally. Pakistan is one of the major beneficiaries of Chinese aid, loans, and grants. In 2006, China reportedly agreed to invest $12 billion in various projects for upgrading railways, ports, highways, mining and agricultural sector, and industrial zones meant exclusively for Chinese businesses in Pakistan.[73] Even though Beijing does not see its client as a "problem state" needing "guidance from other countries," China is part of the "Friends of Democratic Pakistan," a 13-member group formed in 2008 aimed at promoting economic development and preventing the takeover of the country by Taliban. The group collectively has pledged more than $5.28 billion to Pakistan.[74]

According to the Associated Press of Pakistan (September 16, 2009), more than 10,000 Chinese workers are engaged in 120 projects in Pakistan and the total Chinese investment is expected to rise to $15 billion by 2010. Nearly 60 Chinese companies are operating in the oil and gas, defense, information technology, telecommunications, power-generation, engineering, automobile manufacturing, infrastructure, and mining sectors. China's hunger for raw materials to fuel its own economic growth has led to large investments into the Saindak copper and gold project in Chaghm and the lead-zinc mining project in Balochistan's Lasbela district. The proposal to build a railroad and lay an optic-fiber cable along the strategic Trans-Karakoram highway is under consideration. In 2004, Islamabad granted "free market economy" status to China, and Beijing pledged to provide $150 million for Chasma Nuclear Power Plant (Phase II). The total trade volume between Pakistan and China has risen from less than $1 billion in 2000–01 to about $10 billion in 2010. In November 2006, China and Pakistan signed a free-trade agreement (FTA), which will give a major boost to bilateral trade.[75] Under the FTA, Pakistan will gain access to the vast Chinese market, while China will sell Pakistan more and more goods, as well as obtain cheap raw materials and the use of Pakistani ports for the onward export of its goods to world destinations at reduced freight rates.[76] Crucially, Pakistan remains China's biggest investment destination in South Asia. Chinese premier Wen Jiabao signed economic deals worth $35 billion as part of a plan to commercially bind Pakistan closer to the world's second-largest economy. If all goes well, the FTA and the setting up of special economic zones for Chinese businesses, the Gwadar port, and other infrastructure projects would integrate Pakistan into Western China's economy by outsourcing low-tech, basic labor-intensive production and manufacturing jobs, thereby turning it into a giant factory floor for China. Pakistan has been roped in to encourage the worldwide use of the yuan (along with South Korea, Malaysia, Indonesia, and Argentina) by using the Chinese currency in cross-border trade, starting with Xinjiang. Though the two sides have signed several agreements in the areas of agriculture, manufacturing, minerals, energy, environmental protection, satellite purchases, electricity, information and communication technology, service and education, and technical cooperation, a big question mark still hangs over their implementation. Political violence and instability could still unravel these economic arrangements if China and Pakistan fail to pacify and stabilize Xinjiang and Balochistan respectively. Currently, the balance of trade remains in China's favor. China still lags far behind Pakistan's major export destinations in the United States, European Union, and the Gulf states. Chinese goods are considered qualitatively inferior. Beijing's mercantilist foreign policy behavior has created trade tensions between long-term strategic partners. There is opposition to the large-scale dumping of Chinese goods in Pakistan's markets, and China's cheaper textile exports compete against Pakistan's textile manufacturers in the developed world.[77] Despite these concerns, the Pakistani government has no option but to provide preferential market access to lure Chinese investments.

Economically, China's strategy is to integrate South Asia's natural resources and markets into China's national development strategy. Interestingly, Chinese writings on economic development and foreign policy priorities reveal that Pakistan and Burma have now acquired the same place in China's grand strategy in the twenty-first century that was earlier occupied by Xinjiang (meaning "New Territory") and Xizang ("Western Treasure House," that is, Tibet) in the twentieth century. Put it simply, following the integration of the outlying "autonomous provinces" of Xinjiang and Xizang (Tibet) into China, Pakistan is now being perceived as China's new "Xinjiang" (new territory) and Burma as China's new "Xizang" (treasure house) in economic, military, and strategic terms. At the strategic level, the Chinese investments in the

Trans-Karakoram highway and the Gwadar port in the west of India; the construction of the Lhasa railway that will enhance Chinese transport links with Nepal, Bhutan, Bangladesh and northeastern India; and the building of the Irrawaddy Corridor (involving a combination of road, river, rail, and oceanic harbor infrastructure) linking Yunnan province with Burma ports on the Bay of Bengal in the east of India are aimed at drawing South Asia into China's economic orbit. China has also begun a multi-billion-dollar scheme to link Xinjiang, Afghanistan, Pakistan, Kyrgyzstan, Uzbekistan, and Kazakhstan via railroad networks that will not only open up Central Asia to Chinese goods and companies but also serve as conduits for oil and petrol to be brought back.[78] Sinologist John Garver argues that China's great western development effort bears analogy with the opening of the North American west in the second half of the nineteenth century, which created a large market and a superpower: "The opening of China's west—construction of modern lines of transportation, exploitation of western resources, and acceleration of rates of development to achieve levels more nearly approximating China's east—will be crucial to China's successful 'rise' in the 21st century."[79] Since, China—unlike America—has no western ocean, Beijing is applying "modern transportation technology … to link western China to the oceans, transforming the significance of the lands in between."

> These new lines of transportation will be bearers of Chinese influence to Central, South-west and South Asia. Trade flows and inter-dependencies will develop … and China's role in the regions to its west and south-west will increase. From China's point of view, south and south-western Eurasia constitute a littoral giving China's western regions access to the high seas highways of the global economy … As South Asian economies become closely interlinked with the larger Chinese economy, China will be better able to offer rewards for cooperation, and negative incentives for opposing it on key issues. Greater Chinese presence will create Chinese interests that will require protection.[80]

Stated differently, China is embarked on a "hub and spokes economic strategy" for the Eurasian continent, which is somewhat similar to the US "hub and spokes military strategy" in the Asia-Pacific. The success of this geo-economic strategy would allow China to emerge as the hub of all economic development in the Asia-Pacific region and its various railroad and highway transportation networks linking China with Central and Southwest, South, and Southeast Asia will serve as the spokes or arteries that will bring in raw materials and energy resources while exporting Chinese manufactured goods to those regions and beyond. More importantly, Beijing's privileged access to the markets and natural resources of South Asian countries also makes a point on the limits of Indian power. The key point is that the Sino-Pakistan economic dimension, hitherto very weak, has grown in importance since the late 1990s and will have geopolitical consequences.

Global Institutional Partnership

At the UN and other regional and international forums, Chinese and Pakistani diplomats regularly consult and calibrate their stances on global and regional issues in order to advance their interests jointly. Taking a leaf out of Washington's diplomacy book of briefing key allies (Britain and Japan) after each overseas presidential visit, President Jiang Zemin began the practice of briefing Russian and Pakistani leaders after each of his foreign tours in the mid-1990s. Both coordinate their diplomatic strategies to shape international institutions, laws, norms, and treaties to serve their objectives. Pakistan has long supported China on the international stage on all issues (especially those related to Taiwan, Tibet, human rights, trade, environment, and UN reforms) while China backs Pakistani views on Kashmir, Afghanistan, Islamist terrorism, and nuclear proliferation issues. For example, in 2005, both worked closely as members of the so-called "Coffee Club" at the UN to successfully sabotage the "Group of Four" (India, Japan, Brazil and Germany) proposal for expansion of the UN Security Council's permanent membership category. Both help each other gain membership in regional organizations. Pakistan, for example, facilitated China's observer status at the South Asian Association for Regional Cooperation in 2005 while China was instrumental in gaining Pakistan a seat at the ASEAN Regional Forum and Asia-Europe Summit and observer status at the Shanghai Cooperation Organization. Pakistan's President Zardari has spoken of the two countries' "complete understanding" on all issues. Cooperation in regional and global institutions helps Beijing and Islamabad monitor closely India's activities to expand influence and gain advantage or attempts to fill any perceived power vacuum and block India from doing so.

The Pakistan-China Consultations on Arms Control and Disarmament issues are held regularly to adopt common approaches to issues of nuclear non-proliferation, space, and nuclear energy. Whether it is Iran's nuclear weapons program, genocide in Darfur (Sudan), the internal situation in Burma, or the growing Talibanization of Pakistan, Chinese and Pakistani ambassadors to the UN work in tandem to keep these issues off the UN Security Council's agenda and/or dilute the effectiveness of any Security Council action. Over the last decade, China has repeatedly used its UN Security Council membership to ensure that no harm comes to Pakistan for using terrorism against India. In return, Pakistan essentially "carries the water" for China in the Islamic world by acting as a contact point for China's engagement with the Islamic *ummah* (community). Beijing pro-actively courts Islamic countries for their natural resources and support in international forums. Islamabad played a key role in selling China's point of view on the July 2009 riots in Xinjiang, which resulted in 183 deaths. Pakistan has ensured that the Organization of Islamic Countries (OIC) does not pass any resolution condemning China's "strike hard" campaigns (including curbs on the observance of Ramadan) against its Uyghur Muslim minority. Thanks to Islamabad's lobbying, Beijing today has better relations with key Islamic states—Saudi Arabia, Iran, Iraq, Bangladesh, Malaysia, and Egypt—than any other great power. Apparently, the historical memory of defeats of Muslim invaders at the hands of Imperial China has also built into the Muslim psyche a grudging respect for Communist China.

The "Pakistan Factor" in the US-China-India Triangle

During the Cold War, Pakistan was a frontline state against Soviet Communism. Since the 9/11 terrorist attacks, it has been both a frontline ally as well as the battlefield in the War on Terror. It is also fast emerging as the playground for a much larger geopolitical contest between the world's rising superpower (China) and the reigning superpower (the United States) in the twenty-first century. Pakistan is potentially a "wild card." If it does not implode or degenerate into another Iran or Afghanistan (a radical Islamic and/or a failed state), and gets its house in order, Pakistan could emerge as a pivotal player in the triangular relationship involving Beijing, Washington, and New Delhi. It is often said that Pakistan needs China as much as China needs Pakistan. Nonetheless, Islamabad's dependence on US military and economic aid is far greater than its dependence on China. As long-term strategic allies of Pakistan, both the United States and China have built Pakistan into a garrison state to serve their respective strategic interests. However, an unintended consequence has been its retarded political development and lopsided socio-economic growth. For Pakistan, relations with the United States and China have never been an either-or proposition but a simultaneous pursuit of close relations because both Washington and Beijing share interest in strengthening Pakistan, albeit for different reasons. As noted earlier, while China has proven to be a consistent and steadfast ally and a military partner over the last five decades, the pendulum of Islamabad-Washington relations continues to swing back and forth between appeasement/accommodation and acrimony. The challenge for Washington is to consider how to improve US ties with India without alarming Pakistan and how to reduce Pakistani fears of Indian hegemony while waging a common struggle to defeat the forces of *jihadi* terrorism on the Af-Pak border. Another major US interest is to connect the dynamic economies of South and East Asia to markets and energy resources of Central and West Asia in a win-win situation.[81] Conversely, an important factor shaping China's policies concerning Pakistan (and Iran) is its desire to constrain US power in Southwest Asia (by gaining privileged access to resources, markets and bases) without giving Washington a reason to use Pakistan (and Iran) to pressure Beijing.

China's attempts to emerge as the preeminent power in South and Central Asia with a view to deny India its dominant role in its immediate neighborhood as well as the Indian Ocean face resistance from India. The downturn in Sino-Indian ties since the mid-2000s is attributed to the weakening of China's "Pakistan card" against India, necessitating the exercise of direct pressure. As India's power grows, Beijing is devising new strategic, economic, and diplomatic strategies to keep its southern rival in check. In the triangular power balance game, the Sino-Pakistan military alliance (in particular, the nuclear and missile nexus) is aimed at ensuring that the South Asian military balance of power is neither pro-India nor pro-Pakistan but remains pro-China. Beijing fears that an unrestrained Indian power would eventually threaten China's security along its southwestern frontiers. Both enmity and amity between India and Pakistan have significant implications for China's strategic objectives. As in the past, China remains committed to coming to Pakistan's aid in the event of a military conflict between India and Pakistan by upping the ante along the disputed Himalayan border. Conversely, an India-Pakistan rapprochement under a civilian-democratic Pakistani leadership facilitated by closer trade and commerce links would constrain Beijing's options in achieving its grand strategic objectives. It is in China's interests to keep Pakistani fears of Indian dominance alive to keep Pakistan within its orbit.

The "Pakistan factor" is central to the structural dynamics of the US-China-India triangle. As India's strategic competition with China intensifies in the twenty-first century and becomes almost as fundamental a part of the global order as the Sino-American contest, Pakistan's value for China as a geostrategic tool or a bargaining chip in the China-US-India triangular relationship will inevitably increase. Put it simply, Pakistan is likely to become geopolitically more—not less—important to the Chinese. The more Washington gravitates toward India, the more Beijing will tilt toward Pakistan. Apparently, South Asia and the Indian Ocean region is where China's growing power and presence will be felt most as Beijing looks to assert its regional and global leadership and superpower role. If China's economic and military cooperation with Pakistan reaches its full potential, Washington may then find that "it cannot match the 'all weather friendship' offered by Beijing," and will have to "be prepared for the entirely possible eventuality that one day Pakistan may not be an ally at all."[82] China cannot forsake Pakistan in the interest of its relations with India because Pakistan is located at the tri-junction of Central, Southwest, and South Asia where the national security interests of China and the United States intersect in so many ways. Rasul Bakhsh Rais rightly argues that "India has no levers to change the basic structure of the [Pakistan-China] relationship."[83]

Conclusion

It is because of the geopolitical fault line that links Pakistan with Xinjiang and Tibet that Sino-Indian relations have seen so many false dawns. The texture of the China-Pakistan relationship has undergone change over the past two decades. The Pakistan-China alliance relationship that came into being in the early 1960s with the specific purpose of containing India has now expanded into a global multi-dimensional partnership that encompasses the transnational issues (terrorism, SLOCs safety, economic development, resource and maritime security) as well as the old geopolitical concerns (India) and new geopolitical equations (the United States versus China in Southwest Asia). Nearly all Pakistanis welcome China's rise as a global power. Pakistan now serves larger geostrategic and geoeconomic objectives for China, which increasingly relate as much to the Middle East and the United States as to India. Besides, China's economic developmental strategy, driven by hunger for natural resources and access to markets and bases, places Pakistan and South Asia securely in China's orbit.

Beijing prefers a powerful and well-armed Pakistani military as that helps it mount pressure by proxy on India. Just as China's policy is to use Pakistan as a foil against India, Pakistan's strategy is to use the vast Islamist *jihadi* infrastructure to wage terrorist wars while avoiding direct military confrontation with India. However, the limits of both approaches have become apparent with the emergence of Pakistan as

"*Jihad* Central." This has spurred Beijing and Washington to rethink their policies toward Islamabad and the degree of commitment and support to their ally. China has little interest in abandoning its relations with Pakistan, however. US pressure on Pakistan to clear the tribal region of the Taliban and al-Qaeda has had the effect of forcing Pakistan into an ever-tighter embrace of China. The Sino-Pakistan nexus, which has been the anchor of Islamabad's national security strategy for nearly five decades, will remain so in the future as well, despite growing concerns about an increasingly unstable and dysfunctional Pakistani state. Pakistan is likely to remain China's ally in most scenarios in the foreseeable future. Allowing India to do anything that alters the South or Southeast Asian strategic balance so significantly in favor of India is not something that China can swallow without retaliating in kind. And Beijing will take all means possible to ensure that the regional power balance does not tilt in India's favor.

The intensifying Sino-Indian and Sino-American geopolitical rivalries are also likely to increase the significance of China's strategic ties with Pakistan. Islamabad sees itself as uniquely placed to benefit from the "Chinese Century" in the twenty-first century just as it benefited enormously from the "American Century" in the second half of the twentieth century and the US-Soviet and Soviet-Chinese rivalries of the Cold War era. A global power China values the support of powerful regional allies like Pakistan in the new great game. Therefore, China's "all-weather" relationship with Pakistan will remain the most important factor in Beijing's South Asia policy; and this will hinder a genuine Sino-Indian rapprochement. Indian policy-makers' hopes of driving a wedge between Pakistan and China via closer Sino-Indian economic ties are unlikely to be fulfilled. For, if Beijing downgrades ties with Islamabad, Pakistan may become destabilized, completely slide into the American camp, or come to terms with Indian predominance—all three outcomes are detrimental to China's core security interests. Beijing is aware that Pakistan's capacity to protect Chinese interests has somewhat weakened, and that Pakistan's own future trajectory is far from clear. Pakistan's possible futures cover a wide spectrum: from the emergence of a moderate, democratic state to a radical Islamic republic to Lebanonization (being divided into several small pockets). In the worst-case scenario, it may even face disintegration. Should China's long-term asset turn into a liability, a more fundamental reappraisal of Beijing's old South Asia strategy will then be undertaken. Unless Pakistan descends into total chaos and anarchy, and/or is seen as posing a serious threat to China's vital national interests, Beijing will not give up on its "most allied ally" in Asia. Simultaneously, China's (and

Pakistan's) mutual desire to stymie India would be tempered by Beijing's strategic imperative to avoid a policy of open confrontation with New Delhi, because that would only push India closer to the United States and Japan in a "contain China" drive.

Notes

[1] However, the China-Pakistan-type nuclear/missile cooperation, in particular, is unprecedented in the history of post-World War II international relations. The US never shared such a relationship with Britain or Israel.

[2] R. T. McLean, "China heads west," *FrontPageMagazine.com*, March 2, 2006 <http://www.frontpagemag.com/Articles/ReadA...le.asp?ID=21487>.

[3] M. Baabar, "Pakistan: Hu Jintao visit: who, me, worry?" *Outlook*, December 11, 2006; See Asif Ali Zardari, "Sino-Pakistani relations higher than Himalayas," *China Daily*, August 17, 2009.

[4] "China, Pakistan agree to cement strategic cooperative partnership," *Xinhua*, July 8, 2010 <http://news.xinhuanet.com/english2010/china/2010-07/08/c_13390690.htm>.

[5] Y. Klein Halevi, "Islam must challenge its dark doctrines," *Los Angeles Times*, September 13, 2001.

[6] C. Young, "Does Islam foster extremism?" *Boston Globe*, August 19, 2002, 11.

[7] Quoted in *Los Angeles Times,* July 2, 2005.

[8] The phrase "moderate Muslim country" says it all. There is no parallel with "moderate Christian country" or "moderate Hindu or Buddhist country." Likewise, China's notion of "peaceful rise" is an indirect acknowledgement of its neighbors' legitimate concerns about China's past aggressive behavior.

[9] According to the Chicago Council on Global Affairs (CCGA) survey, 68% of Chinese say they do not trust India to "act responsibly" in the world. Agence France Presse, October 12, 2006.

[10] Reuters, "Pakistan trusts China more than US," *Dawn*, November 23, 2006; Fu Xiaoqiang, "Sino-Pakistani ties usher in a vast room for development," *People's Daily*, November 24, 2006.

[11] Rong Ying quoted in P. Aiyar, "Musharraf bolsters China-Pakistan bond," *Asia Times online*, April 24, 2008 <http://www.atimes.com/atimes/China/JD24Ad01.html>.

[12] S. Kondapalli, "The Chinese military eyes South Asia," in A. Scobell and L. Wortzel (eds), *Shaping China's Security Environment* (PA: Strategic Studies Institute, US Army War College, 2006), 197–245; "Is India China's imaginative [imaginary] rival?" *People's Daily online*, March 2, 2005.

[13] Cited in Reuters, "Pakistan trusts China more than US," *The News*, November 23, 2006.

[14] W. van Kemenade, "China and Pakistan: new friends can't compare: the two neighbors have permanent strategic interests," *YaleGlobal Online*, March 12, 2008 <http://yaleglobal.yale.edu/display.article?id=10490>.

[15] Conversation with a Pakistani military officer, August 30, 2006.

[16] See "Aid and the unraveling of Pakistan," *Newsweek*, January 21, 2008; A Report of the Pakistan Policy Working Group, *The Next Chapter: The United States and Pakistan* (Armitage International, US Institute of Peace and DynCorp International), September 2008, 6.

[17] Pakistan's military ruler General Zia-ul-Haq "had dreamed like a Mogul emperor of 'recreating a Sunni Muslim space' between infidel 'Hindustan,' 'heretic' [because Shia] Iran and 'Christian' Russia. He believed that the message of Afghan Mujaheddin would spread into Central Asia, revive Islam and create a new Pakistan-led Islamic bloc of nations," writes A. Rashid in *Taliban: Islam, Oil and the New Great Game in Central Asia* (London and New York: I.B. Tauris, 2000) Chapter 14: "Master or victim: Pakistan's Afghan war,"195.

[18] "Islamabad aims to create a caliphate with the help of the Islamic regimes running from Central Asia to West Asia and Southeast Asia. India stands in the way. Beijing desires to unravel India into multiple parts based on the pre-British model, as it cannot digest the challenge to its supremacy offered in Asia by a liberal union of multi-religious and multi-ethnic States. The truth is that Indian democratic values contradict and thereby pose a threat to the authoritarian philosophy of both, the Communists in Beijing, and the Islamic fundamentalists in Islamabad. It is obvious that if the Indian model wins, autocratic regimes like China and Pakistan lose," writes B. Verma, "India unprepared and unwilling to defend democracy," *Rediff.com*, February 4, 2010 <http://news.rediff.com/column/2010/feb/04/india-unprepared-and-unwilling-to-defend-democracy.htm>.

[19] Quoted in K. Subrahmanyam, "Don't get fooled by China," *Times of India*, August 28, 2007.

[20] Nepal's Maoist leader Prachanda acknowledged ISI's help to his party. See "ISI had offered help to Nepal Maoists," *Indian Express*, November 20, 2006; "India: The Islamization of the Northeast," *Stratfor.com*, April 20, 2007; A. Mukarji, "ISI's main source of funds is now China," *Hindustan Times*, February 22, 2001.

[21] "Terrorism being fanned to destabilise economy: PC," *Indian Express*, March 10, 2010, 1.

[22] C. Kremmer, "Sub-continent fights forces of darkness," *The Age*, December 29, 2001, 1.

[23] Cited in "India's superpower ambition will see strained relations," *Times of India*, April 2, 2001.

[24] See A. Small, "China's caution on Afghanistan-Pakistan," *Washington Quarterly,* 33:3 (July 2010), 89.

[25] The Next Chapter: The United States and Pakistan, 13.

[26] Remarks by a Bangladeshi diplomat, October 2006, Honolulu. "India: Bangladeshi influx fuels growth of Islamic fundamentalism in Northeast," *India–Open Source Center (OSC) Report* SAP20060209025001, February 9, 2006. The Shahi Imam of Delhi's Jama Masjid has declared: "We [Muslims] were rulers here for 800 years. Inshaallah, we shall return to power here once again." "Shahi Imam 'absolves' LeT, blames RSS for Mumbai blasts," *Rediff.com*, July 18, 2006 <http://news.webindia123.com/news/articles/India/

20060718/394446.html>. At the time of the 1947 Partition, the Muslim population in undivided India was about 70 million. Since then there has been a 6-fold increase in the combined population of Bangladesh, India, and Pakistan over the last 60 years, touching the nearly half a billion mark. Over the last 35 years alone, the world Muslim population has multiplied several-fold, from approximately 340 million in 1970 to 1.2 billion in 2005.

[27] Maj. Gen. (R) J. Ayaz Khan, "Coming of Hu Jintao is sweeter than honey," *Pakistan Observer*, December 1, 2006 <http://pakobserver.net/200612/01/Articles01.asp>.

[28] "Treaty of friendship, cooperation and good neighbourly relations between the People's Republic of China and the Islamic Republic of Pakistan," Ministry of Foreign Affairs of the People's Republic of China, April 5, 2005 <http://fmprc.gov.cn/eng/ziliao>3602/3604/default.htm>.

[29] S. A. Hoffman, *India and the China Crisis* (Berkeley and Los Angeles: University of California Press, 1990), 60.

[30] Though China is not responsible for the India-Pakistan hostility and animosity, Chinese strategists early on recognized the enduring nature of that enmity and have exploited it to China's advantage, writes J. W. Garver, "Could it happen again?" *The Rediff.com,* November 2, 2002 <http://www.rediff.com/news/2002/nov/02chin.htm>.

[31] See V. P. Malik, *Kargil: From Surprise to Victory* (HarperCollins, 2006), 297–302.

[32] J. W. Garver, "China and South Asia," *Annals of the American Academy of Politics & Social Sciences*, 519 (1992), 80. 83, 85.

[33] P. Lee, "Beijing broods over its arc of anxiety," *Asia Times online*, December 4, 2009 <http://www.atimes.com/atimes/China/KL04Ad01.html>; Mohan Malik, "China unveils 'the Kashmir card'," *China Brief*, X:19 (September 24, 2010), 6-9 <http://www.jamestown.org/programs/chinabrief/single/?tx_ttnews%5Btt_news%5D=36915&tx_ttnews%5BbackPid%5D=25&cHash=078d3aabd3>.

[34] "Pakistan, China vow to strengthen strategic ties," *Pak Tribune*, July 8, 2010 <http://paktribune.com/news/index.shtml?229306>.

[35] "Multiple crises send Pakistan to the brink," *Agence France-Presse*, October 26, 2008

[36] See "Pakistan: state faces crisis of purpose," *Oxford Analytica*, October 1, 2008 <https://www.opensource.gov/providers/oxan/display.aspx?ItemID=DB145908>.

[37] The argument here is based on *Oxford Analytica* commentary, "Pakistan: state faces crisis of purpose."

[38] The Next Chapter: The United States and Pakistan, 5.

[39] S. Parashar, "Taliban, Qaida trying to take over Pakistan," *Times of India*, October 15, 2008.

[40] R. Callick, "Pakistan violence worries Chinese," *Australian*, July 25, 2007.

[41] "China indicates Uighur terrorists have close links with Pak," *AFP*, October 21, 2008.

[42] See T. Niazi, "China, Pakistan, and terrorism," *Foreign Policy in Focus*, July 16, 2007 <http://www.fpif.org/fpiftxt/4384>.

[43] India's traditionally cordial ties to Afghanistan have been consciously strengthened since 2002, and India is now a major donor to Afghan reconstruction, pledging over $1.2 billion. See Niazi, "China, Pakistan, and terrorism."

[44] Yang Jirui and Sun Jin (eds), *Zhongguo Xibu da kaifa yu Nanya* (*China's Western Development and South Asia*), (Chengdu: Sichuan Publishers, 2004); Liao Yameng, "Expert analyzes the 'balancing' strategies of China, India and Pakistan," *Wen Wei Po*, November 7, 2003, FBIS-CHI-2003-1107, November 13, 2003.

[45] One could also argue that China's "Muslim problem" has never been as serious as India's in Kashmir or Russia's in Chechnya. Being an autocratic state, the Chinese Communist regime has often resorted to strong-arm tactics and mass executions without worrying about critical media scrutiny or public opinion fallout with which democracies like India and Russia have had to contend. Assured of cooperation from Pakistan and other Islamic countries, the Chinese remain confident of dealing with the Uyghur Muslim problem with an iron hand.

[46] Small, "China's caution on Afghanistan-Pakistan," 89.

[47] Discussions with Chinese South Asia specialists, Beijing, Shanghai and Honolulu, 2007–09.

[48] Chinese Defense Minister Cao Gangchuan expressed the determination that such incidents would not affect the friendship between China and Pakistan. General Cao's comments followed those of the Chinese Ambassador to Pakistan, Luo Zhaohui, who warned Islamabad that if Chinese people continued to be targeted, cooperation between the two countries could suffer. See "Recent incident not to shake the bonds of Sino-Pak friendship: Cao," APP, July 19, 2007 <http://www.app.com.pk/en/index.php?option=com_content&task=view&id=13013&Itemid=1>; "China talks tough to Pakistan on security of its nationals," *Pak Tribune*, July 18, 2007 <http://paktribune.com/news/print.php?id=184361>.

[49] Cited in van Kemenade, "China and Pakistan: new friends can't compare."

[50] See P. Musharraf's interview in "The will to cooperate," *Beijing Review*, March 2, 2006, 10.

[51] S. Fazl-e-Haider, "China's growing stake in Pakistan," *Asia Times online*, November 30, 2006 <http://www.atimes.com/atimes/South_Asia/HK30Df01.html>.

[52] J. W. Garver, "Development of China's overland transportation links with Central, South-west and South Asia," 10.

[53] China was initially reluctant to help with the construction of the port, agreed to fund it only after it obtained "sovereign guarantees to the port facilities." T. Niazi, "Gwadar: China's naval Outpost on the Indian Ocean," *China Brief*, 5: 4, February 15, 2005 <http://www.jamestown.org/publications_details.php?volume_id=408&issue_id=3232&article_id=2369262>.

[54] According to *Energy Futures in Asia* (2005), Beijing has established electronic eavesdropping posts at Gwadar, which monitor ship traffic through the Arabian Sea. "Pak offers China monitoring facilities on Makrana Coast," *Nezavisimoye Voyennoye Obozreniye* (*Independent Military Review*) (Moscow), June 29, 2002. <http://www.frontpagemag.com/Articles/ReadA...le.asp?ID=21487>.

[55] Niazi, "Gwadar: China's naval outpost on the Indian Ocean."

[56] The other "pearls" are naval facilities in Bangladesh, Burma, Thailand, Cambodia and the South China Sea. Y. Kumar, "Hu, Pakistan and the 'string of pearls,'" *Rediff.com*, November 28, 2006.

[57] J. W. Garver, "China's South Asian interests and policies." Testimony prepared for panel on "China's approaches to South Asia and the former Soviet states," US-China Economic and Security Review Commission, July 22, 2005 <http://www.uscc.gov/hearings/2005hearings/written_testimonies/05_07_21_22wrts/garver_john_wrts.htm>.

[58] Mohan Malik, "China responds to the U.S.-India nuclear deal," *China Brief*, 6:7 (March 29, 2006) <http://www.jamestown.org/publications_details.php?volume_id=415&issue_id=3670&article_id=2370926>.

[59] "China pleads India-like nuke deal for Pakistan," *Daily Mail*, September 9, 2008 <http://dailymailnews.com/200809/09/news/dmtopstory01.html>.

[60] C. Raja Mohan, "End of long nuke winter," *Indian Express*, December 10, 2006. <http://www.indianexpress.com/iep/sunday/story/18275.html>.

[61] Associated Press, "China to help build 2 Pakistan nuclear plants," *IHT*, October 18, 2008, 1.

[62] "China: walking a fine line in alliance with Pakistan," *Stratfor Today*, October 16, 2008. <http://www.stratfor.com/analysis/20081016_china_walking_fine_line_alliance_pakistan>.

[63] With China's help, Pakistan's navy will have as many frigates as India by 2015. Once India acquires a nuclear-powered submarine and submarine-launched ballistic missile capability, Beijing would ensure that Pakistan will also have one. See "PLAN's Xia Submarine to Pakistan?" *China Defense Blog*, May 14, 2010 <http://china-defense.blogspot.com/2010/05/plans-xia-submarine-to-pakistan.html>.

[64] "Pakistan/China: pragmatism informs Beijing's support," *Oxford Analytica*, October 21, 2008 <https://www.opensource.gov/providers/oxan/display.aspx?ItemID=DB146374>.

[65] Xinhua "Chinese president's visit to further cooperation with Pakistan," *People's Daily online*, November 22, 2006.

[66] A. Siddiqa, "The view: Hu's visit," *Asian Age,* November 27, 2006 <http://www.dailytimes.com.pk/default.asp?page=2006%5C11%5C27%5Cstory_27-11-2006_pg3_4>.

[67] Given Dr. Khan's close links with and numerous visits to the Chinese nuclear establishment, it is inconceivable that Chinese security agencies were unaware of Pakistan's nuclear dealings with North Korea, Iran and Libya. See Mohan Malik, "Dr Khan's China connection," *China Brief*, 4:9 (April 29,

2004)<http://www.jamestown.org/publications_details.php?volume_id=395&iss ue_id=2939&article_id=23663>.

[68] D. S. Rajan, "China: revisiting the 2005 Friendship Treaty with Pakistan," *Saag.org*, Paper No. 2058, December 10, 2006 <http://www.saag.org/papers21/paper2058.html>.

[69] Agencies, "Pakistan will stand by China against US 'siege,' says Rashid," *Daily Times* (Lahore), February 23, 2006, 1 <www.dailytimes.com.pk/ default.asp?page...23-2-2006_pg7_50>.

[70] "Joint military exercises begin," *Dawn*, December 11, 2006.

[71] S. Dasgupta, "China mulls setting up military base in Pakistan," *Times of India*, January 28, 2010, 1; J. Lamont and F. Bokhari, "China-Pakistan military links upset India," *Financial Times*, November 27, 2009.

[72] I. Wilkinson, "China to 'bail-out' near bankrupt Pakistan," *Telegraph*, October 18, 2008.

[73] "China will invest US$12 billion in Pakistan," *Shanghai Daily*, March 9, 2006.

[74] Small, "China's caution on Afghanistan-Pakistan," 89.

[75] Information here is based on "Pakistan/China: pragmatism informs Beijing's support."

[76] Critics claim the FTA was signed in a bit of a hurry and has the potential to benefit China more than Pakistan. The only other county with which China has signed an FTA is Chile. S. Fazl-e-Haider, "China digs Pakistan into a hole," *Asia Times online*, October 5, 2006 <http://www.atimes.com/atimes/ South_Asia/HJ05Df01.html>.

[77] On the challenges facing China-Pakistan economic relations, see Fazal-ur-Rahman, "Pakistan-China economic relations: opportunities and challenges," *Strategic Studies* (Islamabad), XXVI: 2 (Summer 2006), 53–72.

[78] M. Moore, "China extends influence into Central Asia," *Telegraph*, October 17, 2008.

[79] J. W. Garver, "Development of China's overland transportation links with Central, South-west and South Asia," *China Quarterly*, 185 (March 2006), 1.

[80] Garver, "Development of China's overland transportation links…" 2, 18–19.

[81] The Next Chapter: The United States and Pakistan," 21–24.

[82] McLean, "China heads west."

[83] Quoted in Baabar, "Pakistan: Hu Jintao visit: who, me, worry?"

7
Burma: Fulcrum of Rivalry

Burma (now known officially as the Union of Myanmar[1]) has come to occupy centre stage in Asian strategic concerns since the early 1990s. A series of developments, both internal and external, has caused concern about the long-term stability, security, and independence of mainland Southeast Asia's largest country. Burma, with an area of some 676,577 square kilometers (261,228 sq mi) and a population of 47 million, lies at the juncture of three regions within Asia: East Asia, Southeast Asia, and South Asia. It occupies a critical geostrategic position between the two rising Asian giants, China and India. It also shares borders with Bangladesh in the west and with Thailand and Laos in the east. It has a substantial coastline in the south along the Bay of Bengal and the Andaman Sea, which provides access to the Indian Ocean. It is located in a region which has experienced tremendous economic growth over the last two decades.

Burma's potential wealth, natural, and human resources combined with its geostrategic location between South Asia and Southeast Asia suggest that it has the *potential* to be a major Southeast Asian player. However, two decades after the military junta seized power, Burma remains a fractured nation internally and is treated as a pariah externally because of the military regime's systematic oppression of its people. For decades, the Failed States Index has ranked Burma as one of the top five Asian states (along with Afghanistan, Pakistan, Bangladesh, and Nepal) most at risk of failure. Any state failure in Burma would have regional repercussions as its neighbors would be affected by an even bigger flow of refugees, drugs, and weapons than is the case today. To make matters worse, the military junta has abandoned the traditional policy of equidistance between China and India and is *seen* as becoming a puppet of Chinese interests in the region as well as a base for future military operations, thus upsetting the regional balance of power.[2] Consequently, Burma, given its critical strategic position between the two Asian giants, has become a source of competition in the Sino-Indian equation.

Since the early 1990s, several observers have examined the implications of Burma's emergence as the epicenter of China-India rivalry for natural resources, maritime access, and regional influence in South and Southeast Asia.[3] This chapter examines the dilemmas and challenges facing Rangoon by analyzing Burma's strategic culture and fast-changing relations with China, India, and ASEAN. It seeks to answer two key questions: Does Burma have what it takes to be a pivotal player? More importantly, will it be allowed to do so by its powerful northern neighbor, China, the next superpower? It offers a prognosis of Burma's policy options, given its place in China's grand strategy for the twenty-first century. It concludes with a somewhat pessimistic view of the short- to medium-term prospects for Burma's transformation from a pawn in China's regional chess game into a pivotal player. The key argument is that the present and future Burmese leaders would find it very difficult to withdraw completely from China's sphere of influence. Nor would the Chinese government allow them to do so because Burma now occupies the same place in China's calculus of deterrence in South and Southeast Asia that Pakistan does in South and Southwest Asia. More than anywhere else, it is in Burma that Beijing and New Delhi are waging an open and determined struggle for influence and advantage.

History and Strategic Culture

Burma's current predicament and its future role cannot be discussed in isolation from its history or strategic tradition. The way a country's national interests are conceptualized, defined, and defended is influenced by its unique cultural/historical experiences. Political and military elites socialized in different cultural contexts behave in a variety of ways and make different choices, even when placed in similar situations. Strategic culture thus consists of widely shared beliefs, worldviews, traditions, attitudes, symbols, myths, self-image, and identity (in terms of self-representation of the nation and its "proper" role in world politics).[4]

While India's culture and religion have influenced the Burmese way of life over the centuries, China has traditionally exerted geopolitical and strategic pressure on Burma. As Tin Maung Maung Than notes: "Geopolitical ramifications for modern Burma have been overwhelmingly determined by bilateral relations with China," which date back to the early Pyu kingdoms of the ninth century AD.[5] There were periods when powerful Chinese dynasties intervened in Burmese affairs. In 1287, Kubilai Khan, emperor of the Mongol (Yuan) dynasty, sent an army through Yunnan Province (which was until then an independent non-Chinese kingdom called Nan Chao) to conquer the kingdom of Pagan, the "city of ten thousand pagodas." The Mongol incursion effectively brought to an end the first unified Burman kingdom. In the late seventeenth century, Manchu (Qing) armies invaded northern Burma in order to capture the last successor to the Ming throne, Prince Yong-li, who had fled to the Burmese capital, Ava. During the eighteenth century, Burma and Qing China fought over the control of the Shan States, Chiang Mai, and Laos. Between 1766 and 1769, three Chinese invasions were successfully repulsed by Burman and Shan forces led by General Maha Thiha Thura. However, despite winning the wars, General Maha Thiha Thura sought to save Chinese face by agreeing to a *de jure* tribute relationship between Ava and Beijing. From 1885 to 1948, all of Burma was incorporated as a province of British India. British colonial rule led to large-scale migration of hundreds of thousands of Indians to Burma, ranging from civil servants, professionals, and moneylenders to unskilled plantation and dock workers, who went back in the late 1950s and early 1960s as per agreement between the two governments.

Since gaining independence in 1948, Burma has "accommodated China as its 'senior' in a *paukphaw* (kinsmen) relationship, taking great pains at not exercising or even expressing any policies and actions inimical to China's security interests."[6] On several occasions, China posed a threat to the independent Union of Burma (1948–1962) and its socialist, military-ruled successor, the Socialist Republic of the Union of Burma (1974–1988). During the 1950s, bilateral relations were strained due to the spillover of the Chinese civil war between *Kuomintang* (KMT) and Chinese Communist Party (CCP) forces into Burma. Rangoon was forced to allow the People's Liberation Army (PLA) to cross into Burma to crush remaining KMT guerrillas. Attempts to improve relations during the 1960s and 1970s were marred by Beijing's support for the Burmese Communist Party (BCP) and anti-Chinese riots in the wake of the Cultural Revolution in China.[7] Beijing's response to anti-Chinese riots was fast and furious. In 1968, in "an undeclared war that was little noticed because it took place during the Tet offensive in Vietnam, Beijing sent 30,000 heavily armed troops who rapidly occupied swaths of the country and forced the government of General Ne Win to negotiate."[8] The withdrawal of Chinese support led to the breakup of the BCP in April 1989 and removed a major irritant from bilateral relations.

Burma's historical preference has been to steer a middle path between the two rival power blocs and to avoid confrontation with its neighbors. Since independence in 1948, successive governments in Burma have battled around the country's periphery with multiple insurgencies and separatist movements based on ethnic identity which in the past have obtained limited support mainly from China and Thailand. The primary preoccupation of the Burmese armed forces, the *tatmadaw,* has thus been to maintain the country's territorial integrity against threats emanating from within rather than without. As Tin Maung Maung Than observes: "The conduct of Burma's external relations since independence, together with the military's posture and operations, indicate a threat perception dominated by concerns focusing on internal order and stability and border security."[9] The maintenance of national unity and territorial integrity has been accorded such a high priority that regime security has become synonymous with national security.[10] Burma's military junta, especially after the 1962 coup, "has always believed in the legitimacy of its mission as political ruler, guardian of the state and, by extension, of Burmese Buddhist culture."[11] In short, Burma has always understood the harsh geopolitical reality of its long border (2000 km) with China. *Resisting while accommodating* the "big brother" has long been part of the Burmese security culture and will remain the pattern of Sino-Burmese relations in the future too. As for their other neighbors, the Burmese are known to dislike Thailand and do not fear India.

The End of Neutrality and Tightening of China's Embrace

During the Cold War years, the isolationist policies pursued by the Ne Win regime helped to perpetuate Burma's status as a neutral buffer state between India and China. However, the State Law and Order Restoration Council (SLORC) and its successor, the State Peace and Development Council (SPDC), which have run the country since September 1988 when the military violently suppressed pro-democracy protests, effectively has put an end to Burma's neutrality by moving closer to China. In 1990, the SLORC presided over an election in which the opposition National League for Democracy (NLD) won by a landslide but was never allowed to take office. Instead, the military junta placed the Burmese opposition leader, Aung San Suu Kyi, under house arrest, and arrested thousands of NLD supporters and leaders. This sparked worldwide condemnation of widespread human rights abuses and pressure to restore the democratic process. Akin to the pro-democracy uprising of 1988, mass protests led by Buddhist monks erupted again in 2007 and were again met with a forceful response from the junta.

Faced with increasing international isolation and further domestic unrest, the military junta tightened its grip on power. Burma urgently needed foreign exchange, capital equipment, and technical expertise to prevent the collapse of its ailing economy, and it needed assistance in defeating ethnic insurgency.[12] At this point, Chinese interests conveniently synchronized with a range of the military regime's major concerns and the junta in Rangoon moved to establish closer military, economic, and diplomatic ties with the communist regime in Beijing, which had found itself in a similar predicament following the Tiananmen massacre in June 1989. Thus began Burma's slide into China's embrace.

High level visits to each other's capital at regular intervals soon became the norm. Between 1990 and 1998, China reportedly supplied nearly US$1.8 billion worth of arms to Burma, including fighter aircraft, radar equipment, naval patrol boats, heavy artillery, main battle tanks, anti-aircraft missiles, guns, and ammunition.[13] Rangoon relied heavily on these weapons and equipment to end hostilities with insurgents in the border regions. The last two decades have seen the transformation of a poorly-equipped force of 185,000 men and women in 1988 capable only of waging counter-insurgency (COIN) operations into the second largest military of approximately 500,000 in Southeast Asia, behind Vietnam, with a greatly improved capacity to conduct both unconventional and conventional military operations against a wider range of potential adversaries.[14] Much like its Chinese counterpart, the *tatmadaw* also got into running businesses, earning sizeable income from patronage, corruption and the narcotics trade. Burma's economic problems and international isolation led to an upsurge in opium production and cross-border smuggling. Indeed, many of the military junta's peace agreements with ex-communist rebels and ethnic minorities in the northeastern border regions allowed the former guerillas to remain active in the drug trade within the infamous Golden Triangle region across the Burmese frontier with China, Thailand, and Laos. Some Burma-watchers claimed that drug money was being used to finance military hardware purchases from China, Singapore, and elsewhere.[15] Profits from Burma's enormous natural gas reserves (which constitute nearly a third of the country's exports) are funneled to the military junta's paranoid leaders who use them to buy the diplomatic protection of China and others.[16]

China's Shadow over Burma: Key Objectives

Burma-watchers generally agree that the military regime's pro-China tilt was not the result of some "grand design" in Rangoon but because it had nowhere else to go. In contrast, Beijing's forays into Burma are definitely a part of China's grand strategy based on a careful assessment of China's strategic interests and economic needs in the twenty-first century. The significance of Burma's geostrategic location for China's economic growth was outlined first by a former vice-minister of communications, Pan Qi, in an article entitled "Opening to the Southwest: An Expert Opinion" in the *Beijing Review* of September 2, 1985. This article expressed the desire of Chinese economic planners to re-open the old Burma Road to link up the poorer inland provinces, such as Yunnan, which lagged behind the booming coastal provinces, with the fast growing economies of Southeast and South Asia.[17] Beijing sought an overland route through Burma to a port from which it could export cheap consumer goods to mainland Southeast Asia, India, and other developing countries farther afield. Such an outlet would reduce transport time for some of China's trade and make it possible to avoid the Malacca Strait choke point in the event of a conflict in the South China Sea.

The three decades of self-imposed isolation—or what the regime described as the "Burmese road to socialism"—turned the region's once most prosperous country into an economic basket case. Since 1990, the Chinese have found Burma a ready market for cheap consumer goods, industrial, and agricultural products. The annual Sino-Burmese trade exceeded US$2.6 billion in 2008, excluding the lucrative, illicit cross-border traffic in drugs from Burma's side of the Golden Triangle.[18] China has also become the largest donor country to Burma. Several motives underlie China's desire to expand its economic and strategic influence down to the Bay of Bengal and into the Indian Ocean.

Over the last two decades, China has developed substantial economic interests in Burma. To strengthen and increase its trade links with Burma and neighboring countries, Beijing is investing billions of dollars in its southern neighbor's transportation infrastructure (major highway, railway, bridge, and port construction projects) and has emerged as one of the biggest consumers of Burmese raw materials and precious metals (including timber, minerals, and gemstones)—required in ever-larger quantities to fuel China's industrialization and urbanization. Some 69 Chinese multinational corporations are reportedly engaged in at least 90 hydropower, mining (copper, jade, and gold) and oil and gas projects in Burma. Chinese authorities in the southwest province of Yunnan have unveiled plans to build a 1350 km railway through Laos and Burma to Thailand, which will link Kunming with Bangkok. A China-Burma-Bangladesh tri-nation road network is also planned. More importantly, China is establishing an energy corridor through Burma involving an oil pipeline to transship crude oil it imports from the Middle East and Africa. China's pragmatic approach to commercial diplomacy underscores its interest in maintaining Burma's political status quo.[19]

In addition, high ranking Burmese *tatmadaw* and Chinese military officers have strengthened relations both at the personal and official levels. *Tatmadaw* personnel receive advanced training in China. Closer Sino-Burmese ties are now seen as being of "great significance to the national security of China." The Chinese defense establishment has long been concerned about India's ambitions to dominate the Indian Ocean and its increasing military capability to project power. Chinese strategists list India as one of China's most likely opponents in future regional conflicts on China's southern borders (the others being Vietnam and Taiwan). The 1990s saw Chinese strategists increasingly questioning India's view of its status in the Indian Ocean. They viewed India, with its own great-power ambitions, "as the main party [which is going to be] affected by China's naval surges into the Indian Ocean in the next century."[20] A high-ranking PLA officer and director of the Chinese Academy of Military Sciences, General Zhao Nanqi, was quoted in 1993 as saying that China would extend its naval operations farther than the South and East China Sea to check attempts by India to "dominate" the Indian Ocean and other regional waters. Accusing India of seeking to develop a navy to rival that of "large global powers," General Zhao said that "this is something which we cannot accept … we are not prepared to let the Indian Ocean become India's Ocean."[21] Checkmated in North and East Asia by three great powers (Russia, Japan, and the United States), China has long perceived South and Southeast Asia as its "sphere of influence" and India as the "main spoiler" of China's regional supremacy plans there. Contending that "the cases of the Soviet Union and the United States showed that an essential prerequisite for a superpower is the ability to dominate at least two oceans," one Chinese strategic analyst, Hua Di, remarked as early as in 1991 that "China cannot claim to be a truly global superpower unless it has the capability to dominate two oceans, the Pacific and the Indian Ocean."[22] From Beijing's perspective, the Chinese navy's expansion into the Indian Ocean would be the realization of "Beijing's dreams … [to] operate in two major oceans," and thus herald China's emergence as a truly global power.[23] In July 1994, Gen Li Jiulong, then commander of

China's Chengdu military region, which is the command headquarters and major supply base for Chinese troops in Tibet, visited Burma's naval facilities and reportedly persuaded Rangoon to allow China greater signals intelligence access to three islands off the Burmese coast: Ramree south of Sittwe in Western Arakan state; Coco in the Indian Ocean; and Zadetkyi Kyun or St. Matthew's Island off the Tenasserim coast in the southeast, close to the northern entrance to the Straits of Malacca.[24] A bilateral agreement on military intelligence sharing was concluded during Chinese Premier Li Peng's visit to Rangoon in 1997, and in 2003, China helped Burma build an eighty-five meter jetty to naval facilities on Great Coco Island, which lies within 30 nautical miles of the Andaman Islands in India. China is said to have established a reconnaissance and electronic intelligence system on the island, which, along with electronic surveillance facilities at the Alexandra Channel in the Andaman Sea, monitor India's military and missile testing activities in the Indian Ocean.[25] Beijing's Burma policy is thus a manifestation of a long-term Chinese objective to establish a naval foothold in the Indian Ocean.

Since 1993, China has become a major importer of Middle Eastern oil. Resource scarcity in the twenty-first century would see nations engaged in intense competition. In fact, competition for resources has already provoked elbow-bashing in the region, as seen, for example, in the rush to extend claims and counter-claims to the oil and gas that lie under the South China Sea, Sea of Japan, East China Sea, and Central Asia. Historically, major power shifts and wars result in reallocation of "natural resources and living space, often taking them from a declining nation and allocating them to a rising nation."[26] China is both a rising and an expanding power, expanding in economy, energy needs, population, military strength, and strategic frontiers. Growing demand for imported petroleum may well explain Beijing's naval interests in Burma regarding security of shipping routes through the Indian Ocean to the Straits of Malacca and the South China Sea. Given the geostrategic significance of the Spratly Islands for sea-lane defense, interdiction, and surveillance, whoever dominates the Malacca Straits and South China Sea will determine the destiny of the whole region. Arguing that China's sea lanes of communications (SLOCs) are subject to military blockades or interruption in the East and South China seas, Chinese defense planners have been stressing the need for "a route from Yunnan to Rangoon [as] an important transport line for goods and materials."[27] Chinese forays into Burma are thus a reflection of China's transformation from a continental power into a global maritime power increasingly dependent upon external trade, on ever-growing volumes of imports and exports through oceanic routes, and on overseas markets for capital and investments. Nearly 75 percent of China's trade is carried by sea through the Strait of Malacca, the Indian Ocean and the Suez Canal, and the predominance of the Indian and US navies along these sea lanes of communication (SLOCs) is viewed as a major threat to Chinese security. A major hurdle in the Chinese ambitions to secure the Malacca Straits and to ensure the safe passage of goods through the vital sea lanes has been the lack of maintenance bases in and around the Indian Ocean for its naval ships. With Beijing gaining privileged access to Burmese ports for repair and maintenance, a key strategic objective—that is, an opening to the Bay of Bengal/Andaman Sea via China's southwest frontier—may well be realized. China's future naval operations would therefore be undertaken with a view to securing the country's oil supply routes. In addition to Burma, China has been courting other friendly countries, such as Sri Lanka, Pakistan, and Iran, to establish naval bases in the Indian Ocean and the Persian Gulf.

China's future naval plans, which include permanent deployments in the Indian Ocean, are thus an integral part of Beijing's energy strategy. In particular, China's diplomatic thrust is on importing energy from a neighboring country that has estimated reserves of three trillion cubic meters of natural gas and three billion barrels of crude oil. In January 2007, China signed a memorandum of understanding (MoU) to buy 6.5 trillion cubic feet of offshore natural gas over 30 years beginning in 2009. In addition to importing Burmese oil and gas, China seeks to enhance its energy security by building oil and gas pipelines from Burma to Yunnan—a strategy that will enable it to reduce its reliance on the Strait of Malacca—the key maritime chokepoint in Asia linking the Indian and Pacific Oceans. This places Burma in the strategic position as a source of energy as well as a transshipment route for China. An agreement on building US$2.9 billion Sino-Burmese oil pipeline linking the deep-water port of Sittwe on the Bay of Bengal with Kunming in China's Yunnan province was concluded in 2008. This pipeline, ultimately to be extended to Chongqing in Sichuan province, will ship China-bound oil and natural gas from Africa and the Middle East by ocean-going oil tankers across the Indian Ocean to the port of Sittwe in Burma, where they will be taken ashore and then sent by pipeline to China by way of Mandalay in Burma and Ruili in Yunnan before reaching Kunming. To this effect, China is investing heavily in the upgrade and expansion of port facilities along the Burmese coast. While in peacetime, China is emphasizing the commercial uses of this infrastructure, it would serve important military objectives in the event of a conflict with India or across the Taiwan Straits or if a naval blockade of the sea passage through the Malacca Strait is imposed. Chinese strategic positioning in Burma should, therefore, be seen against the backdrop of Burma overlooking vital SLOCs through the Strait of Malacca.

In addition, Beijing has established a robust military relationship with Burma through intelligence exchange, training and supplies of military hardware, including tanks, F-7 fighters, K-8 Trainer aircraft, C-801 ship-to-ship missiles and ship-borne diesel engines for naval patrol ships. Over the last two decades, China has become the junta's biggest arms supplier. In addition, China's long-term allies—North Korea and Pakistan—have emerged as major suppliers of small arms, ammunition, artillery, and missiles to Burma. Growing speculation about nuclear collaboration between Rangoon and Pyongyang has caused a great deal of anxiety.[28] From a strategic viewpoint, Chinese arms sales and military cooperation have always been an important means of funding the PLA's modernization drive and expanding China's influence abroad. Arms sales to friends and allies (such as North Korea in Northeast Asia, first Cambodia and then Burma in Southeast Asia, and Pakistan and Bangladesh in South Asia) have afforded Beijing the unique opportunity to successfully play the dual role of troublemaker and troubleshooter in regional "hot spots." Having equipped the armed forces of Burma and Bangladesh, Beijing offers itself as a mediator whenever tensions flare up between Burma and Bangladesh over their disputed frontiers.

Clearly, both geo-economic and geo-strategic calculations lie behind Beijing's courting of Burma's military regime with liberal economic and technical assistance, cheap loans, trade, and energy deals to the economically embattled nation. That is why China (along with Russia) often uses its veto power in the UN Security Council to block criticism and sanctions against the Burmese junta, allowing it to prop up a dysfunctional economy and resist pressure to undertake political reform. Some argue that Beijing seems to be motivated more by economic reasons (that is, the maintenance of open SLOCs) and the benefit of a secure flank, and less by the need to develop a military base given China's lack of a modern blue water fleet. Others believe that the primary reason for providing diplomatic protection and military aid is strategic. Beijing has taken advantage of Burma's isolation since 1988 to satisfy its own great power ambitions, particularly its desire to counter India in the Indian Ocean, and the approaches to the South China Sea, and to ensure the control of vital sea lanes by drawing Burma tightly into its sphere of influence. Whatever the case, the fact remains that Burma has moved too close to China for India's or ASEAN's comfort. For them, it does not matter whether China's expansion is dictated by economic interests or by strategic interests. What matters is that Beijing's Burma policy is a manifestation of a Chinese *desire* to dominate both the Pacific and Indian oceans. It is also a demonstration of the *potential* for a Chinese naval presence in the Indian Ocean. The prospect of Chinese naval presence at the eastern end of the Indian Ocean littoral adds an unwanted element of unpredictability to the natural resource strategies of resource-poor South and Southeast Asian countries. This realization has brought about a strategic consensus between India and some Southeast Asian countries on the need to counter Chinese expansion into the Indian Ocean. Even if some accounts of China's military presence in Burma are untrue, the fact that they are widely believed in New Delhi, Bangkok, and Jakarta, despite significant improvements in bilateral relations with Beijing, shows the degree of residual distrust and suspicion.

India's Concerns and Response

History shows that peace prevails when large nation-states of the size of China and India maintain and respect buffer states between them. War erupts when one or the other continental-sized nation annexes the buffer state (as China did in Tibet in 1950) or converts it into a surrogate (as China seems to be doing in Burma since the early 1990s). Tibet and Burma were long seen as the two buffer states between the ancient civilizations of India and China. Tibet fell in the 1950s and led to a war in 1962. Will Burma also fall into China's embrace? That has been the key concern of Indian policymakers since the mid-1990s.

The geopolitical implications of a Chinese strategic nexus with Burma were not lost on Burma's immediate neighbors. From India's perspective, it was not the Burmese military build-up in itself which caused concern, but the supplier. Given India's long adversarial relationship with China, anything that promotes China's interests in its immediate neighborhood or expands China's influence worries India. While seeking economic and political engagement with India, Beijing has continued its policy of strategic containment and encirclement of India by forming a ring of regional strategic alliances with India's neighbors. This involves "the building of Pakistan as a counterweight to India, employing Myanmar [Burma] as a strategic observatory and base and gaining a foothold in India's other neighbors—Bangladesh, Nepal and Sri Lanka."[29] The growing military relationship between Beijing and Rangoon not only marked the end of Burma's traditional nonaligned orientation, it also forced New Delhi, for the first time, to pay close attention to events across its eastern frontier with Burma. As one analyst at the New Delhi-based Institute for Defence Studies and Analyses (IDSA) put it: "In dealing with China we have to consider what it is doing in the east rather than see it only as a northern threat."[30] New Delhi reportedly welcomes the reopening of the old Burma Road if the only purpose is to promote trade and economic links between southwest China and South Asia.[31] What worries Indian strategists are the implications of a growing military nexus between China and Burma for India's national security and broader strategic objectives in the northern Indian Ocean region.

Beijing's growing influence and presence over northern Burma could enable it to outflank India in Arunachal Pradesh, which it regards as Chinese territory. It could also facilitate greater Chinese support for insurgent groups in India's turbulent northeastern states.[32] China's inroads into Burma when juxtaposed with its ties with Bangladesh constituted, from New Delhi's perspective, serious encroachments into India's sphere of influence. For India, the worst case scenario would be the emergence of a Chinese-Burmese-Bangladesh axis in the east. Reports of Beijing's involvement in the development of a Burmese naval base at Hianggyi Island and a radar station at Coco Island, southwest of the Burmese coast, thus introduced a whole new dimension to India's threat perceptions regarding its powerful northern neighbor. The location of these naval facilities close to the Indian territory of Andaman and Nicobar Islands in the Bay of Bengal raised the specter of possible future military use by Beijing.[33] Given India's heavy dependence on the Persian Gulf oil and the fact that 97 percent of India's trade is carried by sea, "the Chinese presence at [India's] door step" is seen as a "constant irritant."[34] Therefore, Indian strategists started seeing China as constituting a threat in the north as well as in the east. A "Tibetanization of Burma" is seen as detrimental to India's security interests because Burma also provides the Chinese with an invasion route to India. New Delhi's preference is for a stable, neutral, and peaceful buffer state of Burma between India and China.

These concerns led to the abandonment in 1993–94 of New Delhi's earlier stance of isolating the Burmese military regime and supporting the Aung San Suu Kyi–led pro-democracy movement. Close on the heels of Chinese Foreign Minister Qian Qichen's visit to Burma in early 1993, Indian Foreign Secretary J. N. Dixit paid a low-key visit to Rangoon in March 1993 to hold talks on issues of mutual concern. This first high-level official contact since the *tatmadaw*'s crackdown on pro-democracy demonstrations in 1988 indicated New Delhi's policy shift. Dixit was told that Burmese leaders would "never allow any permanent foreign military presence in their territory." In return for the Burmese army's co-operation in curtailing the drug and arms traffic in India's volatile northeast and maintenance of peace along Burma's 1,600-km border with India, Dixit reiterated the stand of non-interference in its internal affairs. This paved the way for a pragmatic working relationship with the military junta to develop economic and political contacts in order to reduce China's influence over Rangoon. New Delhi also lent its support, albeit belatedly, to ASEAN's "constructive engagement" policy. In May 1998, however, Burma found itself caught up in India-China tensions. Indian Defense Minister George Fernandes singled out China as his country's biggest threat, accusing Beijing (among other things) of building up a military presence along Burma's Indian Ocean coastline, and Indian Prime Minister A. B. Vajpayee gave "deteriorating security environment" as a result of China's strategic encirclement as one of the reasons for going nuclear.[35] During the Indian foreign secretary's visit to Rangoon in March 1999, a broad-based dialogue for understanding each other's security concerns was initiated along with agreement on measures for enhanced security and border management for facilitating foreign trade and future cross-border projects. India offered to step up its engagement in return for the junta's cooperation in flushing out separatist groups using Burma's dense forests as a sanctuary.[36] In October 2004, less than a week after the dramatic ouster of pro-China intelligence chief Khin Nyunt, when Chairman General Than Shwe made his first-ever official visit to New Delhi, the Indian government rolled out the red carpet for the junta leader. Amongst several declarations, the two sides signed a memorandum on non-traditional security cooperation, which was soon followed by coordinated joint military operations against Manipuri and Naga rebels operating on the India-Burma frontier.

The second prong of India's revamped Burma strategy was to find a complementarity of interests with those Southeast Asian countries which shared New Delhi's perception of "the China threat." Historically, Southeast Asian countries had seen "the China threat" as emerging from the east through Indochina and the South China Sea. However, Chinese expansion through Burma into the Indian Ocean amounted to the opening of a new front for Southeast Asian countries in the west as well. It presented New Delhi with an opportunity to establish defense ties and undertake joint naval exercises with Thailand, Malaysia, Indonesia, Singapore, Vietnam, and the Philippines. India's support for ASEAN's "constructive engagement" with Burma also dovetailed well with New Delhi's "Look East" policy of establishing closer ties with Southeast Asia to prevent the region from becoming an exclusive Chinese sphere of influence—an objective shared by the United States and Japan.

With Burma adding a maritime dimension to traditional Sino-Indian rivalry, neutralizing Chinese presence and influence in Burma and Southeast Asia has become a key driver in India's maritime strategy since the late 1990s. If anything, China's maritime expansion into the Indian Ocean validates long-held Indian suspicions about a strong China being an expansionist China. Media reports and interviews with policymakers suggest that ASEAN and Japan also share India's concerns about the implications of Chinese navy's access to Burmese bases. Just as the Indian strategists see the Indian Ocean as India's ocean, Chinese defense planners view the East and South China seas as China's own preserve. Just as China has stepped up its efforts to gain access to the Bay of Bengal and Andaman Sea through Burma and Bangladesh, India has been steadily increasing its naval forays into the South and East China Seas. Since 2000, India has been conducting naval exercises in South China Sea and the Pacific Ocean with Vietnam, Singapore, the Philippines, Japan, and the United States, much to Beijing's consternation. India is also involved in joint patrolling exercises with Thailand and Indonesia and has offered to cooperate with the littoral states in the implementation of the "Eyes in the Sky" program for patrolling the piracy-infested Straits of Malacca. Beijing's "string of pearls" strategy coupled with China's anti-piracy mission in the Gulf of Aden in 2008 have prompted the Indian navy to unveil a three-pronged strategy: fortify its defenses in the Indian Ocean by acquiring privileged access to bases in the Maldives, Mauritius, the Seychelles and Madagascar; conducting joint naval exercises in the East and South China Seas; and launching an ambitious naval modernization program.

If Burma is for China a critical entryway to the Bay of Bengal and the Indian Ocean and a "backdoor to India," for India, Burma is the land bridge that links it with Indo-China and Southeast Asia. In 1996 the Bangladesh, India, Myanmar [Burma], Sri Lanka, and Thailand Economic Cooperation (BIMSTEC) grouping was formed with a view to promoting economic and trade links among these South Asian and Southeast Asian countries. While China is developing a North-South transport corridor along the Irrawaddy River in Burma that will provide Beijing access to the Indian Ocean, rival India is pitching to gain an entry into Indo-China by building an East-West corridor cutting horizontally through Burma toward Thailand and Vietnam.[37] Competition between Asia's rising giants has intensified as both view the Southeast Asian region as a vital source of natural resources and a market for their goods. Following China's lead, India also concluded a free trade agreement with ASEAN. India is now amongst Burma's top five largest trading partners.

The last two decades have seen India proactively wooing the military junta, supplying it with non-lethal military aid, helping with its infrastructure projects, and providing it with low-interest loans. To promote closer economic links, India has become involved in several ambitious infrastructure projects in Burma. In 2001, the Indian Army's Border Roads Organization completed a 200-km road inside Burma between Tamu and Kaleymyo in Sagaing Division, and the two sides began discussions on the possibility of future energy tie-ups to exploit the significant gas reserves in Burma's Arakan region. India provided a soft loan of US$56.35 million to upgrade the Rangoon-Mandalay rail network. Given Bangladesh's reluctance (presumably under Chinese pressure) to grant transit facilities that will improve India's connectivity with its northeastern states, New Delhi is looking to develop a port at Sittwe as an alternative on Burma's northern coast, which links up to the Indian state of Mizoram through the Kaladan River. India offered the junta a $10 million loan for the Kaladan river project, which would connect via a multi-modal transport system its Sittwe and Kaletwa ports with Mizoram and build a 170-feet long "friendship bridge" on the Burmese–Mizoram border to facilitate cross-border trade. The development of this transportation route will also allow India to ship goods from Calcutta to its northeastern states through Sittwe port.

Furthermore, India is competing with China over exploration rights and access to Burma's energy resources. Regardless of India's efforts, however, the Chinese companies have always managed to grab a larger share of the contracts in Burma, either through their diplomatic and financial clout, or by exploiting India's weaknesses. In 2006, China upstaged India when PetroChina, and not India, signed the deal for 6.5 trillion cubic feet of natural gas. After pushing India's GAIL out, PetroChina has established a long-term control over the Shwe gas field reserves even though the shortest distance from the Burmese gas-field to China is three times more than that to India. China also continues to control most of Burma's mineral wealth. Furthermore, it was Chinese pressure on Rangoon that foiled India's designs to be the sole operator of Sittwe port. "Instead of BOT (Build, Operate and Transfer) desired by India, the agreement was eventually signed on the basis of BTU (Build, Transfer and Use)."[38] Historically, whenever there has been a conflict between Chinese and Indian interests, Rangoon has given greater importance to the Chinese interests than to those of India, for the Burmese dare not antagonize China. Not surprisingly, despite intense competition between China and India over Burma's ports, resources, and friendship, China continues to outbid and outperform India.

Most Indian observers and opinion makers concede that "India faces a strategic as well as a moral dilemma in Burma," and that the Indian government's attempts to "imitate China by sucking up to the Burmese generals" without Beijing's ruthlessness to punish or diplomatic and military clout to protect Burma have yielded few results.[39] In this context, Burma's decision in March 2007 to renege on an original deal to sell natural gas to India from two offshore Arakan fields is quite instructive. Even though Indian firms had a 30 percent stake in these fields, Rangoon chose to offer it to China as a way of expressing its gratitude for vetoing the January 2007 UNSC resolution censuring the military junta. The decision was clearly based on political expediency rather than economic logic, confirming the regime's prioritization of survival over prosperity. Such resource deals provide China with an additional incentive to defend the political status quo in Burma and shield its leaders from the wrath of the international community. Not only that, much to India's dismay, the junta has failed to flush out the north-eastern insurgents who continue to operate from Burmese soil with impunity.[40] A senior Indian intelligence officer complained recently that "[a]lthough we have been giving the military regime weapons and vehicles, the junta is not reciprocating in the same manner. We have been pressing for a crackdown on camps inside Burma, but Burma has turned a deaf ear to us."[41] While India has got little from its coddling of the military junta, the latter, in contrast, has gained substantially not only through economic cooperation but from the respectability and legitimacy that association with a democratic India brings. Aspiring to play a greater role on the world stage, democratic India has come under intense criticism and pressure from the international community for its failure to support political reform and for its coddling of Burma's military dictators to pursue mercantilist energy deals and balance of power games against China. Responding to western criticisms of India's "engage Burma" policy, Indian Foreign Minister Pranab Mukherjee retorted: "We have strategic and economic interests to protect in Burma. It is up to the Burmese people to struggle for democracy, it is their issue."[42] Discussions with policymakers and opinion makers reveal 4 key reasons for India's determination to court Rangoon, notwithstanding setbacks and disappointments on some fronts:

- Seek Burma's military cooperation in waging counter-insurgency (COIN) operations in India's northeastern states;

- Counter and neutralize China's growing presence and influence in Burma and in the Bay of Bengal and Andaman Sea;
- Gain access to Burma's market and its natural resources; and
- Use Burma as a strategic bridge to the east as part of India's "Look East" policy to integrate with ASEAN via trade and a railroad network linking India with Indochina.[43]

In short, India's Burma policy is motivated by geostrategic concerns of combating northeastern insurgents and drug-trafficking and weaning Burma away from China and geoeconomic imperatives of exploiting trade, investment, and resource extraction opportunities. It remains to be seen if India and Burma are able to meet the challenge of transforming the present bilateral relationship which is best described as one of "mutual vulnerability" into "mutual interdependence."

ASEAN's Dream: Turn a Pariah into a Player

Just as China and India are closely monitoring each other's moves, so are Southeast Asian neighbors keeping a close watch on developments in mainland Southeast Asia's largest country. Their main concern is that the Burmese military regime could become the new lynchpin of Chinese strategy for the expansion of its influence in Southeast Asia or the cockpit of major power rivalries. Indonesia publicly expressed this concern over the implications of China's reach into the Indian Ocean via Burma. In February 1997, President Soeharto paid an official visit to Rangoon and said that Burma's admission into the regional grouping was necessary to avoid "ASEAN's encirclement by China."[44] Instead of getting drawn into a strategic competition between India and China, or between China and Japan, ASEAN members' interests lie in balancing off one regional power against the other in order to maintain the delicate balance of power. Geostrategic realities also ensure that ASEAN cannot afford to ostracize Burma. Unlike outsiders, neighbors have to live with one another, forever. Arguing that ganging up on Rangoon is counterproductive, as it would push the Burmese further into China's strategic orbit, ASEAN since 1991 has pursued a policy of "constructive engagement."[45] Under this policy, ASEAN has sought to encourage reform in Burma by maintaining commercial and political contacts and resisting Western pressure for sanctions. In July 1994, Burma was invited to join the ASEAN Post-Ministerial Conference as an observer and signed the Treaty of Amity and Cooperation, an essential prerequisite for becoming a member of ASEAN. Vietnam was admitted into ASEAN in 1995, and Burma (along with Laos) became a full member of ASEAN in 1997 (Cambodia joined in 1999). With the inclusion of all regional countries, the ASEAN has finally achieved the vision of its founding fathers, the incorporation of all ten Southeast Asian countries in the regional grouping. From ASEAN's perspective, Vietnam in the southeast and Burma in the southwest serve as two pillars in shoring up the regional defenses, in neutralizing any threat of "Finlandization" of Southeast Asia, and as a bulwark against major power expansion in the long term.[46] Turning a regional pariah into a regional player would be the first step in that direction.

ASEAN's "constructive engagement" policy coupled with economic difficulties and the need to assuage regional concerns about changes in Rangoon's foreign policy orientation have led Burma's military junta to open the door to foreign investment and renew contacts with its Southeast Asian neighbors. Indonesian, Malaysian, and Singaporean leaders have made official visits to Rangoon, and SPDC leaders and officials regularly visit a number of ASEAN countries. Until the collapse of the Soeharto regime, Indonesia was widely seen as a model for Burma's own version of a military-based *dwifungsi* (dual function) socio-political system. The junta has sought to align Burma with the economies and tourist industries of southern China, Singapore, Vietnam, Thailand, Malaysia, and Indonesia. During 2000–09, ASEAN states had invested approximately $4.2 billion in Burma's manufacturing joint ventures. After China, Singapore, Thailand, Malaysia, and India are the top four investors in Burma. Regional trade gives the military government just enough income to maintain its current hold on power. Though this policy has enabled some ASEAN countries to benefit economically, politically it has had no effect. In fact, the military junta has exploited internal divisions within ASEAN and regional fears of the country's pro-China tilt to take the heat off its human rights violations and to further consolidate its rule.

Limitations of "Constructive Engagement"

The "constructive engagement" strategy pursued by ASEAN (and backed by India, Japan, and Australia) has imparted the military regime greater confidence and legitimacy and also won it membership in the coveted Asia-Europe Summit (ASEM) while giving little or nothing in return. It has neither produced national reconciliation nor succeeded in the restoration of the democratic process nor in securing the release of opposition leaders. More generally, the military regime, as its hold on power has become firmer, is increasingly seeking greater international ties and legitimacy on its own terms. Perhaps like Pakistani military leaders' dangerous dalliances with terrorism and proliferation that endanger international security, Burmese generals apparently believe that their impoverished but strategically-located country is also of such great geopolitical importance that it can earn significant "geostrategic rents" and make the international community turn a blind eye to their appalling behavior.[47]

One of the basic justifications for ASEAN's policy of "constructive engagement" with the military regime was to wean it away from China. A majority of Southeast Asian analysts and policymakers now publicly acknowledge that the policy has been a failure. In fact, by raising regional concerns about Burma's strategic alignment with China and offering some economic inducements, the military regime has used ASEAN's engagement to its own advantage. It has helped the junta entrench itself in power and increased the clout of the regime, while the military has cornered all the benefits of ASEAN, Chinese, and Indian investments. During the 1997–99 Asian economic crisis and on several occasions since then, SPDC Chairman General Than Shwe has made it clear that Burma would further develop relations with "big brother" China so as to take advantage of its rapid economic growth. Even the new name of the junta, the State *Peace and Development* Council, sounded very "Chinese" to students of Chinese affairs. While ASEAN set out to change the regime's policies, the regime chose to change only its name. This was a clever move as it created a permanent long-term institutional function for the armed forces as opposed to the temporary "law and order" duty implied in the State Law and Order Restoration Council (SLORC). Pro-democracy activists rightly claimed that SPDC was merely "old wine in a new bottle" on sale to the ASEAN. Even in addressing transnational threats to regional security originating from Burma, such as the cross-border drug trade, smuggling, prostitution, the AIDS epidemic, and environmental problems caused by indiscriminate logging and mining, not much progress has been made either. There is no end in sight to these problems, while the SPDC avoids addressing the underlying issue, which caused the drug-producing insurgent armies to take up arms in the first place: that is, the need for a pluralist and democratic regime in Rangoon.

While the SPDC has withstood all international criticism and pressure, its refusal to change its ways has put ASEAN's cherished consensus diplomacy under pressure. In 1996–97, for the first time in ASEAN history, an open split developed within ASEAN between pro-democracy states (the Philippines and Thailand, supported from the outside by South Korea and Taiwan), which cautioned against rushing Burma into ASEAN's fold and wanted Burma's induction into ASEAN made conditional on the restoration of the democratic process, and anti-democracy states (Indonesia and Malaysia), which cautioned against waiting, while Singapore was somewhere in between, at times tilting toward the military regime. Eventually the latter got their way, but this in turn put ASEAN on a collision course with the United States over human rights issues and with the European Union over Burma's participation in the Asia-Europe Meetings (ASEM).

Clearly, ASEAN could not compete with China either in providing military assistance or in offering trade and investment benefits, especially in times of economic adversity. The organization failed to achieve any of the goals that it set for Burma's incorporation in 1997 because, as Abdul Razak Beginda put it: "The much-vaunted 'ASEAN way' came in the way of regional cooperation on a whole range of issues."[48] Even as ASEAN grew more critical of the junta, China shielded the junta from international criticism, allowing it to prop up an ailing economy and resist pressure to expedite political reform. No other regional government has as much leverage over Burma to move that country toward political moderation as China's because of Beijing's long history of involvement in that country's domestic politics. However, the Chinese paranoia about other countries' designs to checkmate China makes Beijing prefer *stability* to regime change in Burma.

Can Burma be a Pivotal Player?

As noted earlier, Burma is richly endowed with vast natural and human resources, including one of the largest forest reserves in Asia and soils that once produced a considerable proportion of the world's rice. Little of its potential wealth has been exploited. This is a fact not lost upon many of its neighbors. Its size and geostrategic location mean that it has the *potential* to be a key regional player. A non-aligned, neutral, united, democratic, and prosperous Burma will certainly be a stabilizing factor in Asia. However, what are Burma's prospects of defying or escaping from the "tyranny of geography"? This section addresses the problems and prospects of Burma's transformation from a pawn to a pivot. More specifically, it looks at Burma's role in the Sino-Burmese-Indian triangular relationship, especially from the perspective of China-watchers and Chinese strategists, and concludes with some doubts about Burma's ability to be an independent regional player for the foreseeable future.

Burma's Options

Seen from Rangoon's perspective, too much dependence on China is not in Burma's national interests. While the Chinese embrace might have ensured the military regime's survival, it also entailed significant costs. It went against the strategic tradition of self-reliance, ethnic pride, and the Buddhist philosophy of following the "Middle Path." Moreover, it restricted Burma's freedom of action and significantly diluted its national sovereignty. The abandonment of Burma's traditional neutrality has drawn the country into the Sino-Indian rivalry and caused sharp differences within ASEAN. Tin Maung Maung Than notes: "[Burma's leaders] have always been conscious and appreciative of external sensitivities to defense and security issues and have constantly taken great pains to avoid situations which would give the slightest excuse for foreign aggression or intervention in domestic affairs."[49]

In the past, Burma gave obeisance to China in exchange for respect for its independence and minimal intervention in Burma's internal affairs. However, arms transfers and economic ties have now dramatically increased China's influence within Burma. In fact, a few years of trade and military aid have turned the non-aligned state of Burma into China-dependent ally, an objective which the three decades of Chinese support for the BCP insurgency failed to achieve. Not surprisingly, dissatisfied groups accused the powerful intelligence chief Lieutenant General Khin Nyunt (sacked in 2004) of selling out to the Chinese.[50] Burma's markets are flooded with cheap Chinese consumer goods. "Road construction in the north, private investment in north-central towns and cities, and consumer products of every sort all reflect the embrace of the classic big brother-cum-enemy."[51] Burmese nationalist leaders like Maung Aye are reportedly concerned over the Chinese domination of the Burmese economy, the plunder of the country's natural resources and raw materials (timber, jade, and precious stones), a widening trade deficit, and large-scale illegal Chinese immigration. A massive influx of ethnic Chinese into northern Burma, who have taken over houses, hotels, and businesses and forced the local inhabitants to move to the outlying areas, has generated concerns that if unchecked, the changing demographic balance may spark communal violence similar to the anti-Chinese riots of 1967. Nearly 30 per cent of Mandalay's population of around 1.3 million is estimated to be ethnic Chinese, and much of the business in border towns has moved into Chinese hands, creating a potential source of social unrest. Obviously, all is not well between Burma and China behind the bonhomie and façade of "brotherly relations." This was bought into sharp focus in

August 2009 when Burma's military disarmed the ethnic Chinese Kokang rebel group, triggering an exodus of more than 37,000 refugees into China, and prompting an outburst of anger from Beijing.

Historically, Burmese leadership has sought to hedge its bets, playing off friend and foe alike to ensure survival. Burma's national interests lie in counterbalancing China's influence and power through its ties with India, ASEAN, Japan, and the West. Burma is no longer as isolated as it was in the early 1990s. Indeed, the SPDC has been using India as a bargaining chip in its dealings with China. Economic reforms in India and Burma are laying the foundations for stronger economic ties. Both have agreed on joint economic developments in their border regions, construction of a bridge across the river Tiau, to supply Indian electricity to several remote Burmese villages, and to take joint security measures against insurgents and drug dealers. Internally, the regime has succeeded in continuing military control and maintaining the unity of their state by concluding cease-fire agreements with minority groups, building infrastructure, and accumulating foreign exchange earnings (over $5 billion, mostly through gas sales to China and Thailand) after a previous bankrupt regime. That the junta is getting wary of over-dependence on China militarily as well is apparent from their efforts to diversify sources of their weapons acquisition from Russia, India, Pakistan, North Korea, Israel, Poland, and the Czech Republic. Russia has sold MiG-29 fighter aircraft and signed a deal to build a nuclear power reactor.[52] Furthermore, sustained economic growth, greater involvement in regional affairs, and membership in ASEAN and the ASEAN Regional Forum (ARF) provides the Burmese regime with powerful leverage and strong incentives to desist from making policy choices which arouse regional concerns. By resolving the domestic political deadlock, it would not only be able to develop a more balanced policy toward China and India, but also obtain new trading, investment, and financing opportunities in the West and East.

Indeed, the Burmese leadership, extremely sensitive about the country's sovereignty and independence and always suspicious of Beijing's long-term intentions, cannot be happy with a situation which allows Chinese domination of the important aspects of Burma's foreign policy or Burmese society. As Stanley Weiss points out, Burma's intensely nationalistic leaders are paranoid and proud in equal measure.[53] The generals who rule Burma today cut their teeth fighting against Beijing-backed ethnic insurgencies in the 1960s. Despite Beijing's support over the past 20 years, they remain deeply suspicious of Chinese designs on their country. The SPDC remains adamant that it will not allow foreign troops on its soil.[54] Some analysts point out that by exaggerating the *potential* Chinese threat to the region over Beijing's strategic thrust into the Bay of Bengal through participation in military and transport infrastructure, India and ASEAN have already put pressure on the military regime to modify its political stance and distance itself from China.[55] Despite all the hype about Chinese incursions into the Indian Ocean, objective observers concede that given the limited amphibious, sea endurance, and sealift capabilities of China's navy to perform sustained operations in the Indian Ocean, China still has a long way to go before it can think of dominating the Indian Ocean.

Besides, the continuation of the political status quo within Burma itself cannot be taken for granted. The NLD supporters continue to focus international media attention on the military regime's lack of a popular mandate. Remote though it may seem, one cannot rule out the possibility of the SPDC being overthrown by a popular movement for democratic change. Optimists believe that time is on the side of democratic forces worldwide. The collapse of President Soeharto's "New Order" regime in 1999—the inspiration of Burma's military rulers—thoroughly exposed the bankruptcy of the "Indonesian model" of army-directed state building. If Indonesia's today is Burma's tomorrow, Burma is, to borrow a Clintonian phrase, on the "wrong side of history."

In addition, the state of affairs in Burma is making Rangoon's allies, friends, and critics alike ponder the consequences of their policies and actions for regional security. Beijing is under pressure to stop protecting tyrants in its neighborhood and around the world (North Korea, Burma, Pakistan, Iran, Sudan, and Zimbabwe) if China wants to win respect as a responsible global great power. For any violent crackdown on peaceful demonstrators by the junta reflects badly on China itself and its willingness to support dictatorial regimes. Policymakers in India wonder whether the bizarre spectacle of the world's largest democracy courting one of the world's most repressive regimes propped up by the world's largest authoritarian state (China) is in the long-term interests of India's national security.[56] Ultimately, a united, nonaligned, democratic Burma at peace with itself and fully engaged with the wider world is seen as an asset for India in transforming its eastern periphery. Many within ASEAN are pressing for mid-course correction because its policy of "constructive engagement" has started yielding diminishing returns. And the United States and European Union are rethinking their policy of imposing sanctions that has clearly failed to deliver the desired outcome during the past 20 years. The United Nations has repeatedly urged China, India, and ASEAN to use their influence to press for dialogue between the regime and its political opposition. In 2004, this author had proposed that with the UN-brokered talks on political reconciliation having reached a dead end, it might be worthwhile to start afresh with a dialogue framework of ASEAN+3 (ASEAN plus China, India and Japan) on Burma. This would also test China's oft-stated commitment to multilateralism and Beijing's penchant for "Asian solutions to Asian problems."[57] The idea has gradually gained regional and international support. Following widespread protests by the Buddhist monks in Rangoon, Thai prime minister General Surayud Chulanont suggested in October 2007 the creation of a regional forum to solve the Burmese crisis in a One Plus Three framework, comprising ASEAN, India, China, and the UN, modeled on the Six-Party Talks on North Korea. In 2009, the Obama Administration outlined its support for a new "collaborative and constructive" approach to Burma with India, China, and Japan. Cautioning Asian giants against competing with each other for influence in "a mini-version of the Great Game," Jim Steinberg, US deputy secretary of state, said in April 2009 that a better approach would be to persuade India, China, and others to come together in a multilateral forum to engage Burma, along the lines of the Six-Party Talks over North Korea. However, Burma's principal patron—China—seems reluctant to articulate and support such a forum ostensibly for fear of damaging its ties with Rangoon.[58] But then China was initially reluctant to host the Six-Party Talks on North Korea too. It changed its stance once the potential costs of inaction outweighed any benefits. Once a new multilateral approach to Burma begins to take shape, China will not want to be seen as the odd man out on an issue of importance to national security. Nor does political stalemate augur well for the long-term protection of China's interests and investments in that country. Therefore, Chinese pragmatism and interests would make Beijing jump into the fray once a multilateral initiative on Burma gathers momentum both because maintenance of the status quo in Burma is untenable and because Beijing holds a unique capacity to influence its neighbor's future.[59] Besides, as China assumes a greater economic and political profile on the international stage, Beijing is sensitive to the fact that its international behavior, especially its alliance relationships, are coming under greater scrutiny.[60]

If all these conditions are met, and that is indeed a big "if," the negative implications of Burma's recent pro-Beijing tilt can be contained. However, events over the last two decades do not lend much confidence to the junta's ability to play a fine line on issues of national and international importance. Aung San Suu Kyi is of the view that the military rulers "are like a chess player who only thinks one or two moves ahead."[61] This assessment is reinforced by Singaporean statesman Lee Kuan Yew, who has doubts about outsiders' ability to save Burma from itself.[62] Given Burma's dependence on China for military hardware, training, spare parts, financial assistance, industrial equipment, and diplomatic support, Beijing can apply considerable pressure on the regime, be it military or civilian, to prevent its defection from China's camp. ASEAN's "constructive engagement" policy notwithstanding, China still remains Burma's main trading partner, arms supplier, and a steadfast supporter in international forums such as the UN Security Council (UNSC) where Beijing has a veto. Neither ASEAN nor India can compete with China either in providing diplomatic protection or military assistance or in offering trade and investment benefits. Perhaps recognizing this, the Burmese generals always favor Chinese oil and gas companies over their Indian competitors, inking larger deals with China.

Chinese Checkers

As noted above, China, of all the regional stakeholders, has a lot at stake in Burma. Since the early 1990s, Rangoon has come to rely heavily on China—which controls more than 60 percent of the Burmese economy—for support and sustenance. (In 2004 alone, China concluded 33 trade and aid agreements with Burma.) For its part, the military regime values its relations with China more than any other country because Beijing's backing has been invaluable to the regime's survival. For China, the payoff goes beyond geoeconomics to geopolitics, gaining access through Burma to the Indian Ocean. Its intent to steer a more balanced foreign policy notwithstanding, the Burmese junta may not find much room for maneuver. As one Burma-watcher has argued: "China is developing such a hold on Burma's economy and armed forces that it will constrain the Rangoon regime's ability to act independently in the future."[63]

The strategic context in which China views its relationship with Burma is as a close ally both for southward expansion and to counteract the moves of its rival powers. China sees itself as being engaged in a long and protracted competition with other major powers and counts Burma, along with Pakistan and North Korea, as its military allies in Asia. The cozy Sino-Burmese relationship has certainly served to significantly reduce the US, Indian and Japanese presence in a country on China's southern flank. In fact, Burma has now come to occupy the same place in China's calculus of deterrence vis-à-vis India in South and Southeast Asia that Pakistan has long occupied in South and Southwest Asia. A survey of Chinese commentaries shows that Beijing perceives its presence in Burma in zero-sum terms within the larger context of great power politics in the Asia-Pacific.[64] From China's perspective, Burma should be satisfied to gain a powerful friend—a permanent member of the UNSC, and a global superpower who comes bearing gifts of much needed military hardware and economic aid. Since influence over Burma is the key to China's future strategy for South and Southeast Asia, Beijing will use all means available to keep Burma within its orbit. Clearly, Beijing did not provide diplomatic protection, arms, aid, and finance—all on very generous terms—to Rangoon in its hour of need for nothing. China's prospects for economic growth depend on finding raw materials, markets for its goods, investment for its economy and bases to protect them all. Self-interest motivated the Chinese to use their influence in cutting off aid to the Burmese rebels in an effort to gain better access to the resource-rich border region and the accompanying trade benefits.

Proximity and complementarity also work in China's favor. In confirmation of the classic "dependency theory" school of international economic relations, Burma plays the role of exporter of raw materials, timber, minerals, and energy resources while China exports finished manufactured goods, from shoes and rice cookers to electronics, heavy trucks, and railway equipment that conform to Burma's level of development and spending power. To strengthen this economic nexus, more than 1.5 million Chinese nationals, entrepreneurs, and traders have moved to settle down south of the border in the past two decades. Beijing's declaratory policy of non-interference in another country's internal affairs notwithstanding, the Chinese have a long history of interference in Burmese politics either through their support for the opposition parties (the BCP and various ethnic groups) or for government-led forces for more than half a century.[65] As one Burma-watcher has pointed out, since 1990 in particular, "Beijing has disturbed government-society relations by providing arms to the regime and helped to shift the center of political power toward the military."[66] If Burma's attempts to steer an even-handed course undermine China's economic and security interests in the region, Beijing could resume assistance to ethnic insurgents fighting for independence or help engineer a coup by the down-but-not-out pro-China faction within the Burmese military. China, after all, has a reputation for using threats and bluff to force other states (friends and foes alike) to accede to its will. It is worth recalling that following the purge of intelligence chief Khin Nyunt in 2004, Prime Minister Soe Win personally assured Chinese leaders that their interests would be well-protected under the "new" political dispensation. With the weight of cash, muscle and population on the Chinese side, Burma is likely to remain highly dependent on its northern neighbor. And by choice or by necessity, Sino-Burmese relations are going to follow a pattern of Chinese domination.

Last but not least, ideological affinity between the two authoritarian regimes provides the political glue to stick together. Both have a siege-mentality and remain strongly opposed to political pluralism in any form. The bloodbath when the junta seized power in 1988 was matched, less than a year later, by the Tiananmen massacre in China in June 1989. Ironically, the Buddhist-monks-led 2007 "saffron revolution" was followed months later by widespread unrest in Tibet in March 2008. Leaders in both countries combine appeals to nationalism and xenophobia with "cultural" arguments that claim, unpersuasively, that Asians are not receptive to Western-style concepts of human rights and democracy. The Chinese ruling elite has long looked upon Western-style democracy as a potentially subversive force, which could have a disintegrating influence in China—particularly in its peripheral regions such as Tibet. In particular, the Chinese worry that if the Buddhist-monks-led "saffron revolution" ever succeeds in Burma, it would have spill-over effects in neighboring Tibet. To further consolidate its hold over power, the military-dominated constituent assembly has adopted guidelines which grant the military "a leading role in the future political life of the state," and eliminate the possibility that Aung San Suu Kyi could hold office.[67] The "Beijing consensus" model of "development-before-democracy" holds special appeal for Burma's leadership.

The Chinese paranoia about other countries' designs to contain China also makes Beijing prefer *stability* to regime change in Burma. Since China is already encircled by a large number of pro-West democratic states such as Mongolia, South Korea, Japan, Taiwan, the Philippines, Nepal, and India, it is not in Beijing's interests to see Burma becoming a liberal-democratic state. At the most, Beijing would prefer another Pakistan/Bangladesh-like quasi-democratic state where civilians hold power so long as the military tolerates them, and that military is paranoid of its neighbors, and therefore, remains heavily dependent on China for weapons, training, and support. Beijing sees ulterior motives behind Washington's attempts to portray the junta as a threat to international peace and security. As in North Korea, Iran, and Sudan, Beijing would not support UN-backed punitive sanctions or international intervention and a regime change in Burma that might jeopardize its own strategic privileges, commercial concessions, and political interests in Burma. The SPDC's fall from power would constitute a significant defeat for Chinese foreign policy. Although Beijing reportedly backs engagement with Aung San Suu Kyi, it certainly does not want to see her leading a popularly-elected democratic government in her country.[68] For Suu Kyi is known to be closer to India, Japan, and the West than to China. After all, Suu Kyi's NLD blames Beijing's military and diplomatic support to the junta for the current political impasse and sees the provision of access to the Chinese navy into the Andaman Sea as an infringement of Burmese sovereignty. The Chinese fear that political change in Rangoon in the near future, in particular, the coming to power of an Aung San Suu Kyi-led democratic government, could lead to a situation where China is denied access to the very naval facilities and railroad infrastructure it is now building, and this would constitute a major setback for Chinese foreign policy. As Liu Naiqiang observes:

> If the tension and instability persist, once the military regime is overthrown and the pro-Western Aung San Suu Kyi comes into power, the encirclement of China in South Asia by the United States and Britain will be even tighter.... Even if it [the Chinese-Burmese oil pipeline] gets built, its security will be badly compromised and the strategic objective behind the original plan will remain unfulfilled.[69]

Apparently, Beijing would not like to see any political change in Burma that might lead to the installation of a less friendly regime to China. Beijing's topmost priority is to have a Burmese government that maintains patron-client relations and fulfils its economic need for natural resources and its geostrategic goal to seek access through Burma by river, railroad, and port network toward the Bay of Bengal and Andaman Sea.

Conclusion

A realistic assessment of China's strategic and economic needs and Burma's predicament shows that Beijing is unlikely to easily give up what it has already gained in and through Burma. China would want Burma to be securely within its sphere of influence forever. A Chinese Burma expert, Jian Junbo, contends: "Whatever happens, China is unlikely to withdraw from Myanmar [Burma] ... China needs Myanmar's raw materials, and more importantly needs its ports to transport goods to other countries in Africa and Middle East."[70] The increasing Chinese domination of northern Burma's economy has demographic, cultural, economic, security, diplomatic, and political repercussions. Burma's rulers know too well that China is the only Asian great power that has the will and capability to protect its allies and safeguard its interests. No matter how much the rest of the world agitates against Rangoon, the military junta feels at ease under China's protective umbrella and little need to change its ways. Nothing works like oil and geopolitics blended with trade and commerce in inter-state relations. Neither ASEAN nor India nor the United States is capable of imposing penalties or offering rewards to make Beijing give up what it has already acquired in and through Burma.

As noted earlier, Burma has historically accommodated China as its "big brother" by not exercising or even expressing any policies and actions detrimental to China's security interests. If *resisting while accommodating* was the strategic tradition vis-à-vis China in the past, then *accommodating while resisting* the "big brother" may well be the trend of the future primarily for two reasons. First, the regime has not only capitalized on regional fears of the country's pro-China tilt to take the heat off its human rights violations, but has also consolidated its rule and, for the first time, extended its control to cover almost the entire country. Secondly, by moving closer to China, Burma has developed strategic ties with the only country in the world that can seriously threaten (and historically, has threatened) its security interests. Thirdly, since China's extraordinary economic growth has created a nearly insatiable appetite for energy resources, Chinese diplomacy remains focused on exploiting Burma's natural resources and extending Beijing's strategic reach into the Bay of Bengal. In this context, India's Burma policy coupled with growing maritime ties with the South China Sea littorals, Japan, and the United States under its "Look East" policy exacerbates China's rivalry with India. Even a Burma optimist like Andrew Selth seems to agree with this assessment:

> The transition back to a more neutral and economically independent Burma will be neither quick nor easy, *particularly if this shift is opposed by China*. The latter's hold over Burma is already strong, and its strategic weight is steadily increasing as its economy grows and its defence forces are modernised. Also, *the bilateral relationship is developing a life of its own*, and is already affecting areas which may be beyond either the SLORC's [junta's], or China's, ability to control.[71]

Over the long term, though, as China changes, as Burma's political and economic standing improves, and as its economy becomes more integrated with the wider world along with the evolution of regional organizations into an effective multilateral security forum, Rangoon could find greater freedom of action and move a little bit away from Beijing, but still it would not go very far for fear of antagonizing the superpower on its doorstep. Given its place in China's grand strategy in the twenty-first century, Burma is unlikely to play the role of an independent or pivotal player in regional security affairs. In other words, the prospects of Burma regaining its "lost" neutral status vis-à-vis China—this time not as a poor and isolated, but as a fully engaged, democratic, prosperous, and confident nation—do not look very bright. The close and cozy relationship with China is likely to last long after Burma ceases to be shunned by the West. Important geopolitical developments in the region will, of course, affect Burma's internal politics and external orientation. For the foreseeable future, the military seems likely to maintain its iron grip on power in Burma. Unless a vertical split emerges within the Burmese military into pro- and anti-democracy factions along the lines of the Philippines Armed Forces in the mid-1980s, and until Beijing adopts a posture of strict neutrality in Burma's domestic politics, no popularly elected civilian government is likely to emerge in Rangoon. Given China's enormous equities in Burma, Beijing seems unwilling to abandon a winning position in favor of an uncertain multilateral framework to bring about regime change. However, in the event of a sudden political change post-Than Shwe, China can be expected to do a Cambodia on Burma. The sharp U-turn undertaken in the 1990s in Beijing's policy toward the Hun Sen government (China's erstwhile nemesis) in Cambodia to protect and promote Chinese interests could be replicated in Burma too. As in the past, so in the future: Burma will remain an important factor in the Sino-Indian rivalry and regional security calculations.

Notes

[1] In 1989, the Burmese military regime made Myanmar the official English name for Burma; it is a transliteration of the official Burmese language name for the country. The military in Burmese is referred to as the *tatmadaw*.

[2] Editorial, "China's satellite," *The Irrawaddy*, July 10, 2007, 4; B. McCartan, "China's footprint in Myanmar expands," *Asia Times online*, November 1, 2008 <http://www.atimes.com/atimes/China_Business/JK01Cb02.html>.

[3] See J. Mohan Malik, "Sino-Indian rivalry in Myanmar: implications for regional security," *Contemporary Southeast Asia*, 16:2 (September 1994), 137-156; P. Stobdan, "China's forays into Burma: implications for India," *Strategic Analysis* (New Delhi), 16:1 (April 1993); D. Steinberg, "Myanmar as nexus: Sino-Indian rivalries on the frontier," *Studies in Conflict and Terrorism*, 16:1 (1993); A. Selth, "Burma and the strategic competition between China and India," *The Journal of Strategic Studies*, 19:2 (June 1996), 213-230.

[4] P. Katzenstein (ed.), *The Culture of National Security: Norms and Identity in World Politics*. (New York: Columbia University Press, 1996); Y. Klein, "A theory of strategic culture," *Comparative Strategy*, 10:2 (1991), 5-17.

[5] Maung Than, "Myanmar: Myanmar-ness and realism in historical perspective," in K. Booth and R. Trood (eds), *Strategic Cultures in the Asia-Pacific Region* (New York: St. Martin's Press, 1999), 166.

[6] Maung Than, "Myanmar: Myanmar-ness and realism in historical perspective," 166.

[7] D. M. Seekins, "Historical background," in E. M. Bunge (ed.), *Burma: A Country Study* (Washington: The American University 1983), 66.

[8] A. Bezlova, "China cherishes its 'jade kingdom,'" *Asia Times online*, October 3, 2007 <http://www.atimes.com/atimes/China/IJ03Ad01.html>. Analyst Maung Zarni says that "Chinese soldiers wore Burmese Communist [Party] military uniform and they participated in actual battles against the Burmese armed forces." See B. Blanchard, "China casts nervous eye at erstwhile ally Myanmar," *Reuters*, January 25, 2010 <http://www.reuters.com/article/idUSTRE60O0112010012>.

[9] Maung Than, "Myanmar: Myanmar-ness and realism in historical perspective," 173.

[10] Maung Than, "Myanmar: Myanmar-ness and realism in historical perspective," 174.

[11] B. Matthews, "The present fortune of tradition-bound authoritarianism in Myanmar," *Pacific Affairs,* 71:1 (1998), 9, 7-23.

[12] B. Lintner, "Burma: centrifugal forces," *Far Eastern Economic Review* [hereafter *FEER*], February 27, 1992, 16.

[13] W. Ashton, "Chinese bases in Burma-fact or fiction," *Jane's Intelligence Review [JIR]*, 7:2 (February 1995), p. 84; B. Lintner, "Burma: arms for eyes," *FEER*, December 16, 1993, 26.

[14] W. Ashton, "Burma's armed forces: preparing for the 21st century," *JIR,* (November 1998), 28.

[15] B. Lintner, *Burma in Revolt: Opium and Insurgency since 1948* (Boulder, Colorado: Westview Press, 1994), 84; Stobdan, "China's forays into Burma," 25, 27.

[16] S. A. Weiss "Myanmar's neighbors hold the key," *International Herald Tribune [IHT]*, March 7, 2007.

[17] Stobdan, "China's forays into Burma," 34.

[18] B. Lintner, "Rangoon's Rubicon," *FEER*, February 11, 1993, 28.

[19] B. McCartan, "China's footprint in Myanmar expands," *Asia Times online*, November 1, 2008 <http://www.atimes.com/atimes/China_Business/JK01Cb02.html>.

[20] Y. Bodansky, "PRC revives military threat to Taiwan as a prelude to wider expansion," *Defense & Foreign Affairs Strategic Policy*, (July-August 1995), 11.

[21] General Zhao quoted in *Time*, May 10, 1993, 39; "China's plan to build up navy," *Hindustan Times*, January 13, 1993, 14. In the mid-1980s, the Chinese Foreign Ministry toyed with the idea of renaming the Indian Ocean the Afro-Asian Ocean (in August 1986, Zheng Ruixiang, a senior Chinese diplomat

and South Asia expert, asked the author about India's possible reaction to such a proposal). However, the Chinese apparently did not find any takers for the idea at that time. Besides, any proposal to rename the Indian Ocean would have opened a Pandora's box, with some Southeast Asian countries wanting to rename the South China Sea as the Southeast Asian Sea.

[22] Hua Di made this remark at a seminar at the Australian National University, Canberra, in May 1991.

[23] "Beijing expands its navy," *Inside China Mainland* [Taiwan], April 1993, 67.

[24] *FEER,* August 4, 1994, 6.

[25] Testimony of J. Genser, "China's role in the world: the China-Burma relationship," U.S.-China Economic and Security Review Commission, August 3, 2006, <http://www.uscc.gov/hearings/2006hearings/transcripts/aug_3_4/testimony_jared_genser.pdf>.

[26] G. Blainey, "Past and future wars," in R. Thakur (ed), *International Conflict Resolution* (Westview Press & University of Otago Press, 1988), 98.

[27] See Chu et al, "China's national security in the year 2000," cited in L. M. Wortzel, "China pursues traditional great-power status," *Orbis*, 38:2 (Spring 1994), 164.

[28] B. Lintner, "Burma's nuclear temptation," *YaleGlobal Online*, December 3, 2008 <http://yaleglobal.yale.edu/display.article?id=11673>.

[29] B. Chellaney, "The dragon's chicanery behind the smile," *The Pioneer* (New Delhi), October 23, 1996, 5; T. Mapes, "Nervous neighbours," *FEER*, December 12, 1996, 16-17.

[30] N. Mitra, "Corning closer," *Sunday,* August 23-29, 1992, 59.

[31] J. Singh, "Future of Sino-Indian relations," *Strategic Analysis*, 16:2 (March 1994), 1512.

[32] R. Sikri and M. Lall, "Whither India–Myanmar relations?" *Saag.org*, Paper No. 2341, August 22, 2007, <http://www.saag.org/papers24/paper2341.html>.

[33] Jane's Defence Weekly, November 27, 1993.

[34] R. Banerjee, "China: worrying approach," and S. Dasgupta, "The navy: in troubled waters," *India Today*, April 30, 1994, 70-71.

[35] For details, see Mohan Malik, "Nuclear proliferation in Asia: the China factor," *Australian Journal of International Affairs*, 53:1 (1999), 31-41.

[36] The Burmese Army is said to have carried out coordinated operations with the Indian Army since 1995 and again in February 2007. Special Correspondent, "Myanmar to act against anti-India groups," *The Hindu*, October 26, 2004, 1.

[37] C. Raja Mohan, "China's back door," *The Hindu*, April 7, 2002.

[38] See G. S. Khurana, "China-India maritime rivalry," *Indian Defence Review*, 23:4 (July-Sep 2009) <http://www.indiandefencereview.com/2009/04/china-india-maritime-rivalry.html>.

[39] Discussion here is based on discussions and interviews with Indian diplomats, journalists, and military officers in 2006-07. Also see B. Chellaney, "A forward-looking approach on Burma," *The Hindu*, May 14, 2008.

[40] A. G. Noorani, "Very unrealpolitik," *Hindustan Times*, October 22, 2007.

[41] "India-Burma secretary level talks in vain," September 12, 2008, <http://www.indoburmanews.net/archives-1/archive06/323/267/>.

[42] Quoted in J. Kurlantzick, "Burma's buddy—India's craven appeasement in Burma," *New Republic*, October 2, 2007.

[43] On India, China and ASEAN's interests, see Mohan Malik, "Burma's role in regional security," in M. B. Peterson, E. Rudland, R. J. May (eds), *Burma/Myanmar: Strong Regime Weak State?* (London and Adelaide: C. Hurst & Co/Crawford House Publishing, 2000), 241-277; R. Hariharan, "India–China–Myanmar relations," July 21, 2007, <http://www.newdelhireview.com>.

[44] Quoted from Paul Kelly in *Australian,* July 30, 1997, 8.

[45] "Constructive engagement"—defined by *The Straits Times* as "gentle persuasion and quiet diplomacy to prod the regime into political liberalization" - was premised on the idea that, by opening channels of communication and bringing foreign trade and investment into the country's closed economy, Burma would move toward political reform, writes J. Henderson, *Reassessing ASEAN,* Adelphi Paper 328 (London: International Institute for Strategic Studies, 1999), 26

[46] M. Richardson, "China's push for sea control angers ASEAN," *Australian*, July 23, 1996, 6; and "China-Burma ties upset neighbors," *IHT*, April 7, 1995, 4

[47] B. Lintner, "Trade and security trump democracy in Burma," *YaleGlobal online*, October 3, 2007, <http://yaleglobal.yale.edu/display.article?id=9754>.

[48] Author's conversation with Malaysian strategic analyst, 1997.

[49] Maung Than, "Myanmar: Myanmar-ness and realism in historical perspective," 173.

[50] B. Lintner, "Murmur in the ranks," *FEER*, February 16, 1993, 20.

[51] J. Badgley, "Myanmar in 1993," *Asian Survey*, 34:2 (February 1994), 158; A. Davis, "Burma casts wary eye on China," *JIR,* June 1999, 40-41.

[52] A. Kazmin, "Russia to build nuclear reactor for Burma," *Financial Times*, May 15, 2007.

[53] S. Weiss, "Whom do sanctions hurt?" *IHT*, February 20, 2009.

[54] "Myanmar and China: But will the flag follow trade?" *The Economist*, October 8, 1994, 32.

[55] W. Ashton, "Myanmar: Chinese naval base: many rumours, few facts," *Asia-Pacific Defence Reporter*, 19/20:12/1 (June/July 1993), 25.

[56] Critics say India's attempts to catch up with China in courting Burmese generals have yielded few results. Editorial, "India's identity crisis in Myanmar," *Boston Globe*, October 15, 2007; B. Raman, "India should not prove Gandhi wrong & irrelevant in Myanmar," *C3S Paper No.82*, December 5, 2007.

[57] Mohan Malik, "Regime shake-up in Rangoon: a setback for Beijing?" *China Brief*, 5:2 (January 18, 2005), 1-5.

[58] Jian Junbo, "China wary of US-Myanmar 'détente'."

[59] For details, see Mohan Malik, "Resolving the Burma imbroglio" in R. Wirsing (ed), *Fixing Fractured Nations* (Palgrave, 2010).

[60] W. Hoge, "China blocks move to condemn Myanmar, but backs UN envoy," *IHT*, September 27, 2007.

[61] Aung San Suu Kyi, quoted in *Economist*, June 1, 1996, 27.

[62] Lee Kuan Yew quoted in R. Tasker, "Fear of loathing: ASEAN keeps soft line on Rangoon junta," *FEER*, June 20, 1996.

[63] W. Ashton, "Burma receives advances from its silent suitors in Singapore," *JIR*, 10:3 (March 1998), 32.

[64] See Zhang Liwei, "Bai tuo Maliujia ha ixia yilai, kuaisu shi shi xi-jin zhanlue," ["Stop relying on the Malacca Strait, and speed up implementation of look-West strategies"], *Shiji Jingji Baodao*, March 16, 2009, 4; Liu Naiqiang, "China's energy diplomacy faces challenges ahead," *Nanfeng Chuang* [Guangzhou], November 16, 2007, 22-24. Jian Junbo, "China wary of US-Myanmar 'détente," *Asia Times online*, April 17, 2009 <http://www.atimes.com/atimes/China/KD17Ad01.html>.

[65] Bezlova, "China cherishes its 'jade kingdom'."

[66] B. Berger, "Why China has it wrong on Myanmar," *Asia Times online*, October 3, 2007, <http://www.atimes.com/atimes/China/IJ03Ad03.html>.

[67] M. P. Callahan, "Burma in 1995," *Asian Survey*, 36:2, (February 1996), 159.

[68] "China hedges regime bets," *Australian*, 1 October 2007.

[69] Liu Naiqiang, "China's energy diplomacy faces challenges ahead," *Nanfeng Chuang*, November 16, 2007, 22-24.

[70] Jian Junbo, "China wary of US-Myanmar 'détente.'"

[71] Selth, "Burma and the strategic competition between China and India," 226. Emphasis added.

8
The Proliferation Axis

The recent imposition of sanctions by the Bush Administration against Chinese and Pakistani entities for their assistance to North Korea's nuclear weapons and ballistic missile programs have not only once again drawn the international community's attention to the challenges facing the global nuclear non-proliferation (NNP) regime but also made public what has long been common knowledge in the intelligence and policymaking community. Amongst the first-tier five declared Nuclear Weapon States (NWS), the commitment of the People's Republic of China (PRC), the last signatory to the Nuclear Non-Proliferation Treaty (NPT), to the cause of non-proliferation has long been the subject of comment and criticism.[1] Despite Beijing's numerous pledges, assurances and legal commitments to the contrary, intelligence reports suggest that "the China shop" for nuclear and missile technology sales remains open for business.[2] China has been held responsible for aiding, either directly or indirectly, the proliferation of weapons of mass destruction (WMD) on the Korean Peninsula and in South Asia and the Middle East—the world's most flammable regions.[3] The nuclear weapons technology involved in North Korea's program—including large numbers of centrifuge machines to produce weapons-grade uranium—has its origins in Chinese assistance to Pakistan's nuclear program. To make matters worse, long-time recipients of WMD and missile-related technology from China, second-tier proliferators such as Pakistan and North Korea, are now disseminating WMD technologies

---

SOURCE: The body of this chapter was written in late 2002 and published in *The Korean Journal of Defense Analysis*, 15:1 (Spring 2003), pp 57-101. The analysis remains valid, and a postscript at the end of the chapter provides an update on events as of publication.

and expertise to third-tier nuclear aspirants such as Iran, Saudi Arabia, Syria, and Libya.[4]

More importantly, Chinese assistance to Pakistan and North Korea and Islamabad's nukes-for-missiles barter trade with Pyongyang epitomise the emergence of a set of mutually reinforcing proliferation linkages while highlighting the global nature of the nuclear problem and the blurring of the distinctions between Northeast Asian and South Asian security complexes. Proliferation of weapons of mass destruction to and from radicalized and volatile Pakistan or the unpredictable, Stalinist regime of North Korea, Saddamized Iraq, Khameini-ized Iran, or Wahabi-clergy-dominated Saudi Arabia could result in see a proliferation chain being transformed into an interactive, multi-dimensional, interlinked chain stretching from Syria to North Korea in the coming decades. Even more alarming is the prospect of Japan, South Korea, and Taiwan reconsidering their non-nuclear weapons stance to counter what they may perceive as the China-led bloc of nuclear powers.

This chapter discusses major proliferation trends in Asia and analyzes the motivations, objectives, and interests of China, Pakistan, and North Korea behind WMD proliferation. It argues that China and its proxies continue to be instrumental in fueling major proliferation crises large and small, imminent and somewhat more distant. North Korea and Pakistan, with their limited scientific and industrial capabilities and collapsing economies, could not have developed weapons of mass destruction without substantial technical and financial assistance from China and some of the Middle Eastern countries. Nor is it a sheer coincidence that the United States, Japan, South Korea, and India—countries that either see China as their rival or have strained ties with China—find themselves subjected to nuclear blackmail, terrorism, intimidation, and coercion by countries—North Korea and Pakistan—that happen to be China's allies. The last section provides an analysis of the implications of WMD proliferation for the Asian balance of power, especially for the Sino-US-Japanese triangular relationship, Sino-Korean relations, and the future of the global nuclear non-proliferation regime. It concludes that in the absence of great power consensus and coordinated strategy, nuclear and missile proliferation may well be unstoppable in the Asia-Pacific region.

WMD Friendship Store: Dangerous Liaisons

China bears a great deal of responsibility for nuclear proliferation in Asia given the assistance it has provided to Pakistan's and North Korea's nuclear/missile efforts over the years.[5] China's nuclear and missile technology transfers to Pakistan and North Korea have further implications for secondary, or retransferred, proliferation, since these two reportedly have supplied technology to Iran, Iraq, Saudi Arabia, Egypt, Libya, and Syria.[6] Throughout the 1980s and 1990s, the United States sought to persuade China to stop WMD proliferation activities, but to little or no avail.[7] Critics contend that if the so-called "Axis of Evil" ("AoE") countries have one thing in common, it is their "China connection." They argue that going by the "AoE" criteria (non-democratic/militarist regimes, hostility to the United States and its allies, track record in promoting proliferation and/or terrorism, and their capability to do terrible things), if North Korea is a card-carrying member of the "AoE," then Pakistan or China should also be included in President Bush's "Axis of Evil."[8] Unfortuantely, those China-watchers and arms- controllers who have long argued that Washington's confidence in bringing about a change in Beijing's non-proliferation policies and practices was misplaced have been proven right time and again. Neither inducements offered to China by the West (in the form of recognition of its status as a major power and access to world trade, capital, and technology) nor sanctions have succeeded in bringing a complete end to its dangerous liaisons with present and would-be bomb makers. The export of nuclear, chemical, and biological weapons material and missile technology to rogue states and unstable regions now has the potential to unravel the global non-proliferation regime in the early twenty-first century.

China-Pakistan

Of all the nations that China has helped, none has reaped more benefits than Pakistan, often getting materials it could not get elsewhere—highly enriched uranium (HEU), assistance with the building of an unsafeguarded 50-70-MWt plutonium production reactor at Khushab and plutonium reprocessing facility at Chasma, enough uranium hexafluoride feedstock to enable operation of Pakistan's centrifuges, ring magnets, and the machines for the production of weapons-grade uranium for its bombs.[9] All this was in contravention of non-proliferation pacts to which China is a party. It is no exaggeration to say that China was the chief instrument by which Pakistan got its bomb. That is why, soon after carrying out its nuclear tests in May 1998, Pakistan's Prime Minister Nawaz Sharief praised and thanked China for its contribution and help. According to Gary Milhollin, director of the Wisconsin Project on Nuclear Arms Control, "If you subtract China's help from the Pakistani nuclear program, there is no Pakistani nuclear program."[10] US intelligence documents over the past twenty years paint a thorough picture of close Sino-Pakistani cooperation in the nuclear field, which began following the signing of a secret Sino-Pakistani nuclear technology cooperation agreement in 1976.[11] All of Pakistan's nuclear labs—Kahuta, Khushab, or Chashma—have been aided by China. Some US intelligence reports even claim that one or two nuclear devices that Pakistan tested in May 1998 were actually Chinese. This would amount to a violation of the Comprehensive Test Ban Treaty (CTBT) that Beijing has signed, but not ratified. China not only provided Pakistan with nuclear plants and warheads but also their delivery systems: ready-to-launch M-9, M-11 and a number of *Dong Feng*-21 (renamed *Hatf, Shaheen I* and *Shaheen II* respectively) ballistic missiles.[12] China also helped Pakistan build a missile production factory near Rawalpindi. Chinese exports of missiles, components, and related technologies to Pakistan have led to repeated confrontations with the United States and the imposition of sanctions against China.[13]

Information collected by American, Israeli, and Indian intelligence agencies has shown that China is continuing covert assistance to Pakistan. There were unconfirmed reports of China's transfer of some of its tactical nukes to Pakistan and technical assistance for its short-range missiles and its medium-range *Shaheen II* missile during the 2001–2002 border stand-off between India and Pakistan following the terrorist attack on the Indian Parliament.[14] American satellite monitoring of northern Kashmir had detected truck movements of 12 consignments of Chinese missiles on May 1, 2002, via China and the Northern Areas of Pakistan along the Karakoram Highway. These transfers contradicted China's pledge in November 2001 "not to assist, in any way, any country in the development of ballistic missiles that could be used to deliver nuclear weapons."[15] China has also used Pakistan as a front in the arms trade with several Middle Eastern states. Close on the heels of revelations about Pakistani scientists' links with al-Qaeda came the reports of a Pakistani scientist's offer of help to Iraq soon after the 1990 invasion of Kuwait with nuclear weapon designs and bomb components and new allegations of a Pakistan-North Korea nexus. The alleged Islamabad-Baghdad WMD link comes in the wake of allegations that Pakistan helped North Korea go nuclear. Before that, Pakistani nuclear scientists were alleged to have met and offered help to Afghanistan's Taliban regime and Osama bin Laden.[16]

China–North Korea

While China-Pakistan nuclear and missile transfers are well known, well acknowledged and well documented, there is no consensus amongst intelligence agencies on the nature, extent, and duration of *direct* Chinese assistance to North Korea.[17] Though evidence is sketchy, it can be safely concluded that Beijing has contributed a great deal more to Pyongyang's long-range missile program than its nuclear weapons program. However, this assessment raises questions about whether China's nuclear technology has *indirectly* contributed to North Korea's nuclear weapons program through Pakistan, since China is the "principal supplier" to Pakistan's nuclear weapons program. Several hundred North Korean experts were trained in plutonium separation and other nuclear technologies in China (as well as in the former Soviet Union) during the 1960s and 1970s. China is also believed to have directly assisted North Korea's ballistic missile program.[18] Much like Pakistan's *Ghauri* and *Shaheen* (tested in April 1998 and 1999) and Iran's *Shahab* (tested in July 1998), North Korea's *Taepo Dong* (tested in August 1998) medium-to-intermediate range missile has its origins in Chinese CSS-2 missile technology. Pyongyang has produced and deployed as many as 100 *Nodong* missiles with a range of 1300 kilometers, enough to target most of Japan. It also has flight-tested the *Taepo Dong-1*, a nuclear weapons delivery system with possible intercontinental range that can reach the continental United States. Contrary to conventional wisdom, Beijing's growing political and economic ties with Seoul since the early 1990s did not bring an end to Beijing-Pyongyang military collaboration (see Table 8.1). China provides North Korea with food, oil, and other essentials that keep this totalitarian basket case of a country afloat. That North Korea has long served as a conduit for Chinese supplies to other countries was confirmed by a 1999 Pentagon intelligence report, which said "the Chinese are proliferating on a consistent basis without technically breaking agreements with the United States."[19] Beijing, however, has denied US accusations that it provided Pyongyang with missile technology and help for its nuclear weapons program.

According to a CIA report released on January 7, 2003, North Korea tried to buy large amounts of equipment for a uranium-weapons program as late as in 2001 and also purchased raw materials and components for missiles from China. A defense agreement that Pyongyang concluded with Moscow in 2001 will pave the way for arms sales and weapons-technology transfers to North Korea. Reacting to a *Washington Times* (December 9, 2002) report that North Korea was trying to purchase a chemical known as tributyl phosphate (TBP) from China, that is used in purifying uranium and for reprocessing spent plutonium fuel, the chairman of the US-China Security Review Commission, Roger Robinson, announced the establishment of a congressionally mandated commission to hold hearings on transfers of Chinese military goods to North Korea. "There is a burgeoning nuclear crisis unfolding on the Korean Peninsula that demands enhanced export-control vigilance, particularly on the part of Pakistan, China, and Russia," said Robinson.[20] If anything, the TBP transfer once again highlighted the Chinese government's failure to control the export of goods related to nuclear-weapons production and was interpreted as an indication of Beijing's unwillingness to support US efforts to denuclearize North Korea.[21] Nobody in the US intelligence community believes that China was "completely in the dark," as President Jiang had claimed at his summit with President Bush at Crawford in October 2002.[22] Pyongyang's *admission* of a uranium enrichment-based nuclear weapons program in October on the eve of the Sino-US summit may have come as a surprise to the Chinese leadership, but North Korea's nuclear endeavor must have been known to the Chinese intelligence agencies.

In fact, the missiles-for-nukes barter deal between Pakistan and North Korea has a more direct Chinese angle than the fact that these two happen to be allies of China. General Xiong Guangkai, the People's Liberation Army's deputy chief of staff for intelligence (who in 1996 threatened to nuke Los Angeles and San Francisco if the United States intervened on Taiwan's behalf, and the man who calls Pakistan "China's Israel"), is believed to be the broker in the nuclear weapons for ballistic missiles swap between Pakistan and North Korea.[23] Furthermore, the payload and long distance make it highly likely that the C-130s would have refueled at PLA Air Force bases in western China at least twice, once on arrival and once on departure. In the unlikely event that C-130s flew direct without requiring any refueling in China, it is inconceivable that Islamabad would have passed on Chinese-origin nuclear technology in such quantities over such a long period of time to Pyongyang without Beijing's knowledge and consent. As Thomas Woodrow points out, "Chinese technicians working in Pakistan's nuclear and missile facilities would have notified Beijing in any event."[24] If the international community wants to get to the bottom of this matter, then Pakistan, Russia, and China need to be called upon to "detail what nuclear technology and hardware they allowed North Korea to import."[25] At the Sino-US security dialogue in December 2002, senior US defense officials once again urged the Chinese to increase their efforts to stop the export of Chinese technology that could be used to produce nuclear, chemical, or biological weapons in countries like North Korea, Iran, Pakistan, Syria, and Iraq. The Chinese had made no promises, but "asserted that they were *no longer* providing missile technology to North Korea."[26]

Table 8.1: China–North Korea Missile Nexus: The Smoking Gun

YEAR	KEY DEVELOPMENTS
Mid-1970s	- North Korea received Chinese missile technology of Soviet design and was involved in the joint development of the Chinese DF-61, a 1000 km-range nuclear missile that was to be turned over to Pyongyang. Although this program ended in 1978 when its Chinese sponsor fell from favor, by that time North Korea had acquired valuable design assistance from the Chinese. - Chinese assistance helped Pyongyang reverse-engineer a version of the Scud missile it had purchased from Egypt in 1976.
Mid-to-late 1980s	- North Korea arranged for Iranian funding of its indigenous Scud-B missile program in the mid-1980s; these links with Tehran continue to the present day. - North Korea served as a conduit for Chinese transfers of Silkworm anti-ship missiles to Iran to avoid Washington's censure of Beijing. One 1988 transfer reportedly included 80 Chinese Silkworms and 40 North Korean Scud-Bs as part of the same shipment.
1993	- A test-launch of the 1000-km range *Nodong* missile from North Korea evidently "involved no telemetry, reportedly a signature of some Chinese missile tests."
1994	- A missile mockup of the long-range *Taepo Dong-2* resembled the Chinese CSS-2 intermediate-range ballistic missile. - *The Wall Street Journal* published a discovery by the US Defense Intelligence Agency that one stage of the new North Korean missile was a copy of the Chinese CSS-2 missile.
1995	- US intelligence sources claimed that China was both assisting North Korea to develop a family of long-range ballistic missiles and training some 200 Korean missile engineers in China. That family of long-range missiles turned

	out to be the *Taepo Dong*, which Pyongyang successfully launched in August 1998—ten years before the CIA believed it possible.
1997	- A "joint team" of Chinese and North Korean technicians went to Iran to assist in Tehran's ballistic missile efforts. The Iranian *Shahab-3* and *Shahab-4* missiles are variants of North Korean and Chinese missiles. - North Korea likely has used the Iranian and Pakistani missile tests for its own missile program development to circumvent Pyongyang's "promise" not to conduct missile launches (the *Shahab-3* is the *Nodong*; the planned *Shahab-5* is the *Taepodong-2*).
1998	- *The Washington Times* (February, 23, 1999) reported that the US National Security Agency (NSA) suspected in late 1998 that the China Academy of Launch Vehicle Technology (CALT) was working with North Korea on its space program (closely related to missiles) to develop satellites. - The PLA's deputy chief of general staff, Lt-General Xiong Guangkai, visited North Korea in early August 1998, three weeks before the surprising test-firing of a three-stage, medium-range *Taepo Dong-1* missile on August 31.
1999	- An NSA report (March, 8, 1999) suggested that China sold specialty steel for use in North Korea's missile program. - In June, US intelligence reportedly found that Chinese entities transferred accelerometers, gyroscopes, and precision grinding machinery to North Korea (*Washington Times*, July, 20, 1999). - A classified report dated October 20 noted that China's Changda Corp. sought to buy Russian gyroscopes that are more of the same that China supplied to the North Korean missile program earlier that year (*Washington Times*, November 19, 1999). The South Korean newspaper *Joong Ang Ilbo* (November 25) reported that "China had recently sold North Korea massive quantities of military equipment." - In December, the NSA discovered an alleged deal to supply Chinese-made missile-related items to North Korea through a Hong Kong company.
2000	- In October, China invited seven Pakistani and four North Korean nuclear and metallurgical scientists to its Lop Nor nuclear test facility to demonstrate processes to miniaturize nuclear warheads and synchronize missile warhead caps for multiple warhead missile systems. The miniaturization of a nuclear package, advanced guidance components, and

	stage separation mechanisms are critical to North Korea's efforts to develop a nuclear-capable *Taepo Dong*-class missile with a range to target the United States. These are the areas where Chinese assistance is still occurring, possibly under the guise of satellite-launch assistance.
2001	- A CIA report said that North Korea acquired missile-related raw materials and components, especially through North Korean firms in China, in the first half of 2001.
2002	- PLA's Lt-General Xiong Guangkai visited Pakistan in March to sign "Joint Defense" and "Joint Defense Production" agreements and later visited N. Korea in October. - North Korea acknowledged a secret program to enrich uranium to develop nuclear weapons during talks with the United States on October 4. - US intelligence officials told *The Washington Times* that North Korea received a shipment of 20 tons of a specialty chemical known as tributyl phosphate, or TBP, from a Chinese company in Dalian in early December. The TBP can be used to extract material for nuclear bombs from North Korea's stockpile of spent nuclear-reactor fuel and thus raised new concerns that China was secretly assisting North Korea while publicly saying it wanted to see a nuclear-free Korean Peninsula.

SOURCES: Information contained in the above table is based on T. Woodrow, "China opens Pandora's nuclear box," China Brief, *2:24, December 10, 2002 <http://china.jamestown.org/pubs/view/cwe_002_024_001.htm>; S. A. Kan,* China and Proliferation of Weapons of Mass Destruction and Missiles: Policy Issues *(Report for Congress, Congressional Research Service, December 4, 2002), 13-14; L. Niksch,* North Korea's Nuclear Weapons Program *(CRS Issue Brief IB91141); K. Min-seok & Oh Young-hwan, "Iran said to be buyer of North missiles,"* JoongAng Ilbo, *December 19, 2002 <http://english.joins.com/Article.asp?aid=20021219024551&sid=200>; "China in Pak-N.Korea nuclear axis,"* Newsinsight.net, *October 19, 2002; B. Gertz, "Panel to probe China's nuclear-related sales to N. Korea,"* Washington Times, *December 20 2002; E. Timperlake and W. C. Triplett, II, "N. Korea, Pakistan, China,"* Washington Times, *December 8, 2002; B. Gertz, "China ships North Korea ingredient for nuclear arms,"* Washington Times, *December 17, 2002; "CIA says N. Korea tried to buy nuclear gear in 2001,"* Washington Times, *January 8, 2003; M. Ijaz and R. J. Woolsey, "Cut supply lines that fuel Pyongyang's nuclear dreams,"* Los Angeles Times, *January 12, 2003; Author's discussions with South Korean officials and analysts, September 2001-November 2002.*

Pakistan-North Korea

As noted earlier, it is quite a well-known fact that China was instrumental in Pakistan's acquisition of its atom bomb. What is, however, not so well-known is the not-so-secret North Korea-Pakistan nuclear and missile nexus. While Pyongyang has served as a conduit for ballistic missile supplies to Pakistan, Islamabad has shared its weapons-capable highly enriched uranium technology with the North Korean regime (see Table 8.2). In the early 1990s, an insecure Islamic Republic of Pakistan, facing US-imposed sanctions but desperate to counter India's superior military capability, turned to an ostracized and poor, but uranium-rich, communist North Korea, which was feeling cut off from its patrons—Russia and China. Since Pyongyang was engaged in its own nuclear and missile programs, the two became "natural allies" in isolation, supporting each other's WMD efforts. Pakistan reportedly helped North Korea conduct a series of "cold tests," simulated nuclear explosions, using natural uranium, which are necessary to determine whether a nuclear device will detonate properly.[27] Even after General Musharraf sided with the United States in ousting the Taliban in Afghanistan and hunting down al-Qaeda leaders post-September 11, 2001, and the Bush administration's characterization of North Korea, along with Iraq and Iran, as part of the "Axis of Evil" in January 2002, Islamabad continued its murky relationship with Pyongyang.[28] As late as July 2002, US intelligence agencies watched silently as US-gifted Pakistan Air Force's C-130 Hercules aircraft picked up missile parts from North Korea at the height of India-Pakistan tensions amidst talk of the world's first nuclear war in South Asia.[29] Some analysts contend that "China is complicit in this proliferation" because Pakistan could not have flown a C-130 Hercules across China to North Korea without refueling at a PLA air base in western China.[30] Not only did Pakistan supply gas-centrifuge designs and machinery for weapons construction, but a Japanese Korean defector from North Korea, Kenki Aoyama, has revealed that Pakistani engineers helped the North to fabricate bombs intended to threaten South Korea, Taiwan, Japan, and 100,000 US troops in Northeast Asia.[31] *The New York Times* quoted an American official who reviewed the intelligence as saying that "North Korea's drive in the past year to begin full-scale enrichment of uranium uses technology that has 'Made in Pakistan' stamped all over it."[32] Despite protestations and denials by the Musharraf government, sections of Pakistan's nuclear establishment are suspected of helping not only the North Koreans (who openly gloat over Pakistan's tacit nuclear proliferation) but Saudis and Iranians as well. Pakistani nuclear scientists are now considered the weakest link in the WMD proliferation chain. According to the former assistant secretary of state for nonproliferation in the Clinton administration, Robert Einhorn: "If the international community had a proliferation most-wanted list, Dr. A. Q. Khan would be most wanted on the list."[33] Washington's apprehensions about Pakistani nuclear scientists are very similar to its long-standing suspicions about the Russian scientists in the post-Soviet collapse.[34] However, the Bush administration has chosen not to criticize Pakistan publicly or reimpose economic sanctions that were lifted after September 11, 2001, for fear of destabilizing the weak Musharraf government, whose support is vitally important in the War on Terrorism.

Table 8.2: Pakistan's Pyongyang Connection: The Barter Deal of the Century?

YEAR	KEY DEVELOPMENTS
1991	- Islamabad sought Pyongyang's assistance in long-range missile technology to counter India's testing of the *Agni* missile.
1992	- DPRK Deputy Premier and Foreign Minister Kim Yong-nam visited Syria (July 27–30), Iran (July 30–August 3), and Pakistan (August 4–7) to explore areas of bilateral cooperation. - Pakistan's nuclear and missile scientist Dr. A. Q. Khan initiated talks for purchase and transfer of ten to twelve 1500-km range *Nodong* missiles by Islamabad.
1993	- Pakistani and Iranian missile scientists were present for the DPRK's Nodong missile test on May 29–30. - In December, Pakistan Prime Minister Benazir Bhutto visited Beijing and Pyongyang seeking long-range ballistic missiles capable of striking strategic targets within India.
1994	- In April, a DPRK Foreign Ministry delegation headed by Pak Chung-kuk traveled to Pakistan and Iran. - In September, another delegation led by Choe Hui-chong, chairman of the State Commission of Science and Technology, visited Pakistan.
1995	- In November, a DPRK military delegation led by Marshal Choe Kwang visited missile-related production facilities in Pakistan and finalized the agreement on the transfer of about 12–25 Nodong missiles with Dr. A. Q. Khan and Dr. Ashfaq

	Ahmad Khan, head of the Pakistan Atomic Energy Commission.
1996	- Taiwan detained a North Korean ship *Chusong* for misdeclaration of 15 tonnes of ammonium perchlorate, a key missile fuel component that was being shipped to Pakistan.
1997	- Dr A.Q. Khan made three secret visits to North Korea. - The Pakistan government began paying for *Nodong* missiles by providing nuclear know-how.
1998	- Pakistan test-fired a *Nodong* missile renamed *Ghauri* on April 6, prompting the US State Department to impose sanctions against Changgwang Sinyong Corporation (CSC) and Pakistan's Khan Research Laboratories (KRL) on April 24. This was the second time that the State Department had imposed sanctions against KRL. The first time was during August 1993, after Pakistan's acquisition of Chinese DF-11/M-11 ballistic missiles. - One week after Pakistan's first nuclear tests, Kim Sa-nae, wife of a senior DPRK diplomat, was shot dead in Islamabad. Her husband, Kang Thae-yun – who as economic counselor in the embassy worked for Changgwang Sinyong Corporation (CSC) – disappeared soon afterwards. Both were close to Dr. A. Q. Khan. Media speculated that either or both had planned to defect and reveal all.
1999	- In June, India caught a North Korean ship bound for Pakistan loaded with 300 tonnes of equipment and engineering drawings for establishing a plant to manufacture the 300-km range *Hwasong 5* and the 500-plus-km range *Hwasong 6*, both derived from the Scud. The cargo also had Chinese machine components, electrical connectors, and nose-cones for assembling missiles. - On September 16, in his Statement for the Record to the Senate Foreign Relations Committee on *Foreign Missile Developments and Ballistic Missile Threat to the United States Through 2015,* Robert Walpole, national intelligence officer for the Strategic and Nuclear Program, acknowledged that Pakistan's *Ghauri* missile was flight tested with North Korean assistance.
2000	- In October, Pakistani and North Korean nuclear and metallurgical scientists observed the mating of miniaturized nuclear warheads and missile systems at China's Lop Nor nuclear facility in Xinjiang province.
2001	- Dr. A.Q. Khan made two trips to North Korea.

	- A three-member team from Pakistan arrived to work with their North Korean counterparts for six months. Pakistan reportedly shared data from its 1998 nuclear tests with Pyongyang. - In May, US Deputy Secretary of State Richard Armitage said that Washington has "concerns of proliferation" with Pakistan, centering on "people who were employed by the nuclear agency and have retired." Armitage's comment coincided with a week-long visit to Pakistan by the commander of the North Korean Air Force, Colonel-General O Kum-chol, a frequent visitor to Islamabad.
2002	- The *National Intelligence Estimate*, released in January, claimed that "North Korean willingness to sell complete systems and components has enabled other states to acquire longer range capabilities earlier than otherwise would have been possible—notably the sale of the *Nodong* MRBM to Pakistan." - In July, US satellites spotted a US-gifted Pakistani C-130 Hercules picking up missile parts from North Korea at the height of India-Pakistan tensions. - Islamabad dispatched 47 tonnes of special aluminum (which was acquired by KRL from a British firm in Blackburn) to Pyongyang on board a Shaheen Airline flight for its uranium enrichment programme. - In October, US officials publicly confirmed that Islamabad provided gas centrifuges for Pyongyang's uranium enrichment program, in return for North Korea's supply of *Nodong* missiles to Pakistan (*New York Times* and *Washington Post*, October 18, 2002). - On December 29, Japanese daily *Mainichi Shimbun* reported that a sample gas centrifuge used to enrich uranium necessary to produce nuclear weapons was transported by special flight from Islamabad in the coffin of the murdered wife of a North Korean diplomat in June 1998.

SOURCES: Information in the above table is based on S. M. Hersh, "The cold test," The New Yorker*, January 27, 2003; "US confronts Pakistan with N. Korea 'smoking gun,'"* Newsinsight.com*, January 17, 2003 <http://www.intelligenceonline.net/allintelligencefull.asp?id=9365933019391&recno=1681>; E. Ahrari, "Pakistan as proliferator: a view from Washington,"* Asia Times online*, January 14, 2003 <http://www.atimes.com/atimes/South_Asia/EA14Df03.html>; Malik, "China and the nuclear non-*proliferation *regime"; J. S. Bermudez Jr,* The Armed Forces of North Korea *(London & New York: I. B. Tauris*

Publishers, 2001), 270-271; S. Gupta, "Unholy nexus," India Today, *November 4, 2002, 22-23; "Pak informed US of nuclear technology transfer,"* Jiji Press *(Tokyo), December 25, 2002; "China in Pak-N.Korea nuclear axis,"* Newsinsight.net, *October 19, 2002;* Los Angeles Times, *January 7, 2003; "Double-dealing,"* Newssight.net, *November 8, 2002 <http://www.indiareacts.com/fulldebate2.asp?recno=517>; A. Foster-Carter, "Nukes and missiles: the Pakistan connection,"* Asia Times online, *June 5, 2001 <http://atimes.com/koreas/CF05Dg02.html>; PTI, "Pak sent N- material to N Korea in July: report,"* Times of India, *December 7, 2002; D. E. Sanger, "In North Korea and Pakistan, deep roots of nuclear barter,"* New York Times, *November 23, 2002, 1.*

The Proliferation Chain

Even more worrying are the reports of the technological links of China, North Korea, and Pakistan with nuclear aspirants—Iran, Iraq, Libya, and Saudi Arabia. Chinese (and Russian) technicians have assisted Iran in constructing a uranium plant near Esfahan and with other parts of the nuclear fuel cycle, such as uranium mining and processing and fuel fabrication. During the US-China summit in October 1997, China pledged in a confidential agreement to forego future nuclear cooperation with Iran (but not missile cooperation). China has also provided Iran with nuclear-capable ballistic missiles[35] (M-11 and M-9),[36] missile components, and chemicals useful in making nerve gas.[37] China has reportedly "sold Iran 400 tons of chemical agents, giving it the largest chemical weapons stockpile of any Third World country."[38] In December 2002, Iran's President Khatami visited Pakistan and both sides agreed to bury their hatchet from the days of the Taliban's rule in Afghanistan and promote better relations between the two Islamic nations. The Iranians are perhaps hoping that Pakistan will facilitate Iran's clandestine nuclear weapons program as it did North Korea's. The South Korean newspaper *JoongAng Ilbo* reported on December 19, 2002, that Seoul had tracked shipments of weaponry from North Korea to Iran in 2002. An Iranian freighter *IRAN MEEAD* visited the North Korean harbors of Nampo and Songnim multiple times in February and November 2002, where it loaded missiles and rocket fuel destined for Iran. Before calling at the North Korean harbors, the Iranian ship reportedly stopped at China's Tianjin harbour and loaded missile components and Chinese-made heat-seekers. The *JoongAng Ilbo* revelation provided further evidence of North Korea's continuing proliferation activities and military-commercial ties to Iran, while raising concern about China's cooperation on North Korea's weapons program.[39] That same week, US and Spanish forces intercepted and then released a Yemen-bound North Korean vessel also carrying Scud missiles.

A memorandum found by UN inspectors, sent by Section B15 of Iraqi intelligence to Section S15 of Iraq's nuclear weapons directorate, was explicit in stating that Baghdad had received a proposal from "Pakistani scientist Dr. Abdul Qadeer Khan to help Iraq manufacture a nuclear weapon." Iraq admitted to the UN inspection regime that Khan made the offer, but insisted that it turned it down for fear it was a US sting operation. Pakistan, for its part, denied that Khan ever made the offer. Scouring for evidence of Iraq's clandestine WMD program, the United States has stumbled on massive China-Libya links in the construction of Libya's long-range ballistic missiles that can target US forces and interests in the Mediterranean and the Middle East, especially Israel. US intelligence agencies have now discovered that China has helped Libya construct two nuclear-capable IRBMs, called *al-Fatah*, with ranges of 1000–1500 kilometers and 3500–4500 kilometers—and indicate the role of a shadowy Singapore-based Libyan chemical and metals import-export company called *al-Marwa*.[40] Since 1994, there have been intelligence reports of Saudi Arabian funding for Pakistan's nuclear and missile program purchases from China.[41] Prior to September 11, General Musharraf reportedly had reached an understanding on sharing nuclear technology with Prince Abdullah of Saudi Arabia. In return for liberal financial assistance from Riyadh, bankrupt Islamabad was also expected to provide medium-range solid-fueled Chinese M-11s or *Ghauri* missiles which would have replaced 30 *Dong Feng-3* medium-range ballistic missiles that Saudi Arabia had bought from China in 1988 and that were nearing the end of their operational life. Stephen Blank succinctly sums up the nature of the proliferation challenge emanating from the Beijing-Islamabad-Pyongyang axis:

> … the Pakistani-North Korea relationship perfectly epitomizes the phenomenon known as tertiary proliferation, whereby newly nuclear states or new aspirants to that status assist each other, and by doing so obtain technological, military, or financial, as well as political benefits from their relationship. It may also be the case that Pakistan acts as a middleman for a third party, in this case China, that does not want its shipments to North Korea [and other countries] to be directly traceable.[42]

The Proliferation Axis: Objectives, Motivations, and Interests

The following section outlines the objectives, motives and interests behind nuclear proliferation by China, North Korea and Pakistan.

China Pursuing Containment Through Surrogates[43]

Of all the nuclear weapon states, China has perfected the art of proliferation of clandestine nuclear and missile technology transfers as a tool of Chinese national security policy. Increasingly, Chinese assistance takes the form of technology transfer or exports through third parties and missile parts and nuclear components as opposed to complete weapons systems. Evidence shows that Beijing has either paid lip service to the non-proliferation objectives or made only those concessions absolutely essential to (a) mend fences with the West, and (b) to secure access to advanced technology but without accepting terms which would constrain its security policy options or restrict China's nuclear and missile exports. This ambivalence has been accompanied by deliberate attempts to exploit the grey areas ("differences of interpretation" as in the Missile Technology Control Regime case), *ad hoc* decisionmaking, based on mixed or contradictory policy preferences, and poor export controls. This stance also reflects the tension between being a *status quoist* power in terms of nuclear weapons capability and non-*status quoist* power in terms of a rising global great power. The apparent contradiction can best be understood as an outcome of China's tendency to use "the proliferation card" by exploiting loopholes in the non-proliferation regime and contradictions in major power relationships so as to serve its broader national security objectives.[44] To the extent that the United States, Japan, and India are preoccupied with dangers posed by Chinese-supplied conventional and unconventional weaponry in the hands of the mullahs of Iran, the Saddams of Iraq, Kim Jong Ils of North Korea, and the military rulers of Pakistan, those nations are distracted from the threat China itself poses—or at least less capable of dealing with it.

First and foremost is the Chinese strategic objective of limiting US dominance worldwide and countering any moves aimed at the consolidation or enlargement of the US alliance network in the Asia-Pacific. Asia's rising superpower, China, has long viewed the world's reigning superpower, the United States, as its major global strategic rival that needs to be contained and balanced.[45] The Bush administration's national security strategy statements repeatedly warned China that the United States is determined to prevent it from acquiring military forces that in any way seriously challenge those of the United States. From China's perspective, WMD poliferation serves to limit US policy options in Asia and constrains its global ambitions. In 1999, the head of Chinese Foreign Ministry's Arms Control and Disarmament Division, Sha Zukang, had warned that should the United States go ahead with its missile defense program, Washington would "confront a nightmare scenario of nuclear proliferation" and that there would be so many fires around the world that the United States would get exhausted putting out these fires. He did not elaborate as to who will start those fires.[46]

Whenever bilateral relations between China and the United States have deteriorated over issues such as Taiwan, missile defense plans, human rights, and religious freedom, Beijing has retaliated by peddling nuclear and missile technologies to countries hostile to the United States and its allies. As noted earlier, North Korea is also a conduit through which Chinese nuclear and missile technology has been fed to Iran and Iraq—countries that see the United States as their present and future enemy. The United Nations inspectors dismantling the Iraqi nuclear program after Desert Storm found evidence that the plan for Iraq's nuclear bomb was a Chinese design provided by Pakistan. Post–1991 Gulf War, China made a strategic decision to move closer to Iran and to build up its defenses as a counterweight to US influence in the Middle East. From China's perspective, the emergence of additional power centers, albeit far from its borders (for example, Iran in the Middle East), will provide a valuable US hostage and preoccupy the United States, leaving South and Southeast Asia to be dominated by China's growing might. In China's strategic calculations, faced with two or three regional crises simultaneously, the United States would have to choose which one is more important for its national security interests, leaving the other to China to sort out.

Second, and a related strategic objective, is to ensure China's preeminent position in the Asia-Pacific region by "restraining Japan and containing India."[47] China's assistance to the nuclear and missile programs of North Korea and Pakistan has thus been largely motivated by the imperative of Beijing's Asia policy to balance its regional rivals. Since the end of the 1962 Sino-Indian war, Beijing has come to rely on its "all-weather friend," Pakistan, to contain their common enemy—India—and repeatedly broken its promises to halt clandestine strategic transfers to Pakistan in violation of NPT Article I obligations.[48] As for Japan, China's East Asian rival is constrained by its Peace Constitution and the World War II legacy to acquire a full spectrum of military capability befitting of an independent power or a "normal" nation.

To take the heat off its proliferation activities, Beijing has encouraged its military allies, Islamabad and Pyongyang, to establish closer nuclear and missile cooperation links since the early 1990s.[49] As per Sun Tzu's advice of "subduing the enemy without fighting," China has played a double game in South Asia and Northeast Asia, having earlier contributed to their destabilization by transferring nuclear and missile technologies to its allies (Pakistan and North Korea) and later offering to help contain the problem of nuclear and missile proliferation in South Asia and on the Korean Peninsula. Such tactics have buttressed the point that China's "centrality" in regional security issues must be recognised as essential to their resolution. In other words, WMD proliferation has afforded Beijing the unique opportunity to successfully play the dual role of a troublemaker and troubleshooter in South Asia and Northeast Asia. Such a strategy not only obviates the need for China to pose a direct threat to Japan or India but also allows Beijing to wield its prestige as a disinterested, responsible global nuclear power while playing the role of an impartial, regional arbiter.

Yet another motivation is China's strategic need to build a network of close allies (North Korea, Pakistan, Iran, and Burma) because "all great powers have strong allies." Just as the United States can count on the support of its allies (Australia, Canada, Germany, Japan, and the UK) in times of crisis, so the argument goes, China also needs the support of strong allies to secure its interests, particularly in Asia.[50] By building up the military capabilities of allies such as Pakistan, North Korea, and Iran, Beijing seeks to tie down its rivals (India, Japan, and the United States) in their respective regions with multiple security concerns. Alastair Johnston argues that a crucial means of "victory without bloodshed" (*bing bu xue ren*) in Chinese strategic tradition is to intimidate the hostile country into capitulation through provocation, brinkmanship, coercion, and a shift in the balance of power. The objective is to convince the enemy, who is militarily weak and/or tied down with multiple security concerns, that the military situation has shifted to his disadvantage and thus force him to concede.[51] This is evident in the manner in which Chinese-supplied long-range missiles with nuclear capability have been repeatedly brandished by both Islamabad and Pyongyang for coercion and blackmail vis-à-vis India and Japan/the United States. For the past decade, the United States, as well as South Korea, Japan, and India, have sought to improve relations with China, North Korea, and Pakistan. However, their efforts have been repaid with systematic violation of every non-proliferation agreement and commitment Beijing and its allies have signed and clandestine efforts to increase their nuclear weapons capabilities.

In addition to the strategic considerations of countervailing China's rivals and gaining allies, Beijing's nuclear and missile transfers have also been motivated by the need to secure access to critical energy resources, advanced military technology, and diplomatic leverage. For example, a major reason behind Israel's high-tech arms sales to China has been the need to neutralize Beijing's strong support for Arab states and the fear of Beijing's retaliation by means of supply of nuclear and missile technology to Muslim countries hostile to the Jewish state.[52] It was not a coincidence that reports of Chinese assistance to Libya's long-range missile program appeared at the time of intense US pressure on Israel to cancel a $2 billion deal to sell airborne military radar (similar to the US AWACS system) to Beijing that would diminish Taiwan's air superiority. "We don't want to have China hostile to Israel," cautioned an Israeli official, noting that Beijing would send arms to the region, which could harm both American and Israeli interests.[53] Israel's recent announcement of suspension of all contracts on the export of military equipment to China, following some arm-twisting by the Bush administration, is likely to make Beijing retaliate by stepping up WMD proliferation to Israel's Islamic neighbors.[54] Likewise, sporadic reports of Chinese nuclear collaboration with Algeria are aimed at ensuring that the French remain on China's side.

While some transactions may be purely commercial ventures dictated by China's ever-growing energy needs (e.g., the sale of CSS-2 intermediate-range ballistic missiles (IRBMs) to Saudi Arabia for US$ 3 billion), most are meant as leverage or a bargaining chip to extract concessions in the form of military assistance or diplomatic influence and to contain Beijing's rivals. The end of the triangular (US-USSR-PRC) diplomacy of the Cold War years has seen China increasingly playing "the proliferation card" primarily because, unlike the West, Beijing cannot use international financial institutions, such as the International Monetary Fund and World Bank, or the G-8 clout to bring about desired changes in the behavior or policies of other states. For example, Beijing has long linked its nuclear and missile transfers with curbs on US arms transfers to Taiwan and US missile defense plans.[55] In short, Beijing has come to rely on WMD proliferation and non-cooperation on arms control issues to get what it wants.

Notwithstanding Beijing's rhetoric of peace and development, China's strategic posture is based on the realist paradigm of "comprehensive national power" with which it seeks to defend itself and intimidate, aggrandize, and support the enemies of its enemies. It is for this reason that China has been called "the high church of realpolitik."[56] The end result is that China stands out amongst first-tier NWS for its consistent and deliberate use of WMD proliferation as an instrument to advance its grand strategic goals. The roots of Beijing's "containment through proxies" strategy can also be traced to the classic strategic principle of "make the barbarians fight while you watch from the mountain top" (*zuo shan guan hu dou*). This strategy has the additional benefit of plausible deniability. And it undercuts Asian rivals' ambitions to emerge as China's peer competitor and undermines the US influence and presence in Asia. It certainly fits into the pattern of past Chinese behavior. Beijing's customary denials notwithstanding, China's pursuit of grand strategic objectives leads it to undermine the non-proliferation regime.

North Korea Seeking Regime Survival

Several major developments post-Cold War and collapse of the Soviet Union, such as the establishment of diplomatic ties by Moscow and Beijing with Seoul, and the lessons drawn from the Gulf War and the Balkan Wars in the 1990s, contributed to a North Korean perception that its very existence was threatened and that its survival hinged upon the acquisition of nuclear weapons which could be used as a bargaining chip to ensure regime survival. Whilst Washington remained committed to South Korea's defense, North Korea was no longer sure of any security guarantees from its former patrons (Russia and China). Nuclear weapons thus came to be seen by North Korea as the spanners that the world's sole Stalinist regime could poke in the wheels of history to slow down, if not altogether stop, its march. Furthermore, much like Pyongyang's sales of ballistic missiles to Islamic countries, nuclear technology transfer had enormous potential as a foreign exchange earner, thereby reducing the need to look toward "imperialist forces" for aid. Diplomatically, the nuclear card increases North Korea's bargaining power in the reunification negotiations with the South and gives it more room for manoeuvre in its normalization of relations talks with Seoul, Tokyo, and Washington. The nuclear shield also helps the world's most hardline communist regime retain an iron grip over the twenty-first century's only Orwellian state and show a Stalinist-like resolve to quarantine the country from external political, cultural, and economic influences. North Korea's primal fear that it would either be absorbed by the economic might of the South or squeezed by the military might of the United States unless it possesses nuclear weapons means that Pyongyang will not give them up—no matter how many and what agreements it enters into with the United States and other countries.

Many in Pyongyang look to emulate India and Pakistan, recent nuclear weapons states, and they may see the current crisis as their last chance.

Pakistan Seeking Parity with India

Pakistan's quest for parity with a much larger India, the Kashmir dispute, and the history of three wars have made Islamabad highly conscious of its strategic vulnerability. Since the end of the 1971 war, which led to the dismemberment of the Pakistani state, nuclear weapons have come to be seen as a great equalizer to neutralize India's superior conventional capability. From Islamabad's perspective, Pakistan's friendship with the United States has always been one-sided, driven primarily by American security concerns at a given time. In contrast, China has proven to be a consistent and steadfast ally and a military partner over the last five decades. The growing power imbalance between an economically booming, secular, democratic, and increasingly assertive India and a politically dysfunctional, economically bankrupt, insecure, and failing Pakistan during the 1990s further added to Islamabad's sense of insecurity and vulnerability. In this sense, Pakistan's predicament vis-à-vis India was not much different from that of North Korea's vis-à-vis South Korea.

China's Allies: Beijing's Blowback

The preceding section illustrated how Beijing's search for allies to counter US global hegemony and its Asian rivals (India and Japan) has led China into dangerous liaisons with the proliferators of WMD and into the arms of dictators from North Korea to North Africa. Being a permanent member of the UN Security Council and a signatory to nuclear proliferation and missile technology control regimes since the early 1990s, China has used Pakistan and North Korea as fronts in the nuclear and missile trade. North Korea and Pakistan are widely seen as "China's problem children" that would not survive a day without the Chinese life-support system. Both are indeed kept afloat largely by liberal Chinese economic assistance and diplomatic and military support. China alone accounts for 70 percent to 90 percent of North Korea's fuel imports and about a third of all grain imports. Much like Pakistan, North Korea has been working on developing nuclear weapons and their delivery systems for at least three decades. Much like China, North Korea has agreed to abide by non-proliferation treaties and other agreements over the last two decades, but has felt no compunction in violating them if doing so undermined the security of its perceived enemies. In fact, both China and North Korea have used episodic violation as a tool of national security policy, periodically "upping the ante" to produce fresh agreements and fresh economic and technological aid from their neighbors and the United States.[57]

Much like an individual, a country is also known by the company it keeps. North Korea and Pakistan are both militarist regimes, weak and failing states that have initiated military conflicts against their neighbors. Pyongyang and Islamabad also have a penchant for engaging in a game of brinkmanship, belligerence, nuclear blackmail, and coercion to change the territorial status quo (at times with support from Beijing). Both have a history of using nuclear threats, bluffs, military provocations, and belligerence to extract concessions from their neighbors and major powers. While Pakistan threatens a 1000-year war with India, North Korea threatens "1000-fold revenge" if the United States does not concede to its demands. Interestingly, both talk of waging "holy war" against their enemies, though one is an Islamic country and another an officially atheist communist country. Both seem to susbscribe to the "madman theory of international relations": the more unpredictable, more irrational, and more dangerous you seem, the more concessions will come your way. Understandably, the leaders of tottering, fragile countries need to boost their self-confidence with an occasional show of bravado. Adding to the alarm over North Korea's recent admission of nuclear capability was Pakistan President Musharraf's assertion that he was ready to use nukes during heightened tensions with India in May 2002. If anything, Parvez Musharraf and Kim Jong Il's nuclear threats reaffirm a widely held notion that nuclear weapons in the hands of unstable, authoritarian, and failing states spell nothing but trouble.

Pakistan and North Korea also form a different class of proliferators: both are impoverished states that see their weapons of mass destruction as their *only* bargaining chips. Pakistan is, in the words of former Italian Foreign Minister Gianni De Michelis, "the fuse of the world."[58] For its part, North Korea seems to suffer from the Attention Deficit Disorder syndrome. Longtime North Korea-watchers liken the insular, enigmatic country to a petulant child, demanding attention from the West by threatening to resume its suspended effort to develop nuclear weapons. Both have pursued the strategy of negotiation initiation through escalation—Pakistan via cross-border terrorism and North Korea via WMD proliferation. If any country is ever going to use nuclear weapons, it would be either Pakistan or North Korea. A sinking regime in Pyongyang or Islamabad would not think twice about threatening its neighbors. The similarities between the two are indeed stark. While India and South Korea have long worried about their perennially difficult neighbors, it is now the turn of Japan, the United States, Russia, and above all, China to worry about the consequences of the Pakistan-North Korea nexus. Having helped Pakistan (directly) and North Korea (indirectly) to cross the nuclear threshold and equip them with long-range missiles to lob at China's enemies, Beijing is obviously hoist on its own petard. As so often happens in international politics, erstwhile clients and yesterday's friends have gradually developed their own agendas and interests and started biting the hands that fed them.

Apparently, China's attempts to play "the proliferation card" have backfired, revealing a tension between Beijing's two broad policy options: one tends to push China toward supporting non-proliferation for its own self-interested reasons, whereas the other, by accepting the inevitability of nuclear and missile proliferation, would have China steer this process in a way beneficial to its security interests (e.g., by providing nuclear and missile technology to Pakistan, North Korea, and Iran). Though evidence is sketchy, it may be said that China's foreign policy establishment has supported the first option while the country's military establishment lent support to the second option for long-term geostrategic objectives. This tension between two contradictory policies has led Beijing to make several tactical turnabouts on the proliferation issue and reflects the uncertain nature of China's nuclear arms control policy.

A rational cost-benefit analysis shows that Beijing's strategy of "containment through surrogates" has started yielding diminishing returns because China's long-term foreign policy objectives now clash with the imperatives of alliance relationships. The "War on Terrorism" has provided Beijing with the opportunity to join the world's leading responsible nations rather than to be colored with the same dye as rogue nations. In other words, the Chinese would prefer to be on "the right side of history." On the positive side, the present global strategic environment has created a win-win situation for China, despite its violation of the nuclear and missile proliferation regimes. The North Korean brinkmanship has exposed the sole superpower as a "paper tiger," driven a wedge between the United States and South Korea, demonstrated the hollowness of the Bush administration's strategy of preemption and inadequacy of the "two simultaneous wars" doctrine, and above all, has made a mockery of President Bush's zero-tolerance policy toward rogue states acquiring weapons of mass destruction. It also ensures the survival of the Kim regime and further progress on the reunification question on Pyongyang's terms. Moreover, Pyongyang's challenge diverts Washington's attention from the wars in Iraq and

Afghanistan and raises the specter of tying the United States down in a number of theaters. It is worth remembering that the Bush administration came into power proclaiming its intention to take a tough stand on the challenge posed by China and its "nuclear proxies" to both the United States and its regional allies. *Jane's Intelligence Digest* outlines how Washington has lost its focus and reordered priorities post-9/11:

> The Bush administration's major policy decisions to establish missile defence systems; the building of closer strategic ties with India and the re-enforcement of support for its regional allies Japan and South Korea were designed to meet the challenge of the emerging axis in Asia. However, amid current US requirements for Chinese and Pakistani support in its War on Terrorism, the Bush administration has slowed down, at least for the time being, its strategic offensive against the China-led nuclear axis in Asia.[59]

The proliferation and terrorism crises have allowed China to be courted by Washington because of its veto in the UN Security Council. Beijing has also gained influence in South Korea and repositioned itself as an impartial arbiter in the Korean conflict. Always keen to exploit contradictions among their friends and enemies so as to further China's national interests, the Chinese could play the Korean card in Sino-Japanese, Sino-Korean, and Sino-American relations to their advantage. Despite the post–September 11, 2001, improvement in Sino-US ties, Beijing has watched with concern the ever-increasing US presence and influence all along China's periphery in Asia and will be tempted to use the Korean nuclear crisis to extract concessions from Washington in return for pressure, real or imagined, on Pyongyang. In a way, this crisis "foreshadows an eventual power struggle between the United States and China over the Korean Peninsula and the future of the alliance after Korean unification."[60] China's stance—that the only realistic way to resolve the North Korean crisis peacefully is the signing of a non-aggression treaty between North Korea and the United States—is aimed at maintaining the status quo, which invariably gives Beijing a strategic advantage in the region. Although it rails constantly against the crime of a nation divided in the case of itself and Taiwan, China is content with a North Korean buffer state between itself and East Asia's two biggest US allies (South Korea and Japan) and is working to preserve the Peninsula's effective division.[61] Furthermore, Beijing has tried to allay Washington's concerns about Chinese transfers of nuclear and missile technology and made new commitments to nuclear non-proliferation goals.

Against these short-term benefits, however, are several long-term costs. On the negative side, since nearly all of China's allies happen to be weak and failing states (North Korea, Burma, Pakistan), Beijing needs to rethink its alliances. Once close ideological allies, China and North Korea have grown apart over the past two decades— China reforming its state-planned economy and integrating into the global community and North Korea sliding into economic stagnation and political isolation.[62] Likewise, China has advised Pakistan since the mid-1990s against embarking on military misadventures and flirting with terrorism and religious extremism to further its geopolitical interests in Afghanistan and Kashmir. The Chinese know that weak and unstable Pakistan and North Korea can hardly contribute to China's strategic strength; they can only detract from China's strategic strength. Since China has been the North's most crucial benefactor, it is now being called upon to take the lead in taming a monster largely of its own making. But Beijing wields far less influence with North Korea than in years past.[63]

Neither "tailored containment" nor "bold dialogue" can succeed without China's cooperation and support. China is, however, less worried about a nuclearized North Korea than a collapsing North Korea following a possible economic-strangulation strategy. Nor does China want to see any action that undermines North Korea's ongoing economic reforms because that creates renewed problems with North Korean refugees, an issue that perpetually embarrasses Beijing. Already North Korean refugees by the thousands have poured into northeastern China—a region of high and rising unemployment and increasing worker unrest. At the same time, China has a lot to fear from an economic unrest in North Korea and so resists any further tightening of economic sanctions.[64] Despite a recent souring of relations with Pyongyang, Chinese propaganda continues to describe North Korea and China as being as close as "lips and teeth." Apparently, Beijing dreads the prospect of a chaotic collapse of the Kim Jong-Il regime like that in Erich Honecker's East Germany or Nicolae Ceausescu's Romania which could extend US power right up to the Yalu and Tumen rivers. China does not want to see another Asian communist system fall apart and prefers to be surrounded by as many small, weak buffer states as possible. If they are run by corrupt, insecure dictatorships (such as North Korea, Burma, Pakistan, Kazakhstan) where the military is paranoid of its neighbors, thus remaining heavily dependent on China for weapons, training, and support, that is even better.[65] Unfortunately for Beijing, North Korea and Pakistan, where China has made deep strategic and economic investments over the decades, are fast becoming liabilities, rather than strategic assets.

A related cost is the likely deterioration in US-China ties *if* Beijing is seen as unable or unwilling to live up to high expectations in Washington. Serious differences have emerged between Beijing and Washington on the ways and means of dealing with the Kim Jong-Il regime. While Jiang Zemin publicly voiced his desire for a nuclear-free Korean Peninsula, China's state-run media carried commentaries that blamed Washington's "hostile foreign policy" and pointed the finger at Bush's "Axis-of-Evil" doctrine as the main culprit for the nuclear standoff: "North Korea's unexpected revelation that it possesses a nuclear program is a natural response to the hawkish foreign policy of the US government since George W. Bush became the President," said a *People's Daily* commentary on October 25, 2002. An opinion piece in the Communist Party's newspaper in early January 2003 said that since the United States does not dare fight North Korea, fearing large-scale death and destruction, it should talk to it: "It is not that the United States does not want to use force, but rather it fears the consequences will be unimaginable.... Judged from the international macro-environment, an inordinate intransigent US attitude towards Korea is inappropriate."[66] For their part, many conservatives in Washington are urging the Bush administration to seek a regime change in Pyongyang, similar to what the United States is attempting in Iraq. Critics of the Bush administration's China policy have seized the opportunity to embarrass and pressure China. Two influential opinionmakers, William Safire and Charles Krauthammer, of the *New York Times* and the *Washington Post* respectively, have argued that the key to resolving the North Korean crisis on Washington's terms lies with pressuring Beijing—in Safire's words, to "get its client state, its satellite really, in line." Safire observed:

> Beijing cannot escape responsibility for tolerating North Korea's decision to build long-range missiles with nuclear warheads, to be used for blackmailing America or for sale to terrorist nations or groups. China's silence is assent. Communist China is the only nation with diplomatic, economic and military influence over Communist North Korea. It cannot disclaim its salvation and sponsorship of that state on its border.... Perhaps Chinese generals have not thought through the shift in military power in the region.[67]

Citing a recent report that China had sent 20 tonnes of chemicals used to extract plutonium from spent reactor fuel to Pyongyang, presumably making them complicit in Pyongyang's nuclear program,

Krauthammer stressed the need to "tell [the Chinese] plainly that if they do not join us in squeezing North Korea and thus stopping its march to go nuclear, we will endorse any Japanese attempt to create a nuclear deterrent of its own. If our nightmare is a nuclear North Korea, China's is a nuclear Japan. It's time to share the nightmares."[68] Krauthammer was echoing similar arguments that have appeared in American print and electronic media. Others, however, contend that there is no "Japan card" for Washington to play because Beijing calculates, not without reason, that "the United States itself would strongly discourage any 'nuclear breakout' by Japan."[69] The predominant view in Washington is that that since the United States used its influence in the 1970s and 1980s to stop Taiwan and South Korea from developing nuclear weapons, the Bush administration believes that it is now time for China—the only country with leverage or influence over North Korea—to do its part to keep the nuclear "genie" bottled. Statements from China (and Russia) show that they may be more interested in feathering their own strategic nests than in seeking a negotiated end to the North Korean nuclearization.[70] The proliferation crises illustrate how America's historically lackadaisical attitude toward Chinese nuclear and missile proliferation has now come back to haunt it.

For China, what is at stake is the unraveling of Beijing's carefully-crafted grand strategy with potentially destabilizing consequences. Beijing cannot hope to strengthen its ties with Washington as long as North Korea and Pakistan are in serious crises and pursuing policies counter to important Chinese and US interests. For Beijing to continue to have close ties with unpredictable and seemingly irrational regimes that starve and brutalize their own citizens, violate agreements, threaten neighbors, build and export WMD, no matter how genuine China's own security concerns happen to be, has a tremendous potential of driving a wedge between China and the United States. If China wants to escape from its status as a patron of rogue states and emerge as a responsible great power, it will have to distance itself from troublesome allies. China is increasingly uneasy over the growing talk in Washington and Tokyo's policy circles that wants to hold Beijing accountable for Pyongyang's actions or blames Beijing's "indirect strategy" of using allies to thwart American influence and further its own military political aims instead of coming into direct confrontation with Washington over such issues like Taiwan arms sales, the Middle East, or missile defense.

Following the September 11 terror attacks, China was pleased with the pro-Pakistan tilt in the Bush administration's South Asia policy, after a decade of estrangement and abandonment by Washington of China's closest ally. Beijing wants to see closer US-Chinese-Pakistani ties so as to foil New Delhi's designs to align itself with Washington to contain China and Pakistan. That policy is, however, in danger as disenchantment grows with Islamabad's half-hearted measures against al-Qaeda and the widely-held perception in Washington's policy circles that both China and Pakistan are "double-dealing" with the United States: on the one hand they claim to be US allies in the "War against Terror," and on the other maintain ties with North Korea which has exacerbated the current nuclear tensions in Northeast Asia. Many observers argue that Washington may have to rethink its policies if the global campaigns against terrorism and WMD proliferation are to be decisively won. Soon after accusations were leveled against Pakistan for supplying North Korea with equipment for enriching uranium, *The Washington Post*'s Jim Hoagland wrote an article that declared that "[President] Pervez Musharraf's Pakistan is a base from which nuclear technology, fundamentalist terrorism and life-destroying heroin are spread around the globe.... This nuclear-armed country is in part ungoverned, in part ungovernable."[71] Other reports quoted US officials as saying that after Iraq and North Korea, Pakistan would be Washington's next headache.[72] The prospect of the United States exercising greater control over Pakistan's nuclear program, including the command and control of weapons and missile deployment, is equally discomforting for China as it could both reveal and jeopardize the mutually-beneficial Sino-Pakistani military collaboration. Chinese strategists have also expressed alarm over the growing *entente cordiale* between Japan and India based on the understanding that united they contain China and divided they are contained by China and its allies. Beijing is now concerned that Japan and India will seize on the opportunity to play up North Korea's and Pakistan's "roguish behavior" and take additional measures to bolster their defenses against China.[73]

Though preoccupied with the Iraqi and al-Qaeda threats in the short term, Washington will eventually have no other option but to act tough to neutralize the challenge posed by the Beijing-Islamabad-Pyongyang axis. The growing threat of nuclear terrorism post-9/11 has already resulted in the imposition of sanctions against Chinese entities three times in less than a year (September 1, 2001, January 24 and May 9, 2002). Beijing's unconditional support for the "War on Terror" notwithstanding, the US ambassador to China, Clark Randt, describes China-assisted proliferation of WMD technologies as "a make-or-break issue." By openly defying attempts to limit WMD proliferation, Kim Jong-il has undermined the credibility of the US extended nuclear deterrence guarantees throughout the region. And credibility is an integral part of deterrence. The worst-case scenario is a "nuclear domino effect" where an overtly nuclear-armed North Korea forces Japan, South Korea, and even Taiwan to go nuclear, setting off a proliferation race in Asia with serious consequences for China's great power ambitions and the regional stability on which China's economic growth depends. This would profoundly reshape the security environment in Northeast Asia and prompt the United States to accelerate deployment of ballistic-missile defenses. In response, China would likely want to boost its arsenal, which would prompt India to expand its nuclear arsenal, which in turn would spur Pakistan to do the same—and so on and on into an ever more perilous future. Clearly, Pyongyang's nuclear brinkmanship has the potential to derail Chinese objectives of economic development and a peaceful security environment. As Stephen Blank points out: "Despite Chinese support and assistance in the development of those missiles and North Korea's nuclear program, Beijing cannot be interested in North Korea flaunting them, because that ties Japan closer to Washington's missile defence program, justifies US arguments as to its necessity, and restricts China's military freedom of maneuver."[74] Even more worrying is the possibility that North Korea, a long-time proliferator of missile technology, could easily go into the loose-nuke business once it starts churning out the weapons-grade plutonium and enriched uranium. Should Kim Jong-il find out the whereabouts of Osama bin Laden and al-Qaeda, America's worst nightmare would become a reality. Another danger to China is that North Korea-assisted nuclear proliferation in the Middle East and sales of ballistic missiles could solidify an alliance of Israel, the United States, India, and Japan, thereby fulfilling Beijing's own paranoia of encirclement that it claims it wants to avoid.

Not surprisingly, Beijing has urged a return to the Framework Agreement and refused to host Kim Jong-il in China since his last "unofficial"visit in 2001. But the North Koreans seem to be in no listening mood. An indication of this came from a statement issued in Pyongyang recently that basically told the Chinese (and Russians) to mind their own business: "If 'other countries' are worried about its nuclear activities, they should urge the United States to open a dialogue and guarantee North Korea's security. If they do not intend to do that, 'it is better for them just to sit idle.'"[75] Though China has taken the unusual step of joining with Russia in publicly criticizing Pyongyang's nuclear program, many China-watchers suspect that faced with Pyongyang's intransigence and belligerence, China will decide that the path of least resistance will be to persuade South Korea and Japan to accept a nuclear North Korea.[76] Arguing that "both the DPRK and the United States failed to observe the [1994] agreement," Shi Yongming of the China

Institute for International Studies claims that "[t]he price [North Korea] asks is not high, just a legal guarantee of peace and an end of hostility from the United States," and goes on to condone the North's nuclearization: "The international community has reached a consensus on nuclear non-proliferation. However, *we cannot deny a country's consideration of its own security interests*. We can still regard the DPRK's admission of possession of nuclear weapons as an approach to seek an opportunity for peace. *The crux of the matter is how the United States reacts....* It has a tradition of talking with inferior rivals only after they have been disarmed first."[77] Apparently, the Chinese do not want to push the Kim regime into a corner over the nuclear issue.

To convince North Korea to relent on the nuclear issue requires the cooperation of all the regional powers and a joint, coordinated economic and military strategy. But that is asking for too much because China, Russia, the United States, Japan, and South Korea all have different interests on the Korean Peninsula. Each tends to see the nuclear problem through the prism of national interest and as part of a balance-of-power game where each major power is jockeying for influence in anticipation of the eventual Korean unification. Since each country's interests differ, so do their strategies. This explains why several months after the North's enriched uranium program was revealed, there is still no sign of a common strategy even amongst allies—the United States, South Korea, and Japan, not to speak of common strategy amongst all Northeast Asian powers. In Beijing and other Asian capitals, Pyongyang's challenge is also seen as defining limits to American power and hegemony in the Asia-Pacific.[78]

Last but not least, the nuclear crisis could bring about the demise of the global non-proliferation regime and usher in an era of the law of the nuclear jungle. None of the nuclear non-proliferation treaties will be worth the paper they are written on if North Korea succeeds in its nuclear blackmail tactics and goes on to openly produce nuclear weapons and launch missiles in gross violation of its international legal obligations. The crisis also exposes the inability of the non-proliferation regime to enforce compliance. Even as the proliferation crisis in Asia has worsened since the late 1990s, the UN Security Council members have done little to address the problem by reinvigorating treaty commitments in place and undertaking punitive measures. The cases of North Korea and Iraq illustrate that a country's signature on the NPT is by no means a guarantee that it will eschew nuclear aspirations for all time to come. The lesson drawn by Iran and others from Washington's very different approaches to dealing with Iraq and North Korea is that the way to hold off the United States is to acquire nuclear weapons.

Should Pyongyang refuse to denuclearize, it might start a nuclear chain reaction in which previously nonnuclear countries may begin to reconsider their bargain and to hedge their bets and the nightmare vision of a world with 15 or 20 nuclear powers may yet come to pass. There is a general consensus that the NPT would not be able to withstand any more defections.

In short, China's "containment through surrogates" can be a win-win strategy as long as it does not drag China into regional conflicts and/or impinge negatively on China's strategic and economic interests. Chinese policymakers' preference for a balance-of-power approach in inter-state relations has led them to provide military and political support to those countries that can serve as counterweights to Beijing's perceived enemies and rivals. However, Beijing's choice of its allies and balance-of-power politics in the nuclear age has proved to be a double-edged sword; it cuts both ways. The net result is more insecurity for China.[79]

Therefore, the moral of the story is that "[i]f you permit, or even encourage, the proliferation of the deadliest weapons or the long-range missiles with which they can be delivered, such acts are liable to boomerang against you."[80] That is exactly what has happened to China. In 1950, the North Korean leadership dragged China into a war with the United Nations. At the end of it, a million Chinese soldiers had been killed or wounded, including the son of Chairman Mao Zedong. Beijing needs to ensure that history does not repeat itself on the Korean Peninsula. As two China-watchers have pointed out: "Korea could be the crucible that reveals whether China's emerging status as a responsible great power is real or illusory."[81] More than any other power, China has important economic and security interests at stake on the Korean Peninsula and Beijing's policies and posture would make or mar the future of great power cooperation and multilateralism in Northeast Asia for decades to come.

Conclusion

The North Korean–Pakistan nukes-for-missiles barter deal illustrates how China is now facing its own blowback from shortsighted policies. Beijing's Asia strategy lies in tatters. While China's support for North Korea has its roots in the Cold War, Beijing's support for Pakistan has its roots in China's hostility toward and rivalry with India. China's firm belief in the efficacy of raw balance-of-power politics and its provision of nuclear and missile assistance to its regional allies so as to undermine the security of China's perceived enemies has started a spiraling cycle of proliferation which could unravel the entire nuclear non-proliferation regime. Nuclear proliferation through networking among second-tier nuclear states and nuclear aspirants has opened the Pandora's Box of a nuclear arms race. Pakistan's nuclear weapons exports to North Korea not only impinge on US security interests in East Asia but also raise the specter of the likelihood of nuclear weapons/materials/know-how being passed on to the al-Qaeda terrorists. Given North Korea's track record of exporting ballistic missiles to anyone for the right price, one certainly cannot rule out its willingness to export nuclear material, and even nuclear weapons, to other countries and to non-state actors. Beijing must also fear that North Korea's nuclearization could prompt Tokyo someday to shed all its nuclear inhibitions just as New Delhi went nuclear and ballistic in 1998 to counter the Sino-Pakistan nuclear and missile nexus.

On the Korean Peninsula, China is confronted with some very difficult choices. While the Chinese and South Koreans believe that North Korea can be persuaded over time to back away in pursuit of its larger aim of extracting aid, investment, and other concessions, others are less sure. All agree that there is rationality in Kim Jong-il's seeming irrationality. Containment of North Korea can only be accomplished if China and South Korea agree to it. This is not likely, since a cut-off of Chinese economic assistance—along with international sanctions—could bring about the implosion of the Stalinist regime, or a desperate North Korean military could unleash military strikes. It is obvious that Beijing considers it more important to avoid either of these scenarios than to remove WMD from North Korean hands, and as such would prefer to help sustain the Kim regime than let it collapse. The prospect of another war in the region is quite unsettling to all. War prevention rather than nuclear non-proliferation seems to be the objective of all parties. One hopes that North Korea's pressing need for economic ties to the outside world may eventually force the regime to yield on the nuclear question. Otherwise, the world will have to learn to live with a nuclear-capable Korea just as it has lived with the nuclear weapons capabilities of Israel, India, and Pakistan.

***

Postscript

The following information updates the details of nuclear proliferation to the publication date of the book. The theoretical content of the chapter remains current.

The Khan Network

In October 2003, a ship named *BBC China*, carrying Dr. A.Q. Khan–supplied centrifuge components destined for Libya, was interdicted in the Mediterranean Sea in a joint operation involving the US, British, German, and Italian navies. This interdiction resulted in Libya's abandonment of its weapons of mass destruction and long-range missile programs as well as support for terror. More importantly, it led to the dismantling of the A.Q. Khan proliferation network. And it gave birth to the Proliferation Security Initiative (PSI).

The Khan network acknowledged channeling sensitive nuclear technologies to Libya, North Korea, Syria, and Iran for years under the noses of the Pakistani government before it was shut down in 2003–2004. China's initial attempts to play the role of a disinterested, neutral bystander in the fast-unraveling nuclear network came to a halt soon after evidence of the China-Pakistan-Libya nexus turned up in the 55,000 tons of nuclear material and documents that Libya turned over to the United States and which were flown to the Oak Ridge National Laboratory in Tennessee in early 2004. Apparently, the design that Khan delivered to the Libyans in the shopping bag of his Islamabad tailor was of a Chinese nuclear weapon tested on October 27, 1966. The evidence provided proof of Beijing's involvement in Pakistan's nuclear weapons program and insights into the state of both Chinese and North Korean nuclear weapons capabilities. Although the bomb designs sold to Libya were of a 1960s Chinese vintage, an analysis of Pakistan's May 1998 nuclear tests revealed that China supplied more advanced nuclear weapons designs from the late 1980s and early 1990s to Pakistan, which may also have been shared with other countries. Furthermore, it is inconceivable that Pakistani and Chinese security agencies were unaware of Dr. Khan's nuclear dealings with North Korea, Iran, and Libya.[82]

In a departure from the past, Beijing did not deny the report on Chinese-Pakistani links with Libya's nuclear weapons program but launched an "investigation" of its own while reiterating its non-proliferation commitments. Asked to comment on the *Washington Post* (February 15, 2004) report about the discovery of some Chinese language documents in Libya giving detailed instructions for assembling an implosion-type nuclear bomb, Foreign Ministry Spokesperson Zhang Qiyue said: "The Chinese side is seriously concerned by the related reports and we are trying to get more information on this issue." She declined, however, to comment on a *Reuters* report (February 15, 2004) about US officials' claim that "China is still helping Pakistan and Saudi Arabia with nuclear weapons and missile development despite Beijing's promises to control arms proliferation." Interestingly, on March 5, the US State Department declassified government documents on "China, Pakistan, and the Bomb: 1977–1997" which shed new light on three decades of US concern over China's nuclear cooperation with Pakistan. Since Zhang's statement of February 17, 2004, Beijing has maintained complete silence on the outcome of its "investigation" to date. Though Libya became an active participant in the PSI, Pakistan, China, and North Korea have continued with their proliferation activities. The *2004 Report to the Congress of the US-China Economic & Security Review Commission* highlighted the consequences of China's dangerous liaisons with rogue regimes that have made it easier for nonstate actors to acquire WMD:

> The consequence of more than 20 years of China's direct transfers of WMD and related technologies is that the United States now faces enhanced threats from rogue states or terrorist groups that can acquire WMD capabilities. Unfortunately, even in light of overwhelming evidence of the increased threat to global security, *Chinese entities continue to proliferate*."[83]

The *2006 Report to the Congress of the U.S.-China Economic & Security Review Commission* also accused China of failing "to meet the threshold test of international responsibility in the area of non-proliferation" by aiding Iran's nuclear, missile, and chemical programs and refusing to effectively use its leverage to bring North Korea back into nuclear weapons negotiations. The report concluded that "despite its rising power and wealth, China may not be willing or ready to play a responsible role in an international system aimed at encouraging peace and stability."[84] It noted that China in recent years has allowed the transfer of weapons and technology across its territory from North Korea to Iran: "From April to July 2003, China reportedly gave overflight rights to Iranian Il-76 cargo planes that flew to North Korea at least six times to pick up wooden crates suspected of containing cruise missiles. But after a U.S. protest in June 2005, China denied overflight rights for an Iranian plane departing from North Korea." Nonetheless,

North Korean overflights to Pakistan, Burma, and other countries continue. The repeated imposition of US sanctions against Chinese entities for proliferation activities has not deterred "serial proliferators" that "have no fear of government controls or punishments."[85]

Believing that proliferation is inevitable, the Chinese have long practiced what John Mearsheimer calls "managed proliferation": it calls for providing nuclear or missile technology to China's friends and allies (Pakistan, Iran, North Korea) so as to contain its rivals through proxies (India in South Asia, the United States in the Middle East, and Japan in East Asia). Beijing has also engaged in proliferation to pressure Washington to curb its arms sales to Taiwan. As in the past, contradictions between Beijing's grand strategy and nonproliferation objectives, China's security alliances, and commercial goals continue to dictate Beijing's nonproliferation policy. This tension also explains China's reluctance to sign on to the US-led PSI under which countries pledge to interdict shipments of weapons of mass destruction.

Nonstate Actors + Proliferation = Nuclear Terrorism

What we need to worry more about is proliferation encounters of the third kind, which take place through the brotherhood of rogue states and nuclear networking among nonnuclear NPT member states, private-sector companies, scientists, technicians, and terrorists that operate a kind of "Nuclear Wal-Mart." The A. Q. Khan saga illustrated that if the price is right, everything is up for sale. A sort of "yellow pages" directory existed for the supply of Chinese A-bomb designs, nuclear materials, technical expertise, and after-sales service from North Korea to North Africa and northern Europe. Revelations about an illegal international nuclear procurement network run by Pakistani nuclear scientist Dr. Khan, which supplied nuclear materials to Libya, Iran, and North Korea, highlighted the need for global economic, financial, and law enforcement action to counter the sources of support to proliferation. On April 28, 2004, the UN Security Council passed Resolution 1540, which requires all member states to criminalize proliferation by non-state actors and to adopt and enforce effective export controls. In Resolutions 1718, 1737, 1747 and 1803, the Security Council has also acted to deny international financing to North Korea's and Iran's WMD and missile programs.

The IAEA, however, believes that the Khan nuclear network has not been completely dismantled. Therefore, terrorist acquisition and movement of nuclear materials represents a real and growing global threat. A combination of "rogue state" and mass-casualty terrorists is a worst-case scenario that shaped the Bush administration's security policy toward Iraq, Libya, North Korea, and Iran. This concern was expressed in the *Quadrennial Defense Review* released on February 6, 2006: "The prospect that a nuclear capable state may lose control of some of its weapons to terrorists is one of the greatest dangers the U.S. and its allies face." A Taliban–al Qaeda takeover of nuclear-armed Pakistan poses the worst-case scenario for policymakers. More worryingly, the last decade has seen nearly a doubling of Pakistan's nuclear arsenal to more than 100 warheads.[86] According to a classified State Department cable released in 2010 by the Internet site WikiLeaks, Peter Lavoy, the US national intelligence officer for South Asia, told NATO officials in December 2008, that "despite pending economic catastrophe, Pakistan is producing nuclear weapons at a faster rate than any other country in the world." India and the United States have expressed concern over China's sale of two more nuclear-power reactors to Pakistan, as it could erode the ability to stanch the flow of nuclear technologies in unstable regions.[87] By assisting Islamabad's nuclear program, Beijing continues to disregard the Nuclear Suppliers' Group guidelines regulating nuclear trade. The China-Pakistan nuclear nexus is one of the major reasons that "China-India relations [remain] very fragile…and very difficult to repair."[88]

DPRK Won, United States Lost?

For their part, the North Koreans remain defiant, boosting and boasting about their nuclear prowess, provoking and shelling the South Koreans, and selling WMD technologies to "nuclear wannabes" like Iran, Syria, and Burma. In 2003, the Kim regime withdrew from the Nuclear Non-Proliferation Treaty (NPT), expelled IAEA inspectors, and resumed operation of its nuclear power plants in Yongbyon. Since then, it has conducted nuclear and missile tests and disclosed the existence of a clandestine uranium enrichment complex in addition to its plutonium program. Pyongyang is believed to have produced enough fissile material for at least a half-dozen bombs. David Albright of the Institute for Science and International Security believes that North Korea has often procured for its enrichment program either directly in China or by using it as a transit point. Even though Beijing claims that it views the North Korean nuclear weapons program as destabilizing to the region, Beijing is not doing enough to detect and halt such trade.[89] Instead of dismantling its nuclear weapons, Pyongyang is angling to be recognized as a full nuclear power. Following the collapse of the Six-Party Talks in 2007, the change of governments in South Korea (2008) and United

States (2009), and Pyongyang's belligerence amidst political succession from father Kim Jong-Il to son Kim Jong-Eun, the danger of tit-for-tat escalation breaking out into wider military conflict has increased. Since the prospect of another war on the Korean peninsula is quite unsettling to all, war prevention rather than nuclear non-proliferation now seems to be the objective of all parties. So, say goodbye to CVID (comprehensive, verifiable, irreversible disarmament). As Shen Dingli explains:

> After years of negotiations and hand-wringing it has now become clear that the game of containing North Korea's nuclear program has effectively been lost. By exploding a nuclear device in 2006 North Korea has gained an upper-hand that would allow it to have its cake and eat it too: The US and other partners of the Six Party Talks would make concessions while North Korea hangs on to its arsenal. With its inventory of weapons-grade fissile material at possibly eight bombs equivalent, the DPRK wiped out the US policy option of military strike against Pyongyang—because a realist America has no interest in waging war with a nuclear-weapons state.... *So far, it is DPRK rather than the US that is succeeding.*[90]

Post-Iraq, post–A. Q. Khan affair, the United States suffers from a serious credibility problem on the proliferation issue. Bogged down in two wars (Iraq and Afghanistan) and weakened by the financial crisis, the United States is seen as lacking both the clout and the credibility to build a broad international coalition that would dissuade countries from going nuclear. Moreover, the United States is trying to put out the fire with the help of those who started the fire in the first place. But they do not share the US perceptions of the proliferation challenges.[91] What the West sees as a breakdown in nonproliferation is seen by others as a legitimate push for national security. As is well known, America's rogue model is someone else's role model. Dissatisfied powers or rogues assert themselves in times of economic crisis and tectonic power shifts. The Chinese (and the Russians) are also happy that those who want nuclear weapons share their primary objective of limiting US power worldwide. Beijing and Moscow seem more interested in having profitable commercial ties with "nuclear wannabes" and in curbing US unilateralism than in doing anything substantive to curb proliferation. But the proliferation challenge cannot be met in the absence of great power consensus, which is lacking on North Korea and Iran. However, the Chinese are not alone in the proliferation business anymore. In fact, the Chinese have been thoroughly beaten in the proliferation game by their own former clients and allies. Long-time recipients of Chinese

WMD technology, second-tier proliferators (such as Pakistan and North Korea) are now proliferating to third-tier nuclear aspirants (such as Iran, Saudi Arabia, Syria, and Burma). Proliferation through networking among second- and third-tier nuclear states has opened the Pandora's box that has the potential to unravel the nonproliferation regime. The new challenge thus comes from "within" the NPT, as member states (such as North Korea, Iran, Syria, and Burma) abuse their access to nuclear capabilities.

The most likely scenario is that Pyongyang will not give them up—no matter how many and what agreements it enters into with the United States and other countries. Many in Beijing and Pyongyang believe that the world will have to learn to live with a nuclear-capable Korea just as it has lived with the nuclear weapons capabilities of Israel, India, and Pakistan. Many hardliners support North Korea's limited deterrent capability to counter the United States and its allies and interests in the Pacific. Maintaining that "proliferation is America's problem, not China's," they are confident neither Japan nor Taiwan will go nuclear in the future. For example, Yan Xuetong argues that since China is already surrounded by nuclear powers such as Russia, India, and Pakistan, nothing will change as a result of one more nuclear power. They see North Korea's limited nuclear capability as deterring war on the peninsula and posing no threat to China, as its missiles are pointed toward Japan and the US military bases.[92] Beijing's reluctance to force North Korea to abandon its nuclear program indicates that China is persisting with its policy of using proxies to checkmate and undermine rival powers.[93]

That is why China remains steadfast in its refusal to criticize Pyongyang following the sinking of the South Korea's *Cheonan* ship that killed 46 sailors and the shelling of Yeonpyeong Island in 2010, incurring international opprobrium. Though China can bring North Korea to its knees within forty-eight hours if it stops fuel and food supplies, Beijing is reluctant to put pressure on North Korea, whether the issue is nuclear weapons, the sinking of a South Korean Navy vessel, or the shelling of Yeonpyeong Island. Beijing is likely to use its leverage with Pyongyang *only if* a major war threatens.[94] In the meantime, China values its privileged and exclusive access to North Korea's resources and minerals, captive market for Chinese manufactured goods and access to North Korea's Rajin naval base that facilitates the Chinese naval presence in the Sea of Japan for the first time in history. In 2010, Beijing hosted Kim Jong-Il twice and his third son, Kim Jong-Eun, the heir apparent, once. During his official visit to Pyongyang in the same year, Premier Wen Jiabao offered a $10 billion aid package, thereby effectively undermining the UN Security Council-imposed sanctions. Apparently, Beijing considers it more important to maintain stability than remove WMD from North Korea, and as such would prefer to help sustain the Kim dynasty than let it collapse. The diplomatic protection of Pyongyang is also seen as a litmus test for China's credibility as a great power and security guarantor to Pakistan, Burma, and others. Besides, the Chinese fear Korean reunification might lead to a revival of Korean territorial claims to Gando and other areas in China's northeast. A reunified Korean state will certainly deprive Beijing of exclusive access to DPRK's market, vast natural resources, and naval bases.

Not surprisingly, Beijing's relations with South Korea and Japan have chilled over North Korea. China's coddling of Pyongyang has contributed to a further deterioration of the tone and direction of the US-China relationship, already strained over issues such as trade, Iran, currency squabbles, and climate change. In response to the North Korean provocations and apparent Chinese acquiescence, "Washington is redefining its relationship with South Korea and Japan, potentially creating an anti-China bloc in Northeast Asia."[95] Indeed, the North Korean proliferation crisis is going to show if China can play a constructive leadership role in Asia.[96]

Third-Tier Proliferation: Iran and Burma

To other "nuclear wannabes" like Iran and Burma, North Korea's example shows that belligerence—as part of a calculated effort to win concessions—pays. Not surprisingly, both Iran and Burma have stepped up their WMD programs over the last decade, with indirect support and diplomatic backing from China. A WikiLeaks cable reveals that Beijing allowed North Korean sales of 19 long-range missiles (with a range of up to 2,000 miles/3,000 kilometers) in return for hard currency to transit to Iran via the Beijing airport in 2009.[97] Such transfers are in violation of UN Security Council resolutions targeting North Korea's weapons proliferation activities. According to a defector from Iran's diplomatic service, North Korean missile and nuclear technicians have been regular visitors to Iran since at least 2002. Another State Department cable provides details on China's role as a supplier of materials including 25 tons of specialty steel that could be used in building nuclear-related centrifuges for Iran's nuclear program.[98] These deals raise the specter of the export of fissile material in the future. In 2007, Israeli warplanes destroyed an underground facility in Syria that, according to intelligence officials, was being built secretly by North Korea to manufacture and store nuclear weapons. A CIA report to

Congress in 2009 claimed that Chinese companies, both state-owned and private, continued to sell WMD materials to Iran. According to Gary Milhollin, head of the Wisconsin Project on Nuclear Arms Control: "What this shows is that China has been a consistent problem in US efforts to tighten the noose around Iran's nuclear program. Chinese companies have been a conduit for goods going to Iran."[99] At the UN Security Council, Beijing either questions the value of sanctions against Iran or softens their impact, ostensibly to protect its energy investments worth hundreds of billions of dollars in the resource-rich country.[100] While North Korea's military cooperation with Pakistan and Iran is a much closer and older partnership, its WMD partnership with Burma—in clear breach of UN Security Council resolutions and sanctions—is still developing.

While Pakistan—India's neighbor in the west—has long benefitted from the Chinese and North Korean WMD largesse, Burma, which shares a 1,600-mile border with India in the east—is emerging as Pyongyang's new N-buddy in southern Asia. Fears that Burma has joined a clandestine nuclear network linking North Korea, Iran, Pakistan, and Syria have been growing for some time. New evidence collected from satellite tracking and electronic surveillance as well as secret documents and photographs smuggled out of the country indicate that Burmese generals see increased military cooperation with North Korea—possibly on nuclear technologies, as well as on long-range missiles and underground bunkers—as a way of securing their hold on power forever. Concerns over the regime's attempts to develop a nuclear bomb prompted the UN nuclear watchdog, the IAEA, and the US State Department to demand that the ruling junta disclose an inventory of its nuclear technology and allow visits to sites allegedly involved in clandestine nuclear activities.[101] Burma is also emerging as a key transshipment point for North Korean arms going to countries such as Iran and Syria. The US navy has interdicted a number of North Korean ships and cargo planes in recent years that were allegedly moving missile parts and small arms through Burma's waters and airspace.

Conclusion

Despite China's membership in the NPT, Nuclear Suppliers Group (NSG), Missile Technology Control Regime (MTCR), and other control regimes, China continues to provide nuclear/missile assistance to its friends and allies (Pakistan, Iran, and North Korea) when doing so undermines the security of China's perceived rivals (India, the United States, and Japan). Put differently, Chinese foreign policy objectives with respect to Pakistan and Taiwan, Beijing's desire to maintain the status quo on the Korean Peninsula, and its goal to end American hegemony override any interest in pursuing nonproliferation objectives. Should Iran in the west and Burma in the east go nuclear, India—which already faces nuclear-armed neighbors to its west, in Pakistan, and to its north, in China—will be surrounded by Beijing's nuclear clients.[102] Both India and South Korea continue to exercise restraint in the face of grave provocations from their Beijing-backed neighbors. India has responded by boosting defense cooperation with South Korea that includes military exercises, sharing of military expertise, and technology.[103] In addition, India has also established strategic partnerships with Mongolia, Japan, Vietnam, and the United States. Beijing's ham-fisted approach to the proliferation issue and a self-interested "China first" foreign policy approach is driving Asian nations to tighten their security ties with Washington, an outcome contrary to China's long-term policy goals in the region. China's aggressive behavior in disputes over territorial and maritime boundaries has already unnerved its neighbors—behavior that undercuts efforts to sell itself as a benign power. For Washington, China's aggressive behavior not only helps validate American forward military presence in old allies (such as South Korea and Japan), but also attracts new ones (Mongolia, Vietnam, Indonesia, and India), thereby enlarging its strategic footprint in the Asian theater. In short, China's diplomatic missteps have brought the United States, Japan, South Korea, Vietnam, Indonesia, and India closer.

Notes

[1] See S. A. Kan, *China and Proliferation of Weapons of Mass Destruction and Missiles: Policy Issues* (Washington DC: Report for Congress, Congressional Research Service, December 4, 2002) <http://www.fas.org/spp/starwars/crs/RL31555.pdf>; J. Mohan Malik "China and the nuclear non-proliferation regime," *Contemporary Southeast Asia*, 22:3 (December 2000), 445-478; Mohan Malik, "China plays 'the proliferation card,'" *Jane's Intelligence Review* [hereafter *JIR*], 12:7 (July 2000), 34-37.

[2] CIA report to the US Congress on WMD proliferation for the period of July 2001 to December 2001 was submitted in January 2003. See US Department of State, "CIA report documents weapons proliferation trends," January 7, 2003; B. Gertz, "CIA says N. Korea tried to buy nuclear gear in 2001," *Washington Times*, January 8, 2003, 3.

[3] According to the director of central intelligence, the PRC remains a "key supplier" of technology inconsistent with nonproliferation goals–particularly missile or chemical technology transfers. See Kan, *China and Proliferation of*

Weapons of Mass Destruction and Missiles. In its report released in July 2002, the US-China Security Review Commission stated: "China provides technology and components for weapons of mass destruction and their delivery systems to terrorist-sponsoring states such as North Korea, Pakistan, Iran, Iraq, Syria, Libya and Sudan."

[4] According to the CIA, during the second half of 2001, "North Korea ... export[ed] significant ballistic-missile–related equipment, components, materials and technical expertise to the Middle East, South Asia, and North Africa." See M. Lerner, "North Korea weapons a nuclear nightmare," *Washington Times*, January 17, 2003, 1; G. Kampani, "Second-tier proliferation: the case of Pakistan and North Korea," *Nonproliferation Review*, (Fall/Winter 2002), 107-116; A. Iqbal, "US studies Pakistan, Saudi N-ties: report," *Dawn* (Karachi), August 2, 2002, 1.

[5] See E. Ahrari, "Sino-Indian nuclear perspectives," *JIR*, (August 1998), 33; and Mohan Malik, "Nuclear proliferation in Asia-the China factor," *Australian Journal of International Affairs*, 53:1 (April 1999), 31-4.

[6] Information here draws on Steve Doll, "China's record of proliferation misbehavior," *Issue Brief*, Nuclear Control Institute, Washington, September 29, 1997.

[7] *Proliferation: Chinese Case Studies*, Hearing before the Subcommittee on International Security Proliferation, and Federal Services of the Committee on Governmental Affairs, United States Senate, 105th Congress, 1st Session, April 10, 1997, 8, 12.

[8] L. Doyle, "Pakistan is a rogue nation that supports terror," *Independent* (London), December 12, 2002 <http://news.independent.co.uk/world/asia_china/story.jsp?story=360795>.

[9] B. Gertz, "China aids Pakistani plutonium plant," *Washington Times*, April 3, 1996, A4; G. Milhollin and G. White, "A new China syndrome: China's arms bazaar," *Washington Post*, May 12, 1991, C1, C4.

[10] Quoted in R. Windrem, "China gave Pakistan design data, training and nuclear material," *Indian Express*, June 9, 1999, 1.

[11] See J. Garver, "Nuclear weapons and the China-India relationship," paper presented at conference on "South Asia's nuclear dilemma," Weatherhead Center for International Affairs, Harvard University, February 18-19, 1999; T. Weiner, "US and Chinese aid was essential as Pakistan built bomb," *IHT*, June 2, 1998, 1; "Atom arms parts sold to Pakistan by China, US says," *New York Times*, February 8, 1996, Al.

[12] For a confirmation of Chinese supplies of ballistic missiles to Pakistan, see Chinese ambassador to the USA Zhu Qizhen's address to the National Press Club, Washington DC, *Reuters* Transcript Report (June 27, 1991) cited in J. Wilson and Hua Di, "China's ballistic missile program," *International Security*, 17:2, (Fall 1992), 37; D. Lennox, "Control regimes fail to stem the spread," *JIR*, (September 1999), 50-54; R. J. Smith, "China linked to Pakistani missile plant," *Washington Post*, August 25, 1996, 1.

[13] "US says Pakistan has full Chinese missile system," *Reuters*, September 14, 1999, <www.cnn.com/asianow/southasia>; R. J. Smith, "Spy photos suggest

China missile trade," *Washington Post*, July 3, 1995, 1; G. Milhollin, "China cheats (what a surprise!)," *New York Times*, April 24, 1997, A35.

[14] For details, see Mohan Malik, "The China factor in the India-Pakistan conflict," *Parameters*, (Spring 2003), 1-16. "We cannot rule out the possibility of continued contacts between Chinese and Pakistani entities on Pakistani nuclear weapons development," according to the US Department of State, "CIA report documents weapons proliferation trends," January 7, 2003, <http://www.satribune.com/archives/jan13_19_03/P1_targets.htm>.

[15] B. Gertz, "CIA says N. Korea tried to buy nuclear gear in 2001," *Washington Times*, January 8, 2003, 3. Also see US Department of State, "CIA report documents weapons proliferation trends"; *Washington Times*, August 6, 2001; B. Raman, "A warning shot for Islamabad," *Asia Times online*, December 13, 2002 <http://www.atimes.com/atimes/South_Asia/DL13Df03.html>.

[16] J. Bone, "Pakistani scientist 'offered Saddam nuclear designs,'" *Times* (London), December 20, 2002.

[17] M. Hibbs, "No US agency consensus on DPRK nuclear progress," *Nucleonics Week*, January 6, 1994, 10.

[18] L. Spector et al, *Tracking Nuclear Proliferation* (Carnegie Endowment for International Peace, 1995), 49.

[19] B. Gertz, "China still shipping arms despite pledges," *Washington Times*, April 15, 1999, 1. Beijing is reported to have diverted US-manufactured equipment to Pakistan's National Development Centre by disguising the shipment in export documents as "Masada Cookware." J. S. Bermudez Jr, "DPRK-Pakistan Ghauri missile cooperation," Jane's Defence Weekly, May 21, 1998 posted on Federation of American Scientists (FAS) <www.fas.org.>.

[20] B. Gertz, "Panel to probe China's nuclear-related sales to N. Korea," *Washington Times*, December 20, 2002, 3; and "N. Korea seeks aid from China on nukes," *Washington Times*, December 9, 2002, 1.

[21] B. Gertz, "China ships North Korea ingredient for nuclear arms," *Washington Times*, December 17, 2002, 3.

[22] J. Tkacik, "Pollyanna-like on Pyongyang," *Asian Wall Street Journal*, December 2, 2002.

[23] Interestingly, General Xiong's visits to Pyongyang and Islamabad are often followed by serious escalations on the Korean Peninsula and South Asia. Not long after General Xiong's visit to Pyongyang in August 1998, North Korea terrified Japan by firing an intermediate-range ballistic missile. This missile launch was preceded by a serious escalation in South Asia months before with the launching of a Pyongyang-supplied *Nodong* (*Ghauri*) missile by Islamabad followed by tit-for-tat nuclear tests by India and Pakistan in May 1998. Ironically, General Xiong was spotted in Islamabad in March 2002 signing agreements on "Joint Defense" and "Joint Military Production" at the time of heightened tensions between India and Pakistan and later in October in Pyongyang. See E. Timperlake and W. C. Triplett, "N. Korea, Pakistan, China," *Washington Times*, December 8, 2002.

[24] T. Woodrow, "China opens Pandora's nuclear box," *China Brief*, 2:24 (December 10, 2002) <http://china.jamestown.org/pubs/view/cwe_002_024_001.htm>.

[25] H. Sokolski cited in Kan, China and Proliferation of Weapons of Mass Destruction and Missiles, 14.

[26] J. Dao, "US and China resume high-level military talks," *New York Times*, December 10, 2002. Italics mine. B. Gertz, "China's arms sales, stance on Taiwan chill talks with US," *Washington Times*, December 10, 2002, 7.

[27] S. M. Hersh, "The cold test," *New Yorker*, January 27, 2003.

[28] D. E. Sanger, "In North Korea and Pakistan, deep roots of nuclear barter," *New York Times*, November 23, 2002, 1.

[29] Islamabad's "brazenness" in using US C-130 aircraft to transport the secret payload that General Musharraf had personally assured President Bush in 2001 would be used primarily to hunt down al-Qaeda terrorists has not gone unnoticed in Washington's policy circles, writes Sanger, "In North Korea and Pakistan, deep roots of nuclear barter."

[30] Cited in C. Rajghatta, "India imperiled by US ignoring Pak-Korean ties," *Times of India*, November 24, 2002, 1.

[31] "Double-dealing," *Newssight.net,* November 8, 2002 <http://www.indiareacts.com/fulldebate2.asp?recno=517>.

[32] Sanger, "In North Korea and Pakistan, deep roots of nuclear barter."

[33] Quoted in *Los Angeles Times*, January 7, 2003, 1.

[34] Pakistan has reportedly informed the United States that a number of its scientists and military officers were "personally" involved in providing technology related primarily to uranium enrichment and equipment design to North Korea, and have admitted receiving remittances worth "tens of thousands of dollars" as "rewards from North Korea" over "a number of years," Japanese news agency Jiji Press said. "Pak informed US of nuclear technology transfer," *Jiji Press* (Tokyo), December 25, 2002. M. Ejaz, "Washington Diary: Pakistan and Proliferation issue," *The News*, December 22, 2002; AFP, "Musharraf says no barter with N. Korea," *Dawn*, January 13, 2003, 1; A. Iqbal, "Dr Qadeer suspected of links with 'axis of evil' states," *Dawn*, January 8, 2003 1.

[35] Representative T. Lantos, "Chinese ballistic missile sales," Statement before the Subcommittee on International Security, International Organizations, and Human Rights, House Foreign Affairs Committee, May 20, 1993, 4; Senate Hearings on "Weapons proliferation in China," International Security, Proliferation and Federal Services Subcommittee of the Senate Governmental Affairs Committee, April 10, 1997; B. Gertz, "China sold Iran missile technology," *Washington Times*, November 21, 1996, A1. China has transferred short-range CSS-8 ballistic missiles to Iran.

[36] B. Opall, "US queries China on Iran: Fears transfer of missile technology," *Defense News*, June 19-25, 1995, 1.

[37] R. Einhorn, deputy assistant secretary of state for nonproliferation, Testimony before the Senate Governmental Affairs Committee, Subcommittee on International Security, reported in "State Dept. revises report on China's arms sales to Iran," *Washington Times*, April 15, 1997, A3.

[38] M. Yost, "China's deadly trade in the Mideast," *Wall Street Journal*, December 4, 1996, A18.

[39] Kim Min-seok, Oh Young-hwan, "Iran said to be buyer of North missiles," *JoongAng Ilbo*, December 19, 2002 <http://english.joins.com/Article.asp?aid=20021219024551&sid=200>.

[40] "US finds China-Libya missile link," *Newsinsight.net*, December 20, 2002 <http://www.intelligenceonline.net/allintelligencefull.asp?id=04046020410422&recno=1610>.

[41] In May 1999, following the Pakistani nuclear tests, Prince Sultan toured the uranium-enrichment plant and missile production facilities at Kahuta. "If Riyadh's influence over Pakistan extends to its nuclear programs, Saudi Arabia could rapidly become a *de facto* nuclear power through a simple shipment of missiles and warheads," writes T. Woodrow, "The Sino-Saudi connection," *China Brief*, 2:21 (October 24, 2002) <http://china.jamestown.org/pubs/view/cwe_002_021_003.htm>.

[42] S. Blank, "Pakistan bent on proliferation path," *Asia Times online*, January 3, 2003 <http://www.atimes.com/atimes/South_Asia/EA03Df01.html>.

[43] On the enduring interest in not provoking others while China remains weak, see Wang Sheng,"'Taoguang yanghui' bu shi quan yi zhi ji," ("'Concealing one's strength and biding one's time' is not a stopgap"), *Huanqiu shibao* [*Global Times*], August 17, 2001. Also see Mohan Malik, "China's Asia policy: restrain Japan, contain India," *Japan Times*, June 12, 1999, 21; Malik, "China plays 'the proliferation card"; and T. Henriksen and C. Walker, "Seeking surrogates to challenge the US," *Global Beat Syndicate*, April 25, 2001 <http://www.nyu.edu/globalbeat/syndicate/Walker042501.html>.

[44] On taking advantage of the contradictions that exist between these countries, see Hu Yumin, "The US post-Cold War nonproliferation policy," *International Strategic Studies*, (Beijing), 3 (July 1999), 54.

[45] J. Hill, "China offended by US 'threat' theory,'" *JIR*, (September 2002), 10.

[46] Sha Zukang's remarks at a conference in Beijing, September 1999; E. Eckholm, "China says US missile shield could force an arms buildup," *New York Times*, May 11, 2000, 1.

[47] For details, see Malik, "China's Asia policy: restrain Japan, contain India."

[48] Privately, Chinese strategists justify this on the grounds that all NWSs have helped at least one allied state to go nuclear: for example, the US helped Britain, the Soviets helped China, the French and the Americans helped Israel.

[49] "China might be pitting North Korea against Japan in the same way as it is pitting Pakistan against India," wrote T. Delpech, "Nuclear weapons and the 'new world order': early warning from Asia?" *Survival*, 40:4 (Winter 1998-99), 65.

[50] Conversation with Yu Changsen, April 7, 1999. On partnerships as "quasi-alliances," see Ye Zicheng, "Zhongguo shixing daguo waijiao zhanlue shizaibixing" ("The imperative for China to implement a great power diplomatic strategy"), *Shijie jingji yu zhengzhi* [*World Economics and Politics*] No. 1, (2000), 5-10, 9-10.

[51] A. I. Johnston, *China and Arms Control* (Aurora Papers 3, The Canadian Centre for Arms Control and Disarmament, 1986), 13.

[52] See "China silent on whether Iran nuclear sale shelved," *Reuters*, August 26, 1997. On November 28, 1999, Ehud Barak told the Chinese leader Li Peng that Israel was concerned about China's continuing sales of arms to Iran and reminded him of "China's important decision of 1997" to cease such transfers.

[53] B. Barber, "Israel doesn't want US ire over China," *Washington Times*, April 14, 2000, 1.

[54] B. Gertz, "Israel asked to stop arms sales to China," *Washington Times*, January 3, 2003, 1; "US finds China-Libya missile link," *Newsinsight.net*, December 20, 2002 <http://www.intelligenceonline.net/World.asp?id= 363343313604&recno=1610&sub=Ge neral>.

[55] On China's attempts to link non-proliferation issues to the US arms sales to Taiwan, see S. A. Kan, *Chinese Proliferation of Weapons of Mass Destruction*, CRS Issue Brief 92056, *Current Policy Issues*, June 1, 1998.

[56] T. J. Christensen, "Chinese realpolitik," *Foreign Affairs*, 75:5 (September/October 1996), 37.

[57] M. Kelly, "Kick the (Korea) can," *Washington Post*, January 8, 2003, 19.

[58] Cited in F. Sisci, "Mega-NATO: China out in the cold." *Asia Times online*, May 24, 2002 <http://www.atimes.com/china/DE24Ad01.html>; E. Neuffer, "A US concern: Pakistan's arsenal," *Boston Globe*, August 16, 2002, 1. "Pakistan is the new Afghanistan, a privileged sanctuary for hundreds of al-Qaeda fighters and Taliban operatives," wrote A. de Borchgrave, "The new Afghanistan," *Washington Times*, September 2, 2002, 1.

[59] "Asia's nuclear axis," *Jane's Intelligence Digest*, November 6, 2002.

[60] Y. Funabashi, "A Critical Test for Japan's Diplomacy," *PacNet 2*, January 9, 2003.

[61] "China doesn't want reunified Korea," *JoongAng Ilbo*, November 6, 2002, 1. China worries about three kinds of crises once the two Koreas reunify: an emergence of a unified democratic government and the rise of Korean nationalism, a continued US military presence on the peninsula, and Japan's rearming. From a geopolitical point of view, Russia also prefers a divided Korea to one allied with the US or China. As for the United States, it favors the unification of Korea and the end of nuclear proliferation but in a manner that does not destabilize Northeast Asia and reduce its military presence and influence. South Koreans, for their part, seem to resent American meddling more than anything else. They want one unified Korea, and many would not mind if a unified Korea inherits the North's nuclear weapons.

[62] A. Bezlova, "Beijing's influence on North Korea overstated," *Asia Times online*, January 11, 2003 <http://www.atimes.com/atimes/China/ EA11Ad06.html>.

[63] Beijing-Pyongyang relations were further strained in 2002 when Beijing arrested a Chinese-born businessman picked by Kim Jong-Il to run a special economic zone on the Sino-North Korean border and Pyongyang acknowledged a nuclear weapons program on the eve of a Bush-Jiang summit in late October 2002.

[64] Ironically, China now finds itself in the same predicament vis-à-vis North Korea that Pakistan was confronted with post-9/11 when Islamabad came

under external pressure to abandon its pro-Taliban policy and stop all food and fuel supplies to Afghanistan. Much like Pakistan then, China now finds it difficult to comply with the request to stop food and fuel supplies to North Korea.

[65] H. McDonald, "Beijing content with the devil it knows, despite Pyongyang's nuclear threat," *Age* (Melbourne), January 14, 2003.

[66] Editorial, "Why doesn't US 'use force' against DPRK?" *People's Daily online*, January 8, 2003 <http://english.peopledaily.com.cn/200301/08/eng20030108_109768.shtml>.

[67] W. Safire, "An assignment for China and Russia," *IHT*, January 3, 2003, 7.

[68] C. Krauthammer, "The Japan card," *Washington Post*, January 3, 2003, 19.

[69] R. Lim, "Korea in the vortex," *China Brief*, 3:1 (January 14, 2003).

[70] Some American observers have called for the withdrawal of the 37,000-strong US force deployed in South Korea so as to force regional countries to shoulder the responsibility of maintaining security in Northeast Asia and to pave the way for (possible) denuclearisation and reunification of the Korean Peninsula.

[71] J. Hoagland, "Nuclear enabler: Pakistan today is the most dangerous place on Earth," *Washington Post*, October 24, 2002. Also see B. Gautam, "How long will U.S. ignore Pakistan threat?" *Japan Times*, January 13, 2003; T. Anthony, "Alliance with Islamabad shaky from start," *Washington Times*, January 11, 2003, 8; G. Kessler, "Powell says Pakistan warned on N. Korean ties: Musharraf told he will face 'consequences' if nuclear transfers continue," *Washington Post*, November 26, 2002, 21.

[72] P. Bedard, "Washington whispers," *US News & World Report*, January 20, 2003; S. Saleem Shahzad, "The net closes on Pakistan," *Asia Times online*, January 23, 2003 <http://www.atimes.com/atimes/South_Asia/EA23Df03.html>.

[73] J. Mohan Malik, "Dragon on terrorism: assessing China's tactical gains and strategic losses after 11 September," *Contemporary Southeast Asia*, 24:2 (August 2002), 277-280; PTI, "India approaches US, Russia for North Korea-Pak nuke nexus," *Hindustan Times*, December 8, 2002, 1.

[74] S. Blank, "Pyongyang derails Northeast Asian progress," *Asia Times online*, December 17, 2002 <http://www.atimes.com/atimes/Korea/DL17Dg01.html>.

[75] Cited from P. P. Pan, "China treads carefully around North Korea," *Washington Post*, January 10, 2003, 14.

[76] J. Brooke, "China 'looming large' in South Korea as biggest player, replacing the US," *New York Times*, January 3, 2003.

[77] Shi Yongming, "Give peace a chance," *Beijing Review*, November 21, 2002, 15. Italics mine.

[78] D. E. Sanger, "Asia's splits deepen Korea crisis," *New York Times*, December 29, 2002; Mohan Malik, "The Korean Peninsula: conflict or peace?" *Current Affairs Bulletin* (Sydney), 69:12 (May 1993), 4-12.

[79] For example, if media reports about India's nuclear cooperation with Vietnam and missile collaboration with Taiwan are true, New Delhi may have decided to have its own "Israel" to counter Beijing's "Israel." See AFP, "Taiwan, India in secret military cooperation: report," January 2, 2002. Full report in "Wo he Indu mimi zhan kai junshi hezuo," *Lianhe xinwen* [Taipei], <http://udnnews.com/CB/NEWS/FOCUSNEWS/POLITICS/647735.shtml>; R. Puri, "Partnership with Vietnam," *Hindustan Times*, December 8, 1999.

[80] "Nuclear lessons for China," *The Economist*, December 9, 2002.

[81] P. C. Saunders and Jing-dong Yuan, "Korea crisis will test Chinese diplomacy," *Asia Times online*, January 8, 2003 <http://www.atimes.com/atimes/Korea/EA08Dg03.html>.

[82] China, Pakistan, and the Bomb: The Declassified File on U.S. Policy, 1977–1997, <http://www.gwu.edu/~nsarchiv/NSAEBB/NSAEBB114/press.htm>.

[83] "China's proliferation practices," *2004 Report to the Congress of the U.S.-China Economic & Security Review Commission*, 108 Congress (Washington: U.S. Government Printing Office, June 2004), 123–150. Italics added.

[84] C. Giacomo, "China's role in peaceful world questioned," *Reuters*, October 31, 2006.

[85] B. Gertz, "Congressional study cites China as nuc supplier to North Korea," *Washington Times*, October 31, 2006.

[86] K. DeYoung, "New estimates put Pakistan's nuclear arsenal at more than 100," *Washington Post*, January 31, 2011; D. E. Sanger and E. Schmitt, "Pakistani nuclear arms pose challenge to U.S. policy," *International Herald Tribune*, January 31, 2011.

[87] J. Solomon, "China reactors plan fuels U.S. concern," *Wall Street Journal*, July 19, 2010, 8.

[88] Zhang Yan, the Chinese ambassador to India, cited in B. Chellaney, "Troubling China-India ties," *Japan Times*, December 29, 2010, <http://search.japantimes.co.jp/cgi-bin/eo20101229bc.html>.

[89] F. Dahl, "Analysis: did smugglers help North Korea's nuclear drive?" Reuters, December 1, 2010, <http://www.reuters.com/article/2010/12/01/us-nuclear-north-smuggling-idUSTRE6AT1OH20101201>

[90] Shen Dingli, "Revisiting the "Axis of Evil"–Part III," *YaleGlobal online*, August 5, 2008, <http://yaleglobal.yale.edu/display.article?id=11153>. Italics mine.

[91] See A. Olesen, "Why China reluctant to board ships of N. Korea," *Philadelphia Inquirer*, October 18, 2006.

[92] Discussions at the US-China Strategic Dialogue, Beijing and Shanghai, August 2009, June 2010.

[93] J. Bernier, "China's strategic proxies," *Orbis*, 47:4, (Fall 2003), 629–643.

[94] S. S. Harrison, "China's North Korean calculations," *IHT*, January 6, 2011, <http://www.nytimes.com/2011/01/07/opinion/07iht-edharrison07.html?_r=1&ref=global-home>

[94] J. Pomfret, “U.S. steps up pressure on China to rein in N. Korea,” *Washington Post*, December 6, 2010, 1.

[95] J. Pomfret, “U.S. Steps up pressure on China to rein in N. Korea,” *Washington Post*, December 6, 2010, 1.

[96] T. Rubin, “China runs big risks coddling N. Korea,” *Philadelphia Inquirer*, December 5, 2010; M. Landler, “Obama urges China to check North Koreans,” *New York Times*, December 7, 2010, 1.

[97] B. Lintner, “North Korea’s missiles aimed for Iran,” *Asia Times online*, January 12, 2011, <http://www.atimes.com/atimes/Korea/MA12Dg01.html>.

[98] Rubin, “China runs big risks coddling N. Korea.”

[99] Cited from B. Gertz, “Chinese firm tied to steel used in Iran nukes: state warned Beijing on sale,” *Washington Times*, January 24, 2011, 1.

[100] P. Richter, “West worries China may undermine Iran sanctions efforts,” *Los Angeles Times,* June 28, 2010; AFP, “US lawmakers fume over China’s Iran links,” *Channelnewsasia.com,* December 2, 2010, <http://www.channelnewsasia.com/stories/afp_asiapacific/view/1096779/1/.html>.

[101] A. Spillius and D. McElroy, “Burma is working on nuclear weapons programme, experts claim,” *Daily Telegraph* (London), July 26, 2010, 11. Leaked US diplomatic cables published by the website WikiLeaks in 2010 document concerns inside successive American administrations about Burma’s weapons programs and alleged cooperation with North Korea. See J. Solomon, “Myanmar’s links with Pyongyang stir nuclear fears,” *Wall Street Journal*, December 18, 2010, 11.

[102] P. Shenon, “The next nuclear nightmare,” *TheDailyBeast.com*, April 14, 2010, <http://www.thedailybeast.com/blogs-and-stories/2010-04-14/the-next-nuclear-nightmare/>.

[103] “India, South Korea sign five year defense co-operation MOU,” *Asian Defence*, September 3, 2010, <http://asian-defence.blogspot.com/2010/09/india-south-korea-sign-five-year.html>.

9
Multilateral Maneuvers

The liberal school of international relations maintains that participation in international institutions casts aside zero-sum power games and promotes cooperative behavior that is conducive to dispute resolution. For international institutions codify rules and norms in world politics and create arenas for resolving disputes among dissatisfied powers. Liberals believe that the potential for competition and conflict is exaggerated by realists, and they remain optimistic about reducing, if not eliminating, security competition among states and establishing a more peaceful and stable world order. They point to Beijing's policy of engagement and its membership in regional and global institutions as evidence of a thickening web of connections between China and the rest of the world that helps foster stability. The growing Chinese and Indian activism in regional and global organizations post-Cold War has raised hopes of increased dialogue and cooperation that would help overcome their competitive impulses and mutual distrust of each other. Both China and India are active participants in multilateral forums such as the ASEAN Regional Forum (ARF), the ASEAN Defense Ministers' Meeting Plus Eight (ADMM+8), the Asia-Europe Meeting (ASEM), the South Asian Association for Regional Cooperation (SAARC), the Shanghai Cooperation Organization (SCO), the East Asia Summit (EAS), the Group of Twenty (G-20) and the BRIC (Brazil, Russia, India, China) bloc. In addition, China is also a key member of the Asia-Pacific Economic Cooperation (APEC), ASEAN Plus Three (APT) (ASEAN Plus China, South Korea, Japan), the Nuclear Suppliers Group (NSG), and more importantly, a veto-holding permanent member of the United Nations Security Council (UNSC).

However, this chapter demonstrates that far from mitigating their power competition, regional institutions and international organizations have become the new arenas of Sino-Indian rivalry for maximizing relative power and for gaining advantage and influence. Even as both engage in greater interaction and dialogue, Chinese and Indian diplomats continue to engage in one-upmanship in multilateral forums, each side constantly maneuvering for prestige and dominance with the purpose of diminishing or marginalizing the other. Both put forward proposals for multilateral cooperation that seek to sideline or exclude the other. For instance, soon after obtaining observer status in SAARC in 2007, Beijing vowed to "dilute India's hold in the region as a major economic power."[1] In December 2008, China established the Asia-Pacific Space Cooperation Organization (APSCO in 2008), headquartered in Beijing, that has seven member states (China, Bangladesh, Iran, Pakistan, Mongolia, Peru, and Thailand) but excludes India. China has often used multilateral institutions to contain rival India by launching worldwide *undiplomatic*—at times, almost hysterical—campaigns to oppose India's membership of global and regional organizations, whether it is the ARF or the UNSC or the SCO or the APEC or the EAS. Whenever faced with the issue of India's membership, China's initial reaction usually is: "*Yindu bu-xing*" ("Not India"). However, once its "*nyet* diplomacy" fails, Beijing invariably responds by saying "OK, but *not* without Pakistan" to keep India permanently paired with its sub-continental rival. The ARF, the SCO, and the UNSC are a few good examples of this Chinese stance. For its part, India offers solace to those in Southeast and East Asia who remain wary of Beijing's ambitions to establish an "East Asia Co-prosperity Sphere" under China's leadership.[2] The Mekong-Ganges Cooperation (MGC), the Bay of Bengal Initiative for Multi-Sectoral Technical and Economic Cooperation (BIMSTEC), the Indian Ocean Naval Symposium (IONS) and the India-Brazil-South Africa (IBSA) Dialogue Forum are India-led multilateral frameworks that exclude China. The China-India rivalry for relative power gains is also being played out in international financial institutions such as the Asian Development Bank (ADB), the International Monetary Fund (IMF) and the World Bank as well, where each seeks to disadvantage the other.

These two Asian giants' approach to multilateralism validates realist critiques of liberalism; in particular, "the false promise of institutions" in taming or constraining major power rivalries through dialogue, confidence-building measures (CBMs), norms, agreements, and organizations.[3] The multilateral maneuverings of China and India support the realist critique that dialogue and institutionalism alone do not necessarily ameliorate acute security dilemmas or reduce tensions in a significant manner. Asia's regional organizations and global institutions are either too weak to be effective in conflict management or remain susceptible to manipulation by major powers. Instead of developing cooperative approaches to find common solutions to traditional and transnational security threats, multilateral institutions provide Beijing and New Delhi with additional opportunities to air their grievances and subtly undermine each other's regional influence, either through attempts to deny their competitors access to such organizations, or through the launching of contending development and security projects.[4] This chapter outlines the China-India struggle for supremacy and leadership positions in various global and regional multilateral institutions.

Security Council Reform: China Signals Its Veto[5]

Security Council reform has been on the agenda for more than 15 years, spawning countless working groups and task forces and rounds of diplomatic wrangling. Critics have long argued that the council is both undemocratic and anachronistic, and that its effectiveness and legitimacy cannot be sustained unless it is transformed to reflect today's world. There is a consensus that a revamped Security Council should reflect the political, economic, military, and demographic realities of today's world if it is to deal with new threats to international security, notably terrorism, failed states, nuclear proliferation, poverty, and violence. However, UN member states have failed to agree on how big the council should become and whether other nations should be given veto powers. No single proposal has ever won majority support. As a result, the Security Council continues to reflect the global power structure of 1945, when the five Second World War victors (the "P-5") acquired their privileged status. The reluctance of thc P-5 to entertain any change undermining their status has emerged as a major obstacle. The last big push for reform came in mid-2005, soon after a high-level panel of 16 eminent diplomats and public servants (including stalwarts like former United States [US] national security adviser Brent Scowcroft, former Russian premier Yevgeny Primakov and former Chinese foreign minister Qian Qichen among others) submitted its report in late 2004.

Unfortunately, the high-level panel on UN reforms also failed to agree on one proposal and instead suggested two options to broaden the membership of the Security Council.[6] Option A would add six new permanent members—the likely candidates are India, Japan, Brazil, Germany, Egypt, and either Nigeria or South Africa—as well as three new two-year term non-permanent members. Option B would create a new tier of eight semi-permanent members chosen for renewable four-year terms and add one two-year term seat to the existing ten. However, neither option extends veto power beyond the existing five permanent members. That even this panel was unable to agree upon a single model for expansion reflected a wider reality: the politics and the prospects of Security Council reform do not look very promising, especially in light of China's opposition.

Figure 9.1

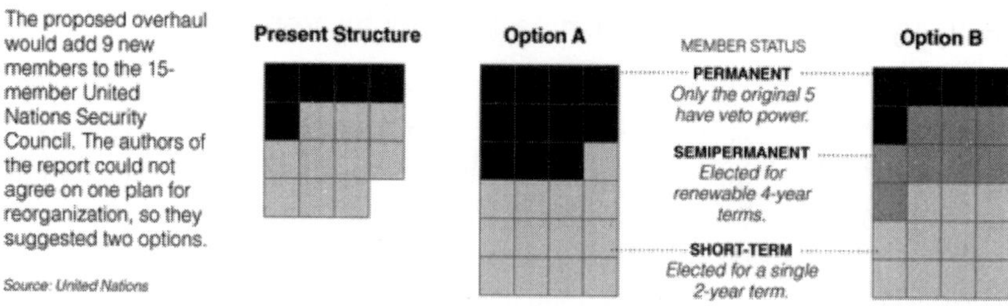

Anticipating the report on council reform, leaders of India, Japan, Germany, and Brazil united to form the "Group of Four" (G-4) in 2004 to back each other's bids for permanent seats. While Japan's bid for a permanent seat had Washington's support, India was backed by three of the P-5: Britain, France, and Russia. Maintaining an ambiguous stance, China, in contrast, deliberately avoided expressing support for any country for a long time while periodically calling for reform of the Security Council. However, in a significant departure, President Jiang Zemin offered encouragement to Germany and Brazil during official visits to those countries in 2002, despite Beijing's stated position that the council is already overrepresented by "rich and white" industrialized nations.

Without commenting on China's stand on countries seeking permanent membership, Chinese Foreign Ministry spokesperson Zhang Qiyue welcomed the high-level panel's proposals on "enhanc[ing] the international collective security mechanism with the UN at its core" and emphasized the need for consensus: "any reform scenario should be discussed by the UN members in a democratic manner so that *extensive consensus can be reached* … there are still many differences in this regard."[7] A valuable insight into Chinese thinking was provided in a commentary in the authoritative *Beijing Review* in May 2004 by the Chinese Foreign Ministry analyst Wu Miaofa, which, for the first time, spelled out "five principles" for reform of the Security Council.[8] These principles were later incorporated into the official Chinese position paper and were articulated by China's UN ambassador Wang Guangya in July 2005.[9] A critical scrutiny of these "principles" (in effect, "conditions") revealed them to be self-serving, contradictory, and antidemocratic—all seemingly designed for the purpose of stalling an expansion of the council that would increase the number of veto-holding permanent members. The "five principles" put in question Beijing's commitment to a multipolar world and contravene the "five principles of peaceful coexistence" (premised on the *equality* of all nations, big and small, first outlined in 1955 during the heyday of Sino-Indian friendship), which are touted by Beijing as the moral basis of interstate relations. At best, the Chinese perspective provides valuable insight into Beijing's insecurities and fears regarding the gathering momentum for UN reform and reflects its core attitudes toward great power relations within Asia. At worst, it is an unconvincing plea for maintaining the status quo.

Geography Matters

According to the first principle, "top priority [should be assigned] to achieving equitable geographic distribution" in the Security Council.[10] This is an admirable position, but the implication is that since Asia is already represented by China, adding representation for Africa and Latin America ought to be the topmost priority. This explains Beijing's public support for Brazil's bid. Admittedly, China's support is in part motivated by its desire to forge closer strategic ties with a major Latin American country in the United States' backyard. Obviously, China could not endorse India's or Japan's bid as it would have the effect of undercutting Beijing's role as the sole permanent Asian voice in the council.

Only Small and Medium-Sized Developing Countries Need Apply

Since developed countries hold a disproportionate number of council seats, the second principle approved "the earnest and legitimate wish of developing countries" for "reasonable representation in the Security Council permanent category." As the council acts most frequently on conflicts in developing countries, it ought to include new members from the bloc that comprises a majority of the 192 UN member states. A strict application of this principle would exclude Japan but favor the inclusion of India, Indonesia, Pakistan, Malaysia, and Egypt. Significantly, this principle was reiterated by the Foreign Ministry spokesperson after the release of the UN panel's report.[11]

However, this formulation did not translate into support for India, the world's largest developing country, despite constant Indian urgings to do so. Far from it: Beijing had long adopted a dismissive and even contemptuous attitude toward New Delhi's bid for a permanent seat. For India, its large size got in the way. As ambassador Wang later clarified (or qualified) in his UN General Assembly speech, "the small and medium-sized [developing] countries in particular should be given more opportunities to enter the Council."[12] A senior Chinese diplomat had confided to his US interlocutor in 2000: "China will never allow India to join the Security Council, certainly not in my lifetime." Chinese diplomats also claimed that giving a permanent seat to India would amount to rewarding it for developing nuclear weapons.[13] In June 2004, in a media interview, state councilor and former foreign minister Tang Jiaxuan was noncommittal about China's position regarding India's bid. However, a few months later, during Tang's October 2004 visit to New Delhi, China's public position softened somewhat, with Beijing now endorsing, for the first time, "a bigger role for India in the international community, *including in the United Nations Security Council*."[14] This statement, later repeated by Premier Wen Jiabao, prompted the Indian media to speculate that China, hitherto ambivalent, was now backing New Delhi's claims.[15] Some observers even asserted that this represented "a significant shift in Beijing's India policy since its 'all-weather ally' Pakistan has gone on record at the UN General Assembly opposing India's bid."[16] However, those who argued that China would not publicly oppose India's bid or gang up with Pakistan for *realpolitik* reasons were in for a surprise. In fact, both Foreign Minister Li Zhaoxing and Premier Wen Jiabao stopped short of publicly supporting New Delhi's bid for a permanent seat.[17]

In their talks with Indian leaders, Chinese leaders reportedly made it clear that China's support for India's seat would come "with strings attached." According to diplomats privy to bilateral negotiations, the Chinese listed three preconditions: India must oust the Dalai Lama, it must not support Japan's bid for a permanent seat, and New Delhi should be sensitive to Beijing's security concerns in building its relations with China's East Asian neighbors.[18] Soon after the release of the high-level panel's report, Li Wei, a Chinese analyst from an influential think tank, the China Institute of Contemporary International Relations (CICIR), spoke of new benchmarks: "one, India should ensure stability in South Asia [translation: resolve the Kashmir dispute to Pakistan's satisfaction]; two, it should have friendly relations with its neighbours [translation: abandon great power hegemonic ambitions] and three, it should contribute towards world peace [translation: cease development of nuclear weapons]."[19] These benchmarks were so broad that no government in New Delhi could accept them as the price for Beijing's support.[20] Were it to do so, any signs of deterioration in India-Pakistan relations, for example, could be exploited to question India's suitability for membership. At any rate, Beijing's conditional support for India's inclusion comes only if the new entrants are not given the right of veto. Commenting on the Indian foreign minister's statement after the release of the panel's report that New Delhi would not accept a seat without a right of veto, Li Shaoxian, Vice President of the CICIR, commented: "If India sticks to this position, I don't see India becoming a permanent member of the United Nations Security Council any time soon."[21]

Until 2004, the Chinese position on India's claim to a seat was deliberately veiled in ambiguity. Beijing continued to reiterate general support for greater representation from developing countries, remained strongly opposed to Japan but said little about India, and seemed favorably disposed toward Brazil and Germany. China-Japan relations, always prickly, deteriorated sharply during 2004–05 due to Beijing's opposition to a permanent council seat for Japan, not to mention their differences over school textbooks and Prime Minister Koizumi's visit to the Yasukuni Shrine commemorating Japan's war dead, where Japanese war criminals are also interred. Reacting sharply to Prime Minister Junichiro Koizumi's push for council membership in his September 2004 UN address, in which the Japanese leader cited Japan's financial contribution to the world body (greater than the combined share of four of the P-5, except the United States), China's Foreign Ministry spokesperson argued that the council was "not a board of directors" and its composition should not be decided "according to the financial contribution of its members." He added: "if a country wishes to play a responsible role in international affairs, it must have a clear understanding of the historical questions concerning itself," referring to Japan's perceived failure to apologize adequately for its aggression before and during the Second World War.[22] In *realpolitik* terms, Beijing believed Brazil and Germany could be leveraged against the United States, but Japan and India could not be. Brazil also attracted China's attention because it was emerging as a vocal critic of the United States on both economic and security issues. Likewise, smarting from its lack of support for the Iraq War (2003), Washington had turned lukewarm to Germany's candidacy. China's more nuanced position on India could also be attributed to Beijing's broader security concerns over preventing an India-Japan alignment.

However, three key developments prompted a rethinking of China's stance: the joint statement issued by the Indian and Japanese foreign ministers in New Delhi in August 2004 on supporting (rather than contesting) each other's candidature for permanent membership, followed closely by the formation of a united front on the reform issue by the G-4 nations in September 2004, and the growing warmth in US-India relations.[23] Seen from Beijing's perspective, the formation of this "Gang of Four" was a major setback for China's diplomacy insofar as it brought together on a common platform two of China's rivals (India and Japan) that Beijing wanted to keep out and two potential allies (Brazil and Germany) that it wanted to bring into the council. Instead of openly opposing India's bid (as in the case of Japan), Beijing initially chose to rely on "spoiler states" like Pakistan, which was waging a diplomatic campaign to scuttle India's bid for a permanent seat.

Small is Beautiful, Consensus Is a Must

Acknowledging the growing clamor for a permanent seat, the third principle cautioned that the council is "an organ of fairly high authority and moderate size," and therefore "its expansion should not go without ceiling or restriction, and that a high degree of diplomatic wisdom and expertise is called for in this regard." While the Chinese insistence upon "a high degree of diplomatic wisdom and expertise" as a prerequisite for permanent membership is disingenuous, if not insulting, to countries with a better record of service to the UN than China, the point about "expansion … without ceiling" is valid. Obviously, no one wants an unwieldy council: in both scenarios outlined by the high-level panel, total membership would not exceed 24. The G-4 calls for addition of six permanent and four non-permanent members. The African Union's proposal called for 26 seats, one more permanent seat than the G-4 proposal of 25, and veto power for new members. The Uniting for Consensus group (UFC, a.k.a. the Coffee Club) led by Pakistan and Italy and backed by China seeks enlargement of the council to 25 by adding ten new members *only in the non-permanent category* elected for two-year terms. The United States does not favor more than 20 against 25 proposed by both G-4 and UFC.

Further, Beijing wants aspirants to hold closed-door consultations in regional groupings "until a final consensus is reached." In the unlikely event that regional consensus were reached, it would require "final UN examination and approval in accordance with pertinent clauses of the

Charter." Intriguingly, the high-level panel's report also suggested that a revamped Security Council would necessitate an amendment to the UN Charter, which in turn would require the approval of the P-5 as well as two-thirds of the 192 member states and then ratification by their legislatures. Since most mid-sized and smaller countries are cool to expansion, that seems like mission impossible.

Not surprisingly, this seemingly impractical demand for resolving the membership issue through consensus in the real world of bitter regional rivalries came in for sharp criticism. India's ambassador Nirupam Sen asserted that the strength of developing nations is their numbers and that "to say that there should be no vote but a consensus is to disarm them [developing nations] of their main weapon." In an apparent reference to Communist China's bid on October 25, 1971, to replace Republic of China (Taiwan) in the UN through a procedural vote, Sen added: "A country that displaced another through a vote is now proposing consensus for others." The Assembly had then rejected Taiwan's credentials in favor of those of the PRC. "After winning the vote by a bare majority, it [China] proposes much above two-thirds majority for others," Ambassador Sen regretted.[24] Proposals that call for expansion in only the non-permanent category or deny large developing countries a place among permanent members are seen as perpetuating status quo and therefore unacceptable.[25]

Besides, Beijing's stance on consensus would further deepen regional hostility. Just imagine India, Indonesia, Malaysia, and Pakistan forever fighting for the one semi-permanent "second-class" (with the single two-year terms being the "third class") seat without veto on the council. This formula would not only disturb regional cohesion but would also tempt meddling by external powers. Latin American countries would have to decide, for example, which would be better at representing their interests: Portuguese-speaking Brazil or Spanish-speaking Mexico. Which Muslim country would have the right to represent the Organization of the Islamic Conference? Since all prospective candidates for seats have regional rivals, the P-5 could exploit these rivalries to their advantage. Worse, it would provoke neighbors' envy. As Secretary General Annan noted in December 2004: "Obviously, there are a group of countries determined to get permanent seats and are campaigning very much for that and there are others in the organization which are determined to prevent them from getting permanent seats."[26] Their identity was no secret.[27] India faced a concerted Muslim campaign led by its bitter foe Pakistan and Islamabad's patron, China.[28] During his 2004 visit to Beijing, Pakistani Prime Minister Shaukat Aziz claimed to have obtained a firm commitment from Chinese President Hu Jintao that Beijing would not let India gain a permanent seat in the council. When pressed to elaborate, Aziz commented: "I cannot disclose what commitment the Chinese side made on the issue."[29] In post-9/11 charm and diplomacy with Islamabad, Dacca, Kuala Lumpur, and Jakarta, Beijing has offered full support for an *Asian* Muslim country's bid for a permanent seat. The Islamic states are pushing for Indonesia, Malaysia, or Pakistan. Given Pakistan's declared preference for Option B (that is, adding a new category of semi-permanent members who would be elected for a renewable four-year term), the Chinese president apparently made a commitment to support the second proposal, which was rejected by India and Japan. In fact, until July 2004, this was the only proposal under consideration by the high-level panel (its chief proponent was none other than China's Qian Qichen), and Option A was included only after strong protests and lobbying by the G-4 nations.[30]

Beijing's stance on *small developing states'* inclusion in the *non-permanent category only* through *consensus* kills two birds with one stone: it undermines Beijing's Asian rivals' bids and it further strengthens China's ties with the Islamic countries on whose energy resources Beijing increasingly relies to fuel its economic growth. Moreover, Beijing remains confident that so long as Pakistan remains Washington's key ally in its war on terrorism, the United States would not upset Pakistan by supporting New Delhi's bid, which is vehemently opposed by Islamabad. As per Chinese calculus, just as Pakistan would react furiously if India were granted a seat, Argentina and Mexico would react the same way if Brazil were to win a seat, and so might South Africa and Egypt if Nigeria were to gain a seat, and so on. The result would be stalemate, and the status quo would prevail.

However, after ten years of seemingly endless debate, UN Secretary General Kofi Annan underlined the centrality of the Security Council to the actual reform process when he stated in March 2005 that "no reform of the United Nations would be complete without reform of the Security Council." Annan also informed UN member states that he wanted a decision on council expansion before the world leaders' summit in September 2005 to consider restructuring the UN. He suggested that if consensus was not possible, the General Assembly president should consider calling a vote. As the G-4 intensified lobbying for tabling a resolution in the General Assembly to meet Annan's September 2005 "deadline," Beijing threw its weight behind the UFC group opposing the G-4 (comprising Pakistan, South Korea, Italy, Mexico, and other countries). On May 16, 2005, India and its G-4 partners circulated a draft resolution seeking expansion of the UNSC. The UFC group opposed this resolution, with China expressing its "resolute opposition to setting a time limit for the UNSC reform, and to forcing a voting on any plan in which major differences still exist."[31] The Chinese ambassador described the G-4 attempt to put the UNSC expansion on a fast track as "divisive," "dangerous" and "immature."[32] Moreover, Beijing vowed to use its veto to block any move to give Japan, India, Brazil, and Germany permanent seats in an enlarged UN Security Council.[33] On June 3, 2005, China publicly joined Pakistan in pushing for more regional representation in the non-permanent category, rather than permanent members, when ambassador Wang expressed support for the UFC group's formula for the proposed expansion of the UN Security Council, stating, "it has many good points."[34] In addition to spewing vitriol and issuing veto threats, Beijing dispatched special envoys to Europe, Africa, South Asia (excluding India and Bhutan), Latin America, and the Caribbean to rally support to delay, deflect, and defeat the G-4 move. More importantly, China's UN ambassador Wang Guangya met his newly installed US counterpart John Bolton to coordinate their efforts to halt the G-4 in its tracks. Beijing seemed quite content to hide behind US ambivalence. Wang took great delight in announcing to the media on August 4, 2005, that China was working with the United States to block Security Council expansion: "*we agreed to work together to make sure our interests are maintained....*"[35] Whereas China was more strident in voicing its opposition, the dilatory tactics adopted by the United States were more subtle and deceptive. While openly endorsing Japan as a potential permanent member of the Security Council, Washington held out an illusory carrot to India in the hope that the two would break ranks with Germany and Brazil. To sow division in the G-4 ranks, China asked India not to make a claim jointly with Japan as part of G-4 if New Delhi wanted Beijing's backing.[36] Ultimately, the great push for UNSC expansion in 2005 failed when African Union (AU) leaders stuck to their demand for a veto-wielding permanent seat and rejected the G-4 formula for compromise (expansion first, veto later). Much to Beijing's delight, the G-4 resolution could not be put to vote in the General Assembly.

No New Vetoes

Unfortunately, neither of the two options recommended by the UN panel dealt with the veto question because panel members saw "no practical way of changing the existing members' veto powers"! The Chinese had already made their position known: The issue of "whether the newly elected permanent members shall be granted the power of veto" will be determined by "consensus among the present five permanent members." Ironically, they advocate limiting the right to veto to the P-5 indefinitely on "historical grounds":

> Since the status of permanent membership is deeply rooted in the historical background in the early days of the founding of the UN and is in the fundamental interests of the UN, it is well reasoned that the veto mechanism should remain as it is. No more countries should be granted the power of veto, which is conducive to efficient and smooth running of the Security Council itself as well.[37]

This demand for keeping "the veto mechanism ... as it is" because it "is in the fundamental interests of the UN" is not only a false claim but undermines the very rationale for reform. Obviously, Beijing wants to have its cake and eat it too. It seems ridiculous for a country like China to suggest that the history of the Second World War alone should continue to be the criterion of veto-wielding power, since Beijing has all along been critical of the machinations of the Western powers and has shown contempt for accords concluded in the pre-1949 era. For Beijing, colonial history appears to matter only when it serves China's interests. Such a stance not only pours cold water on Indian and Japanese aspirations but also is inconsistent with the views of UN members who have long insisted that the veto power has been abused by the P-5. When critics deride the UN as a failed institution, they usually mean that the Security Council cannot find the will to do so, whether through intervention, sanctions, or merely opprobrium. Among other things, the veto has prevented the Security Council from meaningfully addressing Iran and North Korea's nuclear programs and the situation across the Taiwan Strait. It ought to be replaced by a simple majority or two-thirds majority of all members in true democratic fashion. How can the goal of "a just, rational and equitable new international political and economic order," which China espouses, be achieved so long as any one of the P-5 can block the will of the majority of nations without giving more countries a voice, not just representation, on the council?

Apparently, the status-conscious Chinese fear that such reforms would undermine China's position as the sole Asian representative on the council and its claim to great power status. The Security Council is the only international forum where the perception of China as a champion of the developing world and Asia is magnified. Chinese policymakers have long described the veto-wielding permanent seat as a "strategic asset,"[38] and Beijing has not hesitated to use it to defend its interests and keep its rivals off balance. For instance, during the

Bangladesh war of 1971 and after India's nuclear tests of May 1998, China used its "strategic asset" to isolate, intimidate, and contain New Delhi. In 1999, Beijing vetoed a UN peacekeeping operation in Macedonia to punish the latter's coziness toward Taiwan. In September 2004, China threatened to veto any move to impose sanctions on Sudan over the atrocities in Darfur. Beijing has also used its veto to protect the Burmese military junta and to support North Korea and Iran in their nuclear standoff with the International Atomic Energy Agency (ostensibly to protect hard-won resource concessions in these pariah states). Consequently, a squabbling council has given a free pass to authoritarian regimes to pursue repressive policies with impunity. Though many Asian countries would welcome any move that neutralized or balanced China's ascendancy by elevating India and Japan to the same level in the council, China is unlikely to surrender its "strategic asset" and will fight a rearguard battle to keep both out.

It has been suggested that in a revamped Security Council, the P-5 should be able to use their veto only if they have the support of three non-permanent members. The veto could also be diluted by requiring at least two of the P-5 to oppose an action. Limiting or banning the use of the veto, especially in humanitarian crises, would give diplomacy a genuine chance to resolve crises. Another suggestion is that council members should be given weighted votes, based on population and economic and military resources.[39] This system works in the World Bank and the International Monetary Fund. For important Security Council decisions, a "super majority" of the permanent members' votes, say 80 percent, would be required.[40] Given widespread opposition to the creation of a new privileged class of states, another solution might be to take away the veto from the P-5 to fashion a democratic institution where decisions are arrived at through a simple three-quarter majority rule. As Malaysia's Premier Mahathir Mohamad commented in 1993: "We talk of democracy as the only acceptable system of government. Yet, when it comes to the UN, we eschew democracy. And the most undemocratic aspect of the UN is the veto power of the permanent five. The veto must go."[41] However, for China, this seems unthinkable: its power to veto makes Beijing the object of courtship, since Washington needs China's support in resolving regional conflicts in the Middle East, South Asia, and the Korean peninsula and in dealing with transnational threats of terrorism and nuclear proliferation.

No Linkage Between Democratization and UNSC Reform: The Final Nail

The fifth and last principle in effect put a final nail in the UN coffin by delinking the issue of reform and the democratization of international relations: "The concept of permanent membership and that of democratization of international relations belong to two different categories, with no fundamental links between them."[42] Intriguingly, the Chinese contend, "the topic of democratization of international relations deserves full exploration on other occasions," but *not* with respect to Security Council reform.

Divide and Dominate

An assessment of the Chinese perspective suggests that Beijing will do everything to safeguard its coveted status as a veto-holding, permanent member. China has not only become a status quo power as far as the UN system is concerned, but its perspectives on reform are strikingly similar to those of the reigning superpower, the United States. China has indeed come a long way since describing the Security Council "as a tool of big power hegemony" in the 1960s. China's rhetoric about a multipolar world and Asian solidarity notwithstanding, Beijing remains steadfastly opposed to having its Asian rivals—India or Japan—sit on the council *as an equal*. What distinguishes China from India and Japan is both permanent membership and declared nuclear status, thus making it a far more important player in international forums and the sole Asian negotiating partner of the United States on global security matters. In fact, China's vociferous opposition to its Asian rivals' bids is now *the* major obstacle to the realization of their aspirations. Beijing genuinely fears that with India and Japan inside, Washington, when its interests were at stake, could work around Russian intransigence and French resistance and outweigh Chinese opposition.[43]

It has long been said that the Security Council can function only insofar as the United States lets it. The adage now applies to China as well. Just as Washington is seen as using the Security Council for its own ends, Beijing is known for keeping Taiwan and Tibet off the UN agenda and for supporting unsavory regimes (North Korea, Sudan, Zimbabwe, Iran, and Burma) for narrowly conceived geostrategic and energy interests. As the Sino-US rivalry intensifies, each seeks to use the issue of reform to undercut the other. The UN Secretary General's and the G-4 push for reform in 2005 fizzled out mainly due to the divisive games played by the G-2 (China and the United States) and the "neighbor's envy" syndrome. While the United States was only willing to support Japan, China fomented public demonstrations against Japanese membership and backed Pakistan's campaign to scuttle India's bid. The issue is now back in the General Assembly that has opted for inter-governmental negotiation on specific proposals to achieve progress on expansion.

The oft-repeated Chinese "support for Indian aspirations to play a bigger role in international affairs including in the UN" means that Beijing welcomes India occupying a seat in the semi-permanent or non-permanent category only. This position is eerily similar to the Pakistani stance, i.e., more members that are non-permanent should be added rather than permanent ones. Ironically, in the 1950s, India's Premier Nehru declined a permanent UNSC seat—that belonged to China but was held by Taiwan—because he did not want India to be in the Security Council until India's friend, China, was in it too.[44] The Chinese are now repaying India's support by insisting that India should not be in the Security Council (and other international institutions) until China's friend, Pakistan, is in too. A *Renmin Ribao* commentary (February 26, 2009) argued that "reforms should ensure that the large number of small and medium sized nations have more opportunities and can participate in decision-making in the UNSC—reform of the UNSC is not just about increasing the number of permanent members."[45] Obviously, Beijing's interests are better served without New Delhi on the UNSC.

However, this stance puts China in a minority of one in the current P-5 arrangement in opposing any expansion of the permanent membership category. For in sharp contrast with Beijing, Washington, Paris, London, and Moscow support UNSC permanent seat expansion. Unless Beijing changes its attitude with respect to Security Council reform, talk of China-Japan-India triangular cooperation will remain meaningless. If anything, China's opposition brings India and Japan closer into alignment. India continues to call for reforming all international institutions, from the Security Council to institutions of global and financial governance. New Delhi maintains that just as the US opposition to Communist China's membership in the Security Council did not prevent China's rise, Beijing's opposition also will not prevent India's rise as a great power. Though Washington was ambivalent toward India's candidature, things are changing as Indo-US relations continue on their upward trajectory. A number of former Clinton and Bush administration officials had already come out in support of India.[46] Unlike Japan and Germany, whose future trends all point south, India's strategic location and its economic rise mean that its case will strengthen with time. With Russia, Britain, and France already backing India's candidature, India's case has received a tremendous boost, with President Obama himself declaring his support for India's bid for a permanent seat in November 2010. Secretary of State Hillary Clinton's remarks that "India's growing global role requires us to reassess institutions of global governance" signal rethinking, partly to counter China's influence within the Security Council. Such a development would force China to reevaluate its position. More than anything else, China's commitment to a rule-based international order will be tested by Beijing's stance over the UN Security Council reform issue.

However, convincing the United States and China to support the bids of aspirants to permanent veto-holding council seats will be a monumental diplomatic task.[47] Both continue to raise barriers, an endeavor in which they are supported by client states and spoilers. Should the P-5 fail to respond to the demand for a more democratic international order, there is a danger of the UN becoming irrelevant in security matters, as did its predecessor, the League of Nations. If so, the job of resurrecting failed states; of preventing wars, massacres, and genocides; and of constraining tyrants and curbing nuclear proliferation either will go undone or will be done by self-appointed sheriffs with willing and not-so-willing allies, or the pressure to create a possible alternative decision-making body will grow.

Beijing's attitude to the expansion of the UN Security Council is a clear indication that China will not countenance the emergence of another Asian power. However, the UNSC is not the only body where China opposes India's membership. In 2006, when UN Under-Secretary General Shashi Tharoor joined the race as India's candidate for the office of UN Secretary General, it was China that cast the exclusionary negative vote that clinched the fate of Tharoor's candidature. As one senior diplomat put it, "the Chinese would not want an Indian to run the UN."[48] To be fair, the United States also threw its weight behind Ban-Ki Moon, the victorious South Korean diplomat. China was also *the* major spoiler state in the East Asia Summit and the Nuclear Suppliers' Group (NSG) to thwart India's regional ambitions and economic developmental needs.

The South Asian Association for Regional Cooperation: Enter the Dragon

Ever since the founding of the South Asian Association for Regional Cooperation (SAARC) in 1985, Beijing had aspired for its membership in some form. However, India's opposition came in the way, at least until November 2005. A few months after successfully engineering the defeat of the G-4 proposal for expanding the UN Security Council, Beijing scored another major victory over India on the twentieth anniversary of the founding of SAARC. At the 13th SAARC summit held in Dacca in November 2005, India's physical presence was overshadowed by China's invisible presence but growing influence south of the Himalayas. Nothing highlighted this more strikingly than India's volte-face on the issue of China's induction into the grouping as an observer or a dialogue partner. On the first day of the proceedings on November 12, 2005, Foreign Secretary Shyam Saran declared that China could not be inducted as an observer unless it signed a memorandum of understanding (MoU) for being associated with SAARC. In erecting a procedural hurdle on the Chinese request for association with SAARC, India gained support only from Bhutan, which does not have diplomatic relations with China. However, within less than 24 hours, Prime Minister Manmohan Singh was forced (in fact, arm-twisted)—mainly by the pro-China axis comprising Nepal, Pakistan, and Bangladesh—to come out with a statement welcoming China as observer.[49]

India's climb down occurred in the backdrop of the pro-China axis linking the issue of Afghanistan's inclusion as the grouping's eighth member with China's induction into the organization as an observer even though all seven SAARC states had agreed informally to admit Afghanistan *before* the 13th SAARC Summit began. That the decision on Afghanistan could not be taken without a simultaneous one on China came as surprise to many observers. It signaled that India could no longer treat the sub-continent as its exclusive backyard.[50] Apparently, India found itself on the back foot because the Indian foreign policy establishment did not anticipate the response its attempt to induct Kabul into SAARC would encounter from Pakistan and Nepal and underestimated the level of support China enjoyed among other SAARC members. Nepal's King Gyanendra played "the China card" in part to resist India's pressure for an early restoration of multi-party democracy in the Himalayan Kingdom. Beijing, in contrast, had offered full diplomatic and military support to the beleaguered monarchy in Nepal. Finally, a compromise deal was struck, and it was agreed that along with Afghanistan's admission as a new SAARC member, both China and Japan would obtain observer status in South Asia's multilateral forum. New Delhi thus had to eat the humble Chinese pie dished out by none other than Nepal to hold its own on Afghanistan's induction once the two issues were successfully linked by China acolytes within the regional forum. The inclusion of China was seen by smaller SAARC member-states as a useful counterbalance to India's domineering presence and influence in the organization. From Beijing's perspective, its SAARC success marked a culmination of the significant inroads made in India's backyard through cross-border economic and strategic linkages with Pakistan, Nepal, Bangladesh, Sri Lanka, and the Maldives over the decades.

China's presence in SAARC means that Beijing's sphere of influence no longer comprises solely the Asian continent's eastern periphery. Beijing seeks to assert its dominance over the entire continental landmass, including South Asia. To draw smaller South Asian states into China's security orbit, Nepal, Bangladesh, and Sri Lanka are being courted to join Pakistan in concluding peace and friendship treaties with China in the near future. A major reason Dacca would not grant transit rights to India is the undertaking given to China in 1987 (at the time of the Sumdorong Chu valley incident and heightened tensions on the Sino-Indian border), which was incorporated into the defense cooperation pact that rules out the use of Bangladeshi territory by India either during wartime or peacetime. This explains Dacca's refusal for railroad links or the construction of gas pipeline through Bangladesh because that would strengthen India's economic and military logistical position in the vulnerable northeastern states facing China. China is also the largest supplier of weaponry to Bangladesh. Premier Wen Jiabao's offer during his 2005 visit to provide Dacca with nuclear reactor technology in return for access to Chittagong port for Chinese naval assets prompted speculation in India's strategic circles regarding whether Beijing would replicate in Bangladesh the sort of conventional and strategic collaboration it has with Pakistan. Interestingly, South and Central Asian regions are also witnessing a major tug-of-war between Beijing and Washington with both wanting to increase their influence and presence further.

Despite Beijing's success in checkmating India in the SAARC, Beijing was to soon realize that just as India could not keep China out of the South Asian regional forum forever, Beijing could not succeed in excluding its southern rival from pan-Asian organizations comprising China's Southeast and East Asian neighbors. The invitation to India to attend the inaugural East Asian Summit in December 2005, in the face of strong Chinese opposition, was owed partly to the success of New Delhi's "Look East" policy in deepening India's relations with East Asian countries and partly to regional fears about China's growing power.

The East Asia Summit: More Discord Than Accord

The inaugural East Asia Summit (EAS) held in December 2005 in Kuala Lumpur brought together Asia's two fastest growing economic giants, China and India, together with Japan, South Korea, Australia, New Zealand, and the ten Association of Southeast Asian Nations (ASEAN) countries (Brunei, Cambodia, Indonesia, Laos, Malaysia, Myanmar, the Philippines, Singapore, Thailand, and Vietnam). Optimists saw the EAS as the first step toward establishing an East Asian Community (EAC) along the lines of the European Community. However, pessimists pointed to competing geopolitical interests, strategic rivalries and deep-rooted suspicions and ruled out the creation of an Asian free trade zone to rival Europe or the North American Free Trade Agreement (NAFTA).[51] This group is a motley combination of 16 countries, of which eight are democracies, others are dictatorships—either of the military, or of the proletariat—and the rest lie in between.

The EAS began in the backdrop of intense diplomatic maneuverings and shadowboxing and ended with the power games being played out in the open. China and Japan were locked in a bitter struggle for supremacy, with Beijing attempting to gain the leadership position in the planned EAC and Tokyo trying to rein in its rival with the help of other "China-wary" nations in the Asia-Pacific. Although the leaders agreed that the EAS be held regularly on the margins of the ASEAN Summit, the Sino-Japanese feud and the Sino-Indian rivalry, discord over the membership issue, geopolitical fault lines, and wariness about China's emerging power saw some publicly playing down its significance while others wondered aloud if there was much ado about nothing. Nothing illustrated this better than China's proposal for dividing the EAS members into core and secondary categories on the eve of the summit, which cast a shadow over its future. In fact, China's stance provided valuable insights into Beijing's insecurities and fears regarding the gathering momentum for a broader EAC and shifting power alignments within Asia.

The summit was a culmination of an idea first proposed by former Malaysian prime minister Mahathir Mohamad way back in 1991. However, Mahathir's original proposal for an "East Asian Economic Caucus" did not take off largely because it was seen as an East Asian caucus without Caucasians (the Americans and Australians) who countered it with a counter-proposal for an Asia-Pacific Economic Cooperation (APEC) forum, which came into being in 1993 with a major role for the United States and its Asian-Pacific allies.

Almost a decade later, the EAS proposal was resurrected by Mahathir's successor, Prime Minister Abdullah Badawi, at the 2004 APT (China, Japan, and South Korea) meeting and immediately won strong backing from China's Premier Wen Jiabao. Perceiving declining US power due to preoccupation with the War on Terror, a confident and assertive China saw in the proposal an opportunity to steer East Asian multilateralism along the lines of the Shanghai Cooperation Organization (SCO) to serve Beijing's broader strategic goals and further weaken US influence in East Asia. However, Beijing's enthusiasm for an "Asians only" regional grouping alerted those countries that remain wary of becoming ever more divided into Chinese and US blocs in East Asia and/or establishing an "East Asia Co-prosperity Sphere" under China's leadership. Concern about China's ambitions thus led to a campaign to include India, Australia, and New Zealand and to ensure that ASEAN remained at the center of a future EAC. Even after ASEAN decided to make the EAS more broad-based, the membership issue remained a major cause of disagreement with China (keep it closed) and Japan (open it up) on opposing sides.

China, in particular, strongly disapproved of India and Australia's inclusion in the proposed EAS. In early 2005, Beijing dispatched diplomats to Laos (then "country convener for India" within the ASEAN regional grouping) and other Southeast Asian capitals to dissuade them from lobbying for India's membership (albeit unsuccessfully). However, with the exception of Kuala Lumpur, Beijing did not find any takers for its stance. Nearly all Southeast Asian countries supported India's participation in the EAS, seeing it as a useful counterweight to China's growing power.

Having failed to keep India, Australia, and New Zealand out of the EAS, the Chinese Foreign Ministry then came up with another proposal to keep them down. On the eve of the summit, Beijing proposed that the existing APT, and not the new 16-member EAS, should be in the driver's seat for the formation of a future community-building exercise. After arriving in Kuala Lumpur for the summit, Premier Wen insisted that "the East Asian Summit should respect the desires of East Asian countries and should be led only by East Asian countries." China wanted membership of such a group restricted, because a regional grouping that included US friends and allies was seen as diluting its own emerging voice. In other words, having lost the battle to keep the Indians and Caucasians out of the EAS, Beijing insisted that they must not play any role in the formation of an EAC, which should remain the responsibility of the core group comprising APT within the EAS. This proposed EAS division into two blocs—the core or primary states with China as the leading or dominant player inside the APT, and the peripheral or secondary states of India, Australia, and New Zealand (or, "outsiders" as one *People's Daily* editorial described them)—snowballed into a major rift and drew criticism as "a ploy to manipulate, divide and dominate the evolving East Asian Community." However, a *People's Daily* commentary criticized Japan for "trying to drag countries outside this region such as Australia and India into the Community to serve as a counterbalance to China." It claimed, "Japan, Australia and India represent America's influence and interests in the grouping" and would work to "weaken Chinese influence in East Asia."[52]

From Beijing's perspective, India's "Look East" policy and the slew of economic and defense cooperation agreements signed with ASEAN infringe on China's own sphere of influence. Leery of India's great power pretensions and attempts to extend its influence in China's backyard, Beijing sees New Delhi's "Look East" policy as part of a wider "congage (contain and engage) China" strategy unveiled by the Washington-Tokyo-New Delhi axis. The thrust of Chinese diplomacy is to confine India to the periphery of a future EAC and foil India's efforts to break out of the South Asian straitjacket. In a briefing with Southeast Asian diplomats, one Chinese diplomat claimed, "the Indians lack a proper understanding of the 'East Asian way,'" describing them as "too aggressive and arrogant."[53] Even though East Asia has become India's largest trading partner, ahead of the European Union and the United States, China does not want to see India raising its profile in the East Asian region. The CCP's main propaganda organ took a dig at the Indian prime minister's proposal for an Asian Economic Community (AEC): "India hopes to build a free trade area extending from Bombay to New Zealand's Christchurch, and finally expand the area, which covers 3 billion people, into the world's largest of its kind. *But India's proposal is not warmly responded [to] as each country has its own considerations*."[54] Apparently, China's "own considerations" are primarily geostrategic in nature. Beijing fears that India's participation in the core group would make the EAC more balanced and less susceptible to domination by China. Therefore, in the run-up to the EAS in Malaysia, and days after obtaining observer status in the SAARC, China's message to India was clear: "you're not welcome here. East Asia isn't big enough for the two of us." Even though China's economic relationship with South Asian countries is relatively weaker than India's economic and trade relationship with East Asian countries, China sees itself as part of South Asia but claims India has no role to play in East Asia.

Japan felt that the EAS, with more countries participating, would provide a counterbalance to China's growing influence. Therefore, Japan, India, Australia, and New Zealand (backed by Singapore and Indonesia) voiced their opposition to creating a two-tiered, exclusionary, and discriminatory structure within the EAS and favored an inclusive approach based on the principle of equality to promote regional integration and the East Asian Community by all 16 EAS members. This view was also endorsed by Washington. Leading the charge on the other side was China. Backed by South Korea, Burma, Malaysia, and Cambodia (albeit for varying reasons), Beijing was attempting to keep the balance of power in its favor by creating a two-tiered structure with APT forging the core and relegating India, Australia, and New Zealand to secondary status. China assumed that APT—much like the SCO, whose tone and agenda of regional integration is set largely in Beijing—could be made subservient to China's broader strategic interests.

In the end, China won a partial but Pyrrhic victory when Badawi announced that APT, which originally proposed the idea of an EAS, would be "a vehicle for realising the dreams of forming the East Asian Community." However, this support came with one important caveat: ASEAN spurned Beijing's offer to host the second summit, and decided that the EAS will be held annually alongside the ASEAN Summit in Southeast Asian countries only. This means that ASEAN will be the hub of the EAS and the key driver within the APT. The reaction was mixed. An Indian diplomat expressed his disappointment over the decision to entrench the ASEAN Plus Three (Plus Three) framework within the EAS: "To state that ASEAN is in the driver's seat, the passengers have a right to know where they are going." However, Indian Prime Minister Manmohan Singh welcomed the ASEAN initiative to convene the EAS, hoping that a "safe and experienced driver" would take the forum to its destination. Finding Australia relegated to the outer circle, Prime Minister John Howard downplayed the summit's significance relative to APEC. In addition, Japan made clear its preference for the newcomers—India, Australia, and New Zealand—to be more than mere passengers on the road to an EAC.

Realizing that China's original goal of establishing an East Asian version of SCO to counter Washington was a non-starter, Beijing's enthusiasm for the new grouping waned fast. Sensing the setback, the Chinese immediately made a complete U-turn and started singing a new tune in favor of an open and inclusive grouping. Being a distant hegemon, the United States remains the balancer of choice for countries on China's periphery. Of the 16 EAS members, Japan, Thailand, the Philippines, Australia, and South Korea are military allies of the United States, while New Zealand, Singapore, Indonesia, Vietnam, and India are hedgers that worry more about China than the United States. Therefore, on the last day of the summit, the Chinese premier and diplomats suggested that anyone with interests in the Pacific—Russia, perhaps, or even the United States—could eventually take part, a move that would make the EAS indistinguishable from the "talk shop" ARF or mostly ineffectual APEC. By pushing for Russia and other countries' participation in the EAS to make it "open and inclusive," China is seen as trying to subvert the EAS just as the United States diluted APEC's focus by bringing in Russia, Mexico, and Chile.

Clearly, in the absence of a genuine thaw in Sino-Indian relations or great power cooperation, there is little prospect of the EAC taking off because multilateralism is a multi-player game played in a spirit of give and take. If anything, the EAS has had the opposite effect: instead of creating a common bond, it has intensified China's rivalry with Japan as both seek to use the EAS to undercut the other (with Japan backing India and Australia and China throwing its weight behind the APT). The first summit also forced smaller Asian nations to choose sides. Not surprisingly, the EAS remains just another "talk shop" like APEC or the ARF where leaders meet and declarations are made, but little community building is achieved. Interestingly, years after the formation of EAS, China, Japan, and Australia continue to put forward their respective cases for competing ideas of a new Asian economic community. As in Central Asia, Beijing wants to be in the driver's seat of East Asian multilateralism. Seeing itself as the natural core of Asia, Beijing backs an East Asian Community that is essentially the ASEAN Plus Three, thus giving China, with its strengthened economic ties and influence in Southeast Asia, a stronger role compared to Japan. Though ASEAN remains active, its capacity to lead pan-Asian multilateral institutions is thus increasingly being questioned. Neither China nor Japan seems satisfied with leaving the Southeast Asian states in the regional driver's seat. China also remains lukewarm toward Canberra's proposal for a wider Asian Pacific Community (APC) with US and Indian participation. China's opposition to a larger East Asian formulation is indicative of Beijing's desire to curb New Delhi's ambitions to play a "balancing" role in Asia, because "India could prevent the East Asian Community from being dominated by China."[55]

The Shanghai Cooperation Organization: No Pakistan, No India

Of all the multilateral forums, the Shanghai Cooperation Organization (SCO) is in a category of its own.[56] It is unlike any other organization, for example, ASEAN, SAARC or the European Union (EU). It seeks to promote regional economic and security cooperation in Central Asia but is named after a city located on the Pacific Ocean rim, has its headquarters in Beijing, is mostly dominated and led by two great powers, China and Russia, and more importantly, it regularly conducts military exercises not unlike those of collective defense alliances such as the North Atlantic Treaty Organization (NATO). Obviously, the SCO belongs to a different breed of multilateral organizations. It is successor to the Shanghai Five grouping put together in 1996 to resolve China's border disputes with former Soviet Central Asian republics, which has slowly expanded its reach into counter-terrorism, energy, economic cooperation, and defense. With the decline of Moscow's influence, Beijing has sought to rely primarily on the SCO as an instrument to project its power and gain allies in a region that is a source of much-needed strategic energy resources as well as a launch pad for China's larger strategic aspirations in Central and Southwest Asia, and most importantly, to counter the post-9/11 US presence in the region. Beijing's task is made easier by the fact that the SCO is devoid of any democratic and liberal values. Beijing has long touted the SCO as a model template for multilateral organizations.

Through the SCO, Beijing seeks to integrate the smaller Central Asian countries with China's powerful economy via trade dependencies, infrastructure projects, energy pipelines and a communications network with Shanghai as its metropolitan center. The SCO summit meetings routinely endorse a Chinese foreign policy agenda. In 2005, SCO became the first regional forum to oppose the G-4 proposal to expand the UN Security Council's permanent membership and called for an end to the US military presence in Central Asia. This was a classic example of Beijing using a regional institution to prevent reform of a global institution for fear of losing China's privileged position in the UN Security Council. The military exercises in 2005 and 2007 conducted by the SCO member-states led to speculation about the emergence of a "NATO of the East."[57] Rising powers thrive on picking up loose geopolitical change on their periphery. This is what the United States did in the nineteenth century in Latin America by proclaiming the Monroe Doctrine, and that is exactly what China is now doing in Central Asia via the Shanghai Cooperation Organization (and in Iran, Burma, and in Africa, where Beijing faces little or no competition). It is fair to say that the SCO is the power play of China and Russia. Whenever Russian and Chinese interests converge, the SCO looks formidable. However, when their vital interests clash, the SCO looks like a divided house and an inconsequential body. Fissures within the SCO provide others with the opportunity to exploit internal contradictions among member-states to their advantage.

As in other regional organizations, membership is a major cause of disagreement in the SCO as well. The tug-of-war between China and Russia over the membership issue was evident at the 2009 summit when China helped Sri Lanka gain the SCO's "dialogue partner" status, and Russia countered China's move on Sri Lanka by bestowing the same status on Belarus. Of the four SCO observers, Pakistan and Iran have been clamoring for full SCO membership for a long time, while India and Mongolia did not initially show much interest in obtaining full membership in an overtly anti-US organization. Besides, New Delhi resented the SCO's rejection of the G-4 formula for UN Security Council expansion in 2005, and the disqualification of the OVL-Mittal bid for PetroKazakhstan, both under pressure from the Chinese. For its part, Islamabad has offered "an energy corridor and access to warm waters (Arabian Sea and the Gulf)" to its long-time patron, China, and the landlocked Central Asian member states of the SCO, while Tehran has offered oil and gas in exchange for backing for Teheran's nuclear program.

India's main interest in the Central Asian forum is in balancing China. New Delhi is uncomfortable with Beijing's use of the SCO to position itself as the dominant force in Central Asia, a key repository of hydrocarbon resources that India needs to fuel its economic growth. India's aspirations for a greater role in the SCO are backed by Russia, Tajikistan, and some other Central Asian Republics that would like to see India becoming a full member. However, Beijing frowns upon any Indian attempt to secure full SCO membership without New Delhi lifting its bar on China's full membership in the SAARC. India's development of an air base in Tajikistan is an eyesore to the Chinese. Nor would China let India in without Pakistan. However, other SCO members remain wary of having Pakistan—the hotbed of Islamist terrorism and nuclear proliferation—in their midst. In June 2006, the Chinese invited India as well as Pakistan to join the SCO but India declined to take the Chinese up on their offer. Keen on developing stronger economic and strategic ties with Washington and Tokyo, New Delhi appeared wary of being seen in Beijing's camp. Unlike Iran and Pakistan, Indian participation at the annual SCO summits until 2009 was at the energy minister level, not at the head of state level, indicating India's status as an observer and its primary interest in the region's energy resources. However, for the first time in June 2009, Indian Prime Minister Manmohan Singh attended the SCO leaders' summit in the Russian city of Yaketenaburg, which coincided with the hosting of the

Brazil-Russia-India-China (BRIC) summit in the same city a day later.[58] Fearing a pro-Pakistan tilt in the Obama administration's "Af-Pak" policy, New Delhi was warming up to the idea of seeking full membership of the SCO (at the time of writing) in order to work more closely with Russia, Iran, Uzbekistan, and Tajikistan on Afghanistan following the drawdown of NATO forces in 2011.

Chinese Checkers: The NSG and the US-India Nuclear Energy Pact

China's nuclear diplomacy has long sought to deny India entry into the exclusive Nuclear-Five Club and to foil any move that would acknowledge and legalize or legitimize India's status as a Nuclear Weapons State (NWS). That is why China rejects India's overtures for nuclear risk reduction measures (including a bilateral no-first-use pact) that would bestow nuclear legitimacy on a power Beijing likes to pretend is not a rival. While major Western powers have, however grudgingly, acknowledged the reality of India's *de facto* nuclear status, Beijing shows no sign of softening its demand that New Delhi initiate a complete rollback of its nuclear weapons program and unconditionally sign the Comprehensive Test Ban Treaty (CTBT) and the Nuclear Non-Proliferation Treaty (NPT) as a Non-Nuclear Weapons State as per UN Security Council Resolution 1172 of June 6, 1998.

Understandably, Beijing came out in opposition to the July 2005 US-India civilian nuclear energy deal that sought to allow India, once a nuclear pariah, access to civilian nuclear technology to meet its soaring energy needs. China tried discreetly and indirectly to sabotage the deal, and failing that, to ensure that its ally Pakistan got the same treatment. The tone for the official Chinese reaction and critical media commentaries was set by *Renmin Ribao* (October 26, 2005), which accused Washington of being soft on India and warned that if the United States made a "nuclear exception" for India, other powers (i.e., China) would do the same with their friends (read, Pakistan, Iran, Bangladesh, and Burma) and weaken the global non-proliferation regime: "Now that the United States buys another country in with nuclear technologies in defiance of an international treaty, other nuclear suppliers also have their own partners of interest as well as good reasons to copy what the United States did.... A domino effect of nuclear proliferation, once turned into reality, will definitely lead to global nuclear proliferation and competition." In the daily briefing on March 2, 2006, the Chinese Foreign Ministry's spokesperson Qin Gang commented:

> India should sign the NPT and also dismantle its nuclear weapons. As a signatory country, China hopes non-signatory countries will join it as soon as possible as non-nuclear weapon states, thereby contributing to strengthening the international non-proliferation regime. China hopes that concerned countries developing cooperation in peaceful nuclear uses will pay attention to these efforts.[59]

There were two main reasons for Beijing's angst with the nuclear deal. First, it put India on par with China by conferring rights on India that are commensurate with China's in the nuclear domain—the right to have a nuclear arsenal as well as access to civilian nuclear technology despite being a non-signatory of the NPT. Second, it will provide access to advanced conventional weaponry and dual-use technologies from the West that are still denied to Beijing because of an arms embargo dating back to the Tiananmen massacre of 1989. A *People's Daily* commentary alluded to this concern: "The United States has explicitly proposed in the agreement that it would not hamper or intervene in the development of India's military nuclear plan, which will also help the country achieve its goals to be a nuclear power."[60] From Beijing's perspective, once the nuclear deal crossed all the "four big hurdles" (opposition from Beijing-backed left-wing parties in India, negotiations on IAEA safeguards, approval by the NSG, and its passage by the US Congress), it could unsettle the power balance between Beijing and New Delhi.[61] Expressing its disapproval of a pact that could narrow the power gap between India and China, Beijing's stance centered around three themes:

- Using the "double standards" argument to question Washington's commitment to non-proliferation goals in light of its decision to back India's nuclear industry while opposing the right to nuclear energy for Iran and Pakistan[62];
- Insisting that any changes to the NSG guidelines to accommodate the deal must not be "country [i.e., India]-specific" but "universal criteria-based" so that "all countries [read, Pakistan] can benefit from the peaceful use of atomic energy under the IAEA safeguards." This formulation, outlined by Foreign Minister Yang Jiechi, would pave the way for the Chinese construction of the Chashma III and IV nuclear reactors in Pakistan[63]; and
- Seeking assurances that US-India ties are not related to any "contain China" strategy.

What was particularly galling for India was that China—a strategic proliferator in the history of nuclear weapons development—was trying to wreck the India-US nuclear deal by presenting itself as the great champion of nuclear non-proliferation. Apparently, to deflect attention from China's own proliferation activities vis-à-vis Pakistani, Iranian, and North Korean nuclear weapons and missile programs,[64] the Chinese media published speculative commentaries on India's nuclear proliferation to Vietnam:

> If India were to transfer nuclear technology to Vietnam and if Vietnam were to secretly install the technology on the Scud B/C ballistic missiles it acquired from North Korea, then Southeast Asia would face an immense security threat..... It [India] is even bringing about a nuclear threat. India aims to trigger an armaments race in Southeast Asia, creating tension and pushing Vietnam to the front line in confronting China so as to distract China's attention and ease China's pressure on itself.[65]

Even as the Chinese media expressed its angst, Chinese leaders promised verbal support at the official level—as they had done in the case of UNSC expansion—knowing full well that the deal remained blocked for more than a year by the pro-Beijing Communist parties providing parliamentary support to the Indian government. However, once Prime Minister Singh managed to ensure the survival of his minority government and the smooth passage of the nuclear deal in the Indian Parliament after dumping Communist parties opposed to the nuclear deal as ruling coalition partners, Beijing launched a diplomatic offensive to block any changes in the NSG guidelines to accommodate India in the field of dual-use technology. Beijing's opposition emboldened the opponents of the deal on Capitol Hill, where it faced strong domestic resistance.

At the IAEA meetings, China sought to delay the US-India nuclear deal proceedings in a way that would have undermined President Bush's timetable to take the agreement to the US Congress before the November 2008 presidential elections. India's relations with China touched a new low in September 2008 when New Delhi accused Beijing of deliberate prevarication in an effort to stymie NSG approval of a waiver to facilitate the US-India nuclear deal.[66] Despite personal assurances by President Hu and Premier Wen to Prime Minister Singh that Beijing "would not stand in the way," the Chinese played the spoiler with the help of small countries during the NSG meeting in Vienna in September 2008. At the eleventh hour, the Chinese delegation staged a walkout and it took strongly worded demarches by the Indian government in Delhi and Beijing as well as a phone call from President Bush to encourage the Chinese to back down.[67] Faced with China's isolation on the issue in Vienna, Beijing reluctantly relented, and the NSG approval to trade on the international nuclear market was granted. Even then, Chinese diplomats found it hard to mask their displeasure over the failure of small objectors to hold their ground. Cheng Jingye, the head of China's delegation, stated: "It is also China's hope that NSG will equally address the aspirations of all parties for the peaceful use of nuclear power." This was a plea on behalf of Pakistan, which appealed to China for a deal similar to that offered to India by Washington.[68]

Beijing's sabotage, delay, and deny tactics along with its advocacy of a nuclear trade waiver for Pakistan "unmasked China's deep suspicion and hostility towards its southern neighbour's growing status, and a desire to keep India checkmated in its immediate neighbourhood."[69] While the Indian leadership and media expressed surprise over perceived "Chinese betrayal and perfidy," long-time China-watchers felt vindicated by the turn of events.[70] However, after the event, the Chinese claimed that New Delhi would not have obtained the NSG waiver for nuclear trade if Beijing had not "signaled its acquiescence." Hu Shisheng, the director of the South Asia department at CICIR, opined that China's concerns on the issue of nuclear non-proliferation had not been fully appreciated in India: "We have our own concerns and we also have to face pressures from other countries in the region" (i.e., Pakistan, Bangladesh, and others).[71] Since the granting of the NSG waiver to India, Beijing has been arguing that India's case represents a precedent for similar approval to be given to Pakistan—a cause it is now prepared to sponsor. In response to the US-India nuclear deal and one month after the NSG granted a nuclear waiver to India, China and Pakistan signed a nuclear agreement to set up two more atomic reactors, the Chashma-3 and Chashma-4, during Pakistani President Asif Ali Zardari's October 2008 visit to Beijing. Until then, China's assistance with the Chashma-3 and 4 reactors had been under a cloud because all NSG members (China joined the NSG in 2004) are barred from providing nuclear assistance to a non-signatory of the Nuclear Non-Proliferation Treaty.[72] Beijing's decision to build additional nuclear reactors shows China's determination to maintain Pakistan's parity with India, but it ignores global proliferation concerns, undermines the NSG consensus on nuclear trade, and strains its ties with New Delhi.

It is worth noting here that the decisive factor in China's successful defense against India's challenge to its status as the sole Asian permanent member of the UN Security Council in 2005 and Beijing's failure in its rearguard battle to defend its status as the sole Asian Nuclear Weapon State (as per the NPT) in 2008 was the United States: Washington supported Beijing in the UNSC but was arrayed against Beijing in the NSG.

The Indian Alphabet Soup: MGC, BIMSTEC, CoD, IBSA, and IONS

Taking a leaf out of China's book, India has been proactively forming multilateral organizations since the late 1990s with the twin purposes of promoting intra- and inter-regional integration and excluding or diminishing China's presence and influence in its vicinity. In response to China's efforts to keep India out of regional arrangements in Central, East, and Southeast Asia by portraying India as an "outsider" and "interloper," India has been underlining the multi-millennia-old bond of Buddhism, civilizational, linguistic, and cultural links that it shares with its surrounding regions.[73] India became a member of the ARF in 1996, and signed on to the ASEAN Treaty of Amity and Cooperation in 2003. As soon as China launched the Kunming Initiative aimed at developing the Mekong delta region, India responded by unveiling the Mekong-Ganges Cooperation (MGC) project in 2000, which included India's northeastern provinces in a regional cooperation zone with Burma, Thailand, Laos, Cambodia, and Vietnam, but excluded China. Involving exactly the same states as the Kunming Initiative, "the MGC had simply replaced China by India at the head of the project, in a symbolic gesture of defiance that did not go unnoticed by the Chinese."[74] Yet another example of Indian multilateral activism is the Bay of Bengal Initiative for MultiSectoral Technical and Economic Cooperation (BIMSTEC, comprising Bangladesh, India, Burma, Bhutan, Sri Lanka, and Thailand), which also excludes China. A milestone in the burgeoning relationship between India and Southeast Asia was achieved in 2010 with the conclusion of the ASEAN-India Free Trade Agreement (AIFTA)—coincidentally, the same year the China-ASEAN Free Trade Agreement (CAFTA) came into force.

China watched warily India's participation in and co-sponsorship of a US-led initiative, the Community of Democracies (CoD), consisting of 100-plus nations, started at Warsaw in 2000. Apparently, China and its Asian allies, such as North Korea and Burma, see themselves as the major targets of this *Pax Democratica* initiative. More importantly, the coming together in 2003 of three large developing democracies from three continents of Asia, Latin America, and Africa—India, Brazil, and South Africa—to form the IBSA Dialogue Forum was seen as undermining China's claims to be the sole representative of the developing world in global forums. This cooperative trio with impeccable democratic credentials resolved to promote democratic global governance and speak with a common voice on issues ranging from trade, energy, development, and UN Security Council reforms to humanitarian intervention, human rights, and nuclear non-proliferation.[75]

China's unease over India-led regional multilateral initiatives is no secret. In May 2007, Beijing was furious over the first quadrilateral talks involving the United States, Australia, Japan, and India on the sidelines of the ARF meeting in Manila, which were followed by the joint naval exercise in the Bay of Bengal in September 2007—seeing these moves as part of a "contain China" strategy. Indian policymakers frown over Beijing's criticism, given that Beijing has long been forging all kinds of China-centered forums, dialogues, and partnerships. They contend that if the SCO member-states and the Russia-China-India triangle can hold high-level meetings to discuss issues of common concern and hold joint exercises, "then why should India, the United States, and Japan shy away from holding discussions on issues of common interest?"[76] Arguing that China has a habit of protesting too much, a leading strategic affairs analyst asks:

> If India can openly join hands with China and Russia in a Eurasian strategic triangle intended to help promote global power equilibrium, why should it be diffident about partnering other states to seek democratic peace and stability in Asia? When China pursues actions overtly designed to contain India, does it bother to "explain" its actions to New Delhi? Rather, it determinedly presses ahead with steps antithetical to Indian interests, including a "string of pearls" strategy that aims to pin down India.[77]

For its part, New Delhi sees "nothing sinister" in having a common stake with Japan in developing a multipolar Asia to balance China's growing dominance and interprets Beijing's opposition to India's strategic partnership with Japan and the United States as an attempt to establish China-led unipolarity in the region. The US-Japan-India triangular partnership is seen as complementing the Russia-China-India triangular cooperation. Asks C. Raja Mohan, a noted strategic affairs analyst:

> Will they [Japan and India] accept a subordinate status in a Sino-centric order that has begun to emerge in Asia? Or, will Tokyo and New Delhi persist with the construction of a multipolar Asia in the

> face of Chinese resistance at home and abroad? *If Japan and India want a place in Asia equivalent to that of China*, they have no alternative but to impart a strategic dimension to their bilateral economic engagement, deepen their political cooperation on issues ranging from maritime security, high technology transfers, regional stability and global warming.[78]

Concerns about India's pro-US tilt are countered by India's long-standing preference for strategic autonomy in policymaking. The Indian Navy's decision to hold joint exercise with the Chinese Navy in 2006 soon after conducting trilateral US-Japan-India naval exercise in the Pacific Ocean and joint army exercises with China in December 2007 following the September 2007 quadrilateral naval exercises in the Bay of Bengal are cited as examples of India's engagement with all major powers. New Delhi claims to be cautious not to appear anti-China in its policies as China grows stronger. At the same time, "just as China does not want India to object to Beijing's close strategic ties with India's neighbors, seeing them as part of 'normal state-to-state relations,' India hopes China would respect New Delhi's sovereign rights to build strategic partnerships and initiatives based on shared interests with like-minded countries in Asia and elsewhere."[79]

Multilateral Melody: Same Song, Different Tune

The Asia-Pacific of the early twentieth century, home to several rising and contending powers, bears more resemblance to Europe of the nineteenth and early twentieth centuries than to Europe of the early twenty-first century. Unlike Europe's retiring powers, Asia is home to two rising powers—China and India—and a Japan that is increasingly becoming a "normal nation." These three rising powers of Asia are today where Germany, France, Britain, and Italy were at the beginning of the twentieth century. They are increasingly looking outward beyond their immediate regions in search of access to markets, resources, and bases, while jockeying for power and influence and seeking to outmaneuver and outbid each other in different parts of the world. Size, wealth, and power enable Beijing to set the terms of its relationships with other countries. This extra-regional competition amongst Asia's "heavyweights" is invariably reflected in their intra-regional interaction, in their suspicions and perceptions of each other, and in their dealings at multilateral forums. Put it simply, multilateral forums are unable to insulate or curb China-India worldwide competition for resources, markets, bases, and the tussle for diplomatic influence from their community-building projects in the Asia-Pacific. Moreover, Asia is not, like Europe, a collection of nations with common values, but a collection of regimes with *some* common interests. Despite all the talk of a borderless, inter-connected world, Asia is simply too obsessed with sovereignty. Most regional organizations remain essentially toothless "talk shops." While economic regionalism has gained momentum to some extent, there has been little or no progress on regionalism in politico-security spheres. In fact, the proliferation of a large number of multilateral organizations and dialogues is quite telling in itself. It shows the degree of residual or latent distrust, rivalry, and one-upmanship in the region. The fact that ASEAN in 2005 spurned China's offer to hold the second East Asia Summit in Beijing and instead decided to hold the annual EAS summits in Southeast Asian capitals along with the annual ASEAN summits demonstrates the regional grouping's desire not to let Asian multilateralism fall victim to great power rivalries. Asians know that wherever China finds itself in the company of Japan, India, and Australia, it is in Beijing's interests to be on its best behavior. Besides, comprehensive security issues of resource security, climate change, terrorism, nuclear proliferation, and economic development cannot be adequately addressed without their participation. However, cooperation on these issues is clouded by discord over traditional geopolitical issues.

Underneath the veneer of friendship and cooperation, competing interests and divergent motives drive China and India to pursue self-serving approaches to multilateralism. When it comes to "high politics" or geopolitical and security issues, China sees itself in the same league as the United States, without a peer in Asia, and insists India (like Japan) is (and must remain) in a junior league. However, on "low politics" or transnational issues such as climate change, carbon emissions, labor rights, currency, trade, and the world's financial architecture, China defines itself as a developing country in the same league as India. Beijing is willing to partner with India and other poor nations in multilateral discussions as their interests seemingly converge to shield itself from international opprobrium and obligations—despite China's emergence as a financial and trade Goliath.[80] A case in point is the UN summit on climate change in Copenhagen in December 2009 where China deflected global pressure to commit to binding emissions cuts by forging a joint front with India and poor African countries in a triumphant stand-off with the West. However, this does not imply that strategic interests do not influence cooperation on transnational issues. China has shown willingness to use its growing financial influence in international institutions such as the ADB and the IMF to wield veto powers over rescue packages for countries that do not comply with its political demands, especially over issues such as Tibet and Taiwan. As noted earlier, China withheld approval in 2009 for a multilateral development plan for India by the ADB over its long-standing territorial dispute with its southern rival.[81]

Beijing's multilateral diplomacy is dictated by its own vision of a Sino-centric unipolar order in Asia, at the heart of which is China's competitive relationships with India, Japan, and the United States. Many argue that China—a late convert to multilateralism—is using its growing clout in multilateral organizations to define limits to US power, undermine its military alliances, marginalize Beijing's Asian rivals (India and Japan), and mold multilateral institutions to promote its core interests or have its foreign policy agenda endorsed. China's size, historical grievances, level of development, and nationalist aspirations dictate that Beijing only plays by Western rules when those are to its advantage. John Lee quotes Chinese officials as saying "[w]e will work with the Americans when we can, alongside them in rule making and institution building, and replacing them when useful and necessary."[82] Many Chinese believe that the pro-US orientation of countries such as India, Japan, and Australia comes in the way of their efforts to shape existing institutions or build new ones for a post-American world. China's diplomatic energies are focused on creating an alternative pole to democratic-liberal order in international institutions, eroding US power, and driving a wedge between the United States and its allies.[83] Luo Yuan, chairperson of the Strategy Research Institute of the Chinese Academy of Military Sciences, believes that China will soon reach a stage where it will have the power to either mold or discard existing institutions and build a new political-economic international order that will ensure strategic balance and stability.[84] Critics suspect that this "new political-economic international order" would not be much different from the Sino-centric hierarchical order of pre-modern Asia. The Chinese certainly seem far more comfortable with multilateral forums they have constructed, like the SCO, a sort of Central Asian NATO in which China plays the leading role, than with existing global institutions that were created by the United States and its allies and reflect Western values. Given the central role that China plays in giving direction to the SCO, the manner in which the SCO has developed provides interesting clues to the direction other regional organizations, such as APT and EAS, might take if China is allowed to have its way or assume a dominant position. Already, in deference to Beijing's sensitivities, most regional hot spots and hot-button security issues—Taiwan, Burma, competing claims to energy deposits and islands in the South and East China seas, military modernization and maritime expansion, nuclear proliferation, Beijing's river-linking projects that negatively affect the countries downstream in Asia—are all kept off the agenda of regional dialogue forums. With growing global power, and an increasingly nationalistic public opinion at home, China is beginning to rewrite the rules on trade, currency, technology, navigation of the seas, water resources, and climate change, which primarily promote and protect Chinese interests. In short, China operates both within and outside the international system, seeking to mold it to serve Chinese interests while at the same time, in effect, working to establish a new Sino-centric order that will initially exist alongside the current US-sponsored order, and as China's relative power grows, will over a period of time eventually overwhelm and replace it.

Conclusion

Obviously, there is a tension or disconnect between Chinese and Indian approaches to multilateralism.[85] Given their size and power, China in East Asia and India in South Asia generate fear and suspicion ("big state versus small state syndrome") amongst their smaller neighbors respectively and exploit it to each other's advantage. India's South Asian neighbors backed China's admission into SAARC, despite New Delhi's opposition, for the same geostrategic reasons that led China's East Asian neighbors to back India's entry into the EAS and ASEM, Beijing's opposition notwithstanding. The integration and socialization of China and India in multilateral institutions has neither constrained their ambitions nor reduced tensions between them. The Sino-Indian relationship is marked by a "positional" rivalry in multilateral forums—a concern over their relative positions in the regional and global hierarchy—that exceeds the other bilateral great power relations. Both seek to promote multilateral arrangements that exclude or marginalize the other. Each has calibrated its role in multilateral institutions with an ultimate objective to ensure a regional power balance that serves its interests and great power politics that are less hostile to its rise. If China's Asia strategy obliges Beijing to keep India down, if not out, of the evolving East Asian Community, India is reciprocating by seeking to keep China to the periphery of a future Indian Ocean regional community. At the same time, both are keen to demonstrate that their simultaneous rise does not constitute a threat to other countries. The prospects for a cooperative partnership in reforming old and forming new (and effective) multilateral institutions would improve only when China and India avoid mutual containment, mercantilism, and zero-sum power games. Should they cooperate, their combined strength can force a change in the rules of global engagement in ways that that would benefit the two countries and the developing world.

Notes

[1] B. Loudon, “India, China in clash at summit,” *Australian*, April 4, 2007, 7.

[2] Loudon, “India, China in clash at summit.”

[3] See J. Mearsheimer, “The false promise of international institutions,” *International Security*, 19:3 (Winter 1994/1995), 5-49.

[4] I. Rehman, “Keeping the dragon at bay: India’s counter-containment of China in Asia,” *Asian Security*, 5:2 (May 2009), 114-143.

[5] See J. Mohan Malik, “Security Council reform: China signals its veto,” *World Policy Journal*, 22:1 (Spring 2005), 19-29.

[6] W. Hoge, “UN report urges big changes; Security Council would expand,” *New York Times*, December 1, 2004.

[7] Xinhua, “China backs UN reform: FM,” <http://news.xinhuanet.com/english/2004-12/02/content_2287685.htm>; Xinhua, “China to consider UN reform proposals seriously: FM spokesperson,” *People’s Daily Online*, December 6, 2004, <http://english.peopledaily.com.cn/200412/06/eng20041206_166299.html>. Italics added.

[8] Wu Miaofa, “Restructuring the United Nations,” *Beijing Review*, May 13, 2004, 10-13.

[9] “China opposed to forced voting on UNSC reform,” *People’s Daily Online*, July 12, 2005, <http://english1.peopledaily.com.cn/200507/12/eng20050712_195685.html>.

[10] Wu, “Restructuring the United Nations,” 10.

[11] Xinhua, “China backs UN reform: FM,” December 2, 2004, <http://news.xinhuanet.com/english/2004-12/02/content_2287685.htm>.

[12] Ambassador Wang quoted in “China opposed to forced voting on UNSC reform.”

[13] Author’s discussions and conversations with US and Asian diplomats, 2003-04.

[14] S. Srivastava, “Beijing boosts Delhi’s bid for UN council seat,” *Asia Times Online*, October 26, 2004, <http://www.atimes.com/atimes/South_Asia/FJ26Df01.html>.

[15] PTI, “UNSC: China says it won’t be an obstacle for India,” *The Hindu*, July 4, 2005.

[16] I. Bagchi, “China backs India for Security Council seat,” *Times of India*, October 21, 2004.

[17] “‘New phase’ in Sino-India relations?” *Intellibridge Weekly Update*, October 29, 2004.

[18] Discussions with diplomats, September 2004-05. See also, “Out Dalai Lama for UNSC seat, says China,” *NewsInsight.net*, October 23, 2004, <http://www.indiareacts.com/nati2.asp?recno=3002>.

[19] “India’s UNSC entry without veto: China,” *Dawn*, December 15, 2004.

[20] The dominant Indian thinking is not to give in to such “unreasonable demands and conditions” for the Security Council seat, because “the status it

gives may well be more illusory than real." Some point out that Russia's seat did not prevent the Soviet Union's disintegration, nor has it resolved Chechen terrorism. See C. Raja Mohan, "Does the UN matter?" *Indian Express*, November 30, 2004.

[21] "India's UNSC entry without veto: China." This contrasted with Vladimir Putin's position. See PTI, "Putin clarifies remarks on India getting veto power in UNSC," *Hindustan Times*, December 5, 2004.

[22] Quoted in J. Sean Curtin, "Japan-China ties on the ropes," *Asia Times Online*, October 19, 2004, <http://www.atimes.com/atimes/Japan/FJ19Dh01.html>.

[23] S. Shahin, "India, Japan eye new axis," *Asia Times Online*, August 24, 2004, <http://www.atimes.com/atimes/South_Asia/FH24Df03.html>.

[24] Interestingly, Taiwan now supports India's bid for a permanent seat on the Security Council. See PTI, "India deserves UN's permanent seat: Taiwan," *Indian Express*, May 17, 2005, <http://www.expressindia.com/fullstory.php?newsid=14407>.

[25] PTI, "India attacks China on UNSC emasculation," *Indian Express*, July 2, 2005.

[26] Quoted in A. Baruah, "India may accept Security Council seat without veto," *The Hindu*, December 19, 2004.

[27] A group of medium-sized powers, including Pakistan, Italy, South Korea, Mexico, Argentina, and Canada are strongly opposed to creating new permanent seats for fear of their exclusion. They favor increasing longer-term semi-permanent seats as outlined in Option B.

[28] A. Boyd, "India, Japan still shooting for Security Council," *Asia Times*, February 26, 2002. A resolution passed at the 2005 Yemen summit of the Organization of Islamic Conference (OIC) demanded that any UNSC expansion must have the permanent presence of the OIC.

[29] B. Alam Khan, "China, Pakistan to strengthen defence ties," *Dawn*, December 17, 2004.

[30] C. R. Gharekhan, "Join the club," *Hindustan Times*, December 7, 2004.

[31] "China opposed to forced voting on UNSC reform."

[32] "China: UN Council resolution dangerous," *China Daily*, June 1, 2005.

[33] C. Raja Mohan, "China's anti-G4 line may be a lose-lose policy," *Indian Express*, June 13, 2005.

[34] "UN: China supports Italy and Pakistan in Security Council reform," *Dawn*, June 3, 2005.

[35] "Washington and Beijing will unite to block G4 plan," *Associated Press*, August 4, 2005. Italics added.

[36] PTI, "We'll support India minus Japan: China," *Indian Express*, April 15, 2006.

[37] Wu, "Restructuring the United Nations," 12.

[38] See, for example, Qiao Liang and Wang Xiangsui, *Unrestricted Warfare* (Beijing: PLA Literature and Arts Publishing House, February 1999).

[39] G. J. Ikenberry and A. M. Slaughter, "A bigger Security Council, with power to act," *International Herald Tribune* [*IHT*], September 26, 2006.

[40] See M. H. Van Herpen, "Security Council reform: how and when?" October 8, 2003, <http://www.inthenationalinterest.com>.

[41] M. Mohamad quoted in F. Ching, "Reforming the United Nations," *Far Eastern Economic Review*, November 25, 1993, 36.

[42] Wu, "Restructuring the United Nations," 12.

[43] P. Khanna, "One more seat at the table," *New York Times*, December 6, 2003.

[44] *Selected Works of Jawaharlal Nehru*, Series II, Vol. 29, Minutes of meeting with Soviet leaders, Moscow, June 22, 1955, 231.

[45] I. Bagchi, "Pakistan, China gang up to block India's UNSC entry," *Times of India*, March 8, 2009.

[46] R. Wilcox, "Yes, a Security Council seat for India," *IHT*, February 10, 2003. Wilcox was director of United Nations affairs on President Bill Clinton's National Security Council in 2000. "US should back India as permanent member of UNSC: Burns," *NDTV*, June 25, 2009 <http://www.ndtv.com/news/world/us_should_back_india_as_permanent_member_of_unsc_burns.php>.

[47] J. Traub, "The UN's bêtes noires: China and America," *New York Times*, September 1, 2006.

[48] Quoted in M. Chand, "Tharoor exit not surprising," *The Pioneer*, October 4, 2006.

[49] J. Mohan Malik, "China's strategy of containing India," *The Power & Interest News Report*, February 6, 2006, 1-7.

[50] C. Raja Mohan, "SAARC reality check: China just tore up India's Monroe doctrine," *Indian Express*, November 14, 2005.

[51] Mohan Malik, "The East Asia Summit: more discord than accord" *YaleGlobal Online*, December 20, 2005, 1-4, <http://yaleglobal.yale.edu/display.article?id=6645>; "The East Asian summit," *Australian Journal of International Affairs*, 60:2 (June 2006), 207-211.

[52] Commentary, "East Asia Summit: in the shadow of sharp divisions," *People's Daily online*, December 7, 2005.

[53] Interviews and discussions with diplomats, Kuala Lumpur, December 2006.

[54] Commentary, "East Asia Summit: in the shadow of sharp divisions." Italics added.

[55] Remarks by a Vietnamese diplomat, July 2006. Also see Wang Dong, "Asia-Pacific community: reality or pipedream?" *Global Times*, June 23, 2009 <http://opinion.globaltimes.cn/commentary/2009-06/439166.html>; Jia Qingguo, "Realizing the Asia-Pacific community," *East Asia Forum*, July 28, 2009.

[56] See Mohan Malik, "The Shanghai Cooperation Organization" in S. Ganguly, A. Scobell and J. C. Liow (eds), *The Routledge Handbook of Asian Security* (Routledge, 2010), Chapter 6, 72-86.

[57] F. Weir, "Russia, China looking to form 'NATO of the East'?: A six-member group, seeking to balance U.S. power, meets in Moscow," *Christian Science Monitor,* October 26, 2005, 4.

[58] S. Bhatt, "The prime minister's SCO dilemma," *Rediff.com*, May 29, 2009, <http://news.rediff.com/column/2009/may/29/special-pms-sco-dilemma.htm>.

[59] Chinese Foreign Ministry's daily briefings, March 2, 2006, <http://www.china-embassy.org/eng/fyrth/t238267.htm>.

[60] Commentary, "Nuclear agreement and big power's dream," *People's Daily online*, August 30, 2007, <http://english.people.com.cn/90001/90780/91343/6251506.html>.

[61] B. Roy, "123 Agreement and the People's Republic of China," *Saag.org*, Paper No. 2324, August 8, 2007, <http://www.saag.org/papers24/paper2324.html>.

[62] Wang Peng, "The US-Indian nuclear agreement: cooperation or threat?" *People's Daily*, August 11, 2007, 8.

[63] C. Buckley, "China likely to swallow anger over Indo-US N-deal," *Reuters*, August 29, 2007.

[64] For details, see Mohan Malik, "The proliferation axis," *Korean Journal of Defense Analysis*, 15:1, (Spring) 2003, 57-100. Chinese bomb design drawings were recovered from Libya in 2003, and until today the Chinese have not made public the results of their "investigation" launched in February 2004 (*China Brief*, April 29, 2004).

[65] Qin Huaishi, "Indu wuzhuang Yuenan tu ezhi Zhongguo," ["India arms Vietnam to curb China," "印度武裝越南圖遏制中國/ 秦淮仕,"] *Ta Kung Pao*, August 1, 2007, 8.

[66] "India/China: Fears of encirclement gradually mount," *Oxford Analytica*, November 12, 2008, <https://www.opensource.gov/providers/oxan/display.aspx?ItemID=DB146833>.

[67] PTI, "India conveys displeasure to China over NSG role," *Rediff.com*, September 8, 2008, <http://www.rediff.com/news/2008/sep/08chin1.htm>; "India miffed at China's dubious role in Vienna," *Times of India,* September 8, 2008, 1. What particularly irked the Indians was the refusal by the Chinese leadership—both Hu Jintao and Wen Jiabao—to take a phone call from Prime Minister Singh, saying they were "unavailable," even though President Bush spoke to his Chinese counterpart minutes later. India served a demarche to the Chinese ambassador, Zhang Yan, by calling him in the middle of the night. I. Bagchi, "Border talks: NSA heads for Beijing next week," *Times of India*, September 10, 2008, 1.

[68] AsiaInt Reference Library, "India & China pretend friends no more," *SAR*, September 2008, <http://www.asiaint.com/arl/arl19268.asp>.

[69] R. Deshpande, "NSA confirms China's NSG hostility to govt," *Times of India*, September 12, 2008, 1.

[70] See Mohan Malik, "China responds to the US-India nuclear deal," *China Brief*, 6:7 (March 29, 2006).

[71] Quoted in S. Dasgupta, "Anti-Chinese sentiment hampering border talks," *Times of India*, September 19, 2008.

[72] However, Beijing claims to have "grandfathered" the Chashma-3 and Chashma-4 reactors, saying that it has the right to fulfill the contract with Pakistan because it had been signed before China's entry into the NSG. "US

asks China not to help Pakistan build nuclear plants," *Pak Tribune*, November 22, 2008, <http://paktribune.com/news/index.shtml?208224>.

[73] Quoted in I. Bagchi, "Buddhism new obstacle between India, China," *Times of India*, June 21, 2007, 1.

[74] Rehman, "Keeping the dragon at bay," 114-143.

[75] B. Gilley, "Look to Brasilia, not Beijing: the rising challenge to China's great power aspirations," *Wall Street Journal*, April 7, 2009.

[76] B. Raman, "Tawang: some Indian plain-speaking at last!" *Saag.org*, Paper no. 2273, June 22, 2007, <http://www.saag.org/papers23/paper2273.html>.

[77] B. Chellaney, "The quad: Australia-India-Japan-US strategic cooperation," *Asian Age*, July 3, 2007.

[78] C. Raja Mohan, "Two PMs, one problem: China," *Indian Express*, August 21, 2007. Italics mine <http://www.indianexpress.com/story/211558.html>.

[79] Interview with a senior diplomat, New Delhi, March 2007.

[80] See B. Chellaney, "A smoking dragon in sheep's clothing," *IHT*, January 14, 2010.

[81] S. Dasgupta, "China suggests it blocked India's loan efforts at ADB due to border dispute," *Times of India*, April 14, 2009, 1.

[82] John Lee, "The fantasy of taming China's rise," *CIS Foreign Policy Analysis*, 3 (May 6, 2010), 8-9.

[83] On turning the concept of multilateralism on its head into a tool of power projection by China's "neocons" or "neocomms," see M. Leonard, "The rise of China's neocons," *Newsweek*, March 8, 2008.

[84] See Tao Deyan and Zhang Binyang, "Zhuanjia zonglun Zhongguo heping jueqi jinglue" ["Experts discuss China's peaceful rise concept"], *Zhongguo Zhengzhi Xue*, May 18, 2004 (originally published in *Guoji Xianqu Daobao*).

[85] Mohan Malik, "Multilateralism Shanghaied," *International Assessment & Strategy Center*, July 14, 2006, <http://www.strategycenter.net/research/pubID.115/pub_detail.asp>; Chen Xiangyang, "Draw up new 'Greater Periphery Strategy' as soon as possible," *Liaowang* [*Outlook*], No. 29, July 17, 2006, 64.

PART 3

WILL THE FUTURE RESEMBLE THE PAST?

10
Energy Flows and Maritime Rivalries in the Indian Ocean

In the pre-modern era, the Indian Ocean was the main highway of commerce from East to West. The advent, however, of the industrial revolution in Europe and the rise of the United States from 1800 AD onwards led to the dominance of other waterways—first the Atlantic Ocean and then the Pacific Ocean—thereby eclipsing the Indian Ocean's significance in maritime trade and international commerce. Current geostrategic, economic, energy, and demographic trends indicate that the Indian Ocean Region (IOR) could well emerge as the strategic center of the twenty-first century, much as the Atlantic and Pacific oceans played this role in the twentieth century.

This chapter focuses on the geopolitical implications of the ever-growing energy flows through the Indian Ocean and the trade ties between booming Asian economies and the Middle East and Africa. The first half of this chapter examines key characteristics, vulnerabilities, and threats to energy flows in the IOR. It illustrates the Indian Ocean's pivotal status in the global movement of trade, notably of energy resources, from Africa and the Middle East into Europe, South and East Asia, and the world beyond. The second part examines the energy interests and strategies of the major powers, focusing in particular on the Sino-Indian energy competition and maritime rivalry. With their fast-growing economies, China and India are seeking natural resources and markets and acquiring military might and bases. Geopolitical considerations, resource security, and old-fashioned great power ambitions are driving India and China's naval modernization and force expansion programs. China is concerned with: (1) its ability to deter the United States from projecting power in the East and South China Seas; and (2) India's position as a dagger pointing into the heart of sea lanes carrying oil from the Middle East and natural resources from Africa to China. As the Chinese Navy goes south to the Indian Ocean, the Indian navy's interest in the East Asian sea lanes is growing in the new "Great

Game" of the twenty-first century. Interestingly, Alfred Thayer Mahan's prediction made in 1890 that "whoever controls the Indian Ocean will dominate Asia.... In the 21st century the destiny of the world would be decided on its waters" increasingly finds an echo in Chinese strategic analyses that conclude "whichever country controls the Indian Ocean controls East Asia."[1]

The Significance of the Indian Ocean Region

The Indian Ocean (IO) is the world's third largest ocean after the Pacific Ocean and the Atlantic Ocean. Its rim is home to nearly two billion of the world's population, and it acts as a major sealane connecting the Middle East, East Asia and Africa with Europe and the Americas. The IOR, if one defines it as embracing the 33 countries with their feet in the Indian Ocean, stretches (east to west) from the eastern side of the Middle East region (encompassing Iran, Saudi Arabia, Oman, and Yemen) across the Indian Ocean to Indonesia. In its north-south orientation, the region includes large parts of Central Asia, South Asia, and the southern Indian Ocean waters off Australia's coast. It is subdivided into the Arabian Sea and the Bay of Bengal by the southward jutting peninsula of India. It thus spreads over seven sub-regions (Southern Africa, Eastern Africa and the Horn, the Gulf littoral and Arabian Peninsula, South Asia, South East Asia, Australia, and the Indian Ocean islands).

The IOR is distinguished by several key features. A major one, of course, is that contrary to the Atlantic and Pacific as "open oceans," the Indian Ocean is a "semi-enclosed ocean." This is the ocean with the largest number (four out of six) of critically important maritime "choke points": the Mozambique Channel, Bab-el-Mandeb (bordering Djibouti and Yemen), the Strait of Hormuz (bordering Iran and Oman), and the Strait of Malacca (bordering Indonesia and Malaysia). These narrow channels not only serve as the strategic and economic lifeblood of many adjoining nations but also serve as the main arteries for global trade and energy supplies, the majority of which are transported by sea. These choke points in the IO are becoming ever more vital to sustaining the globalized economy.[2]

Second, the IOR is extremely rich in energy resources, minerals and commodities. It is the number one source of global energy supplies. The Persian Gulf region alone contains 65 percent of the world's proven energy reserves and accounts for more than half of the world's oil exports and almost all of Asia-Pacific's imports. The IOR is home to most, though not all, members of the Organization of the Petroleum

Exporting Countries (OPEC) cartel. The IOR holds 65 percent of the world's strategic raw minerals and 31 percent of its gas reserves, holds 30 percent of the world population, and is characterized by fast-growing economies and a large consumer market.[3] It is estimated that the Japanese, European, and US economies respectively import 76, 70 and 25 percent of their crude oil requirements from the IOR. Nearly 80 percent of China's and 68 percent of India's oil is shipped through this region. These two Asian nations, along with so many others, are on the lookout for natural resources in the IOR to fuel their economic growth.

Third, the volume of intra-IOR trade is growing, even if it is still much less than intra-Pacific and intra-Atlantic trade. Currently, only one-fifth of the total IOR trade is conducted among the countries of the Indian Ocean themselves. The economic slowdown in the West, however, has been accompanied by growth in the Middle Eastern, Indian, and Chinese economies.

Fourth, the IOR is at the center of geostrategic and economic seismic shifts currently underway in the world. The search for black gold is bringing distant countries and regions closer, perhaps too close for comfort, creating new tensions and frictions. The Indian Ocean is now inextricably linked to the Western Pacific via deep linkages and interdependencies, whether in energy security, nuclear proliferation, trade and markets, or through economic growth and maritime security. As Pacific Asia becomes closely integrated with Southern Asia and vice versa, the Cold War-era divisions of the region into the Middle East, South Asia, Southeast, and Northeast Asia have broken down and a holistic map of Eurasia is reasserting itself.[4] The strategic consequences of Asia's booming economies becoming increasingly dependent on a wealthy but turbulent Middle East could be unsettling, to say the least.

The Middle East and Asia are also home to the world's largest pools of surplus cash, much of which is managed by six of the top 10 sovereign wealth funds (SWF). Since 2000, trade between China and the Middle East has doubled to $250 billion and is projected to grow severalfold over the next two decades. Thanks to the surge in oil prices, the Middle Eastern capital available for investment is about US$4 trillion—nearly the total size of Japan's annual economic output. Forecasts of continued tight oil supply and high prices in the $80–$100 per-barrel range for several years mean that the holdings of the SWFs of oil-producing nations would almost triple from $3 trillion in 2008 to $14 trillion by 2015. Much of the profit from high oil prices is being spent not on productive sectors of economy, but on military build-ups and on Wahabization (Arabianization or radicalization) of Islam in Asia and the world. Besides, demographic trends indicate that two out of every three people may soon live in the IOR, which will boost the demand for consumer goods.[5] The net effect is that trade, energy flows, investment, and consumption patterns are now binding the Indian Ocean nations and China into a potential new hub of the global economy that Martin Walker calls "CHIMEA" (China, India, the Middle East, and Africa).[6] Walker draws attention to the long-term geopolitical consequences of the seismic shift in wealth and power to "CHIMEA":

> Like all of the great surges of trade in history, the explosion of Indian Ocean commerce is based on mutual needs. China and India need energy supplies from the Persian Gulf states and oil and raw materials from Africa, and Africa needs the financial resources [of] the Gulf states.... The combination of Middle Eastern energy and finance with African raw materials and untapped food potential and Indian and Chinese goods and services looks to be more than just a mutually rewarding three-way partnership. Wealth follows trade, and with wealth comes the means to purchase influence and power. Just as the great centers of Europe clustered first around the Mediterranean Sea until the greater trade across the Atlantic and then the Pacific produced new, richer, and more powerful states, so the prospects are strong that the Indian Ocean countries will develop greater influence and ambition in their turn. In the emergence of CHIMEA as a new factor in global commercial affairs, we may also be seeing the future contours of the world's geopolitical system. Moreover, if one considers most of the projected growth rates for India and China, the CHIMEA connection appears likely to strengthen throughout this century. It could become the catalyst that finally hauls Africa from underdevelopment and poverty.... The new triangular trade of the Indian Ocean sees the Middle Eastern countries export oil to Asia, then use the proceeds to export capital to Asia and Africa.[7]

In short, the coming together of the two most liquid economies—the oil-rich Gulf countries and China—could create a new potent commercial bloc with the potential to reshape the economic order.[8] Should the Middle East see a decline in American (and European) interests relative to Asian powers, it would become an arena of competition among the Asian consumers for influence with the energy suppliers.

Fifth, there exists an enormous ethnic, religious, cultural, political, and economic diversity in the IOR. It contains sovereign states ranging in size from India with over 1 billion people to tiny Seychelles with less than 80,000. On the one hand are the three large economies and navies of India, Australia, and South Africa. On the other are the small island states like the Maldives and Mauritius with weak economic and naval capabilities whose very survival is at stake with rising sea levels.

Sixth, unlike the relatively peaceful Atlantic and Pacific oceans, the Indian Ocean is characterized by incessant interstate competition and numerous conflicts from the strife-prone Horn of Africa through the volatile Persian Gulf and turbulent South Asia. Dubbed the "arc of instability," it is a region marred by geopolitical and religious fault lines. Whether it is the resource crunch or religious extremism (of the *jihadi* terrorist variety) or nuclear proliferation or transnational security problems emanating from weak and failing states (piracy, terrorism, drug and arms trafficking, and refugee flows), IO littoral nations are at the heart of many global threats. This region also happens to be home to the world's greatest concentration of Muslims. An overwhelming majority of the OIC (Organization of Islamic Conference) countries is located in the IOR. Even as the IO facilitates global economic integration, it is fast becoming a chessboard of strategic rivalries and maneuverings of great powers. This is where the maritime interests of the US-China-India strategic triangle intersect. Since both the Middle East and Africa are richly endowed with natural resources from hydrocarbons to minerals and metals, China and India are fiercely competing for influence with IO littoral states, seeking to establish military presence through a combination of direct military footprint and broader security engagement. China is giving massive aid to Indian Ocean nations, signing friendship pacts and security assistance agreements, and building ports and signal intelligence facilities along the strategic sea lanes.[9] Washington and Tokyo seem to be tacitly backing India's role as a counterweight to China, thereby fuelling a maritime rivalry between Asia's emerging giants.[10]

And last but not least, despite its crucial role in providing "maritime connectivity" with other oceans and continents, the IOR has failed to evolve a vibrant regional community for itself. The region has hardly any security bonding. To date, no multilateral forum aimed at promoting region-wide cooperation encompassing the IOR has emerged. The Gulf Corporation Council (the GCC excludes Iran) is barely effective in an unstable region while the South Asian Association for Regional Cooperation (est. 1985) seeks to promote cooperation amongst South Asian countries only. The Indian Ocean Rim Association for Regional Cooperation (IOR-ARC, est. 1997) is the only organization of IO rim countries but has remained dysfunctional due to the competing interests and priorities of major players. Apparently, the IOR's political, economic, and cultural diversity coupled with competing geostrategic interests and territorial, religious, and resource conflicts stands in the way of an Indian Ocean grouping.

Energy Flows in the IOR

Energy is now probably the most important—and divisive—issue facing the IOR because energy security challenges cut across multiple realms—foreign policy, geopolitics, military modernization, nuclear proliferation, economic development, and environmental concerns. Unfortunately, just like the twentieth century, the twenty-first century is also turning out to be "the oil century," with all the attendant unsettling consequences. Oil flows through modern economies in much the same way as blood flows through the human body. The growing surge in energy demand has led to the rise of "energy nationalism" and "resource mercantilism" that is increasingly determining inter-state relations. Major energy producers have long used energy as a foreign policy tool. Iran's nuclear ambitions, the Iraq war, China's worldwide search for energy, the US-India nuclear agreement, and a series of pipeline and maritime infrastructure projects all showcase the increasing importance of energy as a driver of international politics. It seems that in a world of dwindling fossil fuel supplies and rising demand, he who controls not just the production of oil and gas but also the supply will dominate the world.

As noted earlier, the IOR is the world's main medium for the transportation of energy—primarily oil and gas from the resource periphery comprising the Middle East and parts of Africa to the "demand heartland" comprised mainly of India, China, and Japan.[11] More than 100,000 commercial vessels transit through the IOR each year, and crude oil is the biggest single cargo in terms of volume through these sea lanes of communication (SLOCs), which are viewed by energy-dependent states as their very lifelines. At its narrowest point, the Strait of Hormuz is only 21 miles (33.7 kilometers) wide. The Strait of Malacca is only 1.6 miles (2.7 kilometers) wide in the Phillips Channel, creating a natural bottleneck, as well as potential for collisions, grounding, or oil spills. The closing down of either strait will have disastrous consequences for the global economy.

Global oil demand is rising rapidly. It is projected to grow from 82.5 million barrels per day (bpd) in 2004 to 118 million bpd in 2025. India, China, and other industrializing Asian economies will account for 65 percent of the worldwide growth in oil consumption, and Asia will surpass North America as the world's largest consumer. At current rates of consumption, India's oil import dependence, for example, is expected to rise to 91.6 percent by 2020. Despite Beijing's efforts to diversify its energy supplies from different parts of the world, China's dependence on the Middle East will remain in the range of 61 to 77 percent.[12]

Another interesting development is that with more and more national oil companies (NOCs) assuming direct control of energy assets, the global energy trade is steadily regionalizing. A new energy architecture is emerging. Overall, the Middle East supplies nearly 75 percent of Asia's import needs, making the region by far the most important customer. By contrast, about 16 percent of Gulf oil exports are shipped to Europe and only 11 percent to the United States.[13] As North America moves toward Atlantic basin supplies and Europe toward Central Asian, African, and Atlantic basin supplies, South Asian and East Asian energy imports from the Middle East are set to triple by 2025. Asia is thus replacing North America and Europe as the most critical markets for Persian Gulf oil.[14] Therefore, internal instability in major energy suppliers in the future ought to worry Asian consumers more than Europeans and Americans. As Juli MacDonald observes:

> Consequently, the Middle East could become a new arena of competition among the Asian consumers as they vie for influence with the oil suppliers. A competition to watch will be China, India and Japan competing for projects and influence in the Iranian and Saudi Arabian energy sectors. We might anticipate as the Persian Gulf-Asia geostrategic link strengthens, the US and European influence in the region might wane, depending on how events in Iraq, Iran, and Saudi Arabia unfold.... Saudi Arabia and other producers are investing in downstream projects in Asia's major markets to secure future markets for their crude oil. These deals serve to solidify and deepen economic linkages that could take on increasing strategic significance.[15]

Clearly, this "regionalization of energy flows" is likely to result in new geopolitical alliances between consumers and producers. The broad contours of this strategic shift are already evident. Saudi Arabia, for example, is looking for new security partners to its east. And so is Iran. Energy politics will tie China and India much more closely to the Arab and Persian worlds than ever before.

As a natural corollary, maritime transport in the IO, being the most economical means of transportation, is seeing a dramatic increase. Despite all the talk of pipeline projects, Asian countries will remain dependent on sea transportation of energy from the Middle East for several decades. The downside is that the growing number of oil and LNG tankers will increase pressure on already congested strategic chokepoints in the IOR. On the positive side, however, several major ports, numerous small ports, and hundreds of new cities are under construction in Iran, Oman, Saudi Arabia, UAE, Pakistan, India, Sri Lanka, Bangladesh, Burma, and Indonesia. The new Hambantota port that China is developing on Sri Lanka's southern coast alone will boost that country's annual cargo handling capacity from 6 million containers to some 23 million. The energy infrastructure and shipbuilding industries are also booming. The Chinese have planned a fleet of 30 LNG tankers to shuttle between China and its supply sources in the Persian Gulf and the Horn of Africa.

In short, energy and trade trends indicate an unprecedented increase in maritime activities in IO waters, fuelled by demographic changes, integration of regional economies, construction and modernization of ports, and the growing nexus between economic and strategic interests. As a consequence, concerns about assuring future access to energy supplies through the IO sea lanes and critical straits to East Asia are fostering increased naval competition. Major energy consumers show preference for unilateral security measures to protect their interests against both traditional (the classic security dilemma) and non-traditional threats (terrorism and piracy).

Major Vulnerabilities and Threats to Energy and Trade Flows in the IOR

Historically, the rise in sea-borne trade has often led to an increase in vulnerabilities and an intensification of asymmetric threats that challenge the maritime domain. The Indian Ocean waterways, in particular, present a whole range of security threats to energy and trade flows—from maritime terrorism, piracy, arms, and drugs trafficking to conflict within energy-exporting states and instability in failing states. Nearly half of the world's 20 failing states are in the IOR. State failure in a major energy-producing country may necessitate external military intervention to stabilize energy flows. Internal unrest and criminal activity currently threaten a large portion of Nigeria's oil production. The blockage of a choke point, even temporarily, can lead to substantial increases in total energy prices in an increasingly interdependent world. The deliberate sinking of an oil tanker in one of the vital choke points (e.g., the Malacca Strait) or cruising an LNG carrier into a hub-port on a suicide mission is one of the worst-case scenarios. Evidence suggests that non-state actors such as al-Qaeda see the energy transportation sector of the global economy, and the unstable oil-rich countries themselves, as easy targets for attacks. Not surprisingly, since the 9/11 terrorist attacks, there has been a great deal of emphasis on securing ports and shipping from potential security threats involving, among others, "dirty bombs," biological weapons, and even nuclear attacks emanating from non-state actors.[16]

The growing exposure of maritime transportation of energy and shipping routes to threats emanating from pirates and terrorists points to the need for multilateral cooperation aimed at sharing intelligence and building capacity in the IOR. This is so because no single nation, no matter how powerful it is, can alone guarantee sea lanes security from the various asymmetrical and transnational threats that international shipping faces. There have been several hijacks of ships off the Somalia coast. American, Russian, Indian, and Chinese warships have been patrolling off the Horn of Africa in an effort to crack down on piracy off Somalia, where a UN-backed transitional government is struggling to restore order after 15 years of near-anarchy. Then there are disruptions to energy flows from natural disasters (earthquakes, tsunamis, and hurricanes) and man-made disasters (tanker collisions and oil spills) which require contingency planning, capacity building, and rapid response teams. The IOR accounts for around 70 percent of the world's natural disasters. The December 2004 tsunami actually saw the first-ever multilateral relief effort undertaken jointly by the US, Indian, Japanese, and Australian navies cooperating closely in tsunami-hit countries. When Cyclone Nargis battered Burma, leaving thousands dead in May 2008, the US and Indian navies were quick to send relief supplies.

While transnational threats posed by non-state actors or natural and man-made disasters are still manageable and can and do generate multilateral cooperation, land-based ones, in contrast, have historically been more disruptive and damaging to energy flows. In fact, energy supplies have long been hostage to land-based threats (i.e., inter-state wars and conflicts) involving major energy producers (Iraq) or political instability resulting in regime collapse/change in a major oil exporting nation (e.g., Iran). More often than not, it is politics—not economics or geology—that has disrupted energy supplies from the Middle Eastern region. Most of the global economic downturns have had their roots in oil supply restrictions and shortfalls caused by wars and domestic political upheavals:

- 1973–74: the "first oil shock" (the 1973 Arab oil embargo following the Arab-Israel conflict);
- 1979: the "second oil crisis" (following the Islamic revolution in Iran);
- 1980–82: economic recession caused by oil supply disruptions (in the early years of the Iran-Iraq War);

- 1990–91: recession following Iraq's invasion of Kuwait and the first Gulf War; and
- 2007–08: the "third oil shock" and global economic meltdown (wars in Afghanistan and Iraq and growth in oil demand).

At the state level, rising geopolitical tension can lead to attempts by adversaries to deny access along choke points in key Asian sealanes such as the Persian Gulf, the Malacca Strait, and the East China/Yellow Sea. There have been instances when countries have resorted to closure of oil transit choke points either to assert sovereignty over the area or to demonstrate their maritime might. Indonesia, for example, closed the Sunda and Lombok Straits in 1996 to demonstrate a resolve to enforce its interpretation of its archipelagic status. Iran, for its part, has repeatedly warned that any US/Israeli attack on Iran's nuclear installations would endanger the world's oil supplies. Tehran is known to have made contingency plans to block the Hormuz Strait, through which nearly 40 percent of the world's oil passes. Iran's submarines, mines, and anti-ship missiles give it substantial military power over this narrow channel. Many Indian strategists believe that China would use the Gwadar port at the mouth of the Hormuz Strait to block or threaten Indian routes for shipping petroleum from the Persian Gulf in the event of a conflict.[17]

In addition, energy investments in unstable and conflict-prone regions by Asia's energy-hungry economies make them especially vulnerable to naval interdictions or attacks on critical energy infrastructure. Emergency oil reserves in most other Asian countries are either non-existent or far below required levels. Saudi Arabia's oil production facilities are particularly vulnerable. The threat or prospect of nationalization of assets owned by foreign governments and companies has also been disruptive to energy flows. The protection of shipping, energy pipelines, refineries, LNG terminals, offshore exploration, and oil production facilities in the Persian Gulf, the Arabian Sea, and the Bay of Bengal from attacks imposes new mission requirements on regional military forces. For example, production from the Bombay High fields provides more than 60 percent of India's domestic oil and gas supplies. Much of India's domestic oil and gas production and refining capacity is concentrated on India's western coast near Pakistan and well within Pakistan's ability to strike in the event of conflict. As China acquires a robust military and power projection capability, Beijing will adopt a more visible posture along the SLOCs and deploy the forces to defend its energy and trade routes, which may seem threatening to others.[18]

The Age of *Oilpolitik*: Major Powers' Interests and Role in the IOR

Having discussed the growing significance of the IOR and major threats and vulnerabilities to energy flows, this section outlines the energy interests and strategies of the major powers. Energy is at the heart of most of the biggest geopolitical questions facing the world. The IO, where the interests of many major powers intersect and clash, is one of the most politically volatile regions of the world. The world's major economies are competing ferociously with each other to secure the energy imports they need to fuel their future growth. Energy concerns are now a key driver of the security strategies of major energy consumers, resulting in both competition and cooperation. We live in the age of *oilpolitik*. Oil is a powerful weapon of coercion and political influence. Policymakers know that restrictions on energy flows are one of the most potent sanctions available. Furthermore, oil wealth—from Venezuela to Iran—seems to breed contempt for international law, treaties, norms, markets, and rules. We are seeing the rise of "petro-superpowers"—nations that wield disproportionate power in the international system by virtue of their superior energy reserves. Russia, for example, sees energy as a key tool both in regaining its influence on the world stage and ensuring former Soviet republics' alignment with Moscow by punishing those (for example, Georgia) it perceives to be turning toward the West. Cash-rich but energy-hungry Beijing is building pipelines, refineries, railways, highways, and ports to draw small states and middle powers into China's orbit. The cash reserves of OPEC members, Russia, and large energy consumers such as China generate worries in Washington about possible collusion among them. The point is that growing energy needs can be used both as an instrument of coercion and as a means of consolidating regional dominance. Reliance on overseas energy producers can also constrain foreign policy options for large energy consumers. This is the reason China, India, and many other Asian countries are wary of offending Iran and avoiding siding openly with the United States and Europe in their dispute over Tehran's nuclear program. Barring a major scientific discovery or technological breakthrough, *oilpolitik* will not only shape the power and capabilities of the states but also determine the new coalitions of power that will emerge in world politics. Although energy competition alone is unlikely to trigger major conflict, it will contribute to tensions, strains and stresses, particularly in the Middle East and South and Central Asia.[19]

US Interests

Ensuring free and secure energy flows from the Middle East has long been at the heart of the US maritime strategy in the IOR—parts of which now come under three separate US military commands (CENTCOM, PACOM, and AFRICOM). The mission of the US Navy's Fifth Fleet, based at Bahrain, includes keeping the Persian Gulf and Strait of Hormuz open to international shipping, while the Seventh Fleet safeguards the Southeast and East Asian shipping routes. The Malacca Strait, in particular, figures prominently in the US global force posture as American warships, including aircraft carriers, move from the Pacific Command Fleet to the Central Command Fleet and vice versa in times of crises through the strait to reinforce American military presence in the Indian and Pacific oceans. The US naval base in Diego Garcia in the IO has long been central to both military operations and SLOC safety. In the 2000s, the IOR gained greater importance, figuring ever more centrally in US security strategies. As per its new maritime strategy unveiled in late 2007, "the U.S. Navy will shift its attention from the Atlantic to the Indian Ocean and the western Pacific."[20] Currently, US forces are battling in Iraq and fighting al-Qaeda in Afghanistan, and US aircraft carriers and associated warships are deployed in the Persian Gulf. The IOR is also the focus area of two major post-9/11 initiatives: the Container Security Initiative and the Proliferation Security Initiative. Both aim at enhancing regional stability while undermining the nexus between terrorism and nuclear proliferation.

Despite Washington's declining dependence on oil imports from the Gulf, the United States remains the underwriter of the security order in the region.[21] This gives Washington enormous leverage against the major energy consumers in Asia and Europe. This leverage is all the more important because China, India, and Japan are still more dependent on trade with the US economy than they are on a regional energy supplier such as Iran or Saudi Arabia. It is worth remembering that the United States has long used its global naval dominance to threaten or apply energy supply restrictions against nations it has sought to pressure. This has included both enemy states, such as Japan before the Pacific War, and allies, such as Britain and France during the Suez crisis.

Though America's military might still remains unchallenged and unmatched, the US naval presence on the oceans is actually quite thin, mainly due to extensive deployments in the Persian Gulf, Arabian Sea, Mediterranean, and East Asia to support growing commitments in Iraq, Afghanistan, Europe, South Korea, and Japan. In fact, a dramatic increase in military commitments has coincided with a sharp decline in the US Navy force levels from the 1980s highs of a 600-ship navy down to a fleet of 279 naval vessels in 2009. Since 2003, the US Navy has also cut thousands of sailor billets from its rolls. This decline has occurred in the backdrop of the rise in transnational security threats as well as more traditional maritime challenges from Asia's rising powers. Some observers wonder if the US preoccupation with fighting small wars in the Islamic world coupled with the US Navy's declining force levels were behind a senior Chinese naval officer's suggestion in 2007 to PACOM Commander Admiral Keating on "dividing the Pacific Ocean into western and eastern sides, with China controlling the area west of Hawaii and the United States controlling the area east of Hawaii."[22]

At any rate, the United States would like to see Asia's rising stars—India and China, which are contesting the same strategic space in the IOR—engaging in a cooperative burden-sharing arrangement. Since 2000, Washington's India policy has moved from containment to empowerment. In the 2006 Maritime Security Cooperation Framework, the United States and India committed to pursue cooperative efforts to enhance security in the maritime domain, ensure open sea lanes, prevent piracy and other maritime crimes, and build capacity to confront common challenges. The June 2008 *US National Defense Strategy* called on India to assume greater responsibility as a stakeholder in the international system, commensurate with its growing economic, military, and soft power.[23] The "1000-ship navy" concept pushed for an integrated, global partnership of fleets to police the global commons and counter transnational threats short of war, including piracy, terrorism, weapons proliferation, drug trafficking, and other illicit activities on the high seas. While US friends and allies welcomed the "1000-ship navy" proposal, China, Malaysia, and Indonesia remain lukewarm, perceiving it as diluting their sovereignty. Some cynics even argue that this proposal aims at maintaining a coalition of allies under Washington's leadership who would jointly underwrite the costs of US naval superiority, unchallenged since the demise of Pax Britannica. Beijing, of course, views the initiative as yet another instance of disguised American containment that would thwart China's blue-water naval goals and prevent China from establishing itself as an independent naval power on par with the United States.[24] Meanwhile, there has been a dramatic increase in US-Indian defense cooperation. The US now conducts the largest number of exercises with the Indian military, especially joint naval exercises. In 2002, the Indian and US navies coordinated the escort of high-value shipping in the Malacca Strait. During the 2004 tsunami and the 2008 Cyclone Nargis, the US and Indian navies jointly provided disaster relief on very short notice.[25]

Should America's relative decline leave any gaps in securing the global commons in the Asia-Pacific region, there are only two potential candidates to step up and help fill that role: China and India. Both have maintained double-digit increases in defense spending. Based on current trends, the Chinese naval armada is likely to outnumber US ships within a decade or so while India is aiming for a 170-ship navy.[26]

India Energized

India sees itself as the pivotal power in the Indian Ocean. It has vital stakes in the stability and security of the IOR, located as it is at the center of two strategic choke points in an important sea-lane for global oil supplies: the Strait of Hormuz to its west and the Strait of Malacca to its east. The maritime area around India is among the busiest in the world, with over 100,000 ship crossings every year. Currently, 90 percent of India's trade moves by ship. India imports over 73 percent of its crude oil and, according to the IEA's *World Energy Outlook*, its dependence on oil imports will grow to 92 percent by 2020. Nearly all of this is carried by tankers that traverse the narrow straits. Most of India's imported oil comes from the Persian Gulf: 68 percent, followed by 24 percent from Africa, 4 percent from Southeast Asia, and 4 percent from Central America. Saudi Arabia and Nigeria are India's two largest supplier of crude oil, meeting respectively 25 and 16 percent of its annual requirements. Iran is the third largest supplier of oil to India. India's location and dependence on seaborne oil imports makes it vulnerable to supply disruptions and naval interdictions such as piracy, seaborne attacks, or blockades. With its rapidly growing economy and rising demand for imported oil and gas, India is projected to become the third-largest global importer of oil by 2025. Today, some 50 oil tankers sail past Indian shores daily; by 2020, the number is expected to be between 150 and 200.[27] India's extractable coal reserves are expected to run out in 45 years. Although India has ambitious plans to expand its nuclear power generation program, it lacks sufficient uranium even to meet the capacity of existing reactors. Its efforts to secure uranium from overseas through the US-India civilian nuclear deal will take years, if not decades, to come to fruition.

Not surprisingly, India's foreign policy has been energized by energy concerns. New Delhi's growing interest in Southeast Asia and India's relations with the Middle East, Central Asia, and Africa are largely energy motivated. Worried about its excessive dependence on the Middle East—a region of perennial turmoil—India has been scouting for oil outside this region. Much like China, India is becoming increasingly engaged in Russia, Africa (e.g., Sudan, Nigeria, and Libya), and Latin America (Venezuela). India's ONGC Videsh Ltd. holds a 20 percent stake in Russia's Far Eastern Sakhalin-I field. However, India faces intense competition from China and often finds itself at a disadvantage wherever it goes for hydrocarbons—from Latin America to Africa to Asia. China's state-owned oil conglomerates have trumped Indian oil companies in countries ranging from Ecuador to Kazakhstan and Angola to Burma, mainly because China is playing a geopolitical game while Indian oil firms are primarily commercial ventures.[28] Nonetheless, Indian firms have committed over $7.5 billion since 2000 in several countries including Australia, Algeria, Kazakhstan, Indonesia, Burma, Vietnam, Cuba, Venezuela, Libya, Syria, Egypt, Iran, Iraq, Yemen, Ivory Coast, Libya, Nigeria, Qatar, Russia, and Sudan.[29] (In contrast, China's CNPC [China National Petroleum Corporation] alone has made overseas investments of an estimated $45 billion.)

In Africa, India is emulating China as it seeks to lower its dependence on the Middle East even as it raises oil and gas imports. China currently sources 30 percent of its oil imports from Africa. India's energy imports from African countries are expected to reach 20–21 percent by 2020 (up from 16 percent in 2007). Indian investment in Africa's oil and gas sector is growing. As with other interests, India's strategy for building partnerships with Africa in the energy field is also similar to the one adopted by China: courting Africa with soft loans, development aid, arms transfers, and political support to bag lucrative oil projects. In November 2007, India took a leaf out of China's book in organizing a conclave of energy ministers from 25 African countries with a view to raising the level of engagement. The convening of the India-Africa Summit, attended by 14 African leaders in New Delhi in April 2008, is also seen as a response to the first China-Africa Summit.[30] India-Africa trade has grown rapidly in the last 5 years, from $3.4 billion in 2000 to $30 billion in 2007. (China's trade with Africa is more than double the amount of India's.)

More importantly, energy security concerns have prompted a debate in India's strategic circles over the type of capabilities required to secure India's strategic interests in its "extended strategic neighborhood"—defined as the region located between the Malacca Strait in the East and the Persian Gulf in the West, and from Central Asia in the North to the Indian Ocean littorals in the South. India has 7,516 kilometers of coastline and an exclusive economic zone of two million square kilometers which require protection. These include oil and gas resources in the Bay of Bengal, which could be contested by Bangladesh and Burma, as well as waters around the Andaman and Nicobar Islands and drilling sites in the south and west of the country. Having lost out to Chinese competition in Burma and Bangladesh, New Delhi is concerned about Chinese energy firms monopolizing access to the oil and gas resources in Sri Lanka's Mannar Basin, which may hold up to one billion barrels of oil.[31]

Apparently, the Indian Navy is using energy security and sea lane protection priorities to carve out a larger role for itself. In December 2006, then Chief of Naval Staff Admiral Sureesh Mehta employed an energy security rationale to expand the conceptual construct of India's "greater strategic neighborhood" to include potential sources of oil and gas imports located across the globe—from Venezuela in the West to Sakhalin in the East. The arrival from Sakhalin in December 2006 of the first Russian oil consignment on India's shores made naval planners turn their attention to developing plans to defend this new sea lane that originates from Russia's far east and extends through the Pacific Ocean, South China Sea, and Malacca Strait to Indian ports. More than half of India's trade now goes through the Malacca and Singapore straits that link the Indian and Pacific oceans via the Andaman and South China seas.[32] Given this context, a former Indian naval chief has mentioned the need for "creating viable maritime and out-of-country projection capabilities to deal with future extra-regional challenges and to protect India's bourgeoning strategic assets both at land and sea, in particular, critical energy supplies, maritime trade, and the security of the country's recent large-scale investments in the energy sector."[33]

The safety of shipping lanes is a key driver behind the Indian Navy's budgetary allocation and naval doctrine.[34] To this end, a major naval expansion is underway that includes plans to have a fleet of aircraft carriers, long-range maritime patrol aircraft, anti-submarine warfare, anti-ship missiles, amphibious warfare capability, and nuclear submarines over the next decade. Of a projected $100 billion of defense procurement spending in the next 10 years, a substantial proportion will go to the navy. Forty new warships are to be added over the next 15 years. India has already consolidated its naval bases in the Andaman and Nicobar Islands located close to the Malacca Strait. Current plans would see the islands become a nuclear submarine and aircraft carrier base. The United States seems more comfortable with the rise of India than it is with the ascent of China. Official policy documents often express concern over the lack of transparency in China's military expansion. In contrast, the 2010 *Quadrennial Defense Review* hoped that as the Indian Navy's capabilities in long-range maritime surveillance, interdiction and patrolling, and strategic airlift grow, "India will contribute as a net provider of security in the Indian Ocean and beyond" through counterpiracy, peacekeeping, humanitarian assistance, and disaster relief efforts.[35]

Force expansion is being backed by strategic moves in the IO. As a corollary to its "Look East" policy, India has unveiled a "Look West" policy that seeks to pro-actively engage western Indian Ocean littoral states, including Africa and the Middle East, via investment, trade, aid, and security arrangements. India reportedly has established a listening station in northern Madagascar, a large island nation off Africa's east coast. The station is India's first in the southern Indian Ocean and is significant due to the increasing oil traffic around the Cape of Good Hope and the Mozambique Channel. It is also building security relationships with Mauritius and the Maldives, to eventually set up more listening posts and staging areas.[36] India has signed security cooperation pacts with Qatar and Oman and regularly conducts naval exercises with Kenya, Tanzania, and South Africa. To Seychelles, the Indian Navy has offered military hardware and training, partly to counter advances being made by the Chinese. In the north, India has an air base sharing arrangement in Tajikistan and a space monitoring post in Mongolia—both China's neighbors.[37]

Since most of India's oil and gas imports come via sea routes, regular joint naval exercises (with the United States, Australia, Japan, France, China, Britain, Russia, South Africa, Vietnam, and Singapore) constitute the third dimension of India's maritime security. With the United States, the Indian Navy has been carrying out the Malabar naval exercises to promote interoperability since 1992. Since 1995, India has been conducting the biennial MILAN "get-together" involving the South and Southeast Asian navies. In 2002 India and Indonesia began biannual coordinated naval patrols in the Andaman Sea. Since 2006 Indian leaders have repeatedly offered littoral states capacity-building assistance in the Malacca Strait. The navy also makes annual friendly visits to important ports in the region.

As part of "influence-and-confidence building measures" (ICBMs) in the IOR, the Indian Navy is pro-actively engaged in "aid diplomacy": helping littoral states such as Mauritius, Seychelles, and the Maldives in capacity building and providing timely relief during natural disasters. As noted earlier, during the 2004 tsunami and 2008 Cyclone Nargis, the Indian Navy was the first to send relief supplies to the Maldives, Sri Lanka, Indonesia, and Burma respectively, a clear demonstration of its ability to rush aid in times of distress.[38]

Last but not least, in the absence of a multilateral security organization encompassing the IOR, the Indian Navy has stepped forward to fill the void by setting up the Indian Ocean Naval

Symposium (IONS), modeled on the lines of the US Navy-sponsored Western Pacific Naval Symposium (WPNS). The first inaugural summit, attended by naval chiefs from 26 littoral states in the IOR, was held in February 2008 and discussed ways and means to enhance cooperation on issues such as piracy, terrorism, and search-and-rescue operations in the Bay of Bengal, Arabian Sea, and Red Sea.[39] Naval chiefs from 32 littoral states of South and Southeast Asia, Africa, and Oceania attended the second IONS held in Dubai in 2010.

In short, energy concerns are increasingly shaping national security decision-making in India, as New Delhi seeks to exploit its strengths to forge cooperative partnerships with resource-rich states and thereby stem competition within the region from extra-regional powers. Given its growing energy import requirements and the challenges posed by the China-Pakistan duo, maintaining maritime preeminence in the IOR is one of India's three core strategic interests (the other two being preservation of territorial integrity and strategic autonomy based on a credible nuclear deterrent).

Japan's Anxieties

Japan, too, is almost totally dependent on energy supplies shipped through the Indian Ocean. For Tokyo, energy security has always been a matter of national survival. Three-quarters of all Japan's oil needs pass through the Malacca Strait. The world's third largest economy has long depended on the IO sea lanes that are now equally important to China and India.

From Japan's perspective, "resource nationalism" is a major concern. A particular anxiety is the threat of unilaterally imposed measures that deny Japan equal access to energy resources. Tokyo is engaged in a tussle with China/Taiwan over the Senkaku/Diaouyu Islands and worries about China's growing ability to strangle oceanic trade as the Chinese Navy increases patrols throughout the South China Sea region and its warships show an increased willingness to confront regional nations on the high seas and within the contested island chains. Much like China and India, Japan is also looking to Africa to diversify its energy supplies. The Japanese government has offered to double government development aid to Africa. The Japanese keep a close eye on China's activities in the Indian Ocean, particularly the construction of several ports along their vital SLOCs, and are looking to the Indians as a partner to balance China's expanding presence. Since 2000, Japan and India have held joint coast guard exercises focused on piracy and search and rescue, and conducted trilateral (US-Japan-India) joint naval exercises to enhance sea lane security in 2007 and 2009. Tokyo has maintained its anti-piracy presence in the Gulf of Aden, but it has abandoned its at-sea refueling mission in support of coalition operations in Afghanistan. With 119 warships, including 20 diesel-electric submarines, Japan maintains a very potent naval force that is nearly three times larger than Britain's.

China and the Lure of Indian Ocean Energy

China, the world's second largest economy, is redefining the global balance of power with respect to resource consumption. The People's Republic has now turned to the IOR to satiate its critical raw material needs, procuring significantly large quantities of oil and gas, bauxite, copper, iron ore, timber, and zinc from the region.[40] Chinese forays into the IO are a reflection of China's transformation from an East Asian continental power into a global maritime trading power increasingly dependent upon external trade, on ever-growing volumes of imports and exports through oceanic routes, and on overseas markets for resources, capital, investment, and the consumption of Chinese exports. Not surprisingly, China is suddenly everywhere—from Africa to Australia to Argentina. More than 85 percent of China's external trade is transported by sea. China, the world's second-largest energy importer, ferries 70 percent of its oil through the Indian Ocean and the oil-rich Middle East accounts for the majority (about 58 percent) of China's oil imports. The 2008 White Paper on Diplomacy placed energy security as a major centerpiece of China's foreign policy. Should China's GDP continue to grow at a rate of 8–10 per cent a year, China's need for energy is projected to increase by 150 percent by 2020. China's oil consumption is growing by 7.5 percent per year, seven times faster than that of the United States. Chinese state-owned oil companies are currently engaged in numerous international exploration and production projects all over the world. In order to secure access to IO natural resources, Beijing offers aid packages, cheap loans, infrastructure projects, pledges for future increased trade and investment, diplomatic support, and military hardware. China has invested heavily in offshore oil and gas investments in Kenya, Sudan, Iran, Saudi Arabia, Bangladesh, Burma, and Sri Lanka. However, China's efforts to lock up oil and gas resources for its exclusive use at their state of origin have led to heightened competition with other major energy-hungry countries.

Over the last decade, Beijing has redefined its engagement with the Persian Gulf region in general and with Iran, Saudi Arabia, and the United Arab Emirates (UAE) in particular. Beijing has concluded many oil and gas contracts with Iran, making it the largest Middle East oil supplier to China and accounting for 14 percent of China's total oil imports. In 2004, SINOPEC signed a $100 billion deal to buy 10 million metric tons of LNG from Iran annually over a 25-year period. In exchange, SINOPEC secured a 51 percent stake in the giant Yadavaran oilfield in Iran's south, leaving a minority 20 percent stake for a consortium of Indian oil companies led by the OVL. China has also planned a 386-kilometer oil pipeline from Iran to link up with the Atasu-Alashankou pipeline between Kazakhstan and Xinjiang. In 2006, another Chinese company, CNOOC, signed an MoU to develop Iran's massive North Pars natural gas field. Under the $16 billion deal, CNOOC would cooperate with the National Iranian Oil Company to develop and liquefy the field's estimated 80 trillion cubic feet of natural gas. In the same year, another Chinese firm, PetroChina, inked a deal to annually import some three million tons of LNG from Iran over a quarter of a century. PetroChina's parent company, CNPC, followed suit, finalizing a $3.6 billion project to explore and exploit Iran's South Pars gas field. The growing Sino-Iranian relationship not only bolsters China's energy security but also reduces US leverage to successfully negotiate the nuclear issue with Iran.[41] Geopolitically, China sees Iran as a useful counterweight to US allies in the region and is keen to establish a naval presence in the Persian Gulf, through which 40 percent of global energy is transported. After Iran, Saudi Arabia is the Middle East's second largest oil exporter to China. A major deal to explore for oil in Saudi Arabia's Empty Quarter was signed in 2004. The Sino-Saudi relationship has been transformed by regular high level visits in recent years. During King Abdullah's 2006 visit to China, the two countries signed an agreement on energy cooperation that called for increasing joint investment in oil and natural gas fields.

In August 2008, China surprised Western and Asian oil majors by winning the first Iraqi oil service contract since the US invasion in 2003, a deal worth $3 billion. Iraq and China's CNPC renegotiated terms of an old Saddam Hussein-era deal signed in 1997 to pump oil from the Adhab oilfield, whereby CNPC would own 75 percent of a joint venture while Iraq's Northern Oil Company would own 25 percent. The success of Beijing's energy diplomacy in the Middle East is evidence that China today has better relations with the three largest energy suppliers—Iran, Saudi Arabia, and Iraq—than does the United States (or any other major power).[42]

China's involvement in Africa is equally extensive. China now gets more than a third of its total oil imports from Africa, and Angola is second only to Saudi Arabia, supplying China with about 500,000 bpd.

China imports 64 percent of Sudanese oil production. China has also acquired large Nigerian offshore oil and gas fields. China's investment in this civil war–torn country in a 2006 deal was US$2.3 billion. Other energy suppliers from Africa include Algeria, Tunisia, Libya, Congo, Chad, Kenya, Angola, Nigeria, Gabon, Mauritania, Niger, and Equatorial Guinea. In 2006, Beijing hosted a mega-conference of the energy ministers of 36 African nations, promising investment of another $40 billion over the $8 billion already invested on the continent. Beijing's trade with Africa surpassed $100 billion in 2010.

The second dimension of China's energy diversification strategy is the establishment of pipeline networks and railroad linkages involving Iran, Pakistan, Kazakhstan, Turkmenistan, and Burma. The chief motivation is the fear that the Strait of Malacca, through which passes 80 percent of China's energy supplies, can be blocked in the event of a conflict. Reliance on overland pipelines, energy corridors, and railroads is supposed to reduce China's vulnerability. In Burma, China is building an overland pipeline from Sittwe (a sea port in Western Burma) to Yunnan, carrying oil and gas from the Bay of Bengal. The special relationship the Chinese have struck up with the Burmese military junta is founded on that country's geostrategic location and its enormous gas and oil resources. The exercise of UN Security Council vetoes to protect the junta and the provision of massive aid, loans, and military hardware have only one purpose: to allow the Chinese to grab as much oil and gas as they can and to extend Beijing's strategic reach into the Indian Ocean. One Chinese analyst explains Burma's significance in China's energy strategy:

> The plan is to ship China-bound oil and natural gas from Africa and the Middle East by ocean-going oil tankers across the Indian Ocean to the port of Sittwe in Burma … and then sent by pipeline to China by way of Mandalay in Burma and Ruili in Yunnan.… The pipelines will greatly shorten the oil and gas' sea-borne journey and sharply reduce the related costs. Even more important, it will no longer be necessary for a large part of China's oil imports from the Middle East and Africa to sail through the Strait of Malacca, which is highly risky and is under the control of other countries. While this plan is of great help to China's energy security, it may not be something that countries eager to curb China's robust development want to see.… Tension in Burma is not in China's interest.… If the military regime is overthrown and the pro-Western Aung San Suu Kyi comes into power, the encirclement of China in South Asia by the United States will be even tighter. When that comes to pass, the Chinese-Burmese oil pipeline project may never get off the ground. Even if it gets built, its security

> will be badly compromised and the strategic objective behind the original plan will remain unfulfilled.[43]

Likewise, in Pakistan, Beijing plans to build an energy pipeline from Gwadar in the Strait of Hormuz to western China as a way to reduce the time and distance for transporting oil to China from the Gulf region and Africa. The completion of the Gwadar port project will enable the Chinese navy, with its access in Burma, to operate on both sides of the Indian peninsula and reduce China's reliance on the Strait of Malacca. Furthermore, it will enable China's navy to monitor its own as well as Indian, Japanese, and Western energy supplies. It is the western-most pearl in what the Pentagon has identified as China's "string of pearls" strategy, which envisages building strategic relations with several countries to establish a network of bases along the SLOCs from the Middle East to the South China Sea to protect China's energy interests and other security objectives.[44] Critics, however, argue that these projects are not only extremely costly but will not address the problem of interdiction of energy supplies by powerful, hostile navies before their arrival at the Pakistani and Burmese ports. In addition, the success of the Gwadar project remains hostage to internal stability in Baluchistan and Pakistan, while a regime change in Rangoon could jeopardize Beijing's investments and best-laid plans for that country.

The point is that as China's external energy dependency has deepened in the past decade, so has its sense of insecurity or siege mentality. China has a penchant for doing things in small steps and piecemeal; quietly, patiently, and eventually bringing the jigsaw pieces together "when the conditions are ripe." Then the fog suddenly clears, the "string of pearls" emerges, and takes everyone by surprise! But with ever-growing reliance on seaborne commerce, and the world's fourth-largest merchant fleet, it was not realistic to expect Beijing to outsource its sea-lane security to the US Seventh Fleet. The development of an ocean-going fleet coupled with a network of allies along the SLOCs is meant to give Beijing wider options: whether thwarting energy blockades, deterring other powers, or protecting Chinese nationals and interests far away. Large amphibious assault ships, destroyers, plans to build the largest submarine fleet (incl. nuclear submarines), refueling vessels, anti-ship (ballistic and cruise) missiles, and proposed aircraft carriers all will bolster China's blue-water capabilities. So the third dimension of Beijing's energy strategy involves building strategic alliances with IO littoral states.[45] Beijing is, therefore, cultivating comprehensive economic and security relationships with friendly states in the Middle East and South and Southeast Asia, especially those adjacent to the choke points in the IO and the Arabian Sea. In particular, Beijing is increasing its presence in Central Asia, Iran, Pakistan, Sri Lanka, Bangladesh, and Burma so as to ensure safe flow of energy and thwart India's attempts to establish naval dominance in the region. Since 2006, there has been a dramatic increase in Chinese military cooperation with Sudan, Mauritius, Mozambique, the Seychelles, Tanzania, and Zimbabwe. Nearly 90 percent of Chinese arms sales go to countries located in the IOR (mainly Pakistan, Burma, Bangladesh, Sri Lanka, the Middle East, East Africa, and the IO island states).

Clearly, China has developed vital trading, energy, and strategic equities in the IO waters and rim which require protection. In December 2008, the Chinese navy joined the multinational anti-piracy flotilla off the coast of Somalia in response to rising pirate attacks on merchant ships. This deployment was China's first combat-ready ocean expedition since the journeys of the eunuch Admiral Zheng He and his treasure ships in the early 1400s.[46] Exactly a year later, Rear Admiral Yin Zhou, director of the Naval Center on Information Research, floated the idea of China acquiring a permanent naval base overseas to resupply its ships.[47] The suggestion marked a major departure from Beijing's avowed policy of not maintaining foreign military bases or alliances. But it came as no surprise to China-watchers because Chinese probing is often followed by a period of quiet, later broken by new claims and more assertive behavior. In the absence of cooperative maritime arrangements, the Chinese have also floated the idea of carving up maritime zones of exclusive national responsibility in the Indian Ocean to curb piracy and other threats to sea lanes security.[48] However, many see this proposal as a throwback to the Cold War-era zones and spheres. Rory Medcalf, for one, rightly argues that creating national maritime zones by major naval powers "would both reflect and worsen mistrust." If anything, it would imply "the failure of multilateralism, not its success."[49] Apparently, Beijing wants to carve out a larger presence in the IOR but there it warily sees the US and Indian navies working together as "natural allies" with convergent maritime interests.[50] Consequently, China has let it be known that it would brook no interference by another maritime power when it comes to the protection of its trade and energy routes, whether in the Indian Ocean or in the South China Sea. The downside is that an exclusive maritime zone or extended economic zone in the Indian Ocean could bring China and India face to face on the high seas, where a situation could develop into an explosive one in the absence of rules of engagement and confidence-building measures.

Energy Security Spawns Maritime Rivalry: Oil and Water Don't Mix

Asia's two rising continental powers, China and India, increasingly dependent on seaborne energy and commerce for their economic well-being, have set their eyes on the Indian Ocean. Resource scarcity has thus added a maritime dimension to the traditional Sino-Indian geopolitical rivalry in the twenty-first century. As China and India's energy dependence on the Middle East increases, both are actively seeking to forge closer defense and security ties with resource supplier nations, and to develop appropriate naval capabilities to control the sea lanes through which the bulk of their commerce flows.[51] Naval thinkers in China and India seem spellbound by the grandeur of sea power. Mandarins in Beijing wax lyrical about resurrecting China's fifteenth century naval expeditions to the "Western Ocean" (the old Chinese name for the Indian Ocean). According to retired PLA General Xu Guangyu, "China's previous naval absence was 'an abnormal historical accident' that is being rectified."[52] Being among the world's top five energy consumers (China is second after the United States; India is fifth), each has made energy security an essential component of its strategic doctrine. For both, investing in overseas oilfields has emerged as a major strategy to enable diversification and provide protection against random supply shocks in major oil exporting countries.

Consequently, the two are locked in a fierce rivalry for stakes in overseas oil and gas fields all over the world. In this competition, however, China enjoys an overwhelming lead over India economically and diplomatically. China's oil firms have been aggressively scouting for energy sources worldwide as well as beating Indian firms in their own backyard (in Burma, Bangladesh, Iran, and Central Asia), both by combining business and government interests and by exploiting India's weaknesses. According to Cai Xiyou, vice-president of CNPC, "[t]he fight for oil between China and India is getting more intense."[53] Burma is a case in point where India lost out to China on importation of natural gas from Burma's offshore fields, even though Indian state-run firms have a 30 percent stake in those fields, and it would have made more economic sense for Rangoon to send it to New Delhi.

As China goes on to contract most of the emerging and unexplored sources, India—which imports three-quarters of its oil needs—fears being left behind in the race for future energy supplies. A major reason China's state-owned oil companies have outfoxed their Indian counterparts in securing oil deals in a number of countries is that the former can draw on generous lines of credit from the Chinese government, which also offers diplomatic and military support to supplier states. India, in contrast, lacks China's deep pockets (nearly $2.7 trillion reserves), diplomatic clout (in the form of UN Security Council veto), and surplus armaments (both conventional and nuclear), which have proved crucial in swinging deals in Beijing's favor. Furthermore, Chinese oil companies are not averse to entering into uneconomic deals, driven as they are less by market and profit considerations and more by the Chinese government's strategy to establish strategic footholds and lock up resources.

Though the two countries concluded an energy cooperation pact in 2006, China has shown willingness to cooperate with India in the energy sector only if the following three conditions are met:

- Indian oil companies are willing to play the role of junior partner to China's state-owned oil conglomerates.
- Energy resources do not lie in India's immediate neighborhood (Burma, Bangladesh, and Central Asia).
- Energy resources lie in countries or regions (Syria, Sudan, Iran, Venezuela, Columbia, Russia, and Yemen) where China-India cooperation would potentially cause a wedge between India and the United States.

For China, cooperation with India in pariah states such as Iran or Sudan serves to legitimize the Chinese presence there. Such cooperation makes it harder for Western critics to label China's foreign policy neocolonial or mercantilist. Nevertheless, many do see Beijing's foreign policy as mercantilist, driven by the same needs as drove Great Britain and the United States in the nineteenth and twentieth centuries.

Since nearly 80 percent of China's trade is carried by sea through the Strait of Malacca and the Indian Ocean, China views the predominance of the US and Indian navies along these sea lines of communication as a major threat. This is what the Chinese leaders describe as "the Malacca dilemma."[54] Chinese military journals stress the need to protect the country's seaborne trade and energy supply routes, to blunt the US military's overarching superiority in the Pacific, and to disabuse New Delhi of the notion that the "Indian Ocean is India's ocean."[55] A major area of concern is the six-degree channel that lies between India's Great Nicobar Island and Indonesia's Sumatra Island, where China's shipping is especially vulnerable to Indian and other forces. The establishment of a Far East command in the Andaman Islands, close to the Malacca Strait, enables the Indian navy to project power toward the Pacific.[56] As a resident or pivotal power in the IOR,

India enjoys an advantageous position vis-à-vis China. In March 2009, Beijing was miffed over Jakarta spurning China's offer for securing the Malacca Strait and instead inviting rival India to send ships for joint patrols apparently to ensure that "all approaches to the Strait would be safeguarded."[57] Beijing's desire to contain Indian power is no secret.[58] Chinese strategic writings express angst over India's growing military power, its ability to "resist China," and its assertion of influence in the IOR. Of particular concern are India's evolving ties with the United States and Japan.[59] Worried by the growing talk in Washington's policy circles and New Delhi of India as emerging as a counterweight to China on the one hand and the fragile, radical Islamic states on the other, Beijing views a potential US-Indian alignment and the India-Japan global partnership with horror.[60] As noted earlier, shared security concerns about China have already brought Tokyo and New Delhi closer to expand their security cooperation and increase maritime cooperation in the IOR.

Maritime security concerns are increasingly providing the rationale for naval expansion and modernization efforts in China and India. Their navies regard energy security as an explicit part of their mission and are using it to justify budget increases and to acquire more capabilities for ensuring sea lane protection and open navigation of the high seas. Both are pursuing maritime strategies based on the principles of sea denial, anti-access, forward presence, and power projection. Some Chinese officers want to fly the flag ever farther afield as a demonstration of China's rise. They speak of developing three oceangoing fleets: one to patrol the areas around Korea and Japan, another to push out into the western Pacific, and a third to protect the Strait of Malacca and the Indian Ocean.[61] They envisage China undertaking future naval operations with a view to securing the country's oil supply and trade routes. Some hawkish Chinese admirals want warships to escort commercial vessels that are crucial to the country's economy from as far as the Persian Gulf to the Strait of Malacca and to help secure Chinese interests in the resource-rich South and East China Seas.[62] This may seem too ambitious, but China certainly seeks to be the dominant naval power in the region east of the ASEAN group of countries, especially in the South China Sea, just as India hopes to achieve the same capacity in the northern Indian Ocean.

Beijing has laid the groundwork for a naval presence along maritime choke points in the South China Sea, the Strait of Malacca, the Indian Ocean, and the Strait of Hormuz in the Persian Gulf through acquisition of or privileged access to ports in Cambodia, Burma, Bangladesh, Sri Lanka, and Pakistan to protect its long-term economic security interests.

Although these deep sea ports will be for the civilian purposes of trade and securing energy supplies, Beijing could call them in for military or strategic purposes if and when needed by the Chinese navy in the future. Some of these port deals are reportedly accompanied by security- and intelligence-sharing agreements as well. The assumption underlying this strategy is that China's rivals, finding themselves encircled or obstructed by countries aligned with Beijing, will be sufficiently deterred from threatening China's vital economic and security interests. The Gwadar port in Pakistan at the mouth of the Persian Gulf, about 400 kilometers from the Strait of Hormuz, is being developed as a major conduit for global oil supplies to China. It would also allow China to project its might westward, toward the Middle East, western India and eastern Africa, and down into the Indian Ocean.[63] China's new assertiveness at sea is matched by bold official statements and commentaries in state media. Rebuking the peddlers of the "China threat theory," a *Global Times* editorial conceded that the transformation of the Chinese navy would naturally bring changes to a regional "strategic pattern" that has lasted for five decades. It went on to boast that "the time when dominant powers enjoyed unshared 'spheres of influence' around the world is over."[64] As noted earlier, Chinese naval officers and strategic analysts now openly suggest their country, like other great powers, needs "a few military bases" abroad to help the PRC meet the growing expectations placed on Beijing as a global stakeholder. Insists Shen Dingli: "Setting up overseas military bases is not an idea we have to shun; on the contrary, it is our right."[65] This rhetoric has been accompanied by an increase in Chinese defense interactions with IO-littorals through exercises, arms transfers, and port and state visits.

China's 2009 defense white paper acknowledged that the navy was "developing capabilities of conducting co-operation in distant waters." Under China's new naval strategy of "far sea defense" [*yuan hai fang*], forward basing near the Middle East and Africa could assist Beijing to "project military power and sustain forward military operations in other military contingencies, in a region from which the PRC imports much of its oil, natural gas, and other raw materials."[66] This strategy adds a maritime dimension to China's relations with South and Southeast Asian countries after a hiatus of about 600 years. China's cultivation of friendly, pliant regimes via economic inducements and strategic rewards all along the maritime choke points in the Indian Ocean sea lanes is similar to the Ming Court's past attempts to control the maritime lanes by changing political regimes in Malacca, Sumatra, and Sri Lanka so as to facilitate free trade and maritime dominance.

For its part, India discerns real, compelling interests in the Indian Ocean. Like China, it too enjoys seafaring traditions. India's intensifying interest in Africa is driven partly by resource needs and partly by concerns about the expansion of Chinese influence in resource-rich IO states. Security concerns about traditional and non-traditional threats coupled with China's growing naval assertiveness have led the Indian navy to unveil a four-pronged strategy:

- Build new ports (Karwar), modernize old ones, and establish a Far East command in the Andaman Islands;
- acquire access to bases or establish strategic presence in the Maldives, Mauritius, the Seychelles, and Madagascar to fortify defenses in the IOR;
- promote defense cooperation and conduct joint naval exercises with Oman, Qatar, and Israel in the west and with Burma, Thailand, Indonesia, Singapore, Vietnam, the Philippines, Australia, Taiwan, Japan, and the United States in the east; and
- launch an ambitious naval modernization program that includes destroyers, frigates, submarines, aircraft carriers, amphibious transportation, and maritime aircraft surveillance capabilities.

Interestingly, Beijing's "Malacca paranoia" is matched by New Delhi's "Hormuz dilemma," where China is building a major Pakistani naval port (see Table 10.1). This is the maritime choke point through which passes India's 70 percent of oil imports from the Middle East. Indian defense planners worry that Chinese outposts at strategic locations along Indian Ocean littorals (e.g., Gwadar in the Arabian Sea or Sri Lanka's Hambantota port) increase the risk of disruption to India's energy imports.[67] At best, China's commercial links with Indian Ocean littoral states weave a "soft-power web" around India, making it politically costly for India to take action detrimental to Chinese interests in the Indian Ocean. From a military standpoint, Chinese presence in the IO will create new vulnerabilities that could be exploited by the Indian Navy in the event of a crisis. At worse, the "string of pearls" looks a lot like a security perimeter around much of the Asian mainland that will circumscribe India's freedom of action in the waters around the subcontinental plate.

Table 10.1: China's "Malacca Dilemma" versus India's "Hormuz Dilemma"

Malacca Dilemma	Hormuz Dilemma
• "One can say that whoever controls the Malacca Strait, which is China's strategic oil supply channel, has the ability to threaten China's energy security at will."—*Xiandai Jianchuan*, December 2004 • "China's present rapid advance into the world energy market has far outstripped its ability to militarily uphold its global energy interests."—Zhang Wenmu, 2005 • "China needs to adopt a revised oil import strategy because some big countries attempted to control the transportation channel at Malacca."—President Hu Jintao, *Wall Street Journal*, October 2005 • "We should strive to build a powerful navy that adapts to the needs of our military's historical mission in this new century and at this new stage."—Hu Jintao, *Reuters*, January 2007	• Similar to China's "Malacca dilemma" is India's "Hormuz dilemma" because *the Middle East* alone accounts for about 67 percent of India's oil imports. China's growing ties with Iran and Saudi Arabia and the construction of Pakistani Gwadar port in the Strait of Hormuz *could* threaten India's energy security and maritime interests, since 90 percent of India's trade and 75 percent of India's imported oil move by sea. • "Being only 180 nautical miles from the exit of the Straits of Hormuz, Gwadar would enable Pakistan and China to take control over the world energy jugular and interdiction of Indian tankers."—Indian Naval Chief Admiral Sureesh Mehta, *Times of India*, January 22, 2008

India's new naval doctrine aims to influence events around the Indian Ocean—and beyond. Indian warships have confronted piracy, protected multilateral summits in Mozambique, helped Mauritius and the Maldives monitor their territorial waters, interdicted suspected North Korean cargo ships, coordinated patrols with Indonesia and the United States, and rescued Indians and other South Asians from the Middle East.[68] The Indian navy holds joint naval exercises with regional countries at regular intervals. Some naval officers stress the need for India to signal to the Chinese navy that "its future presence in the IO will not go unchallenged because just as the Pacific Ocean is China's frontyard, the Indian Ocean is India's frontyard." They advocate developing their own set of forward base facilities in India's "extended strategic neighborhood."[69] Since 2000, the Indian navy has been steadily increasing its naval forays into the western Pacific. Joint naval exercises with the United States, Japan, Vietnam, and Singapore in the East China and South China Seas have invited protests from Beijing. Just as the Indian strategists see the Indian Ocean as India's ocean, their Chinese counterparts view the East and South China Seas as China's own preserve.

With rising energy imports from Russia's Sakhalin province, Indonesia, and the South China Sea, Indian interest in the East Asian SLOCs is also growing. The fact that India's total trade volume with East Asian economies now exceeds its trade volume with the European Union and the United States imparts a strategic dimension to its "Look East" policy. Apparently, just as China is apprehensive of India's naval strength in the IO and is taking measures to ensure its sea lanes security, India would not want to leave its trade and energy supply routes in the Pacific Ocean to the goodwill of China's navy. As part of its "Look East" strategy, India has concluded over a dozen defense cooperation agreements over the last decade with Southeast and East Asian countries, including those involving limited Indian security assistance and cooperation against piracy and terrorism. As one commentator pointed out: "Though the Indian navy already has an energy sea-lane strategy for the route Persian Gulf–India and also the capability to escort/protect critical energy shipments during crisis/wars; it has to develop a new strategy for the energy sea-lane from East Russia to India via the Pacific."[70]

For both China and India, "forward presence" has acquired greater salience in their national security strategies to achieve "situational awareness" in areas of strategic interest. For Beijing, this means presence in the Indian Ocean; for New Delhi, naval presence in the Pacific Ocean becomes critical for strategic deterrence against Beijing. Sooner rather than later, China's military alliances with India's IO/South Asian neighbors and forward deployment of its naval assets in the Pakistani, Bangladeshi, Burmese, or Sri Lankan ports would prompt New Delhi to respond in kind by seeking access to the Vietnamese (Cam Ranh Bay), Taiwanese (Kao-hsiung), Japanese (Okinawa), and Russian (Vladivostok) ports for the forward deployment of Indian naval assets to protect India's shipping and trade routes in East Asia and access to energy resources from the Russian Sakhalin province to the South China Sea (see Figures 10.1 and 10.2).[71]

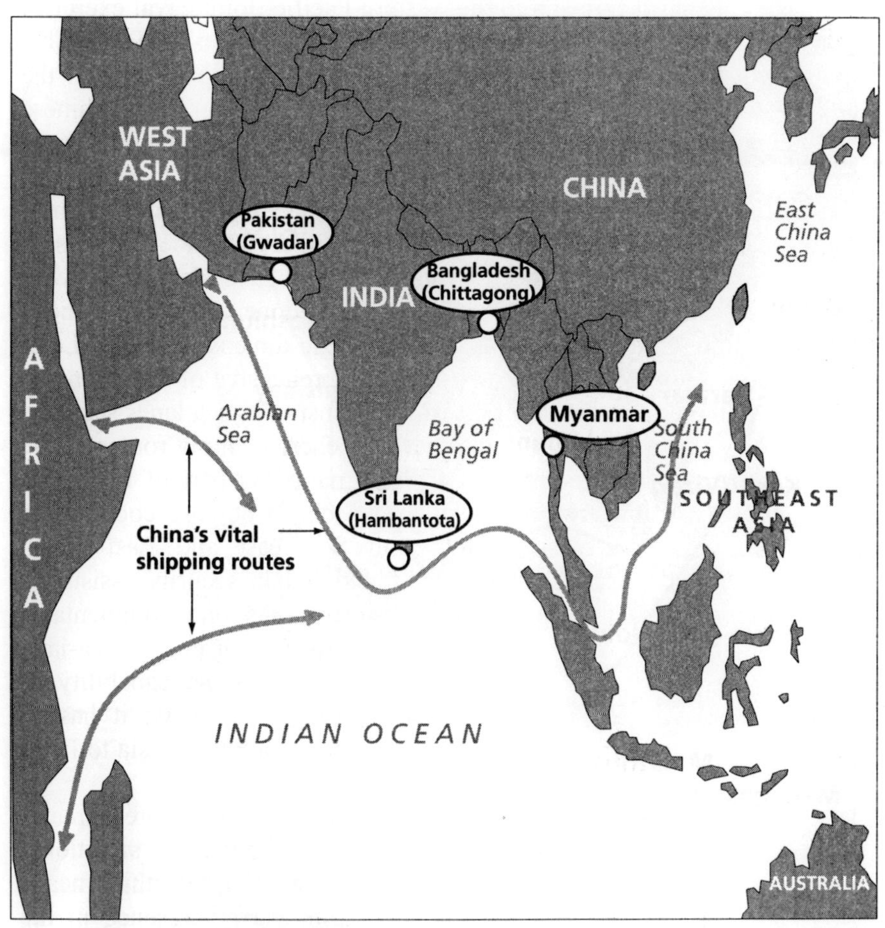

Figure 10.1 Chinese "Pearls" in the indian Ocean: Potential Military Facilities

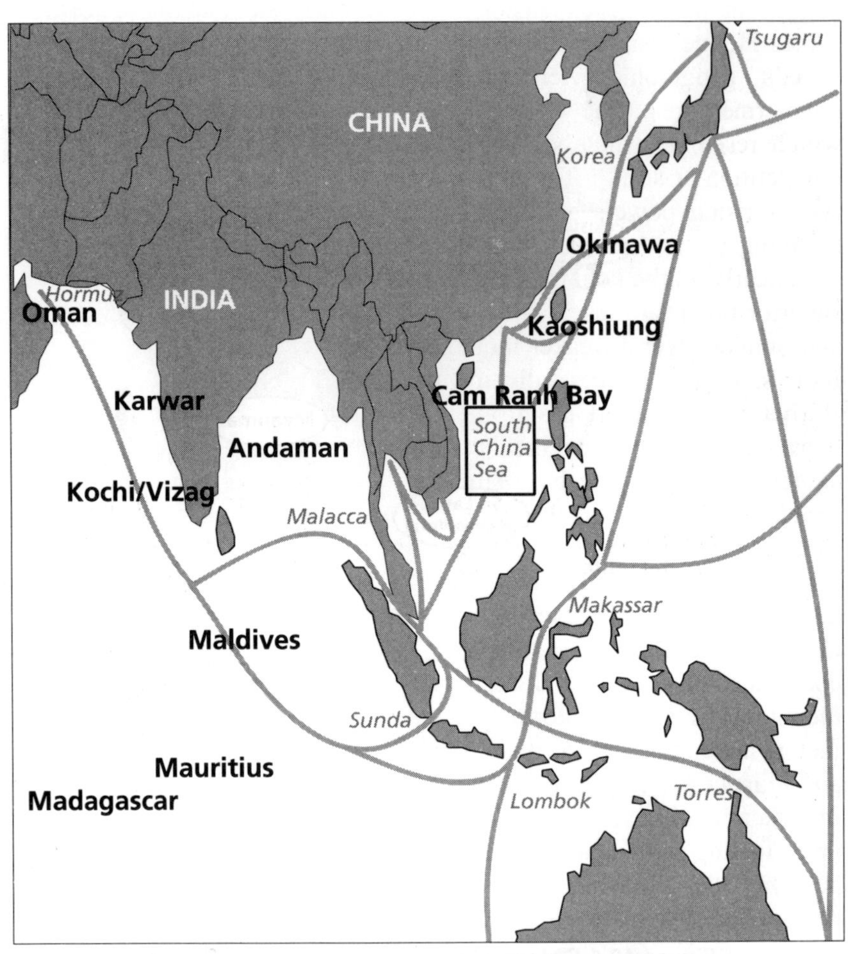

Figure 10.2 India's Maritime-Base Vision

Apparently, resource insecurity provides both with a useful cover to engage in maritime expansion in the Indian and Pacific oceans. As James Holmes has stated: "Any Chinese attempt to control events in India's geographic vicinity would doubtless meet with Indian countermeasures. The Chinese recognize that India's energy needs, which resemble China's own, could impel New Delhi into zero-sum competition at sea."[72] The growing resource competition may well see Asia's rising powers adopting offensive strategies with the intent of targeting rivals' energy security. Beijing maintains solid relationships with nearly all the countries that New Delhi is courting. In fact, China's superior financial muscle and diplomatic clout allows it to easily outbid and outmaneuver a weaker India. China's navy is also leagues ahead of India's. Beijing successfully thwarted India's bids to lease a port in Burma and to import gas from Bangladesh and oil from Kazakhstan. New Delhi, for its part, has been blocking China's attempts to gain a strategic foothold in the Maldives. Indian and Chinese navies are showing the flag in the Pacific and Indian oceans with greater frequency. Their maritime rivalry is likely to spill into the open in about a couple of decades' time when an Indian aircraft carrier will be deployed in the Pacific Ocean and a Chinese aircraft carrier in the Indian Ocean, *ostensibly* to safeguard their respective sea lines of communication. India and China's energy growth is thus unfolding in the middle of a perfect storm: economic, geopolitical, and environmental factors are combining to create new challenges, pressures, opportunities, and alliances. The continuing trend toward higher military expenditure in Asia as a whole is quite evident. The Chinese and Indian naval build-up is fueling a regional naval arms race. The Australian prime minister has warned his country of "an arms build-up across the Asia-Pacific region," and vowed to "ensure the nation's naval capabilities as rising powers such as China and India grew more prosperous and influential."[73]

Last but not least, China's naval forays have also stimulated Beijing's competition with the United States, thereby giving a maritime dimension to the evolving US-China-India strategic triangle. China's penetration of the Indian Ocean rimlands is now reportedly on the agenda of India's bilateral security dialogues with Washington and Tokyo. The more India feels "encircled" by China, the more it will tilt toward the United States and Japan. Should China continue on its current economic trajectory, tensions will increase, given that the US Navy is facing shrinking budgets and increasing responsibilities. Washington is acutely aware that the main thrust of Chinese diplomacy in the Middle East, Africa, South and Southeast Asia is predicated on reducing not only resource dependence, but also US influence in those regions. In capabilities, strategy and doctrine, the Chinese navy is signaling an intent to deny the United States and its allies freedom of action in contested areas, such as the waters around Taiwan. An insight into Chinese naval thinking was given by a top Chinese naval officer, who proposed division of the Pacific and Indian Ocean regions between China and the United States after Beijing launched its own fleet of aircraft carriers.[74] Apparently, a carefully calibrated strategy is needed that would counter Chinese encroachment and strategic gambits without undermining commercial activities. Otherwise, just as a Maritime Asia of the first half of the second millennium, bound by economic interdependence, seaborne trade, trading diasporas at major South and Southeast Asian ports, and preferential trade-cum-tributary arrangements was neither peaceful nor conflict-free, Maritime Asia in the third millennium, bound by economic globalization and trade connectivity, may not be peaceful or conflict-free.

Prospects for Maritime Cooperation

As navies of two rising powers extend their reach and rub up against each other on the high seas, the potential for confrontation—fueled by China's historical nostalgia and an India buoyed by a sense of historical revival—is likely to increase. That tensions are inherent in such a competitive relationship became evident in a 2009 naval incident when an Indian submarine and two Chinese warships on anti-piracy patrol reportedly engaged in rounds of maneuvering as each tried to test for weaknesses in the others' sonar system near the Bab Al-Mandab Strait. The standoff ended when the submarine left the site.[75] With both focusing their naval strategies on each other, the risk of miscalculation and escalation in the future remains high, unless managed skillfully. The history of the IO shows that no single power has ever succeeded in dominating it completely. So, what are the prospects of multilateral cooperation in the maritime domain?

Needless to say, the degree of cooperation and competition between China and India will determine the stability and security of the IOR, which lacks an overarching security system. It is possible that China and India may come to terms with each other eventually in favor of cooperative burden-sharing as their mutual containment policies start yielding diminishing returns, but this is unlikely to happen in the short to medium term. While recognizing the need to cooperate with other major powers in the maritime domain so as to avoid zero-sum competitive games, India's navy seems determined to maintain its regional predominance in the only ocean on the planet named after a country. As for China, the internal debate on the extent to which the Chinese Navy should rely on multilateral cooperative frameworks versus seeking unilateral solutions to maritime issues is far from over.[76] China's preference is for going "solo" at sea but at times in concert with small and medium-sized friendly states in South and Southeast Asia (Pakistan, Sri Lanka, Bangladesh, Burma, Cambodia, Malaysia, and Indonesia). Unlike South Asians, however, Southeast Asian nations are hesitant to accord a leading role for China in the maritime domain. Some believe that over the long term, the inevitable drawdown of US maritime power in the region and interlocking economic interests might help facilitate an enduring multilateral security framework in the Pacific and Indian oceans. Robert Kaplan envisions the United States stabilizing the region in a new order by acting as an "honest broker" in managing the rival ambitions of China and India into a workable security continuum, even as Washington's ability to project naval power recedes.[77] Others, however, discount the possibility of American drawdown of its forces in the region. Not only that, neither Beijing nor New Delhi perceives Washington—regardless of whether its power is declining—as an "honest broker."

For the near term, though, there is an urgent need to frame the rules of engagement and naval confidence-building measures amongst regional navies to promote stability. As things stand, "these navies lack even a basic agreement to stop accidental clashes, like the treaty that helped keep the Cold War cold."[78] Both China and India seem more open to bilateral cooperation than a multilateral arrangement. At the bilateral level, an Incidents-at-Sea-type agreement between China and India (and one between China and Japan) ought to be accorded high priority. Bilateral naval cooperation—joint exercises, exchanges and interoperability—can alleviate tension, and maneuver-space agreements can help avoid needless confrontations. Amidst the growing chorus for overseas bases in the Chinese media, India's deputy defense minister, Pallam Raju, in a significant gesture, offered to collaborate with Beijing to guarantee safe passage of energy supplies. The minister said that India "understands that [China] needed to protect its oil interests." Since the two countries share similar interests to secure trade, particularly in regard to energy and resources, he added that India would be "happy to assist China to keep open vital sea lanes between the Middle East and Asia in order to guard against piracy or conflict."[79] This appeal for collaboration, welcomed by the Chinese media, contrasts starkly with deep-seated anxieties expressed by Indian naval officers and policymakers about the encroachment by China in the Indian Ocean.[80]

At the multilateral level, each of the two Asian rivals tries to minimize the influence of the other. Chinese strategists have called for naval cooperation in the Indian Ocean with Russia, the European Union, NATO, and Japan, but not India.[81] Given Beijing's opposition to India's membership in regional and global institutions, New Delhi is unwilling to grant China associate membership or observer status in the multinational Indian Ocean Naval Symposium (IONS), ostensibly on the grounds that China is not a littoral state in the IOR.[82] This 33-member grouping of Indian Ocean littoral states, established by India in February 2008, seeks to evolve a common security agenda for member states in the seas that wash their shores. Nonetheless, India might be amenable to letting China into the IONS should Beijing end its opposition to India's bid for a veto-holding permanent seat in the UN Security Council. It remains to be seen if the IONS emerges as an effective cooperative mechanism or falls victim to great power rivalries.

The time is right for holding a naval conference of major stakeholders in the Indian and Pacific oceans (mainly navy chiefs from the United States, Japan, South Korea, China, Australia, Indonesia, and India) to chalk out common approaches to challenges in both maritime domains. This inclusive forum would not only bridge the gap between the IONS and the WPNS, but also bring together under one umbrella all the major economies and energy consumers with an interest in ensuring secure sea lanes and stable, affordable energy supplies. Alternatively, a Four-Party Naval Conference involving the United States, China, India, and Japan—the countries possessing the four most powerful navies in the Asia-Pacific—may be convened to focus on sea lane security. Complementing this initiative should be a simultaneous formation of an IO quadrilateral comprising South Africa, India, Indonesia, and Australia, which share oceanic geography and political values. This IO quadrilateral would focus primarily on enhancing small island states' capacity to deal with natural and man-made disasters and protection of their EEZs.

Conclusion

The Indian Ocean is the thoroughfare for nearly half of all global seaborne trade, and the coastal states are home to over 60 percent of the world's oil and a third of its gas reserves. The IO waterways and numerous choke points are becoming increasingly important to the global movement of trade, notably of energy resources. The ever-expanding energy infrastructure throughout the IOR (e.g., refineries, LNG terminals, pipelines, offshore exploration, and oil production facilities) leaves itself open to attacks by non-state and state actors. The fundamental problem all major economies face at present is that none is fully capable of defending and protecting its maritime interests, principally access to foreign markets and overseas energy resources and other natural resources so critical for sustained economic development. In the absence of trust and cooperation, the major powers are taking unilateral measures to protect their sea lanes against piracy or terrorist attacks and ensure free passage for their ships and tankers.

The *oilpolitik* is not only shaping the power and capabilities of individual states but also determining the new pattern of coalitions of power in the twenty-first century. We are seeing a mad rush, a sort of treasure hunt, to gain control of energy resources by China, India, and Japan, especially in those countries which for political reasons are outside the control of major western oil companies. As the economic center of gravity shifts to Asia, a new regional energy architecture is emerging and giving rise to new alignments between consumers and producers, with long-term strategic consequences for world politics. China's pursuit of a policy to secure preferential access to oil and gas resources in politically unstable states is a high-risk strategy that has also resulted in heightened competition with other major energy-importing states. The Chinese military is seeking to project naval power well beyond the Chinese coast, from the oil ports of the Middle East to the shipping lanes of the Pacific, where the US Navy has long reigned as the dominant force. Beijing's resource and security ties with the Persian Gulf and African nations may have the effect of drawing the United States, India, and Japan into a tighter embrace.

Seeking to expand their forward presence, China and India are getting locked into a twenty-first-century version of the competitive Great Game once played by industrializing European colonial powers. Much like China, rapidly-growing India not only needs more oil, it also stands directly in the middle of China's supply route. Thus, the growing resource and trade dependence on the sea lanes has added a maritime dimension to China's strategic competition with India. China and India are merely following in the footsteps of other major global powers, which also established military bases abroad to secure their access to overseas resources and markets. Each is taking diplomatic, strategic, and economic initiatives (such as aid, trade, arms sales, and infrastructural development) aimed at strengthening ties with the littoral states. The Sino-Indian rivalry in the Indian Ocean is also spilling over to the Pacific Ocean. They are also engaged in transfers of sophisticated technologies and weaponry so as to lure resource-rich states to enter into long-term political and strategic alliance relationships with them. As they strive to stamp their authority on the Asian waters, Chinese and Indian fleets may one day maneuver against each other on the Indian and Pacific oceans respectively. Both are acutely aware of their strategic vulnerabilities. While the Chinese see the Strait of Malacca, where the Indian Ocean joins the Pacific, as Beijing's Achilles heel, the Indians see the Strait of Hormuz as their Achilles heel. Unless managed carefully, these shipping lanes, vital for their energy supplies, could be the setting for future confrontation between China and India.[83] For the foreseeable future, though, it is difficult to imagine a scenario wherein either China or India would use its naval forces to conduct expeditionary operations to secure its energy assets overseas. Hopefully, over the long term, China's forays into the Indian Ocean and India's into the Pacific Ocean will create mutual vulnerabilities that may eventually induce both to engage in maritime cooperation. The creation of an open and inclusive maritime architecture in which all work together to keep the sea lanes safe and secure will help to moderate, or mitigate, the security dilemma.

Notes

[1] Shi Hongtao, "China's 'Malacca Straits,'" *Qingnian Bao*, June 15, 2004, Foreign Broadcast Information Service (hereafter FBIS), FBIS-CPP20040615000042; Editorial, "US-Indian alliance against China," *Ming Pao*, August 17, 2005, FBIS-CPP20050817000043.

[2] See "World oil transit chokepoints" (Washington DC: Report by Energy Information Administration, March 2007) <http://www.eia.doe.gov/cabs/ World_Oil_Transit_Chokepoints/Background.html>.

[3] For details, see G. S. Khurana, "Maritime security in the Indian Ocean," *Strategic Analysis*, 28:3 (July-September 2004).

[4] T. Kuehner, "Robert Kaplan on the new balance of power," *FPRI.org*, April 2008 <http://www.fpri.org/enotes/ 200804.kuehner.kaplannewbalanceofpower.html>.

[5] M. Walker, "Indian Ocean nexus," *Wilson Quarterly*, 32:2 (Spring 2008), 21, 21-28.

[6] Walker, "Indian Ocean nexus," 21-22."

[7] Walker, "Indian Ocean nexus."

[8] S. Glain, "The modern Silk Road," *Newsweek*, May 26-June 2, 2008, 32-33.

[9] See K. M. Shoemaker, "Intel brief: China in Sri Lanka," *ISN Security Watch*, May 9, 2008 <http://www.isn.ethz.ch/news/sw/ details.cfm?id=18942>.

[10] G. Rabinowitz, "India, China ships compete in Indian Ocean," *Associated Press*, June 8, 2008 <http://biz.yahoo.com:80/ap/080608/ asia_indian_ocean_intrigue.html>.

[11] See P. K. Ghosh, "Indian Ocean shipping: imperatives of cargo and energy flows." Presentation to the Asian Energy Security Conference, Jackson, Mississippi, October 1-2, 2007.

[12] Ghosh, "Indian ocean shipping: imperatives of cargo and energy flows."

[13] Over the last 15 years, Canada, Venezuela, and Mexico, with their proximity and increasing production rates, have become major sources of imported oil for the United States.

[14] The four major Asian consumers—China, India, Japan, and South Korea—together consume over half of the world's total oil. Japan imports all its oil and 89 percent comes from the Middle East. Singapore, Taiwan, Thailand, and the Philippines each depend on the Gulf for over 70 percent of their oil imports. M. Richardson, "The sea lane & energy security lifeline between the Persian Gulf & Asia." Presentation to the Asian Energy Security Conference, Jackson, Mississippi, October 1-2, 2007.

[15] J. MacDonald, "Overview of global and Asian energy trends." Paper presented at the "Asian Energy Security." Conference at MSU, Mississippi State University, October 1-2, 2007.

[16] Khurana, "Maritime security in the Indian Ocean."

[17] India's Chief of Naval Staff, Admiral Sureesh Mehta, cited in *Times of India*, January 22, 2008, 1.

[18] MacDonald, "Overview of global and Asian energy trends."

[19] "Risks of rivalry: Asia must ensure energy competition does not spark conflict," *Financial Times*, May 3, 2007, 14.

[20] The Marines, too, in their new "Vision and Strategy 2025" statement, highlight thc Indian Ocean as among their main theaters of activity in coming years. Cited from Robert D. Kaplan, "Lifting the bamboo curtain," *Atlantic Monthly*, September 2008.

[21] The US equities in energy and trade in the IOR are far less than all other major powers. Less than 17 percent of US net oil imports come from the Persian Gulf.

[22] Cited from *Washington Times*, August 17, 2007.

[23] Department of Defense, *National Defense Strategy,* (Washington, DC: June 2008), 13.

[24] See V. Sakhuja, "Any Asian takers for a 1000-ship navy?" *Opinion Asia.org*, March 17, 2007 <http://www.opinionasia.org/ AnyAsiantakersfora1000shipnavy>.

[25] Y. P. Rajesh, "US sees India as partner in global naval alliance," *Reuters*, September 7, 2007.

[26] However, Chinese and Indian navies will continue to lag far behind in firepower, technological sophistication, and across-the-board capabilities.

[27] While India now imports around 80 million tons of oil annually, the annual demand for imported oil will grow to an estimated 150 million tons in 2020. R. Maitra, "All at sea in the Indian Ocean," *Asia Times online*, January 21, 2004 <http://www.atimes.com/atimes/South_Asia/ FA21Df02.html>.

[28] J. Leahy, "ONGC enters modern Great Game," *Financial Times*, September 1, 2008.

[29] S. Ramachandran, "India turns its energies on Africa," *Asia Times online*, Nov 10, 2007 <http://www.atimes.com/atimes/South_Asia/IK10Df01.html>.

[30] Agencies, "India woos Africa to check Chinese influence," *Indian Express*, November 1, 2007. Lu Desheng, "'Africa craze' promotes win-win for all parties," *Jiefangjun Bao*, April 16, 2008, 8.

[31] "India: old fears and new spur naval build-up," *Oxford Analytica*, October 19, 2009.

[32] Richardson, "The sea lane & energy security lifeline between the Persian Gulf & Asia." Between 1991 and 2007, the East Asian share of India's trade rose from 18 to 31 percent.

[33] Cited from J. MacDonald, *Energy Futures in Asia: Perspectives on India's Energy Security Strategy and Policies* (June 2007), Prepared for Director, Net Assessments, Department of Defense), 5-22, 23.

[34] For example, an entire chapter of *Freedom of the Seas: India's Maritime Military Strategy* (New Delhi: Integrated Headquarters of the Ministry of Defence (Navy), (May 2007) stresses the need for maritime security of energy resources and offshore assets. It states that energy provides a "rationale for the resurgence of India's maritime military power."

[35] C. Rajghatta, "US more at ease with India's rise than China's ascent," *Times of India*, February 3, 2010, 1.

[36] I. Bagchi, "India looks to ramp up presence in Maldives," *Times of India*, January 27, 2008; "High-level Chinese delegation visits Maldives," *Maldives Chronicle*, June 26, 2008 <http://www.maldiveschronicle.com/high-level-chinese-delegation-visits-maldives/>

[37] "China, Seychelles vow to strengthen military ties," *PLA Daily*, September 14, 2007 http://english.chinamil.com.cn/; S. Srivastava, "China's submarine progress alarms India," *Asia Times online*, May 9, 2008.

[38] R. Sharma, "Indian navy wins friends, expands influence in Indian Ocean region," August 28, 2008 <http://www.newkerala.com/topstory-fullnews-15929.html>

[39] V. Raghuvanshi, "India holding regional naval cooperation conference," *Defence News*, January 21, 2008.

[40] D. Hale, "China's growing appetites," *National Interest*, 76 (Summer 2004), 137-47.

[41] For details, see Suisheng Zhao, "China's global search for energy security," *Journal of Contemporary China*, 17:55 (May 2008), 207–227.

[42] K. L Afrasiabi, "A China base in Iran?" *Asia Times online*, January 29, 2008 <http://www.atimes.com/atimes/Middle_East/JA29Ak03.html>.

[43] Liu Naiqiang, "China's energy diplomacy faces challenges ahead," *Nanfeng Chuang* [Guangzhou], November 16, 2007, 22-24.

[44] The other "pearls" are naval facilities in Sri Lanka, Bangladesh, Burma, Cambodia, and the South China Sea. China is reportedly trying to trump India's military aid program for the Maldives by offering to build a naval base for the tiny island nation. AFP, "US, China, India flex muscle over energy-critical sea lanes," *Yahoo.com*, October 4, 2006.

[45] "An analysis of Chinese and Indian navies' long-distance sea endurance capabilities," ["Zhong yin hai jun yuan hai jian di shi li dui bi de shen du

fenxi"], May 7, 2008 <http://bbs.chinaiiss.org/dispbbs.asp?boardID=78&ID=129008&page=1>.

[46] Although the Chinese sailors had engaged in port visits and joint exercises with the Pakistani navy in the Arabian Sea, the Somali operation represented the first potential combat mission for the Chinese navy outside the Pacific Ocean.

[47] C. Bodeen, "China navy official says overseas base needed," *Associated Press*, December 31, 2009 <http://asia.news.yahoo.com/ap/20091230/tap-as-china-naval-base-bb10fb8.html>.

[48] Commentary, "Navies seeking better ways to battle pirates," *China.org.cn*, November 6, 2009 <http://m.china.org.cn/2009-11/06/content_18838344.htm>.

[49] R. Medcalf, "Chinese naval proposal wrong-headed," *The Interpreter*, November 24, 2009 <http://www.lowyinterpreter.org/post/2009/11/24/Time-to-burst-Chinas-mooted-exclusive-naval-zones.aspx>.

[50] AsiaInt, "China's Indian Ocean goals," *NAR*, March 2008 <http://www.asiaint.com/arl/arl17109.asp>.

[51] S. R. Weisman, "As the price of oil soars, so does its power to shape politics from Washington to Beijing," *New York Times*, July 25, 2006.

[52] General Xu quoted in "China's military objectives reach far beyond Taiwan," *China Post,* May 12, 2010.

[53] Cai Xiyou, "Reflections on international oil trade friction and our country's oil trade policy," *Lilun Qianyan* [Beijing], August 15, 2007, 13-15.

[54] See I. Storey, "China's Malacca dilemma," *China Brief*, 6:8 (April 12, 2006), 4-6 <http://www.jamestown.org/images/pdf/cb_006_008.pdf>.

[55] Commentary, "China's maritime dilemma," *Stratfor.com*, August 2, 2007 <http://www.stratfor.com/chinas_maritime_dilemma>.

[56] See Zhang Xuegang, "Southeast Asia and energy: gateway to stability," *China Security*, 3:2 (Spring 2007), 21.

[57] "Indian navy invited to patrol Malacca," *AsiaInt Weekly Analysis*, March 13, 2009 <http://www.asiaint.com/arl/arl20615.asp>.

[58] Mohan Malik, "China's strategy of containing India," *The Power & Interest News Report*, February 6, 2006, 1-7 <http://www.pinr.com/report.php?ac=view_report&report_id=434>

[59] Lu Jianren, "Is this Asia's century?" *Beijing Review*, April 21, 2006, 18; "US dreams of Asian NATO," *People's Daily online*, July 19, 2003.

[60] "Is India China's imaginative [imaginary] rival?" *People's Daily online*, March 2, 2005.

[61] See G. Fairclough, "As China grows, so does its long neglected navy,' *Wall Street Journal*, July 16, 2007, A1.

[62] E. Wong, "Chinese military seeks to extend its naval power," *New York Times* April 24, 2010, 1.

[63] T. Niazi, 'Gwadar: China's naval outpost on the Indian Ocean,' *China Brief*, 5:4 (February 15, 2005) <http://www.jamestown.org/publications_details.php?volume_id=408&issue_id=3232&article_id=2369262>.

[64] Editorial, "Growing Chinese navy no cause for fear," *Global Times*, April 27, 2010 <http://opinion.globaltimes.cn/editorial/2010-04/526192.html>.

[65] Shen Dingli, “Don’t shun the idea of setting up overseas military bases,” *China.org.cn*, January 28, 2010 <http://www.china.org.cn/opinion/2010-01/28/content_19324522_3.htm>.

[66] R. Weitz, “China tests waters on first overseas naval base,” *World Politics Review*, January 5, 2010 <http://www.worldpoliticsreview.com/Article.aspx?id=4882>.

[67] S. Kondapalli, “The Chinese threat in the Indian Ocean,” *Rediff.com*, May 8, 2008 <http://www.rediff.com/news/2008/may/08guest.htm>; Also see P. Monk, “Sanya base to float Chinese naval ambition,’ *The Age*, May 26, 2008.

[68] R. Medcalf, “India ahoy,” *Wall Street Journal*, April 29, 2010.

[69] Conversation with a senior naval officer, June 2007. Also see G. S. Khurana, “China’s ‘string of pearls’ in the Indian Ocean and its security implications,” *Strategic Analysis*, 32:1 (January 2008). MacDonald, “Energy futures in Asia,” 5-22, 5-23. PTI, “Pak’s new port has strategic implications for India: naval chief,” *Rediff.com*, January 22, 2008 <http://www.rediff.com/news/2008/jan/22port.htm>.

[70] V. Sakhuja, “New Silk Route: As more energy consignment may come from east Russia, India is preparing a blueprint for defending new sea lane,” *Sahara Time.com* <http://www.saharatime.com/NewsDetail.aspx?newsid=277&catid=1>.

[71] Rabinowitz, “India, China ships compete in Indian Ocean”; “Asia’s navies: into the wide blue yonder,” *Economist*, June 5, 2008.

[72] J. Holmes, “China’s energy consumption and opportunities for US-China cooperation to address the effects of China’s energy use,” Testimony before the US-China Economic and Security Review Commission, Washington DC, June 14, 2007 <http://www.uscc.gov/hearings/2007hearings/written_testimonies/07_06_14_15wrts/07_06_14_holmes_statement.pdf>.

[73] “Australian PM flags military build-up as Asian powers rise,” September 10, 2008 <http://www.channelnewsasia.com/stories/afp_asiapacific/view/374915/1/.html>.

[74] M. Pubby, “China proposed division of Pacific, Indian Ocean regions, we declined: US admiral,” *Indian Express*, May 15, 2009; M. Mazza, “China and the lost pearls,” *The American*, April 23, 2010 <http://www.american.com/archive/2010/april/china-and-the-lost-pearls>.

[75] Report, “India, China face-off in the Indian Ocean,” *Rediff.com*, February 4, 2009 <http://www.rediff.com/news/2009/feb/04india-china-face-off-in-the-indian-ocean.htm>.

[76] Commentary, “Navies seeking better ways to battle pirates”; A. Giridharadas, “Land of Gandhi asserts itself as global military power,” *IHT*, September 22, 2008, 1.

[77] H. Chua-Eoan, “Beyond pirates: on the high seas, an India-China rivalry,” *Time*, April 8, 2009; I. Tharoor, “India’s China panic: seeing a ‘red peril’ on land and sea,” *Time*, September 20, 2009.

[78] R. Medcalf, “Securing the sea-lanes: China’s gunboat diplomacy,” *New York Times*, December 28, 2008 <http://www.nytimes.com/2008/12/28/opinion/28iht-edmedcalf.1.18955146.html?_r=1>.

[79] J. Lamont and G. Dyer, "India offers to protect China oil shipments," *Financial Times*, February 17, 2010 <http://www.ft.com/cms/s/0/6788f896-1be8-11df-a5e1-00144feab49a.html>.

[80] Editorial, "India's surprising but welcome message," *Global Times*, February 22, 2010 <http://opinion.globaltimes.cn/editorial/2010-02/506893.html>.

[81] Commentary, "Navies seeking better ways to battle pirates."

[82] P. D. Samanta, "China wants to join Navy initiative on Indian Ocean, MEA says no need," *Indian Express*, April 21, 2009; S. Dasgupta, "China hits out at India's decision on naval symposium," *Times of India*, April 23, 2009.

[83] D. Blair, "India targeting China's oil supplies," *Telegraph*, September 14, 2008, 10.

11
Triangles, Tilts, and Strategic Futures

Geopolitics and geology have one thing in common. Whenever geopolitical shifts occur, they destroy existing power structures, causing havoc and bloodshed in the same way as geological eruptions like an earthquake or tsunami. Geological changes inside the Earth's crust take place constantly, but we notice only when a massive earthquake occurs. Similarly, socio-economic and technological changes are underway in international politics all the time. However, we notice their impact only after they bring about a major tectonic shift, resulting in the collapse of existing geopolitical order and strategic structures. Both geological and geopolitical changes are usually sudden, disruptive, and earthshaking.

At the beginning of the early twenty-first century, we are witnessing geopolitical power transitions of the kind that usually take place once in 50 to 100 years in the international system. Power in the international system is always relative and ever-shifting.[1] It does not stay the same. Changes over time in the distribution of relative power alter the international strategic environment. Historically, long cycles of economic growth, wars, and imperial overstretch inevitably bring about changes in the geopolitical balance of power. No nation remains preeminent forever. The United States (US) National Intelligence Council and the investment banking and securities firm Goldman Sachs Inc. predict that, by 2040, the world's largest economies will be China, the United States, India, and Japan—in that order. Only political disintegration and/or prolonged economic stagnation or war would be their undoing. Economic expansion inevitably leads to overseas military expansion and fuels grandiose geopolitical ambitions. More than a quarter century of exponential economic growth in China has been accompanied by nearly two decades of double-digit growth in its military expenditure. This, in turn, is generating frictions and giving impetus to geopolitical realignments. However, China is not rising in a vacuum. India is also rising, so is Russia, and Japan is increasingly becoming a "normal nation." The Asia-Pacific of the early twenty-first century—home to several rising and contending powers—thus bears resemblance to Europe of the late nineteenth and early twentieth centuries.

Generally speaking, power transitions are usually dangerous periods when an established great power is challenged by the rise of a rival or peer competitors because rising powers are by nature revisionist, not status-quo, powers. The fact that China and India will be both wealthy (in terms of aggregate output) and poor (in terms of per capita income relative to Japan and the West) at the same time could breed dissatisfaction with the international system and resistance to deal with transnational challenges posed by failed states, climate change, and resource scarcity.[2] China's primary rival on the Asian continental landmass is India, another rising power with aspirations for an increased role and status in the international system. Both seek to expand their power and influence in and beyond their regions not only at the expense of established great powers (the United States and Russia) but also at each other's expense. The 2010 Quadrennial Defense Review (QDR) acknowledges this reality:

> The distribution of global political, economic and military power is shifting and becoming more diffuse. The rise of China, the world's most populous country, and India, the world's largest democracy, will continue to reshape the international system.... Whether and how rising powers fully integrate into the global system will be among this century's defining questions, and are thus central to America's interests.[3]

Asia's security dynamics are thus defined by old-fashioned great power politics: two rising powers—China and India—and a status-quo power, the United States, trying to find common ground but moving toward potential long-term competition/conflict over their relative influence and status in the Asia-Pacific region. Old established powers are usually reluctant to cede the prestige and status they have enjoyed over the years. Moreover, rising powers are loath to accept externally imposed limits to their power. No great power goes quietly. No great power arrives quietly. Great powers have great egos, and they often clash. Therefore, the risk of conflict increases (a) if the United States fails to manage China's rise; (b) if China is tempted to precipitate the US economic decline; and (c) if China blocks accommodation of rising India in the regional and international system.

The era of post-Cold War unipolarity—with the United States as the sole superpower—is fast fading into history. When historians look back in a few decades' time, the year 2001 will be seen as marking the beginning of the end of the "unipolar moment" in history. This was the year when the sole superpower, the United States, was challenged by both state and non-state actors—first by China in April 2001 over the EP-3 spy plane incident, and then by al-Qaeda via the 9/11 terrorist attacks. Though the United States still stands as a global colossus—economically, militarily, and culturally—the challenge to US "non-hegemonic primacy" today stems as much from China's rise as from sharpening conflicts over natural resources, the emergence of new economic centers of gravity, ideological differences over democracy or human rights, and challenges posed by a trinity of non-state actors, *jihadi* terrorism, and nuclear proliferation. The 2008 financial meltdown may be the beginning of a global economic rebalancing and turn out to be the harbinger of the permanent loss of status for the United States as the financial superpower. Convinced that US hegemony and Western dominance are now in an irreversible process of decline and final disappearance, Beijing seeks "a diversified currency and financial system" that is no longer dependent on the United States.[4] In short, changes in comparative economic advantages have always preceded political competition in the international system. In the early twenty-first century, the key elements of China's grand strategy can be identified as follows:

- Acquire "comprehensive national power" essential to realizing the status of a "global great power that is second to none" by 2049 (marking 100 years of the founding of the PRC);
- Gain access to global natural resources, raw materials, and overseas markets to sustain China's economic expansion. As an old Chinese proverb puts it, "*yang wei zhong yong*": make foreign resources, goods, and technology help China become strong and powerful;
- Pursue "three Ms": military modernization (including naval presence along the vital maritime chokepoints), multilateralism, and multipolarity; and
- Build a worldwide network of China's friends and allies through "soft power" diplomacy and economic dependencies via free trade agreements, investment, mutual security pacts, arms sales, and bases.

China's pursuit of comprehensive power is aimed at ensuring that no other country in Asia has the wherewithal to undermine what Beijing claims to be its "core national interests." This power maximization drive has already widened the gap between China and its neighbors, especially Russia, Japan, and India. On a normative level, China's growing global influence will empower it to lay down new rules for the post-American international order.

Asian Responses to China's Rise: Three Tiers

The moment a country arrives on the international stage as "a great power of its age," it generates envy, cooperation, opposition, and rivalry. How to adapt to China's growing power and influence is a question that dominates the foreign policy establishment of nearly every country in the world. Among regional countries, China arouses unease because of its size, history, proximity, potential power, and more importantly, because the memories of "the Middle Kingdom syndrome" and tributary state system have not dimmed. As noted earlier, a survey conducted in China revealed that many interviewees thought that "a stronger China will try to restore its traditional vassal system."[5] Historically, there has never been a time when China has coexisted on equal terms with another power of similar or lesser stature. However, with the exception of a few, most Asian countries show little or no desire to live in a China-led or China-dominated Asia. Instead, they seek to preserve existing security alliances and pursue sophisticated diplomatic and hedging strategies designed to give them more freedom of action while avoiding overt alignment with major powers. Being a distant hegemon, the United States remains the balancer of choice for many countries on China's periphery. Most Asian countries are strengthening their security ties with the United States as part of their hedging or balancing strategy even as they become increasingly dependent on the Chinese market for trade, prosperity, and economic well-being.

If one looks at the history of international relations over the last 500 years, the rise of a major continental power—especially one with an authoritarian regime nursing historical grievances with active territorial disputes—has resulted in major geopolitical alignments and led to the formation of a coalition of maritime powers to counter it. China is no exception to this rule. The US hedging strategy, the US-India nuclear deal, the growing warmth in India-Japan ties, the US-Japan-Australia-India quadrilateral (a.k.a. "concert of democracies") are all part of this—an inevitable response to the rise of China. By and large, countries on a rising power's periphery tend to either balance against or bandwagon with the rising power. Some, of course, choose to do both. Given China's centrality in Asian geopolitics, "hedging" or old-fashioned "balancing" vis-à-vis China is becoming the most preferred option, without giving up on the many benefits of engaging Beijing. In the early part of the twenty-first century, the Asian-Pacific states' responses to China's rise can be divided into three tiers:

- *First Tier—Balancing:* India, Japan, Australia, Vietnam, Taiwan, Mongolia, and Indonesia are pursuing a clear balance-of-power or hedging strategy vis-à-vis China by strengthening their security ties with the United States as well as with each other (for example, India's courting of Mongolia, Japan, Taiwan, Vietnam, and Indonesia) to counter-balance China. The first-tier countries are concerned about the strategic implications of China's military modernization program that emphasizes preparations to fight and win short-duration, high-intensity conflicts along its periphery (especially with those countries that have disputed borders with China).
- *Second Tier—Balancing and Bandwagoning:* South Korea, Thailand, the Philippines, Malaysia, Laos, East Timor, and Singapore are both bandwagoning with and balancing against China; in other words, putting their eggs in both American and Chinese baskets. Many of these second-tier countries welcome the return of bipolarity and are already playing the reigning superpower off against the rising superpower to extract economic and security benefits.
- *Third Tier—Bandwagoning:* North Korea, Pakistan, Iran, Burma, Russia, Cambodia, Bangladesh, Nepal, Sri Lanka and some Central Asian countries are, to varying degrees, bandwagoning with China—albeit for entirely different motives.

Against this backdrop of the broader geopolitical scene, this chapter examines the nature and type of evolving partnerships and special relationships, tilts, and strategic triangles in the Asia-Pacific. It concludes with an assessment of the alternative strategic futures of China-India relations in the first half of the twenty-first century.

Bound to Balance

Of all the countries on China's periphery, India is in a category of its own. Since India was never part of the Sinic world order or tributary state system but a civilization-empire in itself, it remains genetically ill-disposed to sliding into China's orbit without resistance. It is the only Asian power that has long been committed to balancing China, especially since the late 1950s. During the Cold War era, India relied primarily on the Soviet Union and its leadership role in the Non-Aligned Movement (NAM) to counter-balance China. While the rest of the world started taking note of China's rise only during the last decade of the twentieth century, India has been warily watching China's rise ever since 1950 when the People's Liberation Army (PLA) troops marched into Tibet. True, India and the United States jointly contained China for a brief period from 1962 to 1965. So did the United States and Japan from 1949 to 1971. But then Washington and Tokyo aligned with Beijing from 1971 to 1989 to contain the common Soviet threat. In fact, much of China's spectacular progress is owed to the massive inflow of US and Japanese capital and technology, which contributed to China's rise as an economic and military power. In contrast, it was the strategic imperative to counter-balance China that drove "non-aligned" India first into the Soviet camp during the Cold War years, then made it gatecrash the exclusive nuclear weapons club in the post–Cold War world, and has made it tilt toward the United States in the early part of the twenty-first century.

As China and India march upwards simultaneously on their relative power trajectories, geopolitical equations and power relations in Asia are undergoing significant realignments. All major powers, including China, are maneuvering for geopolitical advantage and relative gain through new equations, permutations, and formations. The SCO, Russia-China-Iran, and Russia-China-India triangles are good examples. Just as Beijing is seeking friends and allies in Asia and far from its shores, other powers are also working to build new equations and partnerships. The post–Cold War, post–9/11 period of stable, cooperative major power relations may be ending. This means that policymakers will be faced with difficult choices in the era of power transitions, resource scarcity, transnational security threats, economic slowdown, and military expansion. Even as they increasingly cooperate on transnational challenges, the US-China, India-China, and Japan-China security competition is a foregone conclusion. While each values its economic ties with Beijing, Washington, Tokyo, and New Delhi also share a common interest in ensuring that Asia is not dominated by China and that the overall balance of power remains in favor of liberal democracies, not autocracies. Changes in the security environment post–Cold War have brought into sharp focus the growing salience of the US-China-India triangular relationship, which is also influencing the policies of small and middle powers.

The US-China-India Triangle

Notwithstanding customary denials in Washington, Beijing, and New Delhi that "India-US relations and China-India relations have their own compelling logic" or that India (or the United States) is not seeking to "develop relations with any country to counterbalance another," practitioners and academics recognize the growing significance of the US-China-India triangular relationship that has now effectively replaced the US-Sino-Soviet triangle of the Cold War era. Rising powers China and India, with growing economies and growing ambitions, are jockeying for power and influence in Asia, Africa, and Latin America, where Washington, Moscow, and Beijing used to be competitors during the Cold War. Their tandem emergence as major players has evoked countervailing actions by both that invariably influence the security policies of other powers. More importantly, the US military presence post–9/11 in South and Central Asia has made Washington not only the most important strategic factor in the Sino-Indian geopolitical equation but also given it the ability to promote or undermine the interests of China and India vis-à-vis one another or shift the balance of power by tilting in favor of one or the other.

Historical Origins of the Triangle

A strategic triangle exists when three major powers are sufficiently important to each other and each fears alignment of the other two against itself and takes measures to counter any such alignment. Aware of the challenges and opportunities that each presents, Washington, Beijing and New Delhi watch closely the state of their bilateral relations with each other. Both China and India have taken measures to counter an alignment of the other with the United States. In his 2002 study, John Garver argued that the US-China-India triangular relationship came into play in the mid-to-late 1990s.[6] However, its origins can be traced back to the 1971 India-Pakistan War, especially to the Sino-US rapprochement in 1971, if not earlier. In fact, one could argue that the 1962 China-India War laid the groundwork for new geopolitical alignments in South Asia, with Beijing firmly aligning itself with New Delhi's *bête noire*—Islamabad—and New Delhi tilting initially toward Washington and later aligning itself with Beijing's nemesis—Moscow. The state of the Sino-US relationship has always heavily influenced India's foreign policy orientation. For instance, President Nixon's courting of Mao's China in 1971 pushed non-aligned India firmly into the Soviet embrace, leading to the signing of the Indo-Soviet Treaty of

Friendship, Peace, and Cooperation in August 1971, and later influenced New Delhi's decision to carry out a nuclear test in 1974 to prevent potential nuclear blackmail. Throughout the 1980s, India's close ties with the Soviet Union as well as China's quasi-alliance with the United States (forged after the Soviet invasion of Afghanistan in 1979) and military alliance with Pakistan hampered the development of Sino-Indian, Indian-American, and Sino-Soviet ties. Likewise, during the 1990s, President Bill Clinton's attempts to establish a US-China condominium (or "China first" policy, albeit short-lived) with Jiang Zemin's China in 1997–98 encouraged India to openly advance its nuclear and ballistic capabilities in May 1998.

Following the collapse of its Soviet ally in 1991, India began working on new alignments and security arrangements, shopping around for new relationships, demonstrating an unprecedented flexibility in its foreign policy. For the first time in decades, New Delhi started establishing a multi-dimensional engagement with Washington, which suffered a temporary setback following the 1998 nuclear tests. Overt nuclearization was apparently aimed at bolstering India's position in its dealings with China, especially to make Beijing sensitive to core Indian security concerns. In sharp contrast with the Cold War era, India ended its opposition to the US forward presence in the Asia-Pacific, seeing it as premised upon the containment of Chinese influence there—an objective shared by New Delhi, which lacked the means and the capability to influence events in the wider Asian region directly.[7]

In the aftermath of the September 11, 2001, terrorist attacks, Pakistan and China lost no time in reversing their earlier policies and bandwagoning with Washington as soon as India offered its air and naval bases to the US military to overthrow the Taliban regime in Afghanistan. This move had the effect of temporarily slowing down the Indo-US rapprochement underway since President Bill Clinton's visit to India in March 2000 amidst the growing talk of India and the United States as "natural allies," seen in Beijing as an attempt by Washington to rope New Delhi into its "contain China" strategy.[8] On balance, China has played the triangular game ("the US card") to advance its interests over the last three decades more effectively than India (see Table 11.1).

However, the future of the US-China-India triangle is unlikely to resemble the past. The formal understanding that existed between Beijing and Washington since 1971 that "the US would not do anything in South Asia without consulting China" came to an end under the Bush administration (2001–08). Calculations aimed at influencing China's behavior are now a part of the decisionmaking in both Washington and New Delhi. The United States conducts a regular dialogue with India over China and East Asia and holds a separate dialogue with China over India and South Asia.

Table 11.1: Three Phases in the US-China-India Triangular Relationship

PERIOD	TRIANGULAR TILTS	REASONS
1971–1989	The US-China alignment against India	• To maintain the India-Pakistan military balance • To contain the Soviet Union, India's Cold War ally
1990–1999	The US-China alignment against India	• To promote nuclear non-proliferation concerns • To strengthen Washington-Beijing relations
2000–	The US tilt toward India	• To balance a rising China and stagnant Japan in order to establish a strategically stable balance of power in the Asia-Pacific

The tragedy of great power politics is that the more things change, the more they remain the same. Premier Zhou derided the Soviet support for the Partial Test Ban Treaty (PTBT) in 1963 as an attempt "to exert pressure on us at a time when we didn't have nuclear weapons."[9] Three decades later in 1996, India was leveling the same accusation at China, describing Beijing's support for the Comprehensive Test Ban Treaty (CTBT) being made contingent on India's signature on the treaty as an attempt by China to "strip India of its nuclear weapons capability."[10] In 1972, Richard Nixon told Zhou Enlai that "a strong China is in the interests of world peace at this point … a strong China can help provide the balance of power in this key part of the world." Three decades later in 2001, concerned with the rise of a Chinese behemoth, George W. Bush conveyed a similar message to India's Prime Minister Vajpayee: "A strong India can help provide the balance of power in the entire Asian region." His successor President Barack Obama described the US-India relationship as the "indispensable partnership of the 21st century."

Realpolitik rules. For India, which has long regarded China as a strategic adversary, the Bush administration's characterization of China as a "strategic competitor" rather than as a strategic partner was a welcome development. Quite understandably, since 2001 China has become as apprehensive of the Indo-US rekindling of ties as India and the Soviet Union were of Sino-US rapprochement in the early 1970s.[11] In other words, in a complete reversal of roles, it is now Beijing's turn to fear the worst: that India could play the same role in the US security calculus vis-à-vis China (should the Sino-US relationship deteriorate into a new Cold War) that China had played against the former Soviet Union from 1971 to 1989.[12]

Triangular Issues and Interests

The dominant issues in the US-China-India triangle are the territorial claims (Taiwan/Arunachal Pradesh and Kashmir), nuclear proliferation (Pakistan, North Korea, and Iran), China's military expansion, India's "Look East" policy, Pakistan's role in the war on terrorism, trade, resource scarcity, and climate change. India's protracted conflict with China (and Pakistan) and the Taiwan issue make New Delhi and Washington hedge their bets vis-à-vis Beijing. Besides, China's stakes in the non-resolution of the Kashmir dispute are similar to India's stakes in the non-resolution of the Taiwan question: both remain preoccupied on eastern and western frontiers. For a resolution of the Taiwan issue would lead to the deployment of half of the Chinese naval fleet in the Indian Ocean and increase the number of Chinese missiles and other assets deployed against Indian targets. Likewise, a resolution of the Kashmir dispute would lead to the redeployment of India's military assets on the India-China border.

Since the end of the Cold War, the context, tone, and nature of the Sino-US relationship has undergone dramatic change. China is now a global power. As China reaches out for trade, investment, markets, natural resources, and bases, its influence and interests have extended to every nook and corner of the world. Tensions over Taiwan, Tibet, human rights, trade, environment, internet freedom, and Chinese military buildup have made Sino-US relations turbulent. China has also sought to use the 2008 financial meltdown to increase its global influence in ways that will undermine the US dominance over the long term. In an opinion poll in early 2010, more than half of the Chinese people thought that "China and America are heading for a new 'Cold War.'"[13] Many Americans believe that China's rising economic and military power could exacerbate US-Chinese frictions in the years ahead. For Washington would neither reduce its footprint in the Asia-Pacific region nor find it easy to share power with China. Therefore, by default, if not design, the consequence will be strategic competition. In his Congressional testimony of March 25, 2010, US Pacific Command Commander Admiral Robert Willard argued that China's interest in a peaceful and stable environment that will support the country's developmental goals is difficult to reconcile with the evolving military capabilities that appear designed to challenge US freedom of action in the region or exercise aggression or coercion of its neighbors, including US treaty allies and partners. A major US interest post–Cold War has been the prevention of the emergence of a regional hegemonic power or a coalition of states that challenges US dominance and interests in the Asia-Pacific region. In this context, India's economic rise is seen as serving Washington's long-term interests by ensuring that there be countervailing powers in Asia—China, India, and Japan—that prevent the domination of the region by any one power and ensure a stable balance of power by avoiding too much concentration of power in one Asian power.[14] The Bush administration was committed to encouraging India's involvement in a wider Asian security system to balance a rising China and declining Japan. A 2002 declassified report on "US-India Military Cooperation: Expectations and Perceptions" revealed that US and Indian views of China were "strikingly similar." In addition, the twin threats of terrorism and WMD proliferation coupled with growing economic synergy with India, especially in the high-tech sector, and shared values of pluralism transformed Washington's ties with India. While the de-hyphenization of India-Pakistan relations improved the atmospherics, China's rise paved the way for building stronger defense ties with South Asia's preeminent power.

According to former Assistant Secretary for South and Central Asia Evan Feigenbaum, the United States has developed a growing stake in continued Indian reform and success—especially as they contribute to global growth, promote market-based economic policies, help secure the global commons (maritime, cyber, and space), and maintain a mutually favorable balance of power in Asia. The "India factor" is increasingly entering the ongoing US policy debate over China. For India, just by being there as India—democratic, secular, powerful, prosperous, and successful—frustrates China's attempts to establish a Sino-centric regional order. India's democratic development model is also an antidote to China's model of authoritarian development. Secretary of Defense Robert Gates has talked of India's positive role as a "net security provider in the Indian Ocean and beyond."[15] Closer ties between the United States and India could also offset Sino-Russian amity in Eurasia.

For its part, India seeks US economic and technological assistance in facilitating India's rise as a major power. India also needs US support for maintaining its maritime preeminence over the Indian Ocean region. It surely helps that India's long-time security concerns—China and Pakistan—have now also become US long-term and immediate strategic concerns as well. Specifically, India wants to abort Chinese-US cooperation inimical to Indian strategic objectives or prevent US support for a managerial Chinese role in South Asia. Concerns regarding a powerful China have prompted New Delhi to cultivate defense ties with Washington, seeing the US military's forward presence as a factor of stability. Some observers in India's strategic circles see the emerging Indo-US quasi-alliance as providing an opportunity for "payback" to China. As G. Parthasarthy, former ambassador to Pakistan and Burma, stated, "Whether it was the Bangladesh conflict of 1971, or in the Clinton-Jiang Declaration in the aftermath of our nuclear tests, China has never hesitated to use its leverage with the Americans to undermine our security."[16] India's "Look East" policy, which envisions high-level engagement with "China-wary" nations (the US, Japan, Taiwan, Vietnam, Thailand, Indonesia, and Australia), dovetails with the US policy of establishing closer ties with countries beyond Washington's traditional treaty partners to maintain US predominance. US efforts to minimize China's influence or the influence of a coalition of Asian states led by China invariably benefit India. Conversely, US weakness—real or perceived—invites Chinese assertiveness. Beijing's general assessment of the US as being overextended militarily with wars in Iraq and Afghanistan and weakened economically following the 2008 financial crisis has already imbued Chinese policymakers with the confidence to be more assertive on the international stage in ways that are inconsistent with Indian interests. At a time when many countries were relishing US financial troubles, Indian Prime Minister Manmohan Singh, during his November 2009 visit, reposed his faith in the resilience of the US economy and its currency to remain the key to global prosperity.

China is extremely sensitive to major power alignments. Beijing's best-case scenario is that the United States would over time willingly give up its insistence on maintaining the dominant strategic position in Asian, if not world, affairs and reach an understanding with China just as Great Britain did with the United States after World War II. Just as three decades of China's double-digit economic growth has succeeded in making China the largest economic partner of nearly all Asian countries, many Chinese assume that Beijing's growing military power will eventually detach Asians from the US orbit and lead them to switch their allegiance to China in the security sphere as well. However, the prospects of Sino-American accommodation with the US pulling back strategically from Asia as China rises to global leadership or a shared Sino-US (G-2) hegemony or duopoly seem remote. Far from reducing its footprint or walking away from the Asia-Pacific region, Washington is practicing hedging ("power-balancing") strategy as it has vital political, economic, and strategic interests at stake in the region. The US slide into the role of an engaged or offshore balancer would mean that the US-China relations will be characterized by "cooperative competition" at the best of times and "Cold Peace" at the worst of times.

A major objective of Beijing's "peaceful rise" diplomacy is to keep its neighbors from fearing and coalescing against it. The US-Indian strategic engagement coupled with India's expanding naval and nuclear capabilities and huge economic potential have made India loom a lot larger on China's radar screen. At one level, the US-Indian cooperation has the potential to undermine Beijing's ability to use China's ties with smaller South Asian nations as a strategic pressure point vis-à-vis India and the United States. For another, Beijing calculates that India's movement into the US camp would strengthen and prolong US hegemony. In contrast, a weaker, subdued, and isolated India would hasten the arrival of a Sino-centric regional order. Therefore, Beijing seeks to persuade India to disassociate itself from the United States (and Japan) while allowing China's "all-weather" special relationships with Pakistan, Bangladesh, Burma, Nepal, and Sri Lanka to flourish.

Convinced that the US-India security relationship is largely directed against China, Beijing is simultaneously wooing and coercing India to prevent Washington and New Delhi from coming too close for China's comfort. Beijing often plays the anti-West, Asian solidarity, or the "Third World" card to wean India away from the United States. The Russia-China-India trilateral (discussed below) aimed at ending the US "unipolar moment" is a case in point. A China-India bloc that opposes the US imposition of sanctions against Iran or Burma and blocks global agreements on trade, universal labor standards, or carbon emissions is potentially more damaging to India than China in terms of its standing with the United States. For it explodes the myth of democratic India being a "natural ally" of the United States.[17] Chinese interlocutors often call upon their Indian counterparts to foil "Western conspiracies aimed at dividing China and India" and work together to form an "Asian Commonwealth." Chinese leaders and state-run media have been cautioning India and the United States against going too far in working together against China. During 2007–09, the topic of US-India collusion as part of Washington's "contain China" strategy figured prominently in the official Chinese media. *Beijing Review* commented: "Washington … aims to create a balance between China, India, and Japan because it believes that no country should maintain any uncontested domination over this gigantic continent. Therefore, Washington has decided to drag India into its grand strategy of containing China."[18]

To their American counterparts, the Chinese stress that the United States has a far more substantive, multi-dimensional relationship with China than with India. The US economic stakes with China are certainly much higher. Financially, the United States is in debt to China, not to India. On most global economic and security issues, including terrorism, nuclear proliferation, and climate change, and in most multilateral organizations such as the UN Security Council and the IMF, China more often than not works with the United States rather than against it. The global economic crisis once again made allies out of two rivals. Both China and the United States (along with Saudi Arabia) have long shared the cost of propping up Pakistan both economically and militarily—albeit for different reasons. China's long-term objective of becoming the region's preeminent power notwithstanding, a more realistic goal for the foreseeable future is to establish a partnership with the United States in which the US friends and allies are relegated to a subordinate status and the United States and China jointly share preeminence and manage Asian, if not global, affairs.

Fears of strategic encirclement have impelled Beijing to devise new coercive diplomatic and military strategies to keep India in check. The "war talk" in the Chinese official media in 2007–09—reminding India not to forget "the lessons of 1962"—was aimed at raising the stakes in the triangular equation.[19] China's foremost strategic thinker, Shen Dingli, warned, "India has to and is willing to ally with the US so as not to lag further behind China. But it may not be necessarily willing to pay the price. Many Chinese are antipathic [sic] to a closer India-US relationship, especially when the two countries attempt to ally against China."[20] Former Chinese ambassador to India Cheng Ruisheng made it clear that a close alignment with the United States and Japan would be very costly for India.[21] The words matched the deeds: Beijing has stepped up its arming of Pakistan and other South Asian countries, recast the dormant dispute over Arunachal Pradesh as "southern Tibet," re-opened the supposedly "settled issue" of Sikkim, and questioned India's claim to Kashmir by issuing separate stapled visas to Kashmiri residents.

Figure 11.1: China's Position in the US-Soviet-China Triangle, 1971–1989

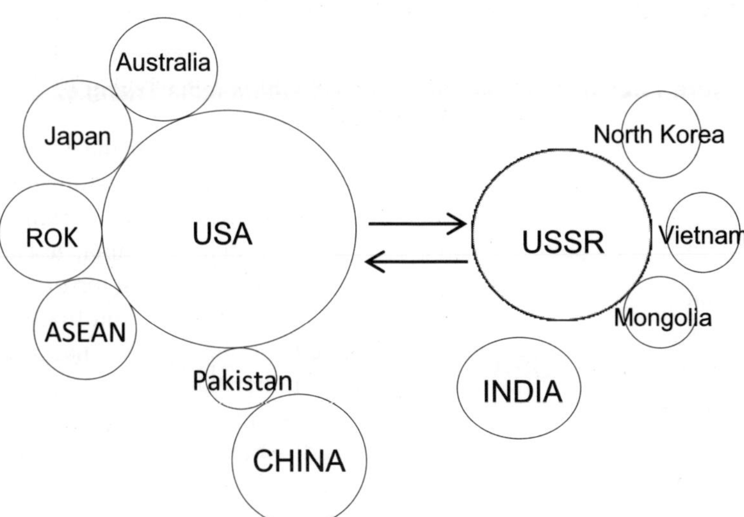

How China and India manage their differences on their border dispute, trade imbalance, Tibet, Pakistan, regional integration, and the UN Security Council reforms will have significant implications on the US place in Asia. Other issues that will determine the nature of the triangular dynamics include economic growth in India, nuclear proliferation, and the state of Sino-US ties. Much as Beijing would like to cooperate with Washington to contain New Delhi, the reality is that there is greater conflict of interests between China and the United States (over Taiwan and the US role in the world) than between India and the United States. Likewise, Beijing's conflicts with India (over the unresolved border, Tibet, and Pakistan) are deep-seated. While Washington sees India as a rising Asian power that needs to be cultivated, Beijing has deep mistrust of India's strategic ambitions and sees India as an expansionist power that must be contained. China views itself as the only rightful preeminent power in Asia and does not want to see India raising its power, profile, and stature. In the Asia-Pacific context, Beijing's vision of regional order is bipolar (the United States and China) and therefore at odds with India's view of multipolarity at *both* regional and global levels. In China, multipolarity is often expressed in terms of "saving others from US hegemony" while in India, multipolarity is expressed in terms of "saving itself and others" from *American and Chinese* hegemony. China's position in the evolving triangle is now the weakest of the three powers (see Figure 11.1), especially when contrasted with China's pivotal position (as a "swing state") in the old Cold War–era Sino-US-Soviet triangle that is now occupied by India (along with Russia) (Figure 11.2).

Figure 11.2: India's Position in the US-China-India Triangle: 2000–present

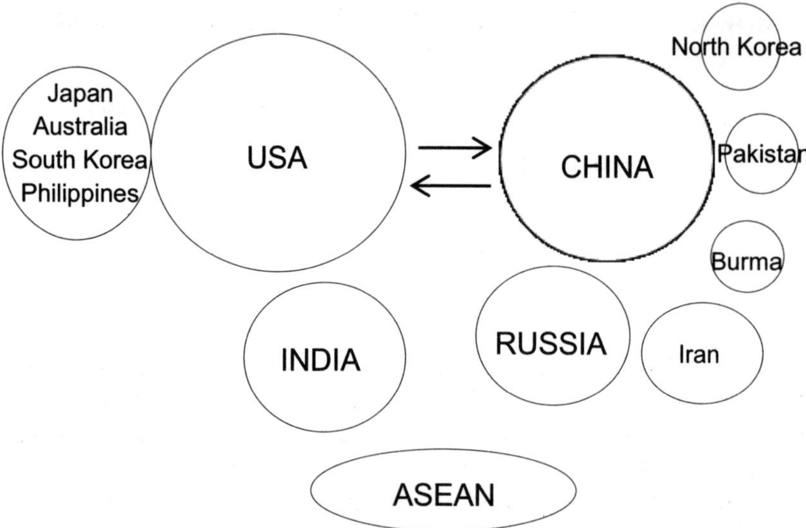

A key feature of the US-China-India triangle is power asymmetry, which works against the creation of a firm alignment of any two of these three countries against the third. For China, the United States is the principal strategic adversary; for India, it is China. India's deterrence capabilities are China-centric, whereas China's are US-centric. Just as Chinese interpretations of American foreign policy view the United States as a hegemonic power driven by the desire for world conquest, India's China-watchers see China as essentially a hegemonic power. Just as the Chinese accuse the United States of pursuing a policy of containment, Indians accuse China of using every opportunity to contain India while publicly professing support for friendly bilateral ties. At the heart of Sino-Indian antagonism is the familiar Indian suspicion that China is seeking to deny India its rightful place in the international system. As Table 11.2 shows, China's complaints and grievances about the United States are a mirror image of India's complaints and grievances about China. It demonstrates that established great powers do not like to see any challenge to their power and status. Stated differently, China's behavior toward India is not much different from US behavior toward China for the simple reason that China is a status-quoist power with respect to India while the United States is a status-quoist power concerning China.

Table 11.2: A Tale of Two Non-Status-Quoist Powers: China and India

CHINA'S COMPLAINTS & GRIEVANCES ABOUT **THE UNITED STATES**	**INDIA**'S COMPLAINTS & GRIEVANCES ABOUT **CHINA**
Recognize the course of history: Status quo is untenable; **China**'s rise is inevitable	Recognize the course of history: Status quo is untenable; **India**'s rise is inevitable
Recognize **China's** sphere of influence to improve ties	Recognize **India's** sphere of influence to improve ties
Don't preach to an ancient civilization	Don't preach to an ancient civilization
Stop sowing discord between **China and its neighbors** and stop arming them	Stop sowing discord between **India and its neighbors** and stop arming them
Dismantle your military alliances with **China's** neighbors and end your encirclement and containment policy	Dismantle your military alliances with **India's** neighbors and end your encirclement and containment policy
Show sensitivity to **China's** core security concerns; Don't exploit/play up differences between **China** and its neighbors	Show sensitivity to **India's** core security concerns; Don't exploit/play up differences between **India** and its neighbors
Recognize **China**'s special historical and cultural ties with **East** and Southeast Asian countries	Recognize **India**'s special historical and cultural ties with **South** and Southeast Asian countries
Bipolarity/Multipolarity is better	Multipolarity is better than

than Unipolarity **in the world**	Unipolarity/ Bipolarity **in Asia and the world**
Be less hegemonic, less arrogant, and share the leadership of the Asia-Pacific region	Be less hegemonic, less arrogant, and share the leadership of the Asia-Pacific region
Shed anti-**China** policies and resolve all outstanding issues to Beijing's satisfaction	Shed anti-**India** policies and resolve all outstanding issues to New Delhi's satisfaction
Strictly abide by the 3 **joint communiqués (1972, 1978, 1982)**	Strictly abide by the 3 **bilateral agreements (1993, 1996, 2005)**
Follow **One-China** Policy; Don't interfere in internal affairs **(Taiwan, Tibet, Xinjiang)**	Follow **One-India** Policy; Don't interfere in internal affairs **(Kashmir, Sikkim, Arunachal Pradesh)**
Accept **China** as your equal and treat it accordingly	Accept **India** as your equal and treat it accordingly

Triangular Dynamics

It is worth noting that the reality of the US-China-India triangular relationship, still in an embryonic stage, is very complex. The relationship among the three powers remains fluid. Short of a major rupture in US-Chinese or Indian-Chinese relations, it is unlikely to crystallize into rigid alignments. China's emergence as the engine of world economic growth means that an explicitly anti-Chinese alignment would be politically a hard sell. Besides, a number of developments in South Asia will have to occur before India will be able to play a significant role in the eventual outcome of the US-China rivalry in Asia; in particular, a significant decline in US military support for Pakistan and sustained growth in India's economy. Despite frequent ups and downs, the US relationship with China remains fairly stable and robust. Although India's relations with China remain far more unstable and competitive, both have sought to reduce tensions in order to focus on internal security and developmental issues. Whenever tensions arise due to divergent strategic objectives, all three countries have enough by way of common interests to keep them out of confrontation.

A pivotal or swing state within a triangle usually enjoys a certain amount of leverage and flexibility, as well as a degree of vulnerability, in its dealings with the other two powers. At the same time, it must constantly remain on guard. Strained US-China relations would make India the swing state in the triangle but tense India-China relations would put the United States in a pivotal position. Beijing's reluctance to adapt its policies to accommodate India's rise and the fact that both China and India value their ties with the United States more than with each other provides Washington with enormous leverage vis-à-vis the two Asian giants. However, the United States would find itself in a disadvantageous position in the event of China-India bonhomie (the Copenhagen Climate Change conference in 2009 was one good example). Furthermore, the country occupying the pivotal position in a triangle benefits as long as the tensions between the other two remain moderate. For example, New Delhi sees some degree of US-China competition as in its interest because it makes India the object of courtship by both Washington and Beijing. However, as Harry Harding observes, "if the relationship between the others deteriorates further—from tension to rivalry to confrontation—then the country that once occupied the pivotal position may be under irresistible pressure to choose between them."[22] Stated simply, all powers in the triangle benefit from a degree of competition but lose if competition turns into overt rivalry and confrontation. One could add that collusion between any two powers can result in the loss of leverage for the third (swing) state. Whenever the Sino-US relationship is characterized by collusion (as in 1996–98 and 2009), India's core interests are perceived as under threat, provoking a visceral reaction from New Delhi. In the triangular power balance game, while India seeks to prevent a Sino-US alignment or US acknowledgement of South Asia as China's sphere of influence, Beijing opposes India's participation in the US containment of China.

Equidistance, Tilt, or Alignment?

The most likely scenario in the near future is that of a weak triangle with ever-shifting, issue-based tilts by each of the three powers. Depending on the particular issue at hand, whether trade or climate change or terrorism or nuclear proliferation or regional security, there will be shifting alignments in bilateral ties and multilateral cooperation.

Ideally speaking, India would prefer to pursue an equidistance policy between China and the United States. The United States is used to relationships where it has the dominant voice. India's historic quest for strategic autonomy, its self-identity as a great civilization, and great power ambitions of its own mean that it will not be the kind of junior ally the United States cultivated during the Cold War. Unlike Britain,

Germany, and Japan in the 1950s, India is a rising, not retiring, great power. India's is also the only large economy that is neither in debt to China nor dependent on the Chinese market for its own growth. Besides, US-India relations cannot be a derivative of the US-China relationship. Regardless of Washington's China policy, India is unlikely to play second fiddle to China in Asia. New Delhi believes that it should enjoy a qualitatively different, more intimate relationship with Washington based on shared political values and common security interests in a way commensurate with its size, its economic and military potential, its security concerns in both South and East Asia, and its global aspirations. In the short-to-medium term, India prefers a US-led unipolar world to a China-dominated Asia—but ultimately seeks a multipolar world with itself as a constituent pole. At a minimum, New Delhi wants to use its strategic ties with Washington to bolster India's position in its dealings with China and in mitigating the dangers posed by its old adversary, Pakistan. Strategically, close economic and technological links with the United States help realize India's power potential. Still, New Delhi would want to avoid any formal alignment with Washington partly because of concern that such an alignment will prompt the Chinese to tighten their embrace of India's smaller neighbors, which, in turn, will exacerbate India's security dilemma. An alignment with the United States might so alienate and antagonize Beijing as to make it overtly hostile to Indian interests. (Beijing's offer to build more nuclear reactors in Pakistan and a nuclear cooperation deal with Bangladesh in 2005 following the US-India nuclear energy deal is a case in point.) And partly there remains a very strong undercurrent of suspicion and fear that Washington is a fickle and not-so-reliable partner and that US priorities and policies vis-à-vis China might change in the future to the detriment of India's national interests.

No other capital in Asia keeps as close an eye on US presidential visits to the Middle Kingdom as New Delhi. For the collateral damage to India's core interests from Washington's pursuit of its short-term goals with China and Pakistan can be as devastating as Beijing's deliberate undermining of them. After all the talk of India and the United States as "natural allies" and "India as a counterweight to China" under the Bush administration, India's enthusiasm for close US alignment dimmed somewhat after the Obama administration came into power believing that the United States and China could live and let live in Asia without stepping on each other's toes.[23] Apparently, the Obama administration's priorities with respect to the war in "Af-Pak" and engagement with Beijing on global governance issues served to elevate Pakistan and China respectively over India in US Asia policy.

This tactical shift in emphasis led some to conclude that Pakistan and China were returning to the affections of the United States. What particularly riled India was the US-China joint statement issued during President Obama's visit in November 2009 offering China a strategic role in preserving "peace and stability in South Asia" with US blessing, which constituted a reversal of George Bush's vision of India playing a role as counter-balance to China in the region.[24] Given China's patron-client relationship with Pakistan, including nuclear and missile transfers expressly to checkmate India and claims on territories in Kashmir and Arunachal Pradesh, New Delhi has never seen China as an impartial, honest broker. In addition, Washington's silence on the Sino-Indian border dispute as Beijing ratcheted up tensions in 2009 coincided with the moves to abandon those aspects of military engagement with New Delhi that could rile China, including any joint army drill in Arunachal state and any further US-India naval maneuvers involving Japan or more parties like Australia and Singapore.[25] The sea lane security in the Indian Ocean was another area where a clear disconnect emerged. Admiral Timothy Keating of the US Pacific Command welcomed the participation of the Chinese Navy in the anti-piracy operations in the Gulf of Aden at a time when New Delhi was expressing concern over this, viewing it as China's muscling into India's backyard.[26] This issue reflected a deeper divide rooted in power asymmetry and reciprocity. The US attitude toward China is clearly that of a stronger power showing magnanimity to accommodate a weaker but rising power. However, any talk of an enhanced role for China in India's backyard raises hackles in New Delhi, which claims that a stronger China has never shown any magnanimity or reciprocity to accommodate a weaker but rising India on any issue. There is also some concern in Indian naval circles over the possibility of a G2-like bargain to carve out the world without the world's reigning superpower and the rising superpower having to clash directly. A senior Chinese naval officer's suggestion on "dividing the Pacific Ocean into western and eastern sides, with China controlling the area west of Hawaii and the Indian Ocean and the US controlling the area east of Hawaii" revived the memories of the 1494 Treaty of Tordesillas under which the Pope assigned areas to the west of a demarcation line in the Atlantic Ocean (South America) to Spain, while areas to its east (Africa and the Indian Ocean) were to be the exclusive preserve of Portugal, the preeminent seafaring superpowers of that time.[27] Much to India's chagrin, Washington was seen as turning a blind eye to a new Chinese nuclear deal with Pakistan as a quid pro quo for Chinese support on Security Council sanctions against Iran.[28] (Strong lobbying from India resulted in American officials asking China to "clarify the details" about its deal to provide Pakistan with two nuclear reactors.) These developments led to speculation in strategic circles—albeit, exaggerated and misplaced—of "the re-emergence of the US-China-Pakistan axis of the 1970s and 1980s."[29] Many argued that a financially broke America kept afloat by China would leave India shortchanged.[30] Cashing in on these fears, the marginalized but vocal (anti-US) minority called for resurrecting India's identity as part of a bloc of developing nations that define their interests in opposition to the West. Pointing to the need to adjust to a China-dominated Asia in which the United States played little or no role, one analyst argued "India's policies need to be fine-tuned to contend as much with US fickleness as with Chinese caprice. The two are in any case not unrelated to each other."[31] Specifically, Indians worry that the United States may not come to India's rescue in times of crisis. Ashley Tellis sums up India's triangular tribulations: "India's long-term concerns essentially pertain to the rise of China, and the thing that New Delhi is most afraid of is that US weakness—or perceptions of current US weakness—might put Washington in a position where it ends up either colluding with the Chinese, or being excessively solicitous of Chinese preferences. Both those outcomes are very dangerous for India."[32]

On the US side, many believe that India's claim to global power is tenuous and over-hyped. Seeing India as both unable and unwilling to share the burden of managing the global commons, they instead advocate a joint Sino-US partnership. With the US share of global economic output declining, they want Washington to cut its losses and cut a deal with Beijing for shared hegemony, instead of shedding US blood and treasure in other people's wars. As David Karl of the Pacific Council points out: "Although Indians dream of their country becoming a rival, economic and otherwise, to China, the gap between ambition and reality is still quite large. And for Americans looking for a new strategic partner to prevent Chinese dominance of Asia, the material basis of Indian power is not as secure as some make it out to be."[33] In this line of thinking, an alliance with India would present far more costs and risks than benefits to each side. A US-India alignment might imply a US commitment to India's security in the event of a Sino-Indian conflict that Washington may not be able to fulfill. In fact, Beijing's paranoia over an Indo-US tie-up, symbolized by the nuclear deal and burgeoning military cooperation, has already resulted in a hardening of China's stance toward India since 2006.[34] Then, there are significant differences between Washington and New Delhi on several issues, including China, "Af-Pak" policy, military aid for Pakistan, climate change, and nonproliferation. More often than not, India's fractious democratic politics (and the presence of a large Muslim population) hinders cooperation on global issues such as Iran, terrorism, energy, trade, and environment. Mitigating the effects of disagreement on such issues to promote bilateral cooperation has not been easy. Given these realities, it is in the US national interests to pursue mutually beneficial cooperative ties with both of Asia's giants without causing offense to the other. Just as India's policy toward China cannot be easily reduced to a single issue or the pursuit of a single objective, US policies toward both China and India require flexible, nuanced, and differentiated strategies. Though economic issues (trade deficit and currency) may have become sources of friction, the prospect of mutual economic gain still holds the United States, China, and India together, mitigating underlying tendencies toward mistrust and strategic competition.

Be that as it may, "the China factor" draws the two closer as much as it pulls them apart. If the triangle was perceived as pro-India during the Bush administration, it was seen as turning pro-China under the Obama administration as Washington tried to placate Beijing to get its support over a whole range of global economic, environmental, and security ("Af-Pak" terrorism, North Korean and Iranian nuclear proliferation) issues.[35] The future scope and shape of the US-China-India triangle will depend on choices made in Washington, Beijing, and New Delhi. Twice in the past—during the 1950s and 1990s—China's and India's supposedly shared interests (such as promoting Asian solidarity, countering the West, and building a more equitable global order) failed to crystallize their relationship into an anti-US alignment. It is unlikely to happen in the future either as the West slides into relative decline with the rise of the East. It is neither in India's interests nor in Western interests to see a single power dominate the whole of continental Asia. Notwithstanding India's desire to remain an independent power, which sometimes results in India's taking policy positions contrary to the United States, there is no enthusiasm for sharing a joint platform with the Chinese against the United States—India's largest source of much-needed capital, investment, and advanced technology.

China and India are engaged in a battle of wits on a range of issues from territorial disputes to maritime expansion to nuclear issues to trade and currency to institutional shadow-boxing. Should New Delhi perceive the dragon running rampant in lands and seas around India, the possibility of a weak Indian tilt toward the United States turning into an alignment against China could not be ruled out.[36] Paradoxically, "the more muscular Chinese approach reinforces the very line of Indian thinking that [engenders] greater Chinese assertiveness—that India has little option other than to align with the US."[37] The threat of a two-front war with Pakistan and China coupled with nuclear proliferation in the neighborhood could also tilt the scales in favor of an Indian-US alignment. Since India is incapable of establishing the Asian power equilibrium on its own because of its relatively weak economic base, fractious polity, preoccupation with internal security issues, and seemingly intractable problems with weak and failing states in its immediate neighborhood, New Delhi will remain on the lookout for credible, like-minded partners—beyond the United States—to help build a stable Asian security architecture.

The China-Japan-India Triangle

Just as India did not rely entirely on the Soviet Union to balance China during the second half of the twentieth century, India is not going to rely on the United States alone to balance China in the twenty-first century. India sees US foreign policies as inconsistent and fears that Washington could trade cooperative interests with India for larger geostrategic interests with China and Pakistan. The worst-case scenario from India's perspective is the emergence of a US-China duopoly where China remains hostile to India and the United States is unavailable as a balancing power. Indian strategists never forget to mention that the United States and China were allies before and during the Second World War and in the second phase of the Cold War from 1971 to 1989. Should Washington in the future reach a strategic accommodation with Beijing, India would then look toward other like-minded countries (such as Japan, Vietnam, Indonesia, and Russia) to ensure a healthy balance of power is maintained in Asia. That could usher in triangular dynamics of a different kind (Russia-Japan-India or Japan-Indonesia-India). Much like India, Japan cannot be certain that the United States and China will not reach an accommodation in the future again and deliver yet another "Nixon shock" if and when the Taiwan issue is settled between the two. Thus, India's drive for "strategic autonomy" and Japan's fear of "strategic abandonment" by Washington is bringing the two closer. While India has been seeking out Japan as a partner to counter-balance China for a long period of time, Japan warmed up to the idea of seeking partners, other than the United States and Australia, only in the 2000s. In October 2008, the Japanese and Indian prime ministers issued a "Joint Declaration on Security Cooperation" that, inter alia, initiated navy-to-navy talks, a regular defense policy dialogue, and bilateral and multilateral military exercises. A year later in 2009, common concerns about energy security, piracy, and sea lanes safety in the Indian Ocean region led to the conclusion of an "Action Plan to Advance Security Cooperation."

Neither Japan nor India is in a position to deal with an increasingly assertive China alone. However, given their geographical location southwest and northeast of China and the impact of Chinese power and ambitions on them, India and Japan are better placed to ensure stable power equilibrium and safeguard vital sea lanes of communication. China's naval forays in the Indian Ocean have been matched by frequent incursions into Japan's exclusive economic zone.[38] New Delhi and Tokyo have countered Beijing's attempts to marginalize and relegate them to the periphery of regional order in Asia. Both India and Japan face hostile neighbors that are armed and backed by China—Pakistan and North Korea.[39] Moreover, both find their bid to be permanent members of the UN Security Council opposed by China. Both prefer a multipolar Asia to a unipolar or bipolar Asia. Both are energy-dependent economies dependent on sea lanes and are looking for ways to cooperate in alternate energy resources.[40] Tokyo has lent a helping hand as India "Looks East" in its quest for greater economic integration with the Asia-Pacific region. With Tokyo's support, India was invited to the inaugural East Asian Summit, and with New Delhi's backing, Japan obtained SAARC observer status in 2005. Tokyo also took the lead in forming a regional quadrilateral arrangement of Japan, India, the United States, and Australia.[41] As China's power grows, the India-Japan relationship could become a key driving force in the construction of new security architecture in Asia based on the protection of democratic values and market principles. By building strategic partnerships with two of China's biggest security concerns, the United States and Japan, India hopes to acquire useful leverage in its dealings with China, which, so goes the argument, will impel Beijing not to trample upon Indian interests.[42] As one commentator observed, "[Diplomatic] niceties apart, Japan and India are telegraphing a message to China—if you can throw a cordon around marking your presence in Pakistan's Gwadar port, erect listening posts in Bangladesh, Myanmar [Burma], Cambodia and the South China Sea and work to politically limit India as a 'regional player' and use history to browbeat Japan, others too can play the game."[43] Obviously, it is not in China's interest to pursue a hard-line approach that could backfire and drive India and its other Asian neighbors into stronger opposition to China and into deeper alignment with Tokyo and Washington, culminating in the emergence of an Asian NATO, an outcome that the Chinese dread most.

India's tilt toward Japan is generating a negative reaction in Beijing. *People's Daily* issued a scathing commentary, deploring what it viewed as an attempt to build an anti-China axis in Asia: "It is absolutely not new for Japan and the US to sit down and plot conspiracies together but it is rather intriguing to get India involved."[44] As with Washington, Beijing's robust economic ties with Tokyo provide China with significant leverage. In addition, India's nuclear weapons program, chronic political instability, and the lack of economic synergy continue to hinder the growth of Japan-India ties. In short, all three Asian heavyweights monitor their relationships with each other closely. To peacefully coexist and prosper in Asia, they need to find ways to reconcile their interests and resolve disputes amicably so as not to exacerbate the security dilemma.

The Russia-China-India Triangle

A major objective of Chinese diplomacy over the past several decades has been to prevent China's neighbors from forging a "united front" to counter China. India's quasi-alliance or "tilted non-alignment" with the Soviet Union during the Cold War was shaped more by Beijing than by Washington. Beijing's friendly overtures to India in the early 1980s were motivated by the strategic imperative to wean India away from the Soviet Union. India's relationship with post-Soviet Russia drifted in the 1990s, as both Moscow and New Delhi recalibrated their policies to changing geopolitical equations in the post–Cold War order. While India sought improvement in ties with China and the sole superpower, the United States, Russia suffered from status deprivation syndrome, harbored an acute sense of insecurity, and feared that the United States was still fighting the Cold War. It was in this context that Russian Foreign Minister Yevgeny Primakov proposed triangular cooperation with China and India in the mid-1990s. Historically, shared desire to build a new international economic and political order has turned out to be a very shaky foundation for China-India amity. Though Beijing shared Russia's fears about a unipolar world dominated by the United States, Beijing initially rejected Moscow's proposal of a Russia-China-India axis because it would have had the effect of elevating India to the ranks of first-tier great powers. Beijing alternatively proposed the formation of a strategic triangle consisting of Russia-China-Iran (or Russia-China-Pakistan) to counter the US-led unipolar order.[45]

However, wary of the Bush administration's overtures to India in 2001, China warmed up to the initiative for a Russia-China-India axis, seeing it as a potential tool to circumvent improvement in the US-Indian relations. Taking note of a "new stage" in US policy that placed special emphasis on ties with India and treated India in the same category as

China and Russia, a *People's Daily* commentary charged that "the US is tipping the balance between China and India, wooing India away from Russia and China and feeding India's ambition to match China force for force by its ever burgeoning arms sales to India."[46] For its part, Russia, increasingly assertive in its foreign policy after a decade of oil-fueled economic growth, is looking for a new role in the world. To achieve its objective of re-establishing Russia as a global player, Moscow has "six cards" to play:

- The "geopolitical card": Russia remains the only truly Eurasian power with the capacity to enlarge its "strategic space";
- The "global power card": As a UN Security Council veto-holding permanent member, Moscow's cooperation is required on all global security issues (Iran, North Korea);
- The "nuclear card": Russia is still a nuclear superpower to reckon with;
- The "arms supplier card": Russia is a major weapons producer arming India, China, and other countries;
- The "energy card": Russia is a major energy supplier to energy-starved, booming Asian economies; and
- The "swing state card": Being a "swing state" or "pivotal Eurasian power," Russia hopes to benefit by making itself the object of courtship by China, the United States, India, and Japan.

Though Moscow shares Beijing's interest in limiting Washington's influence worldwide, Russia also has many geopolitical and economic interests that are congruent with India and the West and at odds with China. The limitations of the US-India partnership arising from the vicissitudes and compulsions of US global strategy have led New Delhi toward adopting "a foreign-policy hedging strategy of 'engaging with all powers but aligning with none.'"[47] More concretely, the dramatic rise of China coupled with the relative decline of the United States in the 2000s is seeing India and Russia resuscitating an old friendship to further their interests. Despite India's efforts to diversify its sources of military supplies, Russia remains a reliable partner on the nuclear energy and defense fronts. Unlike the US-India nuclear deal, the nuclear deal with Russia gives India enrichment and reprocessing rights and provides for uninterrupted uranium fuel supplies from Russia even if it tested a nuclear device. Conversely, the United States can not only terminate its fuel supply, but can also take back the entire stock of delivered fuel. Arms and energy deals distinguish Moscow's relations with India from those of other powers.[48] For its part, Beijing has always countered the Russian-Indian security cooperation by expanding its own nuclear and conventional weapons transfers to Islamabad. Further, India sees Russia (along with Japan) as a partner in creating a multipolar Asia. Nothing gives both jitters more than the prospect of a US-China condominium—the "G-2." Strong Indo-Russian ties can ensure more geostrategic space is not yielded to Beijing or Washington at their expense in South and Central Asia. Both share common concerns about the Talibanization of Afghanistan and Pakistan following the pull-out of NATO forces post-2011. Being a permanent Security Council member, Russia has a role in influencing the course of developments in Afghanistan that Islamabad can neither resist nor resent. However, the Russian-Indian perspective on "Af-Pak" is not necessarily shared by China, which hopes to benefit from the installation of a pro-Pakistani regime in Kabul. The coming years will show how the new "strategic partnership" among the Russia, China, and India triangle pans out to face the challenges of the twenty-first century. For sure, no power is going to put all its eggs in one basket.

However, in contrast with the past, Russia and India do not have a common vision on China. In fact, based as they are on an equal footing, Chinese-Russian economic links are far more substantive and mutually beneficial than Chinese-Indian or Russian-Indian economic ties. Much like India, China covets Russia's enormous oil and gas resources and is investing billions in energy exploration and infrastructure (pipelines) projects. In contrast with the Cold War era, Moscow is now a major supplier of military hardware and technological know-how to China. Given that Russia and China coordinate their stance on several international issues (Iran, Afghanistan, Burma, and North Korea), India can no longer be certain of Russian backing in the event of a confrontation with China in the future. As the projected imbalance of military and economic power between Russia and China grows wider, some analysts advocate promoting better coordination between Russian and Indian policies in Central, South, and East Asia to deal with both China and the United States.[49] However, others do not see Moscow reaching out to New Delhi to balance Beijing.[50] Their priorities are somewhat different too. Russia is miffed by Washington's ties with Eastern Europe and its efforts to penetrate Central Asia, while India is uneasy with the growing Chinese footprint in Central and South Asia, areas where each would like to restore and maintain its influence, respectively. The harsh reality is that a demographically and economically shrinking Russia may have the will but not the power to act as a counterweight to China. Therefore, even as India adds ballast to its old ties with Moscow, it will continue to pursue a policy of vigorous multi-faceted engagement with Washington. While keeping close watch on each other's engagements, all three countries are keen to build stronger commercial ties wherever possible. Neither has an interest in developing their bilateral ties at the expense of relations with the United States. At the same time, given their anxieties about the emerging international order, neither Russia nor India wants to jeopardize its burgeoning links with Beijing. The immutable factor of geography dictates that Moscow will loom large in the US-Chinese-Indian triangular equation.

China and India in 2040: Alternative Futures

Having discussed the various tilts, triangles, and permutations involving major powers in Asia, the following section will lay out five different scenarios of China-India relations to the year 2040.

Scenario I: Asian G-2 Partnership

Power Transitions Theory states that lasting stability can be attained if China, India, the United States, Japan, and Russia join forces in an economic and security arrangement. India and China may be long-term, if not permanent, competitors, but their aspirations appear to be manageable. Just as the United States and the Soviet Union did not go to war to counter each other's power or spheres of influence, India and China need not resort to use of force to neutralize each other's aspirations. The Asia-Pacific region is not only big enough to accommodate both India and China; it is in fact too big for any one country to dominate it without that domination having repercussions at the regional and global levels. The restoration of Tibet's autonomy and a peaceful resolution of the Kashmir dispute could be powerful mitigating factors in the China-India rivalry. Constructing a bilateral relationship based on common security that jettisons the push and shove of balance-of-power politics could be a way out of the security dilemma. Both share an interest in avoiding overt rivalry, confrontation, and conflict given their current focus on acquiring comprehensive national power. The major focus of both Chinese and Indian leaders is on domestic economic development, alleviating poverty, promoting industrialization, and strengthening internal cohesion. Despite no breakthrough yet on finding a solution to the thorny boundary issue, confidence-building measures on the disputed border have been put in place. Both are nuclear-armed nations with enormous stakes in maintaining peace and responsibilities in building a new world order. A degree of pragmatism is informing their view of each other. Trust between the two militaries is being established, especially through holding joint military exercises. History shows that conflictual relations among states often give way to cooperative relations. Even if both seem to assert their interests more actively, there is little to suggest that they will pursue reckless policies.

Hopefully, economic ties would provide the basis for an improved relationship that tides over political frictions. Conceivably, as the relative weight of economic factors vis-à-vis security concerns increases, the reality of the rapidly expanding bilateral engagement and participation in various international organizations and multilateral forums would create sufficient trust and provide a different template for addressing their disputes. Greater exposure and interaction at all levels will definitely help make light of some of history's burdens. While they are competitors for power and influence in Asia, China and India also share common interests in maintaining regional stability (for example, combating the growing Islamist fundamentalist menace; issues of climate change, resource scarcity, and terrorism; maintaining access to capital and markets; and benefiting from globalization). Both cooperate on climate change, global trade talks and in the Group of Twenty. Therefore, the long-term outcome could be a China-India condominium based on a need to focus on social and political stability, strong economic growth and a sense of security so they can concentrate on realizing their potential and avoid the perils of stagnation or decline. From India's perspective, this would be the best-case scenario. This "back to the future" scenario could materialize if the United States and Japanese economies suffer an irreversible decline. By 2040, were China and India to join in an Asian G-2 partnership, they would tower over the rest and Asia would resemble the pre-modern era in history.

Scenario II: Distant Neighbors: Competitors-cum-Partners

Under this scenario, the combination of internal issues of stability, external overlapping spheres of influence, and ever-widening geopolitical horizons forestall the chances for a genuine Sino-Indian rapprochement. Tensions in Tibet and India-Pakistan relations will reverberate in Sino-Indian relations. Asymmetric growth in the Chinese and Indian economies will also have the effect of intensifying their power competition. Simmering tensions over territory, water, energy resources, markets and bases, and rival alliance relationships ensure that the oft-repeated assertion that "there is enough space for the two countries to develop together" will remain more a hope than a conviction. Economic and political engagement and military balancing will remain dual components of India's and China's policy toward each other. Even as a range of economic and transnational issues draw them closer together, old disputes and new frictions coupled with uncertainty over their future strategic alignments will keep them apart. The emergence of an ambitious, nationalist India and an assertive Chinese foreign policy agenda would fuel power competition. As in the past, they will remain distant neighbors, and the relationship between these two Asian giants will be characterized by security competition and economic cooperation. In this scenario, the United States reinvents itself as a green economy and retains its position as the largest economy in the world.

Scenario III: A Sino-Indian Cold War

In this scenario, unless India is willing to play a secondary role to China in a Sino-centric regional order, greater Sino-Indian rivalry is a foregone conclusion. Pessimists point to the territorial, strategic, economic, and geopolitical roots of the India-China divide and paint a bleak picture of the future. The Chinese perception of India as a land of irreconcilable socio-religious cleavages with an inherently unstable polity and weak leadership that is easily contained through proxies aggravates tensions between the two. While Chinese leaders and diplomats chant the mantra of "peaceful rise," their body language makes it clear to everyone to get out of their way. Noted China-watcher Ross Terrill argues that China's long-term strategy is driven by the twin goals of establishing its hegemony in Asia and regaining territories that Beijing feels fall within its sovereignty. The long-term growth of Chinese supremacy in Asia is also contingent upon having smaller and weaker states on China's southeastern and southwestern frontiers.[51] These goals will invariably pit India against China. From Beijing's perspective, an Indo-centric South Asian community would pose a far greater threat to China than a fragmented and divided South Asia. For India, a multipolar Asia is essential to achieving and sustaining its strategic autonomy. But China fears a multipolar Asia would easily degenerate into anti-China alignment. Should China strive for mastery of Asia as a precursor to rivaling the United States as a global power, then it must prevent India's emergence as a peer competitor or as an ally of the United States. At any rate, an unfettered India would constrain the growth of Chinese power and influence in the Indian Ocean region.

Therefore, a new cold war could emerge between any pair of major powers, but one between India and China seems more likely than the

United States and China. The US-Chinese economies are inextricably tied in a symbiotic relationship and US future growth and prosperity is linked to China's. In contrast, given their skewed, lopsided economic relationship, India is the only major economy that neither is in debt to China nor is its current or future economic growth linked to China's economic fortune. Therefore, the logic of economic interdependence constraining competitive state behavior may not apply to the China-India equation. As China's and India's power and ambitions grow, nearly all regions of the world will bear the marks of their competitive economic and geo-strategic outreach. Both will employ strategic maneuvers to checkmate each other from gaining advantage or expanding spheres of influence. New Delhi's efforts to establish closer ties with Southeast and East Asian countries and to emerge as an independent power suggest future tension and friction between India and a China that aspires for regional and global preeminence. Tensions between these giants would drag in all of Asia, and perhaps other regions as well could be divided into something that might resemble "an Asian cold war." A Chinese analyst, Dai Bing, admits, "For the foreseeable future, therefore, while a 'cold war' between the two countries is increasingly likely, a 'hot war' is out of the question."[52] At the same time, leaders in both countries will strive to ensure that tensions and frictions do not overwhelm the relationship as a whole.

Scenario IV: A China-India War?

The probability of another war between China and India, says sinologist John Garver, "is not great. But it does exist." Garver talks of three situations that might, singularly or in combination, lead to an armed conflict on the scale of 1962: "Chinese intervention in an Indian-Pakistan war, a major uprising against Chinese rule in Tibet, and the unresolved border dispute."[53] Chinese strategic writings indicate that as China becomes more economically and militarily powerful, its belligerence toward India, in particular, is likely to increase. Apparently, the fundamental disputes that could trigger a conflict center on the status of Tibet and the territorial dispute that has slid several times into confrontation since 1959. Repeated efforts at negotiated settlement have ended in failure. Brief periods of cooperation have been followed by acrimony and discord. An aggressive patrolling in the Indian Ocean or a sharp reversal in economic fortune (i.e., a Japanization of Chinese economy) could be additional factors in the future. Since the CCP bases its legitimacy on a mix of economic growth, prosperity, unity, and nationalism, it is conceivable that foreign policy belligerence could increase in the event of a sharp economic decline citing other nations as the main culprits. Though the probability is extremely low, should India come close to spoiling Beijing's "party of the century" by outpacing China in economic growth, Beijing could lash out at India and others for its economic woes. More so, if acceleration in India's economic growth coincides with a sharp deceleration in China's economic growth rates. The fear of strength erosion over time and strategic encirclement may induce Beijing to nip the challenge in the bud by force before India reaches the apex of the relative power parity and thus a favorable window of opportunity is closed. Power Transitions Theory postulates that power asymmetry between a rising challenger (India) and the established great power (China) is a major factor that increases the likelihood of war between those states. Countries in a relative state of decline resist ceding their status to rising challengers. A slowdown in power growth relative to a potential challenger can bring about a shift in external behavior "from one that favors engagement and accommodation to one that rewards containment and confrontation."[54]

Great powers in history have often gone to war to prevent the overturning of a particular balance of power favorable to them. The collapse of the Pakistani state or the prospect of loss of control over Tibet post–Dalai Lama would threaten to overturn the South Asian balance of power on which China's security has rested since 1950. Add to these Chinese fears about India being co-opted as junior partner or spoke in the United States' hub and spoke globe alliance system.[55] The fear of major powers collusion to contain China has already led to a harder line toward India. Interestingly, nearly half a century after the 1962 war, strategic analysts in both countries are again seeing parallels between the situation pre-1962 and the situation in the 2000s.[56] Militarily, Beijing perceives India as the weakest link in an evolving anti-China coalition of democratic and maritime powers (the United States-Japan-Australia-India) inimical to China's growth. Some Chinese strategic thinkers feel that a limited war with India would send a resounding message to those who are again courting and counting on India as a balancer or counterweight to China in the twenty-first century.[57] Historically, dissatisfied rising powers have chosen to attack the most vulnerable or weaker power ("easy prey") in order to effect a shattering blow to the rival coalition. After all, a coalition is only as strong as its weakest link. As an old Chinese saying goes, "Kill the chicken to scare the monkey" (*shaji jinghou*)—kill the weaker enemy to scare the stronger enemy. As per this line of argument, the demonstrative effect of a short and swift victory over India would buttress the need for other countries in Asia, especially US friends and allies, to accommodate China's growing power by aligning with, rather than against, China. In short, both power asymmetry and the *prospect* of power parity (the widening power gap between China and India or India overturning the existing power balance) could cause Sino-Indian conflict in the future. Power Transitions Theory holds that at near parity, accommodation is essential to prevent conflict. If accommodation fails, then the possibility of a confrontation cannot be ruled out.

Scenario V: India Capitulates to Big Brother China

Under this scenario, the unequal strategic equation between China and India will eventually force India to capitulate and accept China as its big brother. Unlike China, India lacks the ability to think and plan strategically and mobilize the necessary resources and political will to achieve grand strategic goals. The major objective of Beijing's South Asia policy is to undermine India's will and sap its energy to compete with China by exploiting India's internal contradictions and external vulnerabilities, preferably without striking a blow. This approach signals to Asia and the world that India falls short in being a "balancing power" so that no country looks toward India as a counterweight to China. A crucial means of "victory without bloodshed" (*bing bu xue ren*) in Chinese strategic tradition is to intimidate the hostile country into capitulation through provocation, brinkmanship, coercion, controlled escalation, and a shift in the balance of power. The aim is to convince the enemy, who is militarily weak and/or tied down with multiple security concerns, that the overall "correlation of forces" has shifted to his disadvantage and thus to force him to concede.[58] From Beijing's perspective, Indian capitulation would be the best outcome. As the power gap widens, the costs and risks of resisting or containing China will be too great for New Delhi to bear. The region could be overwhelmed by Chinese economic blandishments to support regimes politically hostile to India. One can conceive of situations that might produce, singularly or in combination, a scenario wherein India accommodates itself to an exponential growth in China's power and accepts Chinese supremacy in the region.

- If China can sustain near-double-digit economic growth, it would enable Beijing to attract most middle and small powers in support of its leadership role.
- If the PLA succeeds in occupying the Tawang tract in Arunachal Pradesh and giving India's military a bloody nose, Indian leaders would then be much more deferential in dealing

with China and Beijing need not worry about the "India challenge" any longer.

- If a sequence of catastrophes weakened India severely: a nuclear conflagration, a two-front war with Pakistan and China, another partition caused by the growing Hindu-Muslim divide, or the success of *jihadi* and Maoist terrorism in unraveling the Indian Union. A "domino effect" could then end in the emergence of several weak and warring states in South Asia—all vying for Chinese aid and support.
- If the US economy goes into free fall, culminating in the reduction or withdrawal of the US forward military presence, and if Japan slides into China's orbit following the return of Taiwan to China's fold. In that event, New Delhi's misplaced faith in the US-Japanese duo to enable India's rise as an equal of China would undergo a quick burial. A weakened Russia may also fall short of great Indian expectations. Devoid of great power backing and left to fend for itself on multiple fronts, New Delhi will want to steer clear of any potential aggravation or competition with Beijing.
- If an isolated India—having fallen so far behind China in relative power terms—chose to cope with the rise of China by bandwagoning with, rather than balancing against, the superpower on its doorstep.

Contending that India is no match for China's economic clout, strategic foresight, and diplomatic influence, some observers have long maintained that the likelihood of India accepting China as the lord of Asia is far greater than China ever accepting South Asia as an Indian sphere of influence.[59] Through a combination of trade, aid, resource extraction and infrastructure development, arms sales, and bases, Beijing is seeking to extend its strategic perimeter in Asia and the Indian Ocean region. Naturally, this makes it hard for China to accept any externally imposed barriers to its growth. Faced with continuing onslaught on its core interests, India may well conclude that the prudent course is to cut its losses and slide under the protective umbrella of Chinese hegemony. The sooner this realization dawns on New Delhi that it can do little to contain China's phenomenal rise and global influence, the better India would be placed to benefit by partnering that growth and sliding into a supporting, junior partner's role. This would require, of course, Indian acquiescence to Chinese leadership in Central and South Asia, Southeast Asia, and the Indian Ocean. India's capitulation to Chinese power would, in turn, propitiate Beijing and prompt it to show magnanimity in settling the territorial dispute with its erstwhile rival turned partner.

Conclusion

As in the past, the major powers will inevitably compete, cooperate, collide, coalesce, and collude with each other in various equations, permutations, and combinations in the multipolar world of the twenty-first century. Asian geopolitics, in particular, will be dominated by the interaction among the United States, China, and India as they compete, cooperate, collide, and collude with each other. Strategic concerns will loom large as China's growing military power and reach run up against the interests of other global and regional powers. The US-China-India triangle is still very much in its infancy. Its future scope will depend on choices made in Washington, Beijing, and New Delhi. There exists a vast power differential between the United States and China and China and India. While the United States is omnipotent militarily, China is omnipresent economically. This power asymmetry deeply influences the strategic orientation of each toward the other and toward India. All three countries will use each other for their own reasons. The United States does not wish to see Asia dominated by a single country; it much prefers the prospect of a balance of peaceful engagement that includes all the major powers in Asia—China, Japan, and India, with the United States continuing to act as an "engaged offshore power balancer." The premise underlying this strategy of forming a range of partnerships is to shape the strategic environment in ways that would induce China to evolve as a constructive and responsible, rather than revisionist or irredentist, power in Asia. For China, its economic relationship with the United States is vitally important as a source of investment and technology and as its biggest export market that facilitates its rise as a global power. For India, its strategic ties with the United States are essential to augmenting its position in Asia. In the triangular power balance game, Beijing fears India's participation in the US containment of China. Conversely, India fears a Sino-US alignment that would allow Beijing to stunt the growth of Indian power or lead to US acknowledgement of the South Asian/Indian Ocean region as China's sphere of influence.

Whether India enters into a soft or hard alignment with the United States (or Japan and Russia, for that matter) will ultimately depend on China's policy toward India. It will largely be determined by Beijing's willingness or reluctance to accommodate India's rise and aspirations. Strategic choices made by China and India will be, of course, critically shaped by the nature and degree of US engagement with both. Both

Beijing and Washington recognize that a weak India would weaken the US position in Asia. Conversely, a strong India might prolong the US hegemony. Over the next 20 years, the United States, China, and India will try to manage peacefully a relationship that is fundamentally competitive. Short of a major crisis, each will form flexible ad hoc partnerships with the others where their interests converge, mobilize the support of one against the other when their interests collide, and checkmate the other two from forming an alignment against it. More specifically, both China and India will pro-actively court the United States, each one seeking to move closer to Washington against the other. The future of the Asian security environment will depend a great deal on how and in what ways the United States manages the rise of China and how and in what ways China, in turn, manages the rise of India and accommodates India's interests. The past record of China's India policy does not give much cause for optimism. Therefore, the decisive factor in this triangle will be China's behavior and policies. Moving away from its Cold War posture of "non-alignment," India is embarked upon a "multi-alignment" strategy to meet the China challenge as well as to facilitate its own rise as a great power. New Delhi is weaving a web of mutually inseparable relationships with an eye to opportunities and balance with great powers and trading partners, while trying to avoid overt alignment and confrontation. Though the US-Indian partnership represents the centerpiece of India's strategy to balance China, India is looking beyond the United States to safeguard its core interests. In a sense, India's strategic ties with Russia, South Korea, Japan, Vietnam, Indonesia, and Australia send a signal to China that India can become part of an anti-Chinese coalition should China take stances that threaten the security of its neighbors. In the meantime, a pro-US, pro-Japan tilt in India's national security strategy—a reaction to the power projection capabilities of neighboring China—will be a defining characteristic of an increasingly globalized India.

Of all the scenarios considered in the last section, the one with the highest probability in the near future is that of a combination of geopolitical competition and selective partnership on transnational issues of mutual interest. The specter of a Sino-Indian Cold War is also looming large. The existence of two economically powerful nations would create new tensions, as they both strive to stamp their authority on the region. Over the long term, the possibility of confrontation cannot be completely ruled out either on their disputed borders post–Dalai Lama or due to Chinese intervention in an India-Pakistan war or because of aggressive patrolling in the Indian Ocean or a reversal in economic fortune. Barring a series of catastrophes that severely weakened or dismembered India, it is inconceivable that India would accept Chinese leadership of the Asian continent without first balancing it by alignment with like-minded "China-wary" countries. Divergent interests between China and India and the United States and China preclude the possibility of a concert of powers emerging in the region. Conversely, Sino-Indian relations could also move in the direction of long-term cooperation. Improvement in China-India relations over the long term will depend upon Beijing's assessment of India's evolving political cohesion, economic growth, and military potential. Self-interest, greater confidence, and pragmatism might see China and India evolving into benevolent hegemons that deal magnanimously with nations near and far. It is possible that economically prosperous and militarily confident China and India might come to terms with each other eventually as their mutual containment policies start yielding diminishing returns, and the two Asian giants will become the co-leaders of a post-American world order. However, this is unlikely to happen in the short and medium term (that is, before the 2040s). History shows that when benefits outweigh costs and common interests override divergent issues, old rivals and sworn enemies do cooperate and become friends.

Notes

[1] In assessing the notion of "national power" in today's world, factors such as technology, education, external respect and reputation, economic growth, and trade are as important as the traditional power attributes of military, geography, raw materials, and population. In other words, "soft power" is as important as "hard power."

[2] J. Kugler et al, "Power transitions and alliances in the 21st century," *Asian Perspective*, 25:3 (2001), 5-29.

[3] Department of Defense, *Quadrennial Defense Review* (Washington DC: February 2010), iii <http://www.defense.gov/QDR/ QDR%20as%20of%2029JAN10%201600.pdf>.

[4] See Chen Xiankui and Tang Wei, "Coming collapse of the hegemonic world," *China Daily*, September 12, 2008, 7.

[5] S. Sartori, "How China sees India and the world," *Heartland: Eurasian Review of Geopolitics*, 3 (Hong Kong: Cassan Press, 2005), 57.

[6] J. W. Garver, "The China-India-U.S. triangle," *NBR Analysis*, 13:5 (October 2002), 7.

[7] P. Sawhney, "Hastening slowly: developing Indo-U.S. relations," *Indian Defence Review,* April 1993, 57-63.

[8] Ren Xu, Qian Feng, and Fang Hua, "Mei Ri dou lalong Yindu: Genben mudi shi ezhi Zhongguo" ["America and Japan rope in India: their basic objective is to contain China"], *Renmin Ribao* [*People's Daily*], April 30, 2001, 4.

[9] Document 3:35 in Malik, "Zhou, Mao and Nixon's 1972 conversations on India," 184-219.

[10] See J. Singh, "Against nuclear apartheid," *Foreign Affairs*, 77:5 (1998), 41-52.

[11] Ren Xu et al, "Mei Ri dou lalong Yindu…" ["America and Japan rope in India…"]; Zhang Wenmu, "Meiguo de shiyou diyuan zhanlue yu Zhongguo Xizang Xinjiang diqu anquan" ["U.S. petroleum-geostrategy and the regional security of China's Tibet and Xinjiang"], *Zhanlue yu guanli* [Strategy and Management] 27:2 (1998), 100-104; and J. Mohan Malik, "China edgy over Clinton's India visit," *The Pioneer*, March 2, 2000, 8.

[12] Jian Hua, "The United States, Japan want to rope in India which cherishes the dream of becoming a major power," *Ta Kung Pao* (Hong Kong), June 4, 2001, trans. in *FBIS-China*.

[13] M. Sheridian "China's hawks demand cold war on the US," *Sunday Times* (London), February 8, 2010, 1.

[14] Z. Khalilzad et al., *The United States and Asia: Toward a New U.S. Strategy and Force Posture* (Santa Monica, Calif.: Rand Corporation, 2001), 203-31. US Department of Defense, *Quadrennial Defense Review Report*, September 30, 2001 <www.dod.gov/pubs/qdr2001.pdf>.

[15] E. A. Feigenbaum, "India's rise, America's interest," *Foreign Affairs*, March/April 2010; R. Gates, "America's security role in the Asia Pacific." Remarks at the eighth Asia Security Summit of the International Institute for Strategic Studies, Singapore, May 30, 2009.

[16] G. Parthasarthy, "Tomorrow's security-missile defence," *The Pioneer*, May 10, 2001.

[17] Garver, "The China-India-U.S. triangle."

[18] Ma Jiali, "Drive for nuclear energy," *Beijing Review*, September 3, 2009, 15.

[19] Mohan Malik, "War talk: perceptual gaps in "Chindia" relations," *China Brief*, IX:20 (October 7, 2009), 6-9 <http://www.jamestown.org/uploads/media/cb_009_52.pdf>.

[20] Shen Dingli, "In diplomacy, ganging up is a very risky move," *Global Times*, November 24, 2009.

[21] Amb. Cheng Ruisheng, "Trends in India's foreign strategy," *Guoji Wenti Yanjiu*, March 2008, 48-54.

[22] F. Frankel and H. Harding (eds), *The India-China Relationship* (Columbia University Press, 2004), 332.

[23] A. Kazmin and E. Luce, "India feels the chill as US warms to China," *Financial times*, November 22, 2009.

[24] Qiu Wei, "India bristles at closer Sino-US ties," *Global Times*, November 20, 2009 <http://www.globaltimes.cn/www/english/world/asia-pacific/2009-11/486614.html>.

[25] S. Dasgupta, "China has tamed India with help from Obama," *Times of India*, November 22, 2009.

[26] IANS, "Disconnect emerges in India-US military views," May 14, 2009 <http://www.thaindian.com/newsportal/uncategorized/disconnect-emerges-in-india-us-military-views_100192531.html>.

[27] *Washington Times*, August 17, 2007. S. Chaulia, "Sino-Indian rivalry and Asian stability," *The Globalist*, June 22, 2009 <http://www.sreeramchaulia.net/Sino-IndiaNavy.pdf>.

[28] G. Kessler, "Questionable China-Pakistan deal draws little comment from U.S.," *Washington Post*, May 20, 2010, A11.

[29] G. Parthasarathy, "The axis of grudging cooperation," *Wall Street Journal*, May 4, 2010.

[30] B. Raman, "Obama & China: the coming shocks," *Saag.org*, October 6, 2009 <http://www.southasiaanalysis.org/papers35/paper3445.html>.

[31] S. Jha, "India uneasy with Obama's Chinese checkers," *UPI Asia online*, November 17, 2009 <http://www.upiasia.com/Politics/2009/11/17/india_uneasy_with_obamas_chinese_checkers/4395/>

[32] A. Haniffa, "India-US ties, the three-card trick" *Rediff.com*, November 24, 2009 <http://news.rediff.com/report/2009/nov/23/india-us-ties-the-three-card-trick.htm>.

[33] D. J. Karl, "Three events tell a tale of two Indias," *PacNet*, No. 67, December 23, 2008.

[34] B. Chellaney, "Tensions in the China-India-US triangle," *Mint*, October 26, 2009 <http://chellaney.spaces.live.com/blog/cns!4913C7C8A2EA4A30!1123.entry>.

[35] L. Polgreen, "Obama's warming to China is seen as slight in India," *IHT*, November 24, 2009.

[36] P. D. Samanta, "Told Obama how China is asserting itself: PM," *Indian Express*, November 26, 2009, 1.

[37] Chellaney, "Tensions in the China-India-US triangle."

[38] Y. Hayashi and J. M. Schlesinger, "Tokyo grows wary of China military," *Wall Street Journal*, May 14, 2010.

[39] B. Chellaney, "Look east, at Japan, not China," *Asian Age*, September 7, 2007.

[40] S. Kondapalli, "Why Japan and India are moving closer," *Rediff.com*, August 23, 2007 <http://www.rediff.com/news/2007/aug/23guest.htm>.

[41] Editorial, "Love with Tokyo," *Indian Express*, August 24, 2007.

[42] P. Bidwai, "Five-nation naval drill presages 'Asian NATO'?" *Inter-Press Service*, September 7, 2007 <http://www.ipsnews.net/news.asp?idnews=39175>.

[43] S. Sirohi, "Japan: the sake is warming," *Outlook*, August 27, 2007.

[44] "A 'goodwill' joint naval drill?" *People's Daily,* April 21, 2007 <http://english.people.com.cn/200704/21/eng20070421_368521.html>.

[45] In the 1990s, both China and Pakistan were under US-imposed sanctions over the Tiananmen massacre and nuclear weapons proliferation respectively. Following the 1991 Gulf War, China made a strategic decision to move closer to Iran and to build up its defenses as a counterweight to American influence in the Middle East. In China's calculus, the emergence of additional power centers, albeit far from its borders (such as Iran in the Middle East), was to preoccupy the US, leaving South and Southeast Asia to be dominated by China.

[46] Li Hongmei, "Indian media stinks up public opinion," *People's Daily online*, September 15, 2009 <http://english.peopledaily.com.cn/90002/96417/6758363.html>.

[47] Parthasarthy, "The axis of grudging cooperation."

[48] N. Lal, "India, Russia and the U.S.: three's a crowd?" *World Politics Review*, April 6, 2010 <http://www.worldpoliticsreview.com/article.aspx?id=5378>.

[49] C. Raja Mohan, "Old friends in a new world," *Indian Express*, March 12, 2010.

[50] P. Sharma, "The new balance," *Outlook*, December 21, 2009.

[51] See R. Terrill, "Inside the Chinese mind," *Wilson Quarterly*, September 2005.

[52] Dai Bing, "India building a security barrier against China," *China.org.cn*, February 8, 2010 <http://www.china.org.cn/opinion/node_7078634.htm>.

[53] J. W. Garver, "Could it happen again?" *Rediff.com*, November 2, 2002 <http://www.rediff.com/news/2002/nov/02chin.htm>.

[54] Kugler et al, "Power transitions and alliances in the 21st century."

[55] Editorial, "Washington draws India in against China," *People's Daily online*, July 7, 2005.

[56] Zhao Bowen, "Zui you keneng yu zhongguo jiaozhan de you na shige guojia?" ["Which ten countries are most likely to have war with China?"] *Nanfang Daily*, January 16, 2009 <http://opinion.nfdaily.cn/content/2009-01/16/content_4848120.htm>; B. Verma, "Unmasking China: China will launch an attack on India before 2012," *Indian Defence Review*, 24:3 (July-September 2009).

[57] "Zhongguo yi ge xiao dong zuo jiu chai san le suowei 'da Indu lianbang'" ["China can dismember the so-called 'Great Indian Federation' with one small stroke"], *www.iiss.cn*, August 8, 2009; On 7 ways to destroy India, see "India wants to compete with China, we have many ways to destroy it" ["Indu xiang he zhongguo dou, women zhengkua ta you duozhong banfa"] <www.armsky.com/BbsJunshi/bbsgaojing/200811/11653.html>.

[58] A. I. Johnston, *China and Arms Control* (Aurora Papers 3, The Canadian Centre for Arms Control and Disarmament, 1986), 13.

[59] J. W. Garver, *The Protracted Contest: Sino-Indian Rivalry in the Twentieth Century* (Seattle: University of Washington Press, 2001), 387.

Bibliography

A Report of the Pakistan Policy Working Group. (2008), *The Next Chapter: The United States and Pakistan* (Armitage International, US Institute of Peace and DynCorp International), September.

AFP. (2002), "Taiwan, India in secret military cooperation: Report," January 2, ("Wo he Indu mimi zhan kai junshi hezuo," *Lianhe xinwen* [Taipei]), <http://udnnews.com/CB/NEWS/FOCUSNEWS/POLITICS/647735.shtml>.

———. (2003), "Musharraf says no barter with N. Korea," *Dawn*, January 3.

———. (2006), "US, China, India flex muscle over energy-critical sea lanes," *Yahoo.com*, October 4.

———. (2008), "Australian PM flags military build-up as Asian powers rise," September 10, <http://www.channelnewsasia.com/stories/afp_asiapacific/view/37495//.html>.

———. (2008), "China indicates Uighur terrorists have close links with Pak," October 21, <http://feeds.bignewsnetwork.com/?rid=18846191&cat=9366300fc9319e9b>.

———. (2010), "US lawmakers fume over China's Iran links," *Channelnewsasia.com,* December 2, <http://www.channelnewsasia.com/stories/afp_asiapacific/view/1096779/1/.html>.

Afrasiabi, K. L. (2008), "A China base in Iran?" *Asia Times online*, January 29, <http://www.atimes.com/atimes/Middle_East/JA29Ak03.html>.

Agence France-Presse. (2008), "Multiple crises send Pakistan to the brink," *Pak Tribune*, October 26.

Agencies. (2006), "Pakistan will stand by China against US 'siege', says Rashid," *Daily Times* (Lahore), February 23, <www.dailytimes.com.pk/default.asp?page...23-2-2006_pg7_50>.

———. (2010), "Terrorism being fanned to destabilise economy: PC," *Indian Express*, March 10.

———. "India woos Africa to check Chinese influence," *Indian Express*, November , 2007.

Aijazuddin, F. S. (2000), From a Head, Through a Head, To a Head: The Secret Channel Between the U.S. and China through Pakistan (Oxford: Oxford University Press).

Aiyar, P. (2008), "Musharraf bolsters China-Pakistan bond," *Asia Times online*, April 24, <http://www.atimes.com/atimes/China/JD24Ad0.html>.

Akbar, M. J. (1990), *Nehru: The Making of India* (Penguin).

Analysis. (2008), "An analysis of Chinese and Indian navies' long-distance sea endurance capabilities," ["Zhong yin hai jun yuan hai jian di shi li dui bi de shen du fenxi"], May 7, <http://bbs.chinaiiss.org/dispbbs.asp?boardID=78&ID=29008&page=>.

Anthony, T. (2003), "Alliance with Islamabad shaky from start," *Washington Times*, January 11.

AP. (1996), "Atom arms parts sold to Pakistan by China, US says," *New York Times*, February 8, Al.

———. (2005), "UN: China supports Italy and Pakistan in Security Council reform," *Dawn*, June 3.

———. (2005), "Washington and Beijing will unite to block G4 plan," *Associated Press*, August 4.

APP. (2004), "India's UNSC entry without veto: China," *Dawn*, December 15.

———. (2007), "China talks tough to Pakistan on security of its nationals," *Pak Tribune*, July 18, <http://www.paktribune.com/news/index.shtml?184361>.

———. (2007), "Recent incident not to shake the bonds of Sino-Pak friendship: Cao," APP, July 19, <http://www.app.com.pk/en/index.php?option=com_content&task=view&id=303&Itemid=>.

———. (2008), "China pleads India-like nuke deal for Pakistan," *Daily Mail*, September 9, <http://dailymailnews.com/200809/09/news/dmtopstory0.html>.

———. (2008), "US asks China not to help Pakistan build nuclear plants," *Pak Tribune*, November 22, <http://paktribune.com/news/index.shtml?208224>.

Ashton, W. (1993), "Myanmar: Chinese naval base: many rumours, few facts," *Asia-Pacific Defence Reporter*, 19/20:12/1 (June/July).

———. (1995), "Chinese bases in Burma - fact or fiction," *Jane's Intelligence Review [JIR]*, 7:2 (February), 84.

———. (1998), "Burma receives advances from its silent suitors in Singapore," *JIR*, 10:3 (March), 32.

———. (1998), "Burma's armed forces: preparing for the 21st century," *JIR,* (November), 28.

AsiaInt. (2008), "China's Indian Ocean goals," *NAR*, March, <http://www.asiaint.com/arl/arl709.asp>.

———. (2009), "India wary of China's friends," *AWA*, June 5.

———. (2009), "Indian navy invited to patrol Malacca," *AsiaInt Weekly Analysis*, March 3, <http://www.asiaint.com/arl/arl2065.asp>.

AsiaInt Reference Library. (2008), "China accused of north-east India terror," *AWA*, December 12, <http://www.asiaint.com/arl/arl20058.asp>.

———. (2008), "India & China pretend friends no more," *SAR*, September, <http://www.asiaint.com/arl/arl9268.asp>.

Associated Press. (2008), "China to help build 2 Pakistan nuclear plants," *IHT*, October 18.

B. Gertz. (2003), "CIA says N. Korea tried to buy nuclear gear in 200," *Washington Times*, January 8, 3.

B. Raman. (2002), "A warning shot for Islamabad," *Asia Times online*, December 3, <http://www.atimes.com/atimes/South_Asia/DL3Df03.html>.

Baabar, M. (2006), "Pakistan: Hu Jintao visit: who, me, worry?" *Outlook*, December 11.

Badgley, J. (1994), "Myanmar in 1993," *Asian Survey*, 34:2 (February).

Bagchi, I. (2004), "China backs India for Security Council seat," *Times of India*, October 2.

———. (2007), "Buddhism new obstacle between India, China," *Times of India*, June 2.

———. (2008), "India looks to ramp up presence in Maldives," *Times of India*, January 27.

———. (2009), "Pakistan, China gang up to block India's UNSC entry," *Times of India*, March 8.

———. (2009), "Chinese media on India-bashing spree," *Times of India*, June 24.

Bajpai, K. P. and Matoo, A. (eds) (1996), *Securing India: Strategic Thought and Practi*ce (New Delhi: Manohar).

Barber, B. (2000), "Israel doesn't want US ire over China," *Washington Times*, April 14.

Baruah, A. (2004), "India may accept Security Council seat without veto," *The Hindu*, December 9.

———. (2009) "'China bashing' in the Indian media," *BBC News*, September 16, <http://news.bbc.co.uk/2/hi/south_asia/825875.stm>.

Basham, A. L. (1967), *The Wonder That Was India* (Fontana, Collins).

Bedard, P. (2003), "Washington whispers," *US News & World Report*, January 20.

Berger, B. (2007), "Why China has it wrong on Myanmar," *Asia Times online*, October 3, <http://www.atimes.com/atimes/China/IJ03Ad03.html>.

Bermudez Jr, J. S. (1998), "DPRK-Pakistan Ghauri missile cooperation," *Jane's Defence Weekly*, May 21, posted on Federation of American Scientists (FAS) <www.fas.org.>.

Bernier, J. (2003), "China's strategic proxies," *Orbis* 47, No. 4, (Fall 2003), 629–643.

Bezlova, A. (2003), "Beijing's influence on North Korea overstated," *Asia Times online*, January 11, <http://www.atimes.com/atimes/China/EAAd06.html>.

———. (2007), "China cherishes its 'jade kingdom'," *Asia Times online*, October 3, <http://www.atimes.com/atimes/China/IJ03Ad01.html>.

Bhatt, S. (2009), "The prime minister's SCO dilemma," *Rediff.com*, May 29, <http://news.rediff.com/column/2009/may/29/special-pms-sco-dilemma.htm>.

Bidwai, P. (2007), "Five-nation naval drill presages 'Asian NATO'?" *Inter-Press Service*, September 7, <http://www.ipsnews.net/news.asp?idnews=3975>.

———. (2007), "Ties with China sour as alliance with US grows," *Inter Press Service*, July 6, <http://www.ipsnews.net/news.asp?idnews=38444>.

Blainey, G. (1988), "Past and future wars," in R. Thakur (ed), *International Conflict Resolution* (Westview Press & University of Otago Press).

Blair, D. (2008) "India targeting China's oil supplies," *Telegraph*, September 4.

Blanchard, B. (2010), "China casts nervous eye at erstwhile ally Myanmar," *Reuters*, January 25, <http://www.reuters.com/article/idUSTRE60O0112010012>.

Blank, S. (2002), "Pyongyang derails Northeast Asian progress," *Asia Times online*, December 7, <http://www.atimes.com/atimes/Korea/DL7Dg0.html>.

———. (2003), "Pakistan bent on proliferation path," *Asia Times online*, January 3, <http://www.atimes.com/atimes/South_Asia/ EA03Df0.html>.

Bodansky, Y. (1995), "PRC revives military threat to Taiwan as a prelude to wider expansion," *Defense & Foreign Affairs Strategic Policy*, (July-August).

Bodeen, C. (2009), "China navy official says overseas base needed," *Associated Press*, December 3, <http://asia.news.yahoo.com/ap/2009230/tap-as-china-naval-base-bb0fb8.html>.

Bone, J. (2002), "Pakistani scientist 'offered Saddam nuclear designs'," *Times* (London), December 20.

Bowring, P. (2005), "China's growing might and the spirit of Zheng He," *International Herald Tribune* (*IHT*), August 2, 7.

Boyd, A. (2002), "India, Japan still shooting for Security Council," *Asia Times*, February 26.

Brooke, J. (2003), "China 'looming large' in South Korea as biggest player, replacing the US," *New York Times*, January 3.

Buckley, C. (2007), "China likely to swallow anger over Indo-US N-deal," *Reuters*, August 29.

Burr, W. (ed) (1999), The Kissinger Transcripts: The Top Secret Talks with Beijing and Moscow: A National Security Archive Document Reader (New York: The New Press).

———. (ed) (2002), *Henry Kissinger's Secret Trip to China: The Beijing-Washington Back-Channel September 1970-July 1971* (National Security Archive Electronic Briefing Book No. 66, February 27), <http://www.gwu.edu/ ~nsarchiv/NSAEBB/NSAEBB66/>.

Cai Xiyou. (2007), "Reflections on international oil trade friction and our country's oil trade policy," *Lilun Qianyan* [Beijing], August 5, 3-5.

Callahan, M. P. (1996), "Burma in 1995," *Asian Survey*, 36:2, (February).

Callick, R. (2007), "Pakistan violence worries Chinese," *Australian*, July 25.

Cao Changching and Seymour, J. D. (eds) (1998), *Tibet Through Dissident Chinese Eyes: Essays on Self-Determination* (New York: M. E. Sharpe).

Chand, M. (2006), "Tharoor exit not surprising," *The Pioneer*, October 4.

Chaudhuri, D. (2008), "China think-tank attacks India, calls it 'arrogant," *Hindustan Times*, April 13.

Chaulia, S. (2009), "Mental slaves," *The Statesman*, May 1, <http://www.thestatesman.net/page.arcview.php?clid=4&id=284531&usrsess=1%20<>.

———. (2009), "Sino-Indian rivalry and Asian stability," *The Globalist*, June 22, <http://www.sreeramchaulia.net/Sino-IndiaNavy.pdf>.

Chellaney B. (2007), "The quad: Australia-India-Japan-US strategic cooperation," *Asian Age*, July 3.

———. (1996), "The dragon's chicanery behind the smile," *The Pioneer*, October 23.

———. (2000), "Jiang Zemin ridicules India: Belligerence Unprovoked," *Hindustan Times*, January 3.

———. (2002), "China frets over Indo-US ties," *Washington Times*, February 2.

———. (2003), "The 100 percenters," *Hindustan Times*, June 19.

———. (2003), "Vajpayee kowtows to China," *Japan Times*, July 9.

———. (2007), “Dragon’s foothold in Gwadar, *Asian Age*, April 11.
———. (2007), “Look east, at Japan, not China,” *Asian Age*, September 7.
———. (2008), “A forward-looking approach on Burma,” *The Hindu*, May 14.
———. (2009), “India’s growing China angst,” *FEER*, September 4, 31-35.
———. (2009), “Tensions in the China-India-US triangle,” *Mint*, October 26, <http://chellaney.spaces.live.com/blog/cns!493C7C8A2EA4A30!23.entry>
———. (2010), “A smoking dragon in sheep’s clothing,” *IHT*, January 14.
Chen Tieyuan. (2001), “People are concerned over India’s ‘dream of becoming a great power’,” *Zhongguo Qingnian Bao* [*China Youth Daily*], May 8, trans. in *FBIS-CHI*.
Chen Xiangyang. (2006), “Draw up new ‘Greater Periphery Strategy’ as soon as possible,” *Liaowang* [*Outlook*], No. 29, (July 7), 64.
Chen Xiankui and Tang Wei. (2008), “Coming collapse of the hegemonic world,” *China Daily*, September 2.
Chen Xiaochen. (2009), “Illusion of ‘China’s attack on India before 2012,” July 17, <http://www.chinastakes.com/2009/7/illusion-of-chinas-attack-on-india-before-202.html>.
Cheng Ruisheng. (2008), “Yindu de waijiao zhanlue zouxiang” [“Trends in India’s Foreign Strategy”], *Guoji Wenti Yanjiu*, (March), 48-54.
Cheung, Tai Ming. (1992), “Smoke signals,” *Far Eastern Economic Review*, November 2, 29-30.
Chinese Foreign Ministry’s daily briefings. (2006, March 2), <http://www.china-embassy.org/eng/fyrth/t238267.htm>.
Ching, F. (1993), “Reforming the United Nations,” *Far Eastern Economic Review*, November 25, 36.
Christensen, T. J. (1996), “Chinese realpolitik,” *Foreign Affairs*, 75:5 (September/October).
Chua-Eoan, H. (2009), “Beyond pirates: on the high seas, an India-China rivalry,” *Time*, April 8.
Coates, A. (1972), *China, India and the Ruins of Washington* (New York: The John Day Company).
Coedes, G. (1968), *The Indianized States of Southeast Asia* (University of Hawaii Press).
Commentary (1993), “Beijing expands its navy,” *Inside China Mainland* [Taiwan], April, 67.
———. (2002), “US finds China-Libya missile link,” *Newsinsight.net*, December 20, <http://www.intelligenceonline.net/ World.asp?id=36334333604&recno=60&sub=Ge neral>.
———. (2003), “China plans to dismember north-east: CIA,” *Newsinsight.net*, November 13, <http://www.intelligenceonline.net/ allintelligencefull.asp?id=305245330241301 1&recno=2419>.
———. (2004), “Out Dalai Lama for UNSC seat, says China,” *NewsInsight.net*, October 23, <http://www.indiareacts.com/nati2.asp?recno=3002>.
———. (2005), “Is India China’s imaginative [imaginary] rival?” *People’s Daily online*, March 2.
———. (2007), “China’s maritime dilemma,” *Stratfor.com*, August 2, <http://www.stratfor.com/chinas_maritime_dilemma>.
———. (2007), “India: the Islamization of the northeast,” *Stratfor.com*, April 20.

———. (2007), "Japan still pushing the 'four-state alliance,'" *Huanqiu Shibao* [*Global Times*], August 6.

———. (2007), "Nuclear agreement and big power's dream," *People's Daily online*, August 30, <http://english.people.com.cn/9000/90780/9343/625506.html>.

———. (2008) "India wants to compete with China, we have many ways to destroy it" ["Indu xiang he zhongguo dou, women zhengkua ta you duozhong banfa"] <www.armsky.com/BbsJunshi/bbsgaojing/2008/653.html>.

———. (2008), "Asia's navies: into the wide blue yonder," The *Economist*, June 5.

———. (2008), "China: walking a fine line in alliance with Pakistan," *Stratfor Today*, October 16, <http://www.stratfor.com/analysis/20081016_china_walking_fine_line_alliance_pakistan>.

———. (2008), "India/China: fears of encirclement gradually mount," *Oxford Analytica*, November 2, <https://www.opensource.gov/providers/oxan/display.aspx?ItemID=DB46833>.

———. (2008), "Pakistan/China: pragmatism informs Beijing's support," *Oxford Analytica*, October 21, <https://www.opensource.gov/providers/oxan/display.aspx?ItemID=DB146374>.

———. (2008), "Pakistan: state faces crisis of purpose," *Oxford Analytica*, October 1, <https://www.opensource.gov/providers/oxan/display.aspx?ItemID=DB145908>.

———. (2008), "Yindu xiang he zhongguo dou, women zhengkua ta you duozhong banfa" ["India wants to compete with China, we have many ways to destroy it"], <http://www.armsky.com/BbsJunshi/bbsgaojing/2008/653.html>.

———. (2009), "India: old fears and new spur naval build-up," *Oxford Analytica*, October 9.

———. (2009), "Navies seeking better ways to battle pirates," *China.org.cn*, November 6, <http://m.china.org.cn/2009-/06/content_8838344.htm>.

———. (2010), "PLAN's Xia submarine to Pakistan?" *China Defense Blog*, May 14, <http://china-defense.blogspot.com/2010/05/plans-xia-submarine-to-pakistan.html>.

Cosmo, Nicola Di. (2002), *Ancient China and its Enemies* (Cambridge University Press).

Curtin, J. Sean (2004), "Japan-China ties on the ropes," *Asia Times Online*, October 9, <http://www.atimes.com/atimes/Japan/FJ9Dh0.html>.

Dahl, F. (2010), "Analysis: did smugglers help North Korea's nuclear drive?" *Reuters*, December 1, *<http://www.reuters.com/article/2010/12/01/us-nuclear-north-smuggling-idUSTRE6AT1OH20101201>*

Dai Bing. (2010), "India building a security barrier against China," *China.org.cn*, February 8, <http://www.china.org.cn/opinion/node_7078634.htm>.

Dao, J. (2002), "US and China resume high-level military talks," *New York Times*, December 10.

Daoxuan: Shijia Fangzhi. (Accounts of the land of Sakyamuni), written in 650, published in 924 by Ye Gongzhuo), juan , 3B, cited in Tan Chung (1987), "The Changing Indian Images in the Chinese Mind During the Nineteenth and Twentieth Centuries," Chapter 4, in Rita Sil (ed), *Images of India in World Literatures* (New Delhi: National Publishing House, 1987), 20, 9-50.

Dasgupta, S. (1994), "The Navy: in troubled waters," *India Today*, April 30.

———. (2008), "Anti-Chinese sentiment hampering border talks," *Times of India*, September 9.

———. (2009) "China suggests it blocked India's loan efforts at ADB due to border dispute," *Times of India*, April 4.

———. (2009), "China has tamed India with help from Obama," *Times of India*, November 22.

———. (2009), "China hits out at India's decision on naval symposium," *Times of India*, April 23.

———. (2010), "China mulls setting up military base in Pakistan," *Times of India*, January 28.

———. (2010), "India to question China on market access, balance of trade," *Times of India*, January 18.

Davis, A. (1990), "Burma casts wary eye on China," *Jane's Intelligence Review,* (June), 40-41.

de Borchgrave, A. (2002), "The new Afghanistan," *Washington Times*, September 2.

de Crespigny, R. (1995), "Tradition and Chinese foreign policy," in Harris, S. and Klintworth, G. (eds) (1995), *China As a Great Power* (Melbourne: Longman, and NY: St Martin's Press).

Delpech, T. (1998-99), "Nuclear weapons and the 'new world order': early warning from Asia?" *Survival*, 40:4 (Winter).

Department of Defense. (2008), *National Defense Strategy,* (Washington, DC: June).

———. (2010), *Quadrennial Defense Review* (Washington DC: February).

Department of State. (2003), "CIA report documents weapons proliferation trends," (Washington DC: January 7), <http://www.satribune.com/archives/jan3_9_03/P_targets.htm>.

Deshpande, R. (2008), "NSA confirms China's NSG hostility to govt," *Times of India*, September 2.

DeYoung, K. (2011), "New estimates put Pakistan's nuclear arsenal at more than 100," *Washington Post*, January 31, 2011.

Dikotter, F. (ed) (1997), The Construction of Racial Identities in China and Japan (London: Hurst and Company).

Document. (2004), *China, Pakistan, and the Bomb: The Declassified File on U.S. Policy, 1977–1997,* <http://www.gwu.edu/~nsarchiv/NSAEBB/NSAEBB114/press.htm>.

———. (2005), "Treaty of friendship, cooperation and good neighbourly relations between the People's Republic of China and the Islamic Republic of Pakistan," Ministry of Foreign Affairs of the People's Republic of China, April 5, 2005 <http://fmprc.gov.cn/eng/ziliao>3602/3604/default.htm>.

Doll, Steve. (1997), "China's record of proliferation misbehavior," *Issue Brief,* (Washington: Nuclear Control Institute), September 29.

Doyle, L. (2002), "Pakistan is a rogue nation that supports terror," *Independent* (London), December 2, <http://news.independent.co.uk/world/asia_china/story.jsp?story=360795>.

E. Ahrari. (1998, August), "Sino-Indian nuclear perspectives," *JIR*, 33.

Eckholm, E. (2000), "China says US missile shield could force an arms buildup," *New York Times*, May 11.

Editorial. (2003), "US dreams of Asian NATO," *People's Daily online*, July 9.

———. (2003), "Why doesn't US 'use force' against DPRK?" *People's Daily online*, January 8, <http://english.peopledaily.com.cn/20030/08/eng2003008_09768.shtml>.

———. (2005), "East Asia summit: in the shadow of sharp divisions," *People's Daily online*, December 7.

———. (2005), "US-Indian alliance against China," *Ming Pao*, August 7, FBIS-CPP2005087000043.

———. (2005), "Washington draws India in against China," *People's Daily online*, July 7.

———. (2007), "A 'goodwill' joint naval drill?" *People's Daily,* April 2, <http://english.people.com.cn/200704/2/eng2007042_36852.html>.

———. (2007), "China's satellite," *The Irrawaddy*, July 10.

———. (2007), "India's identity crisis in Myanmar," *Boston Globe*, October 15.

———. (2007), "Love with Tokyo," *Indian Express*, August 24.

———. (2009), "India's unwise military moves," *Global Times*, June 11, <http://opinion.globaltimes.cn/editorial/2009-06/43674.html>.

———. (2009), "The China tantrum," *Times of India*, April 17.

———. (2009), "Truth about India ties," *China Daily*, September 10, <http://www.chinadaily.com.cn/opinion/2009-09/0/content_8674482.htm>.

———. (2009), "Why India is pursuing military strength," *People's Daily online*, August 20.

———. (2010), "Growing Chinese navy no cause for fear," *Global Times*, April 27, <http://opinion.globaltimes.cn/editorial/200-04/52692.html>.

———. (2010), "India"s surprising but welcome message, *Global Times*, February 22, <http://opinion.globaltimes.cn/editorial/2010-02/506893.html>.

Einhorn, R. (1997), deputy assistant secretary of state for nonproliferation, Testimony before the Senate Governmental Affairs Committee, Subcommittee on International Security, reported in "State Dept. Revises Report on China's Arms Sales to Iran," *Washington Times*, April 5, A3.

Ejaz, M. (2002), "Washington diary: Pakistan and proliferation issue," *The News*, December 22.

Engardio, P. (2007), Chindia: How China and India Are Revolutionizing Global Business (McGraw Hill).

Fairclough, G. (2007), "As China grows, so does its long neglected navy,' *Wall Street Journal*, July 6.

Fazal-ur-Rahman. (2006), "Pakistan-China economic relations: opportunities and challenges," *Strategic Studies* (Islamabad), XXVI: 2 (Summer), 53–72.

Fazl-e-Haider, S. (2006), "China digs Pakistan into a hole," *Asia Times online*, October 5, <http://www.atimes.com/atimes/South_Asia/HJ05Df01.html>.

———. (2006), "China's growing stake in Pakistan," *Asia Times online*, November 30, <http://www.atimes.com/atimes/South_Asia/HK30Df0.html>.

Feigenbaum, E. A. (2010), "India's rise, America's interest," *Foreign Affairs*, (March/April).

Ford, P. (2009), "Rivals China, India in escalating war of words," *Christian Science Monitor*, October 20, <http://www.csmonitor.com/2009/020/p06s04-woap.html>.

Frankel F. and Harding H. (eds) (2004), *The India-China Relationship* (Columbia University Press).

Fu Xiaoqiang. (2006), "Sino-Pakistani ties usher in a vast room for development," *People's Daily*, November 24.

Funabashi, Y. (2003) "A critical test for Japan's diplomacy," *PacNet 2*, January 9.

G. Kampani. (2002), "Second-tier proliferation: the case of Pakistan and North Korea," *Nonproliferation Review*, (Fall/Winter), 107-116.

Garrett, B. N. and Glaser, B. S. (1995/96), "Chinese perspectives on nuclear arms control," *International Security*, 20:3 (Winter).

Garthoff, R. L. (1994), *Détente and Confrontation: American-Soviet Relations from Nixon to Reagan* (Washington, D.C.: Brookings Institution), esp. chap. 8.

Garver, J. W. (1987), "Chinese-Indian rivalry in Indochina," *Asian Survey,* 27:11 (November 1987), 1216-17.

———. (1992), "China and South Asia," Annals of the American Academy of Politics & Social Sciences, 519.

———. (1999), "Nuclear weapons and the China-India relationship," paper presented at conference on "South Asia's Nuclear Dilemma," Weatherhead Center for International Affairs, Harvard University, February 8-9.

———. (2001), *Protracted Contest: Sino-Indian Rivalry in the Twentieth Century* (Seattle and London: University of Washington Press, 200), 2-6.

———. (2002), "Could it happen again?" *Rediff.com*, November 2, <http://www.rediff.com/news/2002/nov/02chin.htm>.

———. (2002), "The China-India-U.S. triangle," *NBR Analysis*, 3:5 (October).

———. (2005), "China's South Asian interests and policies." Testimony prepared for panel on "China's Approaches to South Asia and the Former Soviet States," US-China Economic and Security Review Commission, July 22, <http://www.uscc.gov/hearings/2005hearings/written_testimonies/05_07_2_22wrts/garver_john_wrts.htm>.

———. (2006), "China's decision for war with India in 1962," Chapter 4 in Johnston, A. I. and Ross, R. S. (eds), *New Directions in the Study of China's Foreign Policy* (Stanford University Press), 86-30.

———. (2006), "Development of China's Overland Transportation Links with Central, South-west and South Asia," *China Quarterly*, 185 (March).

———. (2001), The Protracted Contest: Sino-Indian Rivalry in the Twentieth Century (Seattle: University of Washington Press), 387.

Gautam, B. (2003), "How long will U.S. ignore Pakistan threat?" *Japan Times*, January 3.

Genser, J. (2006), "China's role in the world: the China-Burma relationship," Testimony to the U.S.-China Economic and Security Review Commission, August 3, <http://www.uscc.gov/hearings/2006hearings/transcripts/aug_3_4/testimony_jared_genser.pdf>.

Gertz, B. (1996), "China aids Pakistani plutonium plant," *Washington Times*, April 3, A4.

———. (1996), "China sold Iran missile technology," *Washington Times*, November 2, A1.

———. (1999), "China still shipping arms despite pledges," *Washington Times*, April 5.

———. (2002), "China ships North Korea ingredient for nuclear arms," *Washington Times*, December 7.

———. (2002), "China's arms sales, stance on Taiwan chill talks with US," *Washington Times*, December 10.

———. (2002), "N. Korea seeks aid from China on nukes," *Washington Times*, December 9.

———. (2002), "Panel to probe China's nuclear-related sales to N. Korea," *Washington Times*, December 20.

———. (2003), "CIA says N. Korea tried to buy nuclear gear in 200," *Washington Times*, January 8.

———. (2003), "Israel asked to stop arms sales to China," *Washington Times*, January 3.

———. (2011), "Chinese firm tied to steel used in Iran nukes: state warned Beijing on sale," *Washington Times*, January 24, 1.

———. (2006), "Congressional study cites China as nuc supplier to North Korea," *Washington Times*, October 31.

Gharekhan, C. R. (2004), "Join the club," *Hindustan Times*, December 7.

Ghosh, P. K. (2007), "Indian Ocean shipping: imperatives of cargo and energy flows." Presentation to the Asian Energy Security Conference, Jackson, Mississippi, October 2.

Giacomo, C. (2006), "China's role in peaceful world questioned," *Reuters*, October 31.

Gilley, B. (2009), "Look to Brasilia, not Beijing: The rising challenge to China's great power aspirations," *Wall Street Journal*, April 7.

Giridharadas, A. (2008), "Land of Gandhi asserts itself as global military power," *IHT*, September 22.

Glain, S. (2008), "The modern silk road," *Newsweek*, May 26-June 2, 32-33.

Goldstein, L. J. (2001), "Return to Zhenbao Island: who started shooting and why it matters," *The China Quarterly*, 168 (December).

Gopal, S. (1979), *Jawaharlal Nehru: A Biography* (Oxford University Press).

Government of the People's Republic of China. (n.d.) *The Sino-Indian Boundary Question* (Peking: Foreign Languages Press, 965), 39.

Guha, S. (2009), "India and China: A clash of ideologies," *UPI Asia online*, September 6, <http://www.upiasia.com/Politics/2009/09/6/india_and_china_a_clash_of_ideologies/7684/>.

Gumaste, V. (2009), "India and China: It was a stab from the front," *Rediff.com*, August 25, <http://news.rediff.com/slide-show/2009/aug/25/slide-show--a-stab-from-the-front.htm>.

Gupta, S. and Chakravarti, S. (1993), "Sino-Indian relations: vital breakthrough," *India Today*, September 30.

Hale, D. (2004), "China's growing appetites," *National Interest*, 76 (Summer), 37-47.

Halevi, Y. Klein. (2001), "Islam must challenge its dark doctrines," *Los Angeles Times*, September 13.

Haniffa, A. (2009), "India-US ties, the three-card trick" *Rediff.com*, November 24, <http://news.rediff.com/report/2009/nov/23/india-us-ties-the-three-card-trick.htm>.

Hariharan, R. (2007), "India–China–Myanmar relations," July 21, <http://www.newdelhireview.com>.

Harrison, S. S. (2011), "China's North Korean calculations," *IHT*, January 6, <http://www.nytimes.com/2011/01/07/opinion/07iht-edharrison07.html?_r=1&ref=global-home>.

Hayashi Y. and Schlesinger, J. M. (2010), "Tokyo grows wary of China military," *Wall Street Journal*, May 4.

Henderson, J. (1999), *Reassessing ASEAN,* Adelphi Paper 328 (London: International Institute for Strategic Studies).

Henriksen T. and Walker, C. (2001), "Seeking surrogates to challenge the US," *Global Beat Syndicate*, April 25, <http://www.nyu.edu/globalbeat/syndicate/Walker04250.html>.

Hersh, S. M. (1983), *The Price of Power* (Summit).

———. (2003), "The cold test," *New Yorker*, January 27.

Hibbs, M. (1994), "No US agency consensus on DPRK nuclear progress," *Nucleonics Week*, January 6, 10.

Hill, J. (2002), "China offended by US 'threat' theory,'" *Jane's Intelligence Review*, (September), 10.

Hinton, H. C. (1994), "China as an Asian power," in Robinson, T. W. and Shambaugh, D. (eds) (1994), *Chinese Foreign Policy: Theory and Practice* (Clarendon Press).

Hoagland, J. (2002), "Nuclear enabler: Pakistan today is the most dangerous place on Earth," *Washington Post*, October 24.

Hoffman, S. A. (1990), *India and the China Crisis* (Berkeley/London: University of California Press).

Hoge, W. (2004), "UN report urges big changes; Security Council would expand," *New York Times*, December 1.

———. (2007), "China blocks move to condemn Myanmar, but backs UN envoy," *IHT*, September 27.

Holmes, J. (2007), "China's energy consumption and opportunities for US-China cooperation to address the effects of China's energy use," Testimony before the US-China Economic and Security Review Commission, Washington DC, June 4, <http://www.uscc.gov/hearings/2007hearings/written_testimonies/07_06_4_5wrts/07_06_4_holmes_statement.pdf>.

Hu Yumin. (1999), "The US post-Cold War nonproliferation policy," *International Strategic Studies*, (Beijing), 3 (July).

Hua Biyun. (1996), "Yindu lizheng chengwei xia shiji de jingji daguo" ["India: Striving to be an economic power in the next century"], *Xiandai Guoji Guanxi* [*Contemporary International Relations*], 75:1, (January).

IANS. (2009), "India, China not rivals, but partners in emerging Asia: S M Krishna," *Times of India*, July 22.

———. (2009), "Disconnect emerges in India-US military views," May 4, <http://www.thaindian.com/newsportal/uncategorized/disconnect-emerges-in-india-us-military-views_009253.html>.

Ikenberry, G. J. and Slaughter, A. M. (2006), "A bigger Security Council, with power to act," *International Herald Tribune* [*IHT*], September 26.

Indian Ministry of Defence. (May). *Freedom of the Seas: India's Maritime Military Strategy* (New Delhi: Integrated Headquarters of the Ministry of Defence (Navy).

Iqbal, A. (2002) "US studies Pakistan, Saudi N-ties: report," *Dawn* (Karachi), August 2.

———. (2003), "Dr Qadeer suspected of links with 'axis of evil' states," *Dawn*, January 8.

Jacques, M. (2009), *When China Rules the World* (New York: The Penguin Press).

Jagannathan, R. (2009), "The China challenge," *Daily News and Analysis Online*, June 17, <http://www.dnaindia.com/opinion/column_the-china-challenge_1265849>.

Jaishankar, D. (2009), "Foreign policy challenges for UPA 2.0," *Pragati: The Indian National Interest Review*, July <http://pragati.nationalinterest.in/2009/07/foreign-policy-challenges-for-upa-20/>.

Jha, S. (2009), "India uneasy with Obama's Chinese checkers," *UPI Asia online*, November 7, <http://www.upiasia.com/Politics/2009//7/india_uneasy_with_obamas_chinese_checkers/4395/>.

Jia Qingguo. (2009), "Realizing the Asia-Pacific community," *East Asia Forum*, July 28.

Jian Hua. (2001), "The United States, Japan want to rope in India which cherishes the dream of becoming a major power," *Ta Kung Pao* (Hong Kong), June 4, trans. in *FBIS-China*.

Jian Junbo. (2009), "China wary of US-Myanmar 'détente," *Asia Times online*, April 17, <http://www.atimes.com/atimes/China/KD17Ad01.html>.

JID (2002), "Asia's nuclear axis," *Jane's Intelligence Digest*, November 6.

Johnston, A. I. (1986), *China and Arms Control* (Aurora Papers 3, The Canadian Centre for Arms Control and Disarmament), 3.

———. (1995), Cultural Realism: Strategic Culture and Grand Strategy in Chinese History (New Jersey: Princeton University Press).

JPRS (1974), "*Mao Zedong sixiang wansui*" ["Long live Mao Zedong thought"], in *Miscellany of Mao Tse-tong Thought* (1949-1968), 2, No. 61269 (February 20, 1974), Joint Publication Research Service, 573.

Kan, S. A. (1998), *Chinese Proliferation of Weapons of Mass Destruction*, CRS Issue Brief 92056, *Current Policy Issues*, (June 1).

———. (2002), *China and Proliferation of Weapons of Mass Destruction and Missiles: Policy Issues* (Washington DC: Report for Congress, Congressional Research Service, December 4) <http://www.fas.org/spp/starwars/crs/RL3555.pdf>.

———. (2006), "China and proliferation of WMD and missiles: policy issues," *Congressional Research Service* (Library of Congress Report, Order Code RL31555, updated August 8), http://www.fas.org/spp/starwars/crs/RL31555.pdf.

Kaplan, R. (2009), "Center stage for the 21st century: rivalry in the Indian Ocean," *Foreign Affairs*, 88:2 (March/April).

Kaplan, Robert D. (2008), "Lifting the bamboo curtain," *Atlantic Monthly*, September.

Kapur, D. and Subramanian, A. (2008), "Aid and the unraveling of Pakistan," *Newsweek*, January 21.

Karl, D. J. (2008), "Three events tell a tale of two Indias," *PacNet*, No. 67, December 23.

Katzenstein P. J. (ed) (1996), *The Culture of National Security: Norms and Identity in World Politics* (New York: Columbia University Press).

Kautilya. (1987), *The Arthashastra* (New Delhi: Penguin Books), 541-680.

Kaye, L. (1993), "Bordering on peace," *Far Eastern Economic Review,* September 16.

Kazmin, A. (2007), "Russia to build nuclear reactor for Burma," *Financial Times*, May 15.

Kazmin A. and Luce, E. (2009), "India feels the chill as US warms to China," *Financial times*, November 22.

Keating, J. E. (2010), "Beijing's most embarrassing allies," *Foreign Policy*, May 24, <http://www.foreignpolicy.com/articles/2010/05/24/beijing_s_most_embarrassing_allies>.

Kelly, M. (2003), "Kick the (Korea) can," *Washington Post*, January 8.

Kessler, G. (2002), "Powell says Pakistan warned on N. Korean ties: Musharraf told he will face 'consequences' if nuclear transfers continue," *Washington Post*, November 26.

———. (2010), "Questionable China-Pakistan deal draws little comment from U.S.," *Washington Post*, May 20, A11.

Khajuria, K. S. Lt Gen (Retd). (1993), "Security in South West Asia region post-Cold War…," *Indian Defence Review*, (July).

Khalilzad, Z. et al. (2001), *The United States and Asia: Toward a New U.S. Strategy and Force Posture* (Santa Monica, Calif.: Rand Corporation), 203-3.

Khan, B. Alam. (2004), "China, Pakistan to strengthen defence ties," *Dawn*, December 7.

Khan, J. Ayaz, Maj. Gen. (retd). (2006), "Coming of Hu Jintao is sweeter than honey," *Pakistan Observer*, December 1, <http://pakobserver.net/20062/0/Articles0.asp>.

Khanna, P. (2003), "One more seat at the table," *New York Times*, December 6.

Khanna, T. (2008), *Billions of Entrepreneurs* (Harvard Business School Press).

Khurana, G. S. (2008), "China's 'string of pearls' in the Indian Ocean and its security implications," *Strategic Analysis*, 32:1, (January).

———. (2009), "China-India maritime rivalry," *Indian Defence Review*, 23:4 (July-September) <http://www.indiandefencereview.com/2009/04/china-india-maritime-rivalry.html>.

———. (2004), "Maritime security in the Indian Ocean," *Strategic Analysis*, 28:3 (July-September).

Kim Min-seok and Oh Young-hwan. (2002), "Iran said to be buyer of north missiles," *JoongAng Ilbo*, December 9, <http://english.joins.com/Article.asp?aid=20022902455&sid=200>.

Kissinger, H. A. (1979), *White House Years* (New York: Little Brown).

Klein, Y. (1991), "A theory of strategic culture," *Comparative Strategy*, 10:2 (January-March), 5.

———. (1991), "A theory of strategic culture," *Comparative Strategy*, 10:2 (199), 5-17.

Kondapalli, S. (2006), "The Chinese military eyes South Asia," in Scobell, A. and Wortzel, L. (eds), *Shaping China's Security Environment* (PA: Strategic Studies Institute, US Army War College), 197–245.

———. (2007), "Why Japan and India are moving closer," *Rediff.com*, August 23, <http://www.rediff.com/news/2007/aug/23guest.htm>.

———. (2008), "The Chinese threat in the Indian Ocean," *Rediff.com*, May 8, <http://www.rediff.com/news/2008/may/08guest.htm>.

Kranti, V. (2003), "China and the central issue," *The Pioneer*, June 23.
Krauthammer, C. (2003), "The Japan card," *Washington Post*, January 3.
Kremmer, C. (2001), "Sub-continent fights forces of darkness," *The Age*, December 29.
Kuehner, T. (2008), "Robert Kaplan on the new balance of power," *FPRI.org*, April, <http://www.fpri.org/enotes/200804.kuehner.kaplannewbalanceofpower.html>.
Kugler J. et al. (2001), "Power transitions and alliances in the 21st century," *Asian Perspective*, 25:3, 5-29.
Kumar, Y. (2006), "Hu, Pakistan and the 'string of pearls'," *Rediff.com*, November 28.
Kurlantzick, J. (2007), "Burma's buddy—India's craven appeasement in Burma," *New Republic*, October 2.
Ladwig, W. C. (2009), "Delhi's Pacific ambition," *Asian Security*, 5:2, 87-113.
Lai Yuan. (2008), "Injun zai zhongyin bianji…" ("Indian Army on the China-India border"), March 16, <http://www.warchina.com/n53470c4.aspx>; <http://str.chinaiiss.org/content/2008-3-26/262952.shtml>.
Lal, N. (2010), "India, Russia and the U.S.: three's a crowd?" *World Politics Review*, April 6, <http://www.worldpoliticsreview.com/article.aspx?id=5378>.
Lamont, J. and Bokhari, F. (2009), "China-Pakistan military links upset India," *Financial Times*, November 27.
Lamont J. and Dyer G. (2010), "India offers to protect China oil shipments," *Financial Times,* February 7, <http://www.ft.com/cms/s/0/6788f896-be8-df-a5e-0044feab49a.html>.
Lamont, J. and K. Hille. (2009), "Chinese essay sparks outcry in India," *Financial Times*, August 12.
Lamont, J. and Kazmin, A. (2009), "Fear of influence," *Financial Times*, July 12.
Lan Jianxue. (2008), "Zhong yin duiwai zhanlue yitong yu shuangbian guanxi" ["Differences and similarities in foreign strategies of China and India and their bilateral relations"], *Waijiao Pinglun* [*Foreign Affairs Review*] (Beijing), No. 103 (June), 37-43.
Landler, M. (2010), "Obama urges China to check North Koreans," *New York Times*, December 7.
Lee, J. (2010), "The fantasy of taming China's rise," *CIS Foreign Policy Analysis*, 3 (May 6), 8-9.
Lee, P. (2009), "Beijing broods over its arc of anxiety," *Asia Times online*, December 4, <http://www.atimes.com/atimes/China/KL04Ad0.html>.
Lennox, D. (1999), "Control regimes fail to stem the spread," *JIR*, (September), 50-54.
Leonard, M. (2008), "The rise of China's neocons," *Newsweek*, March 8.
Li Hongmei (2009), "Indian media stinks up public opinion," *People's Daily online*, September 5, <http://english.peopledaily.com.cn/90002/9647/6758363.html>.
———. (2009), "Veiled threat or good neighbor?" *People's Daily online*, June 9, <http://english.peopledaily.com.cn/90002/9647/6682302.html>.
———. (2009), "What is beyond the physical line?" *People's Daily Online*, August 2, <http://english.people.com.cn/9000/90780/index.html>.

Li Qiulin. (2009), "Mei In jia qiang junshi he zuo gaibian nanya zhan lue geju" ["Strengthened US-India military cooperation will change strategic pattern in South Asia"], *Xueshi Shibao* [*Study Times*], reproduced in *Qiu Shi*, September 14, <http://www.qsjournal.com.cn/gj/gjgc/200909/t2009094_445.htm>.

Li Yincai. (2009), "Yindu waijiao neng zou duo yuan?" ["How far will India's diplomacy go?"] *Zhongguo Xinwengang*, February 17, <http://world.people.com.cn/GB/4549/887892.html>.

Liang Chen. (2009), "Chinese Web post causes ire in India Source," *Global Times*, August 20, <http://globaltimes.cn/www/english/top-news/2009-08/459440.html>.

Liao Yameng. (2003), "Expert analyzes the 'balancing' strategies of China, India and Pakistan," *Wen Wei Po*, November 7, FBIS-CHI-2003-1107, November 13.

Lim, R. (2003), "Korea in the vortex," *China Brief*, 3:1 (January 14).

Lin Xia. (1993), "Indo-Russian relations enter a new era," *Beijing Review,* February 15-21.

Lintner, B. (1992), "Burma: centrifugal forces," *Far Eastern Economic Review* [hereafter *FEER*], February 27, 16.

———. (1993), "Burma: arms for eyes," *FEER*, December 16, 26.

———. (1993), "Murmur in the ranks," *FEER*, February 16.

———. (1993), "Rangoon's rubicon," *FEER*, February 11.

———. (1994), *Burma in Revolt: Opium and Insurgency since 1948* (Boulder, Colorado: Westview Press).

———. (2007), "Trade and security trump democracy in Burma," *YaleGlobal online*, October 3, <http://yaleglobal.yale.edu/display.article?id=9754>.

———. (2008), "Burma's nuclear temptation," *YaleGlobal Online*, December 3, <http://yaleglobal.yale.edu/display.article?id=11673>.

———. (2011), "North Korea's missiles aimed for Iran," *Asia Times online*, January 12, <http://www.atimes.com/atimes/Korea/MA12Dg01.html>.

Liu Li. (2005), "Gongtong erzhi zhongguo: meiyin qiaoding shinian junshi hezuo" ["Jointly containing China: US and India nail ten-year military cooperation package"], *Dongfang Zaobao* [*Oriental Morning Post*], June 30.

Liu Mingfu, Senior Colonel. (2010), *China Dream [Zhongguo meng]* (Beijing: Zhongguo youyi chuban gongsi).

Liu Naiqiang. (2007), "China's energy diplomacy faces challenges ahead," *Nanfeng Chuang* [Guangzhou], November 16, 22-24.

Liu Xuecheng. (1994), *The Sino-Indian Border Dispute and Sino-Indian Relations* (Lanham, Md.: University Press of America).

Loudon, B. (2007), "India, China in clash at summit," *Australian*, April 4.

———. (2007), "Indo-US military links spook Beijing," *Australian*, April 12.

Lu Desheng. (2008), "'Africa craze' promotes win-win for all parties," *Jiefangjun Bao*, April 6, 8.

Lu Jianren. (2006), "Is this Asia's century?" *Beijing Review*, April 2, 8.

M. Lerner. (2003),"North Korea weapons a nuclear nightmare," *Washington Times*, January 7.

Ma Jiali. (2002), Notice India: A Big Rising Country on the Rise (Tianjin: People's Press).

———. (2009), "Drive for nuclear energy," *Beijing Review*, September 3, 5.

MacDonald, J. (2007), "Overview of global and Asian energy trends." Paper presented at the "Asian Energy Security." Conference at MSU, Mississippi State University, October -2, 2007.

———. (2007), *Energy Futures in Asia: Perspectives on India's Energy Security Strategy and Policies* (June, Prepared for Director, Net Assessments, Department of Defense), 5-22, 23.

MacDonald, J., Danyluk, B. and Donahue, A. (2005), *Perspectives on China: A View from India*, Prepared for Director, Net Assessment, Office of the Secretary of Defense, (Booze, Allen & Hamilton, December).

Maddison, A. (2001), *The World Economy: A Millennial Perspective* (OECD Development Centre).

Maitra, R. (2004), "All at sea in the Indian Ocean," *Asia Times online*, January 2, <http://www.atimes.com/atimes/South_Asia/FA2Df02.html>.

Malik, J. Mohan. (1989), "Hands across the Himalayas," *Pacific Defence Reporter,* (March), 43-45.

———. (1993), "India copes with the Kremlin's fall," *Orbis*, 37:1 (Winter), 69-87.

———. (1994), "Sino-Indian rivalry in Myanmar: implications for regional security," *Contemporary Southeast Asia*, 16:2 (September), 137-156.

———. (1995), "China-India relations in the post-Soviet era: the continuing rivalry," *China Quarterly,* 142 (June), 317-355.

———. (1999), "The India-China divide" *Hindustan Times*, May 24.

———. (2000), "China and the nuclear non-proliferation regime," *Contemporary Southeast Asia*, 22:3 (December), 445-478.

———. (2000), "China edgy over Clinton's India visit," *The Pioneer*, March 2, 8.

———. (2000), "India in a China shop," *Hindustan Times*, February 24.

———. (2001), "South Asia in China's foreign relations," *Pacifica Review*, 13:1 (February), 73-85.

———. (2002), "Zhou, Mao, and Nixon's 1972 conversations on India," *Issues & Studies: An International Quarterly on China, Taiwan & East Asian Affairs*, 38:3 (September), 84-29.

———. (2005), "Security Council reform: China signals its veto," *World Policy Journal*, 22: (Spring), 9-29.

———. "Dragon on terrorism: assessing China's tactical gains and strategic losses after 11 September," *Contemporary Southeast Asia*, 24:2 (August 2002), 277-280.

———. (2005), "Regime shake-up in Rangoon: a setback for Beijing?" *China Brief*, 5:2 (January 18), 1-5.

———. (1991), "Nuclear proliferation in Asia: the China factor," *Australian Journal of International Affairs*, 53:1, (April), 31-41.

———. (1993), "The Korean Peninsula: conflict or peace?" *Current Affairs Bulletin* (Sydney), 69:12 (May), 4-12.

———. (1999), "China's Asia policy: restrain Japan, contain India," *Japan Times*, June 12, 21.

———. (2000), "Burma's role in regional security," in Peterson, M. B., Rudland, E. , May, R. J. (eds), *Burma/Myanmar: Strong Regime Weak State?* (London and Adelaide: C. Hurst & Co/Crawford House Publishing),

———. (2000), "China plays 'the proliferation card'," *Jane's Intelligence Review*, 2:7 (July), 34-37.

———. (2003), "The China factor in the India-Pakistan conflict," *Parameters*, (Spring), 1-16.

———. (2003), "The proliferation axis," *Korean Journal of Defense Analysis*, 15:1, (Spring) 2003, 57-100. 2004).

———. (2004), "Dr Khan's China connection," *China Brief*, 4:9 (April 29), <http://www.jamestown.org/publications_details.php?volume_id=395&iss ue_id=2939&article_id=23663>.

———. (2005), "The East Asia Summit: more discord than accord" *YaleGlobal Online*, December 20, <http://yaleglobal.yale.edu/display.article?id=6645>.

———. (2006), "China responds to the U.S.-India nuclear deal," *China Brief*, 6:7 (March 29) <http://www.jamestown.org/publications_details.php?volume_id=45&issue_id=3670&article_id=2370926>.

———. (2006), "China's strategy of containing India," *The Power & Interest News Report*, February 6, <http://www.pinr.com/report.php?ac=view_report&report_id=434>

———. (2006), "Multilateralism Shanghaied," *International Assessment & Strategy Center*, July 4, <http://www.strategycenter.net/research/pubID.5/pub_detail.asp>.

———. (2006), "The East Asian Summit," *Australian Journal of International Affairs*, 60:2 (June), 207-211.

———. (2007), "India-China competition revealed in ongoing border dispute," *Power and Interest News Report*, October 10.

———. (2009), "War talk: perceptual gaps in 'Chindia' relations," *China Brief*, 9:20 (October 7), 6-9, < http://www.jamestown.org/single/?no_cache=1&tx_ttnews%5Btt_news%5D=35589

———. (2010), "China unveils 'the Kashmir Card'," *China Brief*, X:19 (September 24), <http://www.jamestown.org/programs/chinabrief/single/?tx_ttnews%5Btt_news%5D=3695&tx_ttnews%5BbackPid%5D=25&cHash=078d3aabd3>.

———. (2010), "Resolving the Burma imbroglio" in R. Wirsing (ed), *Fixing Fractured Nations* (Palgrave), 57-82.

———. (2010), "The Shanghai Cooperation Organization" in S. Ganguly, A. Scobell and J. C. Liow (eds), *The Routledge Handbook of Asian Security* (Routledge, 2010), Chapter 6, 72-86.

Malik, V. P. (2006), *Kargil: From Surprise to Victory* (HarperCollins), 297–302.

Mapes, T. (1996), "Nervous neighbours," *FEER*, December 12.

Mathew, T. (2009), "Mighty dragon in the sea," *Hindustan Times*, June 23.

Matthews, B. (1998), "The present fortune of tradition-bound authoritarianism in Myanmar," *Pacific Affairs,* 71:1, 7-23.

Maung Than. (1999), "Myanmar: Myanmar-ness and realism in historical perspective," in Booth K. and Trood R. (eds), *Strategic Cultures in the Asia-Pacific Region* (New York: St. Martin's Press).

Maxwell, N. (1972), *India's China War* (New York: Anchor Books).

———. (1973), "The Chinese account of the 1969 fighting at Chenpao," *The China Quarterly*, 56 (October/December 973), 730-39.

Mazza, M. (2010), "China and the lost pearls," *The American*, April 23, <http://www.american.com/archive/200/april/china-and-the-lost-pearls>.

McCartan, B. (2008), "China's footprint in Myanmar expands," *Asia Times online*, November 1, <http://www.atimes.com/atimes/China_Business/JK01Cb02.html>.

McDonald, H. (2003), "Beijing content with the devil it knows, despite Pyongyang's nuclear threat," *Age* (Melbourne), January 14.

McLean, R. T. (2006), "China heads west," *FrontPageMagazine.com*, March 2, <http://www.frontpagemag.com/Articles/ReadA...le.asp?ID=2487>.

Mearsheimer, J. (1994-1995), "The false promise of international institutions," *International Security*, 9:3 (Winter), 5-49.

Medcalf, R. (2008), "Securing the sea-lanes: China's gunboat diplomacy," *New York Times*, December 28, <http://www.nytimes.com/2008/2/28/opinion/28iht-edmedcalf..895546.html?_r=>.

———. (2009), "Chinese naval proposal wrong-headed," *The Interpreter*, November 24, <http://www.lowyinterpreter.org/post/2009//24/Time-to-burst-Chinas-mooted-exclusive-naval-zones.aspx>.

———. (2010), "India ahoy," *Wall Street Journal*, April 29.

Menon, N. (2008), "State, strategy, power, and policy analyzing China and India," *Indian Defence Review*, 23:3 (July-September).

Meredith, R. (2008), *The Elephant and the Dragon* (W. W. Norton).

Milhollin, G. (1997), "China cheats (what a surprise!)," *New York Times*, April 24, A35.

Milhollin G. and White, G. (1999), "A new China syndrome: China's arms bazaar," *Washington Post*, May 2, C1- C4.

Mishra, B. (2010), "China's positioning on the border is very aggressive," *Rediff.com*, April 3, <http://news.rediff.com/report/2010/apr/03/chinas-positioning-on-the-border-is-very-aggressive.htm>.

Mitra, N. (1992), "Corning closer," *Sunday,* August 23-29.

Mohan, C Raja. (2002), "China's back door," *The Hindu*, April 7.

———. (2003), "Sino-Indian boundary talks," *The Hindu*, October 23.

———. (2004), "Does the UN matter?" *Indian Express*, November 30.

———. (2005), "China's anti-G4 line may be a lose-lose policy," *Indian Express*, June 3.

———. (2005), "SAARC reality check: China just tore up India's Monroe doctrine," *Indian Express*, November 4.

———. (2006), "End of long nuke winter," *Indian Express*, 10, <http://www.indianexpress.com/iep/sunday/story/18275.html>.

———. (2007), "Coonoor cunundrum," *Indian Express*, April 20.

———. (2007), "Two PMs, one problem: China," *Indian Express*, August 2, <http://www.indianexpress.com/story/2558.html>.

———. (2010), "Old friends in a new world," *Indian Express*, March 2.

Monk, P. (2008), "Sanya base to float Chinese naval ambition,' *The Age*, May 26.

Moore, M. (2008), "China extends influence into Central Asia," *Telegraph*, October 17.

Mukarji, A. (2001), "ISI's main source of funds is now China," *Hindustan Times*, February 22.

Musharraf , P. (2006), "The will to cooperate," *Beijing Review*, March 2.

Naidu, G. V. C. (2000), *Indian Navy and Southeast Asia* (New Delhi: Knowledge World).

Neuffer, E. (2002), “A US concern: Pakistan’s arsenal,” *Boston Globe*, August 6.

Niazi, T. (2005), “Gwadar: China’s naval outpost on the Indian Ocean,’ *China Brief*, 5:4 (February 5), <http://www.jamestown.org/publications_details.php?volume_id=408&issue_id=3232&article_id=2369262>.

———. (2007), “China, Pakistan, and terrorism,” *Foreign Policy in Focus*, July 16, <http://www.fpif.org/fpiftxt/4384>.

Nixon, R. (1978), *RN: The Memoirs of Richard Nixon* (New York: Grosset & Dunlap).

Noorani, A. G. (2007), “Very unrealpolitik,” *Hindustan Times*, October 22.

Ojha, I. C. (1971), Chinese Foreign Policy in an Age of Transition (Boston: Beacon Press).

Olesen, A. (2006), “Why China reluctant to board ships of N. Korea,” *Philadelphia Inquirer*, October 18.

Opall, B. (1995), “US queries China on Iran: fears transfer of missile technology,” *Defense News*, June 19-25.

Opinion. (2005), “Washington draws India in against China,” *People’s Daily online*, July 7, <http://english.people.com.cn/200507/07/eng20050707_94676.html>.

Padmanabhan, S. (2009), “China is working towards diverting Brahmputra river away from India,” *Hindu Business*, April 14.

Palit, D. K. (1991), *War in High Himalayas: The Indian Army in Crisis, 1962* (New Delhi: Lancer International).

Pan Yihong. (1997), *Son of Heaven and Heavenly Qaghan* (Bellingham: Western Washington University Press).

Pan, P. P. (2003), “China treads carefully around North Korea,” *Washington Post*, January 10.

Pandit, R. (2007), “China’s growing military clout worries India, US,” *Times of India*, April 10.

Paranjpe, V. V. (2003), “Climb over the wall,” *Hindustan Times*, June 17.

Parashar, S. (2008) “Taliban, Qaida trying to take over Pakistan,” *Times of India*, October 15.

Parthasarathy, G. (2010), “The axis of grudging cooperation,” *Wall Street Journal*, May 4.

Parthasarthy, G. (2001), “Tomorrow’s security-missile defence,” *The Pioneer*, May 10.

Patil, R. (2010), “Chinese think India backward,” *Hindustan Times*, May 16.

Pei, Minxin. (2010), “An assertive China the ‘new normal’?” *The Diplomat*, November 24, <http://www.carnegieendowment.org/publications/index.cfm?fa=view&id=420>.

Pew Global Attitudes Project. (2008), “The Chinese celebrate their roaring economy,” July 22, <http://pewglobal.org/reports/display.php?ReportID=26>.

Pew Research Center. (2008), “Global economic gloom–China and India notable exceptions,” *Pew Global Attitudes Project*, June 12.

Polgreen, L. (2009), “Obama’s warming to China is seen as slight in India,” *IHT*, November 24.

Pomfret, J. (2010), “U.S. steps up pressure on China to rein in N. Korea,” *Washington Post*, December 6.

Proliferation: Chinese Case Studies. (1997), Hearing before the Subcommittee on International Security Proliferation, and Federal Services of the Committee on Governmental Affairs, United States Senate, 105th Congress, 1st Session, April 10.

PTI. (1993), "China's plan to build up navy," *Hindustan Times*, January 13.

———. (2002), "India Approaches US, Russia for North Korea-Pak nuke nexus," *Hindustan Times*, December 8.

———. (2003), "George to raise India's concerns in China," *The Tribune*, January 30.

———. (2004), "Putin clarifies remarks on India getting veto power in UNSC," *Hindustan Times*, December 5.

———. (2005), "India attacks China on UNSC emasculation," *Indian Express*, July 2.

———. (2005), "India deserves UN's permanent seat: Taiwan," *Indian Express*, May 7, <http://www.expressindia.com/fullstory.php?newsid=4407>.

———. (2005), "UNSC: China says it won't be an obstacle for India," *The Hindu*, July 4.

———. (2006), "ISI had offered help to Nepal Maoists," *Indian Express*, November 20.

———. (2006), "We'll support India minus Japan: China," *Indian Express*, April 5.

———. (2008), "24% Chinese view India as an enemy," *Times of India*, July 28.

———. (2008), "India conveys displeasure to China over NSG role," *Rediff.com*, September 8, <http://www.rediff.com/news/2008/sep/08chin.htm>.

———. (2008), "Pak's new port has strategic implications for India: Naval Chief," *Rediff.com*, January 22, <http://www.rediff.com/news/2008/jan/22port.htm>.

———. (2009), "Many Chinese still see India as their main enemy: Report," *Times of India*, September 27.

———. (2009), "Nervous China may attack India by 2012: expert," *Hindustan Times*, July 12, 2009.

Pubby, M. (2009), "China proposed division of Pacific, Indian Ocean regions, we declined: US Admiral," *Indian Express*, May 5.

Puri, R. (1999), "India and the 'Middle Kingdom'," *Hindustan Times*, March 7.

Qiao Liang and Wang Xiangsui. (1999), *Unrestricted Warfare* (Beijing: PLA Literature and Arts Publishing House, February).

Qin Huaishi. (2007), "Indu wuzhuang Yuenan tu ezhi Zhongguo," ["India arms Vietnam to curb China," "印度武裝越南圖遏制中國/ 秦淮仕,"] *Ta Kung Pao*, August 1, 8.

Qiu Wei. (2009), "India bristles at closer Sino-US ties," *Global Times*, November 20, <http://www.globaltimes.cn/www/english/world/asia-pacific/2009-/48664.html>.

R. Gates. (2009), "America's security role in the Asia Pacific." Remarks at the eighth Asia Security Summit of the International Institute for Strategic Studies, Singapore, May 30.

R. Puri. (1999), "Partnership with Vietnam," *Hindustan Times*, December 8.

Rabinowitz, G. (2008), "India, China ships compete in Indian Ocean," *Associated Press*, June 8, <http://biz.yahoo.com:80/ap/080608/asia_indian_ocean_intrigue.html>.

Radhakrishnan, S. et al (ed). (1952), *History of Philosophy: Eastern and Western,* Vol. 1 (London: George Allen & Unwin).

Raghuvanshi, V. (2008), "India holding regional naval cooperation conference," *Defense News*, January 2.

———. (2009), "India sounds another caution on China force upgrade," *Defense News*, July 20.

Rajan, D. S. (2007), "China: media fears over India becoming part of western alliance," *Saag.org*, Paper No. 2350, August 29, <http://www.saag.org/papers24/paper2350.htm>.

———. (2008), "China: military media attacks on India-a Tibet issue fall out?" *C3S* Paper, No. 136, March 28, <http://www.c3sindia.org/tibet/222>.

———. (2008), "China: strategic experts talk about a partial Sino-Indian war," *C3S Paper*, No. 230, Chennai Centre for China Studies, November 24, <http://www.c3sindia.org/strategicissues/49>.

———. (2009), "India is a paper tiger and will be trounced if it uses force against China," experts warn," *C3S Paper*, No.288, June 12, <http://www.c3sindia.org/india/588>.

———. (2006), "China: revisiting the 2005 friendship treaty with Pakistan," *Saag.org*, Paper No. 2058, December 10, <http://www.saag.org/papers21/paper2058.html>.

Rajesh, Y. P. (2007), "US sees India as partner in global naval alliance," *Reuters*, September 7.

Rajghatta, C. (2002), "India imperiled by US ignoring Pak-Korean ties," *Times of India*, November 24.

———. (2010), "US more at ease with India's rise than China's ascent," *Times of India*, February 3.

Ramachandran, S. (2007), "India turns its energies on Africa," *Asia Times online*, November 10, <http://www.atimes.com/atimes/South_Asia/IK0Df0.html>.

———. (2009), "Chinese antics have India fuming," *Asia Times online*, May 5, <http://www.atimes.com/atimes/South_Asia/KE05Df01.html>.

———. (2009), "Indian might met with Chinese threats," *Asia Times online*, July 10, <http://www.atimes.com/atimes/South_Asia/KG10Df01.html>.

Raman, B. (2007), "India should not prove Gandhi wrong & irrelevant in Myanmar," *C3S Paper No.82*, December 5.

———. (2007), "Tawang: some Indian plain-speaking at last!" *Saag.org*, Paper No. 2273, June 22, <http://www.saag.org/papers23/paper2273.html>.

———. (2009), "Chinese military 'greatly displeased' by Indian media campaign against China," *C3S Paper*, No. 354, September 10, <http://www.c3sindia.org/india/853>.

———. (2009), "Obama & China: the coming shocks," *Saag.org*, October 6, <http://www.southasiaanalysis.org/papers35/paper3445.html>.

———. (2009), "Obama's failure to understand Indian distrust of China," *Saag.org*, No. 3511, November 19, <http://www.southasiaanalysis.org/%5Cpapers36%5Cpaper3511.html>.

Ramesh, J. (2005), *Making Sense of Chindia* (India Research Press).

Ranade, J. (2009), "Enter the dragon," *Times of India*, June 11.

———. (2009), "It takes two to tango," *Times of India*, July 16.

Rashid, A. (2000), *Taliban: Islam, Oil and the New Great Game in Central Asia* (London and New York: I.B. Tauris, 2000) Chapter 14: "Master or Victim: Pakistan's Afghan War."

Rehman, I. (2009), "Keeping the dragon at bay: India's counter-containment of China in Asia," *Asian Security*, 5:2 (May), 4-43.

Ren Xu, Qian Feng, and Fang Hua. (2001), "Mei Ri dou lalong Yindu: Genben mudi shi ezhi Zhongguo" ["America and Japan rope in India: their basic objective is to contain China"], *Renmin Ribao* [*People's Daily*], April 30.

Report. (1994), "Myanmar and China: but will the flag follow trade?" *The Economist*, October 8.

———. (1997), "China silent on whether Iran nuclear sale shelved," *Reuters*, August 26.

———. (1999), "US says Pakistan has full Chinese missile system," *Reuters*, September 14.

———. (2002), "Pak informed US of nuclear technology transfer," *Jiji Press* (Tokyo), December 25.

———. (2002), "Pak offers China monitoring facilities on Makrana Coast," *Nezavisimoye Voyennoye Obozreniye* (*Independent Military Review*) (Moscow), June 29, <http://www.frontpagemag.com/Articles/ ReadA...le.asp?ID=2487>.

———. (2002), "US finds China-Libya missile link," *Newsinsight.net*, December 20, <http://www.intelligenceonline.net/ allintelligencefull.asp?id=0404602040422&recno=60>.

———. (2004), "China's proliferation practices," *2004 Report to the Congress of the U.S.-China Economic & Security Review Commission*, 108 Congress (Washington: US Government Printing Office, June 2004), 123–150.

———. (2006), "India: Bangladeshi influx fuels growth of Islamic fundamentalism in northeast," *India–Open Source Center (OSC) Report* SAP2006020902500, February 9.

———. (2008), "High-level Chinese delegation visits Maldives," *Maldives Chronicle*, June 26. <http://www.maldiveschronicle.com/high-level-chinese-delegation-visits-maldives/>.

———. (2009), "India, China face-off in the Indian Ocean," *Rediff.com*, February 4, <http://www.rediff.com/news/2009/feb/04india-china-face-off-in-the-indian-ocean.htm>.

———. (2010), "India, South Korea sign five year defense co-operation MOU," *Asian Defence*, September 3, <http://asian-defence.blogspot.com/ 2010/09/india-south-korea-sign-five-year.html>.

———. (2010) "Pakistan, China vow to strengthen strategic ties," *Pak Tribune*, July 8, <http://paktribune.com/news/index.shtml?229306>.

Representative T. Lantos. (1993), "Chinese ballistic missile sales," Statement before the Subcommittee on International Security, International Organizations, and Human Rights, House Foreign Affairs Committee, May 20, 1993, 4.

Reuters. (2006), "Pakistan trusts China more than US," *Dawn*, November 23.

Richardson, M. (1995), "China-Burma ties upset neighbors," *IHT*, April 7.

———. (1996), "China's push for sea control angers ASEAN," *Australian*, July 23.

———. (2007), "The sea lane & energy security lifeline between the Persian Gulf & Asia." Presentation to the Asian Energy Security Conference, Jackson, Mississippi, October 2.

Richter, P. (2010), "West worries China may undermine Iran sanctions efforts," *Los Angeles Times,* June 28.

Ross, R. S. (1999), "The geography of peace: East Asia in the twenty-first century," *International Security*, 23:4 (Spring).

Roy, B. (2007) "123 agreement and the People's Republic of China," *Saag.org*, Paper No. 2324, August 8, <http://www.saag.org/papers24/paper2324.html>.

Roy, D. (2009), The Pacific War and Its Political Legacies (Westport, CT: Praeger).

Roy-Chaudhury, R. (1995), *Sea Power and Indian Security* (London: Brassey's).

Rubin, T. (2010), "China runs big risks coddling N. Korea," *Philadelphia Inquirer*, December 5.

Safire, W. (2003), "An assignment for China and Russia," *IHT*, January 3.

Sakhuja, V. (2007), "Any Asian takers for a 000-Ship Navy?" *Opinion Asia.org*, March 7, <http://www.opinionasia.org/AnyAsiantakersfora000shipnavy>.

———. (2007), "New Silk Route: As more energy consignment may come from east Russia, India is preparing a blueprint for defending new sea lane," *Sahara Time.com* <http://www.saharatime.com/NewsDetail.aspx?newsid=277&catid=>.

Samanta, P. D. (2009), "China says no but US, Japan help ADB clear India's plan," *Indian Express*, June 16.

———. (2009), "China wants to join Navy initiative on Indian Ocean, MEA says no need," *Indian Express*, April 2.

———. (2009), "Sanctioning jaish chief: UK blinks, China lone dissenter," *Indian Express*, June 25.

———. (2009), "Told Obama how China is asserting itself: PM," *Indian Express*, November 26.

Sanger, D. E. (2002), "Asia's splits deepen Korea crisis," *New York Times*, December 29.

———. (2002), "In North Korea and Pakistan, deep roots of nuclear barter," *New York Times*, November 23.

Sanger, D. E. and Schmitt, E. (2011), "Pakistani nuclear arms pose challenge to U.S. policy," *International Herald Tribune*, January 31.

Sarkar, B. K. (1916), *Chinese Religion through Hindu Eyes* (Shanghai: Commercial Press).

Sartori, S. (2005), "How China sees India and the world," *Heartland: Eurasian Review of Geopolitics*, 3 (Hong Kong: Cassan Press), 57.

Saunders, P. C. and Yuan, Jing-dong. (2003), "Korea crisis will test Chinese diplomacy," *Asia Times online*, January 8, <http://www.atimes.com/atimes/Korea/EA08Dg03.html>.

Sawhney, P. (1993) "Hastening slowly: developing Indo-U.S. relations," *Indian Defence Review,* (April), 57-63.

Saxena, S. (2009), "Why do we fear the Chinese dragon?" *Times of India*, September 13.

Scobell, A. (2002), "'Cult of defense' and 'Great power dreams'," Chapter 3, in Chambers, M. R. (ed), *South Asia in 2020: Future Strategic Balances and Alliances* (PA: U.S. Army War College, Strategic Studies Institute, November), 329-359.

Seekins, D. M. (1983), "Historical background," in Bunge, E. M. (ed.), *Burma: A Country Study* (Washington: The American University).

Selth, A. (1996), "Burma and the strategic competition between China and India," *The Journal of Strategic Studies*, 19:2 (June), 213-230.

Sen, T. (2003), *Buddhism, Diplomacy, and Trade: The Realignment of Sino-Indian Relations, 600-1400* (Honolulu: Association for Asian Studies and the University of Hawai'i Press, 2003).

———. (2006), "The formation of Chinese maritime networks to Southern Asia, 1200-1450," *Journal of the Economic & Social History of the Orient*, 49:4, 448, 42-453.

———. (2008), "The military campaigns of Rajendra Chola and the Chola-Srivijaya-China triangle," Unpublished Paper.

Senate Hearings on "Weapons Proliferation in China." (1997, April 10). International Security, Proliferation and Federal Services Subcommittee of the Senate Governmental Affairs Committee.

Shahin, S. (2004), "India, Japan eye new axis," *Asia Times Online*, August 24, <http://www.atimes.com/atimes/South_Asia/FH24Df03.html>.

Shahzad, S. S. (2003), "The net closes on Pakistan," *Asia Times online*, January 23, <http://www.atimes.com/atimes/South_Asia/EA23Df03.html>.

Shao Zhiyong. (2001), "India's big power dream," *Beijing Review*, April 12.

Sharma, P. (2009), "The new balance," *Outlook*, December 2.

Sharma, R. (2008), "Indian navy wins friends, expands influence in Indian Ocean region," August 28, <http://www.newkerala.com/topstory-fullnews-5929.html>.

Sharma, V. George, V. K. (2009), "China is fishing in troubled waters in Lanka," *Hindustan Times*, April 25.

Shen Dingli. (2008), "Revisiting the "Axis of Evil"–Part III," *YaleGlobal online*, August 5, <http://yaleglobal.yale.edu/display.article?id=11153>.

———. (2009), "In diplomacy, ganging up is a very risky move," *Global Times*, November 24.

———. (2010), "Don't shun the idea of setting up overseas military bases," *China.org.cn*, January 28, <http://www.china.org.cn/opinion/200-0/28/content_9324522_3.htm>.

Shenon, P. (2010), "The next nuclear nightmare," *TheDailyBeast.com*, April 14, <http://www.thedailybeast.com/blogs-and-stories/2010-04-14/the-next-nuclear-nightmare/>.

Sheridan, M. (2009), "China reaches out on 60th anniversary," *Sunday Times*, September 27, <http://www.timesonline.co.uk/tol/news/world/asia/article685084.ece>.

———. (2010), "China's hawks demand cold war on the US," *Sunday Times* (London), February 8.

Shi Hongtao. (2004), "China's 'Malacca Straits'," *Qingnian Bao*, June 5, Foreign Broadcast Information Service (hereafter FBIS), FBIS-CPP2004065000042.

Shi Ren. (2009), "China, India hold border talks to resolve boundary disputes," *Zhongguo Tongxun She*, August 4, 2009.

Shi Yongming. (2002), “Give peace a chance,” *Beijing Review*, November 21.

Shoemaker, K. M. (2008), “Intel brief: China in Sri Lanka,” *ISN Security Watch*, May 9, <http://www.isn.ethz.ch/news/sw/details.cfm?id=8942>.

Shourie, A. (2009), *Are We Deceiving Ourselves Again?* (New Delhi, ASA/Rupam).

———. (2009),“New beginnings?” Speech delivered on the Address of the President, June 8, 2009 in the Rajya Sabha (Indian Parliament’s upper house).

Sibal, K. (2008), “India should stand up to China as an equal,” *Rediff.com*, February 22, <http://www.rediff.com/news/2008/feb/22guest.htm>.

———. (2009), “Talks with China head nowhere,” *Rediff.com*, August 13, <http://news.rediff.com/column/2009/aug/12/talks-with-china-head-nowhere.htm>.

Siddiqa, A. (2006), “The view: Hu’s visit,” *Asian Age*, November 27, <http://www.dailytimes.com.pk/default.asp?page=2006%5C11%5C27%5C story_27-11-2006_pg3_4>.

Sikri, R. (2009), Challenge and Strategy. Rethinking India’s Foreign Policy (New Delhi: SAGE Publications, April).

Sikri, R. and Lall, M. (2007), “Whither India–Myanmar relations?” *Saag.org*, Paper No. 2341, August 22, <http://www.saag.org/papers24/ paper2341.html>.

Singh, J. (1994), “Future of Sino-Indian relations,” *Strategic Analysis*, 16:2 (March).

———. (1994), “Post-Cold War security situation in Southern Asia,” *Strategic Analysis,* 17:1 (April).

———. (1998), “Against nuclear apartheid,” *Foreign Affairs*, 77:5, 4-52.

———. (2003), “The arc in the sky,” *Indian Express*, November 10.

Sinha, P. B., Athale, A. A. with S. N. Prasad, S. N. (eds). (1992), *History of the Conflict with China, 962* (History Division, Ministry of Defence, Government of India).

Sirohi, S. (2007), “Japan: The sake is warming,” *Outlook*, August 27.

Sisci, F. (2002), “Mega-NATO: China out in the cold.” *Asia Times online*, May 24, <http://www.atimes.com/china/DE24Ad0.html>.

Small, A. (2010), “China’s caution on Afghanistan-Pakistan,” *Washington Quarterly,* 33:3 (July).

Smith, D. (2007), *The Dragon and the Elephant* (Profile Books).

Smith, J. M. (2009), “The China-India border brawl,” *Wall Street Journal*, June 24, <http://online.wsj.com/article/SB124578881101543463.html>.

Smith, R. J. (1995), “Spy photos suggest China missile trade,” *Washington Post*, July 3.

———. (1996), “China linked to Pakistani missile plant,” *Washington Post*, August 25.

Solomon, J. (2010), “China reactors plan fuels U.S. concern,” *Wall Street Journal*, July 19.

———. (2010), “Myanmar’s links with Pyongyang stir nuclear fears,” *Wall Street Journal*, December 18.

Special Correspondent. (2004), “Myanmar to act against anti-India groups,” *The Hindu*, October 26.

Spector L. et al. (1995), *Tracking Nuclear Proliferation* (Carnegie Endowment for International Peace), 49.

Spillius A. and McElroy, D. (2010), "Burma is working on nuclear weapons programme, experts claim," *Daily Telegraph* (London), July 26.

Srivastava, S. (2008), "China's submarine progress alarms India," *Asia Times online*, May 9, 2008.

Steinberg, D. (1993), "Myanmar as nexus: Sino-Indian rivalries on the frontier," *Studies in Conflict and Terrorism*, 16:1.

Stobdan, P. (1993), "China's forays into Burma: implications for India," *Strategic Analysis*, 16:1 (April).

Storey, I. (2006), "China's Malacca dilemma," *China Brief*, 6:8 (April 2,), 4-6 <http://www.jamestown.org/images/pdf/cb_006_008.pdf>.

Subrahmanyam, K. (1998), "Understanding China: Sun Tzu and Shakti," *Times of India*, June 5.

———. (2007), "Don't get fooled by China," *Times of India*, August 28.

Sun Shao, Chen Zhibin. (1991), Snows of the Himalaya Mountains: The True Record of the China-India War [Ximalaya shan de xue, zhong yin zhanzheng shilu], (Taiyuan: Bei Yue wenyi chubanshe).

T. Delpech, T. (1998-99), "Nuclear weapons and the 'new world order': early warning from Asia?" *Survival*, 40:4 (Winter), 57.

Tanham, G. (1992),"India's strategic culture," *Washington Quarterly*, 15:1 (Winter), 29-142.

Tao Deyan and Zhang Binyang. (2004), "Zhuanjia zonglun Zhongguo heping jueqi jinglue" ["Experts discuss China's peaceful rise concept"], *Zhongguo Zhengzhi Xue*, May 8.

Tasker, R. (1996), "Fear of loathing: ASEAN keeps soft line on Rangoon junta," *FEER*, June 20.

Terrill, R. (2005), "Inside the Chinese mind," *Wilson Quarterly*, September 2005.

Thakur, R. (1991), "Normalizing Sino-Indian relations," *Pacific Review,* 4:1, 15.

Tharoor, I. (2009), "India's China panic: seeing a 'red peril' on land and sea," *Time*, September 20.

Timperlake, E. and Triplett, W. C. (2002), "N. Korea, Pakistan, China," *Washington Times*, December 8.

Tkacik, J. (2002), "Pollyanna-like on Pyongyang," *Asian Wall Street Journal*, December 2.

TNN. (2001), "India's superpower ambition will see strained relations," *Times of India*, April 2.

———. (2008), "India miffed at China's dubious role in Vienna," *Times of India,* September 8.

———. (2009), "Arunachal can't be parted with at any cost," *Times of India*, September 30.

Traub, J. (2006), "The UN's bêtes noires: China and America," *New York Times*, September 1.

UNI. (2006), "Shahi Imam 'absolves' LeT, blames RSS for Mumbai blasts," *Rediff.com*, July 18, <http://news.webindia23.com/news/articles/India/2006078/394446.html>.

Van Hollen, C., former Deputy Assistant Secretary of State. (1980), "The tilt policy revisited: Nixon-Kissinger geopolitics and South Asia," *Asian Survey*, 20:4 (April), 339-361.

van Kemenade, W. (2008), "China and Pakistan: new friends can't compare: The two neighbors have permanent strategic interests," *YaleGlobal Online*, March 12, <http://yaleglobal.yale.edu/display.article?id=0490>.

Verma, B. (2009), "Unmasking China: China will launch an attack on India before 2012," *Indian Defence Review*, 24:3 (July-September).

———. (2010), "India unprepared and unwilling to defend democracy," *Rediff.com*, February 4, <http://news.rediff.com/column/2010/feb/04/india-unprepared-and-unwilling-to-defend-democracy.htm>.

Vertzberger, Y. I. (1984), Misperceptions in Foreign Policymaking: The Sino-Indian Conflict, 959-962 (Boulder, Colo.: Westview Press).

Wade, G. (2005), "The Zheng He voyages: a reassessment," *Journal of the Malaysian Branch of the Royal Asiatic Society*, 78:1 (2005), 37-58; and "Ming China and Southeast Asia in the 5th century: a reappraisal," *ARI Working Paper* No. 28, July 2004 <http://www.ari.nus.edu.sg/docs/wps/wps04_028.pdf>.

Wake, C. (1997), "The great ocean-going ships of southern China in the age of Chinese maritime voyaging to India, twelfth to fifteenth centuries," *International Journal of Maritime History*, 9:2 (December), 73, 5-8.

Walker, M. (2008), "Indian Ocean nexus," *Wilson Quarterly*, 32:2 (Spring), 2-28.

Wang Dong. (2009), "Asia-Pacific community: reality or pipedream?" *Global Times*, June 23, <http://opinion.globaltimes.cn/commentary/2009-06/43966.html>.

Wang Gungwu. (2000), *Joining the Modern World* (Singapore: Singapore University Press).

Wang Hongwei. (1989), "Zhong yin bianjie wenti de lishi yu 1962 nian Zhong Yin bianjie zhanzheng" ["Historical background of the Sino-Indian border problem and the 1962 Sino-Indian War"], *Yatai ziliao* [*Asia Pacific materials*], No. 1, March 18, 1-13.

Wang Peng. (2007), "The US-Indian nuclear agreement: cooperation or threat?" *People's Daily*, August 11, 8.

Wang Sheng. (2001), "'Taoguang yanghui' bu shi quan yi zhi ji," ("'Concealing one's strength and biding one's time' is not a stopgap"), *Huanqiu shibao* [*Global Times*], August 7.

Weiner, T. (1998), "US and Chinese aid was essential as Pakistan built bomb," *International Herald Tribune [hereafter IHT]*, June 2.

Weir, F. (2005), "Russia, China looking to form 'NATO of the east'?: A six-member group, seeking to balance U.S. power, meets in Moscow," *Christian Science Monitor,* October 26.

Weisenbloom, M. and Spotswood, R. (1998), "China's emerging strategic doctrine," *China Strategic Review*, 3:1 (Spring), 24-53.

Weisman, S. R. (2006), "As the price of oil soars, so does its power to shape politics from Washington to Beijing," *New York Times*, July 25.

Weiss, S. (2009), "Whom do sanctions hurt?" *IHT*, February 20.

Weiss, S. A. (2007), "Myanmar's neighbors hold the key," *IHT*, March 7.

Weitz, R. (2010) "China tests waters on first overseas naval base," *World Politics Review*, January 5, <http://www.worldpoliticsreview.com/Article.aspx?id=4882>.

Wilcox, R. (2003), "Yes, a security council seat for India," *IHT*, February 10.

Wilkinson, I. (2008), "China to 'bail-out' near bankrupt Pakistan," *Telegraph*, October 18.

Wilson, D. (1997), *China: The Big Tiger* (London: Abacus).

Wilson, J. and Hua Di. (1992), "China's ballistic missile program," *International Security*, 7:2 (Fall), 37.

Windrem, R. (1999), "China gave Pakistan design data, training and nuclear material," *Indian Express*, June 9.

Wong, E. (2009), "Uneasy engagement China and India dispute enclave on edge of Tibet," *IHT*, September 4.

———. (2010), "Chinese military seeks to extend its naval power," *New York Times* April 24.

Woodrow, T. (2002), "China opens Pandora's nuclear box," *China Brief*, 2:24 (December 10), <http://china.jamestown.org/pubs/view/cwe_002_024_00.htm>.

———. (2002), "The Sino-Saudi connection," *China Brief*, 2:2 (October 24), <http://china.jamestown.org/pubs/view/cwe_002_02_003.htm>.

Wortzel, L. M. (1994), "China pursues traditional great-power status," *Orbis*, 38:2 (Spring).

Wu Miaofa. (2004), "Restructuring the United Nations," *Beijing Review*, May 3, 10-13.

Xinhua. (2003), "US, Japan, ROK and India want to enter Southeast Asia," *People's Daily*, December 15.

———. (2004), "China backs UN reform: FM," December 2, <http://news.xinhuanet.com/english/2004-2/02/content_2287685.htm>.

———. (2004), "China to consider UN reform proposals seriously: FM spokesperson," *People's Daily Online*, December 6, 2004, <http://english.peopledaily.com.cn/20042/06/eng2004206_66299.html>

———. (2005), "China opposed to forced voting on UNSC reform," *People's Daily Online*, July 2, 2005, <http://english.peopledaily.com.cn/200507/2/eng2005072_95685.html>.

———. (2005), "China: UN Council resolution dangerous," *China Daily*, June 1.

———. (2006), "China will invest US$12 billion in Pakistan," *Shanghai Daily*, March 9.

———. (2006), "Chinese president's visit to further cooperation with Pakistan," *People's Daily online*, November 22.

———. (2007), "China, Seychelles vow to strengthen military ties," *PLA Daily*, September 4, http://english.chinamil.com.cn/.

———. (2008), "China denies selling arms to Indian rebels: Xinhua," November 3, <http://www.chinadaily.com.cn/china/2008-/03/content_76560.htm>.

———. (2009), "China 'dissatisfied' with ADB Document involving China-India border dispute," *China Daily*, June 18, 2009.

———. (2009), "China slams India for protectionism," *South Asia Media Net*, June 26.

———. (2009), "Foreign Ministry spokesman refuses Indian allegations," *China Daily*, May 13.

———. (2010), "China, Pakistan agree to cement strategic cooperative partnership," *Xinhua*, July 8, <http://news.xinhuanet.com/english2010/china/2010-07/08/c_3390690.htm>.

Xu Hua. (2000), "Yindu zhongshi haiyang junshi weishe," ["India emphasizes maritime deterrence"], *Xiandai Junshi* [*Conmilit*], (April), 54-56.

Xu Yan. (1993), Zhong Yin bianjie zhi zhan lishi zhenxiang [True History of the China-India Border War], (Hong Kong: Cosmos Books Ltd.), 28, 29-30, 50, 53.

Yang Jirui and Sun Jin (eds). (2004), *Zhongguo Xibu da kaifa yu Nanya* (*China's Western Development and South Asia*), (Chengdu: Sichuan Publishers).

Yang, Dali and Zhao Hong. (2007), "The rise of India: China's perspectives and responses," Paper presented at the Third International Conference on South Asia "Socio-political and Economic Challenges for South Asia." Meritus Mandarin, Singapore, October 25.

Ye Zhengjia. (1992), "India's foreign policy in the restructuring international relations," *Guoji wenti yanjiu (International Studies),* 3.

———. (1996), "Buru 2 shiji de Yindu" ["India enters the twenty-first century"], *International Studies* (English edition) 61:3, 20.

Ye Zicheng. (2000), "Zhongguo shixing daguo waijiao zhanlue shizaibixing" ("The imperative for China to implement a great power diplomatic strategy"), *Shijie jingji yu zhengzhi* [*World Economics and Politics*] No. 11, 5-10, 9-10.

Yost, M. (1996), "China's deadly trade in the Mideast," *Wall Street Journal*, December 4, A8.

Young, C. (2002), "Does Islam foster extremism?" *Boston Globe*, August 19.

Yuan, Jing-dong. (2001), "India's rise after Pokhran II: Chinese analyses and assessments," *Asian Survey,* 41:6 (November/December), 978-1001.

———. (2008), "Chinese perspectives on a rising India," *World Politics Review*, November 30, <http://www.worldpoliticsreview.com/ article.aspx?id=2983>.

Zardari, Asif A. (2009), "Sino-Pakistani relations higher than Himalayas," *China Daily*, August 17.

Zhang Guihong. (2006), "Competition and cooperation: Sino-India's relations in regional perspectives" *Contemporary Asia-Pacific* (Beijing), (December).

Zhang Liwei. (2009), "Bai tuo Maliujia ha ixia yilai, kuaisu shi shi xi-jin zhanlue," ["Stop relying on the Malacca Strait, and speed up implementation of look-west strategies"], *Shiji Jingji Baodao*, March 16.

Zhang Wenmu. (1998), "Meiguo de shiyou diyuan zhanlue yu Zhongguo Xizang Xinjiang diqu anquan" ["U.S. petroleum-geostrategy and the regional security of China's Tibet and Xinjiang"], *Zhanlue yu guanli* [Strategy and Management] 27:2, 100-104;

Zhang Xuegang. (2007), "Southeast Asia and energy: gateway to stability," *China Security*, 3:2 (Spring).

Zhang Yan. (2010), the Chinese ambassador to India, cited in Chellaney, B. (2010), "Troubling China-India ties," *Japan Times*, December 29, <http://search.japantimes.co.jp/cgi-bin/eo20101229bc.html>.

Zhanlue. (2008), "Zhenggao Yindu zhengfu: Buyao yiyuan baode" ["A warning to the Indian government: don't return evil for good"], *Chinaiiss.org*, March 26, <http://str.chinaiiss.org/content/2008-3-26/262952.shtml>.

———. (2009), "Zhongguo yi ge xiao dong zuo jiu chai san le suowei 'da Indu lianbang'" ["China can dismember the so-called 'Great Indian Federation' with one small stroke"], *www.iiss.cn*, August 8.

Zhao Bowen. (2009), "Zui you keneng yu zhongguo jiaozhan de you na shige guojia?" ["Which ten countries are most likely to have war with China?"] *Nanfang Daily*, January 6, <http://opinion.nfdaily.cn/content/2009-0/6/ content_484820.htm>.

Zhao Gancheng. (2008), "Zhongguo dui Yindu zhanlue qianxi" ["An analysis of China's strategy toward India"], *Nanya Yanjiu* [*South Asian Studies*], No. 1, 3-8.

———. (2009), "India's nuclear plan needs to be transparent," *Global Times*, September 6, <http://opinion.globaltimes.cn/commentary/2009-09/ 46807.html>.

———. (2006), "Commentary," in Symposium on Japan and India: Challenges and Prospects in Asia and Pacific in the 21st Century, March 10, <http://20.63.22.65/region/asia-paci/india/ sympo0603.pdf>.

Zhao, Suisheng. (2008), "China's global search for energy security," *Journal of Contemporary China*, 7:55 (May), 207–227.

Zheng Ruixiang. (1993), "Shifting obstacles in Sino-Indian relations," *Pacific Review*, 6:1, 65.

Zhong Yin bianjiang ziwei fanji zuozhanshi. (1994), [History of the China-India Border Self-defensive War], (Beijing: Junshi kexue chubanshe), 37-40.

Zhu Shanshan. (2009), "90% in online poll believe India threatens China's security," *Global Times*, June 11, <http://china.globaltimes.cn/top-photo/2009-06/436320.html>.

Index

About the Book

Despite burgeoning trade and cultural links, China and India remain fierce competitors in a world of global economic rebalancing, power shifts, resource scarcity, environmental degradation, and other transnational security threats. Mohan Malik explores this increasingly important and complex relationship, grounding his analysis in the history of the two countries.

Malik describes a geopolitical rivalry underpinned by contrasting systems, values, and visions. His comparative analysis covers the broad spectrum of challenges that China and India face. Drawing on his extensive research and on-the-ground experience, he concludes with a discussion of alternative strategic futures for Sino-Indian relations.

Mohan Malik is professor of Asian security studies at the Asia-Pacific Center for Security Studies. His most recent books are *Religious Radicalism and Security in South Asia* and *Dragon on Terrorism: Assessing China's Tactical Gains and Strategic Losses Post-September 11.*